Hall Caine

Hall Caine

PORTRAIT OF A VICTORIAN ROMANCER

Vivien Allen

Sheffield
Academic Press

Published by
Sheffield Academic Press Ltd
Mansion House
19 Kingfield Road
Sheffield S11 9AS
England

Typeset by Sheffield Academic Press
and
Printed on acid-free paper in Great Britain
by Bookcraft Ltd
Midsomer Norton, Bath

British Library Cataloguing in Publication Data

A catalogue record for this book is available
from the British Library

ISBN 1-85075-695-3
ISBN 1-85075-809-3 (paper)

CONTENTS

Preface 7
List of Illustrations 11

Chapter 1 15
Chapter 2 29
Chapter 3 43
Chapter 4 55
Chapter 5 69
Chapter 6 81
Chapter 7 93
Chapter 8 109
Chapter 9 123
Chapter 10 141
Chapter 11 153
Chapter 12 174
Chapter 13 185
Chapter 14 196
Chapter 15 212
Chapter 16 225
Chapter 17 241
Chapter 18 253
Chapter 19 266
Chapter 20 282
Chapter 21 295
Chapter 22 311
Chapter 23 328
Chapter 24 343
Chapter 25 356
Chapter 26 369
Chapter 27 385
Chapter 28 400
Chapter 29 416

Appendix I: The Letters of Dante Gabriel Rossetti and Hall Caine......432
Appendix II: Hall Caine (1953-1931): A Select Bibliography.............433
Appendix III: Caine Family Tree...436

Bibliography 437
Index...440

PREFACE

Mention Hall Caine now and the likely response is 'Hall *who?*' Yet in his day he was so famous he was recognised on the streets of London and New York. This in the days before television, but he and his family appeared on numerous picture postcards. Crowds would gather outside the gates of his home in the Isle of Man and his house in Hampstead whenever word got round that he was in residence, in hope of catching sight of him as he went in or out. Like some other popular writers of his time he was accorded the adulation reserved now for pop stars or footballers and was besieged with begging letters and requests for an autograph. He was more widely read than most other novelists of his time and was frequently the subject of caricatures. Some years before George V began the tradition of a royal broadcast at Christmas the BBC invited Hall Caine to speak to the nation on Christmas Eve. It was said when he died in 1931 that he had sold ten million copies of his novels. As some had been continuously in print for more than thirty years and had been translated into many foreign languages, including Japanese, Finnish and Afrikaans, this could be true. But in a few years rows of books bound in fading red cloth, lying forgotten on bookshelves, were all that remained of his fame.

It was in my grandmother's house, on a wet day during school summer holidays when I was about fourteen, that I found such a collection and dipped into it. She caught me reading *The Woman Thou Gavest Me* and snatched it away, saying it was 'not suitable for young gels' and I could read it when I grew up. I had been grown up for more years than I care to remember before I read it right through but that admonishment was enough to impress the name Hall Caine on my memory and when I moved to the Isle of Man in 1981 I was reminded of him again. Driving with a friend along the Douglas to Peel road we passed a house on a tree-covered hillside and she said, 'That's the house where Hall Caine lived.' My interest was immediately rekindled.

The single most important thing in his life was his association with Dante Gabriel Rossetti. This I had heard of, but who was he? Where did he come from? And how did he meet Rossetti? The first part of this book attempts to answer those questions. The next chapters cover the correspondence between the two of them and the time—less than a year—when Caine lived in Rossetti's house. The rest of the book shows what became of him after Rossetti died in 1882 and traces Rossetti's lifelong influence on him and his work. While this is the story of Hall Caine the shadow of Rossetti is all over it.

I began my researches by trying to find people whose parents knew Hall Caine or who might themselves remember him, though they would have been very young when he died in 1931. I was told some extraordinary stories, many of which were later shown to be quite untrue. For anything to do with the Isle of Man the place to go is the Manx Museum in Douglas. Over more than four years I spent much time in the Museum's Library and would like to thank the staff there, and the Director, Stephen Harrison, for all their help, their continuing interest in the work and their unfailing courtesy. Without their assistance, and particularly that of the present Archivist and Librarian, Roger Sims, this book would never have been finished. I am also extremely grateful to the Manx Heritage Foundation for a generous grant towards the costs of research and illustrations.

In the Manx Museum's collection I found pictures of Hall Caine, the surviving scrapbooks of those kept by his wife and letters to him from Rossetti. From the Archivist I learned that Caine's letters to Rossetti were in Canada. My thanks go to Mr George Brandak and his staff at the Angeli Collection in the University of British Columbia who copied this correspondence for me and also other letters of Rossetti to his family and friends. Caine was a prolific correspondent—at one time he claimed to be writing 'hundreds of letters every month' and told a friend that letters were more important to him than books. Much material turned up in odd places (a collection of telegrams in an antique shop). Information on the plays and films based on his novels came from theatre and film museums in London and the United States. Alan Cleary put out an Internet search for me which revealed important papers in libraries and universities around the world and put me in touch with two of his descendants.

The Manx Museum holds Hall Caine's personal archive. On his death his trustees bundled all the papers they could find in his house into two tea chests and presented them to the Museum with a seventy-year embargo expiring in September, 2001. There is also a small Hall Caine archive, that of his brother William and similarly embargoed, in the Liverpool Public Record Office. Because of these caveats neither collection had been catalogued and no one knew what they contained. I am very grateful to Hall Caine's granddaughter, Mrs Elin Gill, for permission to see them and also for her welcome to Greeba Castle, her grandfather's home. Her kindness and patience, and that of her husband, Mr Charles Gill, in answering my questions, showing me family papers and photographs, some reproduced here, and Mrs Gill's recollections of her grandfather were crucial to the preparation of this book. I would also like to thank Hall Caine's other granddaughter, Mary Hall Caine Burr, and her brother Derek Hall Caine, who both live in America and sent me accounts of their grandparents as they remembered them.

It took well over a year to go through the Manx Museum's archive. As it was not catalogued every scrap of paper, every empty envelope, every bill or receipt, had to be looked at and its contents noted. Caine used old envelopes for memos—on one he wrote a description of the aurora borealis as seen on a visit to Iceland. As many of the letters are well over a hundred years old they are fragile and can only be read with the greatest care. Work is now beginning on cataloguing this archive and putting it onto microfilm in preparation for the end of the embargo.

From the archive the picture gradually emerged of a close-knit, chapel-going, affectionate, working-class family in Victorian Liverpool, of a precociously clever little boy evolving into a mixed-up teenager and then an ambitious young man with literary leanings. The archive covers the years from 1870 to the novelist's death. There are letters from and to his family and young men he had known at school and at work in Liverpool, from girlfriends, from his employers and from odd acquaintances (one or two very odd indeed), the men he hero-worshipped and famous people who became friends, including Bram Stoker, Christina Rossetti and Bernard Shaw.

In addition to the Manx Museum, I must, as in the past, record my thanks to the Librarian and staff of the London Library. Living on an island in the middle of the Irish Sea means one's access to libraries is limited but the London sent me piles of books and checked information for me. On my rare visits, working at the London Library is always a joy, whether digging through ancient copies of *Who's Who* in the basement (with a frisson of fear of being squashed like a fly between the rolling shelves), exploring the vertiginous stacks with their ironwork floors which make one wish one had worn trousers and through which a dropped pencil falls to oblivion, or sitting in the elegant Reading Room.

My thanks are due to Celia Salisbury-Jones, who read my manuscript and made many helpful comments, and to Canon John Gelling, who applied his great scholarship to Hall Caine's *Life of Christ* and gave me a summary of his views. To everyone at Sheffield Academic Press I owe thanks for their enthusiasm for the book and their patience and co-operation. Above all I am grateful to my husband, Archie Atkinson, who read each chapter as it was written, pounced on grammatical errors and restrained the verbiage. As a retired newspaper editor he constantly reminded me that text can always be cut and is usually better for being concise.

In addition I would like to thank the following, listed alphabetically, for their help with various aspects of the research on which this book is based: George Bott; Michael Bott; Miriam Critchlow; John East; Stewart

Evans; Naomi Evetts; Paul Gainey; Anne Harrison; Michael Holroyd; Ann and Angus Luscombe; John and Barbara McGeary; David Leighton; Madeleine Matz; Dr Magnus Magnusson; George Newkey-Burden.

My thanks are also due to the following institutions and their staffs:

The British Library, London.
The British Library Newspaper Library, London.
Douglas Public Library, Isle of Man.
British Film Institute and National Film Archive, London.
Theatre Museum, London.
Keswick Museum & Art Gallery, Keswick, Cumbria.
Museum of the City of New York, USA.
New York Public Library: The Berg Collection, USA.
New York Library for the Performing Arts, USA.
Delaware Art Museum, Wilmington, USA.
City of Liverpool, Brown, Picton & Hornby Libraries.
City of Liverpool, Walker Art Gallery.
National Portrait Gallery, London.
Library of Congress, Washington DC, USA.
Georgetown University Library, Washington DC, USA.
University of Reading Library, Archives & Manuscripts Department.
Central Library, Manchester, Local Studies Unit.
The Fawcett Library, London Guildhall University.
Trinity College Library, Dublin.
Bodleian Library, University of Oxford.
The Master and Fellows of Trinity College, Cambridge.
The South African Library, Cape Town, South Africa.
The Royal Library, Windsor Castle.
The Mander & Mitchenson Theatre Collection.
Greater London Record Office.
Sevenoaks Public Library.
Centre for Kentish Studies, County Hall, Maidstone.
Bexley London Borough, Libraries and Museums Department.

The author wishes to thank the following for permission to quote from letters and published works: Mrs Faith Clarke for the use of letters written by Wilkie Collins; David Higham Associates and Mr Frank Magro for permission to quote from *The Scarlet Tree* by Osbert Sitwell, published by Quartet Books; Mrs Diana St John for permission to quote from her late husband's book, *William Heinemann: A Century of Publishing 1890-1990*, published by Heinemann; The Society of Authors as Executors of the Estate of G.B. Shaw for permission to quote from letters written by Shaw to Hall Caine.

1997 Castletown, Isle of Man

LIST OF ILLUSTRATIONS

Portrait in Oils by R.E. Morrison, presented to the Manx Museum
by Dr Robert Marshall.   frontispiece
   Manx National Heritage.
The Kidnapping of Dr Tumblety.   41
   Courtesy of Stewart Evans and Paul Gainey.
Irving's First Night at the Lyceum, commemorated by the caricaturist Alfred Bryan.   64
   From the Raymond Mander and Joe Mitchenson Theatre Collection.
Bram Stoker, an undated photograph.   66
   Hulton Getty Picture Collection.
The Rossetti family photographed by Charles Lutwidge Dodgson (Lewis Carroll).   94
   National Portrait Gallery.
16 Cheyne Walk.   96
   Greater London Record Office.
Pencil sketch by Caine of Fisher Place.   113
   University of British Columbia, Angeli Collection.
Dante's Dream of the Death of Beatrice by D.G. Rossetti.   119
   *The Board of Trustees of the National Museums & Galleries on Merseyside
   (Walker Art Gallery).*
The Transit of Venus by Ford Madox Brown.   142
   Manchester Central Library Local Studies Unit.
The Dead Rossetti by Frederic Shields.   147
   The Delaware Art Museum, Gift of Samuel and Mary Bancroft.
Wilson Barrett.   166
   Publicity postcard. Author's collection.
Aberleigh Lodge, Caine's home at Bexley.   173
   Libraries and Museum Department, Bexley Directorate of Education.
Hall Caine's House at Keswick.   196
   Author's collection.
Caine in Keswick, 1890, photographed by G.P. Abraham.   198
   Manx National Heritage.
Robert Leighton.   201
   David Leighton.
Caine's study at Hawthorns, Keswick, 1889, drawn by A. Tucker.   206
   British Library.
Caine and his family photographed in Liverpool, 1888.   208
   Mrs Elin Gill.
Caine in his study at Hawthorns by Fred Pegram, 1893.   226
   Manx National Heritage.
Mary in the drawing-room at Hawthorns by Fred Pegram, 1893.   227
   Manx National Heritage.
Greeba Castle in about 1905.   228
   Manx National Heritage.
The Manxman, cartoon of Hall Caine   230
   Vanity Fair.

G.B. Shaw in 1888.   235
National Portrait Gallery.

Hall Caine and his wife with Ralph aged 11 in America, 1895.   242
Author's Collection.

Cartoon by Harry Furniss (1854-1925).   248
National Portrait Gallery.

Viola Allen as Roma in the New York production of The Eternal City, 1902.   259
Museum of the City of New York, The Byron Collection.

Hall Caine aged about 45.   262
Author's collection.

Vesta Tilley, 1905.   270
Author's Collection.

John and Sarah Caine, 1901.   273
Mrs Elin Gill.

Mary Hall Caine with her bicycle, 1901.   276
Mrs Elin Gill.

The Ramsey by-election.   284
Mrs Elin Gill.

Caine and Derwent at Peel Castle.   288
Photograph Collection, Royal Archives, Windsor Castle.
By gracious permission of Her Majesty the Queen.

Caine and his wife skating at St Moritz, 1902.   290
Mrs Elin Gill.

Celebrities Caught—And Bowled, a page from *The Tatler*, 7 September, 1904.   299
British Library.

Lily Hall Caine and George Alexander in *The Prodigal Son*, October, 1905.   308
British Library.

A cartoon of Caine published in *Punch*, 11 September, 1907.   321
Manx National Heritage.

Caine in Egypt, cartoon drawn for *The Tatler* by Charles Harrison,
        19 February, 1908.   324
British Library.

Mattheson Lang as Pete.   330
Author's Collection.

Beerbohm Tree.   333
Author's Collection.

Caine as the Governor General in *The Prodigal Son*, August, 1909.   336
Raymond Mander and Joe Mitchenson Theatre Collection.

Mary Hall Caine in May, 1911, aged 42.   346
National Portrait Gallery.

Photograph of the Jonniaux portrait of Caine presented to him
        by the Belgian Government, 1918.   358
Author's Collection.

Elin Hall Caine, aged 8.   378
Mrs Elin Gill.

Caine with Reginald Farrant in Wengen, Switzerland, in the 1920s.   391
Manx National Heritage.

Essence of Hall Caine. A still from the film of *The Prodigal Son*
        shot in Iceland in 1923.   397
British Film Institute.

Hall Caine drawn by Bernard Partridge, October 1926.   404
British Library.

Mary Hall Caine in the garden of her Hampstead home in 1928
with Lady de Frece, Sir Walter de Frece and Ralph Hall Caine.   407
   Mrs Elin Gill.
Caine talking to the director Herbert Wilcox.   414
   British Film Institute.
A page from Caine's manuscript of *The Life of Christ.*   417
   Mrs Elin Gill.
Caine with Dr Robert Marshall beside the River Jordan.   418
   Mrs Elin Gill.
Caine's study at Greeba Castle.   419
   Mrs Elin Gill.
One of the last photographs to be taken of Hall Caine.   425
   Manx National Heritage.

CHAPTER ONE

Hall Caine emerged from obscurity to become a celebrity and made his way from the back streets of Liverpool to a mock castle in the Isle of Man and a London house on Hampstead Heath. The story of how he did it is in its way as romantic, and occasionally unlikely, as any of his novels.

His father, John Caine, was born in Ballaugh in the Isle of Man in 1821, one of ten children of a share fisherman and crofter named William Caine and his wife Isabella Clarke. William, a cheerful character, dissipated his small inheritance and by the time John was growing up the family was among the poorest in the Island. John Caine had little schooling. He was apprenticed to a blacksmith in Ramsey but when he was out of his time there was no work in the Isle of Man, so—like many other Manxmen when times were hard—he emigrated. He went to Liverpool but had to retrain as a ship's smith before he could get work. He married Sarah Hall, a seamstress. She was the daughter of Ralph Hall, a stonemason from Whitehaven in Cumbria. Her mother was Mary Hall who came from Maryport, also on the Cumbrian coast.

Their first child was born on 14 May, 1853, at 130 Bridgewater Street in Runcorn, Cheshire, a prosaic place for a future romantic novelist to arrive on the scene. Bridgewater Street still remains but there is no longer a No. 130 and it is impossible to be certain which was the house where Hall Caine was born, or indeed whether it is still standing. He was a lusty baby who yelled from the moment he was born and objected to being put in his crib. His father wrapped him in a shawl and carried him to the window. Only then did he quieten down. The family home was in Liverpool but John Caine was working temporarily on a repair job in Runcorn docks. Later Caine laid more emphasis on his Manx and Cumbrian descent than his actual origins, claiming to have got his red hair and Norse characteristics from his mother and his Celtic strain from his father. He was christened Thomas Henry Hall Caine. For some reason he disliked the name Thomas and never used it, though his family and close friends called him Tom.

He was a few months old when the family returned to Liverpool. They rented rooms at 14 Rhyl Street, Toxteth, within easy reach of the docks. The area was chosen not merely because it would be convenient for John Caine's work but because there was a small colony of Manx exiles living there, including some of John Caine's family. At first he could pay only brief visits to his homeland, although it was so close (the Isle of Man Steam Packet Company's boats sailed daily from the Mersey), but in 'the Liverpool Manx' he and Sarah found friendship and a ready-made support group.

A second son, John James, was born on 21 September, 1856, and a daughter, Sarah Jane, on 21 January, 1858. By this time the family had moved along the street to No. 21, where they occupied the whole house. To help his wife after Sarah's birth, John Caine took Tom to the Isle of Man and left him to spend the summer with his Grandmother Caine in Ballaugh. He celebrated his fifth birthday with her.

Isabella had been a widow since 1844. She lived with one of her sons, another William, in a small typical Manx cottage. Tom's uncle farmed 30 acres of rented land, raised cattle, slaughtered them himself and took the meat to market in Douglas. Tom went with him at least once. They made the journey by horse and cart, putting up for the night at an inn on the north quay. The boy shared his uncle's bed in a room where other market men and some sailors also slept. They were out at dawn to set up Uncle William's stall for the market.

However, Tom's stay in the Island was not entirely a holiday. His sensible and God-fearing grandmother despatched him to the village school. She called him Hommy-Beg—Little Tommy in Manx—and introduced him to the Manx language. In the evenings she told him the old myths and legends of the Island. They made a deep impression on him. His favourite was the story of the Fynnoderee, a shy being from the hills who worked by night to help farmers. He had immense strength and could toss huge stones around like chicken feed. There are a number of stories of his doings. When the young Tom returned home to Liverpool it was with the foundations of a life-long attachment to the Isle of Man already laid.

Early in 1862 Tom's family moved the short distance to 5 Brougham Street. The district was known as Toxteth Park but was less salubrious than its name implies. It was a densely packed area with rows of small terraced houses, 'back-to-backs' with courts or narrow sanitary lanes between the rows to allow the 'Lavender Men' access to clear the outside lavatories. In the immediate neighbourhood of the Caine home there were pubs and a public bath house, industrial buildings, the Liverpool United Tramways and Omnibus Depot, a Medical Mission Hall, an Elementary School, a large Roman Catholic church and several Nonconformist chapels.

It was at Brougham Street that another daughter, Emma, was born on 7 April, 1862. Tom was nearly nine. He adored his sister Sarah Jane and the arrival of another little girl pleased him. He and Johnny were settled at the local elementary school where he soon found a delight in drawing.

He had been baptised in the Church of England. Although almost unlettered, John Caine had a good brain and intelligence above the ordinary. The established church did not accommodate his kind of Protestantism so he moved to the Nonconformists, taking Tom with him. First he joined the Primitive Methodists, and, when they failed to satisfy his restless intellect, the Wesleyan Methodists. Still not happy, he joined the Congregational church, finally coming to rest with the Baptists. At his heels followed the small Tom, drinking in the sectarianism of the chapels and conceiving a mature distaste for it. The Myrtle Street chapel became the centre of the family's life. Caine remembered it with affection all his life and as late as 1916 paid a visit to it, many years after he had left Liverpool.

In the autumn of 1862 Sarah Jane joined her brothers at school. With four children finances were strained and the small house was crowded but it was a happy family. Until, that is, the beginning of February, 1863, when Sarah Jane fell ill with a remittent fever. The child weakened and at the beginning of March she developed hydrocephaly—'water on the brain'. With few hospital beds anywhere for the children of the poor, Sarah Jane was nursed at home. After a great deal of pain and distress she died there on 16 March, 1863, aged five.

The death of a child in Victorian Britain was not unusual, even in wealthy families. In the mean streets of the towns and cities it was all too common. Nonetheless the family was stricken, Tom as much as any of them. In May he and Johnny caught whooping cough and gave it to Emma. On 7 June, after a particularly violent paroxysm of coughing, she went into convulsions and died. She was only 14 months old.

Tom was devastated. Terrified by the choking cough, this second death, so soon after the loss of Sarah Jane, marked him for life. Shattered by the double tragedy and worried about the effect on Tom, John and Sarah sent him to the Isle of Man for the rest of the summer to convalesce, in the hope that he would throw off both his cough and the terrors his sisters' deaths had caused. His father put him on a boat to Ramsey with a label pinned on his coat and assurances that his uncle would meet him.

The ferry was delayed by one of the fierce storms for which the Irish Sea is notorious. Bobbing around like a cork in a drain the boat lay off in Ramsey Bay for more than eight hours, unable to reach the quay. Eventually a large rowing boat put out to her. Tom was lifted up, passed over the heads of other passengers crowding the rails and lowered into the bottom of the boat. He was followed by the mailbags. He crouched among them while the rowers heaved on the oars to get them through the surf and onto the beach, where he was safely handed over to his uncle. His grandmother cossetted him but packed him off to the village school for the rest of the term. The storm in Ramsey Bay provided him years later with material for the scene in *The Bondman* where Stephen Orry is cast ashore there.

He returned home in September to a change of school. He was enrolled in the boys' section of the Hope Street British Schools. They had been founded in 1792 by a Unitarian congregation, and were run by a Board of Managers on strictly non-sectarian lines. Parents were charged a small fee, which John Caine could now afford. Funds raised by the managers made up the balance of the costs. The founders had stipulated that 'no catechisms or books should be used in the Schools that taught any points of doctrine other than those general truths about which all sorts of Christians agreed'. There were some Jewish children among the pupils and pains were taken to accommodate them without offending their faith. The standard of teaching was high and many of the boys went on to study at the Liverpool Institute.

Caine spent nearly four years there and they were profoundly important to his development as a person and the growth of his ideas on religion. He was Head Boy for his last year before leaving. 'I was from first to last at the bottom of my class in marks,' he wrote in a letter of 1880, 'pulling up my score in curious corners.'

The headmaster was George Gill, later a publisher of school books, whose ideas on education were in advance of his time. The British Schools were intended only to teach the boys reading and writing 'and the common rules of arithmetic'. The girls were to receive the same teaching with the addition of sewing and knitting. George Gill broadened the curriculum. One of his novel ideas was that all boys should learn to swim. Accordingly they were taken once a week to the Cornwallis Street baths at 1d a head. No wonder he was popular with his pupils.

Tom Hall Caine was influenced by the friends he made at Hope Street as much as by the teachers. His best friend was William Tirebuck. He described him years later as 'a stiff-set little chap with twinkling eyes, a merry laugh, and two round cheeks like rosy apples, fond of mimicry, always in mischief, often in disgrace, frequently going through various forms of punishment and taking his drubbings in the spirit of one who thought they were part of the humour of daily life'. Tirebuck became a journalist and then an author. His early books were about art and artists but later he wrote romantic novels. He died aged 54 in 1900 and with him Caine lost one of his dearest friends and closest confidants.

Caine would not agree that one's schooldays were the happiest days of one's life. His, he said as an old man, had been 'too strenuous' for that. He was undersized, a little odd and precociously intelligent, which never led to any schoolboy being wildly popular with his contemporaries. After Tirebuck, his closest schoolfriend was William Pierce, who became a Methodist minister. These two protected the young Tom as a schoolboy from the teasing that came his way and generally stood up for him. Pierce remained a close friend when they were both in their seventies.

Caine was a serious-minded little boy. When he heard that a new teacher was holding Saturday afternoon Bible classes at the Stanhope Street chapel he immediately joined them. There were about 100 children in the class, most of them ten or twelve years old but many of them well into their teens. The teacher was John Clegg, then 24, who afterwards entered the Methodist ministry. Tom, ten years old, was a bit late the first day. Opening the door quietly he slid into a vacant place at the back and fixed his intent gaze on the teacher, as if his life depended on soaking up everything he could teach him. The stare never wavered or relaxed for the whole class. Although he was so small, at the back and one of so many, Clegg's attention had been caught. Caine made such an impression in the ensuing weeks that more than forty years later Clegg remembered the red-haired boy, though in the interim he had forgotten his name.

Another clear memory stayed with Clegg. When he was about to leave Stanhope Street he set an essay competition for the children, with a book as the prize. Almost all the class joined in so it took him a week to sift the essays. But the winner was never in any doubt from the time he began to read Tom Hall Caine's contribution. A farewell party had been arranged and the prize was to be presented then: the date was 15 January, 1864. There was loud applause when the winner was announced as Master Hall Caine and he made his way to the front. Clegg had one small worry. Holding the book firmly he asked Caine,

> 'My boy, who has helped you to write this paper?'
> 'No one, Sir!' the boy replied instantly and with emphasis.
> 'What book have you copied it from, if any?'
> 'From no book, Sir,' he asserted with obvious honesty. 'It is all my own.'

Relieved, Clegg handed over the prize, suitably inscribed.

'It's a paper which would do credit to a much older youth than you,' he said. 'I congratulate you and wish you success in your after life.'

The party was memorable for more than just the prize giving. At about seven o'clock there was an almighty explosion, the biggest bang Liverpool had ever heard. It shook the building and there was the sound of tinkling glass as almost every window in Toxteth blew out. A ship laden with explosives, called the *Lottie Sleigh*, had blown up in the Mersey. Little of her remained, apart from her figurehead, a substantial wooden carving about eight feet high of the eponymous lady which is now in Liverpool's Maritime Museum, within hailing distance of her epic misadventure in 1864.

In January, 1865, the Caine family moved again, round the corner to 2 Coburg Street. The house was small but they shared it with the maternal grandparents, the stonemason Ralph Hall and his wife Mary. The census of 1871 gives John Caine as the head of the household, not Ralph Hall. Tom adored his Cumbrian grandfather and was fascinated by his craft. His greatest treat was to watch him at work and eventually to be allowed to handle his tools. He absorbed stories of Cumberland life and legend from him and heard about a magical land of mountains and lakes away to the north.

It was while they were all living at Coburg Street that John and Sarah Caine's last two children were born—William Ralph Hall in February, 1865, and Elizabeth Ann, known as Lily, in December, 1869. John Caine was determined his children should have the schooling he had been denied. They were all strictly brought up and encouraged to work hard at their lessons. The family were not well off but neither were they destitute. John Caine was a skilled artisan and their milieu was what the Victorians referred to as 'the respectable working class'. It has been stated that as a boy Tom Hall Caine was a 'street Arab' but this is very far from the truth. Though John and Sarah had to stretch every penny the children were decently fed and clothed and they all went to school, even before the Elementary Education Act of 1870 brought in compulsory free elementary schooling.

Tom stayed at the British Schools until he was 14 and Johnny joined him there. Ralph Hall had steady work—gravestones were in regular demand—but John Caine was only a shipsmith's journeyman on day wages, never sure how long a job would last. However, there were family trips back to the Isle of Man nearly every summer. In his 1908 autobiography, *My Story*, a book as remarkable for what it does not say as for what it does, Caine said he felt his father had sent him so often to the Isle of Man as an ambassador, making the visits he himself would have liked but was too poor to make. As with so much else he says in this book and in numerous interviews with newspapers and magazines, this is romantic nonsense. Family papers give the lie to it, for instance a letter from an aunt in the Isle of Man asking if his parents 'will be coming over this summer as usual as we always like to see them'.

Tom was 12 when Isabella Caine died on 28 January, 1866, aged 73. She had played an important part in his life but he was naturally not as close to her as he was to his maternal grandmother, Mary Hall. He was sad at Grandmother Caine's death but seems to have taken it with equanimity. Her passing meant a change to his holidays in the Isle of Man.

Instead of going to Ballaugh he now went to his father's sister, Catherine Teare, and her husband James. He was the schoolmaster at Maughold, near Ramsey, and Tom enjoyed the company of his young cousins there.

When it comes to the story of his life Caine is not the best witness. He was a chameleon, apt to change colour according to his company and to say what he thought would give the effect he intended. He was also secretive. His Cumbrian grandparents, who were on the spot, were the strongest influence on him as a child and he was also a proud and thorough-going Liverpudlian. When it suited him, however, he became more Manx than the Manx-born and not all of them appreciated it. When word got about in the Island that this book was being planned the present writer was accosted by a staunch Manxman-born with, 'Don't you dare say he was Manx. The bastard was born in Runcorn,' a comment reflecting feelings common in Caine's own day.

On other occasions, as in an interview with the Sketch on 18 October, 1899, Caine gave quite another impression. 'What surprises one most on meeting Hall Caine,' says the writer, 'is to find...that he is not really a Manxman, as is so often stated, but a Liverpudlian, and, what is more, is proud of it. He is only Manx by adoption.' This is a more accurate statement of the facts. In *My Story* Caine acknowledges 'the stoical unselfishness' of his parents to which he owed so much and which gave him and his siblings a sound start in life. This at least is true and he not only remembered it, he repaid it many times over.

In July, 1866, when Tom was thirteen, there was an outbreak of cholera in Liverpool. For ever after he remembered the fear of death that swept through the streets, a fear that was only too well justified. There were funerals in every street, sometimes two lines of coaches at the same time, while the cemeteries were choked with mourners waiting their turn in the chapels. Many of the people of simple faith, particularly the Primitive Methodists, held prayer meetings in Parliament Fields and other open spaces. They prayed and sang with a delirious fervour that seemed almost barbaric to the sensitive small boy hovering on the edge of the crowds, appalled and entranced by their fierce emotion.

In the summer of 1867, when he had just turned fourteen, Tom left school. Further education, in a formal sense, was beyond his family's means but its lack ultimately proved no handicap. For this he had the Liverpool Free Library to thank. Afterwards he said he had been educated by the free library service. A passion for books and a magpie mind that could pick up and retain masses of information, insatiable curiosity to rival that of the Elephant's Child and driving ambition took him to the top.

At fourteen, however, it was imperative that he should start earning. With no clear idea of what he wanted to do but with some talent for drawing he was attracted by an architect's advertisement for a pupil draughtsman. Without telling his parents he applied for the post and was taken on. He did well and was soon promoted to the point where he was actually paid. He gave most of his tiny wage to his mother for his keep.

It was in many ways a momentous choice of occupation. His master, an architect and surveyor named John Murray, was distantly related to Gladstone and a great supporter of the Liberal cause. On the day of the 1868 election, when the Liberals defeated the Tories under Disraeli and Gladstone took office for the first time, Caine was employed in running messages to Gladstone's brother in his office. It was there he saw the great man for the first time.

'He was sitting behind an office table,' Caine wrote in his autobiography, 'a tall man in a stiff-looking frock-coat of the fashion of an earlier day, with a pale face and side whiskers and very straight black hair, thin on the crown and brushed close across his forehead. He was my hero, my idol, my demigod in those days.' This was the beginning of Caine's interest, and occasional involvement, in politics. He saw his hero again a few months later. Gladstone was spending a few days on his property at Seaforth, near Bootle. John Murray had been engaged to survey it and Caine was sent to help the surveyor-in-chief. One morning the man failed to turn up for work and Caine took over. The Prime Minister came out to look on. He was amused to see such a small boy ordering several large workmen around. He asked to see the survey-book and Caine gave him a large explanation of the peculiarities of his estate with the work that ought to be done. Gladstone listened attentively and then, without further remark, patted Caine on the top of his head—which was easy to do—and said he 'would do something some day'.

He must have made an impression for two years later he had a letter from Gladstone's brother saying the Prime Minister wished to appoint him steward of his Lancashire estates. For a boy of his age the offer was a great honour and as he still worshipped Gladstone he was tempted to accept. However, John Murray and other friends, who felt he had the makings of an architect, advised him to decline as it would interrupt his career. Reluctantly he agreed.

Liverpool in those days was an exciting place to grow up in. By the time Caine was out of school the town—it was not created a city until 1880—had been linked to London by rail for forty years, the docks were expanding, the Philharmonic Society at St George's Hall flourished, the British Association met in the town from time to time. There was a Free Library, a Free Museum and the Walker Art Gallery, the gift of the town's mayor.

There were also riots, disastrous fires (not always accidental) and demonstrations by the Liverpool Orangemen, which on at least one occasion ended with fighting and several people dead. The Fenians, precursors of the IRA, were also active—in 1881 they tried to blow up the Town Hall but were foiled when the package of explosives was discovered. Two Irishmen were arrested, tried and condemned to long prison sentences. Never a dull moment in Liverpool.

Books were the teenage Caine's consuming passion. When he should have been concentrating on drawing board and T-square he was devouring every kind of literature he could get his hands on. At 15 he discovered Coleridge's poetry. Until then his chief recreation and delight had been drawing: from now on it was words. *The Ancient Mariner* had him in thrall, the mystery of *Kubla Khan* and *Christabel* enchanted him. Without doubt Coleridge was the first important literary influence on his thought and work.

'The Free Library at Liverpool was my great hunting-ground in those days and surely no young reader ever ran so wild in a wilderness of books,' he said. He worked his way greedily round the Library's shelves with no guidance and no pause for critical consideration. Poetry, history, drama, romance, metaphysics, theology—he galloped through them all, taking out a fresh book about every other day, until his head was crammed with miscellaneous literature. This undiscriminating consumption of books continued for two or three years. When he was older he had to reread many of the books he had raced through before he was twenty.

'The scribbling itch'—his phrase—surfaced but he made no attempt to publish anything. As soon as one item was finished it was consigned to the bottom of an old trunk in his room and he turned to something else. All his life he walled himself in with paper. On the evidence of his personal archive he seldom threw anything away—letters, telegrams, dinner menus, hotel bills, postcards, receipts, were stuffed into drawers and cupboards to emerge a century later in an *embarras de richesse* for a biographer.

In due course the desire to enlighten the world emerged. He and William Tirebuck started a magazine and published it with the help of Tirebuck's elder sister, Maggie, using Caine's home for an office. It was in manuscript and Tirebuck was editor, 'printer', publisher and deliveryman while Caine was the principal contributor. It was a serious publication which undertook to settle the problems of the universe for a select circle of readers. It lasted all of two months. Two issues had appeared when another friend and one of their contributors, Rowland Elliot, not only inherited a small fortune but came into control of it while still in his teens.

'It was bad for the fortune and not good for the boy,' said Caine later, 'but it was decidedly stimulating to our literary ambitions.'

They printed the magazine. They only printed it once. It consisted almost entirely of a very long blank verse poem by Caine and a glowing appreciation of it by Tirebuck. They had ten thousand copies run off but never heard of anyone buying a copy.

This first joint plunge into publication proved a plunge into hot water. When the boy capitalist's fortune sank without trace Tirebuck made a sober assessment of the situation and took a job as a junior clerk in a merchant's office. At home Caine's parents told him to stop playing around and concentrate on his work as an architectural draughtsman. John James was about to leave school but could not be expected to contribute much to the family coffers for a while. Willie was now four years old and the youngest member of the family, Lily, was approaching her first birthday.

Reluctantly Caine returned to John Murray's office but he continued to write. His first published work, apart from the short-lived magazine, appeared in a trade paper, the *Builder*. This, and other similar magazines of the day, carried literary articles and social comment as well as technical news for the trade and gave Caine the platform he was looking for—as well as the boost of small payments for what he wrote. He contributed to the *Builder* for some years while also writing occasional articles for local newspapers, which were sometimes paid for and sometimes not.

On 20 January, 1870, his beloved grandfather, Ralph Hall, died aged 72. He had provided affectionate support for his eldest grandchild, always ready to listen and giving advice only when asked. He had been a steadying influence. Caine was plunged into profound grief. He turned to the solace of poetry. Finally, towards the end of 1870, something snapped. He threw up his job with John Murray and fled to the Isle of Man. It was, he said later, 'the first serious manifestation of the nervous attacks which have pursued me throughout my life'. One of his doctors remarked twenty years later that he was 'a bundle of nerves'. Hectic periods of research and creative work were often succeeded by gloomy depths of exhaustion, frequently prostrating him in a state of 'nervous collapse'. On this occasion the loss of his grandfather, combined with the growing tension between the humdrum work of the architect's office and his growing ambition to be a writer, made him run for cover. This was something he did all his life. Whenever he felt ill or worried or under strain he would opt for that panacea, 'a change of air'. Unfortunately he himself did not change so that he frequently returned home or moved on still feeling exhausted and unwell.

On arrival in the Isle of Man, unannounced, he went straight to his Aunt and Uncle Teare where he received a welcome even warmer than he had expected. Maughold is a small settlement near Ramsey on the northeast coast of the Island. The schoolhouse was on Maughold Head, a bleak spot which was even more isolated then than it is now. When

Caine arrived he soon saw James Teare was ill. He had tuberculosis. To his Aunt Catherine her nephew's arrival was a godsend. She told him he was welcome to stay as long as he liked if he would act as assistant teacher in the school. Nothing at that stage could have pleased him better.

The schoolmaster's accommodation, part of the small schoolhouse, was crowded as the Teares had four children, Alfred, fourteen, Adelaide, who was twelve at the time, the seven-year-old Reuben—'full of life with as much impudence as any boy has a right to have'—and Mona, who was six. The Teares had recently lost another daughter, Ellen, at four months old.

Near the schoolhouse was a tholtan, a tiny, half-ruined cottage with sagging thatch and the door off its hinges. Caine camped in it and, using the stonemason's skills he had learnt from his Grandfather Hall, he restored it. When the work was finished he carved the name Phoenix Cottage on the stone lintel of the door together with the date—8 January, 1871. The brisk Island air and hard physical work, helping his uncle in the school and romping with his young cousins, restored both his health and his nerves. He had seldom been so happy.

He stayed for over a year. Roaming around in his spare time, getting to know the schoolchildren and their parents, he acquired much of the insight into the life and character of the ordinary Manxman which illuminates his Manx novels. The village schoolmaster had considerable status in a community where many were illiterate. He was often asked to make wills, write letters to relatives abroad, even love letters, or to count up a family's income or the value of its livestock. As James Teare became more ill he passed many of these chores on to his nephew. This gave him material which he used to good effect—to the annoyance of many of the Manx—in his books.

He missed the Liverpool Free Library but explored his uncle's bookshelves. They were better furnished than in most Manx homes but contained no fiction, though he does mention *Pilgrim's Progress*. The Manx as a whole did not approve of fiction, regarding anything 'made up' as wicked. Bunyan's book was not considered to be fiction but more akin to the Bible. When Caine first became a well-known novelist, his father was waylaid on the streets of Douglas by an old friend who stood in front of him bristling with fury and disgust and said, 'I hear your son makes his living by telling lies.'

Caine took a lively interest in the Manx newspapers. A number of letters, articles and a satirical poem he wrote were published, including an extraordinary attack on a local clergyman. In those days most journalism was anonymous but both the cleric and Caine's uncle had a shrewd idea who was responsible for these effusions, which included propaganda for Caine's version of Communism, his current political creed. He sent copies of the papers to Liverpool with covering letters in which he poked fun at their lack of sophistication.

A schoolfriend, George Rose, wrote often, once castigating Caine for neglecting to write home. 'Your people have been distressed at this want of news of your health. Your brother called here yesterday to ask whether I had heard from you and he told me how Mr Caine was in great fear that some misfortune had overtaken you.' He went on to tease Caine about the girlfriend he had left behind. Caine thought he was in love with her but Rose said she was stepping out with someone else. It was not true but he hoped the pangs of jealousy would soon bring Caine home. The plot failed.

Rose, as well as other friends, sent papers and magazines so that Caine was not entirely out of touch. It was during this time in the Isle of Man that he first discovered Ruskin, another great influence on him, falling with delight on his letters, *Fors Clavigera*, which were addressed to 'the workmen and labourers of Great Britain', though one wonders how many actually read them. In 1871 Ruskin settled at Brantwood, his home overlooking Coniston Water in the Lake District, where he lived for the rest of his life, and began publishing this remarkable collection of papers, which appeared at monthly intervals up to 1884. They covered a wide variety of subjects but with an underlying motif throughout—the redress of poverty and misery.

He set out his ideas on how this evil had arisen and how it should be remedied. The effect on Caine was to convert him into an eager disciple and admirer until Ruskin's death in 1900. He read everything he could lay hands on that Ruskin wrote and was greatly impressed by the Guild of St George, which Ruskin founded. It was set up on the principle that 'the highest wisdom and the highest treasure need not be costly or exclusive', something calculated to appeal to the young intellectual from a poor background. Members gave a tithe of their fortunes for charitable purposes. Ruskin was practical in his philanthropy, founding several industrial experiments to give work in rural areas, including the St George's Woollen Mills at Laxey in the Isle of Man. They made 'Ruskin Manx Homespuns', endorsed by the great man himself—'An honest cloth made of honest thread'. The Laxey Mills are still working and visitors can see cloth being woven on the old hand looms.

In spite of being part of a loving family, Caine sometimes felt isolated and lonely at Maughold. He was already displaying an intellectual arrogance which could alienate people. 'Let not the sentiments of scorn which you entertain towards so many of Adam's descendants estrange you from two of that large family,' Rose said at one point. Caine had said he did not have the arts of the courtier but Rose reminded him 'of occasions when you exerted charm and flattery so that even the most perspicacious were taken in by you'. Caine kept the ability to switch on the charm. Many years later people were still commenting on it and also on the fact that it could quickly be switched off again.

He had a girlfriend in Liverpool, Florence Waterbury, who had remained faithful. When he heard her parents had died and she was going to America to live with an uncle he made a quick visit to Liverpool to see her and his parents. She wrote from New York, begging him to write and saying she was not going to allow anyone to adopt her—she would get a job and earn her own living. 'All the girls here work.' Caine lost the letter and it was four years before he found it again and replied. Not surprisingly she had lost interest by then.

His father had given him 'a good talking to' about throwing away the chance of a career as an architect. Back in Maughold he told his uncle and Teare wrote to John Caine saying he should not worry about Tom's future because if all else failed he could earn a living by his pen. Caine was grateful but unsure that this would mollify his father. His uncle's increasing weakness and his aunt's distress cast a shadow as winter approached. On 16 December, 1871, James Teare died. He was only 44. Caine, who had in fact been running the school for several months, took it over officially at a salary of £40 a year. In his spare time he carved a headstone for the grave of his uncle and baby Ellen. He wrote to George Rose for advice on the best kind of lettering to use to survive the salt-laden gales. Rose, an illustrator who also regularly designed the lettering for inscriptions, proposed Old English, illustrating his letter with the effects of wear on different styles of the letter E. Caine followed his friend's suggestions and the headstone he carved is still in Maughold churchyard. The lettering is just visible more than a hundred years on. Long after he made it Caine drew on this experience for his novel, *The Manxman*. The description of the gravestone Pete tries to carve for the unmarked grave he believes to be that of his beloved wife, Kate, matches exactly James Teare's headstone. Caine vividly describes Pete working on it and the sound of the stonemason's mallet on his chisel—'*Pat-put! pat-put!*' An evocative piece of onomatopoeia which came readily to someone who had watched a stonemason at work. His description of the stone splitting when Pete, impatient at the slow progress of the work, gives it too hard a whack doubtless came from personal experience.

During his time in Maughold Caine grew up. He also developed an intense affection for that spot on the headland. In May, 1909, he bought a small plot of land high on Maughold Head for his grave, not bothered that it was unconsecrated ground. He paid the Christians of Baldromma Farm five shillings for it. A few weeks before his death in 1931 he went to Maughold with his friend and physician, Dr Robert Marshall of Douglas, intending to visit the site but he could get no further than the top of Maughold churchyard.

'If I can't get up there,' he said, 'other people won't be able to either.'

So he abandoned his original plan and bought two grave plots in the churchyard at the spot he had been able to reach. He was buried there less than a month later, more than sixty years after he became the Maughold schoolmaster.

CHAPTER TWO

One can learn as much about a person from the letters others wrote to him as from those he wrote himself. This is certainly true in Caine's case. The jumble of correspondence he received and stuffed away, mostly in no sort of order, opens windows on a life that was in many ways secretive.

In March, 1872, John Murray wrote a brisk letter telling Caine he was wasting his time in the Isle of Man. His job in Liverpool was still open to him and he should return. Murray must have been a patient and sympathetic man who had a high opinion of his pupil's talent and potential. Caine was nearly nineteen and feeling lonely and bored. He wrote back to Murray thanking him and saying he would be returning. By mid-April he was back in Liverpool.

It was with mixed feelings that he returned to work as a draughtsman. He was determined to be a writer and used his job as a convenience, a method of putting some regular money in his pocket while spending almost every available moment, including time at the office, writing. He put all his energies into his first work of fiction—not a novel but a play. Having completed it, and shown it to William Tirebuck who enthused over it, he approached T.C. Cowper in London, asking for advice as to how it could be put on. Cowper replied describing the process by which a play was read and accepted for production, which took a great deal of work, skill and time. His fee was ten guineas and if Caine forwarded that amount he would read the play and do his best to get it into shape and staged.

Caine was shocked and angry. He was naïve and entirely ignorant of the business of the theatre. Ten guineas was the equivalent of around £500 now and way beyond his means. He wrote back saying he was surprised there was virtual censorship before a play could get onto the stage and that money should be required. He did not have the sum mentioned and could not send it. He told Cowper the public should be the judge of a play. He thought managers would be as eager to get manuscripts to meet the public's constant demand for something new as playwrights were to get their plays performed.

Cowper replied a trifle tartly, having found the letter rude and silly (as it was). Caine, he said, might be a budding Shakespeare but in Shakespeare's time all it took to put on a play was a barn, a crude stage and a notice saying 'A Street in Venice' by way of scenery. Nowadays to put on a full length play in London cost between £300 and £1000. No manager would risk that sort of money on an unknown, untried piece. He suggested that if Caine wanted the public to be the judge of his play he should find the money to put it on himself in Liverpool. 'You will soon be enlightened.'

Thwarted for the time being in his ambition to be a playwright, Caine found other outlets for his intellectual energy. He wrote some terrible poetry. This is the first verse of a gloomy poem covering six sides of blue writing paper:

> My God, it is a dreadful thing
>   And from the swelling heart will bring
> The rending sigh—or deadlier worse
>   The oath—the Heaven recorded curse.
> To stand amid the crowd—alone!
>   An outcast—stranger or unknown!
> To stand a thousand forms among
>   To see a thousand eyelids glazed,
> To see a thousand palmsters meet
>   But not an eye to you be rais'd
> And not an outstretched hand to greet!

'A thousand eyelids', or at least some, probably did glaze when faced with Caine's outpourings. Far from being alone he lived with his affectionate family and was at the centre of a group of close friends. It must be said, however, that he had a talent for upsetting people and getting embroiled in bitter rows. As well as being involved in arguments face to face he fired off intemperate letters without taking much thought and alienated people who were in a position to help him. Someone whose signature is illegible but says he is an old friend wrote a pained letter in 1878, when Caine had attained a prominent position in the intellectual life of Liverpool. He sympathised with his problems but their arguments should not be 'the occasion of deliberate severance from those who, whatever your opinion of their intellectual capacity, held you in respect'. Nearly ten years after George Rose had warned him against intellectual arrogance it was still his besetting sin. The writer added he could 'see no justification for conduct whose sole end, uncloaked, is simply the humiliation of those around us and glorification of self... The tide of ill-feeling will know no ebb while such can truly be said of you.'

Caine volunteered to write reviews for the Liverpool papers. He and Tirebuck were enthusiastic theatregoers, sometimes seeing a different play every night of the week, and critics got free tickets. At least two papers took up his offer. Tirebuck was by this time working on a local newspaper edited by Albert Wainwright. It is difficult to be sure exactly which paper it was—there was a surprising number of them. Wainwright invited Caine to write a theatre column. He complied with alacrity but wrote far more than he was asked for—'Not more than one column should be devoted to your Theatre Gossip,' says an exasperated note from the editor. On another occasion Wainwright summoned Caine to his office because his notice of *The Colleen Bawn*—Dion Boucicault's enormously popular Irish play—was half a column too long. However, Caine's efforts were popular and Wainwright asked for an occasional 'Literary and Fine Arts' column and reviews of art exhibitions as well.

Other papers took note and Caine was soon a busy freelance critic as well as writing numerous articles on everything under the sun, few of which were actually published. He amassed an entertaining collection of rejection slips. An undated one from the editor of the Liverpool *Courier* thanked him for offering them his articles, which they were sure would be of high merit. 'Both Mr Willcox and myself, however, think that on the whole we must forgo the benefit you kindly intend us.' He was so busy he was often late with his copy. His archive is full of cross notes from editors asking him to let them have his copy at once. This continued throughout his working life even after he became a full time writer. Editors, publishers and agents were constantly enraged by his failure to meet agreed deadlines.

Eventually he either strained John Murray's patience to the breaking point or resigned his job. He went as a draughtsman to a firm of builders, Bromley & Son. Here he did not have to go out on site much but spent more time in the office, often on his own, which meant he was as likely to be writing a poem or finishing an article as making the firm's working drawings which he was employed to do. The head of the firm was Israel Bromley but he was getting on in years and his son James was in charge of the day to day business. He was older than Caine but they had much in common and became friends. Caine had a good head for figures and ended up keeping the firm's books.

Together with William Tirebuck and George Rose, he founded a Notes & Queries Society. It first met in the schoolroom under the Myrtle Street chapel but soon grew out of it and forgathered either at the Free Library or at the Royal Institution. It was, according to the brochure, to be a forum 'for the discussion of Arts questions of current interest, new pictures, new music, new plays, new books and good work of every kind'. To begin with they also used it to propagate political ideas, especially Caine's and Rose's theories of Communism, then a live topic among thinking people. Caine's idea of Communism appears to have been closer to a sentimental version of Christian Socialism than to Marxism. Many years later he asserted that he had been a Christian Socialist before the term was generally known.

He and Rose (Tirebuck does not seem to have held the same views) believed that 'the Soil' was given to men along with the power to work and was theirs as of right. It had been stolen by 'the Capitalists', whom they defined as those who do not work. This reasoning declared that 'the earth is the *Lord*'s because *He* made it' so any man who said, 'The land is mine' usurped the prerogative of God.

Both of them approved emigration and 'looked to the day when England holds only as many as the land can support, the factories will close and everyone will have gone back to the land'. They 'hoped that a great part of the population of this country would see the advantages of emigrating', thus leaving more land and work for those who chose to stay—Caine and Rose presumably among them.

The two of them also asserted that the division of labour was a great evil. This showed how much they were influenced by Ruskin. By 'division of labour' Ruskin meant the division between designer and craftsman. The craftsman should make things to his own design, the designer should be responsible for all stages of manufacture. He should not design in isolation and then hand his plans over to others to carry out. This was taken up enthusiastically by William Morris and was a basic tenet of the Arts and Crafts movement.

As membership of the Notes & Queries Society grew, and their political ideas were modified, Caine wrote to Ruskin to ask if he would honour them by becoming their President. He declined. Unabashed, Caine, who had joined the local Ruskin Society, continued to write to his idol. Eventually he was received at Brantwood during one of his Lake District holidays. After that he called and wrote regularly.

The conflict between the tedium of work (even when the evenings were enlivened by the heady delights of discussing Communism) and the life of a writer which he longed for strained his nerves. His urgent desire to strike out on his own and his love for his parents and desire to help and support them combined to drive him nearly frantic. In 1873 the family moved to 59 South Chester Street, Toxteth, a slightly larger house backing onto the Liverpool United Tramways and Omnibus Depot. Caine shared a small bedroom at the top of the house with John James, who was now a clerk with a shipping firm. It provided little space for him to write. The whole of this area of Toxteth has been cleared and none of the houses where the Caine family lived has survived.

That summer Caine fell head over ears in love. He poured out his heart to a close friend, W.W. Jackson, a Liverpool man who was working in London as a journalist. A note of 25 August acknowledges this screed, saying 'It will be no easy task to answer your last (something more than 20 pages!)'. Evidently he had not read it all because a few days later he sent an impassioned scrawl begging Caine to give up all idea of the girl. '*Crush out all* affection for *her*. It's *hopeless—she* loves *him* and thinks highly of him. *He* thinks a *lot* of *her* and the *marriage* may take place any day!' He was sorry for Caine but could not say anything else.

Caine took a knock but he hoarded his feelings and experiences, a hoard he drew on in his novels. He wrote sympathetically of Philip's emotions as he sees Kate Cregeen married to his friend Pete in *The Manxman*.

Caine sent Jackson a play he had written asking for comment. Jackson replied asking why he rewrote plays he had seen, much of it literary rubbish. Why did he not try something original? Caine said he felt hurt at this, to which his friend replied robustly that an intelligent man should not get himself into such states or be so touchy. Caine, however, was to take criticism badly all his life. On several occasions William Heinemann had to restrain him when he wanted to lash out in public at reviewers who had criticised his novels.

In spite of occasional spats Caine continued to seek Jackson's advice. In the spring of 1874 Jackson set up the Jackson and Stimson Standard Dramatic Company. It went on tour briefly and then quietly folded but only after Caine had sent Jackson two or three more of his plays together with some reviews and columns he had written. Jackson replied with detailed and careful criticism but then exploded. 'Your critique on *Genevieve* in my opinion was written very diffusely and your meaning was on several points clouded by superfluous language.' The other reviews, leading articles, notes, jokes and smart paragraphs Caine had sent were 'heart-sickening, brain-muddling ebullitions of crass ignorance linked in the exercise book composition!' He told Caine to read some of his own—Jackson's—critiques to see how it should be done. (*Genevieve* was one of Coleridge's early poems. When he wrote his *Life of Samuel Taylor Coleridge* Caine described it as 'sentimental'.) After the failure of his theatre company W.W. Jackson went to work in Gabon, West Africa. They continued to write to each other. When Caine confided he was in love again, this time with a girl who reciprocated his feelings, Jackson expressed surprise. Caine had disclaimed any suggestion he might some day fall in love again and want to marry. Jackson had always firmly believed 'your *books* would be your bride'. W.W. Jackson never returned to Liverpool, dying in West Africa in 1879.

1874 was an important year for Caine in several ways. In May he turned 21. He told Tirebuck he felt 'quite *Ancient*'. Tirebuck told him he was antique! George Rose wished him a happy birthday in similarly flippant terms and scolded him for being a 'discontented fellow'. He had come of age and among his presents was a letter from his publishers '& still you are not happy!'

This reference to Caine's publishers is puzzling as he brought out no book at this time. It could refer to one of the numerous pamphlets he published, mostly the texts of his lectures. He did, however, found a new magazine. It appeared on 1 July, 1874, and was a more professional publication. He called it the *Rambler* after the periodical Samuel Johnson issued between 1749 and 1752. It was to be a similar compendium of articles, profiles, criticism, etc. Like Johnson, he wrote almost all of it himself. He was so busy with it that he neglected his work for the other papers. He had told none of his friends what he was about. Tirebuck, visiting relatives in Aberystwyth, wrote in astonishment that Caine should have entered on such an enterprise. It did not survive long.

However, the event of 1874 which without doubt had the most importance for Caine was his first meeting with Henry Irving. In the spring of that year Irving was on a provincial tour with Colonel Bateman's company from London's Lyceum Theatre. One of the plays being tried out on this tour was a new production of *Hamlet*, with Irving in the title role and Ellen Terry as Ophelia. Bateman had been reluctant to yield to Irving's pleas for a Lyceum production and had been mean with the money for it. The necessarily simple sets and costumes did not detract from Irving's electrifying new reading of the part. Instead of the elaborate quasi-Elizabethan costumes favoured by Shakespearian actors of his day Irving designed for himself a plain black doublet and hose while Ellen Terry's dress was equally simple.

Irving, who had first played the part in the provinces back in 1862, had refined his performance to great artistic effect, though many playgoers, used to the artificial, declamatory style of his contemporaries, did not know what to make of it. Caine, sent to review it, immediately grasped what Irving was about and was stunned by it. He wrote a lyrical notice and saw every performance while Irving was in town. He haunted the theatre and scraped acquaintance with the company's manager, Henry Loveday.

When Loveday first joined Irving he was inexperienced and unqualified for the job. The two met when he was the first violin in the orchestra at the Edinburgh theatre where Irving played several seasons as an unknown 'walking gentleman' taking occasional juvenile leads. Irving was always loyal to his friends and tended to engage people because they were friends rather than because they were qualified for the job in hand. Loveday, well aware of the importance of publicity and favourably impressed with Caine's review, allowed him backstage and introduced him to Irving.

That summer, as he planned his magazine, Caine cast around for a famous name to help launch it. Still powerfully influenced by Irving he wrote to the actor at the Lyceum asking for a photograph to illustrate an article, 'Irving's Influence on the Theatre of his Day'. Irving replied with a friendly letter dated 16 October, 1874. He did more than that. He had persuaded the reluctant Bateman to open the new season at the Lyceum with *Hamlet*. Now he told him Tom Hall Caine was a respected critic in Liverpool whose work regularly appeared in the papers there, which it did.

A fortnight later, on 31 October, 1874, it was as the accredited critic of the Liverpool *Town Crier* that Caine attended Irving's first London performance as Hamlet. His review was thought by many to be so good and so important that it was reprinted as a broadsheet pamphlet. It was widely circulated, one suspects not least by Irving himself. It was a considerable piece of work for a freelance journalist of just 21, even though he had been writing and lecturing in Liverpool for two years. It was not only remarkable for the critic's youth: it was remarkable as the work of a lad who had left elementary school at fourteen. In later years he referred to himself as an autodidact, which is partly true.

The critique is enthusiastic and favourable throughout. The final paragraph gives the flavour of it:

> We will not say that Mr Irving is the Betterton, Garrick, or Kemble of his age. In consideration of this performance we claim for him a position altogether distinct and unborrowed. Mr Irving will, we judge, be the leader of a school of actors now eagerly enlisting themselves under his name. The object will be— the triumph of *mental* over *physical* histrionic art.

He lectured in Liverpool on Irving's Hamlet and this also became a pamphlet. He wrote articles on Irving and Shakespeare which he offered to the leading national papers and magazines. Mostly they were rejected and his own magazine failed but nonetheless Hommy Beg was on his way.

What was he like, this up and coming young journalist?

In his early twenties he was a passionate intellectual, hungry for knowledge, experience and fame. He grabbed at life with both hands and sometimes he grabbed unwisely, bringing pain and embarrassment, and occasionally financial loss, on his own head. However, experience all is of use, as his near contemporary Ernest Dowson wrote, and use he made of it, eventually transmuting it into his romantic novels.

To look at, he was short—only five feet three inches tall, four at the most. Like many small men he compensated for his stature by snappy, even dramatic, dressing. At 20 he bought himself a pair of shepherd's plaid trousers for 16/4d, a lot of money for those days. When he became rich and famous his trademark was a 'wideawake' hat in soft felt, wide brimmed, high crowned, in white or pale grey in the 1890s, black thereafter. He wore tweed knickerbocker suits—a gift to cartoonists—in the country. For town he favoured smartly tailored suits with striking waistcoats and a loosely tied artist's cravat, all topped off in inclement weather by a swirling black cloak.

Caine's dark red beard and lighter, red-gold hair were fine and rather thin. With his high forehead there was a slight resemblance to the Stratford bust of Shakespeare. He was very proud of this, trimming his beard to enhance the likeness. If people did not remark on it he was apt to point it out. It became an obsession. As an old man he travelled home by boat from a holiday in the South of France with his wife and granddaughter. As soon as they were on board he summoned the ship's barber to trim his beard. The man took too much off, destroying the famous likeness. 'And do you know,' his granddaughter recalled in amusement long after he was dead, 'he wouldn't come out of his cabin for the whole voyage, about five days, until it had grown again.'

The most striking feature of his appearance, however, and the one that people who met him recalled most readily, was the intense, hypnotic stare of his dark brown, slightly protuberant eyes. It shows up in many of the photographs of him taken throughout his life as he chose always to gaze directly at the camera if he knew he was being photographed. It was only in old age that his look became more gentle. For such a small man he had a surprisingly deep and musical speaking voice which he deployed to excellent effect as a lecturer and in addressing meetings. It was often said the stage lost a fine actor when he decided on a literary career but his lack of height would have been against him. No leading lady likes to tower over her leading man though he could have made a good character actor. Not that he would have settled for anything less than the lead. He occasionally took part in special copyright performances of his plays. They were not costumed and were played simply with drapes, the cast often carrying their scripts. Only once did he appear in a proper public production of one of his plays and then for only two performances.

The state of his health was Caine's constant preoccupation. By the time he reached his majority he was thoroughly psychoneurotic. The devastating anxiety attacks to which he was prone all his life, his 'nervous collapses', had already manifested themselves. Over the years he often complained of 'neuralgia' on one side of his head and face. Tension headaches, perhaps, but anyone who suffers from migraine will recognise his descriptions of his sometimes bizarre symptoms. 'If my attack was very serious it was at least short,' he wrote of one such. 'An hour of blinding dizziness with partial loss of sight—a sort of brain and heart storm—and then heart and brain were well again. It was a heart and brain storm to which all literary men and especially all creative writers are subject.'

William Tirebuck, often anxious about his friend, tried to jolly him out of his preoccupation with his health. In a note written in 1875 he said, 'I trust you are as perfectly well as it is consistent for the body of THHC to be.' This obsession with his health led to Caine becoming involved with a strange character often known as the American Doctor, Francis Tumblety, MD, though in America he was called the Indian Herb Doctor as he claimed to have his knowledge of herbs from the Indians. He travelled all over Europe, arriving in Liverpool in 1874. He advertised his services in the local papers. One of the patients he attracted was Caine.

Born in 1833, Tumblety's father was Irish and he was the youngest of eleven children. He disappeared at the age of 17 and when he returned to the family home in Rochester, New York, around 1860 it was as 'a great physician' and apparently wealthy, having practised medicine in Canada. There is some doubt as to whether he was entitled to the letters MD he always put after his name. In fact he was a herbalist, making a lot of money, frequently by dubious means. He quickly earned the undying enmity of the medical profession by publicly opposing the conventional medicine of his day. He claimed that blistering someone suffering from inflammation could only be harmful in that it would add further inflammation to what was already there. Likewise he refused to accept the practice of bleeding a feverish patient, saying that removing a teaspoon of water from a boiling kettle would not stop it boiling, neither would removing a measure of boiling blood help a patient. He used herbs to reduce fever, seemingly with success.

A Washington newspaper of 15 December, 1862, said,

> The Doctor, who, by the way, is a very handsome man, is rather eccentric and odd in his manner, appearing at times on the streets dressed as an English sportsman, with tremendous spurs fastened to his boots and accompanied by a pair of greyhounds lashed together. His skill as a physician, however, is undoubted, his practice in Washington being very extensive and among the higher classes of society.

It ends with a glowing testimonial to his skill as a physician by Thos N. Gray MD who also says, 'I have always found him to be a gentleman, honourable and upright in all his transactions.' This was not the experience of others who encountered him.

Unless the many fulsome testimonials from grateful patients were all forged, and some of them certainly were, he was a good physician who cured people of long-standing complaints. He inveighed against 'the use of metals such as mercury and arsenic' in medicine and could have saved some of his patients from slow poisoning. He also had 'a horror of cutting', referring to surgeons as butchers. As this was before the discoveries of Pasteur or the development of modern anaesthetics he was possibly justified. He prescribed only herbal treatments which he usually made up himself.

In Liverpool he soon gathered a coterie of young men around him and was generally thought to be homosexual. An American lawyer, William P. Burr, who knew Tumblety, said some years later, 'once he had a young man under his control he seemed to be able to do anything with the victim'. When he was about 20 he had married a woman ten years older than himself, only to discover she was a prostitute. This turned him violently against all women and prostitutes in particular.

Caine was attractive to women and attracted by them. Among his friends in 1874 he was supposed to be having a long-running affair with an actress variously referred to as 'Miss Doloro', 'Miss Delaro' and 'Dolores'. (Will Pierce described her as 'the cheap-jewellery and wash-leather-looking girl'.) Caine's friends were worried about this. Tirebuck tried to warn him off while in an undated note Pierce told him that every time he saw 'Delaro' she was with 'a big strong fellow, capable of thrashing 3 or 4 of THHC's!!' In August of 1875 another friend whose signature is illegible sent him the words of a smutty and explicit music hall song and concludes, 'This brings me to the widow; I was glad to hear of your success—yet who could withstand such a power!'

At the same time Caine was attractive to men. There was a strong homoerotic subculture in late Victorian England and many intellectuals and artists were part of it. There was nothing unique about Oscar Wilde except his talent and possibly having a titled lover. In the slang of the day 'Are you earnest?' was the password to what would now be called the gay community, which puts an intriguing *double entendre* into the title of Wilde's most famous play. There is nothing surprising in a sensitive, artistic and attractive young man like Caine being involved in strong male friendships with a homoerotic tinge.

By the beginning of 1875 the American Doctor had made Liverpool too hot to hold him and he went to London. The Liverpool papers attacked him and he replied vigorously. He used Caine to write a pamphlet in his defence and tried to involve him in various odd schemes, some of them very odd indeed. Caine went to stay with him in London several times. In one letter Tumblety made the strange remark, 'You have proved yourself feminine and I feel under a great obligation and hope some time to be able to make some recompense.' Caine did not always accept Tumblety's repeated invitations to visit. On 29 March, 1875, he wrote that he wished Caine was with him for the holiday. He had been to the Crystal Palace, Sanger's Circus and the Cremorne Gardens, the last being 'exceedingly gay'. He thought the Bank Holiday was a great institution. 'The Carnivals at Rome are nothing compared with it, you have missed a rare treat.' He was thinking of starting a business in London manufacturing 'better pills than Holloway's'. He would give away £10 worth of them free, which would create a sensation and break the hold on the market of existing manufacturers. To do this he must have a partner who could share the profits—and presumably the costs. It would be a 'fine speculation' because 'there is no place in the world like England for good pills. The English people all indulge in eating late suppers which produces costiveness and they must have cathartic pills.' Caine should discuss selling the pills with the more prominent chemists in Liverpool. Tumblety would send funds as the money came in. That is, Caine was to bankroll the project.

He went down to London again briefly. The trip, he told friends on his return, had been 'arduous'. It was after this visit that references are first made in Tumblety's letters to Caine going to America with him. He promised to introduce him to some of the leading newspaper people there. He was sure Caine would find plenty of well paid work. 'You are an ambitious enterprising journalist of the first water, and your genius and talent will be appreciated in America... I have...shown your letters to literary gentlemen of your own profession and you are an ornament to it. The newspaper people here want to see you.' Which may or may not have been true. What is fact is that Tumblety wanted Caine with him and used every lure he could think of to get him there. As Caine continued to pay him only fleeting visits and still refused to make any firm decision about going to America he became more open in his blandishments.

'I do wish to see you so much and hope you will pay another visit *soon*,' he wrote in April, 1875. He had told Caine repeatedly to leave Liverpool and go with him. He could guarantee that Caine would make more money if he did. 'If you mean to come with me come now if you like. I have means plenty and if you come with me you shall have everything you want... It amused me very much to read your long letter, how you can delve into the details of anything is a caution.'

Letters were succeeded by telegrams: 'Come here tomorrow evening. I must see you.' Another, signed W.J. Morgan which is almost certainly one of the aliases Tumblety used, reads, 'Dear boy wire at once...wire forty wire wire wire wire wire wire.' A note a few days previously had said, 'Your nervous system is in a most disordered state', which it doubtless was given the Doctor's constant demands for money and his presence.

Tumblety's sister, Bridget, was married to a man named Brady and lived in Widnes, not far from Liverpool. Brady wrote to tell Caine he had not heard from 'the Doctor' for 15 days. He had been to London to look for him but on enquiring at his lodgings 'found he had gone, I know not where. If I can find him I will let you know.'

Tumblety surfaced again on 14 May. Though he had not written for so long he had been thinking about Caine all the time. 'The ultimate friendship which has subsisted between us for so long a period has prompted me to feel lively interest in all that concerns your welfare and happiness.' He wrote from various London addresses and on 4 August he was at the Midland Hotel, Birmingham, writing in a very different vein:

> Dear Caine, Don't trifle with my patience any longer. Send me two pounds to the above address no more nor no less a paltry amount than two pounds and our friendly correspondence shall go on, independent of the little financial matters. Nobody else knows anything about it, there is no fraud being committed on you as I am not in the habit of telling people my private affairs. I got your letter forwarded this morning and felt a little surprised at finding an excuse in it instead of two pounds. I am stopping here for 3 or 4 days don't fail to send a p.o. [postal order].

Though Caine must surely have seen through him by now he evidently sent the money as on the 10th Tumblety wrote thanking him and saying he had really needed it. He had invested what money he had and 'could not get a farthing out of it. I will do you a better favour than this before long. Yours affectionately, FT.'

At the end of August he wrote from London to say he had been called back to New York. Caine must answer his note and send it to the National Hotel, Courtland Street, New York. 'If you have concluded to go to the USA I hope it will not be long before you take your departure... I have just this moment got a ticket & will sail at 10 o'clock tomorrow morning on the *Greece*.' He had repaid the £2 but how much more Caine lost one can only guess.

Tumblety wrote twice from New York and then, after a gap of nearly three months, from San Francisco. Acknowledging a letter from Caine he said,

> It gives me infinite pleasure to hear from you and I should dearly love to see your sweet face and spend an entire night in your company. I feel such melancholy when I read your amiable letter and it brings back the pleasing reminiscences of the past and although eight thousand miles now separate us it only stimulates the affection I have for you.

On 31 March, 1876, he wrote from St Louis, still saying he hoped Caine would join him soon. This is the last letter from the American Doctor. Pinned to it is an undated cutting with no masthead but evidently from an English newspaper. It merely says that Tumblety is in prison in America. It does not specify the charge against him. Caine had had a lucky escape. He was attracted by the idea of America but he was canny enough to refuse the Doctor's invitation and strong enough in character to resist his blandishments. He was also sufficiently loyal to his family and concerned about them to stay where he was. There is no evidence that he had anything to do with Tumblety again after 1876. Tumblety died a wealthy man in St Louis in 1903.

There is a footnote to this story. Tumblety paid a number of further visits to England and was there twelve years later, in 1888. He stayed in

The Kidnapping of Dr Tumblety.

various lodgings in the East End of London at the time of the Jack the Ripper murders. It has recently come to light that he was the prime suspect. He was arrested on suspicion but the police did not have enough evidence to charge him. Forensic science barely existed—it was not even possible to prove that bloodstains on his clothing were human, let alone that they came from a particular person. He was charged instead with 'unnatural acts' under a new law of 1885 and released on bail, which had been set at what the police thought was an impossibly high figure, $1500, but they miscalculated. He was a rich man. He cabled his bank in America and the money arrived within days. He broke his bail, escaped to France and from there took ship for America, travelling as 'Frank Townsend', an alias he had used before. Several British detectives, including a top man from Scotland Yard, went to America, so sure were they that he was the Ripper, but he had fled his lodgings in New York two days after landing there, in spite of being under surveillance by the New York Police. Scotland Yard still had no hard evidence to allow them to charge him with the Ripper murders even though circumstantial evidence, including his grisly collection of human wombs, was overwhelming. The fact that Scotland Yard had Tumblety under arrest and he had escaped was thought so disgraceful it was hushed up and it has only recently come to light.

CHAPTER THREE

By the end of 1875 John James's health was making his parents anxious—he had a persistent cough and occasionally spat blood. The doctor suggested a sea voyage. His employers, the Pacific Steam Navigation Company, were sympathetic and gave him a sea-going job. He sailed in RMS *Polosi* for South America early in January, 1876, writing home regularly in a flowing copperplate hand. Letters reached his parents from a number of ports of call, including Bordeaux, Bahia in Brazil, and Sandy Point in the Straits of Magellan. He complained of prickly heat in the tropics and said sadly he had not lost his cough yet.

He was back in Liverpool by early summer and returned to his job as a clerk in the company's office but was frequently off work. Only his brother Tom, who shared his room, knew how often he woke during the night drenched in sweat and coughing his heart out.

Nominally Caine was still working for Bromley & Son though he was writing so much and had such a busy social life one wonders how much actual work he did for them. He was the centre of a lively group, most of whom had been at school together. There were occasional rows and sometimes they criticised him but they remained friends. Caine was self-centred with an air of intellectual superiority that was often infuriating but he was also a warm and vibrant personality who was forgiven much by those who were close to him. The friends all admired his work and were convinced that one day he would be a great man, an opinion he shared.

He continued to write for the local papers. Journalists then often used a pseudonym—or cognomen as they termed it. Caine wrote as 'Julian', an odd choice for someone with a strong Christian faith: Julian was a fourth-century Roman Emperor who renounced Christianity and declared himself a pagan—hence his nickname Julian the Apostate. Caine may have been thinking of the fourteenth-century English mystic, Julian of Norwich, unaware that this Julian was a woman. Or did he know perfectly well?

At the beginning of March, 1876, Tirebuck was lured away from the Wainwright papers to the *Liverpool Mail*, where he was to be a sub-editor. It was recognition of his solid talent and his next move was to the prestigious *Yorkshire Post*, where he remained until giving up journalism to concentrate on novel writing. His novels, of which the most successful was *Miss Grace of All Souls*, are similar in many ways to Caine's but show a lighter touch, the sense of humour his friend's lacked.

There was a passionate tinge to Tirebuck's friendship with Caine. He was a little younger and at first greatly in awe of him. He was shy and retiring and said he hated 'street acquaintances' but he could stick up doggedly for what he believed in against all comers. Caine was a frequent visitor to his home at 320 Park Road. Apart from his elder sister Maggie, he had two other sisters, Bessie and Kate, and at least two brothers. They were a friendly, hospitable lot who kept open house and Caine was always welcome there. His mother told Tirebuck that she was more fond of Caine than any of his other friends. Long after William Tirebuck's death he remained friendly with the family.

In January, 1876, Tirebuck published a pamphlet. He sent a proof copy to Caine asking if he approved of it. It was addressed to 'My dear one, THHC', and with it was a note, 'What would you say to a new poet? Here are a few lines for which I hold you responsible. Some of them stick in my throat when I give them utterance, so perhaps you can apply a little of the oil of grace to ease the passage.' He would call on Caine the following evening for his verdict. On the back was a dire poem which began:

> I've really a star of my own in the sky
> And nightly it greets me with laughterly eye.

It is terrible doggerel which reads like a love letter. He said he had written to Caine three times on that one day. On other occasions he writes with considerable wit and humour and a pleasingly deft handling of language which makes the poem seem a complete aberration.

He confessed that half the time he was too timid to call on Caine in the way that Caine dropped in at Park Road at all hours. When he plucked up courage, however, he 'felt much the better fellow for it'. Caine's family were as welcoming to him as his own was to Caine, accepting him as their Tom's closest and dearest friend. In a rueful note after one visit to South Chester Street Tirebuck admitted that he must make an effort to get over his fear of treading on people's corns, as he felt so stupid when he found there had been no corns to tread on.

For some time Caine had been working on a long narrative poem, *Geraldine*. He submitted it to Wainwright and it appeared in March of 1876. No entire copy of it has come to light but it was a completion of Coleridge's *Christabel*, something which several other people had attempted. Ever since he had stumbled on his poetry as a schoolboy Coleridge had been a passion with Caine and the unfinished story of Christabel haunted him.

It was Coleridge's conception of poetry which appealed to him and chimed with his own. An additional appeal was the setting of *Christabel* in his beloved Lake District—the poem was begun in Nether Stowey and completed, as far as it went, in Keswick. Caine knew Keswick well and the Lakeland fells like the back of his hand. He often escaped there, catching the train to Windermere and walking on from Bowness. Coleridge introduced the questions of guilt, evil and redemption, which he had been discussing with Wordsworth, into his poetry. These questions were to absorb Caine and influence his own writing for the whole of his life.

Like many other people in the 1870s and 1880s Caine was interested in the supernatural, or paranormal. Spiritualism attracted him and he attended occasional séances but he was not a devotee and retained a certain amount of healthy scepticism. The idea of demonic possession and the brooding atmosphere of evil surrounding *Geraldine* which Coleridge created fascinated him. From the lines which correspondents quoted from Caine's poem there seems to be much harping on death and philosophising over whether it means annihilation or not. 'Life led captive to the shade of Death' is a line much commended, as is 'Grief-stricken yet not hopeless Clarimonde'. One correspondent said he did not recollect ever having read 'such a splendidly chaste description of perfect womanhood as that of Geraldine herself', adding a little oddly that the whole poem was in keeping with the spirit of Greek mythology.

Reaction to the poem when it appeared in print was not all on these lines. Caine was variously charged with obscenity and obscurity. The loyal Tirebuck refuted these accusations but was intellectually too honest to accept the work uncritically. He told Caine that no man could deny there were 'eccentricities, (*perhaps* affectations) of expression' in the poem which might get in the way of its appreciation by some readers, but 'I dread the consequences to your own personal feelings, and indeed, to the work if you pander to a popular vein'. For him one of the joys of poetical language was felt when the mind was kept alert for hidden meanings; there was, he felt, 'a delight in *discovering*'. He thought he saw Caine's religious ideas behind what he had written.

'The subject is a tough one and the teeth of my mind have not yet penetrated it enough to arrive at a definite conclusion,' he continued. He objected to a symbolic God and an objective God, delighting instead in the thought of an all-pervading spirit similar to the Holy Ghost of the Christian faith, perhaps because the idea of an 'all-pervading un-personal God or spirit binds us to the old faith; agrees with evolution; and what is important, with modern spiritualism in the higher sense. This modern spiritualism will, I think, in time have much to do with the character of your religion.' A perspicacious remark. There were paeans of praise from several other friends but from quoted passages the poem seems to have been morbid and sentimental.

It was not only Caine's poetry which the group discussed. They read poems to each other and talked over what they had heard and read much as a group of young people today might discuss pop music and television. Scott, Tennyson, Swinburne, William Morris and Wilfred Scawen Blunt were among their favourites, as well as many minor poets who have been forgotten now. They wrote their own poetry, too. An epidemic of versifying spread among them like 'flu. Instead of coughing and sneezing they wrote poems and sent them to each other.

Will Pierce was another close friend, as the letters that flowed between them when he was away at a theological college show. Pierce and Tirebuck were well aware of the Tumblety affair. Pierce, indeed, seems to have been a little jealous. He wrote wistfully from Caernarvon in April, 1875, at the height of Tumblety's influence, 'You will be at Printing House Square [the offices of *The Times*] soon and I shall lose you altogether.' He depended greatly on Caine. He often sent him skeleton notes of sermons he proposed to preach, asking for help with them, even sometimes asking Caine to write them for him. On one subject they failed to agree: temperance. Caine had joined the movement and let no opportunity slip to promote it. He was not 'teetotal' himself but was always an abstemious man. In later life he would have a brandy and soda before lunch and another in the evening but nothing else. Pierce objected to sermons on temperance and said he would never make them himself. Caine, on the other hand, gave public lectures on the subject.

Will Pierce's letters are affectionate in tone, beginning 'My dear Boy' although they were the same age, and often asking Caine to join him in Wales, where he was studying for the ministry. They discussed theological matters. At one point Pierce was puzzled how Caine could believe in one part of the Christian faith and yet totally reject others. 'You say that you do not believe in the religion that attributes to the very person of Christ a more Godlike sanctity than belongs to the Father. I did not know that that was part of any belief.' Pierce's letters were sometimes despondent and morbid in tone. He referred frequently to 'the load of sin that oppresses us', which of course struck a chord with Caine who all his life was consumed by guilt, although to our way of thinking he had little to feel guilty about. Guilt can be a corrosive and destructive emotion.

Caine was prone to fits of depression. In one of them he wrote to Pierce despairingly. Pierce replied with a fourteen-page screed saying he could understand Caine's 'glooms' because he had suffered from them all his life. He was worried by Caine's interest in spiritualism. Pierce said he could not believe in communication with spirits. There was, he thought, 'an imponderable truth at the bottom of all this nonsense', but his attitude to Mesmerism and Spiritualism was one of curiosity mixed with dread. He warned Caine to be careful. What he hated was 'addle-pated fools' pretending they had found 'the keystone of spirit land. It's a scandal on commonsense and on the memory of dear ones.'

These letters are paralleled by ones from Tirebuck who also had Welsh connections. Staying on a farm near Aberystwyth in the summer of 1875 he gave a lyrical description of the Welsh countryside. He wished Caine were with him to stroll down wooded lanes at dusk. He need not say more as he knew Caine would understand to a nicety the attractions of a summer evening in the heart of the country. 'I only want you to understand that I wish you were here.' In Liverpool he and Caine went to hear Pierce preach on a number of occasions and declared themselves immensely proud of him.

In March, 1876, Tirebuck had a new girlfriend, 'a young but vigorous female', as he described her to Caine. She was a friend of his sister Maggie and her name was Marie Lange. Her father, a German immigrant named Frederick Lange, was a furrier. Marie worked in the office and also made up small items. She made Tirebuck a sealskin tobacco pouch which delighted him with its 'foretaste of future felicity with the pretty hands that made it'. When Caine called casually at the house one evening in April Tirebuck introduced her. This was a mistake. Within a short space of time she had transferred her affections and Caine was in love with her. For a while they tried to keep it to themselves but a friend saw them on one of their secret assignations and gave the game away. There was nothing for it but to confess to his friend. Caine went round to Park Road one evening and getting William on his own told him what had happened.

Tirebuck seems to have taken it philosophically and surrendered Marie without argument. After Caine had gone Tirebuck wrote him a letter.

> I really cannot explain to myself <u>why</u> I turn to my desk on the first floor and scratch this quill until it blotches instead of turning to my bed on the second floor. I have nothing special to write about. I saw you not many minutes ago, and I have a prospect of seeing you tomorrow evening, but I have a species of devil within me which says as plain as the internals ever did say—<u>write</u>! and write I do. I am about as inclined for sleep as a starving tiger.

Marie was now

> 'a lost jewel—a <u>stolen</u> one in short, and glittering with all its powers of brilliance in the bosom of my friend. The jewel & the friend had better be aware, as the desperate side of my character has not yet been seen... Even a 21 ton Woolwich gun will by no means express my sentiments if I am once roused upon a matter of the heart... I fear, your heart has taken your brains by storm

and the furrier trade will supersede the muses. Pray be careful—your brothers
will surely sufficiently perpetuate the name of Caine.

Throughout May of that year the love affair with Marie Lange developed although Caine was spending a great deal of time with Johnny, newly returned from sea. At the end of the month Caine went off to the Isle of Man for a short holiday, taking Tirebuck with him.

It was a time of emotional turmoil. On 22 June, back in Liverpool, Tirebuck wrote another long, intense letter to Caine, beginning,

> I have been upstairs twice…but in spite of myself and the inviting murmurs and snores of a brother or two I find myself here at my desk, & writing to you—writing with feelings I never once thought I would experience, although, at odd times, I have dreaded them and passionately choked them at their first rising.

Now he delighted in them and felt more deeply attached to Caine than ever before. 'My heart has nothing short of affection for you.' He had always been convinced that 'intellectuality' alone would keep them together, 'apart from other attractions', but now he feared he might be losing Caine's good opinion of him because of the changed nature of their relationship. He was terrified of losing Caine's respect and worse still, his friendship. He ended, 'It is the fear of your ceasing to see attraction in me beyond that of the heart, which plagues me and makes me feel desperate. I remember no union of my life which has been as delightful as the union with you.'

There were many alterations and heavy underlinings in this letter which scored the paper, evidence of what it cost Tirebuck to write it. Caine replied within a couple of days and whatever he wrote seems to have come as a relief, as on 24 June Tirebuck wrote to say he was grateful for his answer to 'that no doubt extraordinary communication', which had given him a great deal of misery since the hour he wrote it but now he was 'at peace'.

After this there was much discussion about 'a rural cott' to be rented 'in the salubrious air of Knotty Ash'. It was not for the marriage to her adored Tom which Marie seemed to be taking for granted, but for him to share with Tirebuck. However, these plans fell through, both young men remained living with their families and Tirebuck acquired a new girlfriend. He was wary of introducing her to Caine whom he described as 'a reckless romancer with a bewitching twinkle in those big eyes of his'. He had sad experience of what could happen if he introduced his young lady friends to Caine so he was determined Caine should 'not have half a wink at my fair one from London'. A few days later, however, he decided to take a serious risk. There was to be an informal party that night at the Tirebuck home at which Miss Steele from London would be present and Maggie had invited Marie. 'Now if you can determine that an invitation extended to you will not result in pistols and broad swords a week hence, know by these presents that you may come.' In the envelope with this light-hearted note was a small pressed rosebud.

Throughout July and August notes, love letters and poems (some her own) poured from Marie to 'My dearest and own Tom', or 'My darling'. She soon encountered Tom's black dog, writing on 15 July that she would wait in for him if he promised to come in a good humour, not in one of his fits of despondency.

Occasionally she complained that he had 'stood her up', though when he did it was usually because one of the papers had sent him to review a play or art exhibition at short notice or else needed a book reviewed urgently. Or else he was ill again. One night in August she was expecting him but it was just as well he did not come as she was 'almost frantic with toothache'. She told him she finally fixed it with a mixture of laudanum (an alcoholic tincture of opium) and gin. She had 'a lovely sleep' and felt much better. She was lucky to wake up.

Caine felt smothered by Marie's possessiveness. He was still emotionally immature and unwilling to commit himself to marriage, to her or to anyone else. When Frederick Lange offered to take him into his business he began to feel under intolerable pressure. Reacting in his usual way, he flitted. After giving a lecture on 5 September he took the train to Windermere. He had told Marie where he was going and left an address in Bowness. Evidently he ran short of money while he was there and applied to his mother as on 16 September she sent him a postal order for £1. It was enclosed in a note from Willie asking when he was coming back. Caine had not told Tirebuck. When he found out he had gone to Bowness, Rydal, Grasmere and 'that Caine-lauded place, Derwentwater' without asking him to go along too he was upset. Marie wrote of how she longed to have him home again. She seems by this time to have had some inkling of Caine's ambiguous sexuality because she added an anxious postscript: 'Are you alone or have you some male friend with you?' Her friends were anxious, too. Next day she wrote again saying she had had a difficult afternoon with Maggie Tirebuck and her friend, Mrs Blennerhasset—'another of those disputes, relative to you and me'.

They were right to be concerned. Caine had gone to see 'Poet' Close. John Close was a butcher's son and was brought up to be a butcher but he was convinced it was his destiny to be a poet. He was inordinately vain and at the time Caine knew him used letterheads and cards headed 'Poet Close'. He had published his first book at the age of 16. He made a profit of £30 on his second and used the money to visit London, selling his books and getting orders for his *Chronicles of Westmorland* which finally appeared in 1860. He had set up as a printer in Kirkby Stephen in 1846 and produced several volumes of prose and verse. He was involved in a libel action and tried at Liverpool. The verdict went against him and he was fined heavily.

He was an odd figure, a bit disreputable and wildly eccentric. One is reminded in some ways of Tumblety. Most people believed Close to be homosexual. In the 1870s he was running a bookstall at Bowness, where Caine first encountered him. He sold the *Rambler* as long as it lasted, Caine sending parcels of copies up to him by train. He published an annual Christmas book, usually dedicated to some Lakeland benefactor of his. Anyone who failed to appreciate him and his work was liable to be viciously attacked and lampooned. Supporters, on the other hand, were monstrously eulogised. Caine was never averse to publicity and courted him. He spent at least one night of his holiday with him and told Tirebuck, who had met Close. He replied, 'A night with the poet? Bless me! What a readable heading for a chapter. The poet had you on view, had he, as Julian the Great Unknown? Pray what next?' Well might he ask.

From Bowness Caine took the steamer to the head of Windermere and walked on to Grasmere, where he spent the night. Next day he walked over Dunmail Raise to Keswick where he called on a close friend, Edwin Jackson, a young man of his own age and apparently no relation to W.W. From Keswick he caught the train home via Penrith.

As the winter drew in Johnny's health worsened. Increasingly concerned for his brother, Caine often could not be bothered with Marie. Plaintive notes kept arriving, one calling him 'an unkind fellow'. She had been desperately disappointed on arriving home from work to find a note 'instead of my heart's desire'. Either she was not aware of all his commitments or chose to think them unimportant as she continued to plead for his presence or upbraid him for letting her down when he had promised to see her.

At the beginning of October Irving was back in town. 'How about seeing Irving's Hamlet?' asked Tirebuck, 'I would like to witness his first reception. Have been miserable these few days.' The two friends went together, leaving Marie to pine. On 12 October they were at the theatre again to see the last performance. Caine was delighted to renew acquaintance with the famous actor and introduce Tirebuck to him. It was about this time that what was headlined in the press as 'The Irving-Aveling Mystery' blew up. Edward Aveling was born in 1849 in north London. He was the son of a Nonconformist minister and later became notorious, first as Annie Besant's lover and then for 'living in sin' with Eleanor Marx. He was a brilliant man who preyed on women. At 23 he had married a girl, Bell Frank, with a dowry of £1000. Even his brother Frederick assured everyone he had married Bell for her money. When he had run through it he left her. He had a passion for the theatre and would have liked to be an actor but he became a scientist instead. He tried to join the Savage Club. In his application he claimed to be a brother of Henry Irving. The Club wrote to Irving asking if this was true. Irving said it was totally false and Aveling was refused membership.

It might have rested there had Aveling's father not become involved. Incensed that his name should be linked with an actor of all people, he used an address to the Bradford Conference of the Congregational Union to declare he was not Henry Irving's father, the first time his son's claim had been made public. He said darkly that he had had a 'private interview' with the actor though he did not say where or when. He conceded he had 'learned to esteem him as an accomplished gentleman' but conveyed he was a stranger to Irving and had no knowledge of the eminent actor's career or public persona. He went on from there to thunder against the theatre and warn that a society which tolerated it was 'in danger of degenerating'.

For several months the Liverpool journalist James Ashworth Noble had been preparing to launch a new Liberal newspaper, the *Argus*, and he recruited Caine to write for it as a freelance. Knowing of his acquaintance with Irving, Noble sent for Caine and asked him to get Irving's side of the story while he was in Liverpool and write a piece for the first number of the new paper, which came out on 21 October. Caine needed no second telling. Irving, who liked and trusted him, was glad to give him the facts and the article was duly written. By the time it appeared Irving and the Lyceum company had moved on to Newcastle. On the 20th he sent Caine a telegram asking for a copy of the paper containing his 'Aveling exposé'.

Caine's article referred to 'the objectionable haze which has seemed to enshroud Mr Irving's antecedents' ever since Dr Aveling's extraordinary diatribe at Bradford. It was true, Caine continued, that Dr Aveling had met Irving—he had been to see him at the Lyceum Theatre after a performance, which naturally Dr Aveling had not attended. This had been 'nothing less than upright and honourable' but it was fair to ask why Dr Aveling had not seen fit to disclose the scene of the meeting. Instead he had launched into an attack on the theatre as 'almost incurably evil'. Did he think, asked Caine, that the Congregational Union or his cloth would be 'sullied by supposed connection with the most renowned actor of modern times?' He gave the facts of Dr Aveling's son's application to the Savage Club. After being blackballed he had written Irving an abject apology and begged him 'not to make the shameful disclosures public'. For his father's sake, Irving had kept quiet about it. He was wounded by Dr Aveling's attack but was used to that sort of thing. 'It is the penalty of success to be too "dreadfully attended"', Caine ended his article. He sent a copy of the paper to Irving and it did him no harm with that gentleman. Nor was his reputation as a journalist damaged. James Noble was pleased.

By New Year a quarrel with Marie was imminent. She evidently did not know it was not just Johnny who was increasingly ill. Devoted as he was to his brother this was worry enough for Caine, but added to it was the fear that he too 'had gone into a consumption'. The tubercle bacillus was discovered in 1882 by Dr Robert Kock and the name tuberculosis given to the disease. Before that no one realised it was infectious or knew what caused it. Inevitably, given that they shared a small bedroom and 'night air' was thought to be bad for 'consumptives', Caine caught it from his brother.

He was poorly at the beginning of January 1877 but recovered enough to pay the visit to Marie she had been craving only to find she was out. On the 10th she wrote a pathetic scrawl, blotched with what looks like tears, desperate at having missed him. She might leave Liverpool for a short time. 'If I go it will be to my benefit. I fear to distress my good Father or would go without one moment's hesitation.' She had a short time yet before she must reply to an invitation she had had and begged Caine to call that night. He did not but wrote to her instead. Her reply was pained: she did not want him to renew his vows of love, 'which I hear have been so false'. But she wanted to tell him how she felt about 'the state of things'. It had only just dawned on her how ill suited they were for each other. 'I forgive you the wrong you have done me & only pray you note your heart, if it be love or fascination for a time, before you trifle with an honest girl again.' She had made him her confidant, trusted him with all her thoughts, and now she begged him to 'keep our concerns secret & not make them public'. The letter was several pages long. How cold he had grown: she hoped she would soon be as cold as he. She ended by quoting, or rather misquoting, several lines from a sonnet by Christina Rossetti and put a postscript, 'but I think that you'll remember me'.

That, one would have thought, would be the end of the affair but within days she was 'Yours as of old'. By the end of the month he was her 'sweet love' again and she was 'both now and ever your loving Marie', but on 24 February she addressed him as 'You unkind love'. He had left her sitting alone on a Saturday night which was the worst night of all. However, he turned up on the Sunday, turned on the charm and she wrote afterwards to say how happy the meeting had made her. For these letters she used tiny pieces of paper neatly folded into very small envelopes with a rosebud embossed on the flap. The interesting thing about this correspondence, apart from the fact that Caine kept it to the end of his life, is that he used many of Marie's phrases in the conversations and letters of his romantic heroines, right up to

Bessie Collister in *The Master of Man*, published in 1921 when he was nearly 70.

Marie was still upbraiding him for not coming to see her into March, although at the time he was too ill to go out. He had been terrified one morning to wake and find his pillow soaked with blood. Anxious letters from both Israel and James Bromley showed their concern. James wrote hoping Caine would soon be free of the pains he complained of. There was no need for the doctor to write to him on the subject as he did not wish Caine to come to work until he was fully recovered. By 11 March it had finally been brought home to Marie how ill Caine was and that he really could not dance attendance on her as she continued to demand. She wrote a contrite note saying she had been 'quite unconscious of the serious state of your health'. Since her last letter she had discovered the true nature of his illness and the danger he had been through. 'Therefore I can fully comprehend how cruel and heartless you think me. You say you have spared me pain. That you have, judging from your letters which gave me to believe of nothing serious.'

Others were under the same impression. The family kept to themselves how dangerously ill the two elder sons were. Even now Marie was not really aware of the situation. On the 14th she was still saying she was waiting patiently until he was well enough to walk as far as her home in Crown Street. Although she felt there was 'little prospect of future happiness' for them she still could not really believe it was all over. Caine must have replied making himself entirely clear as on the 21st she wrote a note saying, 'I'm in great pain but tell me, am I to understand you have at last put me from you for ever & won't see me again?' That was exactly what he had meant.

It was the end of their love affair but they did not lose touch. She was still writing to him in 1879—one note arranged to meet him on her return to Liverpool and thanked him for a book he had sent her. She was teaching at a school in Aylesbury. In February 1880 she wrote that she was looking forward to reading his new book as soon as it was published. A man friend had been sending her presents of books and flowers. 'I believe he would do anything and everything in his power to give me pleasure and yet—and yet—can you explain how it is that I don't adore him? Is love the end and aim of all our lives as I have just been reading? Or is it better to love or to be loved? Answer me these questions if you are able but I must confess I sadly doubt your ability— prodigal as you are.' One wonders what if anything he replied to that. She did not know what would become of her as the school was to close and she must look for another job. She hoped he was still enjoying his 'literary correspondence with the round world and all that therein is'.

Marie returned home at the beginning of March 1880. The last surviving letter from her apologised for failing to meet him as arranged and asked if they could meet on Saturday. 'Please <u>don't</u> write. Will tell you why when we meet. Believe me, <u>dear Tom</u> [underlined twice so heavily it has in part gone through the paper], Yours Marie. PS Excuse scrawl but I am half asleep. I hope you appreciate <u>dear Tom</u>.' That is all. Finis Marie. The impression remains that she genuinely loved him. For his part he retained a real affection for her. This love affair, beginning as it did with Caine taking Marie from Tirebuck, and the abortive one referred to by W.W. Jackson, left an indelible mark on his fiction. Almost all his novels are based on the Eternal Triangle—two men in love with the same girl. It could be argued that the one or two that are not are his most interesting.

If Caine had wanted to marry he could well have married his Marie but he was then still firm in his decision to remain a bachelor. It is difficult to know just what to make of his apparent bisexuality. After the visit to 'Poet' Close there is nothing to indicate any further similar adventures. They could have been mere youthful experimentation. He suppressed the feminine side of his nature and was not at ease with it.

To return to 1877, towards the end of March that year Caine rallied but his brother weakened. Dr Bruce called at the house frequently but there was little he could do. On 2 April 1877, John James Caine died aged 21. His mother cut the buttons from the jacket he wore at sea and sewed them up in a piece of flowered cotton material. Later someone, possibly Lily, labelled the jingling small bundle, 'Buttons from the uniform of John James Caine who was in the Mercantile service, brother of T.H. Hall Caine and William Ralph Hall Caine.' They buried him in Toxteth Cemetery beside his two little sisters.

Johnny's death shattered the family and shocked friends, to whom it came as a surprise. Tirebuck sent Caine his condolences after seeing the notice in the paper, concluding it must have been very sudden. Marie wrote a sad note. She could not tell him how deeply grieved she was to hear the news. 'I had not the ghost of an idea of anything so serious occurring.'

The loss of his brother changed Caine. His genuine grief was accompanied by a terrible sense of guilt, guilt that Johnny was dead and he was alive. He consoled himself by reading Tennyson's *In Memoriam*, written after the sudden death at the age of 23 of the poet's friend Arthur Hallam. In a lecture on the poem, which he gave a year after John James died, he called on his audience to 'observe the pang which early death occasions' and after quoting from the poem added a comment on 'the repose which comes with the thought that the powers of the young dead are not lost but bloom in the higher realms'.

CHAPTER FOUR

Caine was in dread of following his brother and succumbing to tuberculosis. The disease had damaged his lungs and he suffered repeated bouts of bronchitis for the rest of his life. More immediately, he felt the increased responsibility for his family without John James to help. Willie was only 12 years old and it would be some time yet before he could contribute much, while Lily was still a little girl. He looked about for better paid work and applied for the post of Assistant Surveyor to the town of Liverpool when it was advertised a couple of months later. He was called for an interview with the Borough Engineer but did not get the job. This failure made Caine think even harder about his future. He was having considerable local success as a lecturer. It was not without cost to him. He suffered agonies of stage fright for two or three days before each event, but the moment he set foot on stage all his fright left him. As he gathered his notes and surveyed his audience he felt in command and began to enjoy himself. His strong instinct to instruct, combined with his dramatic talent, took over and made him a compelling speaker. If it was to be an informal lecture he would merely make notes and 'trust to the angels for the material of the moment'. If, however, the matter was more serious he wrote it out in full. It was the extempore lectures that affected him most, when he approached the talk not knowing the exact words he would use.

The serious lectures were almost invariably published. Many began as presidential addresses to the Notes & Queries Society and were published by them. Others went to magazines and papers, including the *Builder*, the *Graphic*, the *Architect*, the *British Architect*, the *Manchester Guardian*, the *Birmingham Daily Post*, the *Pall Mall Gazette* and all the Liverpool papers together with a magazine called the *Liverpool Lantern*. He was sensitive to the difference between the spoken and the written language, knowing that what was effective on stage would not necessarily read well, and reworked his lectures carefully before publishing them. Between his lecture fees and what he got for his published work he was earning as much again as James Bromley was paying him. Sensibly he did not give up the day job. Too many people depended on his efforts.

Bromley's employed about a hundred men and Caine held a responsible position. His work, at first that of a builder's draughtsman making working plans, had widened in scope and he now had managerial responsibilities as well, especially after the death of Israel Bromley. If Caine's salary was not as much as he might have earned elsewhere he had a substantial perquisite in the form of frequent short holidays and a relaxed attitude to the amount of sick leave he took. He used this time to write his lectures and complete his journalistic assignments. In addition, his private office at Bromley's gave him peace and space to write in, whereas at home he had neither. James Bromley, who knew perfectly well what he was up to, had become a genuine and valued friend. He admired Caine's writing and was sure he had a future as 'a man of letters'. Among all the people who helped Caine on his way to becoming a best-selling author, James Bromley was not the least important. He never flattered. His quiet support and willingness to let Caine make use of him and his business in the way he did were of vital importance to a young man powered by ambition but unsure of himself.

Thanks to his influential patrons and his own growing reputation he was engaged for a series of public lectures through the winter of 1877–1878 which were all published. He began with one on Irving as Richard III and Macbeth. These performances had aroused in Caine a passion for Shakespeare. He read every book on him he could find and studied the plays intently. In October, 1877, he began a correspondence with Edward Dowden (later Sir Edward) of Trinity College, Dublin. He was a noted Shakespearian scholar and had been appointed Professor of English Literature at Trinity College in 1867, at the early age of 24. In 1875 he published *Shakespere, his Mind and Art*, following it in 1877 with his *Shakespere Primer*. Caine wrote to Dowden sending him a copy of his lecture on Irving's Shakespeare performances and asking for comments and advice, thus initiating the 'literary correspondence with the round world' on which Marie later commented.

Apart from his Shakespeare studies, Dowden was a great enthusiast for the poetry of Walt Whitman. In 1871 he defended the heavily criticised writer of *Leaves of Grass* in a paper delivered to a student debating society in Dublin and later published in the *Westminster Review*, a magazine Caine read regularly and to which he later contributed himself. Dowden insisted Whitman was the poet of democracy who 'never degenerated into anything lewd'. Certainly Whitman was a passionate prophet of democracy and saw all the races of the world as one, but poems in the Children of Adam sequence, for instance, with lines such as:

> Bathing myself, bathing my songs in Sex,
> Offspring of my loins

were too much for Victorian modesty—or prurience. To many young men Whitman's work, especially the *Calamus* group of poems, were poems of homosexual love and feelings they had perhaps felt themselves but suppressed. Caine, who may well have been introduced to *Leaves of Grass* by Dowden, became a passionate admirer of Whitman, though he said little about it. He lacked Dowden's confidence or authority to stand up for Whitman publicly.

His surviving correspondence with Dowden is mainly about Shakespeare and about his own career. He told him he was 'engaged in journalism' and was aggrieved at the treatment he received from some reviewers. 'The London critics have handled my essay with, I think, unwarranted severity... I have not yet read your *Primer* but Mr Furnivall tells me any Shakespere [using Dowden's spelling] student may assimilate much from it.' Frederick James Furnivall, whose name crops up fairly frequently in Caine's correspondence, was a colourful and controversial maverick, a scholar and barrister who was interested in social reform and worked tirelessly for the recognition of English Literature as a subject for university study. In his day Oxford and Cambridge both virtually ignored it. He joined the Christian Socialists (though he later turned agnostic). He founded the New Shakespere (sic) Society which is where Caine encountered him.

Dowden was a busy man and could well have found Caine's approach tiresome for he took several months to reply. Caine wrote again on 2 May, 1878, as soon as he received the letter. He was, he said, at a loss to know how to thank Dowden for his 'most interesting and valuable letter' which he had long ceased to expect. 'I love all letters with a deep and constant affection. Letters are more to me than books.' After thanking Dowden effusively for his 'generous appreciation' of his work, he said that since he first began to write he had been 'blamed and ridiculed on the one hand & praised & flattered on the other with equal vehemence & intensity'. This remained the case for the rest of his career as a writer. Dowden told him 'the peculiarities' of his literary style arose from 'excess of deliberation'. Replying, he said it was now clear to him that it was possible to be 'too self-consciously careful & curious', adding the odd remark that he could now see 'a sentence should be written to be read once...as straight & plain as possible'. If his critics were expected to read every sentence at least twice before they could understand it no wonder they panned him.

He went on in convoluted sentences to say he understood what Dowden meant by his criticism: his style was 'far too vivid & unrestrained by judgement, & the colour & cadence which I love in style I am daily striving to subdue'. Dowden would, he was sure, 'understand something of the pang which it costs me to blot out of my MS a rich word that has charm & magic for my ear and mind in order to insert a plain & common one'. One wonders how much he took this to heart when one reads some of his windier efforts. He ended by asking for advice on how to cope with bad reviews which 'hurt me <u>physically</u>'.

When his friend James Ashworth Noble told him he expected Dowden on a visit, Caine wrote excitedly to Dowden, saying he went to Mr Noble's frequently and hoped to meet him there. In an attempt to explain any possible awkwardness on his own part he said, 'My personal enjoyment of anything beyond the common is always at the caprice of a torturing nervous temperament, which, as I am often conscious, transforms me into something quite foreign to the basis of my nature.' This is a candid acknowledgement of a disabling shyness which often made him appear arrogant, aggressive or overbearing. It could account for his repeated failure to get jobs for which he would appear to have been well qualified. He put people off. His friends told him he was his own worst enemy. Self-consciousness combined with feelings of insecurity and inferiority to make him a prey to 'nerves'.

During 1878 Caine founded a Liverpool Shakespeare Society, with himself as President, and engineered its affiliation to Furnivall's New Shakespere Society in London. Papers written for the parent society would be sent to Liverpool in advance so that they could be read to both groups on the same night. However, it soon became clear that there was not the backing in Liverpool for a Shakespeare Society as such so after only a few months of separate existence it was amalgamated with the successful Notes & Queries Society. The aim of the new joint society was to promote the study of the Bard in Liverpool and interest in his plays and to found a Shakespeare Library, in addition to its original scheme of promoting all forms of art and literature. Caine, of course, was elected President. At the same time he was also deeply involved with the local Ruskin Society.

His lectures brought him to the notice of Lord Houghton—the former Richard Monkton Milnes—and his friend Henry Arthur Bright, the merchant and author. These older men, both distinguished writers and reforming politicians, were favourably disposed towards him. Lord Houghton, who was one of the first people to recognise Swinburne's genius and the author of a book on Keats, was influential in getting Caine further lecture engagements and introduced him to other men who could be useful to him. Houghton, a peerless after-dinner speaker, championed the cause of oppressed nationalities, liberty of conscience and the rights of women, all of which Caine espoused in turn. He was often sent to cover Houghton's speeches for one or other of the Liverpool papers. Houghton's influence can be traced throughout Caine's novels and in his later political activities.

The new Notes & Queries was to be launched at a big meeting in July of 1878, at the Royal Institution in Colquitt Street. When he knew Dowden would be in Liverpool Caine wrote, in his most deferential style, to invite the professor. There were several pages of superfluous verbiage before he came to the point: would Dowden honour them by taking the chair at their next meeting? Dowden accepted and the date was fixed for 1 July. The evening was a great success, with the press reporting the presence of the professor in the chair. Caine spoke on 'The Supernatural in Shakespeare', which proved a controversial subject. The Society's standing was further enhanced when Caine persuaded Irving to visit Liverpool specially to preside at the inaugural meeting of the winter season on 21 September. 'The whole thing was very funny and very interesting, in fact quite a unique thing in its way,' he wrote to Dowden. He was keen to stress his friendship with Mr Irving, who was on his way to Dublin. He had told Caine he hoped to meet Dowden there. Probably he did but he also met Bram Stoker, a meeting which proved to be almost as important for Caine as it was for Stoker.

In August Caine awarded himself a short holiday walking in the Lakes, a holiday which had immense repercussions. As usual he started out from Bowness with a knapsack on his back. He crossed Skelwith Bridge and walked the length of Langdale. From there he made the steep climb up the Stake Pass. As he got onto the tops and set off towards Borrowdale along the shoulder of Stonethwaite Fell a thunderstorm was gathering away to his left over Black Sail and Great Gable. It caught him as he dropped down into Borrowdale at Rosthwaite. He followed the winding River Derwent to the village of Grange and the point where it enters Derwentwater. From there it was only a short step to the Borrowdale Hotel where he planned to stay the night.

He arrived at the front porch dripping wet. As he tried to shake off as much water as possible before entering the hotel an elderly gentleman standing there asked him how far he had come on such a terrible day. When Caine told him the route he had taken he was astonished that someone should have come about thirty miles over the fells in such weather. Reference to a modern map shows his estimate of the distance was about right. That Caine could undertake such a walk only a year after a severe illness and take no harm from exposure to cold and wet shows that basically he was, as his friend Reginald Farrant said some twenty years later, 'as tough as old boots'. This was Farrant's response when Caine said to him, 'I'm very frail, you know. I have to take great care.'

After changing into dry clothes (though one wonders how dry the contents of his knapsack could have been) Caine went down to the lounge to wait for dinner. The other guests were gathered there and to his dismay were having a sing-song round the piano. The elderly gentleman who had spoken to him when he arrived was standing apart in the bay window watching the storm, which was now right overhead. He introduced himself, commenting on the view of the lake. The hotel is remarkably little altered from what it was in 1878 but trees and a hedge have grown up to partially obscure the view Caine and his companion enjoyed.

The elderly gentleman was Philip James Bailey, well known then as the author of *Festus: A Poem*, a lengthy work inspired by Goethe's *Faust*. Though forgotten now Bailey was greatly admired by his contemporaries. A chance remark by Caine, as Castle Crag was illuminated by lightning, that only 'poor Tom' and King Lear could enjoy such a storm, 'except as viewed from the ambush of a comfortable hotel', led to the discovery that both men shared a love and thorough knowledge not only of the Lake country but of literature and the world of books and poetry. They dined together and spent the rest of the evening talking until long after the other guests had gone to bed.

This fresh acquaintance knew nearly every prominent author of the day and was happy to talk at length about them. Bailey had known Dante Gabriel Rossetti well as a young man when he was one of the group of artists who called themselves the Pre-Raphaelite Brotherhood. At that time Rossetti, according to Bailey, had appeared to be 'in deliberate revolt against society, delighting in any opportunity to startle well-ordered persons out of their propriety'. Bailey thought he took a wrong turn when he abandoned poetry for painting, though Rossetti himself said he concentrated on painting because it gave better promise of earning a decent living. Bailey talked about him at length, calling him 'a little Italian'. He gave Caine such a vivid portrait of Rossetti and so enchanted him by reciting some favourite sonnets that Caine determined to find Rossetti's poems and study them. Until that evening he had known almost nothing of Rossetti's poetry although he had seen some of his paintings.

The next morning Caine saw Bailey off on the Buttermere coach. After paying his bill he walked on into Keswick. In his book of 1882, *Recollections of Rossetti*, he says he met Bailey at the Derwentwater Hotel. He was writing in London and under pressure from his publisher to finish the book so got muddled. The Derwentwater Hotel is in Portinscale and like the Borrowdale was in business in 1878. Doubtless Caine knew it as well and simply confused the two. This is a classic example of his erratic memory and failure to check details: he had kept the bill from the Borrowdale. He also kept the bill from the Skiddaw Family and Commercial Temperance Hotel in Keswick, where he spent the next three nights. In late Victorian times temperance hotels were common. As a member of the Band of Hope Caine would have had a list of them covering the whole country and he and his family used them whenever possible. When Caine arrived in Keswick's Main Street that August morning he found the Skiddaw Hotel had just been rebuilt and raised from two storeys to four. The impressive frontage—and some of the interior—is unchanged.

Having booked a room he went round the town's bookshops. Rossetti had published only one book of poems, in 1870, and it did not take Caine long to find a secondhand copy. He read it straight through and when he went out for his usual walks took it with him to devour on the way. He was bowled over as much by the mystical element in the verse as by its lyrical beauty. He returned to Liverpool so zealous a convert he felt compelled to spread the gospel of Rossetti far and wide. He decided to devote three of the lectures he was booked to give that winter to Rossetti's poetry.

He was already in touch with William Michael Rossetti, the poet/painter's brother, who was a civil servant in the Inland Revenue Department, a literary man and a critic. William was one of the seven original members of the Pre-Raphaelite Brotherhood and edited their magazine, the *Germ*, writing the sonnet which appeared on its cover. He and Caine had not yet met but they had corresponded occasionally.

On 2 October, 1878, Caine wrote to Dante Gabriel Rossetti for the first time. He enclosed a proof of the prospectus for the newly reconstituted Notes & Queries Society. Writing in formal terms, he said, 'I shall accept it as an honour to be permitted to propose your name on the Honorary Council. We go to press in a few days.' It is not clear whether Rossetti accepted or not. Caine also wrote with the same request to William Michael but he refused.

He had sent a proof of the prospectus to Dowden with his letter of 28 September, asking if he could name him as a member of their Honorary Council too, along with F.J. Furnivall, William Morris and Henry Irving. Interestingly he made no mention of the Rossetti brothers to Dowden nor of the other names to the Rossettis.

1878 saw Caine increasingly involved in what would now be called environmental and conservation questions. James Bromley recruited him into the 'Save Thirlmere' movement. There were plans to dam the lake, which lies beside the road from Grasmere to Keswick, to provide water for Birmingham. Caine, incensed at what he saw as a threat to the heart of his beloved Cumbria, launched himself enthusiastically into getting up a Parliamentary petition to halt the project, which would irrevocably alter the nature and scenery of the valley. They failed: the dam was built and was opened in 1894. For many years public access to the hills surrounding the enlarged lake was restricted and the narrow reedy mere was replaced by the reservoir one sees today. More than a hundred years later it still supplies Birmingham though improved methods of water treatment mean the public can once more go down to the lake shore and walk the hills around it. Concentration on this campaign focused Caine's mind on Thirlmere and the surrounding hills so that he used it as the setting of his first novel, written seven years later.

Caine and Bromley also worked together in the campaign to save old churches from the ravages of the 'restorers' whose alterations, in the name of returning them to their 'best periods', had played havoc with the country's architectural heritage. Caine took a large part in saving Wordsworth's church at Grasmere. He was excited when he heard about the Society for the Protection of Ancient Buildings, founded the previous year. William Morris was the moving spirit. To start with the 'Anti-Scrape Society', as it was affectionately known to its members, and still is, had its offices at 26 Queen Square, Bloomsbury—close to the Temperance hotel where Caine stayed. At one time Morris and his wife Janey had lived there with their two daughters, Jenny and May. When he founded Morris & Co. the business used part of the house but as it expanded it gradually took over the whole premises. Morris kept a small room for himself where he sometimes slept but by 1878 the family was living in Kelmscott House in Hammersmith, overlooking the river. Caine was familiar with Morris's poetry, which he loved, and knew him to be a painter and designer. He joined the Anti-Scrape Society in August, 1878, and remained a member throughout the rest of his life, an unrivalled record of over fifty years' membership.

For some time he had been casting about for a way in which the Notes & Queries Society could be involved in practical work for the arts in general, including architecture. The SPAB might provide the answer. On 6 September he wrote to Morris, who was the Honorary Secretary. He enclosed a circular of the latest session of the Notes & Queries Society, pointing out that 'our scheme has 2 limbs, namely a purely literary one & one purely artistic'. He told Morris, 'We wish to ally ourselves in some workable way with associations for the promoting of art culture or with social associations whose purposes impinge on art.' Most of their patrons and many of the members agreed completely with the ideas of the SPAB and he had himself written an article along those lines.

In short, he wanted to know if his Society and Morris's could be associated in any way. Perhaps Notes & Queries could help the SPAB as 'a kind of North of England centre for the propagation of your principles'. There were plenty of buildings in the neighbourhood of Liverpool—he cited Ormskirk Church as one—to which he and his members had easier access and might know sooner than those in London when they were 'threatened with restoration'.

Soon afterwards Caine went to London for a meeting of the Anti-Scrape Society and met Morris for the first time. They had much in common—their early training as architects (Morris's with G.E. Street), their admiration for Ruskin, a passion for looking at old buildings and a rooted belief in Socialism. Though Caine did not follow Morris into the extremes of the Socialist League or openly espouse Marxism he did occasionally make some fiery socialistic speeches. They both went on to write novels. Morris was now 44 to Caine's 25 and exerted a considerable influence over the younger man. Caine said later that he had a lengthy correspondence with Morris from the time they met extending over five or six years but no letters have so far come to light. It is certain, however, that Morris was important to him, not least in introducing him to the Icelandic sagas.

There was never any formal association between their two societies. Caine, however, was one of two Local Correspondents for Liverpool of the SPAB, a position he held until 1897. The other was James Bromley.

Caine gave his first talk on Rossetti's poetry at the November 1878 meeting of the Notes & Queries Society. On the 15th he had written to William Rossetti to tell him he was booked to lecture on his brother's work and asking for help in dating some of the poems. This information would help him 'materially to understand the poems and their relation to each other'. In a note now with the letter William Rossetti said he gave the information 'with some reluctance, as I knew that my Brother did not particularly like to have anyone intervening in such matters without his express approval'. When the newspapers reported the lecture and quoted Caine as saying he had the dating of the poems from William Rossetti he was considerably upset as he had not expected to see his name published in the newspaper as the informant. His note concluded 'However, there was no real harm done, nor yet intended.'

What astonished and impressed Caine's hearers at this first lecture was not so much the matter it contained as the impassioned fervour of its delivery. Rossetti's *Collected Poems* of 1870 had run through six editions in two years so many of his audience could have been familiar with them. By the time Caine had finished anyone who had not encountered them would surely have wanted to read them. Caine began by saying that some of Rossetti's earliest poems had first appeared in the Germ in 1856. Reminding them of the publication of Rossetti's collected poems so many years later he said, 'This single precious volume, which contains all we know of his music and magic, his sweetness and force and subtlety, contains poems never before published...but from sheer lack of time, their ardency and harmony, and heat of spiritual life have failed hitherto to take rightful grasp of the popular mind.' Caine was about to change all that, at least to his own way of thinking.

The lecture was one long paean of praise. This poetry, he said, should be read with understanding. Poets 'ask in their readers a sympathetic attitude of mind, an impulse that is fervent, an instinct that is right'. Enlarging on this he came to the conclusion, 'if it is asked when and how the poetry of Mr Rossetti should be read, I answer—as it was written, lovingly… Art is a fructifier of august thought, a purifier of exquisite emotion. Wait then, the ardent impulse to turn the leaves of these poems.' He discussed which poems could be read in moments of joy or pain or 'when the glory and sweetness of youth and love swell through our aisles of sense like choral airs down cathedral aisles'.

This first lecture appeared in the *Builder*, leading to a long correspondence in its pages. They also reviewed the second lecture, not entirely favourably. It may seem odd to us that a trade paper should publish essays on controversial contemporary poets but in those days such magazines ran articles and essays on a wide range of subjects. Evidently they expected their readers to be cultivated and educated men (and possibly women) who would have a wide range of interests beyond the professional fields in which they worked.

Irving's First Night at the Lyceum, commemorated by the caricaturist Alfred Bryan. The Prince and Princess of Wales are in the upper stage box. Disraeli is in the box next to them. On stage, Irving exits stage left.

1878 was a crowded year and it ended on a high note. After Christmas Caine went down to London, staying, as he usually did, at a small temperance hotel at 37 Queen Square, Bloomsbury, close to Morris's business. It was also the United Kingdom Headquarters of the Band of Hope. On 30 December he attended an occasion which was a landmark in the history of London theatre—Irving's first night at the Lyceum under his own management. A note on the headed paper of the Royal Lyceum Theatre, Strand, London, reached him at his hotel. It read, 'Delighted to see you tonight. See Mr Bram Stoker—he has a seat in a box for you. Come round afterwards.' It was signed by Irving's stage manager, Henry Loveday.

Over the next two decades Irving's first nights at the Lyceum and the parties afterwards became legendary. That tradition was not yet established but for a young unknown from the provinces to be offered a seat in a box and invited to join the party afterwards on a first night of such importance was quite something. Someone else present was the noted caricaturist, Alfred Bryan. He drew a section of the audience which included the Prince of Wales's box and provided a key identifying some of the famous people in the audience. Among them were Lily Langtry (the Prince's mistress), Disraeli, Wilde, Gladstone, Swinburne, Tennyson, Whistler, Millais, Arthur Sullivan and W.S. Gilbert and the leading critic, George Augustus Sala.

This, however, was not what made the evening another milestone in Caine's life: it was the introduction to Bram Stoker.

Bram Stoker (properly Abraham, 1847–1912) was a slightly eccentric Anglo-Irishman who first encountered Irving in Dublin. At the time he was a civil servant with literary leanings and a passion for the theatre. Invited backstage, Irving treated him to one of his highly dramatic party pieces, reciting Hood's *The Death of Eugene Aram*. Stoker's reaction at the end was as flamboyant as Irving's recitation: he collapsed in hysterics. Gratified by this reception Irving hurried off to his dressing room. He returned with a photograph of himself which he had inscribed, 'God bless you! God bless you! Henry Irving' and pressed it on the overwrought Stoker.

There was some casual discussion about Stoker joining Irving's company as manager but nothing was settled before the actor returned to London. When a letter arrived renewing the suggestion Stoker did not wait for a proper contract. Without knowing what his duties would be or what he would be paid he resigned his job, packed up his home and hurried to London. What his wife thought of this precipitous action is not recorded. She was Florence Balcombe, who was engaged to Oscar Wilde before she married Stoker.

Stoker arrived at the Lyceum in the autumn of 1878, shortly after Irving had taken over from Colonel Bateman, to find the theatre a chaos of workmen and Irving away on tour trying to raise the money to pay for all the alterations and redecoration. Thrown in at the deep end, with little knowledge or experience of the professional theatre, Stoker swam happily and remained with Irving until the great actor's death in 1905.

How he ever found time to write when he was constantly at Irving's beck and call is a mystery but he published several novels. He was peculiarly susceptible to the late nineteenth-century preoccupation with the weird and the erotic. He was influenced by Beardsley, Baudelaire and

Bram Stoker, an undated photograph.

Dante Gabriel Rossetti, whose poetry and paintings he greatly admired. This shared love of Rossetti's work would have drawn him to Caine, apart from Irving's patronage which would have been recommendation enough, but they had something else in common—a love of Walt Whitman's poetry and an admiration for Ernest Dowden. Stoker had been a student of Dowden's during his time at Trinity College, Dublin.

Thus it is no surprise that he and Caine quickly became close friends. They made an odd pair. Stoker was a great bear of a man, well over six foot tall with a magnificent bushy beard and a luxurious head of reddish brown hair. The diminutive Caine with his thin hair and small pointed beard looked like a shrimp beside him.

Stoker is remembered now as the author of *Dracula*, which appeared in 1897. He dedicated it to Caine with the legend, 'To my dear friend, Hommy-Beg', which has puzzled readers not privy to Caine's pet name ever since. Stoker also wrote a two-volume *Personal Reminiscences of Henry Irving* (1906), but it is by his vampire creation, first inspired by Vlad the Impaler, that he is remembered, largely because of the filmed versions and the fashion for vampire stories. There is a definite homo-erotic element in the book. It has been said that Stoker was in love with Irving and that Irving used him like a vampire for 28 years. Stoker would have died for Irving and was treated like dirt in return. In concocting the story of Count Dracula Stoker was perhaps having his revenge. Whether or not there is anything in this, the trio of Irving, Stoker and Caine were intimate friends and without doubt Caine found himself particularly in tune with the other two. Over the years he travelled long distances for the chance of an evening with them. Stoker and Irving shared a sense of the weird and found it also in Caine, whose tales of Manx customs and superstitions, of which he had many apart from those he used in his books, intrigued them both.

Caine was back in Liverpool in time to deliver his next lecture on 28 January in the Free Library. It was titled 'The Poetry of Pre-Raphaelitism' and was a lively occasion. It did not get as much press attention as his previous talks as it coincided with the death of a well-known local clergyman. He sent a report to Dowden with no covering letter, having had the gall to leave three letters from him unanswered. He eventually thanked Dowden for them in a letter of 19 February, apologising for not having written sooner because he was 'quite overwhelmed with work'. Caine acknowledged in another letter that Dowden might think him stupid to take on so much trivial work. 'So it is, and yet such is, I fear, the unhealthy restlessness of my whole nature'—some insight here, he was restless all his life—'that if I were not at all times up to the very eyes in work of one kind or other, I should be the most utterly miserable dog alive... I write hundreds of letters every month.' If he really did, and he could well have exaggerated, it would seem as if he needed constant reassurance of his existence: 'I write letters, therefore I am.' It is consistent with his earlier remark to Dowden that letters were even more important to him than books and would account for the huge number he kept.

Admitting that it was he who had sent the report of his lecture of 28 January he gave Dowden a lively description of the evening which had ended by his being attacked by Philip Rathbone, a member of the Libraries Committee which organised the lectures and a JP. In 1879 he was a power in the city, described as 'a unique figure, a charming personality, an artistic enthusiast, a man of wide culture and generous sympathies'. It was also said that he was outspoken and 'his language was not always chosen with discretion'. He later became an Alderman.

'The lecture hall was crowded with working people (hundreds were turned away),' Caine wrote to Dowden,

> and I had lectured without MS and perhaps said rather extreme things in praise of Rossetti; but when Rathbone began to abuse him I felt as though my lecture were going for worse than nothing and so I became furious. At the full pitch of voice I replied with the bitterest words I could get at and the people, catching the contagion, literally shouted or shall we say yelled their applause. The audience seemed so entirely on my side that poor Rathbone looked utterly crestfallen.

Caine said he tried to smooth things down after this but could see Rathbone, 'though he made a show of good-feeling was unmistakably hurt'. The evening made an enemy of him. 'Alderman Samuelson (a sworn adversary of Rathbone's),' Caine ended, 'told me a week after that the incident was quite the talk among the Council people.'

Lively though this description is it contains at least two terminological inexactitudes. Far from the hall being crowded and 'hundreds turned away', records of the six Free Library lectures between 22 January and 17 March, 1879, of which Caine's was only one, show that 325 people attended, somewhat less than the average of 363. On the previous evening Revd H.S. Brown had attracted 470 people to his lecture on 'The Steady Man' and 480 were recorded at other times. Far from being either 'crestfallen' or 'hurt' Rathbone was angry. He was a man of influence in the artistic and literary affairs of Liverpool and it was stupid of Caine to offend him. Nor were he and Samuelson 'sworn adversaries' or anything like it. Although on opposite sides of the political divide— Samuelson was a Conservative—they worked closely together over many years on the Library, Museum and Arts Committee. Rathbone had helped Edward Samuelson establish the city's annual Autumn Exhibition of Paintings which began in 1871.

Caine's third Rossetti lecture was given in March, 1879. This time he was more widely reported in the press and word of it reached London. It was a general overview of the Pre-Raphaelite movement with special emphasis on Rossetti's work both as poet and painter. When it was over he combined all three lectures into an essay for publication. At the same time he was busy on an assignment for the Ruskin Society. They wanted to publish a set of papers, probably six in number. 'Mr William Morris shall do one, 'the Secretary wrote to Caine, 'and you shall have the others.'

CHAPTER FIVE

In the spring of 1879 catastrophe struck the family. John Caine met with a painful and disabling accident at work. There are no details of what happened but Caine mentioned it in a letter about eighteen months later, giving it as his reason for having stayed in Liverpool when he had good offers of work in London. The census of 1881 gives John Caine as unemployed. As he was 59 when he was injured it is unlikely that he ever worked again. There was no welfare state in those days and the Workmen's Compensation Act did not finally become law until 1897, after years of abortive attempts to get it on the statute book. Caine supported his parents to the end of their lives.

Work in London seemed increasingly necessary if he was to achieve the literary career he wanted. While Liverpool had given him much, the people who mattered were in London and there he was determined to go. However, it never occurred to him to leave while his father was laid low and his mother worried out of her mind. It is his most attractive trait that he remained so loyal to his parents, and indeed all his family, even after he became rich and famous, when he could well have turned his back on his humble origins. Some of his relatives took advantage of him once he had money and battened on him like leeches.

It was frustrating, but Caine never for a moment thought that he had any option but to stay at Bromley's while things were difficult at home. He hoped for work in London that would pay enough to keep him there while supporting his family but would not move until he was sure of it. He needed patronage. The idea had already occurred to him of sending his lecture to Dante Gabriel Rossetti but he hesitated to approach the great man. William had made clear his brother's feelings about people who criticised his work and he knew Gabriel lived a reclusive life. Some years before a vicious attack had been launched on Rossetti and his writing. It was published anonymously but it was soon known that the author was Robert Buchanan. Rossetti's friends were outraged and the poet withdrew into his home in Chelsea's Cheyne Walk and saw fewer and fewer people. He had never got over the shock of Buchanan's attack so that Caine was quite right to tread warily.

In July he went to New Brighton to a boarding house where he often stayed. After cogitating further he finally wrote to William Rossetti on 6 July, 1879, enclosing a letter to Gabriel. Under separate cover he sent a copy of *Colbourne's New Monthly* in which the lecture was printed and asked William to look at it 'before it goes into your brother's hands. In the event of your discovering anything in it which you think likely to hurt his acute sensibility please do me the kindness to retain it and return the letter.'

While the letter to William Michael was addressed 'W.M. Rossetti Esq., Dear Sir', to Gabriel (as his family called him—he had been christened Gabriel Charles Dante) he wrote 'Dear Mr Rossetti'. These niceties meant a great deal in Victorian days. He began the letter, 'I have grown to feel an interest in you and your work so entirely personal as seems to justify the above familiar form of address. If there be, however, anything in it unwarranted by the proper attitude of a student to the poet he loves pray pardon and forget it.' He apologised for an 'imperfect tribute' and added, 'it is to you more than to any other that I owe it that with all the ardour of an earnest and I think intense [crossed out and 'ardent' substituted] nature I "love the principle of beauty in all things"'.

The magazine went astray in the post so William returned the letter addressed to his brother as he was unable to carry out Caine's request. However, Caine had plucked up courage to write to the poet himself. He replied to William on 25 July saying he had sent a second copy of the magazine straight to his brother together with the covering letter William had seen. He asked William, if he saw his brother and heard him speak of his 'little paper', to let him know how Gabriel had taken it.

Gabriel's reaction to the essay was so immediate and so welcoming it must have taken Caine's breath away. In his spiky hand he wrote on 29 July, 1879, from 16 Cheyne Walk, Chelsea, London SW:

> Dear Mr Caine,
>   I am much struck by the generous enthusiasm displayed in your letter, and by the ability with which it is written. Your estimate of the impulses influencing my poetry is such as I should wish it to suggest, and this suggestion, I believe, it will have always for a true-hearted nature. You say that you are grateful to me: my response is, that I am grateful to you: for you have spoken up heartily and unfalteringly for the work you love.
>   I daresay you sometimes come to London. I should be very glad to know you, and would ask you, if you thought of calling, to give me a day's notice when to expect you, as I am not always able to see visitors without appointment. The afternoon about 5 might suit me, or else the evening about 9.30.
>
> With all best wishes,
> Yours sincerely,
> D.G. Rossetti.

When Caine had got his breath back he replied on 2 August saying he had 'the pleasant prospect of a brief holiday' and hoped to take up Rossetti's kind invitation to call. He added that Rossetti might like to know 'what other poetry I love: I mean that I could wish you to feel that my enthusiasm for your work is not at all the freak of a feverish fancy but the serious outcome of a mind that aims to fix its standard high'. Accordingly he was sending a copy of the August number of *Colbourne's* which contained another of his essays, this time on 'The Supernatural Element in Poetry'.

Returning it, Rossetti said he felt it 'a distinction that my minute plot in the poetic field should have attracted the gaze of one who is able to traverse its widest ranges with so much command'. This reads as if he was writing with his tongue firmly in his cheek. The essay is wordy and pretentious and it is difficult to see what point Caine was trying to make. However, Rossetti ended by saying, 'I shall be much pleased if your plan of calling on me is carried out soon—at any rate I should trust it would be so eventually.'

He did not then know how young Caine was. That he meant exactly what he said is indicated by a letter written to his mother on 29 July in which he told her,

> I know you always love all friendliness towards me and my work; so I enclose a letter I got, and will send the Lecture alluded to in a day or two. I shall try to know the writer, who has done his work well, and in the spirit I most wish. I had heard of him already as delivering such a lecture, I believe more than once, but do not otherwise know anything of him.

This was the beginning of a correspondence which continued for about two years. At the start Rossetti was 51 and Caine half his age, 26. The overall impression is of two essentially lonely people happily discussing shared interests, in their case poetry and painting. Gabriel was not an old man in 1879 but he was ravaged by years of addiction to chloral and too much whisky. Too much womanizing in his earlier years had doubtless contributed to both his ill-health and his isolation. He had become alienated from many of his old friends although those that remained were loyal and protective, particularly Theodore Watts (who later changed his name to Watts-Dunton), Rossetti's solicitor who was also a man of letters, and the artist Frederic Shields. Both these men became Caine's close friends for life.

After the initial exchange Rossetti's anxiety to meet Caine cooled. He worried who this excitable Liverpudlian might be and wondered if he was really the sort of man he wanted to invite into his home. No more letters passed between the two for a while. Caine's holiday plans were changed. He had told Rossetti he longed to see the Swiss Alps and Italy. If he was to go there he would have to pass through London and could call at Cheyne Walk. Available time and money, however, would only run to a week in Keswick, where he went in early September with William Tirebuck.

He had another reason for not going too far afield at this time. The Council of the National Association for the Promotion of Social Science advertised for an Assistant Secretary. Caine assembled testimonials and letters of recommendation from everyone he thought could influence his application and prepared a letter containing his *curriculum vitae*. It asserted he was an architect by training and referred to his present job as General Builder's Assistant, adding immediately, 'I have for years been occupied in literary pursuits.' He was, he wrote, familiar with all aspects of printing and publishing which qualified him to edit the Council's publications. His business experience meant he could organise the Council's annual congress and other affairs. He was used to being an Honorary Secretary.

Among his letters of recommendation was a long and detailed one from William Rossetti. While waiting for the result of his job application Caine sent Gabriel Rossetti a list of the council members, asking if he could exert some influence on his behalf should he know any of them. Rossetti replied that he did not know any of them. He thought Caine was sure to be the best candidate 'but too likely to fail in favour of some ass with interest to back him. Never mind if so—you will turn up all right eventually in your true sphere of critical work.' (Like everyone else who knew him at this time he had no idea that Caine would turn into a hugely successful romantic novelist.)

Caine was one of the few applicants called for an interview but he did not get the job. He wrote to Rossetti, 'I have <u>lost</u> the Secretaryship of the Social Science Association. There were 166 candidates and I have just dropped out at the last three. I had set my heart upon living in London, but now that must stand over awhile.' He referred to a paper he had given on Restoration which appeared in the *Builder* and said he was rewriting his Ruskin Society papers for publication in the *Nineteenth Century*. When that was done he had two more lectures to give plus two or three short pieces for *Theatre* magazine and then he was going to concentrate on an important paper on Keats, which he had mentioned to the editor of the *Westminster Review*. Altogether he did not seem to be pining over the latest failure of a job application.

Rossetti sent condolences on losing the job but said it was perhaps no bad thing: it might be all for the better that he should wait until something for which he was more suited came along. Caine had sent him a magazine containing articles he had written. Rossetti warned him,

> One word of advice—just between ourselves. It is really most injurious to put your name to articles printed in such a farrago of absolute garbage as the Magazine of which you sent me 2 Nos. Surely you must know that it holds not even a position as good as the *Family Herald*. What I apprehend seriously is, that, if your name becomes at all familiar in such quarters, you will find excessive difficulty in attaining your true place, even should fortune favour you a little more than hitherto. I only wish I could help instead of offering so barren a counsel.

This arrived in time to stop Caine sending them anything more. He explained he had not been aware of the magazine's nature, giving the odd explanation that he had seen copies of the magazine from fifty years before but no recent numbers and had not realised how much it had changed. In his researches into the Romantic poets Caine had looked for contemporary reviews, intending to compare critical comment in their lifetimes with their standing fifty years later. When he received the copies of the magazine in which his work was printed he was taken aback. He admitted to Rossetti that it was risky to send work to a journal one was not familiar with and added he was now the same age as Keats was when he died.

After Christmas Rossetti wrote, 'You took my advice most kindly and really it was the right thing. I might give a little more in the same line at some time, but not just now. I am truly delighted to hear how young you are: I suppose you are not married. In original work, a man does some of his best things by your time of life, though he only finds it out in a rage much later.' In critical work such as Caine's, however, there were different 'seasons of production, though you have done work already that should honour you yet'. He was sending as a present a copy of his book of translations, *Dante and his Circle*, which Caine received with rapture and effusive thanks.

He wrote to Rossetti much as he had to Professor Dowden. He was seeking someone he could venerate, someone who would help and promote him in his work. Though he remained in touch with Dowden he switched his allegiance, amounting to adoration, to Rossetti.

Through the first part of 1880 they continued to exchange long and increasingly friendly letters. Rossetti often said he was lonely and Caine's letters were a joy to him. In an undated note he said, 'A letter such as yours is always an oasis for me.' On 11 April he returned to the theme, saying, 'I am sometimes very solitary, and then letter-writing brings solace, when one addresses so young and hopeful a well-wisher as yourself.' Caine understood. He also felt lonely in Liverpool where, rather arrogantly, he felt no one else cared about art or literature as he did, they were only interested in making money.

By mid-February Rossetti had dropped the 'Mr' and addressed his new penfriend as Caine, the equivalent to moving to Christian names in a later era, evidently expecting Caine to do the same. He, however, continued to use the more formal address. Eventually Rossetti told him outright to drop the Mr but it was March of 1881 before he could bring himself to write 'My dear Rossetti' to the older man.

Over Christmas, 1879, and the New Year holiday Caine put together a short book on the restoration of old buildings, using his architectural training backed by considerable reading and visiting many of the places he wrote about. He chose the title *Stones Crying Out*, which Rossetti thought 'an admirable title', but he had to drop it when he found it had been used for a volume of sermons. A publisher named Remington offered to bring it out but Caine, as he told Rossetti, did not know whether to accept. Friends in Liverpool said he should print it at his own expense and take the profit. Although he felt it ought to sell he was afraid to risk it. The book was eventually published in Oxford in July of 1880 and Caine sent Rossetti a copy. Whatever new title he chose does not appear in the correspondence and no trace of the book has been found so far.

On 19 January, 1880, Caine replied to Rossetti's letter of 29 December. He reached page nine before answering the speculation as to whether he was married or not. 'No, I am not married. Indeed, I have never yet felt any temptation to marry, or if I have it has been a very prosaic one.' (This appears to be an allusion to Frederick Lange's offer to take Caine into his furrier business if he married Marie.) 'I have observed,' he continued,

> that after marriage my friends have stood closer by their work; and it has some-
> times occurred to me that if I were married and just ten years older than I am I
> should probably be freed from what may be termed the irritating atmosphere
> peculiar to my time of life and conditions. As far as I know my own nature,
> however, I have reason to fear that the same soothing and settling results
> would not ensue in my case.

This is the only acknowledgement of his uncertain sexuality, which was evidently still worrying him.

He left the letter there, as if writing it had exhausted him. Returning to it on 22 January he thanked Rossetti for his comment that he had already done good work. 'I have learned to know the praise which it is worth one's whole heart to labour for,' he wrote, 'and nothing else that could have been said about me by anyone could have given me as much pleasure as I had from the good word you gave me.' It was important to him because for a year he had given up the newspaper work, 'for which journalists here say I have special aptitude', in order to concentrate on other writing 'not for profit or for pleasure or yet (if I know my own heart) from desire of distinction, but mainly from passion'. If he was genuine in denying he was motivated by 'desire of distinction' then he did not know his own heart as well as he thought he did. He was a driven man all his life and what drove him from the beginning was ambition to achieve distinction as a 'man of letters'. That and money. He had seen poverty close to, known the humiliation of having to ask a friend for a loan, and he was determined to put himself and his family as far beyond all that as possible.

Rossetti's praise delighted him because it meant he had made the right decision. 'I have worked under heavy odds. Eight of the best hours of every day, with all that goes with them, are still spent in the merest routine occupations such as make one feel like a horse harnessed to a machine.' As yet he could see no way of escaping that harness but now he had hope that one day he might be able to shrug it off.

They continued to discuss literature and poetry at length, both often writing during sleepless nights. In particular they discussed the sonnet. Rossetti expressed surprise that while Caine seemed to have a good knowledge of Italian and German poets, sprinkling his letters with references to Dante, Goethe, Schiller and less familiar names, which he had read in translation, he seemed to know nothing of French literature.

Caine was fascinated by the sonnet, which he thought the supreme essence of poetry, and Rossetti agreed with him. Rossetti thought sonnet writing was a useful technical exercise for any writer, even if his particular talent lay elsewhere, and he encouraged Caine to persevere with the art. To be able to express rich poetic thought and emotion within the confines of the fourteen lines of a sonnet was the pinnacle of poetic achievement. Caine, who was not a poet, became absorbed in the technicalities of the form. He sometimes rejected sonnets as imperfect because they did not conform exactly to the rules. Rossetti told him to look at what the poet was trying to convey and suggested the greatest poets could and did break the rules without damage to the resulting poem.

Caine disliked the English sonnet form, where the rhyme scheme ended in a couplet. This to his mind produced 'a ridiculous jingling effect' uncomfortable to the ear. As this is the form in which Shakespeare cast his sonnets it was an odd stand to take and Rossetti worked hard to talk him out of it. What Caine admired most, and attempted to imitate, was the Italian, or Petrarchan, form, which divides into an octave and sestet. There is a pause in the thought at the end of the octave with the remaining six lines summing up. Both Milton and Wordsworth wrote sonnets using the Italian rhyme scheme but often did not observe the division at the end of the octave. Caine originally dismissed some of Milton's greatest sonnets on this ground. Rossetti, doing him a notable service, removed this blind spot and brought him round to appreciation of them.

Discussing sonnet form Rossetti said,

> You have much too great a habit of speaking of a special octave, sestette, or line. Conception, my boy, FUNDAMENTAL BRAINWORK, that is what makes the difference in all art. Work your metal as much as you like, but first take care that it is gold and worth working. A Shakespearian sonnet is better than the most perfect in form because Shakespeare wrote it.

There were arguments over Theodore Watts's ideas of a fixed metrical law. Rossetti 'took fire' on this subject, having got the wrong end of the stick with regard to 'Mr Watts's canons'.

He had his blind spots too: one of them was the poetry of Gerard Manley Hopkins. Caine was planning a book about the sonnet—its history and development—and making an anthology to illustrate it. At the end of 1880, when the project was well under way, Rossetti suggested he ask Revd R.W. Dixon for some sonnets. Dixon, it so happened, was in correspondence with Gerard Manley Hopkins and sent two of his sonnets along with his own. These were 'Starlight Night' and 'Caged Skylark'. He urged Caine to write to Hopkins who was working in Liverpool at the time. Greatly impressed, Caine did so and Hopkins sent him three more, including 'Spring'. Caine was bowled over by them and wrote an effusive letter of thanks, promising to use at least some of them. He sent them to Rossetti and the reaction surprised him: 'I cannot in any degree tolerate Mr Hopkin's [*sic*] Sonnets, though perceiving well that he is an able man.' He continued to object so strongly that Caine went back on his promise and left them out. For once Rossetti's influence was malign and could well have caused distress to Hopkins, who struggled for recognition. No complete edition of his poetry was published until 1919 when he had been dead for thirty years.

Caine could not decide whether to include the work of living poets. Rossetti thought he should, and that his sister Christina's work must be included. This led Caine to ask how the poets should be approached. ' "How are they to be approached?"—you innocently ask. Ye heavens!' Rossetti exploded, 'how does the cat's-meat-man approach Grimalkin?— and what is that relation in life when compared to the *rapport* established between the living bard and the fellow-creature who is disposed to cater to his caterwauling appetite for publicity?'

Rossetti was full of suggestions, many of which Caine quietly ignored. He soon learnt that opposing Rossetti's ideas was pointless. He would fly up in their defence, only later to change his mind and agree. Some of Rossetti's proposals Caine had to accept, whatever he thought of them privately, as with the work of his brother, William Rossetti, and Mathilde Blind, the German-born poet, an old friend of the Rossetti family. The same applied to the tedious efforts of Rossetti's long-time friend William Bell Scott. He could not reject any of these whatever their quality and they have not worn well.

Rossetti had a considerable influence over the form of Caine's anthology and the choice of poems. They were to illustrate a long essay but he chose the sonnets first, adding copious notes. At first Caine proposed to intersperse the sonnets through the text. Rossetti's advice that the essay should come first and the sonnets after it, one to a page, was sound and Caine accepted it. Another idea of Rossetti's which he incorporated was that new sonnets published for the first time should be marked with an asterisk in the index.

The book is divided, for the most part, between names unknown today (with good reason when one reads their efforts) and the obvious. Christina Rossetti earns her place, as does Elizabeth Barrett Browning, though she was a controversial choice at the time. There is a terrible sameness about most of the Victorian sonnets in the book, with their 'poetic diction', too much doth-ing and thee-ing and obsession with death, though this last was understandable given the death rate among young people then. Caine chose several sonnets by Theodore Watts, not because he was Rossetti's friend but because of their clear speech and original themes. While some contributions came from poets who have been justifiably forgotten, some whose names have been lost deserve recognition. In particular three sonnets by Philip Bourke Marston repay reading now. Marston, who was recommended by Rossetti, was blind and died in 1887 at the age of only 37.

When, at Caine's request, Rossetti sent him Alice Meynell's address he wrote to her at once. She sent him two sonnets. One was the already published 'My Heart Shall Be Thy Garden'. The other was a new son-net—'Renouncement'—which is now probably her best known poem. He starred it, indicating publication for the first time. It is powerful and affected the young Caine so strongly that in two of his novels he quotes from it (inaccurately) without acknowledgement and possibly uncon-sciously.

Noting at a later date that Rossetti could recite from memory every sonnet of Shakespeare and much else besides, Caine said, 'His memory was exact, too; not like that of most of us (my own in particular) slack and broken, retaining the substance but missing the word.' This rueful admission explains clearly how Alice Meynell's sonnet stuck at the back of his mind and how he could later misquote it without, perhaps, even being aware he was not being original. It is also acknowledgement of the misquotations for which he was often reprimanded by critics. One instance can be found in the Preface to the anthology where he has a word wrong in Milton's famous sonnet beginning 'Avenge, O Lord, thy slaughtered saints'.

Work on the book extended over a year while Caine continued to send poems and 'papers' to Rossetti. He gave a lecture on Politics and Art in Liverpool in March, 1880, during the campaign for an election which was won by the Liberals in April that year. Rossetti commented, 'I must admit at all hazards that my friends consider me exceptionally averse to politics; and I suppose I must be, for I never read a parliamen-tary debate in my life!' Caine asked if he might dedicate the published paper to him but he refused. He thought art so far removed from poli-tics the two could not be linked and artists should not be involved at all. For himself, he said, 'I had better really stick to knowing how to mix vermilion and ultramarine for a flesh-grey, and how to manage their equivalent in verse.'

All this did not stop him discussing the new lecture in detail and praising it. 'It is abundantly rich in spirit and animated truth, and in powerful language too when required. It must do you high credit wherever seen, and when you are able to enlarge your sphere, I look to you as destined to rank among the coming teachers of men.' Praise was mixed with criticism of Caine's prose style. He warned him against repeating such phrases as 'in the same way', 'on the other hand', 'with what', and so on, saying they 'stiffen what is really free and masterly'. The paper was published in the *British Architect* in the spring of 1880.

Rossetti was also impressed by the lecture on 'The Supernatural in Shakespeare'. 'It is truly admirable—such work must soon make you a place.' He was less impressed by yet another on Irving and the modern theatre. He thought the essay 'suffered from some immaturity—moreover if I were you I would eschew modern dramatic matters'. Caine had no intention of doing any such thing. He did not say so and before he could reply Rossetti sent a short note, 'Let me have a line from you. I am haunted by the idea that in declining the dedication I may have hurt you. I assure you I should be proud to be associated in any way with your work but gave you my very reasons.' Caine replied saying he too was haunted, in his case by the fear that he had been taking up too much of Rossetti's time and attention. 'If I could only feel quite sure, once for all, that my letters are never a burden to you... I should restrain less frequently than I do the impulse to write to you.'

This reached Rossetti next day and he sat down at once to write a lengthy reply beginning, 'Let me assure you at once that correspondence with you is one of my best pleasures, and that you cannot write too much and too often for me.' Caine should send a copy of 'Politics and Art' to the *Athenaeum* as soon as possible as they might review it. Rossetti and his brother both tried to get the pamphlet reviewed— Gabriel was adept at getting up a claque—but without success. MacColl, the editor of the *Athenaeum*, refused it saying it was intended to prove that all artists would vote for Gladstone. Caine insisted he meant no such thing. Lord Houghton and H.A. Bright also praised the paper, others—including his friend and contemporary, the poet William Watson— did not like it. Rossetti still thought it obvious there must be 'a veto against the absolute participation of artists in politics', though he conceded that what Caine had written was important and he did not intend to devalue his lecture. 'Too much cannot be said in praise of your brilliant contrasts and flaming English.'

Rossetti had sent Caine some of his own recent work, including translations from Italian poets, and asked him to say what he thought of it. 'All you said in your letter of this morning was very grateful to me,' he wrote after receiving Caine's comments. 'I have a fair amount by me in the way of later MS which I may shew you some day when we meet.'

Caine must have found these references to meeting at some vague future date tantalising.

On 12 March Rossetti returned to criticism of Caine's prose style.

> I think there is <u>some</u> truth in the charge of metaphysical involution—the German element as I should call it, and surely you are strong enough to be English pure and simple. I am sure I could write 100 Essays on all possible subjects (I once did project a series under the title 'Essays written in the Intervals of Elephantiasis, Hydrophobia, and Penal Servitude') without once experiencing the 'aching void' which is filled by such words as 'mythopoeic' and 'anthropomorphism'. I do not find life long enough to know in the least what they mean. They are both very long and very ugly indeed—the latter only suggesting to me a Vampire or Somnambulant Cannibal. (To speak rationally, would not 'man-evolved godhead' be an <u>English</u> equivalent?) 'Euhemeristic' also found me somewhat on my beam-ends, though explanation is here given; yet I felt I could do without Euhemerous:—and <u>you</u> perhaps without <u>humerous</u>. You can pardon me now; for <u>so bad</u> a pun places me at your mercy indeed. But seriously, simple English in prose writing and in all narrative poetry (however monumental language may become in abstract verse) seems to me a treasure not to be forgone in favour of German innovations.

Sound advice, which Caine did not always follow. Rossetti ended with the remark that Caine was very young 'to be so beset with dark moods' as he said he was. 'I am much concerned to hear it. Everyone, I suppose, thinks <u>he</u> only knows the full bitterness of the Shadowed Valley.' Rossetti had suffered from recurrent episodes of depressive illness for years. 'I hope health is whole with you—and then all <u>must</u> come well, with <u>your</u> mind and such energy as yours to make its way. It is very late—Goodbye for tonight.' In a short letter of 23 March he apologised for being so critical. 'I trust you didn't think me too "chaffy" anent the metaphysical Graeco-German vocabulary of our days. You must always pardon me talking some nonsense, for I cannot help it.'

At the same time as he was discussing life and literature with his new friend Caine was keeping up his correspondence with William Morris. He may not have known then of the former close friendship between Morris and Rossetti or of the rift between them. It had been brought about principally by Rossetti's notorious affair with Morris's wife which had begun in the early 1860s when Caine was only a child. Rossetti used Janey Morris as a model many times. She was perhaps his greatest inspiration. It is her face, instantly recognisable, brooding, intense, lovingly painted, which looks out at us from so many of his later works. They were idealised portraits. In photographs she does not look quite the 'stunner' that he paints. It was Janey who posed for what many consider his greatest work, the powerful *Astarte Syriaca* of 1877. She is also *Proserpine*, looking her most sultry and holding a pomegranate. He had fallen in love with her fifteen years before when he and Morris had shared Kelmscott Manor in Gloucestershire. Morris was often away, leaving Rossetti and Janey alone together.

At the beginning of 1880 Caine was following the work of the Anti-Scrape Society with increasing enthusiasm and joining in where he could. One of Morris's campaigns was over proposals to 'restore' Southwell Minster. Plans had been put forward by his old master, the Gothicist G.E. Street, and Morris the purist became involved in a public row with him. Caine went to Southwell to see the minster for himself. Of course he wrote about it to Rossetti. 'To see anything tampered with that is rich with memories is utterly torturing to me,' he wrote in the course of an immensely long letter of 29 February. 'I was at Southwell a few weeks ago & there saw what they propose to do with the splendid arches of the old Norman nave. You may have seen them: they are simple in outline & enriched with bold Byzantine ornament; but it is intended to add some conjectural stuff in every arch.' He sketched the arches as they stood and how it was proposed to fill each of them with a pair of mock-Gothic arches. 'Well, the caretaker was discoursing eloquently on the improvement contemplated when I stopt and startled him & myself by crying out in words more forcable [*sic*] than reverent, "Good God, good God, what next?" Indeed this condition of mind is liable to excess in me.'

He continued to correspond with Dowden, telling him he had refrained from answering the critics of his Rossetti lecture in the *Builder*, as Dowden had advised—he was keeping away from newspaper controversy as much as possible. Discussing modern productions of Shakespeare, he criticised the fashion for over-elaborate costumes and sets. He admitted co-operating in a 'sketch' of himself, possibly the first of a mountain of press interviews during his long life. Tirebuck and some of his other friends were contributing their impressions. He felt a bit ashamed of himself, as well he might when one reads this 'sketch', but as he was not getting much money for what he wrote for the magazine concerned, the *Biograph and Review*, he might as well 'go for the glory'! The article appeared in the first half of 1879 and refers in passing to the year at Maughold. Instead of reporting that he wrote anonymous letters to the local papers, it says 'he became for a time leader-writer to a small biweekly newspaper published there', that is, in the Isle of Man. It is a remarkable eulogy of an almost unknown and very young man from the provinces. The tone is explained by Caine's own co-operation in its production and the contributions of close friends and admirers.

CHAPTER SIX

Caine was absorbed in collecting sonnets for his book. He gave Rossetti a prose version of a sonnet on Keats. Impressed by the exposition Rossetti urged him to 'do it at once' as it 'seems to me most beautiful', but he was disappointed with the result.

> You wished me to say quite frankly what I think of it. Well, I do not think it shews a special vocation for this condensed and emphatic form. The prose version you sent me seems to say much more distinctly what this says with some want of force... Also I must say that more special originality and even <u>newness</u> (though this might be called a vulgarizing word) of thought and picture in individual lines—more of this than I find here—seems to me the very first qualification of a sonnet.

There was more of the same but he smoothed over his critical attack by adding,

> I thought the passage on Night you sent me shewed an aptitude for choice imagery—and so did my brother. I should much like to see something which you view as your best poetic effort hitherto. After all, there is no need that every gifted writer should take the path of poetry—still less sonneteering. I am confident in your preference for frankness on my part.

Whether this confidence was misplaced or not, frankness was what Caine got—and took surprisingly well. At the end of what is another very long letter Rossetti adds, 'I hope what I wrote about your sonnet will not be taken as any discouragement. I know your mind has many embowerings, and that shy bird, the Sonnet, may lodge herself in one of them yet.' Caine had quoted extensively from his juvenile effort, 'Geraldine', which was now torn to pieces. To be fair, Rossetti also criticised Coleridge's poem, saying that apart from a few strong passages 'the rest seems to have reached a fatal facility in jingling'.

Caine did not write again for ten days, not long but enough to bring an anxious note from Rossetti saying he hoped his health had 'not been suffering since I last heard from you, when the report was not a good one'. The explanation, however, was that politics had taken over from art for a while. Parliament had been dissolved on 23 February and an election called for April. Caine was campaigning for the Liberals in Liverpool, writing articles for the papers, canvassing and attending meetings. (The Liberals won with a large majority and Gladstone formed a ministry on 29 April.) On 26 March Caine made up for the gap with a

letter of prodigious length—36 pages. He had to put it in two separate
envelopes to post it.

Much of it was given over to discussion of Keats and his poetry.
Caine was feeling his way towards a major essay on the subject. He
offered to use it as a lecture in aid of the fund for Keats's elderly sister,
Mme Fanny Keats de Llanos, who was living in reduced circumstances.
Rossetti said he should keep half the proceeds as his fee but Caine
refused absolutely. 'The money obtained is sure to be quite little enough
without my keeping back part of the price.' Plans for this lecture and
other means of raising funds for Mme de Llanos were discussed for some
time but were eventually abandoned.

Caine answered Rossetti's criticism of his prose style.

> What you said in your letter anent my numerous Germanisms amused me
> greatly. You let me off very lightly... Those words you quote are certainly
> crushers. The worst is that I can't even plead German precedent for some of
> them. Euhemeristic is actually a monstrosity of my own inventing. I much fear
> that beside being very ugly it is out of all harmony with its Greek original...
> Prof. Dowden says I am fast clarifying my style and I am sure I am trying to do
> so—making it, as far as I can, more simple, manly, English and direct.

Caine did not invent the word euhemeristic: the *Oxford English
Dictionary* records its first use in 1846, before he was born. Euheme-
rous was a Sicilian who lived in about 316 BC. He maintained that the
gods of Greek mythology were deified men and women. The method of
interpretation which regards myths as traditional accounts of real incidents in human history was called euhemerism after him. It is strange
that Caine should claim to have invented the word more than thirty
years after someone else first used it in print. He might coincidentally
have concocted it himself. More likely he had read it somewhere and
when it floated up from his subconscious he genuinely thought it was
his own.

He was grateful for his new friend's solicitousness over his health.
'The fact is, as nearly as I can learn it from the medical diagnosis of my
case, my brain is abnormally large and heavy. This unhappily does not
enable me to see things a whit more clearly than other folks but impov-
erishes most of the other parts of my body, rendering me especially
liable to colds, blood-pressure and the like.' One wonders what his doctor actually said—or meant. In those days there was no apparatus for
measuring blood pressure.

Caine had had a bad fright not long before. 'I went to bed in normal
health but next morning when I awoke I found a stream of blood on my
pillow and my mouth and throat and nostrils half full of blood. I was a
little alarmed.' He must have been terrified, with the memory of John
coughing his lungs out still so vivid. With considerable self-control he
cleared up the mess and said nothing to anyone, going to work as usual.

In the evening he called at his doctor's surgery on the way home. 'I told him calmly about it. I imagine that doctor would expect me to faint if I saw a woman prick her finger, but I verily believe he thinks me a bit of a hero where my own suffering is concerned and I <u>am confident</u> he would frankly have told me if anything had been wrong.' The doctor assured him it was only a heavy nose bleed and nothing to worry about. 'No harm whatever was done—rather good... One day I'll take a long holiday and then all will be well. Travel is good no doubt, but my brother travelled half the world over and came home and died at last. I <u>do not think</u> I shall die earlier than other people and I do not think that hard work hurts me much.'

A friend of Rossetti's who had seen 'Politics and Art' insisted that Caine must be a Roman Catholic. 'Is such the case? Pardon my putting the query...rather abruptly', Rossetti asked. Caine replied,

> That was a good shot at the truth about my being a Roman Catholic and yet I am <u>not</u> one. I sometimes go to the Catholic Chapel on the other side of this street, and more frequently to an Anglican Church of very pronounced ritual. All my friends here are Unitarians, Positivists, Secularists and broad churchmen and my antagonism to all these things and partial sympathy with what is contemptuously called the 'religion of the cross' (as distinguished from the religion of Christ) is notorious and a subject of surprise. I'm not a Catholic, God knows, and yet I feel the beauty of Catholicism in the abstract... I heard a Positivist sermon on Sunday and thought with Emerson if Luther had but known what his act would lead to, he would have cut off his right hand rather than nail up his thesis. It was a passionless ghost of a faith we were taught.

His ideas on religion were to colour almost all of his fiction.

Caine said he accepted Rossetti's comment that he had no real vocation as a sonneteer. 'I had and still have a preference for frankness on your part, and shall feel the pleasure of your praise, whenever again it may come to me, heightened by the assurance that you would not have spared your blame if occasion had required.' He was attempting a dozen or so sonnets and if when they were done he still showed no aptitude for 'that beautiful form of utterance' he would give up. He feared his experiences as a journalist had not helped him when he turned to poetry. His first editor told everyone Caine 'thought vastly too much'. He must have been too slow for newspaper work then but he soon learned to abandon 'excess of deliberation' and write faster than anyone else on the paper, turning out 'a dozen columns of stuff a week' and 'best able to concoct an article out of the slenderest materials fused down to suit the bilious mental appetite of the veriest clod'. He sent Rossetti some of the dozen sonnets he had promised—or threatened— and one or two other poems. When Rossetti took up his pen again after going through them, he was more brutally frank than at any time previously though his criticism was put in a kindly and diplomatic manner.

> Yours just to hand (2 April). You may be sure I do not mean essential discouragement, when I say that, full as 'Nell' is of reality and pathos, your swing of arm seems to me firmer and freer in prose than in verse. You know already how high I rate your future career (short of the incalculable storms of Fate) but I do think I see your field to lie chiefly in the noble achievements of fervid and impassioned prose.

This last remark was perhaps unfortunate. Caine needed no encouragement to write purple passages: his writing is littered with them. Endeavouring to steer his young protégé in the direction where he thought his real talents lay, Rossetti said, 'It would really warm me up much to know of <u>your</u> editing a sonnet book.'

On 5 April Caine wrote, 'I have never had from any other source such letters as I have had from you; I am never likely to have. I feel that they must have an enduring effect upon me.' They did.

He had said a week or two previously that he had not been able to write because he had been involved in electioneering but it was not the whole truth. It was in March of 1880 that Marie returned to Liverpool after losing her teaching job. It was the first time they had met in nearly two years. He was still her '<u>dearest</u> Tom'. What did he feel for her? He said nothing about her to Rossetti but the answer may lie in a few lines of Coleridge which he quoted to him:

> But never other found another
> To free the hollow heart from paining;
> They stood aloof, the scars remaining,
> Like cliffs that have been rent asunder,
> A dreary sea now flows between
> But neither heat nor frost nor thunder
> Can wholly do away I ween
> The marks of that which once hath been.

They could have come to mind after seeing Marie again and haunted him since.

He reverted to his projected book.

> It would be indeed a very splendid thing for me to edit a Sonnet book of a scheme and scope such as you indicate. I feel that it would give me such an assured footing as I could hardly get by <u>any</u> other agency. From a starting point so excellent I might safely go on to numberless further efforts of a kindred nature, such as have long filled my mind and gilded my hope.

His naïveté and inexperience came through in the sanguine remark that 'if it were found possible to do anything of the kind proposed I would go down to London and call on Kegan Paul and others. I feel sure that terms might be made with almost any house.' Writing fiction did not feature in his plans. Several pages of this letter were filled with praise of his friend William Watson, assuring Rossetti he had the potential to be a true poet. He ended, 'I think my health is bettering fast—what a vile phrase! These rivers of morning air do wonders for me. Surely spring is the most life-giving of all the seasons.' Moved by the thought that his own birthday was near he wondered how many poets were born in the spring, 'But you must be weary of my talk.'

Never weary of Caine's 'talk', Rossetti replied on the 11th. 'I am glad your health is feeling the benefit of returning Spring. Is it the season of your birth? (As you remember—you raise the question relative to poets.) I myself was born on Old May Day (12th) in the year (1828) after that in which Blake died.' Both seemed to take a childlike pleasure in the discovery that their natal dates coincided so closely—Caine's of course was 14 May. 'The comparative dates of our births are curious,' Rossetti wrote on 13 April. 'You were born in fact just as I was giving up poetry at about 25, on finding that it impeded attention to what constituted another aim and a livelihood into the bargain—i.e. painting. From that date up to the year when I published my poems I wrote extremely little.'

On his birthday Rossetti thanked Caine for two sonnets. One was a reworked version of Caine's sonnet on Keats and this Rossetti approved, despite his earlier 'swing of your arm' comment. The other, however, left him slightly embarrassed as it was written to him. 'I do not think,' he wrote awkwardly, 'it is only my gratification (which is real because I know you are sincere) which causes me to think it certainly the most poetic piece I have seen of yours.'

There is a copy of it in Caine's handwriting in his archive. As it is dated May 12th, 1880, it must have been intended as a birthday present—it is headed 'Dante Gabriel Rossetti'.

> As when the red ripe harvest newly mown
> Is gathered to a garner where it fell
> And some stout reaper laden all too well
> Bear'st to the barn what grain his fields have grown;
> And, striding through the stubble, feel'st it blown
> In stray small ears, by wayward winds, away;
> And seest the younglings snatch the shreds in play
> And fly in first, and claim them for their own:-
>
> So thou, Rossetti, know'st thy Autumn crown'd
> With the full fruit, and makest many a mate
> Grow great with spoils in steps of thy feet found;
> Yet farest thou best; Well may'st thou choose to wait;
> For lo, strong toiler, thou com'st last though late
> Laden with golden treasure to the ground.

Rossetti commented, 'The image is most complete and thoroughly rendered. In fact the octave is of first rate excellence. I will say no more of my part in it except—thank you.' The only phrase he queried was 'last though late' in the penultimate line. The sending of the birthday sonnet marked a subtle change in the friendship. They still continued their literary discussions but in the background hung the idea that they must meet and soon.

Still no date was set but Rossetti was increasingly curious to see this strange young man who wrote so enthusiastically and at such length but he still held back from naming a day for him to call, not knowing what to expect. Then on 27 May Caine mentioned quite casually that F.G. Stephens was to be in Liverpool on 8 June. 'I am invited to a sort of Conversazione at which, I believe, he is to give a kind of lecture.'

Rossetti leaped at this, replying the next day with a letter that begins, 'As my friend F.G. Stephens is to be in Liverpool, give him (if you like) the enclosed card, and he will be glad to know you for my sake and will learn to be so for your own. This I mean if it proves convenient for you to use it.' Caine was flattered to get such an introduction. For Rossetti it was the opportunity he had been looking for, to have a first-hand report on Caine from someone whose opinion he trusted. He had known Frederick Stephens since the summer of 1848 and the foundation of the Pre-Raphaelite Brotherhood. Stephens was the same age as Rossetti and championed his work from the start. After the Brotherhood drifted apart, and through all the vicissitudes of Rossetti's life, Stephens remained a devoted and loyal friend. One can imagine how anxiously Rossetti awaited his report.

Caine thanked Rossetti fulsomely for the introduction. He thought it was a particular mark of Rossetti's esteem. It was only later he realised he was being vetted before any visit to Cheyne Walk could take place. With this letter he sent the proofs of his 'Politics and Art' essay, soon to be published in pamphlet form. Rossetti thought it 'as fervid and vigorous as anything I have seen of yours. However, your case is serious in one respect. You must really tabulate your memory as regards your own work.' He had repeated something he had used elsewhere—Rossetti marked the passage. Caine thanked him, adding, 'My memory on that subject is most dangerous and is apt to treat me scurvily.' He was full of the thrill of meeting Stephens. The locals had not appreciated his lecture, it was over their heads. He, Caine, who had of course fully appreciated it, would report on it for one of the Liverpool papers. Stephens showed him marked attention, keeping him at his side the whole evening. Caine was particularly pleased when Stephens repeated to him 'some kind words which William Morris had said of me. I was really heartily gratified.' After the meeting ended he walked to the Mersey ferry with Stephens, who was staying in Birkenhead with George Rae, the collector of Pre-Raphaelite art.

As he was not returning to London immediately Stephens wrote to Cheyne Walk. Rossetti's relief bubbles over in the letter he wrote to Caine immediately after receiving the letter.

I am very glad you were welcomed by dear staunch Stephens, as I felt sure you would be. He holds the honourable position of being the only living art-critic who has really himself worked through the Art-Schools practically and learnt to draw and paint. He is one of my oldest and best friends, of whom few can be numbered at my age, from causes only too varying.

Stephens had been surprised at Caine's youth.

Rossetti added a significant remark: 'I have often thought I should enjoy the presence of a congenial and intellectual housefellow and boardfellow in this big barn of mine, which is actually going to rack and ruin for want of use. But where to find the welcome, the willing and the able combined in one?' He had in fact had a 'housefellow' for many years, his painting assistant and paid secretary, Henry Treffry Dunn.

According to William Rossetti, Treffry Dunn had been installed as a professional assistant to his brother in 1867. He describes him as being 'a Cornishman, with a narrow, full-tinted visage, prematurely grey hair, and lively dark eyes. He was an efficient painter, with qualities of execution more solid than graceful, and was of much use to Rossetti in a variety of ways.' The arrangement had worked well for more than ten years but by July of 1880 Rossetti had quarrelled with him and had stopped paying his salary. Eventually Dunn had had enough and retired to Cornwall, refusing to come back to Cheyne Walk until his arrears of salary were paid. He only got his money after Gabriel's death when William as executor paid it out of the estate. It was quite a considerable amount so that Dunn had a right to feel aggrieved after all he had done for Rossetti.

Rossetti went on to ask if Caine was 'aware that at Manchester Ford Madox Brown...is painting frescoes in the Town Hall? Has notice been taken of them in the Liverpool papers? I suppose this must have been the case, as I know they have attracted much attention... FMB is at work there at this moment.' He enclosed a photograph of his newest sketch of either his mother or Christina—it is not with the letter—made when they had spent the previous Christmas with him at Cheyne Walk. He asked Caine what he thought of it and in a postscript wondered, 'Is the S in your address tacked on to an innumerable set of 59's or does it mean South Chester Street?' Caine never wrote 'South' out in full.

One might have expected him to answer this long letter with its exciting hints at once but he was ill again. On the 3rd he escaped to Bowness for three days' convalescence, spending the time, as he wrote to Rossetti, 'clad in blue serge and engaging in the only physical exercise I know how altogether to enjoy, boating'. The weather was fine and rowing out into the middle of Windermere he rested on his oars and drifted, drinking in the peace of sky and water and hills. If only, he said to Rossetti, he could live among these hills he would be 'completely healed'. He had been working hard, he explained, and for several mornings 'received a hint that my circulation of blood was about to kick over the traces: nothing very serious: only some few drops of blood in the wash basin and always clearly coming from my head though coming from my mouth. Vigorous exercise was manifestly best for me (if taken judiciously) and so I ran up to the Lakeland and for 3 superlatively lovely days enjoyed sheer existence as never before.'

He thanked Rossetti warmly for the photograph of the 'exquisite' sketch and apologised for not writing sooner. Although he had intended to keep out of journalism financial pressures meant he was back 'in partial newspaper harness' so he was extremely busy. He was interested to hear of Madox Brown's frescoes which as far as he knew had not been mentioned in Liverpool. He thought he could manage 'a few sticks' about them. 'Would he [Madox Brown] care to have them described? If so, is he still at Manchester and would he be willing to let me look at him as well as his work?'

Once more Caine had given Rossetti exactly what he wanted: the opportunity for one of his trusted friends to run an eye over him and report back. By return of post he sent Caine a note of introduction to Madox Brown. He was 'sure FMB would like to know you and that you should notice his work... You will find him at work I believe all day and even by gaslight until 9 or 10.'

Caine answered Rossetti's enquiry about South Chester Street by giving a description of the area in which he had spent 'eleven twelfths' of his life, 'grudgingly enough, I fear sometimes'. It has been said that he grew up and went to school in the Isle of Man. He may have allowed that impression to arise when it suited him for tax purposes to be regarded as Manx but this statement to Rossetti, which agrees with everything else known of his childhood, gives the lie to it. He hoped to have a short holiday and told Rossetti he would spend part of it in London. Rossetti replied, 'Your letter holds out a welcome probability of meeting you here ere long.'

It was on 25 July, 1880, that Caine went over to Manchester to meet Rossetti's friend. Ford Madox Brown had studied on the Continent and was noted for his paintings of historical scenes and the rich, sombre colours he used. Rossetti had once briefly been his pupil in the early days of the Pre-Raphaelite Brotherhood. His twelve Manchester Town Hall frescoes, which can still be seen, were his biggest project, begun in 1879 and worked on almost until his death in 1893. He and his wife Emma had a son, Oliver, known to the family as Nolly. He was a talented poet and his sonnets were much admired by Rossetti but he died tragically at the age of 19 and Brown was devastated. He never really got over his loss.

Rossetti had warned Caine not to mention Nolly but Brown brought the subject up himself, talking freely about his dead son. Their meeting lasted for five hours. Caine dashed off a note to Rossetti. 'I found the utmost enjoyment in my visit and have now to thank you heartily to whom I owe it.' The two frescoes already completed had impressed him: 'both are soberly-brilliant pieces of colour and vivid examples of characterisation'. Brown had talked at length

> about the men of whom I wished chiefly to hear. What he said of you was very pleasant, and would, I am sure, be grateful to you if you were to hear it. He gave me in that quiet, picturesque way of his that is enchanting, his earliest recollections of you, dating back, I think, 30 years... I should imagine you can have no more passionate admirer or affectionate friend.

In a letter dated merely 'Friday' Rossetti for the first time gave a definite invitation to Caine to go and see him. 'I shall be truly glad to meet you when you come to town,' he said. 'You will recognize the hole-and-cornerest of all existences, but I'll read you a ballad or two, and have Brown's report to back my certainty of liking you. That you would like Brown I knew. He is one of the most naturally and genially gifted talkers I know, but that mention of yours of the biggest of big R's was just the unluckiest thing you could have said, and I myself think that the talk from and about that particular Capital Letter is already about enough for several universes, only don't say I said so, as he is an old acquaintance.' A note in Caine's handwriting on a typed transcript of this letter identifies the 'big R' as Ruskin.

Caine explained his delay in writing as being due to a by-election which had 'eaten up all available energy' for a couple of weeks. In a lordly fashion he said he could not really interest himself in mere by-elections as 'these lesser disputes have little in them to engage my best feelings'. While he was known to have 'eminently radical...almost communistic, convictions' the local Liberal papers 'snarl at me...whilst the Tory papers devote occasional leaders to the praise of my doings'. Towards the end of this letter he said, 'Yes, I hope to be in London before long and then—well, then you must let me see you. FMB gave me such ample accounts of you that I quite feel that I know you.'

The occasion for this visit to London was an invitation from James Halliwell-Phillipps and his wife to spend two days with them in Brighton early in September, 1880. Halliwell-Phillipps was a scholar and biographer of Shakespeare, who was well known to anyone interested in the Bard. How Caine got to the point of being invited to stay with him at Hollingbury Copse, his Brighton home, no one knows but Professor Dowden may have had a hand in it.

However the invitation arose Caine accepted it with alacrity. He arranged to take a train to London on Monday, 6 September and stay at his usual hotel for that night. He would travel down to Brighton on the Tuesday afternoon, returning to London on the Thursday for another

overnight stay, going home on Friday, 10 September. He waited after his
initial letter to Rossetti saying when he would be in London but no invitation arrived from Cheyne Walk. By this time he knew Rossetti well
enough, both from their correspondence and from what Stephens and
Madox Brown had told him, to realise that if he wanted the meeting he
had to propose himself for a definite date. At the last minute he sent
Rossetti his travel arrangements, gave him the address of his hotel—the
temperance one at 37 Queen Square, Bloomsbury—and asked permission to call on the Monday evening. The actual letter has not come to
light but Rossetti's reply shows it was written and that it threw him into
a tizzy. On the Friday he wrote, 'Do I understand that you are to be in
London only on 2 separate days? This would seem rather difficult to deal
with as to appointments, yet I should be sorry indeed to miss you when
you do come to town. The evening is my only fit time for seeing
friends—the day is too scattered.' He might have added that his day
rarely began before noon. 'I would propose that you should dine with
me at 8.30 and spend the evening. But you must let me know what further you can about it.' There were two postscripts. The first said, 'Of
course if an evening's impossible, I'd be pleased at your just looking in
on me one afternoon any time after 3,' and the second, 'Of course when
I speak of your dining with me, I mean tête à tête and without ceremony of any kind. I usually dine in my studio and in my painting coat!
D.G.R.'

This reached Caine on Saturday, 4 September, and he set out early on
the Monday morning thinking everything was arranged. Rossetti, however, was on the dither again and on the Saturday night wrote a further
note asking,

> Is Friday evening free with you in London? If so, it happens to suit me better
> than Monday, though Monday would do. In either case, better come about
> 7 on Monday or 5.30 to 6 on Friday (if feasible with you) that I may try to shew
> you a picture by daylight. I judge this will reach you in time tomorrow for a
> note to reach me on Monday probably. But if not and you turn up on Monday,
> all will be well. Telegrams I hate.

That Rossetti could think a letter written on a Saturday evening in
London might reach Caine in Liverpool on a Sunday is a neat comment
on the postal services of those days.

Of course this last note missed Caine but on checking into his hotel
he found a postcard from Rossetti asking him to call at Cheyne Walk so
he turned up on the Monday evening as arranged. Before that he had
been to the offices of several national newspapers seeking freelance
work. That evening both he and Rossetti were as nervous as any
penfriends meeting for the first time. Caine's shyness and awkwardness
has already been mentioned. When meeting new people he was

self-conscious and insecure, more like an awkward teenager than a young man in his mid-twenties who had been out in the world of work for more than ten years. Rossetti, at this stage of his life, was always reduced to a state of shattered nerves by the prospect of meeting someone new, even someone with whom he had been corresponding regularly over the previous nine months. However, the occasion was made easier for both of them by the presence of the faithful William, who always dined with his brother on a Monday.

Caine has left a detailed account of this first meeting. His book, *Recollections of Rossetti*, was published exactly two years later. While it is the best available account and is broadly a true record it must still be treated with circumspection as some of the details are patently not correct. Whether this is because his memory was treating him 'scurvily' again or because he set out to deceive it is hardly possible to say.

16 Cheyne Walk is still standing and still bears the name Tudor House on the gatepost. An earlier owner chose it because he thought it had at one time been the home of the Tudor Princess Elizabeth, but this is not possible as the present house is an excellent example of eighteenth-century London town architecture. It was built on the site of the home of Sir Thomas More. Rossetti had moved in as tenant in 1862, after his wife's death, as he could not bear to stay in the home they had shared. His brother William lived with him, as did George Meredith and Swinburne, who both had rooms there at one time, though this arrangement did not last long. Rossetti endowed his palatial new home with a raffish Bohemian splendour. While Rossetti was never conventional, Swinburne's wild behaviour was too much even for him. Swinburne, very drunk, sliding naked down the bannisters, was more than he could take. And definitely more than the staid William was prepared to put up with. Swinburne left.

Rossetti continued to live there in shabby splendour, filling the place with mirrors and making a shrine to his wife Lizzie with her paintings and drawings on the walls. He insisted she had great talent but no one else agreed. He made a fine collection of blue and white china. For years he kept a menagerie in the garden with many strange animals including a wombat. He loved that animal dearly and would nurse it on his lap upside down while he tickled its tummy. Morris drew a cartoon of it. Rossetti was distraught when it died. He alarmed his friends at one point by insisting he was going to buy an elephant and train it to wash the windows but he was persuaded to drop the idea.

Approaching the house Caine viewed it with an educated eye. He approved its façade, which looked to him as dating from the Queen Anne period, but he thought the addition of two bay windows had 'much mutilated' its classical purity. William Rossetti, on hearing this comment, remarked that from the inside they were a great improvement to the large drawing room, running the full width of the house. From the style of the house, with its big stone gateposts and paved courtyard in front and solid end walls, it looked to Caine as if it had originally stood alone. In Rossetti's time it was, as it is now, part of a terrace facing the river. Cheyne Walk when first built had meandered along the banks of the Thames with the water not far from the iron courtyard gates but the building of the Chelsea Embankment meant it now stood well back, divided from the river by trees and the busy road along the new river wall. The house looked neglected, as it had been for some time, with peeling paint and rampant ivy which threatened to cover some of the windows, though they were so filthy with the dust and grime of years it would not have made much difference if it had. Weeds grew through the chinks in the courtyard paving. The large garden of about an acre at the back of the house was an overgrown wilderness. By the time Caine first arrived on the doorstep the animals had been long gone and Rossetti was about to lose the greater part of his garden as the landlord intended to build on it.

A servant answered the door to his ring and led him into the entrance hall, which looked at once fine and shabby. There were statues in two recesses, a handsome grandfather clock and a beautiful marble floor, but the walls needed painting and much of the floor was covered with frayed coconut matting. It struck him as odd that there was no sign of a staircase, only three doors leading off the hall and a corridor on either side. The central door opened and Rossetti advanced on him with both hands extended and the cheery 'Hulloa' with which he greeted all his friends.

CHAPTER SEVEN

Gabriel turned and led his visitor through the third door, which was the entrance to the studio. William was waiting there and Caine shook his hand. Although he had met many distinguished men, including Henry Irving, Lord Houghton and William Morris, this meeting with the Rossetti brothers almost overwhelmed him. There were other men who were important and helpful to him in his career and a number he counted as friends but Gabriel Rossetti might have been from another planet, so far above anyone else was he in Caine's estimation and affections. Quite simply, he idolised him.

In a letter to Dowden written after his return to Liverpool Caine described Gabriel as he saw him that evening.

> A man of medium height; inclined to corpulency; with a full round face that ought to be ruddy but is deathly pale; large black eyes, very brilliant at times and then lapsing into laziness of expression; a massive forehead with strong lines over the eyebrows suggestive not of severity but boundless power; intensely nervous, and occasionally of an irritable manner which he struggles hard to control. His hair (now grown thin) and long beard are streaked with gray; his walk is painfully weak and shaky and the whole outward seeming is that of a man grown old long ages before his due time. He talks rapidly for a while and then the last few words fall lingeringly: his voice, which in conversation seems thin and almost fretful, becomes organ-toned when he reads poetry, which he does as I never heard man read before... We sat up until all hours and he read me whole volumes of his unpublished poetry, all or much of it in my opinion greater in every way than any contained in his book [the collection published in 1870].

This first impression gives a better picture of Rossetti in 1880 than the over-written and sycophantic description which Caine put into *Recollections of Rossetti*, written after his subject's death. The later writing has been sanitised, with all comment that might be construed as critical omitted. Caine was not too overcome by the occasion to note the details of the studio. It was 'a large room probably measuring thirty feet by twenty, and structurally as puzzling as the other parts of the house. A series of columns and arches on one side suggested that the room had almost certainly been at some period the site of an important staircase with a wide well, and on the other side a broad mullioned window reaching to the ceiling.' There was a large fireplace at one end and a number of fine chalk drawings and water colours on the walls. Several easels carried oil paintings in various stages of completion. There was not much room for furniture but there were a couple of armchairs, a small writing table and cane chair in a corner by the window, a bookcase with a copy of the Stratford bust of Shakespeare on top of it and a large sofa. Gabriel flung himself down on this 'with his head laid low and his feet thrown up in a favourite attitude on the back, which must, I imagine, have been at least as easy as it was elegant.' As Caine describes it it sounds neither.

Gabriel opened the conversation by remarking on how 'robustious' Caine looked (a word even then archaic but which deserves resurrection) compared with what he had been led to expect from repeated references to 'uncertain health'. This is further confirmation that most of the illnesses Caine complained of were psychoneurotic in origin and that he was basically fit and strong.

The Rossetti family photographed by Charles Lutwidge Dodgson (Lewis Carroll) in the garden of 16 Cheyne Walk on 7 October, 1863. Left to right: Dante Gabriel, Christina, Mrs Rossetti, William Michael Rossetti.

William watched, saying little. The family were worried about this latest arrival on the scene. Gabriel had attracted a succession of younger men whom he took up enthusiastically, championing them as God's gift to poetry or art and often raising the eyebrows of his contemporaries. William suspected that Caine was 'on the make' and only after what he could get from his brother in the way of advancement. He modified this view on acquaintance and was later grateful to Caine for the unselfish way in which he abandoned his own work to look after the increasingly ailing Gabriel.

Returning to that September evening in 1880, Caine's account says that the three men adjourned to the small, green dining-room hung with round mirrors, despite what Gabriel had said in his letter about dining in the studio. Gabriel was in high spirits. He 'rattled off two of the rhymes, now called "Limericks", at the making of which nobody who ever attempted that form of amusement has been known to match him'. He ridiculed some of his best friends in this form, including Bell Scott:

> There once was a painter named Scott,
> Who seemed to have hair, but had not.
>   He seemed to have sense,
>   'Twas an equal pretence
> On the part of the painter named Scott.

If he was unkind in rhyme to his friends he did not spare himself either, as in this, composed after he had attained fame and distinction:

> There is a poor sneak called Rossetti,
> As a painter with many kicks met he—
>   With more than a man—
>   But sometimes he ran,
> And that saved the rear of Rossetti.

Caine's remark about Rossetti's limericks is not mentioned in his first *Recollections of Rossetti*. It comes from the 1928 revised version. By that time Caine himself had also been the subject of at least two of these comic verses.

Over dinner Gabriel talked about his friends, the two Caine had met and others such as Theodore Watts whom he had not. Watts, said Gabriel, had a head like Napoleon, adding with a chuckle 'whom he detests', while Frederic Shields was 'as hysterical as Shelley'. Shields was also a great draughtsman, 'none better now living, unless it is Leighton or Sir Noel Paton'. Rossetti likened Ford Madox Brown to Dr Johnson in that he was equally sententious. Caine had reservations on that judgement, having got on famously with Brown and found him an easy talker.

After the meal they settled in the studio for an evening of poetry. Rossetti wore spectacles, and when he was reading put a second pair over the first. In his *Recollections* Caine comments that Rossetti was dressed in a manner which seemed to him 'rather negligent than otherwise'. He was wearing a knee-length 'sack-coat', buttoned to the neck and with large vertically cut pockets at the sides. This was the famous 'painting coat' which Gabriel wore most of the time. It was one of several garments which he designed and had specially made up.

As Gabriel read Caine looked up at the drawings and watercolours on the walls and thought how right Gabriel had been when he had written that the feeling in his paintings was the same as in his poetry—there was a strong affinity between the two. He ended with a new ballad, 'The White Ship'. Some discussion followed of Gabriel's sonnets. Caine said he admired most the sad one, 'Without Her'. 'I cannot tell you at what terrible moment it was wrung from me', said Gabriel. He had written it after his wife died from an overdose of laudanum which could have been accidental but might have been suicide. A verdict of accidental death was returned at the inquest.

16 Cheyne Walk.

Eventually, well after midnight, William insisted it was time to go and Caine rose with him. Gabriel asked Caine when he would be back from Brighton. He insisted he must dine with him again on the Thursday and sleep the night at Cheyne Walk. He should come early so that he could see some pictures by daylight.

In his first version of this meeting Caine ends there. In the later account he says that Gabriel came to the door to see them off and William offered him a lift. They hailed a hansom and William dropped him 'at the door of the "hole-and-cornerest" of all hotels, which, as a young countryman I had somehow ferreted out'. It is difficult to understand why he should have said this. Far from being a simple young countryman he had been coming to London for years, knew it well and had no difficulty in 'ferreting out' a temperance hotel. As the national headquarters of the Band of Hope, 37 Queen Square hardly qualified as a 'hole-and-corner' hotel even if it was not very grand. Caine said he remembered the cab ride with William because of 'a dazed sense of having seen and spoken to and spent an evening with what I thought one of the gods of the earth. That is a delicious sensation that only comes once perhaps to any of us, and then in our youth; and it was after my first meeting with Rossetti that it came to me.' And remained with him for fifty years.

Still in a daze he caught a train to Brighton next day and was welcomed by Halliwell-Phillipps who, he told Dowden, was 'a great big old boy who never talks about books and won't let anybody else talk of them'. He found him delightful company and was introduced to some of his friends. He called them 'good old Shakespearian dry-as-dusts'. On the Wednesday the note Rossetti had fired off at the last minute about Friday night being the most convenient arrived, forwarded from Liverpool. Caine hardly knew what he was expected to do—should he stick to Thursday as arranged or should he go on Friday? He sent a hurried note to Cheyne Walk saying he knew Rossetti hated telegrams but unless he heard by noon next day he would take an afternoon train and arrive at 6 that evening as arranged.

He need not have worried. Rossetti welcomed him as cheerfully as before, though Caine thought he looked tired and unwell compared to the previous Monday. In his 1882 account of the meetings he glosses over the time between them and runs the story of the two evenings together so it is difficult to work out what Rossetti was supposed to have said on each occasion. By 1928 Caine was airily saying he had been to Brighton for 'two weeks for my health' rather than two days. No mention of Halliwell-Phillipps. Letters written at the time give the true picture.

On this second visit Caine and Rossetti were alone together and again the evening passed in literary talk and reading poetry. Caine has left what appears to be a detailed account of the conversation on both the Monday and the Thursday evenings, rather on the lines of Boswell's records of Dr Johnson's talk. He later insisted he took no notes but was able to assemble his account from letters he wrote to friends at the time and it was a genuine record of what took place.

They sat up until 4 am, nothing unusual for Rossetti, as Caine was to discover. He almost reversed the normal pattern of waking and sleeping. Rossetti referred to this 'idiosyncrasy' by saying, 'I lie as long, or say as late, as Dr Johnson used to do. You shall never know until you discover it for yourself, at what hour I rise.'

To Caine's discomfort, Rossetti started questioning him about the lecture when he was challenged by Philip Rathbone. He tried to change the subject, knowing how such criticism could upset his host, but Rossetti insisted and wrung the full details of what had been said from a reluctant Caine. He listened attentively, saying at the end that it was the old story, which had begun ten years before with Buchanan's attack 'and would go on until he had been hunted and hounded to his grave'. Caine was startled by Rossetti's intensity and appalled that what had seemed to him merely an error of critical judgement should have been taken so personally. He tried to reassure him that this was just one man against the many who praised his work and nothing personal had been intended. Rossetti said kindly, 'It was right of you to tell me when I asked you... But of this conspiracy to persecute me—what remains to say but that it is widespread and remorseless—one cannot but feel it.' Caine endeavoured to persuade him that no such conspiracy existed but it is indicative of Rossetti's mental state at the time, induced by his drug addiction, that he stuck to his persecution complex. It was this which kept him so much indoors. If he did venture out he felt sure everyone was staring at him with contempt and wanted to attack him. It also led to his refusing to admit any but a few of his most cherished friends to the house. He was certain his enemies were planning to invade it. About a year before Caine's first visit Rossetti complained bitterly about the noise from his neighbours which he said was coming through the studio wall and was deliberately intended to stop him working. Nobody else could hear a thing. William said the noise was a hallucination caused by the chloral his brother was taking and he was probably right. However, to try to keep Gabriel happy Watts and Treffry Dunn spent a whole weekend building a false wall at the end of the studio and filling the gap with wadding to stop the 'noise'.

Unaware of all this, Caine insisted there was no conspiracy and Rossetti had many ardent supporters, but he just shook his head and said Caine must know what he asserted was true. Growing impatient with this delusion Caine told him this was depression induced by isolation. Rossetti admitted he had hardly been out of the house for years. 'Your brain has meanwhile been breeding a host of hallucinations, like cobwebs in a dark corner,' said Caine. 'You have only to go abroad, and the fresh air will blow these things away.' With his love of fresh air and exercise Caine could not understand what chains bound the older man. He continued to plead with him and was upset when Rossetti's only reply was to name as enemies three or four men whom Caine knew admired his work and supported him in every way. He insisted they had not called recently because their work had kept them too busy. This was not entirely true. Caine did not know at this stage how Rossetti's odd behaviour had saddened some of his oldest friends and kept them away.

This exchange set Caine's nervous guts reacting—'an attack of the mullygrubs', as he called it, which spoilt the evening for him. Eventually even Rossetti was ready for bed. He told Caine he was to sleep in Watts's room. 'He comes here at least twice a week, talking until four o'clock in the morning upon everything from poetry to the Pleiades, and driving away the bogies.' As he lived at Putney Hill a bed was kept for him. Rossetti suggested that before Caine went to his own room he should have a look at his. On the way to it he opened a door to the drawing-room, a large room smelling musty with disuse. The candles they carried glittered in the crystals of three large chandeliers. On the walls were a number of small watercolours in oak frames. Caine walked round looking at them.

'I should have thought the man who painted these pictures was rather a poet than a painter—who was it?' he asked.

Rossetti answered in a low voice, 'It was my wife. She had great genius.'

They moved on to Rossetti's room, further down the same corridor. It was reached through a smaller one, his breakfast room. It was bright and cheerful with a chandelier which once belonged to David Garrick. From the tapping of trees against the window Caine supposed it looked onto the garden.

The inner room, however, was contrastingly dark, with heavy tapestry hangings on the walls and round the bed. There were thick velvet curtains and the candles they held scarcely penetrated the general gloom. Their voices sounded muffled. An enormous black oak chimney-piece filled most of one wall, nearly reaching the ceiling and dominating the entire room. It was strangely carved, with an ivory crucifix on one of its many ledges. At the foot of the bed was a couch with a table in front of it bearing a wire lantern with a spare candle beside it. As Rossetti lit the candle in the lantern from the one he held, Caine remarked that he probably burned a light all night. Rossetti admitted he did, saying his curse was insomnia. He often got up in the night when he could not sleep and lay on the couch reading by the light of the lantern—Caine noticed he had taken a volume of Boswell's *Johnson* from the studio bookcase as they started for bed. Were Rossetti's references to Dr Johnson and the deliberate choosing of his bedtime reading meant as a hint that he saw Caine as his Boswell?

Also on the table were two small bottles, sealed and labelled, and beside them a measuring-glass. Caine asked if that was his medicine.

'They say there is a skeleton in every cupboard,' Rossetti said quietly, 'and that's mine; it's chloral.' Caine was shocked but forbore to comment. Chloral is an oily, colourless liquid produced by the action of chlorine on ethanol, with a characteristic pungent smell. Mixed with water it becomes chloral hydrate which is a powerful sleep-inducing drug. It is also strongly addictive, something not appreciated by the early Victorian doctors who prescribed it. Rossetti had been given it at the time of his wife's death eighteen years before and it had taken its inevitable toll, producing the morbid condition in which he now found himself.

Watts's bedroom turned out to be as gloomy as Rossetti's own. Caine described it as 'heavy with hangings and black with antique picture panels'. The ceiling was so high it was beyond the light of the single candle he had been given. Seeing Caine's reaction Rossetti said it never worried Watts who was entirely unaffected by his eerie surroundings and slept soundly. 'But on myself,' Caine wrote later, 'I fear they weighed heavily, and augmented the feeling of closeness and gloom which had been creeping upon me since I entered the house.' The room was full of bric à brac which Rossetti had found on his rambles around Chelsea, together with some very strange old books. Carved heads and grinning gargoyles, together with Burmese and Chinese Buddhas 'of every degree of placid ugliness' seemed to have been left about with the sole purpose of murdering visitors' sleep—or at least frightening the chambermaid. For a young man from the back streets of Toxteth it must have been akin to sleeping in the Chamber of Horrors.

Caine got into bed and as he was young and healthy and it was past four in the morning he was soon drifting off to sleep. At that point Rossetti came back, ostensibly to ask if he had enjoyed his visit. Caine replied that he would never forget it.

'If you decide to settle in London I trust you'll come and live with me, and then many such evenings must remove the memory of this one.'

Caine laughed at so remote a possibility.

As he left the room Rossetti said, almost boasting, 'I have just taken sixty grains of chloral. In four hours I take sixty more and in four hours after that yet another sixty.' Caine, who knew what that meant, was shaken. Rossetti said he had taken more chloral than anyone else. His doctor had told him that if he went to a Turkish bath he would 'sweat it at every pore'.

When Rossetti had gone Caine was left to contemplate this revelation. It accounted for what had puzzled him about Rossetti's delusions. The drug 'had blighted half his life'. Which was true. However, Rossetti was not actually taking the enormous amount of chloral he thought he was: his doctor had ordered the chemist to dilute the mixture before dispensing it.

When Caine woke next morning there was no sign of his host and he breakfasted alone. It was a fine day with the first hint of autumn. With nothing to do he went out into the garden. An avenue of limes opened onto a large open space. The grass was long and rank, weeds everywhere. Evidently the tenant was completely indifferent to the wild state of his garden. Considering he knew he was shortly to lose most of it this was not surprising.

Returning to the house Caine browsed through the library. Though not large it contained valuable books dating back to the sixteenth and seventeenth centuries. Rossetti had bought them more for their illustrations than their text. Ruskin's work featured there and books in French and Italian.

Caine waited as long as he could to say goodbye and thank Rossetti for his hospitality but eventually he gave up as he had other business to see to before catching the Liverpool train. He left a note saying he had 'slept soundly, never better'. The refrain of Rossetti's ballad 'The White Ship' was, he said, still with him and he could remember much else of what he had heard, though he was 'confoundedly angry with the Fates that I should have had that miserable ache while you were reading'. He made a request he had not felt able to voice the night before: could he please have a copy of the sonnet 'Without Her'?

Time was pressing as he had an appointment with a possible publisher for his anthology. 'In case he thinks favourably of the proposal,' he added to his note, 'I believe I shall on the strength of it, and of some reviewing work that is offered me, come down to London to live, and in the lecturing season look up the lecturing brotherhood and see what can be done. I shall be warmly prompted to bend all energy in that direction by the recollection of last night and the prospect of other nights of the sort at intervals.' He was worried about the impression he had given, being ill at ease much of the previous evening due to 'that d-d gut's ache'. He was disappointed though not surprised that Rossetti was not up to see him off. Leaving his note in the studio, he let himself out. On the doorstep he took a deep breath of fresh air and shook off the gloom of the house behind him. With its mediaeval furniture, dark panelling and collection of ancient artifacts, censors, crucifixes and lamps, Caine had found the atmosphere of the aptly named Tudor House 'heavy and unwholesome.' But his visit had cemented his affection for this 'most magnetic of men'.

His business that morning took him to Paternoster Row, the centre of the printing, publishing and bookselling business. He was headed for

No. 53, the offices of Elliot Stock. The firm had been founded by the eponymous Mr Stock in 1859, specialising in non-sectarian religious works and periodicals, although by 1880 he had expanded the scope of his list considerably. He had set aside a writing room for the use of ministers and clergymen of all denominations but it gradually became a centre and meeting place for antiquarians and bibliophiles. In 1873 he founded the *Baptist*, which was how Caine came to hear of him. Early in 1880 he had founded another magazine, the *Antiquary*, edited by Edward Walford. Caine had contributed to it from the start but it was not magazines he had come to discuss, it was his sonnet book.

Stock had a long-standing interest in the Pre-Raphaelites. He had published the work of several of them, including Bell Scott, so his visitor's remark that he had come from staying the night at Mr Gabriel Rossetti's house was a good introduction. Stock was interested in Caine's proposal and took little persuading to publish a book which came with Rossetti's recommendation. Royalties were not usual in those days, publishers more often buying the copyright. At least an author knew what he was getting but if the book was a success and ran into several editions he was the loser. Stock preferred what was known as the joint-share method of publishing, with the author agreeing to buy up all unsold copies, but he offered Caine a royalty of £2.2.0 per hundred copies sold after the first 250. His usual print-run for a book of verse—he had recently brought out one by Philip Bourke Marston—was 1000. While delighted at the chance of publication in London by a prestigious house Caine was not sure whether he should accept and asked for time to think it over. He felt such a novice in the world of book publishing that he wanted to seek advice before signing a contract. He would have preferred a lump sum for the copyright. Royalties seemed too uncertain and might not provide the money he needed if he was to move to London.

Caine's intentions for the immediate future were now fixed: to get to London come what may. Back with his T-square and drawing board in the small office allotted to him, looking out onto the yard full of carts and men coming and going, the contrast between the life of a builder's draughtsman and the sophisticated world of art and letters he had glimpsed was painful. With this first visit to Rossetti comes a change in his attitude to life and his own work. His horizons were broadened and ambitions raised. From this point he began, consciously or subconsciously, the process of reinventing himself. T.H. Hall Caine, the T-square wielding builder's assistant and part-time provincial journalist, became Hall Caine the Great Author and Man of Letters, as he saw himself, the commercially successful romantic novelist as the world saw him. His first move was to drop the spare H in his signature, as he pointed out in one of his letters to Rossetti. For the next six years all his work was signed T. Hall Caine. After that, with the publication of his first novel, the remaining initial was discarded and he became Hall Caine. It took a little longer for the rest of the world to recognise this.

Apart from dropping initials he would have to discard the architectural draughtsman. This meant giving notice to James Bromley and sinking or swimming by the aid of his pen alone. It would have been a big enough step had he only been responsible for himself. With parents, a younger brother and a little sister to support it was a very serious step indeed. Rossetti, pondering the note Caine had left him, saw that and was worried he might be held responsible for encouraging Caine to take the risk. 'I should welcome your advent in London warmly,' he wrote,

> but of course I do think it a step requiring an infinity of forethought, and one which no friend has a right to urge on you over strongly. I know a man who has command of the best journals in an average—I may say a high average—way, and who I know states that £400 or £500 a year is the utmost to be made by a successful journalist. Of course you would be far from needing so much as this at present—but how far might you be (during dangerous interval of delay) from making even as much as you make now? I only say, ponder it well.

William and his wife Lucy had been spending the evening with him. Both had spoken warmly of Caine, particularly William. 'Now, by the bye, what would <u>he</u> have done without his permanent berth?' Gabriel added. 'He never realised one half per annum by literature of the sum named by my friend whom I quoted,—and his usual income from that source must have been ridiculously below the half. Nevertheless I do not want to write in an ominous tone, and no doubt you have too much experience to act rashly.'

This reached Caine on the Monday morning after his return from London and that night he sat down to write a long reply. After four pages of the usual literary criticism he said, 'I've not heard yet from the Publisher about the contemplated Sonnet book—I can't think what occasions the delay.' As he had only seen Stock the previous Friday morning this must have amused Rossetti.

'I am writing as fast as I can lots of stupid sketches for guineas each. Of course I despise the work, indeed I loathe it, but the money is needed and (when each sketch is finished) is forthcoming, so I go ahead.' Several pages further on he replied to Rossetti's anxious comments on his plans.

> My dear Mr Rossetti, I thank you heartily for your letter intended to warn me against too rashly leaving Liverpool… I do not think there is much danger of my acting hastily: the opposite is my weakness, and indeed I go on ruminating upon any step I contemplate until I appear to lose the power of carrying it out… I have now other interests to consider than my own merely: a painful accident which occurred about one and a half years ago leaving invalided the head of our household. My own needs would be ridiculously small and you

would smile if I were to say how inconsiderable a part of £500 a year would, if quite assured to me, take me away from here, but I cannot and must not rid myself of a responsibility which makes the necessity for a certain sum a lasting one. I shall not trouble you with the facts, painful enough to me at the best and always hampering. So you see I'm not likely to run away heedlessly... London today seems more remote than it did a fortnight ago, and yet come what may I <u>must</u> bend all my energies in that direction.

Rossetti replied that he was sorry to hear 'of obligations impeding your career. Their nature is no business of mine, but merely that you are hampered.' He hoped he would soon have a good offer from Stock 'but I know how flighty is the memory of publishers'.

The publisher concerned had already written, repeating the offer discussed in his office. It arrived on the Tuesday morning and Caine, not knowing what to do, sent the letter on to Rossetti. He in turn showed it to William, who 'viewed it as a curiosity'. Gabriel himself thought it was no offer at all—the results of any sales being so 'problematical' that 'the question remains whether a start in this form might or might not be worth your while, *loss* positive being avoided'. He added that William would ask Swinburne for some sonnets and Caine should write himself to his sister, Christina. He thought on the whole Caine should go ahead though he still said the offer was not fair. Stock thought the book would contain only new poems and shied off this. When he realised it was to range from Shakespeare to established contemporary poets he made a fresh offer. Caine signed a contract for a down payment of £25 plus a small royalty, which seemed fair as he was only the editor, though his introductory preface was long and there were copious notes.

The correspondence with Rossetti continued with renewed fervour. The title of the book was much discussed. Rossetti headed Caine off calling it 'The Sonnet Castaly', which would have been incomprehensible to most potential buyers: 'too euphuistic', as he put it. The word is of Greek derivation and comes from the name of a spring on Mount Parnassus sacred to the Muses. Rossetti's own suggestions were not much of an improvement, being long-winded and awkward. It was Caine himself, with a little prodding from Elliot Stock, who came up with the final title, *Sonnets of Three Centuries*.

Work piled up that autumn. As they had paid him well previously Caine sent more articles off to the various architectural journals, hoping to net enough for him to be able to give up the newspaper work once more. He was also booked to deliver three lectures, 'Curiosities of Criticism'. These, he explained to Rossetti, would be based on literary criticism from magazines from 1800 to 1825, giving contemporary opinions on the leading poets of the day. Rossetti thought it a splendid idea and said it would go down well in London. Caine worked hard on the lectures and sent a synopsis to Stock. The response delighted him. 'Elliot

Stock asks me to be sure to send him the MSS of my lectures when I have done with them,' he told Rossetti on 21 October, 1880, 'and he will see if he can make me a proposal for their publication. I am to have £10 for them from the Corporation here, and I hope to get as much in Manchester and also in Leeds; so that if at the end of the winter Stock offers me another £10 I shall have made as much out of the lectures as I have any right to expect.'

The lectures were successful and Stock did even better for him than Caine expected. Rather than putting out yet another pamphlet he got Caine to rewrite and extend them into another book which he published as *Cobwebs of Criticism* in 1883.

Anxious to get on with the lectures, Caine wrote from 6 pm until 2 am one day and, after only four hours' sleep, from 6 am until 9 am the next, when presumably he went to the office. 'I wrote 40 closely-penned pages of letter-paper,' he told Rossetti, 'and the work has something of the beat and force of a swift march, but I fear I have paid a little too dearly in intellectual energy for what I've done... I am still writing my weary sketches, whereof the only joy comes of the guineas they bring.'

Rossetti was shocked and wrote back saying, 'I do think you try yourself too rashly... Do be more cautious.' The editor of the *Builder* had offered to print his latest work and he intended to give up writing the profiles he found so time-wasting. These 'sketches' were reprinted up and down the country, he told Rossetti. 'They bring me invitations too, but I grudge the time spent at some dinners, and I hate the ceremony and so I don't always accept them.' Ford Madox Brown asked him to spend a couple of days with him and his wife in Manchester but reluctantly he refused as he had too much work on hand to get away. Rossetti thought the 'sketches' might be no bad thing and could be useful socially, 'for it is quite a mistake to keep personally in a corner when young'. Caine could hardly be said to have 'kept in a corner' when young, or when he was older for that matter. Rossetti was still anxious on his behalf. 'The account you gave of your fagging habits of work is to me absolutely frightful: it will kill you if you do not draw in.' Caine kept up the 'fagging habits of work' but lived to a ripe old age.

When he finally got to Manchester his brief stay with the Browns was a treat. In the autumn of 1880 Madox Brown had begun painting the third fresco, *The Expulsion of the Danes*. Caine sat for one of the minor figures. He is probably the warrior in the middle of the picture staggering after being hit on the head by something thrown from a window above. While he painted Madox Brown talked about Rossetti and the early days of the Pre-Raphaelite Brotherhood. Caine was amused by a more recent story. The *Danes* picture is a large and elaborate one and includes the burning of a pigsty with a piglet getting under the feet of the fleeing marauders. Like all the Pre-Raphaelites Madox Brown painted realistically detailed scenes of things that never were, using models and props of all kinds. He was working on the *Danes* panel high up in the Town Hall behind a canvas screen. Having borrowed a piglet as a model he set to work with someone holding it in position. It objected loudly to the indignity, disrupting with its protesting squeals an organ recital that was going on in the hall. When it escaped, squeezed under the screen and caused havoc among the audience painting was suspended for the day.

Madox Brown was corresponding with Rossetti at this time. In November of 1880 Rossetti wrote,

> Young Caine paid me two visits when in London, and I liked him extremely. He seems modest, yet not likely to miss a chance that can be duly seized. He now seems to have sufficient chance of London literary employment to induce him to entertain some thoughts of settling there; but I warned him how serious a step that would be. Still, I should like to know he really had any prospect in such directions, as he must be much too good for his present work.

Another undated letter but from its contents written a month or so later says, 'I hear sometimes from Caine, whose project for a sonnet book interests me. A collection from the living only by one Waddington has just appeared. It is poorly got up and not particularly well edited, so I think Caine will have the pull. I think you should let him print that Boccaccio sonnet and find another if you can.'

The appearance of Waddington's book alarmed Caine as he thought it might make Stock change his mind about publishing his own. He could not help feeling relieved when Waddington's book, which contained only new material, drew bad reviews and failed to sell. Stock was confirmed in his opinion that Caine's anthology should cover established poets, mostly dead ones and only a few of those still living. Rossetti backed him, saying, 'known names would better things'. Madox Brown began promoting Caine's book among his friends, which was helpful as he knew, according to Rossetti, 'so many bards'. By this time Caine had written and published his article on the Town Hall frescoes. Rossetti criticised the style of it but Madox Brown and his family were 'thoroughly pleased with the enthusiastic spirit'.

The lectures on criticism were given before Christmas of 1880 and were well received. Proudly Caine sent copies of the newspaper reports to Rossetti who picked him up on a mistake he had made. Caine admitted it was one of his too frequent blunders. 'I am confident I am at times the densest-headed mortal the sky looks down on... I should think there never has before been anyone whatever who could see so vividly as I am sure I can sometimes see and who yet could usually be so utterly blind and muddle-brained as I am eleven hours out of twelve.' Too much work undertaken too hastily probably accounted for it.

He tried to husband his strength through the winter of 1880–81 by working only every other evening. The evenings between were used for visits to the theatre, long walks or seeing friends. One of these was William Tirebuck, who came on a brief visit to his family in Liverpool that November. He was now assistant editor on the *Yorkshire Post*. Caine recited several of Rossetti's sonnets to him and eagerly showed him the collection for his book. Tirebuck was still, and remained till his death, a close and trusted friend to whom Caine could confide anything.

A young artist in Liverpool invited Caine to his studio. Several other painters were gathered there and the talk turned to Madox Brown and the Manchester frescoes. Someone suggested Liverpool ought not to be outdone by Manchester but should buy one of Madox Brown's paintings for the new Walker Art Gallery. If Brown, thought Caine, then why not Rossetti as well? The others agreed in saying Rossetti was the greatest colourist since Titian and an idea dawned. He, Caine, would somehow persuade the city fathers to buy one of Rossetti's works.

The first step was to ask what was available. Caine, having learnt that the best way to approach Rossetti on any question was sideways, told him there was a move to buy one of Madox Brown's pictures for the city and added it would be nice if they could have one of Rossetti's as well. On 7 December, 1880, Rossetti wrote, 'I should be very glad if you succeeded in selling a work of Brown's to the Liverpool Society. As to myself, I happen to have one just now which would be chiefly dispensable as a gallery picture: viz: the full-sized version of the "Dante's Dream", of which you saw the reduced version. The large one is fully equal and of course more important.'

Originally painted in 1871 it was—is—very large, roughly seven feet high by ten feet wide. It was commissioned by William Graham, at the time MP for Glasgow, a connoisseur who had a fine collection. He found the picture too overwhelming once it was hung in his house and asked Rossetti to paint a smaller version. It was almost finished when Caine paid his first visit the previous September. He had been impressed by it and had described it with passionate fervour to his artist friends in Liverpool. As soon as he read Rossetti's letter he determined that somehow he was going to get the full-size *Dream* for his home town. This was a godsend to Rossetti. The smaller version had been sent to Mr Graham and the large version returned to Chelsea where it was cluttering the studio with little possibility of another private sale. As Mr Graham had generously agreed to a straight swap Rossetti was prepared to sell the big one to Liverpool for a reasonable price.

This was the start of negotiations lasting about nine months. Caine was without doubt the moving spirit and in all the hassles and arguments he displayed considerable tact and diplomacy, unexpected in a young man not known for either. One of the first complications Caine

had to face was Philip Rathbone—Rossetti called him Ratsbane! He
went first to Alderman Samuelson, asking him to back the idea and put it
to the other members of the Libraries, Museum and Art Committee,
Rathbone included. An added, and considerable, complication was
Rossetti's attitude to the business. For many years he had refused to
exhibit any of his work and would only sell from his studio. The
Liverpool council had a rule that they would only buy from exhibitions.
Faced with Rathbone's enmity on one side and Rossetti's sensibilities on
the other Caine did a notable egg dance for months on end.

Quite reasonably, Samuelson said the city could not buy the work
unseen. He proposed that he and one or two other members of the
committee should go down to Chelsea to see it. Rossetti agreed fairly
willingly but backtracked when he learnt that Rathbone was to be one
of the party. Having heard only Caine's side of the events at the lecture
on Pre-Raphaelite Poetry he had taken an intense dislike to the man
without ever seeing him or knowing anything else about him. He
refused absolutely to have him in his house and Samuelson refused to
come without him. A great part of the surviving correspondence
between Caine and Rossetti during 1881 is taken up with the ensuing
negotiations.

Eventually a deputation led by Samuelson and excluding Rathbone
viewed the picture and agreed to buy it but that was nowhere near the
end of the affair. The Liverpool city fathers were still adamant they
would only buy the picture if it was first exhibited in Liverpool while
Rossetti insisted he would never show work before it was sold. One can
sympathise with Rossetti, who thought he was faced with the expense
of sending such a large picture north without any certainty that it would
be sold. It was Caine who with a flash of inspiration broke the impasse:
he would nominally buy the picture, put it into the 1881 Autumn
Exhibition displaying the red star meaning it was sold and the city could
then buy it off him. And that, almost a year from the first move, is what
happened.

CHAPTER EIGHT

Dante's Dream runs like a leitmotif through 1881. Many of Rossetti's letters refer to it and Caine's position as contact man between the painter and the Library, Museum and Arts Committee absorbed much of his time. At the beginning of the year, far from any plans for London there were family discussions about Caine moving to New Brighton, both for the sake of his health and to give him more space and quiet for his work than the crowded terraced house in Toxteth could afford. Willie and Lily were growing up and needing space of their own, though now that Sarah Caine's parents were dead—Mary Hall had died in 1875—the pressure was relieved a little.

Caine wrote to leading poets asking for sonnets. He told Rossetti who replied that he doubted

> the wisdom of writing without introduction to such men as you mention. A superior man runs the risk by doing so, of being confounded with those who are perpetually directing correspondence to everyone whose name they have heard—and the bibliographic and autograph hunting tribe whose name is legion... I know the sort of exclamation that rises to the lips of a man as much beset by strangers as (say) Swinburne, when he opens a letter and sees a new name at the end of it.

Did Caine remember that twenty years later when he himself was 'beset by strangers' and pestered by autograph hunters?

Rossetti was wrapped up in the proposals for *Dante's Dream*. He would gladly show the larger version of the picture to Alderman Samuelson, he told Caine, but would need notice as it was stacked at the back of the studio and would take a couple of hours to move. Apart from being so big it had an ornate, heavy frame carved to a symbolic design of his own which had cost him £100. His charge for the picture would be 1500 guineas, including the frame, so Liverpool was preparing to lay out a substantial sum—the equivalent of about £75,000 today. Caine was confident the money could be found. When they met at a dinner party Samuelson told him that the city made £2000 every year from their Autumn Exhibitions and used the money to buy works for their permanent collection. Whatever price Rossetti got he promised to pay Caine the commission already agreed between them. When the sale was concluded he handed over the handsome fee of £100 (about £5000 today). Without Caine's efforts the sale would never have gone through.

The big version of the *Dream* was not exactly the same as the one Caine had seen—the two figures at the bottom did not appear in the larger painting. In making the reduced version he had improved it by altering the drapery of two of the figures, Beatrice and one of the pall bearers. He intended to make the same changes to the bigger painting but of course had not got round to it. Spurred by the possibility of a sale he drew the cartoons ready for tracing onto the canvas. This was a cause of further hiccups and delays but the changes were made before the picture went to Liverpool.

Alderman Samuelson went to see Rossetti with another committee member named Galloway. Caine was in agonies at the prospect, desperately worried as to how they would be received, but relaxed when Rossetti wrote that they were both 'the nicest of fellows'. Samuelson had spoken 'most cordially and admiringly' about Caine. He 'was very anxious about your not overworking, as are all your friends'.

'You are right that he [Samuelson] is a capital fellow,' Caine replied. 'I can't conceive how I should have got along in Liverpool without him.' Rossetti said Samuelson had mentioned Rathbone 'as being a good fellow at bottom and of course I shewed no rancour. I did not mention that he should take care the bottom at which he is a good fellow does not happen to get kicked.' A later comment on Galloway was that he was 'the handsomest man I ever saw. One feels he ought to be seen in armour!'

Galvanised by the thought of reselling *Dante's Dream*, Rossetti was also doing other work. He told Caine he was 'painting a picture of modern life begun long ago, and when I finish it, <u>may</u> be shewing some things in one way or another. This again in thine ear.' A note in Caine's handwriting with this letter identifies the picture as the one named Found and links it with the poem 'Jenny' which tells the same story of a country girl lost in the city.

In January, 1881, Caine spent a weekend with the Madox Browns. He asked if he could include a sonnet by Oliver in his anthology and they agreed. His admiration for Nolly endeared him to Madox Brown as much as anything. He also asked for two of Madox Brown's own sonnets but was refused. 'His objection to publishing any of his verse seems insurmountable', he told Rossetti. Making the final selection was turning into a nightmare. Word having got round, he was being inundated with unspeakably bad poetry. Some sonnets he received were 'passionate and rather powerful, and the rest—O God, such knock-kneed cripplings. The thought of what to do with them gives me a touch of a cold sweat.' Rossetti's sensible reply was, 'I would not be too anxious were I you about anything in choice of sonnets except the brains and the music.' Caine wrote to Matthew Arnold who replied that he would like to write something for the book if his school duties allowed him the time—he was a schools inspector. (His father had been the famous headmaster of Rugby.) Rossetti commented cynically that Caine would be highly unlikely to get anything out of him, but he did.

He was almost overwhelmed with work. 'I have written nearly 30 magazine pages this month already,' he said in the same letter. 'I get a lot of reviewing that I have to set aside.' He had enjoyed the previous Saturday to Monday with the Browns. (The word 'weekend' had only just been invented and was not in general use in 1881.) 'Really he is one of the most unselfish of men. He speaks cordially of nearly everyone... I do think his stories of Swinburne and others kept me in one continuous roar of laughter; yet he never seems to make one laugh <u>at</u> anyone.'

Rossetti said he hoped Caine was not showing his letters to anyone else. As Caine had several times been in trouble for showing private correspondence to a third party or revealing confidences in public one wonders if rumours had reached Rossetti. Caine dismissed his anxiety in a few words—he had only ever read a letter of his once to anyone and that was to James Ashworth Noble when Rossetti had mentioned his work. 'And O, I remember shewing to [William] Watson something relating to himself.' It sounds as if he had a guilty conscience.

Rossetti sent Caine a sonnet by William Sharp suggesting he ought to use it. The letter in which Caine acknowledged it was far more stilted and less friendly than his usual tone, as if he sensed a rival and was jealous. His praise of the sonnet was lukewarm and he suggested altering a line of it. Sharp was another youthful protégé who threatened to rival Caine in Rossetti's affections, without succeeding. He was two years younger than Caine and an aspiring poet. After spending two years in Australia for his health he returned to London in 1878 where he worked as a clerk. Encouraged by Rossetti, he gave it up for a literary career. Like Caine he became a romancist. He also wrote several biographies and in the 1890s began to write mystical prose and verse under the pseudonym 'Fiona Macleod'. There were also some plays under the same name, including *The Immortal Hour*, which was set to music by Rutland Boughton. *The Faery Song* is about all that is now remembered of it, as much due to Boughton's haunting melody as to the words. Sharp kept the secret of his *alter ego* until his death in 1905 at the early age of 50, when even close friends were astonished to find that he was 'Fiona Macleod'. At first mutually suspicious, he and Caine became close friends.

One contemporary writer caused Caine a tricky problem: Oscar Wilde. In November, when the book was more or less complete, Edmund Gosse wrote to Caine to say he had learned from Watts that the book would include a contribution from Wilde.

I hope you will not think me disagreeable if I say that this absolutely precludes me from the pleasure of appearing in it, and that I must ask you to remove my name and to exclude all my contribution. This decision, if you will pardon me for saying so, is final. I have no personal acquaintance with Mr Oscar Wilde, but I have formed a very distinct idea of the quality of his productions. I look upon his so-called Poems as the appendage of a social reputation with which literature has nothing to do and as the illustration of vagaries that are hateful to every studious and unaffected mind. Had they been published anonymously, or under some obscure pseudonym, not a newspaper in the kingdom would have devoted three lines to their consideration... I cannot expect you to share my views, and I therefore, with many sincere regrets, must deny myself the pleasure of appearing in your book.

Reference to the anthology shows that nothing by Oscar Wilde was included but there are five sonnets by Gosse.

Caine was now approaching the biggest upheaval in his life so far. He was contracted to Stock for one book and a second was in view. Lecture engagements were being offered him in several towns besides Liverpool. He had commissions for articles from magazines and newspapers, including the Liverpool *Mercury*. The new editor, John Lovell, admired him and thought he had a great future. Even with his appetite and capacity for hard work there was no way he could fulfil all these commitments and continue to work for Bromley & Son. He knew he was going to have to resign at some point but worried and dithered over it. It was not just that he needed the money. Bromley had been a good friend to him and he knew how much he owed him. In early February, 1881, he broached the matter and said he wanted to leave. James Bromley's reaction staggered him. He begged him to stay and told him that, having no children of his own (there is no mention of his being married) he had left the business to Caine in his will. When he was dead Caine would have an assured income from it which would allow him to devote himself to writing as much as he liked. Bromley was older than Caine but still only forty and in good health. He came from a long-lived family and was likely to live a good many years yet. Staying chained to work he increasingly disliked while waiting for dead men's shoes formed no part of Caine's plans for his future but he could hardly say that to Bromley. He tried to refuse the inheritance without wounding him, pleading his literary career could not wait. He was 25 already, and the strain of trying to keep up two jobs at once was destroying his health. Bromley compromised by suggesting he took a month's sick leave to finish his book and carry out the journalistic assignments he had been given and then they would review the situation.

*Pencil sketch by Caine of Fisher Place, the house in the Vale of St John,
near Keswick, where he stayed with Rossetti in 1881.*

Caine said nothing to Rossetti at this point except that he was going to
Grasmere for about a month 'for his health'. He felt ill with the strain
and feared it might be tuberculosis again. He left Liverpool at the end of
February and spent a couple of days at a hotel in Ambleside before moving on. Instead of Grasmere he went to a farmhouse at the southern end
of the Vale of St John, not far from Keswick. He had stayed there once
or twice before on his walking tours. It was called Fisher Place and was
new, having been built in 1875. It is still there and recognisable from a
sketch Caine made of it a few months later. At some time afterwards the
original house was extended on either side and then divided up into a
row of separate cottages. The central part, where Caine stayed, is now
Nos. 3 and 4. The fell rises up steeply behind the house and Fisher Ghyll
tumbles down close to it. The sound of the ghyll, which in February
would have been flowing strongly, filled the house. Caine found it
soothing. The farmer's wife, Mrs Keighley, who catered for summer visitors, must have been delighted to let a bedroom and a sitting-room in
the depths of winter. She fussed over him and fed him well. For ever
after he remembered the kindness of 'the farm people' at Fisher Place.

His plans had been carefully laid and he had no intention of going
back to live in Liverpool. He tried to break this to his mother as gently as
he could. He had some money put by and could afford to live and work
at Fisher Place for some months at least. He wrote to his mother from
there in March—the letter survives in his brother's archive in the
Liverpool Record Office. In large, clear writing he said,

My Dear Mother,

Enclosed you will find a £5 note. Change it and spend it at 15/- or 20/- weekly. You need not hesitate to use £1 weekly if necessary as I have several notes left and can send you another when it is done—but let me know. I am not certain what course I shall take but I think I shall remain here some months and then go to London. I am not under great expense, I have plenty of work to do when I am fit to undertake it, and now I am daily feeling stronger.

Yours very truly and affectionately,

T.H. Hall Caine.

A postscript scrawled across the corner of the last page says, 'Of course if I determine not to return to Liverpool it shall make no difference in the money I send you.'

His work included commissions which came as a result of Rossetti's recommendation. Among others he had given Caine's name to the editor of the *Magazine of Arts* who asked for an article. Rossetti had also shown his review of Madox Brown's frescoes to the editor of the *Academy*. Caine wrote to thank him, saying, 'The Editor seems to have taken up your proposal heartily, for he asks for a long article.'

The question of going to London still bothered him. Though he had work in hand which would bring him to the notice of literary and intellectual London he could only afford to settle there if Rossetti confirmed his invitation to live with him. He did not dare tell him he had gone against his advice and thrown up the day job already, nor that he had left Liverpool with no intention of returning, but if Rossetti did not know this he was unlikely to press his invitation. Neither could he ask Rossetti straight out if he could come. Caine was not aware that Treffry Dunn, whom he never mentions, had left Rossetti's employment and the household was sinking into chaos. To share the home of his idol would be wonderful but, having seen inside 16 Cheyne Walk, his feelings about living there were ambivalent to say the least.

He pushed the dilemma aside with work and walking on the fells in all weathers. When he told Rossetti he was coming to London to see Stock Rossetti invited him to spend a week with him over Easter. 'I shall be greatly glad to set eyes on you and the sonnet work in London soon, as I hope. Of course make these your quarters.' Caine simply hoped that somehow things would arrange themselves while he was there. Rossetti's mood had lifted considerably and he was encouraging. 'You are the friendliest of fellows, as dear old Brown, now back, loudly avers.' A postscript to that letter said, 'My ballad of The King's Tragedy is a ripper, I can tell you!'

When the proofs of his book arrived Caine was thrilled and sent them on to Rossetti, who replied, 'What beauties they are!' He was eager to see Caine again as soon as possible. 'I am expecting you, and would like your advent to be not later than tomorrow or Sunday. Communications come thick for you.' A day or two later he wrote, 'We will talk of your sonnet book and of everything in the circle but not of <u>outside matters of any kind</u> which I do not entertain at all.' Rossetti's recurring melancholia was drawing a veil round him, cutting him off from many of his friends and the outside world. He was becoming increasingly quarrelsome and irascible so that some of his oldest friends now seldom or never visited him. Even Bell Scott who lived only a few doors away hardly ever called in at No. 16 any more.

Bromley was still refusing to accept Caine's resignation when he left for London. He found Rossetti less well than when he had last seen him, appearing thinner, his walk more halting, but he was still full of enthusiasm both for his own plans and for Caine's. Stock had sent the manuscript to Cheyne Walk and they set about checking the proofs together. Concerned over Rossetti's health Caine suggested he join him for a holiday in the Vale of St John. A change of air and scene would be sure to do him good. His garden was being taken away from him and a high wall was to be built. The developer told Rossetti he could continue to walk in what had formerly been his garden until the actual building began but Rossetti refused. All the exercise he had taken for some time had been to walk daily six times round the big square of rough grass. If he could no longer do this and was to be disturbed by building work Caine feared his health would be even worse. Rossetti agreed he would like a holiday and the sound of the retreat Caine had found appealed to him but of course he could not, or would not, make up his mind.

Mrs Rossetti and Christina had spent five days with Gabriel at Cheyne Walk during Lent. It had not been a very happy visit. Christina, who had a new book of verse due to be published that summer, had turned up with a bundle of manuscripts of her latest work. She was looking forward to reading the poems to Gabriel and discussing them with him but he showed no interest, sweeping her work aside to read them his own latest ballad. This was odd as he had previously been such a champion of her work. He had told Caine the previous autumn that his sister had no new work and no sonnets available, which was not true. Eventually he had given Caine her address and when he wrote to her she replied cordially and sent a poem.

Caine was anxious to meet more of the Rossetti family, though he did not meet either Christina or her mother for several months more. Neither did he see anything of William and Lucy during his visit. They were otherwise occupied. Lucy had given birth prematurely to twins, Mary Elizabeth and Michael Ford, which completed their family of five children.

Having corresponded with Theodore Watts for several months Caine expected to see him in person, knowing he often visited Rossetti, but he had been ill and did not come. Instead, to Caine's great pleasure, Watts invited him to spend the whole of Easter Saturday at his home, The

Pines, Putney Hill. Thus he would meet Swinburne as well. He took the proofs and Watts looked over the work done so far, making a number of helpful suggestions. He also offered to check the final proofs, a job he did so thoroughly that Stock complained that the cost of so many author's corrections was going to eat up his profit.

Watts and Caine took to each other straight away, talking non-stop for most of the day. Swinburne impressed him but there was not the same rapport as with Watts. After he got back to Liverpool Caine wrote to thank Watts for 'an extremely pleasant day', adding, 'I believe we hold many opinions in common, and (which is much more assuring) I believe the bias of my mind is not unlike that of your own.' It was the beginning of a firm friendship which lasted until Theo Watts's death in 1914.

Discussions with Stock went well. Frederic Shields was to design the cover and endpapers for a special edition, 100 copies printed on hand-made paper and numbered. Rossetti grumbled that the money would have been better spent on good quality paper and type for the whole printing, but was pleased that Shields was involved. His enduring friend-ship with Caine meant much to them both.

The most important outcome of the Easter visit was that Rossetti renewed his invitation, insisting Caine must come to live with him and soon. In return for free board and lodging Caine would give intellectual companionship and conversation in the evenings. He could concentrate on his work and treat the house as his own. It was a generous offer sin-cerely meant but did not turn out as planned. It was intended to allow him the freedom to earn his own living and was worth a lot to a young man in Caine's position. There is no record that he was ever paid a salary.

The return to Liverpool, on Friday, 22 April, was exhausting: the train was delayed and the journey lasted six and a half hours. The prospect of the office on Monday was too much for him. Though still hesitating to accept Rossetti's offer he told James Bromley he could not go on. Bromley still refused to agree to his resignation and told him his place would be kept open for as long as necessary, but he never went back. They parted on good terms and remained friends.

Caine wrote his bread-and-butter letter to Rossetti on the Sunday. 'I have visited London countless times, but never under such delightful conditions as recently.' He was working on 'a full scheme for a maga-zine as we talked of, and if Stock takes it up I shall no longer hesitate to go permanently to London.' Watts had advised against it, telling him a man could make a name for himself more quickly in the provinces than in the metropolis, but Caine argued that provincial success was worth little: only recognition in London counted.

'If the publisher takes warmly to the proposal,' he continued, 'I shall be able to leave behind me (out of past husbanding) what may keep things square for half a year at home and surely six month's start <u>ought</u> to do something for any man of energy. As to what you so generously proposed anent my possible residence—I can hardly trust myself to write at this or any moment: it is so much too much of a kindness.'

He ended the letter with his new signature, 'T. Hall Caine.' A line from it leads to a note, 'I've dropped the <u>H</u> and the dismembered signature looks to me like the pig in the proverb!' He began the letter, as he always had, to 'Dear Mr Rossetti'. A peremptory postscript to Rossetti's reply, written on 26 April, reads, 'Do drop <u>Mr</u> for the future in writing me.' In his next letter he obeyed.

On 28 April, 1881, Rossetti wrote,

> I can see no likelihood of my not remaining in the mind that, in case of your coming to London, your quarters should be taken up here. The house is big enough for two, even if they meant to be strangers to each other. You would have your own rooms, and we should meet just when we pleased. You have got a sufficient inkling of my exceptional habits not to be scared by them. It is true, at times my health and spirits are variable: but I am sure we should not be squabbling. However, doubtless you have no intention of a quite immediate move, and we can speak further of it.

At the beginning of May Caine was back at Fisher Place and writing to Watts. 'I don't know if you have heard that I have given up business connections in Liverpool—that is to say I have resigned, though my resignation is not yet accepted. The step seemed inevitable, and I took it reluctantly, but my health admitted of no prolonged parley.' He had plenty of work for the present and was grateful to Watts for his promise to give him a 'lift' wherever he could.

Rossetti's new book of poems was about to be published. Caine was helping with the proofreading. He promised Rossetti he would put everything else aside to do a lengthy review and 'philosophical analysis of your claims to front rank as a poet'. The editor of the *Academy* was asking for it but he knew Rossetti wanted the *Athenaeum* to be first in the field.

With most of his garden taken from him and the threat of building work disturbing him Rossetti was thinking of moving. He wanted Caine to come and see estate agents for him. He had heard of a house with a large garden available in Brixton—could Caine go and look at it for him? Caine replied he had heard the locality was a healthy one. 'If…you think my presence in London for a time would be helpful to you I trust you will not hesitate to command me.' He told Rossetti about his resignation not being accepted and about James Bromley leaving the business to him. 'Doubtless you think this looks tempting, but what can it ever be worth?' Bromley was wealthy enough to retire already 'but he won't'. He was in robust good health and 'it is <u>not possible</u> that I can outlive him. The chief value the circumstance has in my eyes is that of a splendid testimonial to one of the youngest men (out of 100) in the employ. There are two great obstacles to my return: my health, (which though improving is still uncertain) and my unconquerable love of literary pursuits.' He had now put his cards on the table and told his friend exactly how things stood.

There was a flurry of letters to and fro. On 11 May Caine suggested Rossetti should join him at Fisher Place. 'Finer mountain scenery I cannot conceive: the landscape is constantly changing aspects. Doubtless the actual presence of these hills would give you a great freshness of inspiration. I could arrange everything for you.' This shows how little he knew or understood Rossetti, who was an inveterate townee, a Bohemian and a real Cockney in his attachment to London. He had never evinced any liking for the countryside or spectacular scenery.

Caine had mentioned some time previously that if he could be assured of ten lectures a year he would move to London. He now asked if Rossetti could suggest to Samuelson that the Library Committee should give him a contract. 'I have it much at heart to further your lecture scheme,' Rossetti replied. 'I suppose this could be carried out by journeys, even were you to settle in London.' This was the heyday of the railways. They made it possible for a young man like Caine to contemplate living in London and lecturing regularly in the North of England and for him to suggest that Rossetti could easily travel from London to Cumberland. Having said he would raise the matter of the lectures straight away Rossetti did nothing. Instead he worried about Caine's plans. He wrote reassuringly that if Liverpool did buy 'the big daub', as he called *Dante's Dream*, he had already decided that Caine's commission should be at least £100 as he was 'the only cause of its sale'. The offer of a room in Cheyne Walk was renewed, Rossetti insisting Caine would be under no obligation. 'Obligations do not exist between those who sympathize.'

During a brief visit to Liverpool Caine spent a pleasant day with George Rae and his wife in Birkenhead. They told him, as he reported to Rossetti, that the Library Committee had 'within the past week appointed an intolerable Oxford noodle, who can lecture about as intelligibly as a jackdaw, to deliver them a course of lectures in the autumn—this mainly because he has a long array of letters affixed to his name and because he has the countenance of his university.' This was a blow to Caine's hopes. He was acutely aware of his own lack of a university education and his jealousy of the 'Oxford noodle' shows. Soon afterwards he was writing to Rossetti to say he might shortly be appointed to lecture in English literature at a university but this was wishful thinking when he had not even matriculated. Nothing more was heard of this idea but he was awarded a contract for three lectures at the Liverpool Library that autumn, despite the interloper.

*Dante's Dream of the Death of Beatrice. D.G. Rossetti's painting
which was acquired for Liverpool through Caine's mediation.*

George Rae told Caine that in his view *Dante's Dream* was 'the cheapest picture in England'. It was only its excessive size which prevented him buying it himself for his collection at his home, Redcourt. Caine told Rossetti this, adding that Mr and Mrs Rae had talked about 'that Jesuit who wrote the funny sonnets as a friend of your sister's', meaning Gerard Manley Hopkins. 'He has sent me a 20-page letter,' Caine continued, 'very clever, very conceited, very cheeky,—and very flattering withal.' This is unkind, given that he had originally read Hopkins's sonnets with delight and admiration. It smacks of toadying to Rossetti, who hated Hopkins's work and told Caine he should not use it. One wishes Caine had had the courage of his convictions.

Continuing his letter, Caine referred to Rossetti's invitation to live with him. He was so overwhelmed he could only say 'Thank you'. About the building at the back of the house, he said with an eye to the main chance, 'If your owner happens not to have had his plans prepared I believe I could devise a good scheme for him: I could speedily acquire a knowledge of the London bye-laws and work it out.' Like so many of his more far-fetched plans, this one came to nothing. He said he would like to help with 'minimizing the nuisance of workmen's noises—that might to some extent be done, but only if one were in some sort of command as Clerk of the Works, an office requiring perhaps an hour's or 2 hour's labour daily—scarce otherwise I fear'.

Apart from a short note of 15 May, that is the last of Caine's surviving letters to Rossetti. He seems to have stayed on at Fisher Place with occasional forays back to Liverpool to deal with 'the matter of the big daub'. Rossetti wrote as frequently as ever. There are three notes which show he sent Caine £25, a fair sum for those days. Rossetti commented on 16 June that he supposed 'the stoppage of your old means of livelihood was at last a necessity'. In an undated note he said, 'I shall be most happy to do as you wish. I suppose a cheque would be unavailable so will send for the money to the bank and post it tonight to you. I know you must have reflected well on the step, so will not think of remonstrance. No need at all to trouble about repayment at present.' 'The step' must refer to Caine's having resigned from Bromley & Son. In a further short letter Rossetti said he had sent two notes, one for £20 and the other for £5, and gave their numbers. He was anxious they might have gone astray. Caine telegraphed that they had arrived, apologising for not acknowledging the money sooner. When Rossetti died Caine retrieved his letters from Tudor House before William could see them. He would not have wanted it known that he had solicited a loan, especially if it was still outstanding, in which case William, who was his brother's executor, could have demanded that the debt to the estate be repaid. It is not unreasonable to suppose that Caine himself destroyed those particular letters.

On 20 June Rossetti referred to his new volume of poetry which was 'hanging fire' but Caine would have one of the first copies when it came out. He asked a touch plaintively, 'How long is your holiday?' He had sent him a copy of a narrative poem, *The Bride's Prelude*, begun some years before and left unfinished. He was 'much pleased' with Caine's verdict on it and supposed he 'must set to and finish it one day—old as it is'. On 24 June he wrote about the upheavals around him but insisted he must stay in central London to 'keep in the market circle, therefore make at present little doubt or none that our mutual house-mating arrangement can come off'. He ended with 'Let me hear from you', so something was preventing Caine from writing as often as usual. It could well have been that he was still in two minds about accepting the invitation, still hoping to be able to go to London independently.

The start of building on Rossetti's garden loomed and he felt thoroughly unsettled. Perhaps a holiday in Cumberland would be the answer after all. He asked Caine if he would like to come to town in a couple of weeks and escort him to Fisher Place. 'Of course all expenses would be mine.' A few days later Rossetti was dithering again.

> I would much like to reach your side, but there are preventives at present… I certainly do love quiet, and a farmhouse suggests noisy operations. Moreover, wherever I go I find I must carry my mattress with me, which is ridiculous, but I can never sleep on any other. Not that I like a very <u>soft</u> bed. I hate it… Of

course no small amount of painting apparatus must come too... My present
idea is to seek another London house with large garden, in which you might
help me eventually.

His next letter thanked Caine 'for the information as to your Shady Vale
which seems a vision—a distant one, alas!—of Paradise. Perhaps I may
reach it yet in time.'

The building began and what Rossetti still referred to as his garden
was being 'torn up and everything in it destroyed'. On 3 July he said, 'I
think before many posts go out I may be asking you to come to London.
I am in the midst of many inconveniences—the monstrous heat, the
destruction going on at the back...and now my housekeeper threatens
to leave', and on the 12th, 'How soon could you come up?' Caine must
have said something about repaying the £25 because he continued, 'Let
that matter you mentioned as being due be quite forgotten between us.
When I am poorer than you are, I will remind you of it.'

By the end of the month he was saying, 'I shall be glad to see you
here soon. My housekeeper is gone away, though coming back, I believe,
and everything is desolation.' He was cross with Caine for telling
Samuelson that he was 'possibly coming into Cumberland' and might
'turn up in Liverpool'. He would do no such thing, nor did he want
Samuelson or anyone else turning up and disturbing him at Fisher Place.

After a delay caused by having to see the committee in Liverpool to
smooth over a new row Rossetti had created, Caine said he would arrive
in London on the first Saturday in August, 1881. By this time Rossetti
seems to have made up his mind that Caine was going to move in permanently. He had already discussed the idea with his sister Christina—
they were always close. In a letter to her he said he was glad she
approved the plan. Caine was good company and never talked politics.
If indeed he never talked politics with Rossetti it amounted to self-control on a heroic scale as Caine was a political animal if ever there was
one. Playing on his sympathy and anxiety over his health Rossetti wrote
to Caine, 'I will hope to see you in town on Saturday next... We will
then set sail in one boat. I am rather anxious as to having become perfectly deaf on the right side of my head. Partial approaches to this have
sometimes occurred to me and passed away, so I will not be too much
troubled at it.'

Meanwhile, on 3 August, 1881, Rossetti wrote to his mother,

Dunn has been away since New Year's Day and I am now parting with him
altogether... You may have heard of a young man named Hall Caine, who has
shown himself very well disposed towards me. I am going to try the experiment of having him to live in the house and so shall have more society... Caine
has tastes similar to my own, and is a reading man. He follows literature. He is
likely to be coming here by next Saturday. He is going to do Christina's book
for *The Academy*.

Rossetti knew perfectly well that Dunn would not return unless his arrears of wages were paid but he seems not to have told his mother the full circumstances. People have said Rossetti treated Dunn badly, throwing him out to make room for Caine. He did not actually throw him out but undoubtedly he made things so difficult for Dunn that he left, though at the time there was no clear intention of replacing him with Caine. Dunn's employment was not formally terminated for several months. Rossetti complained he had deserted him. In a way he had, but it is understandable. When Caine looked like being a more malleable and suitable companion Rossetti told Dunn not to return to Chelsea, without paying what was due to him. Shortly before his death he admitted to William that were he to die Dunn would have a substantial claim on his estate, as would Watts for work as his solicitor.

When Caine arrived at 16 Cheyne Walk, Rossetti flung open a door to the left of the hall and said, 'This is your sitting room.' Caine was embarrassed to find that this and the bedroom he was shown to—not 'Watts's room' on the half landing—had been freshly cleaned out and refurbished for him. Watts later told him they were the rooms Swinburne had used when he shared the house with Gabriel, William and, for a short time, George Meredith, in 1862. Rossetti made clear to Caine that this was to be his home from now on. He settled in gratefully, an unlikely Boswell from Liverpool.

CHAPTER NINE

Caine thought he was going to spend his days writing and his evenings in pleasant conversation but he was soon disillusioned. Almost at once he found himself secretary, companion, housekeeper, general factotum and eventually nurse with hardly a minute to himself. On top of it all he was the butt of Rossetti's bad temper. Most of the time Rossetti was as genial and friendly as ever but sometimes he gave way to unprovoked outbursts of startling rage. He had always had a tendency towards manic episodes and vast depressions but he was good hearted and when he realised he had upset someone would make deeply felt apologies for his 'sulks' and bad manners. Which did not stop him from acting in exactly the same way again. He was well aware of how badly he sometimes treated Caine and full of remorse afterwards. Once he said to him, 'I wish you were my son, for though then I should still have no right to address you so, I should at least have some right to expect your forgiveness.' He was forgiven just the same.

For a green young man from the provinces life at Tudor House must have presented some awkward moments and he must sometimes have been amazed that Rossetti's complicated life did not unravel completely. Domestic problems were the first to be thrown in his lap. Apart from the cook-housekeeper there were two housemaids. One by one they left and Caine had to find replacements. There was nothing new in this—Rossetti could never keep his servants. A postscript to a letter to Frederic Shields dated 21 July, 1879, said, 'I write from a house servant-less and so far blest. The last of the lot went out today, and tomorrow I expect two new ones—promising decency at any rate.' A year or so previously he had invited Shields to dinner saying it would have to be cooked by the butler as his cook had left!

In all that he wrote about Rossetti's home, Caine never mentioned the kitchen premises, though he ventured down there soon after his arrival at the beginning of August, 1881. The basement area housed a large kitchen, a scullery, a wash house and a warren of vaulted cellars and store rooms. The story went that at one time a tunnel had led from the basement to the river bank but it has never been traced. In Tudor times, when the river was close to the door, there may well have been a water gate. The Thames was a busy thoroughfare and a boat the obvious way to reach any building on the riverside.

Caine's biggest problem, however, was Fanny Cornforth. She was a street girl who became an artist's model. Rossetti told Caine he picked her up in one of the London pleasure gardens one night in the late 1850s. She was a buxom girl with a mass of corn-coloured hair and as they passed each other she cracked a nut between her strong white teeth and threw the shell at him. Without doubt she was what the Pre-Raphaelites called 'a stunner'. She posed for several of them but soon became Rossetti's particular property and his mistress. Her raucous laugh and strident Cockney accent irritated Caine intensely but amused Rossetti. He called her the Helephant, a comment both on her weight and on the fact that her h's were strewn with abandon through her talk and never where they ought to be.

At first she thought Rossetti would marry her and when he became engaged to another of his models, Lizzie Siddal, she still expected to get him back. When he and Lizzie were married and honeymooning in Paris Fanny went through agonies of misery and jealousy. After Lizzie's death she appeared again and became part of Rossetti's Chelsea ménage. A photograph taken in the garden of Tudor House in 1862 or early 1863 shows her surrounded by Gabriel, his brother William and the young Swinburne. She was looking plump even then. She did not move in but was sometimes found breakfasting at the house by Rossetti's friends. She took advantage of her position to cheat and steal from him. Before Treffry Dunn arrived and put his affairs in order Rossetti never had a bank account. He kept his money, and he was earning a great deal, stuffed into a drawer of his desk which he did not bother to lock. Fanny helped herself whenever she liked. When Rossetti caught her at it he only laughed.

She was disliked and mistrusted by his friends and drove many of them away. Ruskin said, 'I don't object to Rossetti having sixteen mistresses, but I won't have Fanny.' Rossetti admitted to Caine that she had been his mistress at one time but by 1881 had long ceased to be. He also said he had been impotent for years as the result of 'a horrible accident', though Caine does not give details. Given the state of his health, his drinking and his addiction to chloral he could well have been impotent anyway.

At the time Caine met Fanny she was running the Rose Tavern in Jermyn Street with her former lodger, John Schott. She had recently married him, afraid she would get no more out of Rossetti. She was his evil genius and even after her marriage continued to turn up at Tudor House, upsetting everyone when she did so. Caine was at a loss as to how to deal with her. He knew Dunn had got on the wrong side of her and suffered for it so he moved cautiously. He tried taking Rossetti for walks by the river of an evening or sitting up late talking to him in an effort to prevent him seeing too much of her.

This worked to a certain extent but there was nothing he could do about another lady in Rossetti's life, Janey Morris, William Morris's wife. Whenever she was going to call she wrote saying what time she would arrive and how long she would stay. Rossetti would send Caine a polite note. One of them, undated, reads: 'Dear Caine. The lady will dine with me at 8 in the dining room, and as she is not well, perhaps I will ask you to dine alone today. Pray excuse, and choose your own hour. Yours DGR.' Thus Caine never saw her.

Rossetti had been passionately in love with Janey for many years and their affair had been notorious, Morris appearing a *mari complaisant*. As Rossetti had been so famously indiscreet for so long it seems at first sight strange that he should have been so coy about her with Caine. It is reasonable to suppose that he wanted to be undisturbed when she came to see him but he could also have been merely tactful. He was aware that Caine knew Morris and wanted to save him the embarrassment of meeting his friend's wife on an assignment with her lover. They were no longer lovers in the modern sense by 1881—some say they never were and that Janey was more in love with being loved than in love with Rossetti. This seems unlikely, given the times they spent alone together and that everyone accepted them as a pair, including Morris. Whether or not she truly loved Rossetti, he adored and worshipped her.

When Caine was summoned to London the idea had been for him to take Rossetti back to Cumberland within a few days but the days stretched to weeks and they were still in Chelsea. Gabriel was busy with the proofs of his *Poems and Ballads*, which Ellis published in September. Caine soon found that organising Rossetti's holiday in Cumberland was akin to getting a circus on the road.

On Caine's arrival as a resident in Cheyne Walk some of Rossetti's friends thought his intense, almost hypnotic stare could mean he had mediumistic powers. They arranged a séance when they would put him to the test. When he told Rossetti he was going out and what was planned Rossetti got into a terrible state, telling him such things were dangerous as he knew from his own experience and pleading with him not to go. Caine, sorry to have upset his friend and not caring much whether he went or not, said at once he would stay with him for the evening. Biographers have speculated what this unhappy experience of Rossetti's might have been. No one has yet come up with the complete answer but it is known that at one time he went to a number of séances with Janey Morris. Bell Scott told William Rossetti, who seems to have been inclined to believe in spiritualism, that séances were held at 16 Cheyne Walk after Lizzie's death and she often 'manifested' by rapping out messages. If true this would have been enough to upset and distress the widower but it seems odd that William, who was living in the house, did not already know about them. However, he had spent much of his time back in his old home with his mother and sisters so might have missed what was going on.

On 8 August Frederic Shields called to see Rossetti. It was probably the first time he and Caine met in person, though they had heard of each other from both Rossetti and Madox Brown. They quickly became close friends. Shields noted the occasion in his diary: 'To Rossetti's; Caine established there.' He called frequently throughout that August, anxious and full of foreboding as to Rossetti's health. It was their common concern and affection for him that drew Shields and Caine together. They also shared the notion that art should teach, should present the great moral truths. Shields was highly strung and intense, with the same tendency as Caine to be morbid, but unlike Caine he had a sense of humour and could be entertaining company when he chose. He had had a desperately poor childhood. His parents died young and in his teens he not only had to look out for himself but be responsible for his siblings, all of whom died young of the tuberculosis which killed their parents. Shields could have made a successful portraitist, judging by the superb heads he drew as a young man, but he was obliged to churn out popular watercolour landscapes and similar work which eventually earned him a lot of money.

Caine occasionally thought he was dealing with a madman and he possibly was. Janey Morris certainly believed Rossetti was mad and said so after his death. He had suffered a serious mental breakdown in June, 1872. The immediate cause had been Buchanan's attack, published in October, 1871, under the title 'The Fleshly School of Poetry,' and the controversy which followed it. It began as an indictment of Swinburne and Morris—in the latter's case totally without justification—for indecency in their verse and ended by labelling Rossetti as the leader of a band of dirty-minded versifiers. Rossetti replied in the press and arguments and insults flew until the following summer. On 1 June, 1872, the *Saturday Review* renewed the attack on the 'Fleshly School', sneering at 'their sickly self-consciousness, their emasculated delight' and 'their unmanliness which is...so disgusting'. The Victorians placed great emphasis on manliness. Even before all this began Rossetti had been showing signs of mental instability and the persecution mania which he had demonstrated to Caine. It was clear to Rossetti that Buchanan had led the conspiracy against him but one of the saddest things was that he also turned against some of his best friends. He drove away his faithful physician Dr Hake and his son George, who in the months following Rossetti's collapse travelled with him and looked after him with great kindness. Rossetti even took against the inoffensive Revd Charles Dodgson—Lewis Carroll—insisting his *Hunting of the Snark* was a personal attack and a cruel lampoon when it had nothing to do with him at all. But it was the final insult in the *Saturday Review* which tipped him over the edge into insanity. It is to be questioned whether he ever recovered completely.

How much of all this Caine knew, including what seems to have been a failed attempt at suicide with laudanum, is doubtful. Shields and Madox Brown had told him much about Rossetti's early life and the beginnings of the Pre-Raphaelite Brotherhood but would not have discussed intimate details of his health, particularly his mental health. By the time Caine moved into Cheyne Walk Rossetti was a wreck, sick in both body and mind. He told Caine a great deal in confidence about his marriage, his mistresses and his impotence but one cannot imagine he admitted to being mad. He was still a powerful and magnetic personality and, to Caine as to many others, a genius. He was the greatest painter-poet after Blake and as such has not been surpassed.

After considerable procrastination, the mountain of things Rossetti considered essential for a country holiday was packed and they were almost ready to leave. Shields called round on that Sunday morning, 16 September, 1881, and seems to have been surprised to find him about to set out for the Lakes with Caine. He did not think him well enough for the journey. Rossetti sent a note to William while Shields was there, telling him not to make his usual Monday evening call as he was off to the country that day. After Shields had left he dropped his bombshell—he had invited Fanny to go with them. Did Caine object? He was appalled but could only say, 'Not a bit.' He knew he was unlikely to win any argument over Fanny. Rossetti told him to take a cab to Jermyn Street and fetch her. There was nothing he could do but obey. In Cumberland she was introduced as Rossetti's nurse and nobody questioned this. When he came to write his *Recollections* Caine referred to 'the nurse' without identifying her, greatly to the Rossetti family's relief.

They left Euston at nine o'clock that Sunday evening with the famous mattress, a mass of artist's impedimenta and enough books to keep them amused for a year. They travelled in a reserved carriage attached to the Glasgow train which was uncoupled at Penrith and hooked onto a train of the Cockermouth, Keswick and Penrith Railway. They alighted at Threlkeld in a grey dawn to be met by their host, who drove them through the Vale of St John's to Fisher Place. As the fells rose up round them Caine's spirits lifted as they always did but Rossetti was still too drugged with the chloral he had taken in the train to notice anything.

Next day Rossetti was better and delighted with the peaceful scenery. To Caine's astonishment he announced he was going to climb Great Howe. This is the hill that stands alone at the head of Thirlmere, not far from Fisher Place, and is just over 1000 feet high. Caine refers to it as

Golden Howe. Never thinking Rossetti would get even half way up he agreed they should go, Fanny tagging along with them. With many pauses, ostensibly to look at the widening view, Rossetti made it to the top where they sat for an hour looking at the scene before them. When they started the descent he slipped on the steep path and slithered a fair way down before Caine could catch him while Fanny above them fell about shrieking with laughter. Rossetti insisted with dignity that he always went downhill on his 'fundament' and it was far the best way.

It rained that afternoon but he ambled about outside for a while and in the evening wrote to his mother to say they had arrived safely and were 'housed in the most comfortable quarters possible'. The food was good and the house 'so clean as to seem as if no one had ever inhabited it before, and the beds and attendance are most excellent'. He was feeling better for country air already.

> The scenery is grand in the extreme—mountains rising on all hands... I have said several times to Caine how much you would enjoy this place. The quiet is more absolute than I have ever met with elsewhere... Christina will be interested to hear that, as I was leaning over a bridge today, an old snail came up out of his shell and submitted to be stroked, after which he retired... With love to all,
> Your most affectionate Gabriel.

He also wrote to Shields, evidently pleased with himself about his climb. 'That I am not absolutely limbless was proved yesterday by my ascending the Great Hough [*sic*], which is a steep wooded height of 1200 feet, and this without particular fatigue.'

For the first weeks of their stay Rossetti did indeed seem much better. In the evenings he talked about old friends and the times they had had together. He spoke of Carlyle, George Eliot, Ruskin and Longfellow, all of whom he had known at one time. He painted a little, beginning a small replica of his picture of Janey Morris as Proserpine. 'I found it one of my best pleasures to watch a picture growing under his hand,' Caine wrote in his *Recollections*, 'and thought it easy to see through the medium of his idealised heads, cold even in their loveliness, unsubstantial in their passion, that to the painter life had been a dream into which nothing entered that was not as impalpable as itself.'

He had brought the proofs of his anthology to work on. Before leaving London he had given the preface to William for his comments. William sent it on to Fisher Place with a long and appreciative critique which cheered Caine as he respected William's opinion. He sent him the syllabus of twelve lectures on literature he was soon to give in Liverpool, so it would seem his influential friends had ousted the 'Oxford noodle' and seen to it that Caine got the contract which was so vital to him, providing the only income he could be assured of for the coming winter. At this time he was seriously considering a career as a lecturer and critic which would have made the new contract doubly important to him. He asked William to show the syllabus to Madox Brown so he could see he was going to talk about Nolly. 'Your brother is delighted with the Vale of St John,' he added.

> I have never seen him in such spirits. He says the place is the most romantic and sublime he ever beheld. He finds perpetual surprise on every hand. The seclusion he considers perfect: the house extremely pretty and comfortable. Indeed…he is constantly declaring he will take a house and live here 'for ever'. Every half hour he tells me how vastly his mother would enjoy residence here. He says he seems to hear her saying, 'O, look, Christina, look at that lovely ghyll!'

To pass the time Caine made a pencil sketch of the house where they were staying.

Rossetti followed his usual routine of lying late in the mornings so for two or three weeks Caine breakfasted alone with Fanny every day. She talked incessantly, mostly about friends of Rossetti she had met in the years following Lizzie's death. They had all 'sucked his brains', she said, and profited thereby. Morris, Burne-Jones, Brown, Swinburne—according to Fanny they would never have amounted to anything if it had not been for Rossetti. She returned again and again to Janey Morris, about whom she was vicious and waspish. She accused her of all sorts of things but Caine knew she was lying. Coming down earlier than usual one morning Rossetti walked in unexpectedly and overheard some of this. Instead of defending Janey he merely laughed and with a glance at Caine said, 'But who believes anything said by the Helephant?'

At first she tried to ingratiate herself with Caine but it only made him wonder what she was up to. One morning Rossetti, while he and Caine were out for a walk, asked him to draw up a will leaving everything to Fanny. Caine refused. He thought he saw a look of relief in Rossetti's eyes as if that was the answer he had wanted to hear.

In preparation for his new lectures he was re-reading some of the classics. Once the curtains were drawn and the lamps lit Rossetti, whose eyes were troubling him, could no longer paint or read so he made Caine read his study books aloud. He sat at the table close to the lamp and read by the hour. For most of the time Rossetti tramped up and down the small room, as he had been used to do in the studio at home, with his hands thrust into the pockets of his painting coat. From time to time he would throw himself into an armchair, sighing deeply. When a book was finished he discussed it in detail, analysing it with insights which impressed Caine. He was amazed that a man who had spent his life painting and writing only poetry should have such an intuitive grasp of the art of fiction.

Until that time Caine had not been interested in writing novels though he had ambitions as a playwright, but during this stay at Fisher

Place he thought over the tales of old Cumberland his Grandfather Hall had told him when he was a boy. One rather eerie story set around Thirlmere struck him as the basis for a novel. He told it to Rossetti but he thought it too tragic and lacking in 'sympathy' to make a successful book. Far better, he said, for Caine to use some of the Manx tales he had talked about. To be 'the Bard of Manxland' would be a fine thing. To use the Isle of Man as a setting for fiction would be something entirely new and likely to appeal to the reading public. To Caine the Bard of Manxland would forever be T.E. Brown, whose dialect poems he admired and whose *Fo'c's'le Yarns* had just come out. Between reading and talking they were sometimes up so late the first pre-dawn light was showing through the little window on the stairs as they took their candles and went to bed.

On 10 October, 1881, Rossetti wrote to his mother again. He said he was not very well and had no news except that his book was out. Watts had given it 'a fine critique' in the *Athenaeum*. He had asked some friends to give favourable reviews in all the leading literary journals before anyone unfriendly could get their hands on it. 'I have sought for loneliness,' he continued, 'but here the solitude and silence are absolute—a magic spell. Still, Caine is good company... [He] is excessively attentive and friendly, and is really quite an abnegator of self. He went the other day and delivered a lecture at Liverpool (on Richardson) with immense success.'

Before they left London Rossetti's doctor had given Caine a supply of chloral. It was in small phials and Caine's instructions were to give Rossetti only one a day. They were in a locked travelling cabinet of which he kept the key—and kept it hidden. The drug gave Rossetti about four hours' sleep so Caine was glad to stay up late in the hope that by the time it wore off it would be daylight. However, there were nights when Rossetti came to Caine's room at three or four in the morning pathetically begging him for another dose. When he was refused he found the key to the cabinet and stole into the room to take another bottle when Caine was asleep—he found the extra empty under Rossetti's bed next morning.

This seemingly increased dependence worried Caine until he hit on a plan. He poured away part of each bottle, replacing it with water before giving it to Rossetti. Gradually he poured away more of the chloral until the point was reached where the phial Rossetti took was pure water. As the chloral was colourless and tasteless when diluted Rossetti drank the dose and went off to bed unsuspecting. Caine waited for a little while and then tiptoed into his room. He was fast asleep. To Caine, perhaps naïvely, it seemed that the terrible addiction was beaten, but he reckoned without Fanny. Unfortunately she had seen what he was doing. She told Rossetti. It was a cruel trick and the effect on Rossetti was terrible. His demands for more chloral than the doctor had prescribed became increasingly furious and urgent so that Caine, sick with worry, gave him more.

He was reluctant to leave him but had to fulfil his engagements in Liverpool. The statesman—the Cumbrian term for a yeoman farmer—always met him off the train on his return with the words that he would be welcome back. On the third occasion he was met with an emphatic, 'You'll be *very* welcome, Sir.' Seeing Keighley's expression he asked if anything was wrong and was told 'the nurse' had gone and Mr Rossetti had drunk a great deal of whisky. He was sending for a bottle a day from the Nag's Head and it was finished by morning.

It did not take long to get what had happened out of Rossetti. Taking advantage of Caine's absence Fanny had returned to the subject of the will. She had demanded that Rossetti make one in her favour—a lawyer could be fetched from Keswick if necessary. When he refused she packed her bags and flounced off back to London. Caine was furious with her and with himself for not spotting what her game was all along. She must have wheedled the invitation to join them with only one idea, to get Rossetti to make the will she wanted. She rightly saw Caine as an obstacle and when she caught him substituting water for chloral she thought she had the means to discredit him and get her way. She reckoned without Rossetti's trust in and affection for Caine and his feeling for what was right. Leaving all he possessed to a trollop and ignoring his family and friends would be wrong. He was fond of Fanny but he was not going to embarrass everyone by making her his heir.

The days were closing in and the weather turning wet and wintry, which did nothing to help Rossetti's state of mind. At first he had seemed to benefit greatly from the holiday but now his melancholia returned and his health worsened again. It must have come as a relief to the distracted Caine, overburdened with the responsibility of looking after the addicted invalid who was continuing to drink large quantities of whisky to add to his problems, when Rossetti announced he had had enough of the Lakes and was returning to London.

Caine packed their belongings and telegraphed for a reserved carriage to be ready at Threlkeld. This way, as on the journey up, they would not have to change trains. For the whole of the long overnight journey south Rossetti sat bolt upright in coat, hat and gloves, as if getting off at the next station. Caine, who was dropping with exhaustion, forced himself to stay awake, peering through the curtains at intervals to see how far they had got. It seemed an endless night and during it Rossetti told Caine more of his early private life than he had ever told anyone else. He talked of his remorse over Lizzie's death and revealed the contents of the note she had left, something he had not disclosed to anyone else. He also went over the story of how he had put the poems in her coffin touching her cheek, even saying how he had wrapped her long titian hair round it. As he had been alone in the room no one had seen exactly what he had done. He was full of remorse over the exhumation of her body to retrieve the poems, making no excuses. Tantalisingly, Caine's discretion in his account of these revelations means that we do not know exactly what was said. He disclosed some of it in a letter to Bernard Shaw in 1928 but he told no one, ever, what was in Lizzie's note.

When they arrived at Euston before dawn it was drizzling and chilly. An omnibus had been ordered to meet them and when it drew up outside Tudor House all the blinds were still down which seemed to Caine a dreary home-coming. Rossetti, however, though so feeble that Caine had to help him up the front steps, said heartily as he stood in the hall, 'Thank God! Home at last, and never shall I leave it again!' They had been away for a month.

Rossetti was increasingly difficult to deal with, snapping at people who bored him, restless and irritable. There were no more letters to or from Janey Morris after the return to Tudor House. She was ill and he never saw her again. What Caine wrote of this period for publication is discreet to the point of misinformation. He says Rossetti's old friends all came round to see him and his mother and sister were there a great deal. It is true they wanted to visit him but Rossetti refused to see anyone except by appointment and even then they could be turned away. Eventually, tired of appointments being cancelled, Mrs Rossetti and Christina took to turning up unannounced. Christina got herself invited to dinner with the Bell Scotts and went briefly to see her brother. She was upset to find him ill and alone. It must have been one of Caine's lecture nights. He went up in the afternoon and came back by the first train next morning so was away for less than twenty-four hours. Two days later Christina returned bringing her mother. They were both anxious about Gabriel's health but relieved to find Caine in attendance and Watts there too. Despite what Caine wrote and what William Sharp later said, other friends had stayed away, apart from Madox Brown, who came when he could but was in Manchester most of the time. Even Shields did not call for a while.

Watts was the most welcome visitor of all but that autumn he was ill and unable to leave The Pines for a time. When he could come he always cheered Gabriel enormously. William, on the other hand, was becoming impatient with what he saw as his brother's hypochondria. In fact Gabriel was now genuinely ill. On the evening of 24 October, 1881, the day after their return, William dined at Tudor House as usual on a Monday. Caine took the chance to slip out, promising to be back by 10.30 when William was to leave. He was delayed and missed him. As soon as he got back he wrote a note saying he was sure William would have guessed that as well as his 'acknowledged purpose in going out' he had intended to scc Rossetti's doctor, Dr Marshall. 'This I did and he has said he will be here at 6 pm tomorrow. When I told him the full quantity of chloral and whisky taken he did not seem at all alarmed, but assured me twice as much of both had been used previously. Nevertheless he thought I had done well in calling and would take measures to have the strength reduced.'

Dr John Marshall was one of the great surgeons of his day and Rossetti had tremendous faith in him. He had entered the Pre-Raphaelite circle early on as an admirer of their work long before being asked to treat Gabriel following his suicide attempt in 1872.

Next evening, when Caine had finished unpacking his own things, he found the sketch he had made of Fisher Place and sent it to William. On the back he wrote that as William had spoken about the farm he might like to see what it looked like. Dr Marshall had been to see his brother 'and now there is a nurse in the house'. This was a considerable relief as Caine felt he could not otherwise have left Rossetti. A week after getting back he was on the train north again. This time it was not to lecture but to represent Rossetti at the installation of *Dante's Dream of the Death of Beatrice* in Liverpool's Walker Art Gallery. It still hangs there. It was 3 November and the Mayor had invited him to give a 'Disquisition'. It was a moment of personal triumph and for his parents of enormous pride, fully justified as it had been Caine's idea in the first place and without his considerable efforts the picture would never have got there. It was due to be despatched shortly before they left for Cumberland but at the last minute Rossetti came up with fresh objections to the arrangements, in spite of a telegram from Samuelson saying everything was as he wished and the sale complete. Caine had to send an urgent note to Watts asking him to come and persuade Rossetti to let the picture go.

Back in Tudor House Caine was full of the event and the praises heaped on Rossetti and was eager to tell him all about it. It should have been a good time for Rossetti, a major picture sold and on view in a public gallery, his new book of poems well received and soon to be reprinted, but he was sunk in gloom and despondency. To Caine's intense disappointment he showed little interest in hearing about the Liverpool showing or in reading reviews, however laudatory. Caine acknowledges wryly at one point that with his own lugubrious turn of mind and tendency to depression he may not have made the best companion for Rossetti. For a few days the strain became too much for him and he was in bed with a fever.

Although Caine said in his book that they saw nothing of Fanny after their return from the Lakes until the end of January it seems she turned up several times. Caine would send her away but she knew when he would be in Liverpool and came then. She quarrelled with the nurse and interfered in her regime for the patient. Rossetti sent an urgent note to his brother asking him to get rid of her which he did and there was peace for a while. However, Rossetti was tiresome and difficult and eventually the nurse left. This threw all responsibility onto Caine once more.

Rossetti wrote Shields a note in a feeble scrawl saying he was going 'daily from bad to worse, I am quite exhausted now, and really don't know how it may end. I have been seeing Marshall.' Evidently this did not bring Shields round at the run as he had hoped so he sent a further note on 22 November, 'William has told you that I shall be alone tomorrow. Let me implore you to come. I am still very ill.' Caine also wrote to Shields begging him to visit Rossetti. There was a touching reunion, tearful on Shields's side, when he came on 26 November. According to his diary he had seen Dr Marshall on his way to Cheyne Walk and had also been 'to town on Rossetti's business to get him a nurse'. This was Mrs Abrey, a kind and capable soul who stayed with Rossetti to the end.

Shields was an emotional man but he may have stayed away not because he had taken offence at anything Rossetti had said or done but because he could not bear to see him in such a state, knowing the prime cause. Years before he had himself been hooked on chloral, innocently recommended by Madox Brown as an effective sleeping draught, when he had been under great stress and suffering from insomnia. He had broken free from it but he more than anyone else would have understood and sympathised with Rossetti.

Rossetti felt his sight was failing and tormented himself that he would never paint again and that he was faced with dire poverty. Had he lived longer than he did this might have come true. At the height of his powers he had earned a large income but none of it had been saved or invested. This was a lesson Caine took to heart. William tried to reassure his brother, telling him, 'If the worst comes to the worst, you will come to my house and stay there as long as either of us lives.'

In the long hours of his sleepless nights Rossetti confided in Caine that he thought he was dying and how much he feared it. With no religious faith he believed it would mean total annihilation and he dreaded it. Caine tried to reason with him and Shields pleaded with him to turn to God, but neither of them had much effect. One day when he was particularly poorly and William and Watts were there he astonished them all by asking for a priest to make his confession. Watts reminded him of his lack of belief, but William, who was an atheist, as was Lucy, said that if his brother wanted the comforts of the church he should have them.

Two people Rossetti was always glad to see were the young blind poet, Philip Bourke Marston, and his father. On the evening of 11 December they spent an hour or two with him. Rossetti seemed more restless than usual, tramping around the studio where they were all gathered. After a bit he threw himself down on the sofa in his usual posture and for a while seemed more cheerful, almost his old self. Suddenly he called out to Caine that he could not move his left arm, and then that he had lost the use of that leg as well. Knowing how Rossetti's mind ruled his body, Caine said he was sure nothing was really wrong but when he went to help him up he found it was only too true. Rossetti had suffered a mild stroke. Dr Bourke Marston went to Caine's assistance and between them they half carried Rossetti up the twisting stairs at the back of the studio to his bedroom and got him into bed. His mind was clear and Caine was aware of his terrible humiliation at having to be helped in this way. Philip, unable in his blindness to be of use, sat in the studio. Dr Marshall was summoned.

In the weeks leading up to that night Rossetti's craving for chloral had grown. Caine did all he could to check it but was out of his depth. In his typically florid style he wrote later, 'I could as easily have checked the rising tide; and where the lifelong assiduity of older friends had failed to eradicate a morbid, ruinous and fatal thirst, it was presumptuous if not ridiculous to imagine that the task could be compassed by a frail creature with heart and nerves of wax.' Dr Marshall might not have put it like that but would doubtless have agreed. He took drastic steps, saying that the use of chloral, which had caused so much damage, had to stop at once and completely. He called in Dr Henry Maudsley, the leading psychiatrist of the time.

Maudsley stayed in the house for several days, supervising Rossetti's treatment and injecting morphia when the terrible withdrawal symptoms became too painful. Caine watched horrified throughout Rossetti's ordeal. For hours on end he was delirious. It seems strange that a sick man who had just suffered a stroke should be subjected to 'cold turkey' like this but it worked. On the fourth day, after his first sleep for a long time not induced by drugs, Rossetti woke lucid, calm—and grateful. Though weak the patient was a great deal better and Dr Maudsley was able to leave. Caine felt he was seeing the real Rossetti for the first time. The delusions, the suspicions, the hallucinations were all gone. The transformation was dramatic.

News of his seizure had got about and many old friends called whom he had not seen for a long time. One evening Edward Burne-Jones came to sit with him for an hour, looking thin, pale and ill himself but full of affectionate solicitude. Afterwards he dined informally with Caine in the studio and talked about the early Pre-Raphaelite days and his admiration for his old friend. There were unfinished works on easels about the room. Looking at one of them he said, 'They say Gabriel cannot draw, but look at that hand. There isn't anybody else in the world who can draw a hand like that.'

Caine was kept busy replying to letters enquiring after Rossetti and from people proposing to call and see him, all of whom had to be politely put off. One of these was the Russian novelist Turgenev, who was on a visit to London. There were few men Caine would have liked to meet more but he had to put him off along with the rest. Turgenev, who was ten years older than Rossetti, died in 1883 and Caine never again had a chance to meet him.

Knowing that Rossetti always spent Christmas with his family and set much store by it, William and Laetitia Bell Scott invited Caine to share their Christmas dinner. He accepted thankfully and was looking forward to it but when Christmas Day came Rossetti was still bedfast and not able to join his family. He hated being alone at any time but this day most of all. He begged Caine to stay with him, 'for I cannot fairly ask any other'. Of course Caine stayed. This was his first Christmas in London away from his own family and he knew how Rossetti was feeling. He also suspected that this could be Rossetti's last Christmas.

'We dined alone,' he wrote, 'he in his bed, I at the little table at the foot of it, on which I had first seen the wired lamp and the bottle of medicine; but later in the evening William Rossetti, with his brotherly affection, left his children and guests at his own house, and ran down to spend an hour with the invalid.'

Church bells had upset and irritated Rossetti for as long as Caine had known him but as they rang out that Christmas night they did not worry him at all. Indeed he listened to them with pleasure. He talked of his sister Maria, who had died of cancer five years earlier, and how his mother and Christina had been supported in their loss by their religious faith. 'Are you a believer like Shields?' he asked. Caine, who had diplomatically kept off the subject, admitted he was. Thinking back in later years Caine concluded Rossetti's position had been that of the agnostic, rather than the atheist stand taken by his brother and sister-in-law. From then on there was no more morbid brooding on death or fear of poverty.

It was natural that Rossetti should talk much about the past, having shut himself off from the present for so long. One day he said to Caine, 'To marry one woman and then find out, when it is too late, that you love another, is the deepest tragedy that can enter a man's life.' He spoke with such intensity that Caine was sure he spoke of his own experience, but he did not elaborate and Caine could not question him as to what he meant.

One subject they did discuss was the problem of prostitution, 'the age-long problem of the poor scapegoats of society who carry the sins of men into a wilderness from which there is no escape', as Caine puts it in his usual elliptical way. Rossetti insisted rescue was almost impossible but Caine thought it had to be attempted. Years later he gave a lot of money to missions for 'fallen women'. This problem was one Rossetti had dealt with many years before in his poem *Jenny*, and in his painting, *Found*, which tells the same story. In the picture a young man grasps the wrists of a girl, evidently a prostitute, who crouches against the wall of a highly symbolic churchyard, turning her face away from him in shame. In the background is the farm cart containing a netted calf on its way to market, the errand which has brought the farm boy to town and which symbolises the fate of the girl. Caine admitted that he had met a street walker, a girl of some refinement and education who had been driven onto the streets by personal tragedy. Rossetti asked Caine to fetch a copy of his first volume of poems, containing *Jenny*. When he brought it he wrote the girl's name in it with 'a few touching lines' and told Caine to give it to her, which he did, but after that Caine never saw her again and never knew what became of her.

Watts now came to Cheyne Walk every day, lightening the claustrophobic atmosphere of Rossetti's room. It was probably through him that Rossetti received a present which meant a great deal to him. It was a romance, *God and Man*, which was dedicated 'To an Old Enemy'. The author was Buchanan, now filled with remorse for what he had done to Rossetti and converted to a huge admiration for the poetry he had once decried as 'fleshly' and decadent. Under the dedication were two verses in which he took back all he had previously said:

> I would have snatched a bay-leaf from thy brow,
>   Wronging the chaplet on an honoured head;
> In peace and charity I bring thee now
>   A lily-flower instead.
>
> Pure as thy purpose, blameless as thy song,
>   Sweet as thy spirit, may this offering be;
> Forget the bitter blame that did thee wrong,
>   And take the gift from me.

It was as public and complete a recantation and apology as Buchanan could have made. At first Rossetti could not believe the verses were meant for him but Caine repeatedly told him Watts had said they were and he had it from Buchanan himself. When he at last accepted it Rossetti was reduced to tears. Caine was deeply grateful that this old wrong should have been righted. Not long after Rossetti's death he got to know Buchanan and they became quite friendly. He told Buchanan how good it was that his retraction had come before it was too late. Though he had been so much moved Rossetti never mentioned it or Buchanan again.

In January, 1882, in the midst of his anxiety over Rossetti, Caine's anthology was published by Elliot Stock. Shields said in his diary that he spent two or three days at the end of the previous November, when he was particularly busy, designing the front cover and on 29 December he went to the binders to check on its production. His work was not acknowledged in the book. Perhaps he did not want his name mentioned for some reason.

This should have been a great occasion for Caine, the appearance of his first proper book between hard covers instead of the paperbound pamphlets he had brought out so far, but it fell rather flat. Early reviews were lukewarm but then George Saintsbury praised it in the *Saturday Review* while the *Athenaeum* was kind, along with one or two other papers. As a result the book began to sell quite well. Another critic to praise it was Professor Dowden but it was Saintsbury's commendation which really counted. A former schoolmaster, he was famous at this time as an active and highly respected critic.

Poetry was a live issue to the Victorians in a way that is hardly comprehensible today. Swinburne, Tennyson and Rossetti, as well as many lesser poets, were the subject of much discussion and critical review. Stock's usual print run for a book of verse was 1000 copies. Caine was able to write to William a year or so later, 'My sonnet book is now sold out.' It was not, however, reprinted. Gabriel was delighted with it and sent a copy to his mother.

He never recovered entirely from the paralysis caused by the stroke and was confined to his room for about three weeks. After that he managed to get down to his studio but was so weak it became clear he was not recovering as well as they had all hoped. The mountains had done him no real good the previous autumn. Now, in late January, it was decided that he should try the seaside for a change of air. An old friend, Tom Seddon, who was an architect, called on him. He was designing a development of holiday bungalows and houses at Birchington, on the Kent coast. He had built a large bungalow for himself and offered Rossetti the use of it for as long as he liked. Caine had a look at it and reported favourably. Rossetti agreed to go, though of course it took some time to get him there.

Caine then made a surprising request. Lily, now twelve years old and still at school, had been ill with bronchitis. She was recovering but a spell at the seaside would do her a world of good—could she come with them? Rossetti, who was fond of children, said he would be glad to have her. Wildly excited at the prospect of her first trip to London, Lily was put on the train at Liverpool, travelling alone. At Euston the crowds frightened her until her brother found her and whisked her off to Cheyne Walk in a cab. It seems odd now that Caine should have introduced his little sister to this strange household and the company of a dying man but in January of 1882 no one, with the possible exception of Dr Marshall, had any idea that the end was so near. Rossetti's nurse, Mrs Abrey, seemed happy to look after the child and so she entered Tudor House.

Ten years later, when he was working on a memoir of his brother and Lily was a rising young actress, William Rossetti asked her to record her memories of Gabriel, telling her that a child's impressions of the great man and his home would be of much interest. She obliged, writing in an exercise book which is now in her brother Willie's archive in Liverpool. It was published in the *New Review* in September, 1894.

She found the entrance hall of Tudor House dark and intimidating although it was so spacious, the whole house 'heavy and dull'. To a child who had spent her life so far in a succession of small terraced houses the sheer size of the place seemed extraordinary. She could quite believe a princess who became a queen had lived there. Caine led her down a corridor to the room she was to sleep in. It was 'so dark that I found myself coming into collision with old oak chairs and cabinets which were so shaky on their foundations as to totter for minutes after they were touched'. The 'faded splendour' of the drawing room as they passed it impressed her and she noted the silver candlesticks were quite black for lack of polishing.

A couple of hours after her arrival Caine took her to the studio to meet Rossetti. She looked around at the stacks of unfinished paintings, the elaborate mantelpiece surmounted by a study of Dante's Beatrice and at the enormous, overgrown chairs and sofa. The furniture struck her as out of date without being really old. Rossetti had a collection of plaster casts and lay figures. Lily 'suddenly saw a headless woman. That object filled me with terror, and I verily believed that I had got into Blue Beard's secret chamber when I caught sight of the collection of heads on the floor.' Then a voice said, 'Is that you, Caine?' She looked round to see who had spoken and saw Rossetti deep in one of the big armchairs.

Caine replied that he had brought his sister. 'Ah,' said Rossetti, 'What's your name?' Lily was almost too dazed to speak and riveted by the sight of the black glove Rossetti was wearing on his left hand, which still remained partly paralysed and always felt cold to him. She managed to say she was Lily and in teasing fashion he pretended not to hear.

'Oh, yes, Minnie,' he said. 'No, no, Lily.' 'Ah Jenny.' 'No, no, my name is Lily.' 'I've got it at last,' he said laughing. 'Lily, that's a very pretty name.' And the ice was broken. Rossetti was at his best with her, chattering gaily and more relaxed than with anyone else. After dinner the nurse came to take her to bed. Her room was hardly arranged for a child. A glowering bust of Cromwell frightened her—it was standing just where she could see it as she lay in bed. Mrs Abrey made up a story about it to calm her fears and settled her for the night.

For the next week or so Lily played happily about the house while Rossetti changed his mind at hourly intervals as to whether he would go to Birchington or not. Someone, probably one of the servants, told Lily about the ghosts in the house. One was a woman who appeared at the top of the second flight of stairs and then retreated into the bedroom overlooking the river. It has often been said that Lily saw the ghost but she does not expressly say so. She evidently asked Rossetti about it and found this was one subject on which he never joked. He told her that there were some things that no one could explain and that he himself had seen and heard people who were dead. Caine offered to sleep in the top bedroom without a candle to disprove the story of the haunting but Rossetti would not let him do it.

CHAPTER TEN

It was 4 February, 1882, when they all set off for Birchington—Caine, Lily, Nurse Abrey and the protesting Rossetti. The usual pile of luggage went with them. At the station Rossetti announced he was not going anywhere. Somehow Caine, who was in the middle of sorting out the luggage with the porter, soothed him down and Lily distracted him.

'When we left for Birchington,' Lily wrote later, 'I was delighted with Mr Rossetti's companionship. I had never met a man so full of ideas interesting and attractive to a child.' But then he had always been good with children, including Jenny and May Morris when they were small. He talked to Lily all the way in the cab from Cheyne Walk to the station, telling her stories about everything they passed. When he saw a barrel organ with the organ grinder churning out his raucous tune at top speed he said, 'Now you don't tolerate those things in Liverpool, do you?' 'Oh yes!' said Lily, 'we do and rather enjoy them.'

They travelled by the London, Chatham and Dover Railway. 'As the porter was labelling our luggage,' said Lily, 'Mr Rossetti took me by the hand. We were interested in the porter's operations and Mr Rossetti was amused at the company's initial letters: LCDR. "Why Lily," said he, "They knew we were coming. That stands for Lily Caine and Dante Rossetti."'

Caine must have blessed his little sister as he shepherded his party onto the train, ignoring Rossetti's objections. Of course as soon as they arrived at their destination Rossetti announced it would not do at all and he was going home. As they walked up to the door of Westcliffe Bungalow he bent down and said to the child, 'Lily, I don't think think this looks like a house, do you? It's more like another LC & DR station.' Caine told him they had to stay for Lily's sake as it was for her health as well as his they had come. Grumbling, Rossetti said he would give it a week. He was not to leave it again alive.

Caine managed to keep the subject of when they should return home at bay by creating excitement, aided by Lily, over the choice of rooms to sleep in. Rossetti chose his first and then said it was too small. Nurse Abrey took charge of him, firmly telling him this was the one that would suit her best if she was to look after him. Rossetti sat grumpily watching the trunks being brought in. When the last one was unloaded, according to Lily, he changed his mind once more. 'He said he needed no change and asked crossly why he had been brought there—a place like that! He could see neither beauty nor comfort anywhere.' However, after much fuss about finding somewhere with a north light, his easel was set up and he was mollified by the possibility of being able to paint.

At first he managed a few short walks—Lily told him he <u>must</u> come and see the cliffs—but far from the change improving his health he weakened steadily. He tried to paint a little but the hand was losing its cunning. He was restless and irritable with everyone except Lily. He wanted to go home because no one came to see him. Caine wrote to several friends asking them to come down for a day or two. Watts came and so did young William Sharp and one or two others but Rossetti asked for Shields. Caine sent him a rather incoherent note saying, 'Rossetti threatens to return at once unless someone comes out to see us. Such is the condition of things. When can you come? He says you promised to come—do try to do so, or something of the kind.' Shields did not respond immediately as he was being pressed to complete a commission. Madox Brown was in London working on the cartoons for his next Manchester Town Hall fresco, *Crabtree Watching the Transit of Venus*, and managed to get down for a few days. While there he asked Caine if he would sit for the figure of Crabtree and used the opportunity to make some preparatory sketches of him.

The Transit of Venus, one of Ford Madox Brown's frescoes in the Manchester Town Hall. Caine was the model for Crabtree.

Rossetti's walks got shorter and shorter until they were merely a turn about the garden. After the first week he hardly ever went outside at all but listened attentively to what Lily had to tell him about the sea, the shore, the cliffs and the flowers growing so early in the year—it had been a mild winter.

All along he had insisted he would only stay if his mother and sister came with him. They arrived on 2 March and were saddened to see him failing but he was far happier with them there and calmed down considerably. He amused himself and everyone else by writing a ballad about a character he named Jan van Hunks who engaged in a fatal smoking-duel with the devil. When he lost the devil trundled him off to hell in a barrow, soul and body. An odd choice of subject for a man who seems to have been well aware of his own approaching death. According to Lily he 'laughed with us as he read it bit by bit every night'. He clung to his shabby old 'painting coat' and when he could manage it would shamble backwards and forwards across the drawing-room in his slippers as he used to do at home but he walked unsteadily, his head thrust forward, looking like a very old man.

When friends came he presided cheerfully over dinner. 'When he was in the humour,' said Lily, 'he would rally me about my objection to oysters. He said I should get over that in a few years. And he spoke truly. His own appetite for oysters was quite voracious.' Although Nurse Abrey put her to bed fairly early she remembered listening avidly to Rossetti reading after dinner, in particular Edgar Allen Poe's *The Raven*, which stirred her imagination. 'His voice was so deep and strong it seemed to my childish fancy to come from under the floor.' One day he found her reading *The Arabian Nights*. 'Put the book away, Lily, and I will tell you the stories.' Which he did in enthralling manner. He also told her a story which struck her as quaint.

> A poor old man who lived much alone in the great heart of London lay dying when a neighbour, wishing to render him a good service, sent for the clergyman. The minister took a chair, sat down at the bedside and asked in the manner of the person beginning a discussion, 'Do you know why Christ died?' The man in a half childish way replied, 'Oh sir, is this the time to ask conundrums?' And Mr Rossetti would imitate the weak and exhausted voice of the dying man.

The story may have struck Lily as 'quaint' but to the adults it seemed odd that he should tell it at all.

He was eventually confined to bed, sitting up for only an hour or two a day. Nurse Abrey confided to Caine that she was becoming deeply concerned. The local doctor diagnosed 'softening of the brain', but Dr Marshall, who came down several times, dismissed that and said there was now serious kidney failure. In fact Rossetti had Bright's Disease, a generic term used then for a group of chronic and acute kidney diseases. At last it dawned on Caine that this was not the place for a little girl to be. On Friday, 10 March, 1882, he took Lily up to London and put her on the Liverpool train. Before she left Nurse Abrey took her to say good-bye to Rossetti, whom she had not seen for a week. She was shocked to see how much thinner and more shrunken he looked. 'Although he was very weak he bade me goodbye with all his old warmth,' she wrote. 'He had many a good wish for me... His eyes with a fixed glassy stare were still on me as I was leaving the room.'

She was sad to go. She felt Rossetti was as much her friend as her brother's. In the short time they had been together she had also become fond of Mrs Rossetti, remembering her later as a sweet old lady with a deep religious faith, walking about slowly on her daughter's arm. Although frail she never missed church—Lily admitted to seeing her coming in from the early service just as she herself was getting down to breakfast. 'Miss Rossetti too evoked my affection by her gentle ways', she added. When she was older she was 'honoured and delighted to grow more intimate with my dear and greatly-gifted friend'. Christina gave Lily a present of a small portable writing desk, writing her own name and the child's inside the lid. Lily used it well and it got marked and ink stained but the bold signature of 'the great English poetess' remained clear. The desk was Lily's dearest possession for the rest of her life.

Throughout the first week in April Rossetti's state worsened. On the Wednesday morning, 5 April, he asked for Caine. He was propped up in bed and dictated two sonnets which he had just composed, telling Caine to give them to Watts for publication. The next morning Caine found his speech thick and blurred but in spite of this 'he talked long and earnestly...it was our last real interview'.

'Can you understand me?' he asked abruptly. Caine said he could. 'Nurse Abrey can't,' said Rossetti sadly.

When they were alone together for a few minutes, Rossetti brought up the subject of Fanny. She had arrived at Tudor House one day in January when he was ill in bed and insisted on going up to his room, shutting the door in Caine's face. Some time later Rossetti called for him and asked him to fetch the cheque book. Caine had charge of it, writing the cheques for the bills and giving them to Rossetti to sign. He told Caine Fanny was badly in need of money and asked him to write a cheque in her favour for £200—several thousand at today's values. Caine refused absolutely and Rossetti did not press him. Caine led Fanny away and she ran down the stairs in front of him. When he got down to the hall she came out of the studio carrying one of Rossetti's drawings. Caine did not say anything, simply opened the front door and ushered her out.

Now Rossetti whispered, 'Have you heard anything of Fanny?' 'Nothing at all,' Caine replied. 'Would you tell me if you had?' 'If you asked me—yes.'

'My poor mistress,' Rossetti murmured and Caine, moved at such loyalty and unable to say anything more, left the room.

In his book Caine did not give Fanny's name, simply putting a dash to represent it and another in place of 'mistress'. There was a great deal of speculation as to who it was that Rossetti remembered on his death-bed. Many thought it was Janey Morris. Caine never published the name but he told Bernard Shaw who it was in a letter written in September, 1928.

After some discussion with Mrs Rossetti, Christina and the nurse, Caine telegraphed Dr Marshall, William Rossetti and Watts to say Gabriel was failing and they should come at once. Mrs Rossetti, although much distressed, insisted on sitting up with her son in her usual turn. Caine stayed with her until the small hours when Christina came to relieve them. Rossetti sat up in bed most of the night. He was free of pain—he told them 'a sort of stupefaction' had removed it. He crooned odd lines of poetry. 'My own verses torment me,' he said. Later he began to half-sing, half-recite, snatches from Iago's songs from *Othello*, commenting that they were strange things to come into one's head at such a time. Caine told him his brother and Watts would be with him next day. He summoned other close friends as well.

William and Watts arrived next morning, William complaining of the problems of travelling on a Good Friday with a Sunday train service. Brown was back in Manchester and did not receive his letter in time. On the Saturday morning Watts drew up a will for Rossetti to sign, giving it to Caine to make a fair copy. When the dying man had signed it with a shaky hand Caine added his name as one of the witnesses. Gabriel wanted everything to go to his brother and sister but Christina protested vehemently, insisting her mother's name should be substituted for hers. Rossetti remembered his closest friends. They are listed as Ford Madox Brown, William Bell Scott, Edward Burne-Jones, Theodore Watts, Algernon Swinburne, Frederick Leyland, Frederic Shields—and 'Thomas Hall Caine of 16 Cheyne Walk'. All of them were to receive such drawings and articles as they might select from his house as mementoes, subject to William's approval as executor.

That same morning Caine telegraphed an urgent plea to Shields to come to Rossetti and he arrived in the evening. Leyland, who was staying at Ramsgate, came over during the day and Dr Marshall arrived to confer with the local practitioner, Dr Harris.

On 9 April, Easter Sunday, Rossetti had an easier day and in the evening Nurse Abrey gave such a good report of her patient that they all gathered in his room in cheerful mood. The doctor had ordered hot packs to be applied to his back and groin. As Mrs Abrey prepared to give the treatment Mrs Rossetti and Christina went to their room across the passage, William to the drawing-room and Watts, Shields and Caine to the dining-room where they sat chatting, happier than for some time. At about nine Watts went into Rossetti's room and returned saying he was comfortable and 'very bright'. They began to dare to hope but as they were laughing together they heard a terrible scream and the sounds of running footsteps and a banging on every door.

'We hurried into Rossetti's room,' Caine wrote, 'and found him in convulsions. Mr Watts raised him on one side, whilst I raised him on the other.' His brother, mother and sister rushed into the room while Shields fled away to fetch the doctor. 'There were a few moments of suspense, and then we saw him die in our arms.' Just at that moment Lucy Rossetti arrived from Manchester.

This account of Gabriel's last moments does not tally exactly with others, in particular with William's diary. The next day he made a succinct entry: 'He died 9.31 pm. The others—Watts, Mother, Christina and nurse in room; Caine and Shields in and out; Watts at Gabriel's right side, partly supporting him.' Caine claimed repeatedly to the end of his life that 'Rossetti died in my arms', but that is not what William reported. He was a civil servant, a careful, unimaginative man, accustomed to taking accurate minutes of meetings. He always reported scrupulously on what he saw and was not given to speculating on what he had not seen. 'Caine and Shields in and out' does not corroborate Caine's claim. On the other hand it was a moment of tension, alarm and grief, the whole family and the nurse were crowded round the bed and next day, exhausted and harassed with preparations for the funeral, William may not have recollected as accurately as usual. Shields certainly was not 'in and out'—he went for the doctor. Likewise Caine, who rushed to his beloved friend's side when he was already unconscious, may have convinced himself he was holding him at the moment he died. Everyone agrees that Watts was there all the time. 'Watts is a hero of friendship' were almost the last words Rossetti said.

Dr Harris—Marshall had returned to London saying there was nothing more he could do—arrived quickly and only added to the confusion by saying at first that Rossetti, though unconscious, was still alive, and then almost immediately that he was dead. Whatever the exact facts of the matter Caine was convinced of the truth of what he claimed. It marked him for life and he never for a moment forgot it.

Although it cannot have been unexpected, the group of friends were devastated by Rossetti's death. When the news reached Madox Brown, back in Manchester, he wrote a touching letter to Shields. 'I don't know how you feel this sad event; to me it is the greatest blow I have received since the loss of our dear Nolly. I cannot at all get over the idea that I am never to speak to him again.'

Substitute 'Johnny' for 'Nolly' and he could have been writing for Caine. The bottom had dropped out of his world and above all he was now without a home, without employment and without his patron. It is impossible to exaggerate the importance of Rossetti to Caine. He had

The Dead Rossetti, drawn by Frederic Shields in Chalk on Paper,
from the copy made for Frederick Leyland.

opened doors for him to take a place in the London literary scene which
he might never have attained on his own. It was Rossetti's patronage
that launched him.

The morning after the death Shields, at William's request, drew Rossetti
on his death-bed, sobbing convulsively as he worked. Afterwards, still in
tears, he made three copies, one of which was given to Caine and
another to Frederick Leyland, Shields keeping the third. At Mrs
Rossetti's insistence a professional firm was brought in to make a death

mask. It did not turn out well and none of the family wanted it. William
Sharp said it was 'alike misleading and unpleasant'. Caine, however,
received this ghoulish object with gratitude and it was displayed prominently wherever he lived for the rest of his life. Of his own family only
Lily would have known whether Sharp's judgement was correct but
they all hated the thing and after his own death it disappeared mysteriously, probably into the dustbin. In 1928 Caine still owned Shields's
pencil drawing of the dead Rossetti but that has likewise disappeared.
Leyland's copy is in an American collection but there seems no record
of the third.

A family conference decided Rossetti should be buried at Birchington—he had told William he did not want to be buried in the family plot
at Highgate Cemetery where his wife lay. Caine did not know this and
thought it strange that the family chose Birchington, but that windswept
spot within sight and sound of the sea seemed appropriate. The funeral
was fixed for the following Friday and a plot chosen near the church
porch. In the interim Caine went up to London to check that all was
well at Cheyne Walk and pay the servants. As he walked into the studio
it struck a chill in him but he went through Rossetti's desk to retrieve
his own letters, or all he could find of them, and put them in his bedroom before returning to Birchington.

The funeral was a private one with only the family and a few friends
present. Watts and Shields, who had both gone home earlier in the
week, returned for the ceremony and stood with Caine by the grave.
Madox Brown was ill and could not leave Manchester. They heard later
that Ned Burne-Jones had set out to join them but had felt ill on the way
to the station and gone home. Shields stayed the night at the bungalow
with Watts and Caine. They remained a week or more, packing
Rossetti's possessions to take back to Cheyne Walk and generally clearing up. Caine, having caught a bad cold and worn out with the strain of
the past weeks, collapsed into bed. News of this reached Christina who
wrote, 'My Mother is quite sorry to think of you ill and alone at
Birchington, without any of those you cared for to care for you.' She
seems not to have realised Watts was still there. 'Perhaps soon we shall
have the pleasure of hearing directly or indirectly, that you are well
again and are no further involved in our troubles than your own kind
heart necessitates.' Evidently she had been discussing her work with
Caine because she adds, 'Were you not a little curious to know what I
should get for "Resurgam"? 2 guineas only, I assure you, so you see I am
not particularly enviable. My dear Mother...sends you best remem-
brances and wishes, and has often thought of you.'

Before he left to return to Cheyne Walk Caine began negotiations
with the vicar on behalf of the family for a memorial to Gabriel. Mrs
Rossetti and Christina gave the church a stained glass window, designed

by Shields, and William provided the headstone for the grave. Taking a last look at the grave before leaving Caine was surprised and touched to find it strewn with fresh flowers. He and Watts travelled up to London again with the trunks. Caine felt Rossetti's death drew them closer to each other, as in life he had brought them together in the first place.

Caine arrived at 16 Cheyne Walk on 24 April to find a letter from Lily. Now Mr Rossetti was dead, she asked, would he be coming back to Liverpool? His parents were anxious as to how he was going to manage. In reply he told her,

> Don't be the least anxious about me. I am all right. My health is excellent. O no, I shall not be going to live in Liverpool. I am remaining in London. I shall stay on here for a while (2 or 3 months) and then perhaps go into chambers in the Temple (where Goldsmith lived when he became a swell). I am all right. You must not (any of you) say anything about me in Liverpool except that I am in London as a journalist and doing very well. I have a salary from the Liverpool Mercury that is alone quite enough to keep me, and a mite like you too. Say nothing of this, however, and never say anywhere that I have anything to do with the Mercury: mind that.

This is an early but typical example of Caine's secretiveness, which in the next few years was to become even more pronounced. Willie, now 17, had left school and was secretary to John Lovell, the manager and editor-in-chief of the *Mercury* since 1880. It was thanks to Lovell that Caine was in the happy position he described to Lily. While they were at Birchington he wrote a profile of Bell Scott, whom he thought had been unjustly neglected as a poet and deserved to be better known. He sent it to the *Mercury* who published it. This made Scott into an implacable enemy until his death in 1890. The article was laudatory and he ought to have been pleased but he was touchy and bad-tempered and was furious with Caine for not consulting him. But it reminded Lovell of Caine's existence. He replied with a letter that began, 'I have for some time thought of asking you to join our staff as an outside contributor.'

It was surely the most extraordinary assignment in the history of journalism and the most generous. Lovell agreed to pay Caine £100 a year (later he increased it to £125, then £150). For today's values multiply those figures by at least 50. In return Caine was to write as much or as little as he liked for the *Mercury* about anything that took his fancy—the theatre, literary life or any newsworthy event he came across. If he wrote nothing he was still to get the money. In addition to this retainer he would write book and theatre reviews, profiles of people in the public eye (referred to as biographies) and 'memoirs'—obituary notices. These last he found easy and lucrative. He trawled the London papers for obituaries, then rewrote those he thought appropriate to give them a Liverpool angle and sent them off to Lovell. For this work, including the reviewing, he was paid 21/- a column. For any number of words up to half a column he got 10/6d. Generous terms for those days. Small wonder that he did not want Lily or his brother to let on about it. It would have made him unpopular with former colleagues and old friends on the paper. His work, of course, was unsigned.

With this behind him he was quite happy to stay on at Cheyne Walk for a while to help William sort out the contents of the house. Though Gabriel had sold parts of his collection during his lifetime, Tudor House was still crammed with furniture, pictures, carvings and objects, from fine china and porcelain to the head of Cromwell that had frightened Lily. Once the friends had selected what they wanted arrangements were made for a sale on the premises. It was held on 6 July and raised a substantial sum, which was as well, as Rossetti had left a lot of debts. Apart from what was owed to Treffry Dunn and Watts, the chemist presented a bill for a year's supply of chloral, the butcher wanted his outstanding account settled and then there were the doctors' bills and Nurse Abrey to pay. Not to mention the servants.

For his mementoes, apart from the death mask, Caine chose the vast sofa in the studio on which he had so often seen Rossetti lounging. He also begged for the old oak armchairs. As all were in poor shape William was quite happy to let him take them. In addition Caine chose a large oak cupboard and a number of small things—a book rest, a watch stand, a china candlestick and a few other bits and pieces which had been in Rossetti's bedroom or which particularly reminded him of his friend.

During this clearing up period Caine went down to Birchington on a day trip to look at the grave. He found the thyme and violets planted on it in flower and a stream of visitors looking at it. He was pleased to see that both Westcliffe Bungalow and the road leading to it had been renamed after Rossetti and wrote to Christina to tell her. She wrote back at once to thank him. 'Of course we did hope either to see you or to hear from you: thank you for not disappointing us, and for doing all you had done for us.'

Caine did not sit back and merely live off Lovell's generous help. He provided a huge amount of copy for the paper and had other irons in the fire. As soon as he was back in Chelsea he went to see Elliot Stock and proposed to him a book to be called *Recollections of Rossetti*. Stock jumped at it and gave him a contract. Caine told him he was also planning a biography of Coleridge and another book. Stock expressed interest in them too but urged him to concentrate on one thing at a time and put the rest aside until the Rossetti book was finished. He was a kindly man and a good friend to the young writer. He had worked himself up from relatively humble beginnings and enjoyed helping other young men do the same. He lived at Gospel Oak and invited Caine out to his house. The first occasion was in May of 1882 after a postponement forced by Mrs Stock's spring cleaning. He sent instructions as to how to get there from Chelsea by train, with a sketch map showing the house. 'Coleridge was not buried in the Highgate Cemetery but in the church-yard of the parish church,' he added. 'We will stroll up to it after dinner and talk of our book on the way.'

On 27 May, 1882, he wrote from Tenby, where he was on holiday. Watts had told Caine that Stock's offer for the book was too low. Stock said he appreciated all the work Caine would have to do on his 'Rossetti memoirs' and would like to pay him more but did not think there would be any great sale for a book about someone who was not known to the general public. However, he would pay £40 down and a royalty of £1 per 100 sold. He hoped to publish it by November but could not promise to have it ready before any others which might be in prepara-tion. One of these was being written by Sharp who, hoping to be first in the race, had been to see him about it.

William Sharp was liked by the family and Christina agreed to talk to him. He had first met Gabriel in the autumn of 1879. His book opens with a bland memoir only 38 pages long and taken entirely from pub-lished sources. The rest of it discusses Rossetti's work from the incep-tion of the Pre-Raphaelite Brotherhood to his death and, while pleasantly written, does not say anything fresh.

'I shall not publish Sharp's book,' Stock said, 'but now he knows I have another in hand (he does not know by whom but I have had to tell him).'

Worried by the threat of Sharp's book to Caine's sales Stock wrote again a few days later, 'Pray remember that time is the essence of the contest.' He added another suggestion: 'Keep the reader in your mind's eye throughout and give him what he will be interested in, remember-ing that in 99 cases out of 100 he (or she) did not know Rossetti person-ally and wants to know all he can about the man and his work.' He hoped that Rossetti's early friends such as Holman Hunt and Ruskin would help him, 'for their period will be one of the most interesting to present day readers'.

That was not the sort of book Caine was planning, however. It was to be more personal, the story of a great friendship, and the core would be the letters. When William heard of the project he was appalled. Caine knew far too much. He might publish things that would upset and embarrass the family. Stock continued to urge Caine on with the work as 'others are in the field'. The first to get into print was none other than Caine's Liverpool friend, William Tirebuck. His book, however, was a slim essay on Rossetti's art with little about his life. It came out in June, 1882, and William dismissed it as of no importance as the writer had not known Rossetti personally and was himself unknown.

In June Caine went up to Manchester for two or three days to sit for Madox Brown who was now working on the *Transit of Venus* panel. He painted him in profile, wearing a sort of dressing-gown and staring at the trace made on a board by the beam of light coming through a telescope to the right. Behind him sits his wife with their two children. With one hand she grasps the arm of the little boy to stop him running into the beam and destroying his father's vital observation while on the other arm she holds her baby girl. The model was Brown's daughter, Lucy Rossetti, and the children his grandchildren.

Back in London and working hard on his book Caine was faced with moving out of No. 16. The big, dark house was depressing, he missed Rossetti desperately and the task of sorting through his possessions and making ready for the sale depressed him. Not surprisingly he fell ill again. Not wanting to bother William, who had enough problems of his own, he sent a note to William Sharp asking if he would get him some patent medicine which had done him good before. Sharp replied at once on 15 June with a kindly letter, 'I will obtain 2 more bottles of Hydoleine for you with pleasure... If you are feeling seedy it would perhaps be better for me to come to you than vice versa, so I will endeavour to turn up at No. 16 at the earliest opportunity... Hoping you will soon be all right again. In extremity of haste, Yours ever.' The medicine must have done the trick because soon afterwards Caine went to Manchester briefly to pose for Madox Brown again.

CHAPTER ELEVEN

On his return from Manchester in early July Caine went into rooms in the old Clement's Inn—No. 18—and began his independent life in London. In his biography, *My Story*, published in 1908, he also said of this period that it was the time when he became a journalist, which is arrant nonsense: he had been writing for the press professionally for more than eight years. He also said,

> With my income of a hundred a year, I had to be my own cook and housemaid (making my own bed and breakfast)... It may be enough to say that I was rather poor and very lonely, having few friends in London, hardly any houses to call at, and little to live for except my family, who were far away, and my work which was always with me.

This portrait of a young writer struggling and alone in London is as much fiction as any of his novels. In fact he was not living alone but sharing the Clement's Inn rooms with an academic friend, Eric Robertson. He was seeing Sharp quite often and he had a wide acquaintance among influential people with whom he dined and talked. Robertson, who had been to university and was an MA, had a great many friends. Someone who knew the pair at this time wrote years later that the whole of intellectual London gathered in their rooms, 'the younger unknown part at any rate'. The two of them made great play of having to make their own beds and prepare their own breakfasts. If not invited out to lunch a bit of bread and cheese sufficed. In the evenings they had a meal sent in from a coffee shop in nearby Clare Market, then an area of 'rookeries', overcrowded slum tenements. The food was brought by two girls who worked there, one of them called Mary Chandler. At first they left the dishes and took them away when they brought a fresh meal the next evening. Before long, however, they took to waiting while Caine and Robertson ate and then went back to the coffee shop with the empties. The young men found them amusing and they stayed later and later, joining in the fun when friends called. A merry time was had by all with no thought of any consequences.

The bomb fell one evening in September. Instead of the girls with their meal the two fathers, or in the case of Mary Chandler the stepfather, arrived. Their daughters, they claimed, had been 'ruined'. When did the young gentlemen propose to make honest women of them? That either of them had been ruined in the Victorian sense is highly unlikely—nothing but a bit of flirting had taken place—but no doubt the fathers, seeing their girls 'taken advantage of' by young men they assumed to be wealthy toffs, saw the chance of getting them off their hands and well settled. They were not to know that Caine and his family were probably little better off than they were. Robertson and Caine were horrified: the girls were very young. One of them, Mary Chandler, was 13, and her friend not much older. The young men pleaded for time to see what could be done. Robertson seemed willing to marry the older girl. His family rallied round and provided £1000 for a smart wedding and to rent and furnish a house at Chislehurst in Kent.

Caine was left to find the rent of 18 Clement's Inn on his own and cope with the ominous figure of Mary Chandler's stepfather. The girl was pretty but she was only a child. She had had little schooling. He was now 29 but his thoughts on marriage had not changed since he had written to Rossetti two years previously saying he had never 'felt any temptation to marry' and did not think he would be happy if he did. Child brides were nothing unusual in Victorian times and not illegal. In 1882 the age of consent was 13 and had been only 12 not long before. Caine knew Shields had married Cissy when he was 40 and she was 16. He also knew that the marriage was unhappy. Indeed, Cissy left her husband about a couple of years after this and they lived apart for the rest of their lives. Ellen Terry had likewise married the painter G.F. Watts when he was 47 and she was barely 16. Within a year that marriage too had broken up. Neither case would have encouraged Caine to think there was any chance of happiness in marriage with a girl 16 years younger than himself. Mary may have been almost Juliet's age but Caine, ambitious, serious-minded, pedantic and sexually ambivalent, was at 29 no Romeo.

Legally there was no bar to his marrying Mary, any more than there had been to Robertson marrying the other girl, but other things, apart from Caine's inclinations, stood in the way. A vigorous political campaign was going on in 1882 to have the age of consent raised to 16. It had begun in 1871 and in 1875 a compromise was reached when the age was raised from 12 to 13. The subject was back in the news in 1880 with the activities of several noted campaigners for 'social purity' and a flurry of concern about an alleged traffic in young girls between Britain and Belgium. Prostitution was a major problem: in 1880 there were about 10,000 prostitutes on the streets of London and around 3000 brothels. Whitechapel, Shadwell, Spitalfields and adjoining areas were the centre of the vice trade. The degradation of the women and young girls was terrible. They would 'oblige' a man for 4d to buy a tot of gin or a pint of beer. They were often assaulted by their customers—beaten up or even murdered. Many were at the mercy of brutal pimps. Caine, who had begun visiting the East End and its police courts in search of copy for the *Mercury*, was fully aware of the facts.

By the autumn of 1882 pressure was growing for a new Protection of Minors Act that would change the age for consent to sexual intercourse to 16. It was intended to outlaw child prostitution and prevent young girls being sexually exploited. Caine, who was concerned by all aspects of prostitution, had publicly supported this movement. One of the people involved was Christina Rossetti. The following spring she collected signatures for a petition to Parliament on the subject. In the face of all this, how could he openly marry a child of 13?

Mary's stepfather, a man named Ward, continued to dog him. Later he told his brother Willie that Ward had insisted he take the girl on any terms he cared to name. Doubtless Ward wanted to be rid of the burden of another man's child and possibly her mother wanted a nubile teenage daughter out of the reach of her second husband. Caine protested that he had to go to Liverpool to deliver some lectures, which was true. Rather than travel up and down as he had the previous year he fled out of reach of the man Ward and arrived in Liverpool harassed and exhausted. He stayed in lodgings out at Aigburth rather than with his family in Toxteth, pleading he needed space and quiet to work but doubtless glad to avoid too much questioning.

While all this was going on Caine was busy with the proofs of his book. He asked William Rossetti, in a letter from Aigburth, if he could send them to him as he would be grateful for his comments. 'I am compelled to say frankly that you will not enjoy my book unless you read it from my individual standpoint,' he ended. 'I believe I have written the exact truth in every particular but it is the truth as it came to my mind, and I had but one informant on matters that did not come within my personal experience and that was your brother himself.' He added he was 'staying in very delightful countryside', a measure of how much Liverpool has grown since 1882.

William was relieved when he read the proofs—Caine had been a great deal more discreet than he had expected. He did not much like the book but as far as he was concerned it could have been worse and he was pleasantly surprised by Caine's tact and loyalty. Caine knew too much and William heaved a sigh of relief at how circumspectly he had dealt with matters which he feared were about to be published in regrettable detail. Christina did not particularly like the book either but was generous in her judgement, saying to Lucy Rossetti that considering the circumstances of Caine's friendship with her brother she considered the book 'neither unkind nor unfriendly'. She would have preferred to see her brother's biography written by someone who had known him longer but her generous spirit would not allow her to criticise Caine too heavily. Like William, she was deeply appreciative of everything Caine had done for Gabriel.

The style of the book is florid and turgid which makes it difficult reading today and it smells of hagiography. Whether Caine saw himself as Boswell to Rossetti's Johnson one can only guess but the way in which he reverently records Rossetti's conversation and letters suggests that he did. He knew Gabriel liked Boswell's *Life of Johnson*, having seen him read it. William must have shown the proofs to his wife—and Lucy was furious. They arrived as she was leaving to visit her parents in Manchester. She simmered all the way to Calais Cottage, Crumpsall, which Ford Madox Brown was renting, and from there on 29 September, 1882, she loosed off eight pages of rage, invective and threats. The trouble was something Caine had written about her adored dead brother, Oliver, indicating that some people, including Gabriel, might have thought him less than a genius. She ended her letter, 'I am sure you will be glad to have this correct information and will repress these misleading statements, which would be far too painful to us all and which we are particularly anxious...should not reach my father's or my sister's ear.'

Caine must have written back promptly and at his most emollient because in a second, shorter letter from Manchester Lucy acknowledges his apology and thanks him for his promise to remove the offending remarks. Her feathers were still ruffled, however. She remained unforgiving and no doubt influenced her husband to distance himself from his brother's protégé. On the evidence of this letter Lucy seems to have had quite a temper and she was a good hater. To be fair, however, it must be said that her health was poor and she found bringing up her young children a struggle.

The book came out in October, 1882, and sold tolerably well. It brought interesting reactions from some of his friends. Gosse wrote from his club to say he had read it with 'much interest and admiration'. The book was 'notably honest and courageous'. He had been prejudiced against it, wondering how Caine would tackle such a difficult subject, but Caine's frankness and the interest of his story had disarmed him.

Caine acknowledged that a full biography of Rossetti ought to be written by an older friend. Gabriel himself had asked Watts to take it on. William repeated the request after his brother's death and Watts agreed. To William's distress, Watts continually put off doing anything while saying he was working at it. William waited thirteen years and then in despair of Watts ever providing what was wanted wrote his own *Memoir of Dante Gabriel Rossetti*. He was brought to the point by the death of Christina on 29 December, 1894, which brought 'a flood of not undeserved but assuredly fervent praise; and in the eulogies of her were intermixed many warm tributes to my brother'. 1894 was a terrible year for William: Lucy Madox Rossetti died in Italy, where she had gone for her health, on 12 April. She was only 50. Her father had died a month or two previously. By the end of the year, with Christina gone too, William had lost all his siblings, his mother and his wife. (His father had died in 1854.) Writing his Memoir of his brother may have been some solace.

The time had come to put right what he saw as inaccuracies in Caine's book. He had been not unnaturally put out when he found Caine was rushing into print in 1882 so soon after the death. He gave the book only qualified approval but acknowledged that Caine had submitted the manuscript to him and agreed to omit two or three passages which he did not like because they might upset people still living at the time—that is, Lucy, though he does not say so.

Referring to Caine's description of Rossetti putting his poems in his wife's coffin, William said he remembered the incident well. Several friends had assembled in a room in Chatham Place. The coffin, not yet closed, was in another. Gabriel had gone alone into the room where the coffin was and put the MS into it. He had then gone back to the other room and told Madox Brown what he had done. 'I have often been writing at those poems when Lizzie was ill and suffering,' he said, 'and I might have been attending to her, and now they shall go.' Madox Brown disapproved of this sacrifice and appealed to William to remonstrate with his brother. William refused, saying the feeling reflected well on Gabriel and they should let him do as he liked. By making this very real sacrifice William said Gabriel not only lost the chance of poetic fame, 'which had always been a ruling passion with him', he also gave up publication of a volume which had already been advertised. William added, 'I do not know from whom he [Caine] obtained his details; where they may be considered incompatible with my reminiscence, I abide by my own.'

He quoted from Caine's account, which said in part,

> On the day of the funeral he walked into the room where the body lay, and...spoke to his dead wife as though she heard, saying, as he held the book, that the words it contained were written to her and for her, and she must take them with her for they could not remain when she had gone. Then he put the volume into the coffin between her cheek and beautiful hair.

Caine must have had this account of putting the poems in Lizzie's coffin from Rossetti himself. As no one else was in the room no one else could have told him in such detail what took place. Exactly how the book was placed was only discovered when the body was exhumed after a few years for the poems to be recovered and then it was not talked about. An account of the exhumation corroborates what Caine reported Rossetti as having said. It could be that William was jealous of Caine, albeit unconsciously, for having received this confidence when he himself had not. As Rossetti talked of Lizzie and his marriage during the long train journey from Cumberland back to London it is reasonable to suppose that this was part of what he told Caine that night. Note that William Rossetti only says 'I do not know from whom he obtained his details.' He does not accuse Caine of inventing them. The train journey had been less than a year before Caine wrote his book so his memory of those confidences would still have been vivid.

Caine has been criticised by some biographers of Rossetti, but others, such as Rosalie Glynn Grylls, writing in 1964, were kinder. Remarking on how the offer of bed, board and conversation had turned into an unpaid job as agent, companion and nurse, she commented on how gladly Caine had taken it all on, abandoning his own work without knowing when his service might end. She considered he had displayed tact and discretion in making use of what he had learned and had 'often been unfairly treated'.

The way he published some of Rossetti's letters has been attacked by at least one writer since they became available to the public. It was unscholarly in that Caine put bits of different letters together as if they were one and failed to mark ellipses in the usual way—a row of dots indicating something has been left out. He was also accused of not dating the extracts he used but this is hardly fair in that many of the letters are undated. Working under pressure he would have had little time to sort out dates from internal evidence or his memory of the sequence of events. He was trying to show that this was a great body of letters, rivalling any other literary correspondence, but that view is hardly justified. The most interesting parts are those where Rossetti touches on personal matters and the business concerning the sale of the big picture and these Caine excluded. He wanted above all to celebrate his friend.

William Sharp reacted somewhat differently. He sent his congratulations on 'a most fascinating volume' but went on to pick it to pieces, noting a number of mistakes. He was sore that he himself was only mentioned once and thought he should have been given more credit as he saw Rossetti frequently from the autumn of 1879.

Hitherto almost unknown outside Liverpool and Rossetti's circle, Caine's book brought his name before 'that part of intellectual London' which was very well known indeed and if it did not make his reputation it did not kill it in infancy either.

Caine returned to London from Liverpool early in December, 1882. The showdown with Ward was imminent. Clearly he would have to do something about Mary Chandler. Marrying was not an option as far as he was concerned but he was sorry for her and perhaps an offer to send her to school would fend off the aggrieved stepfather. Exactly what happened when he and Ward met no one now knows for sure but his brother, to whom he later told the full story, always maintained it had overtones of blackmail. Undoubtedly Ward was after money. He would have known that girls as young as Mary were bought and sold in the 'White Slave Trade', as W.T. Stead demonstrated in his 'Maiden Tribute' campaign in the *Pall Mall Gazette* soon afterwards. Having little money, Caine put his offer to have the girl educated and it was accepted but it seems Ward went further. As far as can be made out, he dumped the child at Clement's Inn, making Caine solely responsible for her. He was left with the options of adoption or marriage.

His plan of educating Mary with only the vaguest idea of what would happen afterwards may have seemed reasonable to him but he reckoned without two factors. The first was that Mary Chandler was as over-whelmingly in love with him as Juliet with her Romeo. She adored him and it showed. Although he was arranging to send her to school she could not start until after Christmas. Ward had turned her out and she had nowhere else to go. Well aware of what could happen to a girl of that age thrown onto the streets of London Caine kept her with him at Clement's Inn.

The second factor to upset his plans was that friends dropped in. Seeing Mary they jumped to the conclusion that they were married. After all, Eric Robertson had married her friend. They addressed her as Mrs Caine. Although in the 1880s Free Love had its advocates it took more than ordinary bravery and defiance of convention openly to set up house with a partner out of wedlock. It took an Eleanor Marx, who was living with Edward Aveling. Neither Caine nor Mary was capable of act-ing like that. They both kept quiet, never admitting they were not mar-ried. Caine got over his political difficulty by telling his friends Mary was 17.

Someone who knew them then described her as 'a girl with petal-like skin, deep blue eyes and hair like heather-honey. She was a shade over five feet in height—her waist was a fairy's, her shoes size two, and her gloves five and a half. She was like a girl painted by Fragonard. But her greatest charm was her voice. No man who ever heard it forgot it.' That she was so small of stature must have appealed to Caine who was not above five feet three or four himself. The same informant—in an unsigned newspaper article—said 18 Clement's Inn was a tiny house, crammed in a corner.

Caine swore the friends who met Mary to secrecy. He confided the full truth only to Watts. His family were told nothing and Mary was smuggled away from Clement's Inn before too many people could see her. He took her down to Sevenoaks. There was a private school for girls there which could possibly have taken her as a boarder. It is more likely that she stayed with a retired governess prepared to coach her intensively for six months, which was the time she spent there, and teach her some of the refinements necessary to fit her for something better than the Clare Market coffee shop. Her own father had been a

poulterer in Walthamstow, which in those class-conscious days would
have assigned her to the respectable lower middle class, or 'shopkeeper
class'.

Caine said he came from the lower middle class himself (though artisan would have been nearer the mark), once adding that it was the most
difficult niche from which to rise. It could be done, however. England in
the last quarter of the nineteenth century may have been classbound
and snobbish but at the same time society was more fluid than ever
before. Socially correct behaviour was a minefield for the upwardly
mobile but there were plenty of guides to see them safely through it.
Etiquette books had been around for a long time and proliferated in the
1880s and 1890s. It is easy now to laugh at such instructions as, 'Ladies
should take tea in their hats', but that was perfectly comprehensible and
eminently sensible to those for whom it was written. All ladies wore
hats. When paying a formal call ladies kept them on because politeness
decreed formal calls should be short, a quarter of an hour or twenty
minutes. To be asked to remove your hat was an invitation to relax and
make yourself at home.

All the pitfalls of the dinner party were likewise detailed, including
how to cope with an unfamiliar array of cutlery and glasses. A rule of
thumb was to wait for your hostess to begin eating and see what tools
she picked up. One etiquette book said sternly, 'Only one small piece of
food on the fork at a time, for ladies a _very_ small piece, and only one
kind of food at a time.' Then there were the rules about when a girl
'came out', putting up her hair and lowering her skirts from ankle to
floor length. This was at 18 or when she married, whichever came first.
Mary obeyed this one scrupulously.

Why did Caine choose Sevenoaks? There may be a Rossetti connection
as Christina and her mother stayed there occasionally. It is possible that
Christina, who had friends and relatives who were or had been governesses, was able to recommend someone to Caine. The matter is not
mentioned in her friendly and affectionate letters to Caine but there are
references to how much her 'dear Mother' and she had enjoyed his visits to their home in Torrington Square. On one of these visits he could
well have asked her advice about schooling for a girl he wished to help,
without telling her the full details. It was just the sort of 'rescue' work to
appeal to her and she would have been glad to help if she could.

However it came about, Mary settled in Sevenoaks and concentrated
on learning enough to make her a fit wife for a rising intellectual and
author, for wife she intended to be. Those familiar with Caine's novels
will recognise Kate Cregeen trying to teach herself French to become
enough of a lady to marry the young Deemster. More telling still is the
story of Bessie Collister in *The Master of Man*, who also had a step-

father and was sent to stay with two elderly sisters, retired teachers. Caine describes her burning her candle down to the stump every night as she worked at her grammar and spelling to make her worthy to be the wife of the young advocate, Alec Gell.

Having seen Mary settled in, Caine returned to London with a sigh of relief and threw himself into his work. On 20 January Christina sent him a ticket for the exhibition of Rossetti's work which was being held at the Burlington Club. The ticket was made out in her mother's name, one of a dozen they had been sent for their friends. Caine told Christina he felt William no longer wished to know him as he had not called or written. Christina asked why he did not call on William, 'if you value his acquaintance'. She made excuses for her brother.. 'Don't you think that as a family man allowance may fairly be made for him if he is not very sedulous in returning visits? I can safely say that I know of no reason on his side to bar your friendship.' She was right in saying William bore Caine no ill will but the implacable Lucy did.

Caine was sure there was a deliberate conspiracy to freeze him out of literary circles in London, despite Saintsbury's championing of his sonnet book and praise from H.A. Bright. The book sold out but it was not reprinted. The Rossetti book did not improve his literary standing as much as Caine had hoped, though this did not discourage him from completing *Cobwebs of Criticism*. He hurried it on after Watts tipped him off that someone else was planning a similar book. Neither he nor Stock wanted to be forestalled again. When he wrote to thank Watts and tell him Stock had definitely accepted the new book he told him of his future plans. He would finish his Coleridge book, and he was already

> casting about for fragmentary data towards a book to be called *The Companions of Shakespeare* treating of the works and social life of the forgotten contemporaries of the national dramatist... If both my volumes were already published and favourably received I think I would even venture to offer to write a biography of Keats or Leigh Hunt, about whom I possess a lot of inedited information.

Stock brought out 'the criticism book' in August, 1883. It is subtitled 'A Review of the First Reviewers of the Lake, Satanic and Cockney Schools.' Caine had trawled through early nineteenth-century magazines to see what contemporary reviewers had said about Coleridge, Keats, Leigh Hunt, Byron and others, and how right or wrong they had been in their judgements. His love of the Lake Poets started him on the project. He had met a number of people in Cumbria who had known Coleridge and his son Hartley well, while others could tell him about Wordsworth. 'Coleridge,' he said, 'appears to have been <u>loved</u> by the hillsmen, and Wordsworth <u>reverenced</u>.' An old farmer at Grasmere told him, 'Master Col-e-ridge was gran' at a crack'—a gossip!

In the introduction Caine said he chose the period 1800–1825 because it was the age in English literature he knew and loved best. His starting point was *Lyrical Ballads*, the mould-breaking collection of poems by Wordsworth and Coleridge first published in 1798 and reissued in 1800. This was the start of the Romantic Revival, with which Caine was so much in tune. He began by looking at the literary magazines of the time for comment on this landmark in the history of English poetry but drew a blank. Wordsworth and Coleridge had been ignored in favour of Dr Parr's *Spital Sermons* and Wood's *Optics*.

When he did come across reviews of his heroes it was to find Wordsworth reviled and Coleridge pilloried. *Cobwebs of Criticism* consisted of essays on each of the poets covered, with quotations from magazines of their time. It showed a wide knowledge of his subject, way beyond what one would expect from a young man who had left school at 14 and gone to work in a world far removed from that of literature. He divided the book into three sections. 'The Lake School' covered Wordsworth, Southey and Coleridge. Under 'The Satanic School' was one name: Byron. The third part looked at 'The Cockney School', so called because the poets concerned, including Keats, were all Londoners. *Blackwood's Magazine*, founded in Edinburgh in 1817, attacked them cruelly. Another magazine said, 'it was reserved for the foolish and profligate Cockney school to raise the banner of an insensate and black ambition whose only aim was to ruin society'. This at the time of the Regency, not in Victoria's heyday in which Caine was writing in praise of these poems. Caine was mining a rich vein. The book was well received but not widely noticed.

Even with Eric Robertson married and living in Chislehurst Caine had a full social life, whatever he said to Christina Rossetti about his solitary existence. He saw a lot of Watts, who often called at Clement's Inn. They had long, rambling talks which Caine later recalled with pleasure. When in return he visited The Pines he enjoyed seeing Swinburne. Lord Houghton had a London house and at his dinner table Caine met others who could be useful to him—he met R.D. Blackmore there for the first time. When Houghton died in 1885 he lost a valuable patron. Other new acquaintances included Matthew Arnold and Robert Browning. He saw Madox Brown when he was in London and Shields often came to Clement's Inn. Caine was still in touch with William Morris though they began to part ways over politics when Morris's socialism became too radical even for Caine. Both were so busy they had little time to meet but Caine still valued Morris's friendship. And William Sharp, earlier animosities forgotten, was a close friend.

It was all a long, long way from 59 South Chester Street but he did not forget his family. He continued to send regular sums of money—

sometimes a cheque, sometimes a £5 note—to his mother.

Large packets of copy went to the *Mercury* every week. He decided the paper should have the same service as the London ones when it came to theatre reviews and Lovell agreed. He went to first nights as the *Mercury*'s representative, telegraphing his reviews to Liverpool where they were printed next day. This made him popular with theatre managements when he gave good notices. Most productions toured after London and a favourable critique from a local paper could bring in audiences when they got to Liverpool. Caine also wrote regular Literary and Theatre Notes. It occurred to Lovell that when famous people died papers often had difficulty in bringing out substantial obituaries straight away. He therefore commissioned Caine to write 'obituaries' of people who were still alive which could be filed for instant use when they died—a common policy nowadays but apparently unheard of then. Caine obliged delightedly, starting with his own literary friends and acquaintances and enlisting their help. The idea of writing their own obituaries tickled their fancy and 'Caine's post-mortems' became a joke.

One of the most important of his London friends, after Rossetti, was Henry Irving. His dining club was a rich source of congenial company, influential acquaintances and useful copy. The famous Beefsteak Room was backstage at the Lyceum, with a private entrance from the lane behind the theatre. It took its name from the eighteenth-century Beefsteak Club which stood approximately on the site. It was here that Irving, during his reign at the Lyceum, entertained lavishly with Ellen Terry as his hostess. The catering was done by Gunter's and for twenty years the Lyceum became part of the social history of London. A long list of celebrities fêted there included the Abbé Liszt, for whom Gunter's provided his favourite dish of lamb cutlets, mushrooms in butter and lentil pudding. Statesmen, explorers, ambassadors, foreign princes and potentates, poets, novelists, historians, philosophers, scientists and Irving's old friends from his early days in the theatre all swept in through the Lyceum private entrance to enjoy Irving's legendary hospitality and among them came Hall Caine.

To have the entrée to the Beefsteak Room during the 1880s and 1890s, when the scale of Irving's entertaining backstage matched that of his performances on stage, was to have arrived socially, at least in artistic and intellectual circles. For an unknown young journalist from the provinces to have been among those invited to supper in the panelled Beefsteak Room, dominated by a portrait of Irving, was a notable accolade and Caine was one of the circle from the start. It was another big move forward in the process of reinventing himself.

Intimate Beefsteak suppers were usually for 36 people, but the supper parties on opening nights were princely in scale with up to 350 people crowding onto the stage. By contrast, there were evenings when only a handful of friends foregathered after the show. Someone who was always there was Bram Stoker. He became devoted to Caine and was his closest friend for many years. If Irving's friendship had done nothing more than introduce Caine to Stoker it would have been of singular importance to him but there were other introductions of great value.

The company at Lyceum first night parties was often led by the Prince of Wales, later Edward VII, and the Princess of Wales. Caine, who was reviewing for the *Mercury*, was at one of these on 31 March, 1883, and he went to many more. No exact record remains of when Tom Hall Caine from Toxteth first met the Prince of Wales informally, as opposed to being briefly presented at an opening night, but it was in the Beefsteak Room. The Prince would sometimes arrive unannounced and *en garçon*, accompanied by only a few close members of his entourage. The Prince was far from being an intellectual and was easily bored. The old aristocracy and his mother's courtiers tired him. He preferred the company of self-made men, high-flying achievers and pretty women. All who knew him dreaded seeing the royal fingers drumming on the table, the sign that his patience was wearing thin. Caine did not bore the Prince, he entertained him and became in a minor way a friend of his future king. He had the good taste and sense never to talk about this.

The idea that fiction might possibly be his real métier was beginning to dawn on him. In a letter to Watts in the spring of 1883 he said, 'I wish someone would give me a romance to write.' His exploration of the East End and hours spent listening to cases in London police courts meant that before long he had an encyclopaedic knowledge of the seamier side of London life. He was ostensibly looking for stories for the *Mercury* but he was also garnering a rich fund of characters and anecdotes. He remarked in his autobiography that the best training for a novelist was to work as a journalist first. One case he watched gave him the opening to his second novel, *A Son of Hagar*.

It must have been about this time he wrote a story called *Danny Fayle* and submitted it to Lovell who published it as a weekly serial. The idea was that it should come out in book form afterwards but neither Caine nor Lovell could persuade anyone to take it and it disappeared. Parts of it could well have survived in his published work. He never wasted anything. Newspaper and magazine short stories were recycled as incidents in novels. Failed plays reappeared as short stories. A novelette called *She's All the World to Me* was brought out as a paperback in New York in 1885. Only about 80 pages in length, it was No. 13 in Harper's Handy Series. Caine had intended to publish it in England also but under the lax laws from which Dickens had also suffered, he forfeited the copyright. He was unable to use it as it stood and had to shrug off the loss but the bulk of it resurfaced a few years later, incorporated in his third novel, *The Deemster*.

A surprise visitor at Clement's Inn soon after he had left Mary at Sevenoaks was Robert Buchanan. Because of the honourable amends he had made to Rossetti Caine had forgiven him his earlier attack. He liked the man—they had much in common. Buchanan had called to invite Caine to dinner and asked him to tell Watts how much he and his wife would like to see him too. Caine passed on the message, saying he had hinted that Watts might not feel able to accept. 'Of course I appreciate your position and realise the delicate nature of my own, but the truth in this case affects us differently I think. I like the man and the Rossetti people have (with one exception that is really important to me) practically turned their backs upon me. Why therefore should I not follow my inclination?' The 'notable exception' was Christina. She also remained interested in Lily and when she came to London was always glad to see her too. He did not see William Rossetti though they corresponded at intervals about Gabriel's letters. Lucy never forgave him for his perceived slight on her brother. For the sake of domestic peace William kept his distance. Lucy was a tiger when it came to her father's and brother's reputations. William Sharp felt the rough side of her tongue too, as he told Caine. 'I caught it from Mrs W.M.R. for my "*unqualified abuse*" of Madox Brown in re his etching.'

Caine could hardly have been referring to Rossetti's circle, as opposed to the family, in his remark to Buchanan. Watts, Shields and Madox Brown all remained his friends, as did George Meredith, and Swinburne was cordial to him. Bell Scott had 'turned his back', as we have seen, for another reason. By the time Caine met Buchanan the latter was an established poet and novelist. He had satirised Swinburne and attacked the Pre-Raphaelite school of painting before launching the assault on the Fleshly School of Poetry which caused so much trouble. He was a combative character and won a libel action against Swinburne in 1875. No wonder he was *persona non grata* with the Rossettis and their friends. He came from Glasgow where he had imbibed socialism from his father. Given Caine's twin passions for socialism and the theatre it is no wonder they became friends.

One result of Caine's work as a theatre critic was an introduction to the actor-manager Wilson Barrett. They met in 1883. Barrett saw Caine's review of one of his own productions and did not like it. After finding who had written it he wrote to Caine protesting. He asked him to call and explain himself. At the end of a long and disputatious interview he shook hands and said, 'And now I've told you what I think of your article, I wish to tell you what I think of yourself. I think you could write a play.' If he hit on a suitable subject for Barrett he was to let him know.

Wilson Barrett

This was the beginning of a fruitful co-operation but it was not without its rocky moments. Barrett was a real old ham and a rival of Irving. Louis N. Parker, another of Caine's collaborators, said of Barrett after his death in 1904, 'People may sometimes have smiled at some of his idiosyncrasies; but always the smile was sympathetic. His foibles were inherent in his calling, and, considering how he was adulated, it is astonishing that he had not more of them.' Although their association at one time descended into acrimony and threatened lawsuits Barrett was an important figure in Caine's career as a playwright.

Busy as he was, Caine did not forget about Mary Chandler. He spent the weekend at Sevenoaks when he had no business or social engagements in town. Mary waited eagerly for his visits and was desperately disappointed when he cancelled them at short notice, as he occasionally did. On 2 February he wrote to his brother Willie, adorning the top of his letter with a drawing of a row of trees numbered one to seven. At first he took lodgings at 7 Bessel's Green. Whether or not this was where Mary was staying it is impossible to say. From about April he stayed at Lennard Lodge, Chevening.

In July Caine went to the Lakes—posting a card to Willie from Ambleside on the 11th. It was written on the steamer from Bowness. 'How delicious this is! The sun is shining, music is playing on board, there's a soft westerly breeze and everything is lovely. Kent is not a match for Westmoreland.' He also spent a day or two in Keswick with his friend Edwin Jackson who had a house there. Mary was left studying her grammar in Sevenoaks. On the way back Caine called on his parents. Lily had just finished school for the summer and he begged to be allowed to take her south for the holidays. He was back in Lennard Lodge by the end of the month. His concern to give Lily a good holiday was mixed with concern as to what he was going to do with Mary whose lessons were also finishing. The solution was to instal Lily at Sevenoaks to keep Mary company while he went back to London to work. Goodness knows how he explained Mary to Lily but he swore her to secrecy. No breath of Mary's existence was to reach Liverpool. It was a heavy burden to put on a child of 13 but she adored her eldest brother and was happy to do whatever he said. Mary had turned 14 the previous May—Lily's birthday was in December. Luckily the two girls liked each other on sight. They remained affectionate friends until Lily died in 1914.

Stock spent a few days at Lennard Lodge to discuss Caine's current book and future plans. The day he left Caine wrote to Watts, 'Can't you come out for such another weekend?... I promise you lovely country and the heartiest welcome.' It is noticeable that he said 'he' would be glad to see him, not 'we'. He complained of not hearing anything for weeks but supposed 'the dark-eyed charmers' were keeping him busy. Watts had met George Borrow in 1872 and from then on had a great interest in gypsies. He wrote a number of poems about them which appeared in the *Athenaeum* and they figure largely in his novel *Aylwin*.

Relieved to have company for Mary, Caine returned to London to see *Cobwebs of Criticism* through the press. He had a backlog of book reviewing to do and began work on his life of Coleridge. He joined the two girls at Lennard Lodge whenever he could. Lily stayed with them for three and a half months. She returned to Liverpool at the end of October and Caine took Mary to the Isle of Wight. The literary associations appealed to him—Keats had written *Lamia* while staying in Shanklin. Sea air always did Caine good and he had heard the winters there were mild. Several writers lived on the Isle of Wight, notably Tennyson, as well as artists and the photographer Julia Margaret Cameron, but they were over on the more fashionable—and expensive—southwestern corner of the island. Queen Victoria, of course, was often at Osborne. Caine rented a small bungalow of only three rooms, Vectis Cottage, near Sandown on the east coast. It stood alone in a small garden only yards from the cliffs and the sea.

A long letter to Willie of 5 November, 1883, began, 'Here I am after many buffetings settled (I trust) for the winter.' The house was comfortable and suited him because 'it was not overlooked'. Willie, as yet knowing nothing of Mary, did not appreciate why privacy should be so important. Vectis Cottage was six miles from Ventnor. 'I think this will suit me well, but if not, I can remove in a week to the ends of the earth if necessary... I have much more to do this winter than I can possibly get through.' Willie had spoken about a reporter's job coming vacant on the paper and thought he might apply for it. Caine urged him 'not to think of it. You'll do much better where you are yet awhile, I'm sure. Work diligently at that.' One suspects Willie was more use to him as Lovell's secretary than he ever would be as a reporter. 'I'm missing Lily very much,' he ended. 'Being with me daily for three and a half months one naturally misses her, but it was far better for herself that she should return to get again to school.' Lily attended the Granby Street Board School in Liverpool and was being prepared for the examination that would lead to a job in the Post Office. Caine kept reminding her of the need to earn her own living, emphasising both the cachet and the security of working for the Post Office. Lily, however, had other ideas.

Meanwhile his work went well. On New Year's Eve, 1883, Lovell wrote, 'I break a long but I hope you will not think curmudgeonly silence, first, to wish you a prosperous New Year as much in reputation as in pocket and secondly, to gather up a few loose ends before the old year closes.' He enclosed a cheque for £25 and said another was on the way. Caine had written a long 'post mortem' on Queen Victoria. Lovell continued, 'What to do with the Queen I don't quite know. One thing, however, is clear and that is that we shall never be able to find room for much more than half of it.' He proposed to pay for it as for ten columns but as the old Queen outlived Lovell by twelve years he never had the problem of how much of it to use.

Lily might have been back at school but any further schooling which Mary received was at Caine's hands. He made out a reading list for her and encouraged her to write accounts of what she read but he was so busy himself he could not have had a lot of time for educating Mary. She, however, was blissfully happy. At last she had her beloved Tom to herself and could keep house for him. The inevitable happened. By the spring of 1884 Mary was pregnant. She was still only 14.

As Mary is never mentioned in his letters of this period one cannot know what Caine thought of this latest complication in his life. Their tenancy of the cottage was coming to an end and in March Caine heard that his much loved Clement's Inn was to be pulled down to make way for new developments at the Law Courts. 'I'm all at sixes and sevens about chambers,' he wrote to Willie. His bachelor quarters were important to him but having Mary and a baby there was out of the question. He had to have somewhere to entertain his family and any friends who did not know of Mary's existence. By April he had found new chambers at 5 New Court, Lincoln's Inn. They were up four flights of stairs at the top of an old building. Lovell, visiting him, complained bitterly of the climb. When he eventually heard about Mary he insisted he had never seen her at either Clement's Inn or New Court and knew nothing of her.

If she could not come to New Court where was Mary to go? She could not live alone and would need someone to look after her. The someone was a Mrs Bell. She stayed with Mary at Vectis Cottage while Caine made arrangements for them in London. On 14 April, he wrote to Lily from New Court, 'My rooms are perfectly delightful. I read some three chapters of my story to some writers here the other night and they pronounced it superior to anything by any living novelist.' Well, they would, wouldn't they, in the classic phrase. They were hardly likely to accept his hospitality and then abuse his work to his face, but one must allow that it could have been their honest judgement. The story concerned was *Shadow of a Crime*, his first published novel. Continuing his letter Caine told Lily that there was not much likelihood of his getting up to Liverpool soon. 'The great "M" comes to London tomorrow.' Lily would know that M stood for Mary.

Caine solved his problem, temporarily at least, by renting a house called Yarra in Worsley Road, Hampstead. (It was destroyed in an air raid in the Second World War.) Mrs Bell and Mary were installed there with a maid. This proved useful when he came to describe the secret 'love nest' in Hampstead known to only a few close friends in *The Christian*. It looks like a fair description of Mary in Worsley Road with Mrs Bell. Caine visited her when he could. Just in case he was seen so far from his usual haunts by someone who knew him and might pass the news on to Liverpool, he said to Willie on a postcard of 22 April, 'I sometimes go up to Hampstead Heath as it is splendidly bracing up there'!

He told Willie to ask their mother 'how her cash progresses. I could without inconvenience send her more at any time.' He must have been earning steadily over and above what he was paid by the *Mercury* or else he could never have kept up both his chambers and the Hampstead house with money to spare for his parents. Willie had been ill. Tom told him not to worry about 'the sweats'—which could have meant tuberculosis. They were nothing serious. 'After a hearty supper and glass of hot whiskey I sometimes experience something of the sort. I merely give myself a downright good scrubbing with a rough towel and put on a fresh singlet.'

A couple of days later he was back on the subject of Willie's health, advising 'hot flannels on the chest and stomach again and again' and telling Willie to 'wear a second waistcoat and two pairs of drawers. A second singlet might be good. Don't walk too fast and make yourself perspire.' This to a strong lad of 19. Another note said, 'The weather is unsettled. Thicken your clothing at once.' On 14th May he supposed the current hot weather 'would make you sweat a lot'. No wonder if Willie was still wearing all those extra clothes.

Caine did not stop at advice. He arranged for his brother to have two weeks' holiday at a boarding house in Ventnor in May of 1884, paying his expenses. The weather was evidently fine because Tom sent a post-card to Willie saying, 'If the heat affects you take belladonna.' Casting the odd clout would have been better.

Willie spent the night of 18 May at New Court on his way to the Isle of Wight and stayed there again on his way home. He neither saw nor heard anything of Mary but years later said he had felt 'something was wrong' and that his brother was not being quite frank with him. Being twelve years younger he was never completely in Tom's confidence but knew him well enough to suspect he had a secret. Tom's generosity to him extended to telling him he must say if he was 'insolvent at any time' because he could help a little. When Willie returned to work he began doing theatre reviews. Tom sent him copies of his own reviews of plays which were to transfer to Liverpool, telling him, 'you might fairly use up the ideas and some few of the phrases, etc.' Another time he said in lordly fashion that if Willie cared to send him some of his reviews he would comment on the style and offer improvements.

Despite the secrecy there were friends who came to Worsley Road in the summer of 1884. One of them was William Sharp. He sent a note to Caine at Worsley Road on 16 June 1884:

> My dear friend, If really not inconvenient, could you put me up tomorrow night? I have had, this afternoon, a narrow escape from rheumatic fever and must leave here at once. I think I have fought it down but I must not risk such another durance. I have been crouching over a large fire and with my medicine having got the better of the cursed complaint.

He was waiting to move into a flat in Inverness Terrace, off the Bayswater Road, but it was not available for a few days so he had nowhere to go. 'I am so chilled and pained I can hardly hold the pen.' Caine told him to come at once and Mrs Bell and Mary looked after him. In August he went up to Scotland and on the 26th wrote from the Isle of Arran to tell Caine that his long engagement was drawing to a close and he and his fiancée, Lillie, were to be married soon. 'Is the hour of paternity drawing nigh? I wonder if MacColl would accept for the *Athenaeum* a sonnet on "Caine's First-born"? I must try. If a boy, please call it Abel, or in case this would give rise to too many poor jokes, what do you say to *Tubal*. Most people would simply think you had called him after "that fellow, you know, in one of George Eliot's poems"'! (In Genesis iv, 22, Tubal-cain was 'the instructor of every artificer in brass and iron'.)

Sharp's health was never good and Caine was always sympathetic. In 1887 he wrote a long letter to Caine describing his ill-health and the pain he suffered from angina. '"Snake in the breast" gives some idea it is not pleasant.' His doctors had told him he could die at any time (but he lived to fifty). The pain, he said, was appalling. 'You are the only one of my friends to whom I have written thus—but you drew it from me by your brotherly sympathy and now having read my words destroy and forget them.' Instead Caine kept this one with Sharp's other letters.

Mary's baby was born in Hampstead on 15 August, 1884, when she was 15 years and three months old. It was a boy and Caine had no hesitation in choosing a name—Ralph, after his beloved Grandfather Hall. His letters to friends give no hint that anything as important as the birth of his first child had occurred. Nothing interrupted the flow of his apparently bachelor life at Lincoln's Inn. Only a few intimates knew about Worsley Road and what had happened there.

A few days after Ralph's birth Lily wrote a long letter about the forthcoming wedding of two family friends in Liverpool, evidently hoping that 'our Tom' would get round to marrying Mary, though whether or not she was aware of Mary's pregnancy is not clear. Tom's reply is revealing. His main comment on the 'splicing' was that the people concerned were spending a lot of money. 'All right if it won't hamper them in coming years. They'll have a nice place, no doubt.' He then added, 'I will try to do as father and mother say. I'll think it over.' His parents probably thought it was high time he married and presented them with grandchildren.

Still he made no move to legalise the situation and Mary's child was illegitimate. He did not register the birth for a month, wrestling with his conscience as to what he should do. Finally on 15 September the baby was registered as Ralph Hall, son of Thomas Henry Hall Caine, journalist, and 'Mary Alice Caine, formerly Chandler.' This was perjury: she was still Mary Chandler. He gave his address as 'Yarra', Worsley Road, Hampstead, which was also recorded as the place of the baby's birth. Later he propounded the theory that once a man had slept with a woman he was married to her and 'bits of paper' made no difference. In God's eyes he and Mary were man and wife. If the law thought differently the law was an ass. This point of view is put into the mouths of several characters in his books over the years but most forcefully in *A Son of Hagar*.

Ralph's birth produced an instant metamorphosis in Caine. Against everything one would have expected he became a doting parent who adored both this son and the next and spoilt them thoroughly.

Mary, however, did not consider herself married. She did not put her hair up but continued to wear it in one long, thick plait, nor did she lengthen her skirts. As an old man Caine said with a chuckle, 'She used to walk around with her hair down her back and a baby in her arms. No wonder people were puzzled.' In September they moved to Bexley Heath, to Aberleigh Lodge in Red House Lane. Why Bexley Heath? This time the connection is not with the Rossettis but with William Morris. He and Janey had rented Aberleigh Lodge for a year while the Red House was built to Morris's design. It was completed in 1860. The grounds of the two houses march together. Aberleigh Lodge had a large garden with a big orchard and the Red House was built on part of it. It still stands and is open to the public. Aberleigh Lodge, a pleasant square red brick house with three bedrooms, was pulled down in the 1970s. It is quite possible Caine heard about it from Morris.

Caine found it convenient for 'running up to town'—they were a mile from Bexley station. He continued to spend a lot of his time at his chambers while Mary stayed at Aberleigh Lodge with the baby and a servant. It was a pattern of life she had to get used to but they were very happy at Bexley Heath. For the rest of their lives they said Aberleigh Lodge had been the nicest house they ever had.

Aberleigh Lodge, Caine's home at Bexley. He is sitting in the deck chair with Ralph beside him. Mary stands at the front door wearing one of the big hats she loved.

CHAPTER TWELVE

Now he had a son Caine worked harder than ever, if that were possible. The first number of *Shadow of a Crime* appeared in the Liverpool *Mercury* in the autumn of 1884, when he had only the first three or four chapters ready. Like Dickens, he wrote at white heat, rushing each chapter off to Liverpool in the nick of time. He kept up a running commentary to Willie. In September, after he and Mary had moved to Aberleigh: 'I suppose you consider the title very strong and attractive? Do you suppose it will fetch 'em?' He hoped to have it finished by the end of November 'and then go on to dramatise it'. This was at Buchanan's instigation, but there is no record of *Shadow of a Crime* ever being performed in a stage version. Caine was still full of advice for Willie, telling him to 'keep away from the reporting fraternity. They are a rummy lot in more than a single sense.' Willie should avoid going to the Liverpool Press Club, 'which would be a very tenth rate club in London'. If he had any spare time it would be better spent in taking exercise or reading a good book.

By the end of October Lovell was 'speaking warmly of the book and its effect on circulation' while Caine worked flat out to finish it. There was a pause in the spate of advice to Willie until at the end of November he wrote to apologise, saying he had not had time for anything but work. 'For one thing I am just finishing the story and that takes it out of me in time and thought... I trust you are liking the "Shadow". I have just written a chapter on the death of Garth which beats everything else: it will make your hair stand on end. Ralph before the judges is also one of my favourite bits.' A few days later he reported that he had worked until 2 am reading and reviewing a book. 'Thus the book was read and reviewed in some 5 hours. What the article was like I cannot imagine. I'm not sure I dare look at it.' *Shadow of a Crime* was finished on time at the end of November. It was in essence the story he had told to Rossetti at Fisher Place but he ignored Rossetti's advice not to publish it.

He showed the first draft to Lovell whose reaction was, 'I suppose you want my candid opinion?' Diffidently, Caine said yes. 'It's crude,' Lovell replied, 'but it only wants sub-editing.' Caine rightly took that as advice to revise the whole book. When Lovell looked at it again his only caveat was that the book ended in tragedy. This sparked the first of a lifetime of arguments over what Caine called 'the problem of the happy ending'. It was a tragic story, he said, and had to have a tragic ending, but Lovell stuck to his point. 'The death of your hero will never do. If you kill that man Ralph, you'll kill your book. What's the good? Take no more than the public will give you to begin with, and by-and-by they'll take what you give them.'

It went against the grain but Caine did as he was told. In response Lovell took a chance on the novel, paying Caine £100 for the serial rights. His readers backed his judgement. This time a book publisher was quickly found. It was not suitable for Elliot Stock's list but someone introduced Caine to Andrew Chatto, of Chatto & Windus. Caine sold it to him outright for another £100 and he published it in February, 1885. It was dedicated to John Lovell. The *Saturday Review* said it stood comparison with Blackmore's *Lorna Doone*, while the *Academy*'s critic wrote, 'This book is no ordinary novel; to treat it as such would be an injustice... It is a character-study of a high order of merit... Mr Caine has produced a work of art which will live in the memory.' As reviews were never signed in those days we cannot be sure which of them was written by Watts, but his must have been on similar lines as Caine wrote to him, 'My very heartiest thanks. No sane mortal could expect or desire more full, serious, prompt and generous handling. Chatto will be delighted and for my poor part I am deeply grateful.' It was a good start and sales were healthy despite competition from Rider Haggard's *King Solomon's Mines*, which came out about the same time. Chatto was so pleased that he made at least two *ex gratia* payments to Caine over and above the contract price.

The setting is a hamlet at the head of Thirlmere in the seventeenth century. The heroine, whose mother died at her birth, is the daughter of an elderly Statesman. When her father dies one of her admirers who, obviously to anyone except the heroine, has more of an eye to her inheritance than her charms, arrives at the cottage to say she can't stay alone, 'would she not come to him?' This apparently sends her weak at the knees.

> It was the force of the magnet to the steel. With swimming eyes she looked up into his strong face, tender now with a tremor never before seen there; and as he drew her gently towards him her glistening tears fell hot and fast over her brightening and now radiant face, and, as though to hide them from him, she laid her head on his breast. This was all the wooing of Angus Ray.

She has two brothers—Willy and Ralph. (One notes the difficulty Caine always had in choosing names for his characters as he draws heavily on his own family.) Both brothers are in love with the same girl—the theme of most of Caine's novels. The plot is convoluted and the attempt to portray Cumberland life of the period awkward. The all too accurate rendering of the local dialect makes it difficult to read in places.

Liverpudlians may have taken it in their stride but metropolitan readers were baffled. Caine was surprised and upset. Having grown up with the Cumbrian dialect as spoken by his mother and grandparents he had genuinely not realised that southerners would not be able to make sense of it.

It is a strong tale of love and treachery told with emotion and an effective use of suspense. Chatto kept it in print into the next century and it still had its admirers when Caine was an old man. It launched Caine on a career as a romantic novelist of huge popularity which was to span forty years and produce fifteen novels.

With *Shadow* he completed the metamorphosis of Tom Hall Caine the blacksmith's son. Having dropped one initial he now abandoned his Christian name, which for some reason he hated. From then on he was plain Hall Caine, the Great Author, All that was needed to complete the transformation was a title but that had to wait a while.

At this point Mary began a project which would engage her for the rest of her life—her scrapbooks. Caine subscribed to a cuttings agency and bits of paper had piled up in drawers and cupboards. Mary sorted them all out and made herself responsible for a record of Caine's career. Thirteen of her scrapbooks, mostly huge leatherbound volumes, are in the Manx Museum in Douglas. She pasted in everything, good reviews and the howlingly awful ones, reports of Caine's speeches and of his opening of public buildings and memorials, menus of formal dinners, passenger lists and dinner menus from various liners, cartoons both cruel and kind, and even in the early days the receipted bills from the cuttings agency. It makes a fascinatingly detailed account of his public life. Two or three of Mary's scrapbooks have been lost. In a letter to her husband of 8 December, 1924, she said that two lent to William Heinemann had not been returned after his death a few years previously. In addition the first one of all, on loan to Bram Stoker when he was writing his life of Irving, never came back to her. 'I suppose we shall not see it again now,' she added sadly. Stoker had been dead for twelve years. The first of the surviving ones starts with the publication of Caine's fourth novel, *The Bondman*, in 1890, apart from some minor items from 1887 which she must have missed while at work on the first book.

Elated by the good reviews of *Shadow* and shrugging off the bad ones Caine made plans for his literary future. He had a head full of stories and hardly knew which one to deal with first. In January of 1885 he went to the Isle of Man, staying at the Peel Castle Hotel. He met 'a leading member of the Legislature' and was expecting an invitation to Government House but told Willie, 'in default of a tail-coat it is doubtful if I can go. Peel is an interesting little place, but dirty enough. Tomorrow I dodge about among the fishermen.' After visiting Sulby he walked from Peel to the southern extremity of the Island and after looking at Castletown walked on to Douglas to stay a few days at the Peveril Hotel. From this it is clear that a Manx story was brewing.

At the same time he was writing another Cumbrian novel. 'The new story gets along <u>very</u> slowly but I trust finely. It becomes extremely exciting. I'm fearing almost too much so.' No wonder it went slowly if half his mind was on the next book but one. It also went slowly because he was continuing to research the laws on marriage and illegitimacy in Scotland, which he had found were different to those of England.

In April of 1885 Caine caused a sensation in Toxteth: he wrote to his mother and told her about Mary and Ralph. He had known it would be a terrible shock to his God-fearing, chapel-going parents to find their eldest son was 'living in sin' with a young girl and that they had an illegitimate grandchild eight months old. This particular letter is not in the archives, nor the one that Lily wrote to tell Tom what happened when it arrived, but writing to Willie on 25 April he said,

> Judging by Lily's letter the sensation occasioned by my letter to my mother must have been enormous. If it is true that Lily talks 2 volumes a day on an average I'll wager she has talked 4 volumes a day since the arrival of my letter. However, though important it is not so terrifically so that it need occasion an earthquake. And moreover there is no immediate pressing crisis. I am very busy just now but will write later on. Meantime tell me how the event is regarded.

Now that she was released from her vow of silence one can well imagine the 15-year-old Lily pouring out everything she knew about Mary and describing their time together. What none of them knew was when, or even if, Caine would marry her. Mary would be 16 the following month and it would have been legal then even under the new law but Caine made no move. It is hard to understand why, as he seemed committed to Mary and their son. Those friends who knew about Mary thought they were already married so any public ceremony would be difficult to explain but it could have been done quietly—as eventually it was—but he did not fob his parents off with a lie. They were not married, he said so and that is how matters remained.

It was a long letter to Willie. Nine pages remain and the end of it is missing. It is only on page 5 that he gets round to mentioning 'the earthquake' and says no more than what is quoted above. Now that it was all out in the open he invited Willie to spend his forthcoming holiday with them. He told him Aberleigh Lodge was small with only three bedrooms but 'the garden is marvellously beautiful and large and very rich in fruit, and we are within half an hour of Cannon Street and only one mile (nominally) out of London. But as much in the country as if we were at Sevenoaks.' The rest of the letter is taken up with his work. There had been offers from several newspapers to serialise his new story and the editor of the *Graphic* had asked him to write something about Russia, 'if this present trouble can be settled without war'. (Russia attacked Afghanistan in a quarrel over borders and many died in a battle on 30 March. Russia agreed to arbitration by Denmark over the border question and a war involving western European powers was averted.)

Until 1883 events in his own country and the progress of his career had absorbed Caine entirely. He first became interested in foreign affairs with the upheavals in Egypt. There was panic among the 37,000 Europeans in Egypt in June of 1882 when riots in Cairo and Alexandria threatened their safety. Gunboats and soldiers were sent and the country subdued. When the troops returned to London in October, 1882, they were received by rapturous crowds. True to his socialist ideals and his belief in the right of countries and peoples to self-government Caine was uneasy over the British subjugation of Egypt. There was nothing of the jingo in him. Chaos and financial collapse reigned in Cairo in April, 1884. The London Conference of the six Great Powers of the day was convened at the end of June to decide what should be done about Egypt but it achieved nothing and adjourned *sine die* on 2 August. From then on Caine watched developments with interest but his one novel set in Egypt, *The White Prophet*, did not appear until 1909.

Once over the shock of her son's news his mother wrote him an affectionate letter and plans were made for her to visit them. At the end of April, 1885, the owner of Aberleigh Lodge died suddenly at the public house he owned in London. Caine was worried. They loved the Lodge and had thought they were settled. Nightingales were singing in the garden for two nights before the news came but now the house could be sold or the new owner move in. Either way Caine's lease might not be renewed when its five-year term expired.

Among the friends who came to stay at Aberleigh was Edwin Jackson, from Keswick. In return he invited Caine to stay at Hawthorns, his Keswick home, and at the end of July Caine went there, leaving Mary and the baby in Bexley. In the autumn Lily came down to Aberleigh and they all went to the Isle of Wight for a month at Vectis Cottage.

A shortened version of *Shadow of a Crime* was published as a paperback in New York, followed by *She's All the World to Me*. Both Watts and Andrew Chatto had advised Caine against publishing the latter as it was not up to the standard of his other work but he needed the money and wanted exposure in America. One of the two men in love with the heroine of *She's All the World to Me* is called Danny Fayle, so it could well be the story of that name published by the *Mercury*. The account of a night's fishing trip reads more like a young reporter's notes for a piece on the fishing industry than an episode in a romantic novel.

Although the story builds up to a fairly strong climax the writing is diffuse and nowhere near his best.

At the same time he rushed into an unwise contract with Tillotson's Newspaper Literature, intending to give them only serialisation rights in his work, but he had not read the small print and found Tillotson's claiming rights to hardback publication as well. It took a long time and, in due course, all the skills of Bram Stoker and the famous lawyer Sir George Lewis (who defended the Prince of Wales in the Tranby Croft Affair), to extricate him. Lewis was legal adviser and confidant to many of the leading artists and writers of his time, including Oscar Wilde, Sir Edward Burne-Jones, Sir Lawrence Alma Tadema and John Singer Sargent. It was said of him that he 'knew enough to hang half the dukes and duchesses in the kingdom' and he was without doubt the most eminent, as well as the most discreet, lawyer of late Victorian times, so Caine's affairs were in good hands.

In spite of these distractions Caine finished the new book before the end of the year and *A Son of Hagar: A Romance of Our Time* was serialised in several newspapers. Chatto & Windus brought it out in three volumes early in 1886, on the same terms as his first novel: that is, they bought the copyright. He dedicated it to R.D. Blackmore and sent him a copy. Blackmore thought highly of it.

In this way Caine began a course he followed with each of his subsequent books—sending advance copies to eminent people. Many of the recipients replied with nothing more than a brief note of thanks. With others it was the beginning of friendships that were as prized by Caine on a personal level as for any publicity value. This was the case with Blackmore. Caine revered him and admired his work. In return Blackmore's letters show a liking for the younger man and appreciation of his work.

Caine started at the top in his despatch of books to notable people. In April of 1884 he sent a book to Queen Victoria at Osborne. The Private Secretary replied thanking him and saying he had 'laid it before Her Majesty with great pleasure'. Whether Queen Victoria took great pleasure in reading it, if she read it all, is another matter.

One recipient of *Shadow of a Crime* was Wilkie Collins. Caine sent it on 1 June, 1885, with a cringingly grovelling letter, hoping the author of *The Woman in White* would deign to accept it. One would expect such a letter to lead to a brush-off but instead we find increasingly friendly, even affectionate, letters to Caine from Collins. For instance, on 22 June, 1888, he wrote from his home in Wimpole Street, 'Dear Hall Caine'—note the informal address—'Of the friendly motive which has associated me with you, I will only say that it adds to my reasons for specially remembering the lucky day (for me) when I became personally acquainted with you.' Earlier he had told Caine to call whenever he was in town—'You won't interrupt me if you find me at my desk.' Caine was deeply shocked on one visit to see Collins knock back a whole wine-glassful of laudanum, a dose which would kill any ordinary man and had indeed killed a manservant who had tried it in emulation of his master. Caine must have been painfully reminded of the problems of Rossetti's addiction. Collins had suffered from painful rheumatism for years.

Caine admired both his ability to write a gripping story and his prose style. Collins had known Dickens and collaborated with him on stories for *Household Words* and Caine drank in all the older man could tell him. He only got to know Collins during the last few years of his life. Like Rossetti, he was one of Caine's heroes who was lost almost as soon as found.

His persistence at this time, when he was in his early thirties, in attaching himself to older men in a quasi father-and-son relationship indicates continued emotional immaturity. One notes also his friend-ships with Theo Watts (born 1832), George Meredith (born 1828), Frederick Shields (born 1833) and William Holman Hunt (born 1827). This group were all associated with the Pre-Raphaelites and Caine met them through Rossetti. However, he remained close to good friends from his old school in Liverpool, William Tirebuck, Will Pierce and Robert Leighton. Bram Stoker, who was devoted to him, was only six years older.

In his preface to *A Son of Hagar* Caine apologises for making a bad man the subject of a book. 'For me there has been a pathetic, and I think purifying, interest in looking into the soul of this man and seeing it cor-rode beneath the touch of a powerful temptation until at the last...it rises again in strength and shows that the human heart has no depths in which it is lost.' Victorian novelists genuinely believed it was the writer's duty to give moral instruction to the reader and Caine lays it on with a trowel in this book. It is, he says, 'a plea for the natural rights of the bastard... In England alone have the rights of blood been as nothing compared with the rights of property and it is part of the business of this novel to exhibit these interests at a climax of strife.' Judging by sales readers were quite happy with this sort of thing, indeed expected it. During the course of his career as a novelist friends urged Caine to aban-don prefaces and let his stories stand or fall as such rather than as vehi-cles for propaganda, but he could not always resist the temptation. In *A Son of Hagar* he is blatantly propagandising. Some of the writing is powerful, particularly the opening scene in a London police court in 1845 where a pathetic girl and her illegitimate baby have been dragged from the Thames and she has been charged with attempted suicide.

Caine was a good reporter and he must have come across such a case while haunting the London courts for the *Mercury*. He tortured himself with thoughts of what might have happened to Mary had he not stood by her, or to Ralph had he not given him his name, albeit illegally. At the back of his mind, with the reference to the would-be suicide's once fine dress, would have been the gently born prostitute he had told Rossetti about.

Knowing as we now do that his first child was born before his marriage to the boy's mother it is clear where the inspiration for this book arose. Later he attempted to suppress it, excluding it from both the Collected Editions of his novels because it was 'an unworthy book'. More likely he feared he had been too close to home and his and Mary's secret would be deduced from it. Many of his literary friends considered it to be a strong work and one of his best.

A secondary theme of *A Son of Hagar*, which recurs in other works, was inspired by what he knew or guessed of Rossetti's marriage to Elizabeth Siddal, that of the man who betroths himself to one woman only to find he really loves another.

Originally Caine had planned to set the book on the Cumbrian coast around his mother's birthplace of Maryport. He toyed with the idea of including a mine disaster but settled for a catastrophic fire and located the story in the beautiful Vale of Newlands, near Keswick. The dialect is less impenetrable than in the previous Cumbrian novel. He is learning his craft, but the rural scenes are contrived, country traditions are dragged in by the hair of the head—local over-colour, one might say. Dialect still comes thick as porridge, as in 'Dunnet gowl, Aggy. Mappen I'll be maister mysel' soon.' In an important scene a stalwart young man of 28 wins a bout of Cumberland wrestling against the local champion and as Paul Ritson is hailed as a true son of his father. No one knows he is illegitimate. Later in the story he falls in love with a girl, neither of them realising they are half-brother and -sister. The mother confesses:

> 'Paul, my son, my darling son, you think me a good mother and a pure woman. I am neither. I must confess all—now and to you. Oh, how your love will turn from me! How you will hate me! How every kiss I have given you will seem to leave blisters on your lips!'... A strong shudder ran over her shoulders and she sobbed aloud. 'You are not your father's heir,' she said; 'you were born before we married... But you will try not to hate me, your own mother? You will try, will you not?' 'Do you mean that I am—a bastard?' he said in a hoarse whisper.
>
> Before God at that moment he was his father's son. If the world, or the world's law, said otherwise, then they were of the devil, and deserving to be damned. What rite, what jabbering ceremony, what priestly ordinance, what legal mummery, stood between him and his claim to his father's name?

One can only wonder what Mary thought of this passage when she read it. She was one of the sternest critics of her husband's work and in due course a knowledgeable and useful one. The subsequent marriage of the parents did not legitimise offspring born out of wedlock until

1927. It was a theme the author returned to in several novels. He lived to see the law changed and possibly his propagandising affected the issue. At the least he may have been responsible for some 'consciousness-raising' in influential quarters.

One of the more striking incidents in this book is the story of Mercy Fisher, the blind mother. Caine was not particularly original or inventive though he could embroider fancifully once he found an idea. Thus when one comes across such a vivid incident one looks for where he got it. Indeed, in old age he said his books were 'all true' and he had simply disguised people and events. The disguise is often thin. In the case of the blind mother the inspiration can be traced to an incident when he was a boy of about ten in Liverpool. He was attending the Infirmary there when he saw a young woman sitting waiting with her eyes bandaged. He was told she had had an operation for the removal of cataracts and been warned not to remove the bandages for two weeks or she would lose her sight altogether. She was impatient at this restriction because she had a child born before the operation whom she had never seen. The drama of the girl's situation so impressed itself on the boy's mind that more than twenty years later he incorporated it in *A Son of Hagar*. However, his urge for the melodramatic and love of tragedy led him to enlarge on the story. The girl in his book tears off the bandages because her child is ill and she fears it will die before she sees it. The child does die and she is left blind.

In 1890 when a leading French author, Octave Feuillet, died, it was pointed out that he had used an identical story in a novel published in the 1830s or '40s and Caine was accused of plagiarism. Though there were times during his career when such a charge might have stuck this time he had drawn on something he had himself seen.

Watts wrote a glowing review of this second novel in the *Athenaeum*, saying that with it Caine had established his position as a leading writer. The episode of the blind mother was 'almost too painful for art'. He compared it to *Les Misérables*, 'that terrible picture of power and pathos', hinting that the character of Mercy was based on Mary. Caine confirmed this. 'My wife—who is much touched by your article—never suspected that Mercy meant herself until your words drove the idea into her head. And yet 50% and more of Mercy's sayings are right hot from her own lips!'

Naturally the *Mercury* praised the book lavishly and even the *Whitehall Review* pronounced it 'a powerful and unique work, with the stamp of genius marked indelibly upon it'. But there was at least one dissenting voice. A certain London critic three years Caine's junior, George Bernard Shaw, took a bilious view of the romantic novels of his day with their ridiculous plots often hinging on earthquakes, train smashes and similar disasters, their villains, their handsome heroes and swooning maidens. When *A Son of Hagar* reached him its three volumes seem to have been the last straw, and, as Michael Holroyd recounts in his definitive biography, he boiled over. Shaw suggested there should be a guild of contemporary authors 'with their imaginations out of long-clothes and fairly grown and educated—all sworn to write hence forth according to rules'. He listed sixteen for consideration. One said that fictitious persons should not be criminals, another that no two characters should be so alike as 'to make a mistake of identity possible'. They must all have 'lucid and fairly cheerful intervals at least once in every five chapters' and take their disappointments in love 'with reasonable fortitude' and 'find something else to talk and think about after a lapse of a week'. If the hero was given to fisticuffs when irritated, 'he shall be thrashed by the villain in a fair stand-up fight at least once in the third volume'. Surplus characters must 'be got rid of without railway accidents, colliery disasters, or cataclysms involving the destruction of many innocent persons'. All marriages must be legal and not take place in Scotland. Finally Shaw insisted 'that books shall not be written at all except under irresistible provocation... Under these conditions a civilized school of novel and drama might be formed, and the lives of reviewers almost indefinitely prolonged.'

Had Caine obeyed Shaw's strictures he would have written no more novels. Yet in time the two not only became good friends but many years later Caine wrote one which Shaw praised and defended in the press when others condemned it.

Although he was able to prevent *A Son of Hagar* from appearing in Heinemann's first Collected Edition of his novels, which came out about 1904, Caine was not able to stop Chatto licensing it to Thomas Nelson and Son in 1907. They printed it in the Nelson Library, a collection of popular novels abridged in one volume.

In April of 1886 the Royal Literary Fund offered to nominate Caine as a steward. This was flattering and showed he had acquired status as a writer but he feared that to accept would be expensive so he refused. Shortly afterwards he was elected a member of the London Library, which had been founded two years before. He was proposed by H.T. Mackenzie Bell, a fellow writer who was related to him by marriage and was to be Christina Rossetti's first biographer. Caine remained a member until his death 45 years later. He was apt to hoard the Library's books: a terse card from the Librarian in the 1890s asks him to return the twelve he has had out for nearly three years! Nowhere near a record for the time books were detained but possibly a record for the number. He was notorious for borrowing books and not returning them. George Meredith, in a note saying he hopes Caine will come to see him while he is in London, adds drily that he could use the opportunity to return some books he has had for some time.

Research for *A Son of Hagar* had shown him how he might marry Mary without publicity or fuss. The solution was the Scottish marriage scorned by Shaw, 'by declaration before witnesses', but the problem remained of how to get himself and Mary to Scotland without betraying the true purpose of their journey. Irving provided the answer. He was on tour and would be playing Edinburgh. In the past Caine had travelled all over the country for the chance to see Irving and Stoker so no comment would be aroused if he went to Scotland while Irving was there. Leaving Ralph with his grandparents Caine and Mary took the train north, arriving in Edinburgh in mid-August. They stayed at 83 Princes Street. Residential qualifications and legal arrangements took a little while but on 3 September, 1886, T. Hall Caine, journalist and bachelor, married Mary Chandler, spinster, 'by declaration in the presences of Angus Campbell, Coachman, and John McNaughton, Hotel Waiter'. No one else other than the Registrar knew a thing about it. Caine's age is correctly given as 33 but Mary's is entered as 23. She was in fact 17. No mention of their two-year-old son. Mary put her hair up and let her skirts down to a matronly level. For a honeymoon Caine took her to Torquay.

CHAPTER THIRTEEN

Caine's marriage marked the start of the most successful, productive and happiest years of his life though there was a small blip at the start. Back at Aberleigh Lodge he put the finishing touches to his *Life of Coleridge*. For several years publishers had turned it down but then a White Knight arrived in the shape of his friend Professor Eric Robertson. He had been engaged by the publisher Walter Scott to edit a series of 'critical biographies' under the title Great Writers. Robertson himself was writing the first, a life of Longfellow, and knowing how long Caine had worked on the subject of Coleridge asked him to provide the second. The books were short—Caine's is only 154 pages—so he had to cut a lot of what he had written but he was greatly excited by the commission. This was the recognition he craved as a Man of Letters and the book would make his reputation as a literary man, not just a romantic novelist: the term was often pejorative then as now. After his usual flurry of last-minute work he sent the proofs to Watts who had agreed to read them. He asked Watts if he could dedicate the book to him. The reply must have been a shock. On 17 October, 1886, in a long letter from The Pines, Watts refused brusquely. He addressed it to Caine at Lennard Lodge, Chevening. He seems to have been so cross he forgot Caine had moved!

'I should not care to have this book dedicated to me, even as one of the best of a bad lot,' he wrote. 'It is best to be entirely candid on such a matter with a friend who I believe and hope will be a friend as long as life lasts.' In what he had written Caine had had every opportunity to acknowledge Watts's work by quoting from it. Watts claimed that no one had studied the neo-Romantic movement as he had. Perhaps Caine had not referred to it because he did not wish to appear partisan. Watts approved of this, but when Caine went on to 'damn us all as nincompoops, forgetting that in so doing you damn me by implication among the rest', he got angry. Trying to neutralise this treatment with a friendly dedication was what he did not like.

Caine must have dealt with this as the word 'nincompoop' only occurs once in the book and refers to one named person—Street, the editor of the *Courier* for which Coleridge worked for a time. He attempted to smooth Watts's ruffled feathers by quoting two lines of his poetry but there is no dedication. As he was genuinely fond of Watts so many pages of complaint and wounded pride must have hurt. By the next day Watts had repented his diatribe and wrote again, saying he thought he had been 'too hard' in his objections. He conceded the book was 'very interesting' and 'exceedingly well laid out' but there were many points he disagreed with and its general tone did not appeal to him. It had 'a certain presumptuousness' which surprised him when it was 'the work of so unpresumptuous and amiable a man'. He had often noticed that a man's writing might not reflect his character. This was a wise comment. It would be wrong to judge Caine's character solely by his novels. He was a professional writer and wrote—sometimes under protest—what his readers wanted. While some events of his own life went into the novels and some traits, such as his seriousness and lack of humour, are reflected in them, he wrote a vast amount in addition, much of it quite different to his romantic fiction. The real man behind this huge output of words cannot be deduced from the printed page alone.

Watts ended by saying he feared his candour might offend, 'but without honesty friendship is a humbug'. Caine valued Watts's judgement, something his friend William Sharp did not always agree with. 'I was with George Meredith at Browning's funeral,' he wrote in March, 1890, 'and there I met and shook hands cordially with Watts. Still—what a poseur he is!... However, it doesn't matter. He is a good fellow below it all.'

When the *Life of Coleridge* came out early in 1887 it was a damp squib. What few reviews appeared were unenthusiastic. Caine had set great store by it—it was to justify his claim to be a real author. Instead it fell flat and did not sell. The prose style was clear and literate but the overall effect was dull and failed to bring Coleridge to life. His account of Coleridge's lapse into opium dependency was sympathetic and understanding, which could have prejudiced the book in the eyes of the sanctimonious Victorian public. It shows how much he had learnt from coping with Rossetti's addiction and seeing what it had done to him. To Caine's contemporaries Coleridge was a cad and a bounder who had deserted his wife and children and sunk into degradation and addiction. Caine showed how he had fought it and eventually broken his opium habit. Caine acknowledged that Southey had had to help Mrs Coleridge and her children and had paid for the elder boy, Hartley, to go to Oxford, but emphasised that by the time the second boy, Derwent, was ready to go to Cambridge Coleridge was cured and working and met the fees himself. This cut no ice with the critics.

Caine also showed sympathy for Coleridge's youthful ideas of socialism, approving the theory of Pantisocracy he developed with Southey in the wake of the excitement roused by the French Revolution. This was the concept of a settlement in America 'quite outside the range of governments, and therefore untroubled by laws and taxes'. It was to overthrow 'the tyrannical wickedness of the existing order of society'. Its aim was Aspheterism, which meant 'the generalization of individual property'. This would have been unlikely to endear either Coleridge or his biographer to the general reader in 1887. Pantisocracy had been intended as 'the nucleus of a great socialistic regeneration', an idea close to Caine's heart.

Fears that the French Revolution might spread to Britain, common during Coleridge's lifetime, had abated by the 1880s but socialism of any kind was not a widely popular cause, as William Morris was finding. The whole scheme of the settlement in America was so hare-brained as to be almost laughable and it was never taken up.

The failure of his long-cherished biography of Coleridge upset Caine badly. If the life of the literary intellectual he hankered for was denied him he would prove himself as a serious novelist. In a fury of the hard work of which he was capable he completed his third novel, *The Deemster*, in time for it to be published the following November. At last he took Rossetti's advice and set the new story in the Isle of Man, where judges are called deemsters. Well aware what the reaction of the locals might be he tried to defuse it by giving it an eighteenth-century background. It did not work. There was uproar in the Island.

Bram Stoker, in an introduction to a later edition, said the book was written in Douglas, during a stay of seven months. Somehow he had gained the wrong impression. The work certainly took seven months but Caine had a comfortable home at Aberleigh Lodge and sufficient income to pay the rent and that was where he worked, as his letters show. He knew where to turn for help with the background of the story and wrote to both the poet T.E. Brown, then still a master at Clifton College, Bristol, whom he knew and admired, and his brother, the Revd Hugh Stowell Brown in the Isle of Man, outlining the plot and asking them to check some of the details of local colour. Both were Manxmen by birth, which Caine was not, and steeped in the folklore and history of their Island. Both begged Caine to choose another setting, saying the reading public cared nothing about the Isle of Man, which was true then, and that the story was far above the small insular life of the inhabitants who would be sure to be upset by it. T.E. Brown suggested the tale be set in the Alleghennies. Having asked their opinion Caine ignored it. He also consulted A.W. Moore, a Manx lawyer, for advice on legal points, and Sir James Gell, another lawyer and later deputy governor of the Isle of Man.

In September he went to the Island for a week or so, talking to friends and his remaining relatives, and visiting the scenes described in his story. Back home he saw Andrew Chatto. He argued for royalties but as he needed money badly he agreed to the same arrangement as before, selling the copyright to Chatto & Windus for £150, the equivalent of around £8000 now. The contract was signed on 27 September, 1887. In it Caine reserved 'all stage rights in perpetuity, the American book rights, and the rights of serial publication'. Caine was dealing with Andrew Chatto because William Windus was very much a sleeping partner. He lived for some years in the Isle of Man and took little part in the business.

The rapid completion of so long a book amazed Caine's friends. They did not realize that much of the material came from his novel published in America, *She's All the World to Me*. He used the incident of the fatal fight, with the body being taken out to sea in a fishing boat only to float back to land, but it is far better handled than in the earlier book. Starting from this point it was no problem for him to finish the novel before the end of the year. Indeed, he found time to read Rider Haggard's *She* when it came out that summer and write to the author to congratulate him. Haggard replied from Cairo in September, 'I am glad you think that I am a success. Often without affectation I think myself a dismal failure. But I did and do believe in *She*. It is the only thing that I have done that I care for.'

While waiting for his book to come out Caine took Mary and Ralph to the Isle of Man. They stayed in a boarding house on the front at Douglas for sixteen days in November, 1887. He had looked forward to introducing Mary to the Island but the visit was not a success. Mary turned out to be a very bad sailor which upset Caine, who was seldom if ever seasick, and dreary November weather did not show the Island to advantage. More than thirty years later Mary wrote to her husband, 'I remember the east wind in Douglas. It gave me neuralgia.' Those familiar with the place in winter will sympathise with her.

Caine was nervous ahead of publication day. It was a crucial point in his career. With wife, child and elderly parents to support he desperately needed a big success. He got it. The reviews were excellent and sales astonished him. It eventually ran through more than fifty editions in English and was translated into French, German, Dutch, Danish, Swedish, Russian, Spanish, Finnish and Bohemian. *Punch* christened it 'The Boomster' and the name was also applied to the author as his fame grew—and his talent for self-publicity, or log-rolling as it was known.

The Deemster may have made his name but he lost heavily over the copyright sale compared to what he would have had in royalties. However, as soon as Wilson Barrett read it he decided Dan Mylrea was a part tailor-made for him. He bought the stage rights and began work at once on a dramatised version with the title *Ben-my-Chree*—the name of the hero's fishing boat and Manx for 'Girl of my Heart'. Caine had hoped to interest Irving but he was touring in America so he opted for the bird in hand. At the end of April, 1888, Irving returned and immediately offered to stage it but to Caine's embarrassment it was too late. Barrett's first night was already announced for 17 May, at the Princess's Theatre, Oxford Street. Despite some dodgy reviews it was a success and was revived a number of times over the next twenty years or more, making Caine a good deal of money in the process. It was pure melodrama which, as Barrett well knew, was what audiences wanted.

The dramatisation, on which Caine and Wilson Barrett collaborated, twisted the story for melodramatic effect in such a way as to make it completely ridiculous instead of merely improbable. The title was changed because the ending was altered. The problem was that Barrett was a real old ham and all he wanted was big scenes for himself and he did violence to the story in contriving them. Had he played the character as Caine created it all might have been well.

In the book the narrative is vigorous and carries the reader along for most of the time. There are some strongly written scenes such as the account of Dan's efforts, with the help of some of his fisherman friends, to dispose of Ewan's body. They take it out to sea in the *Ben-my-Chree* and dump it, only to have it washed ashore next day. The account of Dan's solitary struggle with his conscience over seven years and his agonising over the possibility of atonement for his cousin's death, for which he now accepts responsibility, is well done even if sometimes mawkish.

The play ends with Mona protesting her innocence on a charge of immoral conduct when Dan appears unbidden. He corroborates the maiden's oath but by speaking he sacrifices his own life, having been sentenced to life-long silence on pain of death if he breaks it. Mona dies of shock, the Governor is handed over to the police for laying false evidence and Dan throws himself across his sweetheart's body while waiting for the hangman. Death separates the lovers in the book, but only after a loving reconciliation and after Dan has received the news that he has been proposed as Deemster.

In 1888 Caine was on increasingly good terms with Wilkie Collins. In February Collins wrote to say he was 'suffering the domestic agonies of moving' but if Caine did not mind a room without carpet or curtains he would be delighted to see him and give him all the information he could. This concerned copyright problems. He warned Caine that English copyright law allowed 'any scoundrel with a pot of paste and a pair of scissors' to steal their novels for stage purposes unless the authors had themselves produced a stage version before the novel was published. He would tell Caine more about this when they met. Caine was grateful for the advice. In future all his novels were given a 'copyright performance' ahead of publication to protect his dramatic rights.

A couple of weeks later Collins wrote from his new home. 'Let us drop the formality of 'Mr' and let me set the example because I am the oldest.' He had waited to thank Caine for *The Deemster* until he had time enough to read the book right through. He wrote now not as a critic but as 'a brother in the art'. Caine had written a remarkable work of fiction, to his way of thinking. It was a great advance on *The Shadow of a Crime*, a powerful and pathetic story. He thought the characters vividly drawn 'and set in action with a master hand'. Collins was particularly impressed by the description of fishermen taking the dead body out to sea in the hope of concealing the murder. In describing the motives assigned to the men and the way they talked, Collins said, Caine showed he had a knowledge of human nature which placed him 'among the masters of our craft'. He had avoided the conventional treatment of the tale in a way he, Collins, could not praise too highly. For a long time he had read nothing that approached what Caine had done in this new book. However, he advised him for the future to consider whether his tendency to dwell on the grotesque and the violent did not need discipline. Caine's power as a writer sometimes misled him into forgetting the value of contrast. 'Next time I want more of the humour which breaks out so delightfully in old Quilleash. More breaks of sunshine in your splendid cloudy sky will be a truer picture of nature and will certainly enlarge the number of your admiring readers.'

Caine valued Collins's judgement but his skies stayed cloudy and his stories short on humour. Collins was by this time ill and aging. He was used, he said, to the strain of writing a story for weekly publication, but when on top of this he had a fight, in the new house, 'with every form of decorative bad taste which the average Englishman can stick on the walls and paint on the doors and drag up the staircase—then the test of endurance becomes heavy in the case of a man who numbers four years on the wrong side of sixty.' He begged Caine to come and see him whenever he was in London with time to spare as he wanted to hear about Caine's new play. This was *Ben-my-Chree* and Caine had invited Collins to share his box at the opening night. Collins politely declined. A first night—and especially a friend's first night—was no pleasure to him. 'The malice of enemies and the stupidity of fools, among the audience, and the stage fright behind the curtain, are tests which my nerves are not strong enough to sustain.' Once Caine's play was successfully launched on a long run, as he did not doubt it would be, he would 'try to get well enough to go and enjoy it'.

After a short run Barrett took *Ben-my-Chree* on tour. Houses were good, as he hastened to tell Caine, and the play was having more success in the provinces. Wilkie Collins was not surprised. He thought the average London audience was 'the stupidest audience in England'. He made

a dreadful confession. I am at work again—hard at work—furiously at work—nearly a third of the way through a new story... A devoted friend has discovered a very good reason for the obstinacy of the ancient novelist in refusing to let go of his pen. 'I'll tell you what it is, Wilkie, you are a canny fellow and a clever fellow and you contrive to hide it from most people—but I tell you, you're mad!' This is my only excuse for being just as incapable (when a story comes to me) of resisting the temptation to write it, as I was forty years since!

Collins was a sick man when he wrote in February the following year, 1889, wishing Caine good luck for another first night when *Ben-my-Chree* returned to London, and saying he was sorry he could not be there. 'My room still holds me a most unwilling prisoner.' The writing is blotched and scrawled with a note, ringed, 'Here is a letter all post-scripts. I have been taking Ether and am "fuddled"!' By the end of May he was writing cheerfully that he was again hard at work in spite of ill health with nothing but native obstinacy to keep him going. 'Do come here when you are next in London. Is it a new play? or a new novel? I am sorely in need of a new novel to read which shall be also a work of art.' This was his last letter. He died a few months later and Caine went to his funeral.

In 1888 Caine enjoyed a reputation among his friends as a successful playwright. On 4 March William Sharp wrote that he was delighted to hear Caine had achieved financial success with his plays,

> though I honestly admit that you, with your high abilities, should be working at more enduring stuff than ordinary melodrama. We need a true dramatic writer, and you have it in you to be the man—but!—I have your reputation so truly to heart that what you yourself say is good news to me...though the financial aspect, with a man like you, ought to be—and in your case is—of secondary import.

He planned to 'run down to Bexley' to discuss this and other 'artistic matters'.

With royalties coming in he took Mary and Ralph for a seaside holiday. They spent most of August, 1888, at Aldeburgh. That autumn, as the end of his lease of Aberleigh Lodge loomed, Caine had to face the problem of where they were to live. He heard of a house in Putney and wrote to Watts asking if he could come to dinner when he went to look at it. Watts replied saying Caine was welcome to dinner and Mary too but if he wanted to look at a house how could he judge it by moonlight? This exchange is typical of the way Caine sometimes acted as if he had forgotten he had a wife. He invited only himself to dinner—it was Watts who included Mary.

The Lakes pulled and he wondered whether he could not live in Keswick. In October he rented Castlerigg Cottage, close to where his friend Edwin Jackson lived, and went there with Mary and Ralph. He was working hard on a new play in collaboration with Wilson Barrett but they stayed for nearly two months. They left at the end of November and called on the family in Liverpool. With real money in his pocket at last the first thing he did was to buy 59 South Chester Street in his father's name and present it to him, thus assuring a roof over his elderly parents' heads. When they were both dead it reverted to him and he owned it until the 1920s, leasing it to a series of tenants.

They returned to Aberleigh where he put the final touches to *Good Old Times* and attended rehearsals. The idea for this play had been Barrett's but he left the writing of it to his collaborator. It is set in Cumberland and Tasmania. The hero takes the blame for a crime he has not committed and is deported. He is reunited with his wife after prison escapes, brawls and robberies along the way. It opened at the Princess's Theatre on 12 February, 1889. The first night was a success but reviews were poor. Receipts fell short of the 'get out' figure and it was taken off. It was too long and the complicated story difficult to follow. However, it was revived in October the following year at the Pavilion Theatre, Whitechapel, with John M. East, a good character actor, in the cast. East's chief claim to theatrical fame is that from 1892 to 1904 he ran a stock company at the Lyric Opera House, Hammersmith. Built as the Lyric Hall in 1888, it became a theatre two years later and was extensively rebuilt as a home for melodrama in 1895. East staged a revival of *Ben-my-Chree* there in 1896, with his brother Charles in Barrett's part of Dan Mylrea. In melodrama there was a happy tradition of audience participation. When Charles East as Dan uttered the immortal line, 'My disgrace is complete. Will nobody speak to me now?' a voice from the gallery replied, 'I will, guv'nor. How are you keeping?'

John East was a sociable man. He lived in Chiswick and his house was famous for Sunday and 'after theatre' gatherings. Caine often joined them. Other regulars were Tyrone Power, father of the film star and known as Fred, and the noted theatre critic, Clement Scott. Caine liked East and remained in touch with him. When his novel *The Manxman* was filmed in 1916 he asked for John M. East to play the part of Caesar Cregeen, the heroine's father. During his time at the Lyric, Hammersmith, East produced several of Caine's plays.

When it came to house hunting Caine was adamant he must live in the country—the hustle and bustle of the city exhausted him and he could not work there. This is amusing when one remembers his earlier eagerness to get to London. He had to go to town on business and to see friends quite often and hotels were expensive and did not suit him. Therefore he must have a *pied à terre* in town. The Lincoln's Inn chambers had been given up a year or two previously as no longer suitable. At this juncture his relative Mackenzie Bell introduced him to a widow,

Mrs Blanchard, who had a flat at Albert Mansions, 114 Victoria Street, not far from Westminster Abbey. It was too big for her and she was anxious to let part of it to 'a literary gentleman'. She wanted a writer as sub-tenant because the part of the flat she had available included her late husband's book-lined study with a large writing desk. She felt only a serious author was worthy of this accommodation. Caine took it immediately and first stayed there in July, 1889.

The problem of a permanent country home solved itself. Edwin Jackson, who was in banking, wrote to say his work was increasingly taking him away from Keswick and he wanted to sell Hawthorns. Was Caine interested? It was hardly necessary to ask. After losing Aberleigh the idea of owning his own home appealed to him. A price was soon agreed though the house was not available until October.

1889 was a full and crowded year and there was much to do before they moved to their new home. In August Caine and Mary went to Iceland. That statement looks surprising but such a visit was not unique. A number of travellers regularly made the voyage north—Rider Haggard also went to Iceland that summer and William Morris had been on two expeditions, in 1871 and 1873. Whether or not he had given Caine the journals of his travels in Iceland to read it is likely that it was Morris who first interested Caine in the country. Morris was absorbed by the world of the sagas. He taught himself Icelandic and in 1876 published a translation of the *Saga of Sigurd the Volsung and the Fall of the Nibelungs*, on which he had collaborated with the Icelandic scholar Erikur Magnusson. It is a monumental work in four volumes of anapaestic couplets. It was his greatest book—many consider it his best. Caine was entranced by it. The drama and romance of the sagas appealed to his deepest feelings, as they did to many of his contemporaries. Artists and intellectuals throughout Western Europe were looking to the northern lands, their sagas and their gods. Wagner's cycle of four epic music-dramas, *The Ring of the Nibelung*, was given for the first time at Bayreuth in August of 1876. While there is no evidence that Caine ever saw Wagner's *Ring*, the influence on him of Morris's epic was enormous and led directly to his interest in Iceland and to his creation of Icelandic heroes and heroines in two of his novels. Some of his best descriptive writing is of the Icelandic landscape.

Morris's *Volsung* epic is roughly the same story as Wagner's *Ring*. The complex, romantic tale of treachery, murder, vengeance and remorse was exactly to Caine's taste and it is easy to see how it fired his imagination as much as Morris's brand of socialism influenced the development of his political ideas. Morris went on to produce a series of novels based in the remoter regions of northern Europe and published them in the 1890s. His death in 1896 at the age of 62 was a great grief to Caine.

Iceland also appealed to him because of the links with the Isle of Man. Both islands had been occupied by Norse settlers who had set up assemblies or parliaments, the Althing in Iceland and Tynwald in the Isle of Man. Thingvellir, the open arena where the Althing met, was established in 930 AD, the world's oldest parliament, but Iceland came under Scandinavian rule in 1262, not becoming independent from Denmark until 1944. Although founded earlier than Tynwald, the Icelandic parliament was not allowed to meet for many years, being revived only in the nineteenth century. Tynwald on the other hand has had a continuous existence for over a thousand years. When he returned to fiction writing Caine soon began to brood on a novel which would combine the legends and history of both islands. What emerged was his fourth novel, *The Bondman*.

By August of 1889 the story was complete and already appearing in serial form but Caine determined to see Iceland before he allowed it to appear as a book. Sarah Caine came down to Aberleigh to look after Ralph. An agent in Leith kitted Caine and Mary out for their trip and made all the arrangements, including the provision of a guide and interpreter. They travelled north to Leith, the port of Edinburgh, where a note was waiting for them from John Caine wishing them a good journey. He was following the serialisation of *The Bondman* and thought that week's episode 'the most touching yet'. They sailed next day on the SS *Magnetic*.

It was their first journey abroad together, the first of many, but it started inauspiciously for the 20-year-old Mary. The first port of call was Bergen on the Norwegian coast. Although it was August there was a storm in the North Sea and she was devastated with seasickness. Her husband did not feel too good either. A fellow passenger who happened to be a doctor dosed both of them with opium, a surprising cure but it worked. From Bergen they sailed round the north of Scotland and called at the Faroes before arriving in Reykjavik.

Caine was enraptured by the bleak beauty of Iceland. The small wooden houses with corrugated iron roofs looked strange to him but the 'potato gardens' everywhere were familiar. The people lived on fish and potatoes, exactly as the Manx did. Most households kept animals to support the family, in particular cows for milk. Otherwise the place was completely foreign to Caine, more so than he had expected. He found Iceland to be northern in latitude but Mediterranean in national character, a curious mixture. The influence of the bleak landscape was paramount. A romantic view of the country is knocked out of anyone who spends a winter in Iceland but Caine saw it only in summer so did not get this necessary corrective. The Icelanders of that time made the most of the long summer days outdoors and in the winter sat round the fire and read or told stories. It was this tradition of story-telling which had kept the sagas alive. They also drank—drink was a real problem, not surprisingly when there was not much else to do in the long dark nights and short gloomy days of the Icelandic winter. Wealthier families sent their children away to Denmark to school or college and the Danish influence is still felt today. The Icelanders have a strong musical streak with a particularly rich heritage of choral singing. Caine noted these facts and incorporated them in one of his novels.

He had arrived with introductions to leading people in Reykjavik and was invited to ride with the official party to Thingvellir for the opening of the Althing. Mary, who was not used to riding, remained with their hosts. For Caine this was the most impressive part of the trip, with echoes of Tynwald in the ceremony. How much more he saw of the country is not clear—certainly he did not travel as far as Morris had done as they were able to stay for only two or three weeks before sailing home. Caine, at least, was determined to return one day.

CHAPTER FOURTEEN

As soon as they reached Aberleigh Lodge they packed up and moved to Keswick. Caine leased Castlerigg Cottage again as the sale of Hawthorns was not yet complete and the house needed redecorating. He and Jackson signed on 23 October and Hawthorns, the first house he ever owned, was his. He paid £1650 for it, part of which was a mortgage of £600 at 4% given him by Jackson, the balance being paid in cash. Caine was also to pay 6d a year for the right to draw water from adjoining land belonging to Mrs Stanger, a popular old lady who did much for local charities. She was a niece of Raisley Calvert, Wordsworth's benefactor, which at once interested Caine. Her late husband, Joshua Stanger, was a member of an old local family.

Hawthorns is a square, stone-built house with a large porch, standing on the north side of the Penrith road, just above the junction with Chestnut Hill. The lane which runs up to the Stone Circle was the original way to Penrith. When the new, wider, road was driven through, not many years before, it cut the Hawthorns property in two. The house

Hall Caine's House at Keswick.

was left standing with its stable block at the apex of a small triangle, the end wall close to the road. Two thirds of its land was left on the south side. It was less than they had had at Aberleigh Lodge but still enough to keep a cow. Mary learnt to milk it and to make butter and cheese.

Caine loved this house. It was the position as much as anything which appealed to him. The house faced west with a glorious view over the little town of Keswick in the valley below. Set in the garden wall near the front gate is a milestone, Keswick 1 Mile. The story goes that if Caine saw the telegraph boy approaching he would rush out and meet him on the Keswick side of the stone. That way he was entitled to receive his telegram free. More than a mile from the telegraph office and he had to pay 6d. People laugh now at such apparent meanness but with no telephone Caine was sent a large number of telegrams, and 6d a time added up to a substantial amount. 6d was, after all, the cost of his water supply for a year.

The literary associations pleased him too. Close by on Chestnut Hill was the cottage where Shelley had stayed with Harriet. On a knoll above the town he could see Greta Hall, the home of Coleridge and Southey. Beyond it lay the parish church of Crosthwaite, just visible. In the distance a glimpse of water and on the skyline the fells above Derwentwater and Bassenthwaite. From the side windows he looked out on Latrigg and Skiddaw, while at the foot of the hill on which the house stood the River Greta chuckled over its stones, a sound which carried to his study window when it was open. The land on that side belonged to Colonel J.J. Spedding, a peppery gentleman who also belonged to an old Cumbrian family. He was active in local affairs and a JP but was a difficult man to deal with.

There were pleasant walks in all directions. One of Caine's favourites led up the lane past the Stone Circle and over Naddle Fell to the lonely church of St John's in the Vale. Another went the other way, across Chestnut Hill and over the fields to climb Castle Head. At the top he loved to sit among the rocks and contemplate the panoramic view of Derwentwater and the fells. He soon became a familiar figure in and around Keswick with his flowing red hair, striding along in his Inverness cape and the boots and breeches he favoured for country wear. He often went down to the boat landings near Friar's Crag and talked to the boatmen. They held the same interest for him as the Peel fishermen in the Isle of Man. One of them was a local worthy called Thomas Telford, a preacher as well as a boatman, who wrote a good deal of mediocre verse. He and Caine became firm friends. He helped Caine develop the garden at Hawthorns and looked after the property when the family was away. He and Caine were the same age. Telford died at 79 in May, 1932, when the local paper described him as a friend of Hall Caine.

Caine in Keswick, 1890, photographed by G.P. Abraham.

In the midst of domestic upheaval Caine was preparing his new novel for publication. As soon as the legal business of the house purchase was completed he went back to London and immersed himself in work. On 18 November a note came from Wolcott Balestier: 'Imagine your being engaged on four plays! It makes me tired to think of it.' The diligent researcher, looking at the evidence of all Caine did in the months and years following his return from Iceland, will feel with Balestier. Bram Stoker had introduced Caine to him not long before. He was a young businessman who was about to go into partnership with William Heinemann to found the publishing house which still bears the latter's name, though now as part of a large international group. Heinemann was looking for a blockbuster novel to launch the new imprint. Stoker and Balestier both thought *The Bondman* was the book.

As to the four plays, one was *Ben-my-Chree*. Caine was tinkering with it to meet some of the criticisms. He also started on the dramatisation of *The Bondman*. This was a big job as it is a long, complicated story. It was given a copyright performance in Bolton one afternoon in November, 1892, without scenery and the cast reading their parts, but it was not formally staged until September, 1906, when Arthur Collins mounted it at Drury Lane. The varied sets its five acts demanded and the large cast were daunting to a theatre manager. It was not until Caine had had several successful plays produced and the public would go to anything with his name attached to it that any manager was brave enough to take it on. Wilson Barrett wanted to produce it in the autumn of 1890. Stoker drew up an agreement but Barrett could not raise the money and gave up the idea. Lily got wind of this when she saw Barrett's company on tour. She wrote to her brother that Miss Eastlake had said Barrett was dropping the production of *The Bondman* in his next London season in favour of a play by someone unknown. Both the women thought this a calculated insult to Caine and that he should insist on holding Barrett to his contract but finance held the key.

The third play in progress was originally titled *Mahomet* while the fourth was probably *Good Old Times*, which needed much work done on it before its revival. Irving had for some time wanted to mount an 'Eastern play' and the part of the Prophet attracted him. A play was published in France by de Bornier on the subject. That gave Irving the idea such a production would be possible, and he asked Caine to write the script. Caine jumped at the chance. Not only had he long wanted to do a play for Irving, he was also keen to produce one with an Eastern theme. He was planning a scenario at the time Balestier protested about the amount of work he was doing.

He was still loyal to Chatto & Windus and began discussions on terms for *The Bondman*. He insisted that this time he was going to have royalties and would retain the copyright. He also wanted a substantial advance. The argument went on through November until on 6 December Andrew Chatto said that, after looking through the sales records for *The Deemster*, he did not think the large advance Caine was asking would be justified, nor was he willing to agree to royalties 'in the congested state of the book market'. He was, however, prepared to give a higher price, £350, for the copyright, exclusive of the American rights. He was not to know that Heinemann and Balestier had already made a better offer, including an agreement on royalties. Caine turned down Chatto's proposal. He replied with a note saying he was sad not to have the new book and wishing Caine luck. Perhaps he would be able to publish him again in the future. They parted on good terms, which was just as well. Chatto & Windus continued to control the copyright of Caine's first three novels, which caused some minor problems when the questions of a collected edition and film rights came up, but matters were dealt with amicably. Years later Caine bought the three books back in order to sell the film rights. Only *The Deemster* was actually filmed.

Between June and November, 1889, *The Bondman* was serialised in the *Isle of Man Times* as well as several provincial papers on the mainland. All this had been organised under his contract with Tillotsons' Newspaper Literature. On 28 October they wrote to congratulate him 'on the completion of your great work "The Bondman"... For the sake of yourself and the great future before you, we trust you will take a period of repose before attempting to win further laurels.' Repose was the last thing he allowed himself.

He had made notes in Iceland and incorporated some of what he had seen in *The Bondman*. His note-taking was thoroughly disorganised. He scribbled on any odd bit of paper that came to hand, mostly old envelopes or the backs of letters. On one he noted a description of the Aurora Borealis which he saw for the first time in Iceland. How he kept track of these notes is a mystery.

As usual he sent the first proofs of the book off to a friend for comment but this time it was not Watts but Robert Leighton, now living in Scotland with his wife, Marie Connor. Earlier that year Caine had met the Leightons in London and told them the story of *The Bondman*. He was still unable to grapple with a contemporary novel and this one is set vaguely around the turn of the eighteenth century. Leighton did a conscientious job. His knowledge of history was much sounder than Caine's and he was able to save him from some veritable howlers. He returned the proofs on 7 November, 1889, saying he wished they were not so far apart as there was so much about the story he wanted to discuss. He thought it a great novel but feared critics would say Caine had 'taken improbable liberties with circumstance'. Caine made it natural enough, for instance, that fate should keep the young men apart, 'but Jason rushing about Reykjavik in search of Sunlocks and being always defeated by opposing fate almost reminds one of Japhet in search of his Father'. He thought it a trifle overdone but would not say so to anyone else. He was puzzled by the chronology of the story, pointing out that the narrative referred to events in 1793, 1820 and then back to 1801 and some of

Robert Leighton

Caine's historical facts were wrong. Caine took notice and put most of it right. Despite the historical inaccuracies Leighton thought the book was one 'for all classes of readers. It is so grand that the highest intellect will be elevated by it. It is so simple that our shepherd's boy out here might read it and be thrilled by every line of it.'

Once the contract was signed Caine started fussing about whether Heinemann had planned sufficient advertising. He wanted the book announced two weeks in advance but Heinemann thought one week better. It came out at the end of January, 1890, and was an immediate and spectacular success, launching both the author and the new firm into orbit. The book is dedicated to 'My Son, Little Sunlocks'—Ralph, so called because of his blonde hair. According to his father this was an Icelandic nickname for the very blonde. The leading character in the book is named Michael Sunlocks. So great was the success that Heinemann chose 'Sunlocks, London' as the firm's telegraphic address and so it remained until telegrams were superseded by fax. The book was translated into eleven languages and a second, one-volume, edition came out in October, 1890. It was continuously in print until the 1920s. Caine was well served by his translators, especially the Swedish and Russian ones. They made his books into the fine literature he thought they were. This accounts for his high standing among authors and critics in both Sweden and Russia compared with how he was seen at home.

At Caine's request Heinemann sent a copy of *The Bondman* to Gladstone. Delighted with the Grand Old Man's response, he assured Caine that he would give the widest possible publicity to Gladstone's opinion, which was: ' "The Bondman" is a work of which I recognise the freshness, vigour and sustained interest no less than its integrity of aim.' *The Times* was equally quotable from a publisher's standpoint. 'It is impossible to deny originality and rude power to this saga, impossible not to admire its forceful directness, and the colossal grandeur of its leading characters.' Other critics were agreed that there had been nothing like it in recent fiction. In many ways the novel is similar to *The Deemster*, as if written to a previously successful formula. It is packed with chunks of the history of Iceland and the Isle of Man and their myths and legends. Parts of it read like a tourist brochure. The action is divided between the two countries, reflecting Caine's fascination with the parallels between the islands. In interviews he said the book was intended as a reworking of the story of Esau and Jacob 'but in my story sympathy attaches to Esau'. This seems disingenuous nonsense considering the author's introduction to the book. He continued to insist over the years that his stories were biblical in origin though it is frequently difficult to see the connection. As his later stories were increasingly attacked for their subject matter he asserted ever more strongly that they were based on the Bible, hoping to deflect the damaging charges of 'moral obloquy' flung at him. In the case of *The Bondman* the obvious inspiration is the Icelandic sagas.

The novel is in three sections, 'The Book of Stephen Orry', 'The Book of Michael Sunlocks' and 'The Book of Red Jason'. This drags the reader to and fro between the two islands and backwards and forwards in time, so that the story is not always easy to follow. As the headings suggest, the main characters are firstly, Stephen Orry, a handsome ne'er-do-well of Reykjavik, who bewitches Rachel, the daughter of Governor Jorgensen. He marries her, treats her badly and deserts her after their son, Jason, is born. He becomes a seaman on an English boat but jumps ship in Ramsey, in the Isle of Man. He has problems because he speaks only Icelandic and is on the run from English crewmen of his ship. The Manx, however, see no reason for aiding their ancient enemy, England, and several of them help Stephen escape detection, including Adam Fairbrother, who is to become Deputy Governor of the Island. Stephen is finally taken in by Liza Killey, 'the island drab', who lives in a wretched hut on Maughold Head (remember Caine had been schoolmaster at Maughhold and had lived there in what could well be described as a 'wretched hut'). Stephen marries Liza bigamously and she has a son, Michael, whom his father christens Sunlocks because of his fair hair. Liza dies and for a time he brings the boy up on his own.

Meanwhile back in Iceland Rachel has also died. On her deathbed she begs Jason to find his father and kill him in revenge for his treatment of her. She dies and holding her hand Jason swears, 'I will hunt the world over until I find that man and when I have found him I will slay him.'

The complicated story has intrigues galore and much hatred between the half-brothers. Jason arrives in the Isle of Man. He dramatically rescues Stephen from a storm at sea without realising this is the father he had come to kill. In the nick of time all is revealed, he cannot do the deed and Stephen blesses his son with his dying breath. Jason decides his half-brother Michael Sunlocks will have to be sacrificed instead. Both brothers fall in love with Greeba, the daughter of Adam Fairbrother. Michael, who marries Greeba, returns to Iceland where he mysteriously first becomes governor and is then destroyed by a plot against him and sentenced to work in the sulphur mines. The devoted Greeba follows with their baby and Jason returns as well.

Michael has gone blind and therefore does not know that Greeba, who chooses not to reveal her identity, is near. Michael is condemned to death and a posse sets off from Reykjavik to carry out the sentence. A conscience-stricken Jason brings Sunlocks and Greeba together and helps them to escape by sea to the Shetlands. He takes Michael's place and is shot in his stead.

A sample of the overheated style may be taken from Chapter V of The Book of Red Jason. Greeba has learned that she is to be reunited with Michael Sunlocks:

'Two years I have lived alone in the solitude of a loveless life and the death of a heartless home. My love has been silent all this weary, weary time, but it is to be silent no longer. At last! At last! Yes, yes, my hour has come at last! My husband will forgive me for the deception I have practised upon him. Only think, how can he hate me for loving him to all lengths and ends of love?' Then from crying she fell to laughing, as softly and as gently, and as if her heart grudged her voice of the joy of it.

Jason makes his final sacrifice in similar manner, writing a letter to his brother telling him, 'She has loved you, you only, all the days of her life.'

The book is hopelessly sentimental and melodramatic and not his best work, despite its enormous success when published. The shine was taken off this success, however, when a legal row broke out with Tillotson's. It began in March of 1890 when Heinemann arranged for Tauchnitz to bring out a German edition only to find that another publisher was before them. Heinemann wrote to them saying they had pirated the book but received a bland reply that they had bought the rights from Tillotson's. Stoker, who by this time had qualified as a lawyer but never practised, found a loophole: the agreement with Tillotson's had been for 'The Maid of Mona', the original title for *The Bondman*. There was much unpleasantness and legal manoeuvring, however, before the matter was settled and a new contract with Tillotson's, for short stories and serialisations only, signed. Stoker had his work cut out to stop Caine writing angry letters to Tillotson's which would have made matters worse. He insisted Caine send all letters through him.

By January, 1890, Caine had worked out the scenario of his 'Mahomet' play. He spent the last Sunday of that month with Bram Stoker and his wife Florence, after a trying morning dealing with a press interviewer. Work, however, as Stoker commented, 'was always a stimulant to Hall Caine'. In his memoir of Henry Irving Stoker gives an account of Caine telling his story of *Mahomet* which brings the man vividly to life.

In the dim twilight of the late January afternoon, sitting in front of a good fire of blazing billets of old ship timber, the oak so impregnated with salt and saltpetre that the flames leaped in rainbow colours, he told the story as he saw it. Hall Caine always knows his work so well and has such a fine memory that he never needs to look at a note. That evening he was all on fire. His image rises now before me. [He was writing in 1906.] He sits on a low chair in front of the fire; his face is pale, something waxen-looking in the changing blues of the flame. His red hair, fine and long, and pushed back from his high forehead, is so thin that through it as the flames leap we can see the white line of the head so like to Shakespeare's. He is himself all aflame. His hands have a natural eloquence—something like Irving's; they foretell and emphasise the coming thoughts. His large eyes shine like jewels as the firelight flashes. Only my wife and I are present, sitting like Darby and Joan at either side of the fireplace. As he goes on he gets more and more afire till at the last he is like a living flame.

We sit quite still; we fear to interrupt him. The end of his story leaves us fired and exalted too.

He was quite done up; the man exhausts himself in narrative as I have never seen with anyone else. Indeed when he had finished a novel he used to seem as exhausted as a woman after childbirth. At such times he would be in a terrible state of nerves—trembling and sleepless. At that very time he had not quite got through the nervous crisis after the completion of *The Bondman*. At such times everything seemed to worry him; things that he would shortly after laugh at.

This description says almost as much about Stoker as it does about Caine. The next morning the two men went to see Irving in his office at the Lyceum. Caine told him the story of the play, with less flamboyance but almost equal effect. Irving was delighted and agreed to do it. However, the censor stepped in and forebade it, even though they changed the title from *Mahomet* to *The Prophet*. The censor's argument was that to stage any play dealing with the founder of Islam 'would give offence to many of Her Majesty's subjects'. It was a desperate disappointment but Caine did not waste the material: he published the playscript and a year or two later used the material again in a novella.

Caine had a gift for friendship. One of his favourite Shakespearian quotations was from Polonius's advice to Hamlet—'The friends thou hast, and their adoption tried, Grapple them to thy soul with hoops of steel.' Once he had so grappled a friend, as he did Bram Stoker, there was no limit to the pains he would go to to help them. He could be generous with his money but more importantly he was generous with himself. While he was nervously awaiting the public's verdict on *The Bondman* and working feverishly on his 'Eastern' play, Bram asked for help and he gave him his time. Bram had turned to novel-writing and desperately wanted Caine's verdict on his first book. Putting everything else aside Caine read it carefully and then wrote several pages of praise and comment. Bram said this letter had given more hope, pleasure and encouragement than he knew how to express. He had waited anxiously for his friend's verdict, not expecting a good one. Caine must know how hard it was to judge the value of one's own work. He had believed in his judgment already but found his criticism to be

tender as well as most searching and its spirit is truly *brotherly*. What a world it would be if critics had all such sympathy. I shall try to do better work & believe me old fellow that if it be better it will in great part at all events be due to you. Your letter has left me in a tumult and you must pardon my seeming incoherency... I assure you that my heart feels very warm to you and I am truly grateful to you for your sympathy and encouragement.

Caine had left Mary to supervise the move into Hawthorns, to unpack and to arrange everything the way she knew he would like it. Though she would rather have had him at home she was not unhappy about this. She dedicated her life to making a home for Caine, wherever they might be, and protecting his writing time. She was a devoted wife in every way. She became closely involved with his work, reading everything as he wrote it and often able to give useful criticism and advice. She was his first secretary. When many years later he withdrew from her to such an extent that she did not even know what the book he was working on was about it nearly destroyed her. Sarah Caine came up from Liverpool to help with the move and keep her company. Ralph's contribution was to go down with measles.

Caine's study at Hawthorns, Keswick, 1889, drawn by A. Tucker. The bust of Shakespeare on the desk originally belonged to Rossetti. The chair designed and made for him by William Morris is on the left. On the right, a carved oak chair from Cheyne Walk.

Following the meeting with Irving and the book launch, which involved numerous press interviews, Caine finally went home to Hawthorns. The room he had chosen for his study was crammed with memorabilia of Rossetti. The death mask stood on top of a book case while the mantelpiece and a small table were crowded with bits and pieces from Cheyne Walk. Also there was one of his most cherished possessions, a chair designed and made for him by William Morris when he moved to Aberleigh. Morris had noted that his friend preferred to write on his knee rather than at a desk. He designed a low chair with a long seat so the author could sit with his legs stretched out and write with ease. The chair still belongs to his family and is both sturdy and extremely comfortable. Morris covered it with one of his typical upholstery fabrics, in a special blue he favoured shot with gold. Mary made a chintz cover to protect it.

February saw an event of domestic importance: the breeching of Ralphie, now four years old. In those days little boys were at first dressed in skirts, for understandably practical reasons. Dressing a boy in his first pair of trousers took on almost the air of a barmitzvah. Ralphie's delighted grandparents wrote from Liverpool. His grandmother said, 'How do you like your trousers is it could [cold] can you play out? Hav you gon to scoull [school] yet?' With this missive is a long letter from Father to Tom, Mary 'and Little Breeches with Buttons'. Lily, shrugging off all suggestions of working in the Post Office, had gone on the stage in 1888 and had already taken small parts in provincial tours. According to her father, at the time of the 'breeching' she was in London in rehearsal. She had had two free days and indulged in shopping. Her purchases included 'a pair of gutta percha shoes' to cover her boots in wet weather! Their father had seen Tom's letter in the *Athenaeum*—it is interesting that he read the magazine. 'It was a fine review of "The Bondman" in the Mercury', he added.

Lily read the book while on tour. From Rochdale she wrote to her brother, 'I am raving about The Bondman. How I should like to play that death scene of Rachel's!' The strain of touring was beginning to tell and she said she was 'not quite as strong as I should be but don't repeat this and I can't go for very long walks so I should like to do some copying for you. I reserve my strength for night.' Her clear and attractive handwriting was often useful to her brother.

On 21 February a telegram brought the news that John Lovell had died suddenly after only a few days' illness, aged 55. Though shocked and upset Caine sat down at once to write a long obituary of his friend and patron. He telegraphed it to the Liverpool *Mercury* which printed it on the 22nd. He wrote of Lovell as 'A cheery, bright, humorous, strong soul, not to be deluded by any false show, always hopeful...always calm in a sure faith that things which seemed to go awry would work themselves out for the best in the end. It was an education to know him, a tonic to be with him, a stimulant to work by his side.'

He went to Liverpool for the funeral on the 24th. The *Mercury* gave a long account, in which they mentioned that Mr Hall Caine was in the fourth carriage of the long funeral procession, the one immediately behind those carrying members of the family. Among men listed as representing the paper was 'Ralph H. Caine'. This was Caine's brother Willie. He was William Ralph but preferred to use the name Ralph professionally. He was Willie to his family to the end of his life. Now 25 and as yet unmarried, he was still Lovell's secretary. After Lovell's death Willie joined the editorial staff of the *Mercury*, becoming a leader writer

Caine and his family photographed in Liverpool, 1888. Standing, Lily and William Hall Caine (brother and sister). Seated, left to right, Tom Hall Caine, Sarah Caine (mother), Ralph Hall Caine (son), John Caine (father), Mary Hall Caine (wife).

and reviewer. He had already published an anthology of humorous poems and was working on *Love Songs of England*, published in 1893. He wrote primary school 'readers' in geography and history and eventually several other books, but his style was stodgy and dull and he had nothing like his elder brother's success. He lived under Tom's shadow all his life and resented it. At the time of the funeral he was bored with Liverpool and looking for an opportunity to move to London.

Caine must have been already working on his next book, *The Scapegoat*, as serialisation began in April, 1890. The editor of the *Graphic* wrote in February trying to arrange a price. He understood Caine had reserved American rights but what about India and Australia?

> With regard to other people's prices, I have heard that [R.L.] Stevenson, taking things all round, obtains £10,000 for his novel. The present value of Haggard, taking serial rights only, is about £1500, that of Blackmore £1000, and Besant less. Curiously enough Hardy, whom I together with many others look upon as our greatest living English novelist, does not appear to command so high a figure... The prices of novels have considerably gone up of late years.

It would be interesting to know where Caine stood on this scale but there is nothing more on the subject.

Wisely Caine selected a completely fresh setting for this new book. He chose Morocco and in March went on a visit for local colour. He sailed from Liverpool to Gibraltar, where he caught a ferry to Tangier and stayed at the French Hotel. Mary remained at home. At that time Tangier was a popular winter holiday resort for Europeans, especially the British. The tourist part of the town was modernised and sophisticated with good hotels, comfortable but not much help for Caine's purposes. Despite anguished warnings from the British Consul he wandered alone around the Kasbah and through the narrow streets of the 'native quarter', talking to anyone he could. He found a guide and interpreter who arranged an expedition into the desert, faithfully described in the ensuing book.

The main theme of *The Scapegoat* is the persecution of the Jews. Caine hated anti-Semitism and did all he could in his work to counteract it. It was strong and widespread in the 1890s. Ever since the old days in Liverpool, his friendship with Yussy bar Ely and the gatherings in Yussy's café The Persian Depot, Caine had had many friends among the Jewish community. Once settled in London his Jewish acquaintance broadened. They included Dr Herman Adler, the Chief Rabbi, and Israel Zangwill, author, philanthropist, teacher and then journalist. Zangwill discarded his Jewish religion but clung fast to his Jewish identity and people. His style is delightful, showing that lighter touch which Caine lacked. In his novels he handled the Jew with knowledge, affection and justice and established a solid reputation. From 1896 he flung himself wholeheartedly into the Zionist cause and converted Caine to it, although one can see from letters that Caine had already begun thinking along the lines of a national home for the Jews in Palestine as early as 1888.

A secondary theme of his new novel was the position of women in society. Caine himself said it was the story of Samuel and Eli 'with Eli in my story being a girl'. As with most of his books where he quotes a biblical story as the basis the connection seems tenuous. Many discerning critics have considered *The Scapegoat* to be the best thing Caine wrote. It is certainly different to most of his other novels, many of them having a certain sameness about them. (He was known to complain that he wanted to write great literature but his public wanted his romances.) *The Scapegoat* is a weirdly haunting story and aspects of it linger in the mind after even a cursory reading.

He still does not tackle a contemporary story as the action deals with events of forty or fifty years previously. The central characters were said to be inspired by the Mahdi and his wife. Caine met them on his visit to Morocco and was deeply impressed by them. Most readers assumed they were the couple described in the preface to the book. However, a Mr V. Abrahams wrote to Caine in October, 1890, as if he was the character referred to. Whoever Caine based his portraits of Israel ben Oliel and his daughter Naomi on they are beautifully drawn. Most likely Israel is a mixture of the Mahdi and Abrahams. The girl is born blind, deaf and dumb but is described as a happy, laughing child. Her mother dies at her birth and Israel, who is a tax collector for the local Moorish Sultan, brings his daughter up alone. He comes to see how his extortion of taxes for his master, Ben Aboo, urged on by the ever-growing demands of his greedy and vicious wife Katrina, have impoverished the people, using Israel as his tool. Revolted by Ben Aboo's excesses Israel, in disguise, gives away all his wealth and returns his seal of office. He says, 'For what I did long ago of my own free will and intention to oppress the poor, I have suffered and still am suffering.' He is the Scapegoat and he sees Naomi's affliction as the sins of the father visited on the child. Israel makes a kind of pilgrimage and on his return finds that Naomi can hear—and it terrifies her. In a later and dramatic scene she follows her father to the Kasbah and hears Ben Aboo's cruel attack on Israel and a decree of exile. In the shock she realises she can see. Then she begins to speak as well. Drummed out of town, Israel and Naomi are helped by country people and settle in a cabin built earlier by 'a renegade Irishman' who escaped at Gibraltar from the ship transporting him to Australia. Israel cultivates the land round their cabin and they live in rural bliss. There is a moving and sympathetic description of how gaining her sight affected Naomi and how she adapted to the change.

Israel watches his burgeoning daughter: 'a beautiful phantom of Naomi's future would rise up before him. Love would come to her. The great mystery, the rapture, the blissful wonder, the dear, secret, delicious, palpitating joy.' This quintessence of romance is at the heart of all Hall Caine's fiction.

Ben Aboo discovers Israel's hiding place, captures him and throws him into prison. When she finds what has happened Naomi sets out to take him food but she too is captured and taken to Ben Aboo. The book opens with this scene and a visiting Englishman catching a glimpse of a beautiful and apparently English girl (her mother was English) being dragged to the Kasbah, and tells her story in flashback. Caine had historical precedent for this mixed marriage. In 1884 the Grand Sharif of Wazan had married an Englishwoman. He had freed the slaves and carried out other reforms but his opponents harried him and forced him to leave the country for France. In the book the Englishman falls instantly and passionately in love with the unknown girl. A Spanish army attacks the town and again Caine had historical precedent for his tale—there had been many battles between Spanish cavalry and the Moors since 1844. In the fictional account the Kasbah is burnt, the hated Ben Aboo is stoned to death by the mob and the Englishman rescues Naomi. They escape together to the cabin where Israel, released from prison, lies dying, the Scapegoat in the desert. They arrive in time for the old man to recognise his daughter and to commend her to the Englishman who promises to marry her and take her to England. Israel dies happy as the people of the city, having found he was in the end their benefactor, arrive to honour and to bury him.

The book was a critical success but worried Heinemann as it did not sell as spectacularly as *The Bondman* had. It went well enough, however, to run through four reprints in the first year, and then continued to sell steadily in one-volume form for a long time, although it was never dramatised or filmed. Evidently Caine had made good use of his three-week stay in Tangier. V. Abrahams, thanking Caine for a copy of the book, said, 'Jewish readers are unanimous in approval. My cousin, a young man born in Morocco where he has passed much of his life, pronounces the novel a marvellously life-like picture of Moroccan scenes.' Someone else (with an illegible signature) who said he was from Morocco wrote praising the book as accurate apart from one or two minor points. Caine had got the feel of the country and used translations of Arabic expressions beautifully.

The Scapegoat was the first of his novels to bring him a considerable correspondence. Not all of it was as pleasant as the above. Some letters were anonymous, some abusive. He was shocked by their viciously anti-Semitic tone and indeed of that of some reviews. One unnamed critic wrote, 'Who cares about these nasty Jews? Who will read this trash? The Jews are a doomed and d-d race, let them perish with this detestable book which we reserve the right to slate.' Another, more serious and showing some knowledge of the subject, advised the author, 'Embark, then, for Russia, develop your experiences, evolve a new epic of humanity. A stern people is purging itself of an alien element which, like an interminable tape-worm, has for some time past been preying upon and draining the internal vitality of its populace.' Some of the letters came from Germany. When Caine went to Berlin he was disturbed to find the level of anti-Semitism there as bad as anywhere. It was a relief to turn to letters calling down a blessing on him for what he had tried to do.

CHAPTER FIFTEEN

Now that he was living in Keswick one might expect Caine to produce another Cumbrian novel. Instead he spent the rest of 1890 working on three lectures he was to give on the history of the Isle of Man. He had plenty of unused research material and a fascination with the past of his father's homeland. Heinemann wanted a book a year but having no theme for a novel he buried himself in his 'History'. The lectures were given at the Royal Institution in Liverpool on 22 and 29 January and 5 February, 1891. Heinemann published them as a book with the title *The Little Manx Nation* in June. Caine dedicated it to T.E. Brown who had given him so much information on Manx legends and ballads.

The portrait painted of the Isle of Man is an affectionate one but, as the title indicates, rather patronising. It is not a dispassionate history—facts are presented as Caine saw them. This is particularly true of the chapter on Illiam Dhone, 'Brown William', as William Christian was known. To many of the native Manx he was—is—a martyr and national hero, to others, including Caine, a traitor. He certainly betrayed his employer, the Countess of Derby, at the time of the Civil War, and is said to have turned his coat as often as the Vicar of Bray, but the argument advanced in his favour is that he did it in an attempt to free his native land from the grip of English colonial rule. He was shot on Hango Hill, by the sea at Castletown, when a pardon was already on the way from London. Tragically, it arrived too late. The event is still commemorated each year at Hango Hill in early January. Caine's taking the 'English' viewpoint over Illiam Dhone was another black mark as far as the Manx were concerned.

At one point he says, 'It is an odd thing that woman plays next to no part whatever in the history of the Island. Surely ours is the only national pie in which woman has not had a finger.' This reads oddly given that women were given the vote, on a limited franchise, in the Isle of Man in 1882, though the successful campaign was organised by two English women. Their aim was to show that the skies would not fall if women voted so that the British Government would soon follow suit. However, it was 1918 before the London government accepted votes for women and 1928 before they won the full franchise.

A copy of *The Little Manx Nation* was bought in July, 1891, by 'A. Kelly', who signed his name on the flyleaf. As Kelly is to the Isle of

Man as Smith is to England it is impossible more than a hundred years later to say who he was. At the head of the chapter on Illiam Dhone he wrote, 'Read carefully and above all consult other and greater authorities, few of whom would endorse this indictment. It is difficult for a Romancist (or Novelist) to be a true <u>historian</u>. Consult Train.' It would seem Mr Kelly had not bothered to read the dedication in which Caine says that apart from Brown his main source had been Train, 'our only accredited chronicler'.

After the lectures he took Mary and Ralph to London, renting a house in South Hampstead near several of his friends, including William Sharp and Mackenzie Bell. Lily stayed with them while once more rehearsing for the tour of a new play. (She made her London début in a leading part the following year.)

Overwork was catching up on Caine. He was bothered with bronchitis and elected to take his usual medication of 'a change of air'. He went back to Tangier on his own, staying this time at the Continental Hotel. Soon after he sailed a tremendous storm broke out which lasted for several days. His father wrote crossly that he should have telegraphed his safe arrival and not left his parents to read in the papers of the SS *Mirzapore* reaching Tangier after a rough voyage. At home there was heavy snow. Lily, heading for Exeter with the theatre company, was snowbound in a train overnight. She wrote from Plymouth on 16 March that the town had been 'cut off from the world for a week... My landlady here asked me was I related to him as wrote *A Son of Hagar*. Because she saw me with a pen in my hand she thought I <u>must</u> be.'

While her husband was away Mary took Ralph to see her family. She wrote from Newington Causeway, near the Elephant and Castle. There is no direct evidence that she maintained contact with her mother but this could well have been her home. Mary did keep in touch with her younger sister, Jenny, who later married a man named Mandeville and lived in South London. Mary was glad to tell Caine that 'our darling's cough is much better but I dare not let him out of his room yet'. She was giving him 'strong beef tea', that great Victorian nostrum. She also mentioned the heavy snow and said she did not know how she was to get home.

In Tangier Caine met the Mahdi again, as well as other local leaders. In 1889 rebel Moorish tribesmen had murdered a number of people connected with a British-owned factory at Cape Juby. In August, 1890, the Sultan defeated the rebel tribes and allegedly beheaded many prisoners. Just before Caine arrived, the Sultan agreed to pay the British Government £50,000 reparations for the British deaths. The able ambassador, Sir William Kirby Green, who had negotiated the deal, died suddenly on 25 February. His replacement was Sir Charles Euan Smith, with whom Caine dined. In places the country was still turbulent.

Caine never wasted time on pure holiday-making. In Tangier he gathered material for articles which he telegraphed to London papers.
Mackenzie Bell saw one of them and wrote that he was sorry Caine had
formed 'so poor an opinion of the internal state of the country. But I am
not surprised. My own conclusions were the same. Owing to international jealousy there is little immediate hope of better government in
Morocco. Do you find that your "Mahomet" is known, and, if so, do you
go much about in dark streets at night?'

Back in London again Caine was involved in committee work. He had
for a year or two past been on the committee of the Authors' Syndicate,
with Walter Besant, Jerome K. Jerome and Maurice Colles. He was now
persuaded to join the Society of Authors, which had been founded by
Besant in 1884, and was soon on their committee too. He remained a
member, active for much of the time, until his death.

Even when he was not writing novels he wrote stories for magazines
and newspapers, including a serial called *St Bridget's Eve* which
Tillotson's placed for him. He was much in demand. The future Lord
Northcliffe, then still plain Alfred Harmsworth, wrote from 107 Fleet
Street, 'I am afraid I shan't capture you but faint proprietor never won
crack author so here goes.' He offered £160 for a 30,000-word story in
eight parts. He suggested this length hoping to tempt Caine from his short
stories. If his price was too low he would have to wait 'and come at you
again some years hence when I can better afford you'. He was 'delightfully ignorant' as to whether the £160 he was offering was a good or bad
price but it was the most he could afford to set aside for the fiction part
of his plans for a new kind of journalism which he would like to discuss
with Caine one day. Whether or not Caine accepted this offer, in due
course Harmsworth was well able to afford him and Caine wrote many
stories and articles for his papers. The two became good friends.

During the summer of 1891 Caine arrived in Edinburgh to see Irving
and Bram Stoker on tour. After a performance they had supper and
talked for hours. Caine said if Shakespeare had had modern theatre
equipment he would not have needed to put in his long descriptive passages. Irving retorted drily that it would be good for modern playwrights
if they learned a few lessons from Shakespeare. From the Bard they
turned to what Stoker called 'weird subjects'. Caine told an eerie story
of looking in a mirror and seeing a reflection not his own. They bandied
tales of the occult until four in the morning.

In September Caine met Dr Adler, the Chief Rabbi and chairman of
the Russo-Jewish Committee. Adler, who had been favourably impressed
by *The Scapegoat*, asked him to go on the Committee's behalf to look
into the situation of the Jews in Russia and Poland. There were terrible
pogroms going on, many Jews were fleeing from Russia and Dr Adler
was sure no Jew would be admitted to that country. Also the Committee

had raised a large sum of money which it sent to Russia to fund schools for Jewish children. They were anxious to find out how this money was being used. Dr Adler suggested that Caine, with his known sympathy for the Jewish cause, might find material for a book that would help them, but was insistent that no word of any connection between the Committee and any novel Caine might write should get out. Caine discussed the project with Heinemann, who was enthusiastic and promised help with setting up the journey. He suggested Caine should first spend some time in Germany and Austria to look at the problem of the Jewish refugees. Heinemann had many connections there and gave Caine a number of introductions, including one to Count Tolstoy in St Petersburg.

Word got out and stories appeared in the press with talk of the proposed book, nearly wrecking the project. Caine offered 'Letters from Russia' to various papers—the editor of the *Daily Graphic* was one who accepted—but this angered both Dr Adler, who wanted no publicity until after Caine returned, and Heinemann, who thought such premature announcements could lead to the Russians calling off his trip altogether. He wrote furiously to Caine telling him not to write letters to anyone, nor promise them. One of the first stories appeared in the *Manchester Evening Mail* on 25 September. It said Caine had agreed to go to Russia at the request of Dr Adler to investigate the condition of the Jews 'and it is presumed he will write a book on the subject'. On 10 October the *Illustrated London News* published an article headed 'Mr Hall Caine's Mission to Russia'. This was even more dangerous from the Russo-Jewish Committee's point of view as it recalled the part that Harriet Beecher Stowe's *Uncle Tom's Cabin* was reputed to have played in ending slavery in America and mentioned the treatment of Jews in Morocco. Caine's usage of the subject in *The Scapegoat* had, they said, been much praised 'by the most intelligent and influential members of the respectable Jewish community in London'. The Committee were looking to Caine's 'candour and veracity' to find out the truth about Russia's treatment of its Jewish population and use the power of his pen to bring it to a wide readership.

The source for these reports was probably Caine himself. Perhaps not directly, but if he talked indiscreetly it would soon have been passed on. The article said Caine would go to Russia free from any commitment and had 'declined to write any special newspaper correspondence' but Dr Adler was furious. He threatened to remove his support if anything more was said. After his return Caine told the papers he had sold the idea for a novel based in Russia and received an advance but when he had seen the country and realised its vastness and its problems he had felt inadequate to cope with the subject and abandoned it. Behind the scenes Dr Adler was insisting he should not write any such book.

Now he was famous Caine was news. With his talent for publicity he was seldom loth to be interviewed. Articles about him had appeared in the Liverpool papers for years. From the appearance of *The Bondman*, however, the stories came thick and fast and were seen in national papers. Not everything came from interviews with Caine or was even sanctioned by him. For years to come he complained about the untruths the papers wrote about him, putting words in his mouth. One amusing example comes from 1891 or 1892—the cutting in the family papers carries no masthead or date. It is a brief review of Caine's career and is illustrated by four photographs claiming to represent him at the ages of 6, 25, 33 and 38. The last two are clearly pictures of Caine but the one at 'age 6' is not of him at all but Ralph. He had brought the child an embroidered Moroccan robe and a round, tasselled cap from Tangier and had him photographed wearing them. Photographers reckoned to make money out of pictures they took of celebrities then as now and the less scrupulous did not bother to seek permission. Whichever magazine it was that got hold of this picture of Ralph immediately jumped to the conclusion that it showed the Great Author himself as a child. The second picture, 'age 25', is not of Tom either but his brother Willie. There is a family resemblance but it is obviously not the same person as the last two pictures. In black and white Caine's red hair photographed very dark, almost black. The second picture is of a fair-haired man with no beard.

Newspaper reports were still suggesting up to November that Caine would be leaving for Russia shortly. Two things delayed his start. One was another bout of illness, the other the birth of his second son on 12 September, 1891. They called the boy Derwent, the name Coleridge had given his younger son. A few days before the birth Caine took Ralph down to his grandparents in Liverpool. He himself paid a brief visit to the Isle of Man. An intriguing puzzle remains as to where else he may have gone. On 28 September George Meredith wrote to say he hoped to leave in a day or so 'to go with you to Tunis and have my feast of oriental colour'. If he thought Tunisia was the Orient his geography was unsound. There is no proof as to whether or not the Tunisian trip took place but Meredith was by this time prematurely aging and already feeling the effects of the spinal trouble that only a few years afterwards paralysed him. It seems unlikely that he would have been fit to make such a journey but Caine could well have invited him to go along and then abandoned the plan when Meredith was not up to it.

Mary wrote to her husband in Liverpool asking him to 'bring home a pretty swing-cot' for the baby. Had Caine bought Ralph 'an overcoat and a Mackintosh? You see what it is to be the father of two boys.' Leaving Ralph in Liverpool Caine went to stay with Bram Stoker in Chelsea. Heinemann planned to reprint *The Scapegoat* in a one-volume edition.

Caine worked at high pressure to revise the book. He was delighted to find, when he saw Heinemann, that 6000 copies had already been subscribed. 'Stoker has been most kind about the business matters,' he wrote to Mary, 'getting me better terms. I am to remain with Heinemann.' There had evidently been further shopping requests, as he asked anxiously how much a baby carriage for 'Babs', their pet name for Derwent, would cost!

He was longing to get back to Hawthorns—'London is very trying.' How trying was proved by a 'nervous collapse', possibly a severe migraine attack, as soon as he arrived home. Caine often dramatised the state of his health but he could well have been exhausted with over-work and the emotion of the arrival of the second baby. He was back on his feet by 22 October and registered Derwent's birth. The papers reported alternately that he was about to leave for Russia and that he was too ill to go. He was well enough to go to London in November, however, as he dined with Irving and Stoker in the Beefsteak Room after the show on the 19th. It was a quiet night with only one other guest present, the musician Alexander Mackenzie, the principal of the Royal Academy of Music. Caine took Ralph, aged eight, with him. Eyebrows were raised but Stoker comments that the boy was quiet and well behaved and no one took exception to his presence. Caine used every possible opportunity to put his boys forward from then on. Doting on them both himself, he took it for granted that everyone would be glad to see them on all occasions. After Mackenzie had left he told Irving and Stoker the outline of a novel to be set in Cracow and said he intended going there during his forthcoming journey. Irving was 'hugely inter-ested', seeing the possibility of a play on the subject, but none was written.

Caine arranged to start for Russia immediately after Christmas. However, in December a terrible famine began there which led to riots and the organisers of his visit thought it would be wiser to wait. Left at home in Keswick Caine worked on a number of journalistic assignments and on a new book, *Cap'n Davey's Honeymoon*, a collection of three stories due out the following autumn. Maps and books about Russia piled up as he did the necessary background research before setting out. For some reason hard to fathom his handwriting changed completely. Up to that point it had been well formed and legible. Overnight it turned into a tiny crabbed script that became increasingly illegible as he grew older.

Even so far from London journalists beat a path to his door. One came from the magazine *Black and White*, which was edited by a London friend Oswald Crawfurd, in March, 1892, though the article was not published until 23 July. The reporter was Raymond Blathwayt, an old friend from Caine's Liverpool days. He brought with him an artist,

Arthur Tucker. The two of them stayed at Hawthorns for several days. Tucker drew a view of the house and the scene from the study window. He also drew Caine's study showing the William Morris chair and a chair of Rossetti's. The paper used a photograph of Caine taken by the up and coming Keswick photographer G.F. Abraham, later to be famous for his photographs of the Cumbrian mountains. Blathwayt commented that it was not in London that one saw the real Hall Caine.

> He is a son of the people...and coming of the soil in a more literal sense per-haps than is the case with any other notable man of letters now living. The peasant and the student, the man born to write books, and yet half fitted by nature for the life of the hills, a certain ruggedness of exterior (loosely, almost untidily, dressed) with a real delicacy of physique, the head of an Elizabethan, having a perfectly startling resemblance at some moments to the portraits of Shakespeare—it is certainly a curious and striking blend of personality.

Caine had written a play and he read it aloud in the drawing room one evening, wearing his dressing-gown—a Moorish djellabah—and looking 'as unlike a modern Englishman as any such could be, frequently passing his long fingers through his long hair upwards from the forehead and reading with strong feeling'. Many people commented on this gesture of pushing back his hair, including Stoker. His reading reminded Blathwayt of hearing Mark Twain read his own work. 'His voice, like the written style of his best books, seems to tingle with passion at the great moments.' The reading went on for an hour and a half, the audience consisting of Mary, Lily and Ralph apart from the two visitors. 'I wish I could be free to speak of the play,' said Blathwayt. 'All I can say is, wait, there's something coming, and if I know chalk from cheese it's something worth waiting for!' Going by the date this was most likely the 'Mahomet' play which never reached the stage. Heinemann printed only 600 copies of what he called 'your Prophet pamphlet' and even then advised Caine not to talk to the papers about it.

The most surprising revelation Blathwayt made, one he was sure his readers would not be prepared for, was that Caine had been working for several years on a Life of Christ. 'I read some of it and saw its *raison d'être* instantly. It was to present the personality of Jesus as vividly, as realistically, as closely as any great figure in modern biography; or, not to put it irreverently, as any grand figure in serious romance.' The astonished Blathwayt asked when the book would appear. Caine shrugged. 'Years hence, if at all—the public wants me as a novelist, and not as a prophet.' How right he was.

Caine was far from being alone in his choice of subject. It seems as if half the Victorian population was engaged in writing books about their own particular view of Christ. For instance, Mrs Sarah Heckford, a philanthropist and traveller, had, in 1871, written *The Life of Christ and its*

Bearing on the Doctrines of Communism, urging her readers to discard the dross but 'keep the real gold which is the heart of Communism'. As early as 1849 Millais had caused a furore with his painting, *Christ in the House of His Parents*, showing the Christ Child as an ordinary boy—no halo—with his carpenter father at work, the scene drawn in loving Pre-Raphaelite detail down to the wood shavings on the floor. Caine, who with his affinity for the Pre-Raphaelites must have known this picture together with Holman Hunt's *The Scapegoat*, took the same line.

It may be that in making this disclosure to Blathwayt, an old friend whose sympathy he could count on, he was trailing his coat to see if anyone would react favourably to the idea. If this was his intention it failed. Friends told him to forget it while Heinemann was appalled. The argument rumbled around for some time. T.E. Brown summed up general opinion in a letter two years later to a friend in the Isle of Man.

Hall Caine, he said, had been a great success but he was anxious about him. Brown remembered that some years before Caine had been 'coquetting with a wild notion of writing "A Life of Christ"!' Recently his brother had told Brown he was still determined to do it. Brown wanted to get at him and tell him it would be a terrible mistake. The world expected great novels from Caine 'but a "Life of Christ", a novel! Heaven help us! Yet what could he make it but a novel?' Brown thought that if he went ahead he 'would simply degenerate into a first-class scandal, and be made the bugaboo of the orthodox and the laughing-stock of the scoffers'.

For some time after the appearance of the *Black and White* article publishers, including several American ones, wrote asking when the book would be ready. Newspaper editors were also interested. Although he worked on it for the rest of his life he never published it. After his death his friend Robert Leighton and his devoted secretary put the enormous and barely legible manuscript into shape. It came out in 1937 to a notable lack of interest.

He left Keswick for Russia on 15 June, 1892. He confidently expected to be travelling through the country for at least two months and to be away for three to four but not everything went according to plan. He stopped over with Bram and Florence Stoker in London for a couple of days and at once sat down to write home. His parents and Lily were staying with Mary so she did not lack for company.

'The Jews are very kind and doing all they can,' he wrote to his wife. 'They talk of voting a sum to pay for an interpreter. Tomorrow I am to lunch with [R. Golding] Bright and Jerome. *The Idler* offers £40 for the article I wrote last week. Good pay for 3 days' work, isn't it?' He would let the family know where they could write.

> Keep me well up in all home news. That is what I shall be anxious about—
> nothing else. So don't fail to keep everything right, so that I may be content
> and get through my work. Don't have any fear for me. I have not the slightest
> fear that the Russians will do anything to me. They may turn me back but I
> don't think they will. Remember that all your letters to Russia will be opened.

He went first to Brussels and then on to Berlin, where he stayed at
the Kaiserhof. Heinemann cabled his safe arrival to Mary. The Keswick
telegraph office scrambled it and the telegram read, 'Mr Hall Caine
arrived safely at Bertha', leaving the two girls puzzled as to where he
could be. The promised interpreter, who lived in Lübeck, was not there
to meet him due to a mix-up over dates. This man spoke fluent Russian
and Yiddish, necessary if Caine was to talk to the people he hoped to
see. He also spoke German, which Caine did not, though he later learnt
a little of the language. However, he had several literary friends in
Berlin, including the Russian-born Karl Emile Franzos, who spoke
English. He and his wife had been in London for the launch of the
English translation of his best-seller, *The Chief Justice*, and Heinemann
had introduced them to Caine and Mary. In Berlin Caine discussed
Jewish affairs with Franzos. Baron Hirsch was arranging for Russo-Jewish
refugees to settle in the Argentine. Caine thought the scheme miscon-
ceived and everyone could see it was being bungled in execution.

Were there no Jews left who dreamed of a return to the Holy Land?
he asked Franzos. Very few, was the answer. Franzos poured cold water
on Caine's Zionism, telling him that Palestine was a primitive, desert
country and there was nothing for the Jews there. However, he sent
him to see a Jewish doctor who supported Zionism. Speaking no
German and dressed in his usual untidy manner Caine was mistaken for
a beggar and sent packing! He later told this story against himself with a
rare flash of humour.

He missed his family badly and wrote home almost daily. When no
letters came from Keswick he turned peevish.

> You are indeed a precious lot of beauties! Are you not ashamed of yourselves?
> Where are your letters? Since the letter written this day last week I have not
> had a line from you. And yet I am only 24 hours from London! What will hap-
> pen when I am farther off?... If you knew how I wait for a letter, and how
> when it does not come I am disturbed the whole day you would surely have a
> little more consideration... Write immediately,

he ended on a peremptory note. 'Thursday—Friday—Saturday—
Sunday—Monday have passed without your putting pen to paper! Why?
Why? Why?'

Mary was stung into a prompt and spirited reply.

> It is really too bad of you for writing us such a scolding letter. You may be sure
> that we should write or telegraph if there was anything wrong at home. You

should always take no news as good news... You have been from home three weeks and I must say that I don't much care about being a <u>Grass Widow</u>.

There was more about the children and general family news to cheer him up. Mary's liveliness, her humour and her outgoing personality were a healthy antidote to her husband's seriousness and self-absorption. He was further mollified by letters from Lily and from Willie, saying all was well. Lily told him,

> We all thought it best to sell the calves as they would have taken all the milk the mother gave. Grandpa got the best price for them £1 each—a week old they were... The cow's all right—we're selling six quarts of her new milk per day. Mary made butter on Tuesday last—two and a half lbs of butter in three days and that was supplying the calves as well for they were here then—well done cow!

This domestic news was what Caine needed and he replied at once but with another gap in letters he convinced himself the children were ill, possibly dying. Telegrams rained on Mary who took steps to reassure him. His next stop was Hamburg. Bravely she set out for Germany with Ralph so that his father could see the child was perfectly well. They stayed several days with him in Hamburg. Greatly heartened and at last with his interpreter at his side he set off for Austria and the Russian border. Reaching Breslau he found a letter from Heinemann saying he really must not write to everybody in England telling them where he was. Caine had written to a friend giving his impressions of Berlin and the man had published it. 'You are all the while attracting the attention of the enemy to your acts. For God's sake! my dear fellow, do use more strategy. Let no one in England know where you are except those who really must know.' Heinemann was strongly of the opinion that Caine would see a great deal more persecution of the Jews in Berlin than he ever would in Russia. He advised him to travel south through Hungary to the Black Sea, take a ferry to the Crimea and enter Russia that way. This dismayed Caine as he was aiming for St Petersburg and the promised meeting with Tolstoy but it was not to be. He travelled almost the whole length of the border but cholera was raging and the way to the interior was barred for fear of spreading the contagion.

He saw a number of villages in the Pale and met many pathetic Jewish families, some packing carts ready to move out, others terrified and not knowing what to do. He was touched by the way they met together in intensity of prayer which reminded him of Liverpool in time of cholera when he was a boy. Having seen all he could he reluctantly turned back towards Berlin just as the Germans closed their borders to the Jewish refugees. This shocked him, as did the degree of anti-Semitism he saw in Germany. It struck him as worse than much of what he had seen in Russia—Heinemann had been right. It was an abortive trip and, with no book, largely wasted time. He had seen little of Russia and failed to meet Count Tolstoy though he did see him later. His Russian translators were good—Tolstoy admired his books, as did Gorky. When the latter visited London some years later a grand reception was held for him to meet England's leading literary men, including Hardy, Shaw, Wells, Bennett and Edmund Gosse. Entering the room Gorky glared round the company assembled to welcome him and then demanded, to the embarrassment of his hosts, '*Where* is Hall Caine?'

Caine was back at Hawthorns in September. On 6 October Tennyson died and his son Hallam Tennyson sent him a ticket for the funeral in Westminster Abbey on 12 October. Caine's seat was in the Triforium. The ticket said, 'Gentlemen Only—Ladies Not Admitted', which looks odd to us but in those days ladies did not go to funerals. The ceremony was grand but he thought it less impressive or moving than it should have been. Remembering descriptions of Wordsworth's quiet funeral at Grasmere with a handful of mourners, he wrote an article comparing the funerals of the two Poet Laureates which was published by *The Times* on 17 October, 1892, and much praised. He sent a copy of it to Ruskin at Coniston. It was promptly acknowledged by Ruskin's cousin, Mrs Joan Ruskin Severn. She and her husband had moved into Brantwood to look after the old man who, she said, had found the article most interesting. Ruskin's health was failing and he never wrote himself, even to old friends, 'tho' he is much gratified by your having written to him and giving him the pleasure of seeing your interesting letter, as he does not see *The Times* tho' he reads your stories!' The arrival of a letter from Caine had created much excitement. Gordon Wordsworth, the poet's grandson, who had also been at Tennyson's funeral and was now staying at Brantwood, agreed with all Caine had written.

Although while he was away in Europe and Russia he had been anxious to get home to Keswick Caine stayed on in London after the funeral to work on his new book, *Cap'n Davey's Honeymoon*. Heinemann had had two of the stories for several months with a view to publishing in September that year. However, Stoker, who was editing the book, thought the last part of the title story should be re-written and held it over until Caine returned to do the revision and add a third story as the book was rather short. Heinemann was in two minds about this—he wanted to get something of Caine's out while he was in the news but was not sure that the book as it stood would do. Caine agreed with Stoker and worked hard to revise *Cap'n Davey*. When that was done he wrote a new story, *The Last Confession*. It is an overwrought, emotional pot-boiler. Stuck for inspiration he wrote a thinly disguised account of his second visit to Tangier, using items from his and Mary's letters to each other. There are episodes in this—rather bad—story which were rcused to much better effect in a later book.

He was eager to see Ruskin again and wrote back to Mrs Severn, sending an advance copy of *Cap'n Davey's Honeymoon*. She replied that she would always keep his letter 'amongst my autograph ones!' On Ruskin's behalf she thanked him for the book 'with the pretty inscription. It is such pleasant print and always a treat to him having a new book—and I left him with it to enjoy in his study in his arm chair by a nice fire, on this dull damp day which you have greatly helped to brighten for him.'

Heinemann published *Cap'n Davey's Honeymoon* in January, 1893. It was dedicated to Bram Stoker as follows:

> When in dark hours and in evil humours my bad angel has sometimes made me think that friendship as it used to be of old, friendship as we read of it in books, that friendship which is not a jilt sure to desert us, but a brother born to adversity as well as success, is now a lost quality, a forgotten virtue, a high partnership in fate degraded to a low traffic in self-interest, a mere league of pleasure and business, then my good angel for admonition or reproof has whispered the names of a little band of friends, whose friendship is a deep stream that buoys me up and makes no noise; and often first among those names has been your own. Down to this day our friendship has needed no solder of sweet words to bind it, and I take pleasure in showing by means of this unpretending book that it is founded not only on personal liking and much agreement, but on some wholesome difference and even a little disputation. *The Last Confession* is an attempt to solve a moral problem which we have discussed from opposite poles of sympathy—the absolute value and sanctity of human life, the right to fight, the right to kill, the right to resist evil and to set aside at utmost need the letter of the sixth commandment. *The Blind Mother* is a somewhat altered version of an episode in an early romance, and it is presented afresh, with every apology, because you with another friend, Theodore Watts, consider it the only worthy part of an unworthy book, and also because it appears to be at all points a companion to the story that goes before it. Of *Cap'n Davey's Honeymoon*, I might perhaps say that it is the complement of the other two—all three being big stories of great and consuming love, father's, mother's and husband's—but I prefer to confess that I publish it because I know that if anyone should smile at my rough Manx comrade, doubting if such a man is in nature and now found among men, I can always answer him and say 'Ah, then, I am richer than you are by one friend at least,—Cap'n Davey without his ruggedness and without his folly but with his simplicity, his unselfishness and his honour—Bram Stoker!'

This effusion deeply embarrassed Bram. He was thankful to escape to Scotland for a couple of weeks' holiday at his beloved Cruden Bay, north of Aberdeen, hoping desperately everyone would have forgotten about it by the time he returned to London. A few years later he returned the compliment when he dedicated Dracula to Caine but the form the dedication took—simply 'To my dear friend Hommy-Beg'—looks like a gentle reproof for Caine's embarrassing effort. Dracula has never been out of print, unlike Hall Caine's novels, but the form of the dedication kept the identity of the author's friend secret from most people.

Cap'n Davey was largely passed over in silence. It did not sell and in June 1908 it was being remaindered. The surprise is that it had not been pulped long before.

CHAPTER SIXTEEN

While on the surface all seemed happy and settled at Hawthorns, when Caine returned home at Christmas, 1892, he had been dealt a blow which enraged him and led to furious conflict with his neighbour, Colonel Spedding. There had been arguments over their common boundary before this but now there were plans to build a terrace of tall houses which would not only overlook Caine's house and garden, they would block the view over Keswick Vale he loved so much. He raged but he could not stop it. An idea of moving to the Isle of Man had lurked at the back of his mind for some time. What had prevented him moving there so far was the fear that he would not be able to get to London easily. There was a good train service from Liverpool but 72 nautical miles of unpredictable Irish Sea lay between his home town and the Island. There was also the problem of schooling for his sons. A year or so earlier he had made preliminary enquiries for a country house to rent furnished for six months to see if it would be possible to live there. One house in particular attracted him: Greeba Castle.

It had belonged to Edward Windus, son of Andrew Chatto's partner William Windus. Edward died in his early forties and the house passed to his widow. She did not want to stay on there as their children were growing up and would soon leave home. Caine got in touch with her and they had some correspondence but came to no agreement. Now a year later he wrote again and reopened negotiations, with much haggling over the rent and conditions of tenancy. Was there, he wanted to know, a room 'entirely out of the reach of noise, and a lawn or grass plot where one can sit out in the hot weather to work unobserved by passers-by?' He also wanted to know if the house was 'within reach of a telegraph station'. Mary was anxious about servants. They went across to meet Mrs Windus and look over the house. Back in Keswick the letters flowed once more. Caine found that one wheel of their phaeton was unsound and the harness damaged—the Hall Caines were carriage folk now. Could Mrs Windus lend them her harness and leave 'the dog cart' at Greeba while he had the phaeton repaired? By the end of April everything was settled and on 1 May, 1893, they moved into Greeba Castle for six months.

Many years later Caine told his family that as a little boy, staying with his grandmother in Ballaugh, he had passed Greeba in his Uncle

*Pen and ink drawing of Caine in his study at Hawthorns by Fred Pegram,
1893.*

Pencil drawing of Mary in the drawing-room at Hawthorns by Fred Pegram, 1893.

Greeba Castle in about 1905.

William's cart. Seeing the house, which stands above the Douglas to Peel road, he announced that he would live there one day. As there were no trees screening it from the road then he could well have seen it but his initial letters to Mrs Windus indicate he knew nothing about the house and was vague as to where it was. Castellated but never a real castle, it was built in 1849 for William Nowell, a gentleman from Manchester who settled in the Isle of Man. The architect was a local man, John Robinson, who also built the Bank of Mona in Douglas, now the seat of the Manx Parliament.

There is a legend that William Nowell staked his house on a game of cards and lost. Next morning, when he had sobered up and realised what he had done, he went to the winner and tried to buy it back but the man would not part with it. Whether there is any truth in this story is impossible to prove now but it is true that Nowell bought the land adjoining the Castle on its eastern side and got Robinson to design him an almost identical but slightly smaller house, Greeba Towers.

Caine made a mound of difficulties over the tenancy of Greeba Castle, telling Mrs Windus he had been offered a number of larger and finer houses. Mary hated the place. Stone-built, it was covered in ivy which harboured creepy-crawlies and she said it was like a morgue. She was worried by stories that there had been 'a fatality' at the house and that it was haunted. It was also a sea journey from her beloved London.

Thomas Telford had been left in charge of Hawthorns which was to be let from 1 August. Several of Caine's letters to Telford are in the Keswick Museum. In September he told him, 'We have decided not to remain at Greeba Castle but whether we shall take another house in the island or go to live in London is still quite uncertain.' He told Mrs Windus the expense of their rented London house, 48 Ashley Gardens, which was essential as he had to go to London frequently, was such that he could not afford Greeba Castle as well. After another meeting with Mrs Windus, however, he changed his mind and on 16 September wrote saying he would take 'the house and field' for a further two years, provided Mrs Windus made the roof watertight. At the end of the month he went to London with his family. The Ashley Gardens house was given up and they took a large, self-contained flat in Whitehall Court, which is a substantial block between Whitehall and the Victoria Embankment, behind the Banqueting House. They kept it for several years.

In spite of his assertions that his 'deepest interests' lay in London and that it was where Mary was most at home, Caine made up his mind to go back to the Isle of Man. He had still not been able to come to an agreement with Mrs Windus. Instead of returning to Greeba Castle he took a house in Peel, 4 Marine Parade, a substantial red stone house facing the sea. They were still living there the following summer when the Keswick house was sold. A subsequent owner of Hawthorns changed the name so that when land at the back was sold off for building a row of 'artisans' dwellings', the developer was able to call it The Hawthorns. Caine's old home is now known as Ashtree House.

During the summer of 1893, while renting Greeba Castle, Caine wrote one of his most successful and best-known novels, *The Manxman*. At the end of the year serialisation began in the *Queen*. This landed him in dire trouble with Tillotson's as, despite the agreement he had signed

The Manxman, *cartoon of Hall Caine by Bernard Partridge, published
in* Vanity Fair, *2 July, 1896.*

with them, he had gone over their heads and negotiated directly with the *Queen*, which was one of their clients. He had also made arrangements with a number of provincial papers, including the *Manchester Evening News*, without consulting them. He sent them a short story, 'Little Jan', which they agreed to handle, but it was not the end of the affair and Bram Stoker still had much work to do to extricate Caine from his problems in that direction. Less contentiously, Caine wrote a guide for the Isle of Man Steam Packet Company, *The Little Man Island: Scenes and Specimen Days in the Isle of Man*, published for the summer season of 1894. In April that year he presided at the Shakespeare Birthday Dinner in Fleet Street. In May he joined the Board of Directors of the Authors' Club. Oswald Crawfurd, CMG, the editor of *Black and White* and a former diplomat, was the Chairman.

Heinemann published the *Manxman* on 3 August, 1894. It was an immediate and huge success, already reprinting on the 17th. By mid-September it had sold 34,000 copies. Caine wrote in awe to Heinemann, stunned by the way the money was rolling in, far more than his previous books had earned. By 1913 the book had sold half a million copies and been translated into 12 languages. It was published simultaneously in New York by Appleton's and had an enormous success in the States, making Caine a household name there.

Only four of his books are set entirely in the Isle of Man and this is the second of them. In it for the first time he does not hide in a mythical past time but writes of his own day. There is a dichotomy at the heart of the book in that it has two heroes. There are two young men, cousins and friends since childhood but now aware of differences in their social positions. Philip Christian is the son of the Deemster while Pete Quilliam is the son of a fisherman. Inevitably, as this is a Hall Caine novel, they both fall in love with the same girl, Kate Cregeen, the daughter of a publican who is also a Bible-thumping preacher, Caesar Cregeen.

At the start Pete is the central figure, then he disappears. He is too poor to marry Kate so he goes off to the South African Diamond Fields to make his fortune, entrusting Kate to Philip's care, not realising he too loves her. Kate transfers her affections to Philip, seduces him and becomes pregnant. At this stage Philip Christian appears to be the book's hero. News reaches them that Pete has died in South Africa and Kate prepares to become the wife of the new Deemster—Philip's father has died and he has succeeded him. But the news is false. Kate receives a telegram from Pete saying he is on his way home. Having indeed made a fortune at the Diggings he intends to marry her as soon as he gets back. They meet and 'Kate shuddered with a new fear. It was clear that in the eyes of her people the old relations with Pete were to stand. Everybody expected her to marry Pete.' Philip makes no move. Out of loyalty to Pete, though desperately in love with Kate, he stands aside so that she can marry the man to whom she is pledged, not knowing she is carrying his child. Feeling betrayed by Philip, Kate, in a state of misery, goes through with the marriage.

When the baby, a girl, is born Pete thinks it is his and Kate keeps quiet but in the end things become too much for her and she runs away, leaving the baby with Pete. Gallantly he covers up for her, telling everyone he has sent her away for a holiday. When he does not hear from her he buys a present for the child and pretends its mother has sent it. Philip comes to see him, intending to tell him that Kate has come to him and is being hidden in his house, but Pete, who is illiterate, sets him to write a letter to Kate on his behalf, thanking her for the present 'she' has sent the child. Under protest Philip does as he is asked and then rushes from the house, overcome with remorse.

He is appalled at his own treachery and at what he is doing to Kate. He cannot acknowledge her openly nor can he bring himself to send her away. Eventually he tells Pete she is dead. When Pete wants to see her grave he shows him an unmarked one in St George's Churchyard, behind his house in Athol Street, Douglas. Pete sets about carving a headstone for it. Failing to persuade Philip to acknowledge their love and longing for her child, Kate throws herself into Ramsey harbour in despair. She is rescued and hauled, dripping, into court, charged with attempted suicide, so that the book ends where *A Son of Hagar* began. The man who sits in judgement on her is Philip Christian. At first he does not recognise her and, when he does, conceals it. Kate is consigned to the Island's gaol in Castle Rushen, while Philip is consumed with guilt that he has sat in judgement on the victim of his own sin.

Pete discovers the truth in the end. He surrenders the child and leaves the Island and Kate. Philip stands up before the Governor and Tynwald, confesses and resigns his position as Deemster. He claims Kate and leads her out of Castle Rushen before a crowd of people.

Although it is a love story the main strength of the book is in the portrayal of the two young men, the Deemster and the fisherman. There are some splendid dramatic scenes of which the best is the fishermen's petition to the Governor at Tynwald when Philip averts a riot. This part of the story is based on historic fact. The description of the open air parliament is well done and there is even a touch of humour in the account of Caesar Cregeen selling his long-horned cow, which has started to have fits, at the Tynwald Fair and then being tricked into buying it back with its horns sawn off. There is another strong scene involving Caesar when his inn burns down and he marches round it blowing on a ram's horn, finally gone mad.

Caine's readers may have tumbled to the fact that he used real people and places for his books and the Manx looked round for a local man to fit the part of Pete. One claim to be the model was made by John Kinnish, born in Maughold in 1839. When an illustrated edition of the book was being prepared a photographer went over to take pictures of local scenes. He chose Kinnish's cottage to represent Pete's cottage and most local people jumped to the conclusion that John Kinnish was Pete Quilliam. The author denied it frequently but to no avail and John Kinnish made a cottage industry out of playing the part. Picture post-cards had become a craze and he was often photographed for them in the character of Old Pete until his death in September, 1906. Once the old boy had died Hall Caine wrote a wry and amused letter to the *Isle of Man Times* in which he asserted that he had not even known John Kinnish at the time he wrote his book. He described the idea that Kinnish could have been the original for Pete as 'an interesting fiction'. The man who inspired the character, said Caine, was a friend who had nothing to do with the Isle of Man. The character is a development of Cap'n Davey and he, as Caine had already said, was based on Bram Stoker.

If any Manxman contributed to the character it would have been Joe Mylchreest, 'The Diamond King'. He left his home in Peel at the age of 18 and went to Australia. After some years he moved on to South Africa and struck riches in Kimberley, eventually selling out to De Beers and returning home a wealthy man. His career could have given Caine the germ of an idea—that a young fisherman could go out to the Diggings, as people called the South African Diamond Fields at that time, and return rich beyond the dreams of most Manxmen. Apart from that there is nothing to link the real life Mylchreest with the fictional Quilliam. Picture postcards bearing John Kinnish's photograph were around years after his death and the Manx continued to believe his story, not the author's.

The Manxman is one of Caine's best novels and the most accessible. Anyone coming to his books for the first time would be well advised to start with it. The unity of space compensates for the spread of time it covers. The powerfully sustained narrative is as close to Dickens as he ever came but the tale got him into trouble on the Island. Some of the Manx still hold it against him. He was accused of traducing the Island's maidens. No Manx girl could possibly behave as Kate Cregeen did—they were all chaste and virginal to a girl, it was asserted. Evidently those who made this claim had not looked through their parish registers and seen the number of births entered with only the mother's name. One vicar in the last century pencilled in the names of the boys he thought responsible. In one case he wrote, 'Gone to Australia'!

Caine made much of his friendship with the Peel fishermen. He joined them in their pubs for a smoke and a drink, asking them about their work. They were shrewd enough to know what he was up to but many of them were angry when they found he had used their actual words and their yarns in his books. But when one of their number, known as Charlie the Cox, died in 1894 leaving a widow and several small children, Caine headed the list of subscribers to a fund for their relief. He wrote *A Life Poem*, the story of Charlie the Cox, which was widely published and often recited at amateur entertainments.

The reviews of *The Manxman* must have warmed the cockles of Heinemann's heart. The critics were almost unanimous in declaring it a great novel. Sir Arthur Quiller Couch ('Q'), writing of the book in *The Speaker*, said, 'As I read, I began to say to myself, "This is good"; and in a little while, "Ah, but this is very good"; and at length, "But this is amazing." If he can only keep this up, he will have written one of the finest novels—English or foreign—of his time.'

Robert Barr, coeditor of the *Idler* with Jerome K. Jerome, told Caine he had instructed their critic 'to write a rattling good review of it'. (Which he did, rating it as even better than Hardy's *Tess of the D'Urbervilles*.) Barr had been to New York and on the day he arrived the papers were full of sensational accounts of the suicide of a well-known man,

> because he was in somewhat similar position to one of the principal characters in your story. He had read the book and suicide seemed to him the correct dramatic ending for whatever mistake he had made in his life... 'The Manxman' is, of course, as everybody has said, the greatest literary production of the year, and in fact I should be puzzled to know to what year in the past to go to find its equal.

Lord Rosebery, then Prime Minister, wrote from 10 Downing Street to thank Caine for a copy of *The Manxman*. 'It will rank with the great works of English fiction...consummate skill...art which is pitiless. The delightful originality of Caesar is a drop of water to the tongue. Were there but a single Pete or Caesar left in Mannland I would hurry to the island.' He may not have done so but tourists in droves poured into the Isle of Man to see where the Manxman had lived and loved. In due course they included Queen Alexandra. 'The visiting industry', as Caine called it, had been growing for some time but this novel electrified it. Unpopular as Caine was with many Manxmen even the most churlish would grudgingly admit that his novels put the Isle of Man on the map as a tourist destination.

Caine scored an undoubted triumph with *The Manxman*. George du Maurier's *Trilby*, George and Weedon Grossmith's *Diary of a Nobody*, Anthony Hope's *The Prisoner of Zenda* and Kipling's *Jungle Book* all came out about the same time but Caine outsold them all. The difference is that they are still remembered, whereas Caine is largely forgotten. He even outsold Marie Corelli, thus attracting her undying enmity. Writing from his Cornish home on 8 October, 1894, Quiller Couch admitted he had compared Caine to Marie Corelli. Now he apologised but added a warning about judging work solely by the number of books

G.B. Shaw in 1888.

sold: 'Critics may be amazing asses...but if injustice has been done, it is always the critical few that first perceives it. Wordsworth was at first derided by the general public...but critics reinstated him. And numbers of the greatest writers—to take a single instance, Ben Jonson—live by the suffrages of a very few in each generation.'

However great the success of the book, in the theatre it was another matter. *The Manxman* has the distinction of being dramatised in two different forms. The first version, under its own title, was quickly made by Wilson Barrett and opened at the Grand Theatre, Leeds, on 22 August, 1894, barely three weeks after publication of the book. There was a long provincial tour before it opened in London, at the Shaftesbury Theatre, in November, 1895, under new management. It survived for only 13 performances. Barrett's version was a disaster. He cast the charismatic matinée idol Lewis Waller as Philip Christian instead of Pete and gave him all the good lines, which completely skewed the story. The critic of the *Standard* said the play had 'the almost inevitable faults of a dramatised book: the spectator feels he only half understands what is in progress'. Which was not surprising given that the play started halfway through the book when Pete had already been abroad for several years and Philip was wooing Kate.

Shaw panned the production and Caine wrote to protest. In a reply dated 17 December, 1895, typed in green ink, Shaw said no criticism of his had ever been put forward as a just judgement.

> A play which you have not repudiated, and of which you would have had nearly all the credit had it succeeded, has been put forward at a London theatre as a dramatization of a well-known novel of yours. In my notice of it I said that it was the worst play ever written—the worst that ever could be written—the worst that could even be conceived as unwritten. I cut that out for your sake...and in observance of my own point of honor as a critic, expressed what I did not cut out in such a way as to shew the temper in which I was writing. I did not pretend to be impartial or to have read your book. I said what I thought of it; and I exulted openly, in another article entitled 'Told You So', when the play met the fate it deserved.

He had gained the lowest possible opinion of Caine as an artist. If he wanted to save something from the failure, he had better write a good play. Caine had made the excuse that he had not read the play and did not know how much of his own writing was in it. 'Writing is your business: it is not Mr Wilson Barrett's. Yet you hand your novel over to him to turn into his well-known notion of a drama, with Pete Quilliam as the central figure. Then you allow this to be rehashed so as to make Christian the central figure.' Why had he done this? Was he just a simpleton or merely thoughtless and lazy? Perhaps he did not care what happened in the theatre as long as he got his royalties. 'If so, why should I, the watchdog of the theatre, spare you? You ask me whether it occurs to me that if anybody has been hurt it is you. It certainly has not occurred to me.' The actors and stage staff thrown out of work had been hurt. 'I am not aware that anything has happened to you except the shame which, if you had the artistic conscience to feel, you would not have incurred.' Caine had no right to pity or Shaw's sympathy, nor should he complain about Shaw not having read his novel when he admitted not having read Shaw's review.

> What sort of a man are you?... I could understand your writing to me or to the public to apologize for your gross negligence, and your Esau's sale of your literary offspring to be mutilated by an actor-manager; but to write to me to tell me that you are not angry with me, and to gently reprove me for my injustice to you 'as between man and man' (have I lived to be coupled in this fashion with the author of that confounded play?) is beyond all bearing.

Any fool could write a novel 'though many wise men cannot'. Few people could write plays. 'When you have made enough money by novels to do some work for its own sake—or before that, perhaps, for it is dangerous to wait—write a play yourself, if you can... If you do your best, I shall be civil to you, whether it fails or succeeds. At present you have not the smallest claim to my consideration.'

There was more in the same vein and it could well have killed their nascent friendship but oddly enough it did not. However, it stung Caine into making a better drama out of the book himself, working in collaboration with Louis N. Parker. They gave it the title *Pete* to distinguish it from Barrett's version, making Pete the central character. Mattheson Lang played the title part and his wife, Hutin Britton, Kate. It was far more successful and the Langs played it off and on until 1916.

While *The Manxman* was the great event of 1894 for Caine he was busy with much else besides. A year or two previously Jerome K. Jerome had invited him to contribute to a series he was running in the *Idler* on 'My First Book'. Caine wrote for him an illuminating account of how he came to write *The Shadow of a Crime*, including a description of his stay at Fisher Place with Rossetti. In 1894 Jerome re-issued the series in book form. Caine's contribution has a number of illustrations, including a drawing of himself reading to Rossetti by lamp light. There is a portrait drawing of Caine by George Hutchinson, and also a photograph of him in his study sitting in one of the oak armchairs from Rossetti's home. Mary is shown in her drawing room writing a letter with a toy drum at her feet.

Later Caine said he spent from the autumn of this year until the spring of 1896 researching his next book. He may well have done but it did not occupy all his time. At the end of September he was in Keswick to settle the sale of Hawthorns. Back in Peel he wrote an important lecture which he delivered in November to the Edinburgh Philosophical Society at their inaugural meeting. The title was 'Moral Aim in the Novel and the Drama'. He sought the views of dramatists and authors among his friends. Among those who replied Pinero said he had 'never written on the subject of the moral aim of the Drama—feeling that a great deal too much has been, and is, written about the Drama by those whose business it is to write the thing itself. I look forward with anticipation of pleasure and profit to your Edinburgh lecture.' Henry Arthur Jones said he had read Caine's lecture with 'the greatest interest and agreement throughout. When my essays come out I think you will be struck with the general similarity of our views on these matters... I am just starting a new play—delightful agony!' A PS says 'Christian and not Pete ought surely to have been made the hero of the play?' The opposite conclusion to that reached by other critics.

On 4 December Oswald Crawfurd, as chairman of Chapman & Hall, wrote to say his firm were about to launch a fiction magazine and wanted Caine to contribute to it. Among others he listed Brett Harte, Stanley Weyman and Anthony Hope as already signed up.

> I know that you are at present interested in a periodical of your own, and that you will not therefore be able to write for other periodicals but my admiration, I may almost say my delight, in your work is so great I cannot resist the temptation of at least asking you for a contribution…if for no other reason, to prove to the public my own high esteem of your admirable work.

An ambition Caine had cherished for some time was to relaunch Dickens's magazine, *Household Words*, and it was this that Crawfurd referred to.

The Christmas, 1894, number of the *Christian World* contained a story by Caine, 'The Mahdi: A Story of Love and Race, A Drama in Story'. It was based on the material he had gathered for his 'Eastern play'. Much of it was incorporated fifteen years later in the novel he set in Egypt. He was so pleased with the story he had 100 copies reprinted for private circulation.

Early in the new year he visited Ruskin at Brantwood. He was preparing a magazine article and wanted to question the old man about his boyhood in London. Ruskin, who was now 75, had been his earliest inspiration, the first of his 'demigods', and Caine's admiration of both the man and his work only increased as the years went by. Ruskin's influence on British life and letters was profound and enduring. From Coniston Caine returned to London to rejoin Mary and the children who were staying in Belsize Road, Hampstead.

On St Valentine's Day, 1895, he published a Manx Ballad, *Graih my Chree*, which means Love of my Heart. Despite the title it is written in English—Caine did not speak Manx. It is an eerie story and a fine ballad. Young love is thwarted—the couple part, the boy giving the girl one part of a ring he has broken in half. She promises to join him if ever he sends the other half to her. She waits for years and then marries another thinking her first love must be dead. Sitting one night rocking her baby's cradle she hears her lover's voice and the other half of the ring comes flying in at the window to drop at her feet. He appears and begs her to go with him in his ship and in the end she does. But he, the ship and its crew are ghosts. He had been sailing back to her, his ship full of gold, when it had sunk off Italy in a storm. When the ghost ship reaches the spot it too sinks and the girl drowns.

Caine was not in the Isle of Man for the publication of the ballad. On the evening of St Valentine's Day he had supper with Irving and Stoker in the Beefsteak Room. Irving had just returned from a successful tour of America. Caine had written a narrative poem called *The Demon Lover*, which he thought might make a play for Irving. According to Stoker, Irving 'had a great opinion of Caine's imagination and always said that he would write a great work of weirdness some day. He knew already his ability and his fire and his zeal. He also believed in the convincing force of the man.'

Immediately after that evening Irving and the Lyceum company set out on a tour of the north of England before disbanding for a holiday. Caine mulled over various possible plays for Irving while continuing his usual London life—speaking at dinners, joining committees. In May it was Jerome K. Jerome's Gallantry Fund, inaugurated to provide awards for the 'unsung heroes', the ordinary people who did not get peerages or knighthoods. On 29 May his editor at Heinemann's, Sydney Pawling, took Caine to the Derby. For Caine this was less a day out at the races— he deeply disapproved of gambling—than a research project for the new book. Pawling sent a note of the arrangements which gives a neat vignette of the Derby in the 1890s.

> I hope to call for you quite early tomorrow morning, say as near quarter to 9 as I can manage and we can go down from Whitehall Court together. We shall find it dusty—very—and we are going in old clothes and round bowler hats, so that we can go about among the booths and riff-raff without attracting notice: the drive will be tiring but one sees more of the real traditional Derby by road than rail. We have a landau & shall take food, drink and ice.

During this day out Caine discussed the new book and confessed to Pawling that he was stuck with it. The public argument with Marie Corelli and some press attacks on him were undermining his confidence. He was doing a lot of background research into the London scenes he intended to use but somehow the story would not gel. Pawling wrote a kind letter after he reached home.

> I hope you are now safely back with your face to the sea and happy with all your family around you. I shall be glad to hear more about your new story—its aim, grip and go… As a book it shall have all the help we can give it and critical as your position now is I have no doubt you will again have a great success. It is the people of England—not the press of Grub Street—you are writing for and to and success there is after all the permanent and real one.

He added the hope that after the 'time of stress and storm' they have been having the atmosphere has been cleared 'and we shall hope to be your publishers far on in the next century'. Caine had had an almighty row with William Heinemann over his percentage and Pawling was doing his best to smooth things over.

Another project which yielded material used in more than one book and a raft of newspaper articles was Marriage Law Reform. It was Holman Hunt who drew him into the organised movement. On 29 May, 1895, he wrote a long letter to Caine beginning,

> Perhaps you know what a wicked man I am, in that I married my first wife's sister after I had lost the former some years. Perhaps it adds to my enormity that I am altogether unrepentant and in fact find every reason to glory in the act. But the law as it stands imposes penalties upon my children of the second wife which I am very anxious, as are all in my position, to have annulled, so I make a point of supporting the Society which advocates a change of the law in all practicable manner. The Secretary of this society (entitled The Marriage Law Reform Association) Mr Paynter Allen, now writes to me explaining that in Jersey legislative measures to make this marriage legal are in full progress.

Without knowing the truth concerning Caine's marriage and Ralph's illegitimacy he had struck the one note that would resonate with Caine and ensure his help. Holman Hunt said that if Caine and Revd T.E. Brown

> could express a favourable opinion of the object we have at heart, any existing prejudice would quickly disappear and then we might have every hope of success... If you agree that the present law is foolish and iniquitous I will not scruple to ask you to use your influence in the Isle of Man. It would increase the strength of the arguments against the present anomalous state of the Marriage Law, which make a family, which in the Colonies and dependencies of the Empire are altogether under the protection of the law, illegitimate in the mother country.

This was no new cause: the Marriage Law Reform Association was formed on 15 January, 1851, to work for the introduction of a law such as Holman Hunt wanted. One passed the Commons in July of that year but was thrown out by the Lords. The two houses played shuttlecock with the bill for years, one rejecting, the other passing it. The Lords voted for it in May, 1879, by 101-81, with the Prince of Wales and the Duke of Edinburgh approving it, but the following year it went down in the Commons. However, the majorities against it were getting smaller. By the time Hall Caine joined the Association the bill had twice reached a second reading only to be slapped down by the Lords and that was how things still stood when Holman Hunt wrote enlisting Caine's support. Marriage to a deceased wife's sister did not become legal until well into the twentieth century—neither Caine nor Hunt lived to see it. The two of them discussed it over dinner at Holman Hunt's house in Fulham and found they were in complete agreement.

Caine and Mary took the boys back to the Isle of Man. Whatever the inconveniences he had come to love the Island so much that he was determined to make it his permanent home, if possible in Greeba Castle. Meanwhile he was still renting the house in Peel. On Tynwald Day, 5 July, the Island's National Day when the open air parliament is held at St John's, Caine attended the ceremony. He was reported in the papers as 'being prominently seated on the Mound', the parliament hill. From then on he made a point of being present on Tynwald Day every year if he could possibly get there, often organising house parties for the occasion.

CHAPTER SEVENTEEN

Leaving Mary and the children to enjoy the summer on the beach at Peel, Caine returned to London at the end of July. For some time the problems of copyright in North America had been exercising those who represented authors in Britain. The matter was brought to a head by the news that the Canadian Government was about to enact a Copyright Bill which would have the effect of legalising the pirating of works published in Europe. The Canadian market on its own was not of great importance but the American one was. Publishers there and in London were worried that this much greater market would be flooded with cheap Canadian editions which would be paying no copyright fees. The greatest losers would be English writers. The Society of Authors, with the backing of the Government, arranged for someone to go to Canada to negotiate with the authorities in Toronto for amendments to their 1889 Copyright Bill which had not yet come into force. The man chosen for this delicate task was Hall Caine. He also carried a letter from Joseph Chamberlain recommending him to the Canadian Government.

After talks with civil servants and the chairman and committee of the Society of Authors, which everyone concerned was anxious to keep out of the papers, Caine returned to Peel. Ralph, now 11, was to go with them to America but Derwent, who was only four, was too young for the trip. He was also a handful, given to temper tantrums of epic proportions. His long-suffering grandparents came from Liverpool to look after him. John Caine wrote regular reports to his parents while they were away. In one of them he said Derwent had been good most of the time—'today only in one little temper'!

Caine left Peel for Liverpool with Mary and Ralph on 21 September, 1895, the start of their first visit to the States. (Family letters of June, 1893, suggest that Caine was about to leave for California then but something must have happened at the last minute to stop him going.) Next day they sailed for New York in the White Star Line's RMS *Teutonic*. From the ship he wrote to a friend to say how he hated to leave the Island, 'the sweet little spot', even for a short time. 'The last glimpse of the Island very nearly broke me down. Never have I met in any other place so many staunch and loyal friends, such hearty human sympathy, such warmth of genuine affection.'

*Picture postcard of Hall Caine and his wife with Ralph aged 11
in America, 1895.*

They arrived in New York on the 25th. William Appleton, his New York publisher, was there to meet them. So were the cohorts of the New York press. The crush of reporters anxious to speak to the Great Author frightened Mary while she was thrilled that her dearest Tom should be getting such a great reception. The reporters dismissed Mary as 'a pretty little Englishwoman' apparently much younger than her husband. One of them even had it that 'Mr Hall Caine is travelling with his daughter and his little boy'. Mary was 26, Caine 42. For some obscure reason Ralph, small for his age, was wearing a mortar board with an Eton suit. In the throng it got constantly knocked askew but as often as this happened he straightened it with great aplomb. The Rotary Photo postcard company published a card of the three of them, with Ralph wearing his mortar board, to celebrate the visit.

Before they could leave the docks the press had to be allowed to get their interviews. Caine told those who could hear him that Mr Appleton had invited them to stay at his home at Lake Placid in the most beautiful part of New England. Appleton was a neighbour and close friend of President Cleveland and Caine was looking forward to being introduced. His appearance was vividly described by all the papers with remarks on his lack of inches, comment he was not accustomed to in England. 'The famous Manxman is a short, stocky little fellow, about 5'4" tall at the most, and wears a bristling, reddish beard and moustache and long, yellow, golden hair falling in ringlets upon his shoulders,' said one paper. 'He wore a broad brimmed white felt hat and a suit of light-coloured tweed,' said another, adding that Mr Appleton was tall and thin and 'his shoulders were about on a level with the top of Mr Caine's hat.' *The Deemster*, it was asserted, had had almost as wide a circulation as *Trilby*. 'By its setting in the Isle of Man it opened up a new domain in literature as surely as Scott, Dickens and Thackeray had in their day. His [Caine's] winter house is in London, where he is a social lion. His summer home was for some years in the Lake District, loved and sung by Wordsworth, but lately it has been in a romantically situated villa in the Isle of Man, his own native place.'

Bram Stoker was on a tour of America with Irving, now Sir Henry, and met Caine in New York. Stoker tells the story of how he and Caine joined the great Sunday promenade down Fifth Avenue. Before they had gone far Caine was recognised and a crowd began to follow them. They tried to outpace the fans but their way was blocked when they came face to face with the great pianist Padereweski, who was walking towards them with a friend, hotly pursued by a similar attendant train. They stopped to talk—they both knew Paderewski well from his visits to the Beefsteak Room—and were immediately trapped as the crowd closed in around them. The four of them were only able to escape by ducking into a hotel with the aid of the doorman. After a little while they sneaked out by a side door.

Stoker introduced Caine to Elizabeth Marbury, an influential person in American theatre who headed the Miss Marbury Theatrical Agency and represented Irving in America. She now took on Caine as well. In the course of talks with publishers and politicians Caine found that in America the Canadian copyright demands were seen as just as dangerous as they were in London. A report in *Harper's*, published as Caine arrived, said, 'There can be little doubt that if the absolute right of Canada to legislate upon copyright is admitted by the Imperial Government, the US International Copyright Law cannot long endure and British authors will suffer in consequence.'

Stoker urged Caine and Mary to come down to Boston as his guests to see Irving perform. The papers reported Caine in a box with Ralph at the theatre but made no mention of Mary. Appleton had already assured Caine that sales of *The Manxman* were excellent, 'especially in Chicago', but he lost no opportunity to talk to the press wherever he went. Publicity was the breath of life to him. A long interview in one of the Boston papers described Caine as 'slender and spare, active even to restlessness, but short. His beard is redder than his hair.' He told them he often went four or five days without sleep 'and his old enemy was insomnia'. He pointed out that his son's name was pronounced Rafe, not Ralf.

From Boston they travelled to New England to visit Mr Appleton. Mary and Ralph stayed on there while Caine went to Toronto for the real business of their journey. After much haggling and argument he brought the Canadians round to his way of thinking and an agreement was reached. They had been threatening to withdraw from the Berne Convention but Caine persuaded them not to. There were arguments as to whether artists, sculptors, photographers and photo-engravers, as well as authors, were to be included in the new copyright law. The whole business was enormously complicated. Caine reported to William Appleton who urged him to make no more newspaper comment until the whole matter was settled, which would not be until Caine had returned to New York.

With most of the work done Caine sent for Mary and Ralph. They all had a week or so together in Canada. From Toronto they went to Ottawa, going on by train to New York on 2 December, 1895. They returned to Liverpool as they had come, on the *Teutonic*, sailing at 7 am on 4 December. Caine kept the menu for 8 December, 1895, which must have been their last night on board, labelling it 'Our First Visit to America' above the picture of a White Star Liner in the Mersey. The meal began with 'Oysters on the Half Shell, Olives and Salted Almonds' and went through soup, fish, entrée, roast, a 'remove' of Mallard Ducks and Currant Jelly and Paté de Foie Gras to desserts headed by Plum Pudding, Brandy and Hard Sauce, ending with a savoury—Herring Roes on Toast. Even when one allows for the fact that only small portions were served of each course one wonders how they managed to get through that lot.

During the voyage Caine put the finishing touches to 'Mr Hall Caine's Report to the Society of Authors', intended for publication in the *Author* in January, 1896. From the boat they took the train to London where Caine reported the success of his trip. The agreement he had reached on behalf of the Society of Authors had been submitted to the Dominion Ministers at the Copyright Conference held at Ottawa on November 25, 1895. He could congratulate himself on a job well done but it was some time before the new Copyright Bill was law. They were back in Peel on Christmas Eve.

In the New Year Caine returned to haggling with Mrs Windus over Greeba Castle. Her situation had changed in that she had remarried. Her new husband, a Mr Jacques, lived in England so she was at last willing to sell the house rather than let it. Despite his previously expressed sympathy for her widowed state Caine beat her down until he got the house on his own terms and at his own price. To start with she had asked over £1000 for it. The house was mortgaged and she wanted a profit to hand to her young son.

There was a great deal, apart from his work, to distract Caine from the business of Greeba Castle. Edmund Gosse wrote to him on 6 January, 'Like you, I feel the future to be so vague and so perilously uncertain that I hardly like to make any long engagements. In calmer times you will remember, will you not, that you owe me a slice of your London leisure?' Looking back now the 1890s seem a golden age but to those living then they did not appear to be any such thing. South Africa was boiling. 6 January, 1896, was the day that Dr Leander Starr Jameson surrendered to President Kruger's men at the end of his ill-judged raid into the Transvaal which lead to Cecil Rhodes's resignation as Premier of Cape Colony. The Transvaal and the Orange Free State entered into a military alliance and the German Kaiser sent his famous telegram of congratulation to Paul Kruger which caused outrage in London. Many people thought war in South Africa inevitable. In France the Dreyfus Affair was causing dissension. Italy, which had gone to war in Abyssinia the previous year, suffered a tremendous defeat and was about to withdraw. Trouble too in the Sudan where Kitchener was launching his campaign against the Mahdi. 1896 did not start auspiciously.

On 28 January Gosse wrote again: would Caine be in town on 24 February? If so, would he come to dinner? 'The witty old Bishop of Gloucester and Bristol' would be dining with him that night at eight, and Lord Wolseley had promised to be there also. 'Won't you say yes?'

He could well have done as the whole family were back in London staying at 27 Harley Street, which Caine had taken for a month or two. Lily was getting married. Her husband to be was George David Day, described on the marriage certificate as an author though it has proved difficult to trace anything he wrote. He was 31. Lily's age was given as 24—she was actually 26. The 'Rank or Profession' of both fathers is given as 'Gentleman'! Lily had arranged token lodgings at 25 Hanover Square so that she could be married in her 'parish church', the fashionable St George's, Hanover Square. The wedding took place on 5 March, 1896. Her brother signed the register together with Mackenzie Bell and Charles Warner—he had been a leading actor in London for twenty years, particularly successful in melodrama, and well known in America.

The whole Caine clan foregathered. Willie, who had left Liverpool the previous year, was living in London and running an office set up by a group of Manx businessmen to promote tourism to the Isle of Man. He was also working as a freelance journalist. Everyone else stayed in Harley Street with Tom and Mary. John and Sarah Caine came down from Liverpool as did Lily's cousin Adelaide Teare, who was chief bridesmaid, and her family.

St George's was crowded for the occasion with literary, intellectual and theatrical London, from Dr Adler to Israel Zangwill. The *Queen* and other society papers carried full reports with pictures of the bride and bridesmaids and the bride's going-away gown. Lily is referred to as 'the sister of the author of *The Manxman*', not as an actress. Amusingly, Caine used almost verbatim the description of the ceremony in the *Queen* for the wedding of Polly Love in his next book, *The Christian*, down to the bride and groom standing under an arch of potted palms to make their vows, lilies decorating the chancel and details of the bride's dress, trimmed with Brussels lace.

For the former blacksmith's apprentice from Ramsey, giving his only daughter away in such surroundings, with his famous elder son and an array of notabilities present, must have been a tremendous occasion. He was a dignified old man and would have had no problem with carrying out his part. Sarah Caine found it all a little overwhelming. The society papers said the reception afterwards at 27 Harley Street was hosted by Mrs John Caine 'assisted by Mrs Hall Caine'. Mary, who loved entertaining, was more than happy to help her mother-in-law and behind the scenes do all the organising for her. For 'our Tom' it was a great joy to see his sister so splendidly wed. What Mary thought, as they waved the happy couple off for their Paris honeymoon, about the contrast with her own hole-in-corner wedding ten years before, can only be guessed. Perhaps she did not envy them at all and thought her own far more romantic.

The wedding over, they hurried home to Peel. Caine had kept in touch with Mrs Windus. She had written in an undated letter about the plans her late husband had had for Greeba Castle, admitting it was in a bad condition due to years of neglect. Her husband had mortgaged it for £950 but she was now willing to let Caine have it for £800 if he would send a cheque for £50 or £100 immediately. 'Then it is yours.' This left her out of pocket with nothing to pass on to her son but they signed the agreement on 10 March, 1896. Greeba Castle remained his home for the rest of his life.

Work on the house went on for years. They stayed on in Peel for a few months while structural repairs, including putting the roof right, were done but by midsummer they moved in. Using his early training, Caine was his own architect. The original front door was in the middle of the south front, above a steep flight of steps. One of their first visitors fell down them and broke her arm so Caine ordered the door to be replaced by a large window and the steps removed. A new entrance was made by building a balustraded terrace along the west front—they called it 'the piazza'—approached by a shallower flight of steps. A new front door was installed in place of the window of a small room which became the new entrance hall.

As he had done with Hawthorns and just about everywhere else he lived, Caine set about recreating the gloomy, cluttered atmosphere of Tudor House. It took time. Dark oak panelling was put in throughout the ground floor. An oak beam with an archway was built across the entrance hall and on it Caine carved a quotation from Amiens' song in Shakespeare's *As You Like It*: 'Here Shall Ye See No Enemy But Winter And Rough Weather'. He signed it HC and dated it 1897. He also put in two huge and elaborately carved overmantels, one in the entrance hall and one in his study. He designed them himself from sketches made in Rossetti's home years before. The larger one caused a problem when it arrived by ship at Douglas in an enormous crate—there was no cart on the Island big enough and strong enough to transport it to Greeba so it had to be taken apart.

A large conservatory was built on the side of the house. Double doors with stained glass lights led into it from what was then the dining room. There is more stained glass in the rest of the house. The style is typical of the Arts and Crafts movement but as no bills or correspondence concerning it have turned up one cannot be sure who designed it. Frederic Shields could have been involved but he was ill and unable to work much at this time. Or it could have been designed by the architect Baillie Scott, who was living and working in the Isle of Man then and designed stained glass for houses he built there and elsewhere. William Morris died in 1896 so was not personally involved but Caine and Mary

Cartoon by Harry Furniss (1854–1925).

chose all the carpets and soft furnishings for the house from Morris & Co. The sofa from Rossetti's studio, re-covered in material designed by Morris, was placed in front of the study fireplace.

As Caine's fame spread people came from literally all over the world in the hope of seeing him and if he was away they would just gaze at his house. One excited visitor in 1908 sent home a postcard with the message, 'I have SEEN Hall Caine!' A girl wrote to admit she had been one of a group who had waited by the gates in the rain for more than an hour, hoping to see him come out. She hoped he did not mind.

A succession of journalists interviewed him and wrote articles about 'Hall Caine at Home'. One, who arrived during that first summer of 1896, was Gerald Cumberland, a well known gossip writer. He was there when T.E. Brown called, as he often did. The three men were sitting chatting amicably in the drawing room when a servant announced that a party of twelve Americans had arrived and she had shown them into the library. Caine went to talk to them and give them tea. After an hour he returned looking tired but pleased. It was, he said with a weary sigh, one of the penalties of fame to have to deal with such invasions.

Brown smiled and remarked that Caine was not the only one to suffer from his fame. 'I am constantly besieged by American journalists, who come to me for private information about yourself.' One woman had asked if he was educated! Caine roared with laughter and asked what he said. 'I asked her what she meant by education and she replied "Is he at all like Matthew Arnold?" '

A disturbing letter reached Caine early in June. It was from Bram Stoker, writing from the Adelphi Hotel in Liverpool where Irving was appearing. 'My dear Hommy Beg, There is a matter which I want to ask you about and I write instead of speaking as I wish you to be quite free in the matter.' He was in serious money trouble and needed to borrow £600 urgently. A long-standing debt had been called in rather sooner than expected, he had invested more than he could afford in Heinemann and Balestier's business and then bought the leasehold of his house, using a loan from Coutts. They would advance him no more until he had paid off this loan. 'Now my dear old fellow if you would rather not care to do this do say so freely for I would not for all the world have you let anything to do with money (of all things) come in any way between us.' He only mentioned it 'because you are closer to me than any man I know... Of course if the new book comes out well at all the first money I get will go to pay the debt.' (The book was *Dracula* which must have restored his financial position.) He ended by saying he hoped that if Caine did not care to help him he would still treat him, Stoker, as a friend 'and say so frankly—as frankly as all things have been—and please God ever shall be between you and me. In any case you must not let the matter worry you by a hair's breadth.'

Caine understood completely—he remembered too well being in the same position, though never for so much money. Irving must have been paying Stoker a pittance for him to have got into this state. Caine sent a cheque by return of post and on the 6th, still from the Adelphi, Stoker wrote, 'Your letter is like yourself and that is saying all.' He was not going to say much about it as he knew Caine would not like it but he felt truly grateful. 'I am rejoiced that I was right in thinking or rather knowing that I might speak to you frankly... Believe me my dear old fellow I shall not forget your brotherly kindness.'

They met shortly afterwards in Manchester, the next stop on Irving's tour, Caine staying with Bram in his lodgings. He showed him the scenario of a play on the theme of the Flying Dutchman and a completed new play, *Home, Sweet Home*. Next day they went to see Irving at the Queen's Hotel. Caine read him the 'Dutchman' scenario and outlined the new play. The three went on a carriage drive and discussed both projects. Although he seemed interested at first Irving turned them both down. He said he was too old for *Home, Sweet Home* and while he was the right age for the Flying Dutchman, 'There is no general sympathy on the stage for tall old men'! Caine also told them the story of his new novel. He called it 'Glory and John Storm', a title Stoker thought would not do. In the afternoon they went to Bellevue Gardens, taking Ellen Terry, to see the famous chimpanzee, Jock, who rode a tricycle, ate with a knife and fork and drank port and lemon.

From Manchester Caine went to London. His copyright agreement was threatening to unravel due to political upheavals in Canada. He had urgent talks with the Society of Authors and the government representative in charge of negotiations. It began to look as if nothing would be settled until after the looming Canadian general election.

Heinemann had given him an introduction to someone in Soho and Caine followed it up in his search for accuracy in the background of the new story. He wrote later that he visited all the scenes he intended to use.

> This method of preparation took me into many bright and beautiful places, but also into the purlieus of the publican and sinner as well as the cell of the religious devotee and I saw a good deal in these haunts of the children of darkness that was painful and perhaps shocking... In choosing to present my facts in this form, not for themselves but only as the background to a spiritual drama that is imaginative, I trust I have nowhere done wrong to the purest spirit that may read my pages.

There were places, however, which were closed to him. He was not received in some of the high society circles where Heinemann could go and he appealed to him for help. Heinemann replied he would be happy to supply information on the setting for a big society occasion in the book. He gave Caine a detailed account of the home of a Mrs Mackay in Carlton House Terrace, overlooking the Mall. With it he enclosed plans of the ground and first floor reception rooms and 'the very grand staircase at the top of which Mrs M. receives'. In a later letter he reminded Caine that the house he described for him belonged to Mrs Mackay. Caine's calling the character Mrs Mackie really would not do and he must think up another name. In the completed book he has a description of a grand ball at 'Mrs Macrae's', which was still perilously close, though he placed the house in Belgrave Square. Heinemann's description is all there, down to the very grand hostess receiving at the top of the stairs, the parquet floor, the palms and the chandeliers, but Caine's description of the guests is unkind to the point of being vicious.

Throughout the summer at Greeba Caine worked hard to complete *The Christian*, in time for the start of the serialisation, which began overseas in *Munsey's Magazine* in November. At home it ran in the *Windsor Magazine* from January to June of 1897. At this stage neither editor had seen the completed story and there was a lot of trouble when they found how long it was. Cuts had to be made which upset the author, though they were restored in the book version.

In November, perhaps to take his mind off the business and certainly to earn some ready cash, he set off on a lecture tour of Scotland. The talk, which he gave at Dundee on the 9th, followed by Glasgow, Aberdeen, Greenock and Edinburgh, was billed as 'Home, Sweet Home, (A Spoken Novelette) By Mr Hall Caine, Novelist'. It was more of a one-man dramatic performance than a lecture. Sydney Pawling wrote to say the firm had done everything possible about copyrighting the new book and it would be registered at Stationers' Hall. He added advice about copyrighting *Home, Sweet Home*. Pawling, who was Caine's editor, was working slowly but carefully through the 'printed slips' of *The Christian*. These were proofs of the opening episodes of the serial. 'I can only say at present that I am sure you have touched upon the greatest theme any novelist has ever attempted, and my main feeling is now an intense desire to see and read the development of the characters and possibilities.'

If neither the theme nor the telling of this story are to present-day tastes one can see how powerful a book it was in its time and how it achieved the enormous success it did. The two central characters of Glory Quayle and John Storm are among Caine's best creations. Both come from the Isle of Man though the action is set almost entirely in London. He drew deeply for this book on his knowledge of the seamier side of London life from his time as a journalist. *The Christian* marks his first attempt at metropolitan scenes. From the early books with pastoral settings in Cumbria, through the Manx novels and the Moroccan scenes of *The Scapegoat*, he moves on now to high life in the big city and therein lies its weakness. Most critics agree that so long as he stuck to peasant characters—fishermen and the kind of people he really knew—his work had merit but when it came to portraying society folk and the wealthy upper classes his touch was far less sure.

The Christian did nothing for his popularity with the Manx people, who resented his portrayal of a Manx girl giving up her worthy work as a nurse to go on the stage and her treatment of John Storm. She is described as a redhead. To readers of Victorian romance red hair was a code for 'no better than she ought to be', in the phraseology of the day. Though decorous to us, Hall Caine's frank treatment of sex worried his fellow islanders, and, to be fair, others as well. In his delineation of the clergyman John Storm, Caine gives a moving study of a tormented man sinking into religious mania.

He was often accused, not without a grain of truth, of putting his friends and even his family into his books. His account of Glory's trials at the hands of a shady theatrical agent and her struggles for engagements and success reflect his knowledge of the theatre of the 1890s and his friendship with such people as John M. East and Wilson Barrett. He also drew on his sister's experiences. Lily made her first recorded appearance on the London stage in 1892 and later appeared in several of her brother's plays. His telling description of a rehearsal in a seedy theatre is clearly drawn from life—probably one in which he was involved as author. He was a good reporter of what he actually saw. The character of Glory Quayle owes a lot to Lily, although she played Glory's friend, Polly Love, in the first London production of the stage version. Later she appeared as Glory Quayle on tour.

Some people took exception to the ending of the book. There was uproar at the apparent implication that Glory slept with Storm before their marriage. John Storm, on the edge of madness, goes to Glory's rooms with the intention of killing her to save her soul from damnation. It is late at night but she is not there. He waits for her but when she comes home, far from killing her he declares his love. Many people read it as saying that the two of them had sex that night. It is certainly the impression the scene gives today, backed by the account of Storm's agonised wandering about London next day, but Caine furiously denied that he had intended any such interpretation. He could never have suggested that they went to bed together before they were married—such a thing could not occur. Guilty conscience, perhaps.

CHAPTER EIGHTEEN

In the spring of 1897 Caine and Mary were staying in Wimbledon. Caine proposed a visit to Shields, who was living at Merton. 'Whether "we" means your good wife and yourself, or your brother, I shall be most glad to see "we" whenever you please to turn up,' Shields replied. He had been stuck in bed for weeks with an unpleasant leg ulcer. It is interesting that a close friend could not take it for granted that 'we' meant Caine and Mary.

While they were away the grandparents stayed at Greeba Castle to look after the boys. In one letter to his son John Caine said that Derwent had gone fishing 'and taken Mother with him'! Ralph was educated at home until he was 12 but had been a boarder at Ramsey Grammar School since the previous September. The Headmaster, A.S. Newton, wrote after Ralph had returned from the half term holiday in his first term that the boy was working hard and his conduct was exemplary. As a reward he was allowing him to sit up till 9.30 'for recreational reading and conversation'. Ralph seemed happy and went to Ramsey on his own by train with no problem while his grandfather was in charge. However, after his parents returned he started whingeing and whining and refusing to go. Mary had to travel with him to get him back to school at all. As soon as his grandfather heard about this he wrote, 'I hope when he returns home you won't make any fuss of him. He cannot stand it. Be firm and come with little notice and if he whimpers to go threaten him with a stick to his back. He is too big now to have Mary trouble with him.' Ralph was nearly thirteen that summer term. In September, 1897, he transferred to King William's College at Castletown, where he was in School House.

From the start of *The Christian* serial in January of that year, letters began to pour in. Caine received more correspondence concerning this book than any other he wrote. Much of it was fan mail praising the book in extravagant terms but many other letters pointed out his mistakes. One man wrote presciently, 'I see that this is going to be an eye-opener to many, consequently it will bring you many enemies.'

There were indignant letters from doctors and nurses pointing out where he had gone wrong. One letter said delicately, 'Have you not made slips in clinical matters?' The silliest he made was to have the nurses at his fictional hospital (clearly modelled on Bart's—he even calls it 'St Barthimaeus') hold their annual ball in the operating theatre. 'Oh, shades of Lister!' said one critic. Caine took note of this and when the book appeared the nurses' ball had been shifted to the lecture theatre. However, some of his errors were fundamental—there was no possibility that things could have happened as he wrote them. They could not all be corrected or there would have been no story left: he would have had to tear it up and start again. Given that the serialisation had begun and the book was with the printers that was not an option. However, despite the mistakes most readers loved the book and took Glory Quayle and John Storm to their hearts, writing of them as if they were real people, a credit to his characterisation. Caine answered all the letters of criticism, usually asking humbly for more detail so that he could put things right before the book version appeared.

One of the scenes Caine had visited in the course of his research was the West London Mission in Soho. It had been established by the Wesleyan Methodists in Fitzrovia, Marylebone and Soho in response to the general social distress of the period, working in much the same way as Toynbee Hall and the Women's University Settlement. Its first leader was Hugh Price Hughes. As the work developed it became more associated with the problems of prostitution. Price Hughes's wife Dorothy founded 'The Sisters of the People' whose aim was to rescue girls and women from the streets. This was the part of the work which Caine particularly espoused and he gave a lot of money to it over the years. Eventually Mrs Price Hughes was able to set up a 'rescue flat' in the heart of the West End with her Sisters in charge. It was a refuge to which girls could go and be protected from their pimps, an early example of a 'drop-in centre'. It was rumoured that Caine had in fact bought the flat and presented it to the Sisterhood. He may well have done although there is no proof.

The 'Woman Question' in general absorbed Caine's attention and coloured much of his writing. As people understood it in the 1890s it was not just a matter of the suffrage. It covered the whole field of woman's position in society: equality (or inequality) with men both sexual and intellectual, marriage, prostitution, equal opportunities in business, the professions and the arts. There was much solemn debate on whether or not women should expect to be completely fulfilled by marriage and child-rearing and whether or not they had any right to enter the world of men. By the 1890s the New Woman, complete with bicycle, had arrived on the scene but the 'Woman Question' had not been settled. A century later it still has not been—only changed in emphasis.

In *The Christian* Caine highlighted the problems a young woman— Glory Quayle—encountered in trying to live an independent life and follow a career. This aspect was brought out more in the various versions of the play than in the novel. A noted feminist of the time, Sofia Bevan, wrote to him on 7 November, 1897, thanking him for the way he had taken up the Woman Question. *The Christian* was a book which should be read by all young people. They should be made aware of 'the depressing circumstances which surround a woman's life' if they were to work out their own salvation. 'It is easy to see that the Woman Question is the man's question also: the future of the race depends upon its right solution.'

This was the first of his books in which Caine tackled the Woman Question head on, though heavily sugar-coated with romance and melo-drama. His good friend and fellow writer, Robert Leighton, enjoyed it immensely. 'There is gigantic force and virility in "The Christian". Glory is splendid. Storm is absolutely right and firm, a perfect Man.' He had no doubt that it was by far Caine's greatest work. Everyone, he said, was talking about it. 'People don't buy the Windsor Magazine, they buy "The Christian".'

A great many clergymen wrote to Caine, most of them commenting on errors in ecclesiastical matters. The only clergyman who gave the book an entirely favourable review was Dean Farrar, the Dean of Canterbury and a former pupil of King William's College.

Altogether he was not short of advice: someone writing from Port Said pointed out that he had got the titles of his aristocratic characters wrong. By and large the clergy wrote more in sorrow than in anger though a few sounded very cross indeed. Most liked the story. They wanted it to succeed and not be laughed out of court for silly slips. Several old Liverpool friends wrote in praise, one saying how John Caine was enjoying all the excitement. Doctors and, especially, nurses were the ones who protested most. Caine was accused of defaming the noble profession of doctor in his description of the conduct of young house-men at the hospital. However, in a letter from Glasgow one doctor said many surgeons did behave as Caine described.

> In one of the large infirmaries of this city the house surgeons were one year a particularly jovial lot. On one special night they passed a merry evening with a doctor friend from the infirmary of a neighbouring town. So merry were they that he missed the last train and had to be brought back by them to their own quarters. These they reached about half past eleven in a cab which one of them, a prominent minister's son who was pretty 'far gone,' insisted on driving round the infirmary square, at the same time howling lustily. This was a by no means uncommon occurrence and what the effect on the patients would be can be readily imagined. You may make what use you like of this so long as you do not mention my name!

Caine used this scene in the book.

As publication day approached a flurry of letters from both Pawling and Heinemann brought last-minute corrections. Heinemann thought the book 'magnificent and great—how great I will only say when I have read it again'. News from America was excellent, Caine was 'very strong' there and Munsey pleased with magazine sales. The Bishop of New York sent an appreciative letter which Caine offered to Heinemann for publicity. Pawling said they would keep it in reserve for use if 'any so-called religious papers' took exception to the book. 'We could then set up against that the Bishop's charming note. It is well known that he is one of the most saintly [crossed out and 'influential' substituted] men in America.'

On Saturday, 7 August, 1897, a 'copyright performance' was given at 11 am at the Grand Theatre, Douglas. It was a reading rather than a proper staging and the cast consisted of Caine's family and friends. The tickets were an exorbitant £1 but the theatre was well filled with both visitors and locals curious to see the Great Author. Caine himself read John Storm while Lily read Glory Quayle and Mary was Polly Love. Master Ralph Hall Caine read Brother Andrew. A surprise member of the cast was William Heinemann who read the Father Superior. Two days later the novel was published simultaneously in London and New York.

Caine sent Gladstone an advance copy. On 11 August he replied from Hawarden Castle, Chester, congratulating Caine on covering 'things unseen as against those which are seen'. Caine sent him samples of the reviews. Gladstone's comment was, 'I am not surprised to hear that you are run in upon by those whose concurrent notions you have sharply disturbed.'

The reviews were mixed, to say the least. W.T. Stead blasted *The Christian* in the *Review of Reviews*. Caine was furious and upset and wanted to answer back, alarming Heinemann who fired off a telegram to Greeba: 'For heaven's sake leave them alone you can afford to let them bark they won't hurt you and you can't afford to take notice.' The 25-year-old Max Beerbohm was another who panned it. Heinemann followed up his wire with a soothing letter. 'I've had my fling at that little squirt Beerbohm... The book is going magnificently and it's good—very good. So don't you bother and just let 'em howl.' Caine did bother, however, and Heinemann was alarmed to hear his touchy author wanted to reply to the critics in the press and was also seriously considering legal action against one paper which had printed a defamatory article. 'I write to urge you, with all the conviction possible,' said Heinemann, 'that you will make a terrible mistake if you enter the arena.' If a book was sent for review, no legal action could be taken because criticism had been invited. Caine must ignore the critics as Ibsen did. Meanwhile Heinemann wrote to the editor of the offending paper but Caine's ire was not soothed. 'I'll be delighted to be your champion,' Heinemann wrote next day, 'only you must sheath your own sabre.' 70,000 copies had been sold in three weeks and Heinemann enclosed a cheque for

£1000, the second for that amount since publication. Sydney Pawling told Caine, 'The great British reading public is with you', so there was no need to say anything.

On 28 August *Punch* joined in the fun. When *The Manxman* proved a best-seller they had published a cartoon of Caine by Bernard Partridge. Now they published a funny but rather unkind cod coat of arms for 'Hall Caine, 1st Lord Manxman'. Friends took to referring to Mary as 'Lady Caine'. The first quarter of the shield showed 'three human legs conjoined at the thigh and flexed in a triangle garnished and hygienically knickered proper running gaily through several editions'—making fun of Caine's famous knickerbocker suits and the movement for 'hygienic' and 'rational' clothing in which Bernard Shaw was prominent. The second quarter depicted a Christian emerging from a printing press with a flourish of trumpets and the third showed a 'bondman' leading a scapegoat (with spots). The fourth quarter had 'two Manx cats passant with sensational tales aperted'—flourishing tails were shown separated from the animals. The motto was: Through the Press to the Front! The crest consisted of a profile of Caine gazing at a sprig of bay while the supporters were 'an ancient statesman void of guile inveigled drawn and exploited to the full'—a dig at the wide publication of Gladstone's letter—and 'a dignitary of the church radiant in approbation scenting purple patches for delivery in a rural diocese arrayed proper to the nines'.

In fact numerous sermons were preached on *The Christian*, not only in London but as far afield as America and South Africa. In Liverpool the preacher at the Myrtle Street chapel spoke on the story of John Storm and Glory Quayle. John Caine wrote next day, 30 August, to tell his son about it. The chapel was packed—'so very seldom seen there now'. The preacher, the Revd John Thomas, MA, said, 'Mr Caine would be heard all over the world in the defence of women.' His text was: 'The fashion of the church and the fashion of the world—Hall Caine's splendid protest.' The preacher had opened by saying he did not often preach from a book not the Bible 'but to pass this book unheeded he felt he would not be true to his profession as a Minister of religion'. He went on 'amid breathless attention' to say the novel was 'such a treat as he never heard before'. He told the congregation to buy it and read it carefully and then read it again. He admired the Author for his courage in making known evils in high places and his noble defence of Christianity. 'Mother said she never heard such a sermon. She came home in a complete torrent of rain not 10 years but 20 years younger, very wet but got her clothes off at once so I think she hath little harm... Mr Gladstone's letter is much spoken of.' Willie in London had heard nothing but talk of the new book. 'It hath caused great delight among Dissenters and among low Churchmen,' said their father.

A public attack was launched on Caine by his rival and contemporary, Marie Corelli. She had published her first novel in 1886, the same year that Caine published *A Son of Hagar*. She resented the fact that his sales were bigger than hers. On 25 September, 1897, she sent an open letter to the papers.

> Sir, I have read your 'Bondman' and the impression left upon my mind is, that it would make a good 'Penny Thriller', or 'Shilling Shocker'. It is of the morbidly sensational order, and evidently written with a view to its being adapted and dramatized for the Stage. Several of the dramatic situations...remind me, when a boy, of seeing such pieces at the Old Victoria Theatre New Cut in the 'Bravo Hicks' days and at the Surrey. Why not try your hand at an Adelphi drama?... If the 'Bondman' is fairly representative of your genius (?) as a Novelist, I hope I may be spared the infliction of reading any more of such utter bosh and nonsense.

She signed the letter 'Pro Bono Publico'. In spite of the pseudonym and 'when a boy' it was common knowledge who had written the letter.

A friend, Douglas Sladen, asked if Caine was going to reply to it. 'Thank you, no,' was Caine's answer. 'I have never had a literary quarrel in my life and I do not think I can begin one now, least of all on such provocation. There is nothing in the lady's letter which needs an answer from me. I must leave her mistress of the field.' Which must have been a relief to Heinemann. In 1900 Corelli published a novel with the title *The Master Christian*. Caine was furious and wanted to have a go at her. Heinemann agreed it was a dirty trick and an attempt to profit by the success of Caine's similarly named book but Caine had no grounds for a case against her. He advised him to ignore it and Caine agreed reluctantly. He encountered a good deal of jealousy among other less successful writers. Owning a castle in the Isle of Man did nothing to make the eye of jealousy less green.

John Caine took the five-year-old Derwent to Liverpool for a holiday at the beginning of August, 1897. Three weeks later Caine took Ralph to Liverpool to fetch Derwent and to see his sister—Lily's first child, David, had been born in July and she and the baby were visiting her parents. At the time the press were reporting that Caine was too ill to leave the Island, indicating that he sometimes used his health as an excuse to avoid things he would rather not do. It was a rough voyage home. John Caine was anxious—the Isle of Man Steam Packet's new boat, he said, was 'awful, like a huge bag in the water, nearly shoots everybody off the deck. When it becomes to be known the people won't go with her, besides she was four and a half hours in crossing.'

That autumn Caine began dramatising *The Christian*. The strain of fending off the critics of the book became too much for him. He went to Rome with Mary early in December to escape the pressures and the worst of the English winter. Mary fell in love with the city and it was her favourite place for ever afterwards. They stayed at the Albergo Hotel. He completed the play and began sketching the plot of the new book. He had seen *The Christian* as a play first and a novel second and the two versions were different in many ways. As soon as the script was finished he sent it to an American producer in Chicago who had asked for it. However, when Mr Willard received it he cabled Caine in Rome saying, 'Don't wait for me.' While Caine was wondering who next to approach he met an American who told him a rising young American actress, Viola Allen, was exactly the right person to play Glory Quayle. For ten years she had been the star of Charles Frohman's Empire Theatre company. The Caines broke their holiday at the end of January to return to the Island where he had been invited to speak at a banquet in his honour. By an odd coincidence the first message he got on arriving in London was a cable from Viola Allen asking for the play. It was sent to her and she agreed to do it.

Viola Allen as Roma in the New York production of The Eternal City, 1902.

Viola Allen was the same age as Mary. Her father was from an old New England family and her mother English. Her father was an actor and drama teacher and named her after Shakespeare's Viola. She grew up in Boston and, like Ellen Terry, began her career as a child actress. She was not quite 13 when in July, 1882, she starred in the title role in *Esmeralda* at the old Madison Square Theatre. She never looked back. She kept up her studies for the next few years, coached largely by her father, while continuing to appear in leading roles. She was a star at 15 and was described as 'the girl who left her nerves in the dressingroom'. She grew into a dark-haired beauty and a polished and accomplished actress who was a favourite with audiences and never out of the limelight until her retirement in 1918. In 1898 she was at the height of her powers.

Negotiations for the production did not go smoothly. Caine offered the part of Glory to Viola Allen but Charles Frohman wanted impossible terms, including the sole rights to produce the play in London as well as in America. In the end Caine concluded an agreement with the Liebler Company and Viola Allen left the Empire Theatre to join them with a contract to play Glory Quayle in New York and on tour. As a result the play was performed in America over a year before it was staged in London.

Caine presided at the banquet in Douglas for which he had broken his holiday. His after-dinner speech of thanks was well received. One of the organisers, writing next day to congratulate him, said his speech had made a deep impression.

> You are the theme of general admiration here and there is now a genuine desire to do fitting homage to you. Those who were your chief detractors in the street and the hotel last week are today loudest in their appreciation and readily admit their previous judgement was founded upon want of knowledge respecting yourself. Today you are the most popular man in the place and long may you continue to be so.

This was gratifying given that he had been criticised and the object of envy since settling in the Island. In spite of this he had made a number of good friends there. One of these was his next door neighbour in Greeba Towers, Reginald Farrant, although he was more than twenty years Caine's junior. He was a lawyer, called to the Manx bar in 1899 and later to become First Deemster. Caine also greatly liked and admired another lawyer, Sir James Gell, who had helped him with advice over *The Deemster* and whose son, James Stowell Gell, became his friend as well. Another friend, an exact contemporary, was Arthur Moore. He came of an old Manx family and went to Rugby and Cambridge, where he took a first in history. He entered his father's business in the Isle of Man and was elected to the House of Keys, in due course becoming Speaker.

These were men with whom he could have the sort of intellectual conversation he had had with Rossetti. However, his closest friend on the Island was without doubt Dr Robert Marshall, only six years his junior and his personal physician. He trusted no other doctor as he did Robert Marshall. If he felt ill while on his travels he would summon him. Marshall had somehow to find a locum and journey to wherever Caine happened to be languishing. He could unburden himself to Marshall as he could to no one else except Bram Stoker. He and Marshall had similar tastes and interests and talked far into the night when they were together. When they met Marshall was a bachelor. He married in April, 1901, at the age of 42, and took his wife to Rome for their honeymoon, where Caine and Mary happened to be staying at the time.

After the Douglas banquet Caine returned to Rome with Mary, staying there until early April when they went to London. Martin Conway, the chairman of the Society of Authors, wrote to Caine privately from his home at The Red House on Campden Hill, asking how and when he would be prepared to report on his work in Canada to a meeting of the Society and accept a vote of thanks for it. Walter Besant had suggested the time was ripe. Conway wanted to know if Caine agreed or whether he would sooner wait until the legislation had been passed and the job could be seen as complete. 'Personally both Besant and I feel very keenly that authors owe you a warm expression of thanks for your very hard work.' Caine was pleased but for once in no hurry to step into the spotlight. He was still having considerable correspondence with the people in Toronto and was afraid to be seen rejoicing when things might still go wrong.

Lily was about to return to the stage after an absence of nearly two years. Louis N. Parker, who thought she had the potential to be a big star, cast her in his play, *Change Alley*. It opened at the Garrick Theatre on 25 April. Also in the production were Lillah McCarthy, Fred Terry and Julia Nielson among others who went on to stardom but it only ran for twelve performances.

The most important event of April, 1898, however, as far as Caine was concerned, was the arrival in London of Viola Allen. They had been corresponding for several months on business and details of the script. Now she came to see him to discuss her performance as Glory Quayle and to rehearse with him, for he was to direct despite a total lack of experience. From letters Viola Allen wrote later they must have gone to Greeba to work on the play. It was not a happy time for Mary. She felt excluded. Viola was not only a far more sophisticated young woman with a powerful personality, she was a ravishing dark-eyed beauty. Mary would have had to be superhuman not to be jealous when her husband spent hours closeted with this amazing creature. One matter discussed between them was at what stage of rehearsal Caine should go to New York. Viola wanted him to go soon and to bring Mary with him. Mary refused to go.

Hall Caine aged about 45,
from a publicity postcard.

By the end of April Viola was back in America and writing long letters about the play and its presentation. Caine was making difficulties over the business side of things. She had a clear grasp of theatrical affairs and acted to smooth things over between him and Tyler, manager of the Liebler Company.

In May Gladstone died. Caine at once sent a letter of condolence to his son, Herbert Gladstone, who had succeeded to the viscountcy. He replied with a friendly letter thanking Caine and hoping he would be able to join them at the Abbey for the state funeral on the 28th. He enclosed a ticket signed 'Norfolk, Earl Marshall' and over-printed FAMILY. Caine was given Gladstone's large fob watch which ever after had pride of place on his study mantelpiece at Greeba.

Negotiations with Tyler about the production of *The Christian* continued through the summer when Caine was mostly at Greeba Castle. He was also involved in business, buying properties in the Isle of Man and at Southport, on the Lancashire coast. He was investing cannily, determined that neither he nor his family should face the shadow of penury which had clouded Rossetti's last days. He was generous to Mary, though, buying her jewellery and beautiful clothes. He had her photographed at a fashionable London studio during the summer of 1898. She was 29 but the pictures show a girl who looks much younger, more like a shy débutante than the mother of a teenaged son. She wears an evening dress lavishly trimmed with lace, a long rope of pearls and what looks like a diamond necklace. In one shot she wears an ermine cloak. She does not look happy, rather as if the clothes did not belong to her and she was being forced to dress up against her will. She peers from under the hood of the cloak as if weighed down by it.

Caine continued to work on his play, simplifying the story and emphasising the relationship between John Storm and Glory Quayle. Letters flowed between him and Viola Allen, she with suggestions or queries, he sending changes to the script. She thought it would 'act beautifully'. Nothing was shown of Glory as a nurse, the play moving straight into her career on the halls, which meant Viola had to sing. She asked for a copy of the music of 'John Peel'—she had all the other songs. Incidental music for the play included a waltz specially written by William Fürst. It was agreed with Tyler that the programme should say the play was 'Produced under the personal supervision of the Author.' He was helped by Frank J. Keenan who arranged the crowd scenes—the cast included over fifty 'Footmen, commissionaires, servants, etc.' Caine's inexperience as a director showed and caused one critic to write that 'Mr Hall Caine is not so good a stage manager as he thinks he is.' (Stage manager was the term used then for what we now call the director.)

Viola wrote continually urging Caine to come over, adding in one letter, 'I still have hope that Mrs Caine may come too', but when Caine
sailed for New York early in September he travelled alone.

He arrived in America in time for a last hectic week of rehearsals
before a preview in Albany. *The Christian* opened at the Knickerbocker
Theatre, New York, on 10 October, 1898. Viola Allen gave a performance which clinched her position as the greatest star of the American
stage of her day. Caine appeared before the curtain at the end, responding to cries of 'Author! Author!' He made a graceful and emotional
speech hoping his play would cement the ties of friendship between his
country and America. Nationality had nothing to do with it, snorted one
critic. 'Mr Caine might come from Piccadilly or else right down the pike;
if he brought a good play with him it would be endorsed as such here-
abouts. And "The Christian" is emphatically worthwhile, for it is a discussion exciter.'

A vast number of column inches were given over to the reviews.
Many noted that there would be huge numbers of people eager to see
the play as the book had sold over one million copies. Adding together
English and American sales and taking into account the numerous translations and colonial editions this could well be true. Claims that it had
sold between three and four million were probably exaggerated. From
the reviews it is clear that the enormous success the play enjoyed, making fortunes for all concerned, was due less to the quality of the play
than the quality of the acting. The men—Edward J. Morgan in the lead
as Father Storm with John Mason as Horatio Drake and Jameson Lee
Finney as Lord Robert Ure—were all good but Viola Allen was superb. It
was her night and it was because of her that the play did so well. It ran
for twelve weeks in New York and then went on a lengthy tour. In the
summer of 1899 there was a two month break, which Viola Allen spent
holidaying in Europe, and then started on another tour with substantially the same cast.

Caine had told Mary he would be back in six weeks. This would have
meant sailing immediately after the opening night, getting home to
Greeba Castle by mid-October. Had he done so he would have been
in time to attend the funeral of T.E. Brown, who died suddenly on
29 October, 1897. However, soon after his arrival in New York Caine
was offered a lecture tour of America. Tyler urged him to accept as it
would be valuable publicity for the play. It would also earn Caine a substantial sum of money as the fee was £60 per lecture, the equivalent of
£3000 at today's values. He was exhausted from the strain of working
on the play and directing rehearsals but felt it was too good an offer to
turn down. He wrote to his wife and to his parents—his mother was
with Mary at Greeba, or so he thought—saying he would be delayed
until early December.

Unknown to her husband, Mary had left Greeba soon after he had to stay with friends in Southport, where she caught a chesty cold. Instead of returning home she went to London. Willie met her at Euston and recommended the Brunswick Hotel in Jermyn Street as comfortable and quiet. She settled in there to await her husband's return. He had written affectionately to his 'darling girl' as soon as he arrived in America, wishing she was with him, but he had been offered a lucrative lecture tour. 'When are you coming home?' she replied. 'I hope you won't attempt to lecture. I know you would make a pile of money but what's the good of it if it undermines your health?' She explained why she was in London: 'I am so afraid of my lungs.' Caine had infected her with his neurotic attitude to health. She ended her letter, 'Now there's a darling come home to me, I want you so badly and really I cannot wait very much longer, I feel so disappointed that you have not kept your promise. You said you would be home in six weeks... Make haste there's a darling and come to me. I feel so lonely without you.'

On the same day John Caine wrote to Tom in New York. Mother was 'very much troubled that she hath nothing hardly to do' at Greeba. Derwent had a cold. 'I told the boy that Grandmamma was sorry that he was not getting a better boy. He said that Grandmamma should mind her own business... He is very serious that I shall not tell you anything.'

John Caine and his wife were both extremely worried over Mary and could not think what she was up to. John Caine in particular was equally concerned over how his younger grandson was turning out. On 23 November he wrote to Tom again, telling him his mother was in London to see what had become of Mary. Derwent had been sent to school in Ramsey as a boarder but his grandfather had no sooner taken him there than he came home again, with some tale about the cooking. Like many spoilt children he was faddy over his food. When Tom comes home 'where you are much wanted' he must watch carefully what is going on, not only with his property but with his family. 'I hope you will pardon me in what I am going to say as I am ignorant of why Mary is staying so long in London when she hath a house and servants here and two boys. I am sure it would occupy the whole of her time to see to this one house.' Much wanted doing on farms Tom owns 'of which I know every part'. One farm is particularly neglected and another tenant is behind with his rent.

He agreed reluctantly that Caine should stay on in America if he was well and able to bear the strain. 'I would say to you Lecture away and make money while you have the chance but do not trust the Yankees too far.' He was feeling ill and might have to go home to Liverpool but 'I should like to remain here till you or Mary comes back. I think I am of some little service to keep things straight.' As indeed he was.

CHAPTER NINETEEN

In 1899 Caine reached his forty-sixth birthday and he had lost his way. As long as he stuck to Cumbria and the Isle of Man and the ordinary people he knew well his work was good though not, by and large, to the taste of succeeding generations. Once he attempted to depict the life of cities and society people he floundered. His plots had never stood close examination and were sometimes frankly ridiculous but he could spin a good yarn and induce what Coleridge called 'that willing suspension of disbelief'. He always said a novel had to have 'grip and go'—if it did not grab the reader with the first few pages it had failed. His enormous popular success proves he met his own criteria.

After *The Manxman* he was on the crest of the wave, the darling of critics and public alike. After *The Christian* he was suddenly the most excoriated of writers. That his readers still loved him and bought his books by the million did not really console him for the loss of critical acclaim and he let it show. Jibes such as 'Mr Hall Caine's highly-coloured view of Christianity' hurt. Up to this point he had exhibited faint traces of a sense of humour but now the last vestiges were lost. He was soured and on the defensive. One suspects that wealth and success had spoilt him.

He faced the approach of the new century without so many of his early friends, patrons and advisers, the men on whom he had depended. He had lost Wilkie Collins, Lord Houghton, H.A. Bright, John Lovell and Ford Madox Brown. Within another year R.D. Blackmore, Ruskin and the dear friend of his youth, William Tirebuck, had also died. But above all he had lost Rossetti. Dante Gabriel had been his lodestar and he mourned him for the rest of his life.

In addition his marriage came under strain for the first time. The gap in their ages began to tell. While her husband was middle-aged Mary, at just 30, was still a young woman. Apart from being wrapped up in his writing, which dominated everything, business affairs took more and more of his time. Greeba Castle was occasionally a bone of contention between them. Mary never liked it and longed for a London house. She regarded Greeba as a holiday home for the summer months, while for Caine it was the centre of his life. It had importance for him beyond that of a loved home: it was his proof of Manx domicile. Today the Isle of Man has a low rate of income tax but in those days there was none at all.

As the money from his books and plays rolled in the UK Receiver pursued him ever more relentlessly despite his insistence on being Manx. The Receiver said that as he was born in England and had only settled permanently in the Isle of Man in 1896 English tax was due on the whole of his income. His accountant told him he must never be seen to pursue his avocation of writer in England—all his writing must be done in the Isle of Man or abroad. Early in 1899 Caine totted up his cash savings on the back of an old envelope—they amounted to over £3000 deposited in five separate banks in London, Paris, Liverpool and the Isle of Man, a useful sum then. The arguments led to a bruising encounter with the tax authorities in 1902 after which an uneasy compromise was reached. Meanwhile the London flat was given up and for a while they stayed in hotels or with friends when they went to town.

It is significant that four years separated the publication as a book of *The Christian*, and his next novel, *The Eternal City*. In 1899 the only book he produced was a small paperback guide to the Isle of Man for the Steam Packet Company. Of course with his name to it it became a highly sought after souvenir and was in print for a good many years but it was not what his public expected of him. There were problems too in America. In August William Appleton wrote to say that pirate firms were binding copies of the serial version of *The Christian* in hard covers and selling them without permission and nothing could be done about it. Caine's American sales were being considerably harmed. Appleton thought it might be better to abandon magazine publication in future.

At the same time trouble blew up with Wilson Barrett. He had been on a prolonged tour of Australia during which time he had made and performed his own dramatisation of *The Christian*. Back in London he tendered Caine part of the payment he had received for it from an Australian manager, claiming that Caine had made an agreement with him that they should jointly adapt the novels for the theatre. Caine was furious. He returned the money and sued Barrett for stealing his copyright. Barrett tried to make peace, sending his manager to see Sir George Lewis, who had been retained by Bram Stoker on Caine's behalf, saying that as it was clear Caine did not wish Barrett to play in *The Christian* he no longer wished to do so. 'I think Mr Barrett wants somewhat to climb down,' Sir George wrote to Caine. Barrett hinted that an arrangement might be made by which Caine would give him a percentage of the profit of *The Christian* and so end the litigation. The threat of this lawsuit was holding up negotiations with Charles Frohman for the production of the play in London and they finally fell through. Sir George thought it very doubtful that Barrett would go for an injunction but Frohman was not prepared to risk it. The business rumbled on until August, 1899, when Barrett finally provided Sir George Lewis with documents which he said proved his claim. They did nothing of the sort. The trouble was that in the excitement of getting *The Deemster* staged as *Ben-my-Chree* Caine had never signed a contract or agreement of any kind with Barrett. Stoker went up to Greeba Castle to discuss the problem and the case was eventually settled out of court. Meanwhile a whole year had been lost in staging *The Christian* in London and with it had gone the chance of Viola Allen playing Glory there, a bitter disappointment to her and to Caine. There is no record of her ever appearing in London.

Caine did not need this distraction from his work on the 'Roman book'. It seems as though he could not decide whether he was a playwright who wrote novels or a novelist first and foremost. As a dramatist his forte was melodrama but he came on the scene twenty years too late. He could have made a great career out of melodrama but by the end of the Nineties the taste for it was waning. Ibsen and Shaw were changing the theatre for ever, aided by Pinero and Wilde, among others. Even when they wrote comedies theirs was the Theatre of Ideas and what Shaw called Unpleasant Plays—plays that dealt with social and political problems. Caine tackled them in his own way also but it was as a writer of romantic novels that he was most successful.

He called himself a Man of Letters but he was so much else besides and that is what makes him interesting. In particular he was increasingly involved in politics. From his teens he had been a political animal but now it threatened to take over. Not only did he follow the politics of the Isle of Man and Westminster closely, he interested himself in the cause of oppressed small nations everywhere, following Lord Houghton's example in believing in their right to rule themselves. In the summer of 1899 a Finnish woman, Mrs Aino Malmberg, visited him at Greeba Castle to seek his help for her country, which was then a province of Tsarist Russia. She had come from Finland, where Nationalists were struggling for independence, specially to see him. Caine gave her a warm welcome. He asked for a detailed account of her homeland. She was gratified by his interest and on her return home she and her husband travelled throughout Finland for several weeks while she compiled her report.

She began by telling Caine the politicians could not and would not help the Nationalists. Their only hope was that great men, bearers of great ideas, would teach the world right from wrong. They well knew what the sympathy of such men as Caine and Count Tolstoy meant. Finnish singers, artists and writers had given their services free to raise money for the Nationalist cause. Famine threatened but a worse danger was the Russian Governor, General Robrikoff. Russian newspapers were saying openly that the best way to subdue Finland was to ruin it economically. The burden of the occupying army was heavy. Censorship had recently been made tougher than ever, no societies were allowed any more, spies were swarming round the country. The people remained hopeful even though the Tsar had refused to meet a European delegation which wanted to put the case for Finland's independence. Caine offered their National Theatre the Finnish rights to *The Christian* on behalf of their cause and Mrs Malmberg translated it. She asked if she could tell the papers his next book would be set in Rome, 'and would you allow me to translate it into Finnish as soon as it is published in English? Perhaps I shall have finished *The Manxman* before that.'

Caine maintained his interest in Finland. In August 1903 he offered the Finnish Theatre the stage rights to his next book. Mrs Malmberg thanked him but feared the censors would never allow it to be performed. She thought it a miracle his novels had been allowed to appear unaltered but censorship of drama was more severe. She thanked Caine for his 'moral assistance' and described a sorry state of affairs. 'About 50 of our best men are sent into exile since May (without trial, of course) and everybody who dares to utter fearless words has to expect the same fate. Matters are growing worse day by day, and oh! there are so many who do not ask any more, what is right? but only what is political?' General Robrikoff had been given dictatorial powers by the Tsar as Governor of Finland and had removed officials he did not like, replacing them with Russians. Finland had much to endure before it became independent. There was civil war in 1918 and a Russian invasion in 1939. The Finns were forced to cede valuable territory when they sued for peace.

When *The Christian* finally opened at the Duke of York's Theatre on 16 October, after a preview in Liverpool, it was with an English cast. Lily played the part of Glory's friend, Polly Love. The reception was lukewarm. The production staggered on for 62 performances and closed on 16 December. This was not entirely the fault of the play. The opening coincided with the outbreak of the Boer War in South Africa and Londoners had too much on their minds to think much of going to the theatre. Caine from the outset was bitterly opposed to the war which drew accusations that he was 'Pro-Boer' and a traitor to his country. Far from the mark but damaging.

In the middle of all this he continued to work on *The Eternal City*, set in Rome. On 26 February, 1899, he met Cardinal Vaughan, the Roman Catholic Archbishop of Westminster. He had originally intended to portray John Storm as a Catholic but had been persuaded that this would be unpopular so had made him a High Church Anglican instead. However, he was determined to set the new story within the ambit of Catholicism. He discussed his intentions with Cardinal Vaughan, asking for advice. When he returned to Rome Caine had a private audience

Postcard of Vesta Tilley in costume for her song,
'Good Luck to the Girl Who Loves a Soldier' 1905.

with the Pope, which Cardinal Vaughan could well have arranged for him.

Caine and Mary spent two or three months in London, staying at the Hotel Cecil, going to the theatre and seeing friends in the evenings. During the day Mary went shopping or to see her sister while he worked. He now had a desk at the *Daily Telegraph*, which he retained until about 1916. He was supplied with letterheads which had 'Reply to: Mr Hall Caine' in the top left-hand corner and wrote regularly for the paper.

About this time they got to know the music hall artiste Vesta Tilley, famous for her male impersonations. In 1890 she had married Walter de Frece, a Liverpool man who, like Caine, began as an apprentice architect. He abandoned this to follow his father into theatrical management and after their wedding he managed Vesta's career. Off stage she was the apotheosis of femininity. She and Mary Caine struck up a friendship which lasted until Mary's death. It was because of this that Vesta Tilley included the Isle of Man in her hectic touring schedule for a couple of weeks each summer.

The Eternal City was the only one of Caine's books to be conceived as a play. When the script was ready he looked for a theatre. He thought it would be easy to place it but no one was interested. He laid the script aside and serialised it for a magazine before finally turning it into a novel. Appleton had already advised him to accept $7500 offered for the American serial rights.

Caine wanted to see R.D. Blackmore before they went back to the Island but he was away. Blackmore wrote from North Wales of his disappointment at missing them. He had hoped for a long time to see Caine again 'and it is very grievous thus to lose the chance'. He had been stuck at home for more than four years, he said, but had been persuaded 'to run off (by way of a forlorn hope) from my long and painful illness, which makes life an hour of groans. This foe, of course, stuck fast to his pillion and means to go home with me next week.' If Caine was still in London then he would be delighted to see them both at any time. In July he wrote to Caine at Greeba. Far from his Welsh holiday having done him good he was worse than before and not allowed to see anyone. 'I hope you are very well but not <u>too</u> active, as your nature urges you to be.' A week later he sent a letter which was smudged and straggling and in parts illegible, saying he wished he

> had ever done anything to deserve your largesse of good will... I am truly grateful for your friendly thoughts of me... Your great work is yet to come, if my dull old brains have forecast correctly. Take your time, take hold of rapid emotion or drift of the public's rotten tastes; but work to your best mark... I would gladly see your kind face again.

Because of his accountant's instructions not to work in England, and Dr Marshall's that he should not winter in the Isle of Man because of his tendency to bronchitis, Caine planned to spend several more months in Rome where he would write the book. He and Mary travelled there by way of Paris, where they stopped for a few days. Passing through London Caine saw Blackmore for the last time—he died a month or two later.

Derwent, who had been for a few terms at Ramsey Grammar School, had become too much of a handful for his elderly grandparents. He had developed asthma and Dr Marshall advised a school on a warmer coast. Accordingly before his parents left for Rome they had installed him at a leading prep school in Eastbourne, St Cyprian's. The Headmaster's wife, Cicely Vaughan Wilkes, was ambitious for the school to win scholarships to the major public schools. Accordingly the older boys were crammed for the Common Entrance examination, often helped by a good whacking from Mr Vaughan Wilkes to stop their attention flagging. According to accounts of the school written by old boys the regime was tough. The day began with a plunge into an icy swimming pool followed by PT before breakfast. It is difficult to imagine Derwent, a spoilt little Mummy's boy, taking kindly to this. However, Cicely Vaughan Wilkes wrote reassuringly to his parents. The first page of her letter is missing so it cannot be dated exactly but what remains starts, 'I think it extraordinary he did not have an attack of asthma on the spot!' She thinks he 'should play plenty of football but no swimming this term' so he was let off the morning plunge at least for a time. 'I think a quiet regular life without excitement is what he wants most and to be taken out of himself. He has really been very good so far this term and most amenable but I do think he is inclined to be over-anxious and hysterical about his own health.'

The boys joined their parents in Rome for the Christmas holidays, giving Caine an idea which surfaced in his novel *The Woman Thou Gavest Me*, published in 1913.

Caine was still in Rome on 3 February, 1900, when a major disaster hit the Isle of Man: the collapse of Dumbell's Bank, a private institution which controlled many major concerns in the Island. Unwise speculation and a series of business failures had caused uneasiness for some time but too many people in high places were involved and insolvent for any public disclosure. When there was a run on the bank it closed its doors and a great many people were ruined. Firms large and small shut down and unemployment rose. Caine had £500 deposited with the bank, which he lost, but he had been wise enough not to put all his eggs in one basket, unlike many others. The economy of the Island was seriously damaged and it took years to recover.

John and Sarah Caine, 1901.

In August, 1899, Caine had bought a fifth farm on the recommendation of his father, who had been over it for him. Now he took advantage of the situation to buy up mortgages and more property, including the Mooragh Hydro Hotel in Ramsey. A lot of people were grateful to him for helping them out of their difficulties but many of the Manx were increasingly envious. His father had always kept an eye on things when he was away but John Caine was now old and ailing and could no longer go to the Island whenever his son happened to be away, nor could he be responsible for so many scattered properties. Caine appointed a bailiff, or business manager, Thomas Cowley, a Ramsey man, whose duties were to deal with tenants, collect rents and act as Clerk of the Works at Greeba, where improvements to the Castle and its grounds continued.

Partly because of his indecision as to whether *The Eternal City* should be a play or a book and partly because part of his mind was on his Manx investments the work went slowly in Rome. Serialisation began in the *Lady's Magazine* in England and others around the world, putting more pressure on him. Viola Allen in America was worried. He had promised her the lead in his next play and she wrote and cabled him several times with no reply. Finally, at the end of July, 1900, when Caine was back at Greeba, she wrote again from Long Island, New York.

> Why don't you send me some word???... I believe the worst and I am heart-lessly deserted. I am sure something must have occurred but I am at a loss to know what... Why don't you write me something? You really must not sell my birthright without letting me know, should you?... The weather is boiling and my brain sizzling with anxiety. Warmest remembrances to all the family.
>
> Faithfully yours, Viola Allen.

No wonder he had not written to her. He was in trouble with the magazine publishers Pearson's over the serialisation. The story was far too long and he had failed to deliver parts of it on time. They were threatening to stop publication and sue him for £1000 damages for breach of contract. Stoker and Sir George Lewis took on the case but warned him he might lose and it would be better to settle out of court. At the same time he was involved with the provincial tour of *The Christian*. Lily, who had played small parts in plays by Ibsen and Henry Arthur Jones in the capital, had her first big London success as Polly Love but this had not been enough to save the production. The poor reception and relatively short run of a play which had wowed the whole of America was a disappointment for her, as for everyone else concerned. Her husband, George D. Day, 'took the matter in hand' and set up a tour under the management of the impresario Wentworth Croke. Caine revised the script, distracting him from the new book, and Lily starred as Glory Quayle. In what was virtually a new version of the play she did so well that the tour played the circuit of suburban theatres where it was reviewed by the London papers. The critics cried 'Peccavi' and praised it this time round.

It opened in Douglas on August Bank Holiday, 1900. Caine made his usual curtain speech and visitors and locals packed the theatre for the two-week run. With that out of the way Caine got back to work on the serial version of *The Eternal City*. It looks as if this serialisation gave him more trouble than any other but once it was complete he rewrote it as a book. Bram Stoker, a regular visitor, arrived at Greeba Castle on 1 October to read the manuscript. He suggested corrections and improvements and—just as important—cuts. Caine had tinkered with it so much it had become far too long. After the problems he had encountered with *The Christian* Caine, whenever he had finished a book, commanded the presence of his Heinemann's editor, for many years Charley Evans. He would be invited to stay for anything up to two weeks, when he would go through the manuscript checking for errors and knocking it into final publishable shape. Sometimes his wife came with him and they made a holiday of it.

In January, 1901, Caine set out with Mary for another stay in Rome, where he intended to write the final version of *The Eternal City*. They took a few days in town for Caine to consult Heinemann. He was by now one of the 'sights of London'. Frank Swinnerton described him as 'like a huge thrilling black moth'. Osbert Sitwell, who as a young man before World War I remembered seeing him, drew a similar picture. In the second volume of his autobiography, *The Scarlet Tree*, he says he would often pass the well-known figure in the street

> and always found a certain pleasure in it, equivalent to that, it may be, of identifying a rare bird. He was usually on his way to his publishers... I remember one of the partners in the firm...talking to me about him, and stressing how impressive he was as a personality, and how misunderstood as a writer. Money, in spite of the vast sums he made, my acquaintance averred, always came second with him.

This man—Pawling? Heinemann himself?—recalled an occasion when Caine had called at his office. As he sat down he noticed one of his own books lying on the publisher's desk.

> The author had taken it up, with a certain diffidence, and then, opening it, his eye had lighted on a passage so effective, and so full of moral grandeur, that he had begun to read it aloud in his fine voice, rolling and resonant. The paragraph ended with some such words as 'So, ladies, though your fate may be different, be not hard upon a fallen sister.' As he finished, he was quiet for a moment, then commented, 'Beautiful, beautiful,' and added, as an afterthought, 'and money in every line of it!'

If money did not come first with him it came a close second.

They were in Rome by mid-February, staying near the Spanish Steps. Awaiting them was an invitation for Caine to call on Tolstoy's daughter at her hotel, where, she was careful to point out, she had a sitting room. They were joined at the end of April by Dr Marshall and his wife—on their honeymoon. Mary went home at the beginning of May but Caine

Mary Hall Caine with her bicycle, 1901.

spent a week or so in Paris. The Pearson's lawsuit was still hanging over his head. He was involved in the law in another way: in 1901 he was appointed a JP of the Isle of Man. He sat on the Peel Bench—when he was at home—almost to the end of his life.

The Eternal City was finally brought out by Heinemann in August, 1901 and proved to be his most successful novel—it sold more than a million copies in English alone and there were editions in 13 other languages. It out-performed *The Christian* and remained in print until his death. It was Mary's favourite of all his books. When it became clear that this was a runaway best-seller there were demands for a stage version from the very people who had previously turned it down. The author promptly provided the script and the play opened at His Majesty's Theatre, London, on 2 October, 1902. It ran for 117 performances, a long run for those days, but it was not the huge theatrical success some of his other books achieved, despite featuring Beerbohm Tree as Baron Bonelli, Constance Collier as Donna Roma Volonna, Nancy Price as Princess Bellini and Brandon Thomas (on the face of it an unlikely casting for the author of *Charley's Aunt*) as Pope Pius X. Mascagni wrote the incidental music for it. Caine loved music and going to concerts. He reworked the play later for a revival as *The Eternal Question*. It was filmed twice, the second version starring the young Lionel Barrymore. The original production was sufficiently successful for it to spawn a 'theatre edition' of the play—forerunner of 'the book of the film/TV series' today. For this version Caine removed all the political and religious propaganda, leaving only the central love story and reducing the work from 600 to 400 pages. It was published, as usual, by Heinemann in London and Appleton in New York, both agreeing to withhold the original version for a while.

The seeds of this story lay with Rossetti and in particular in his poem, *The Last Confession*. This Caine considered Rossetti's 'highest mastery of the narrative form' in poetry, far exceeding that of Scott whose 'great gift of reality inclined him merely to reproduce the material furnished by his eye and memory, without regard for its ethical significance; and Byron's pruriency of instinct forbade his vivid perception to sound the depths of passion'. This criticism, contained in his lecture on Rossetti's poetry, encapsulates Caine's literary aims with the emphasis on 'ethical significance' and passion without prurience, the Victorianisation of Romance.

Rossetti, whose father and grandfather were Italian political refugees, had told him about the Italian community in Soho and what had driven them from their homeland. This supplied the material for the opening chapters of his book. While in Rome he absorbed the atmosphere of the city and did meticulous research into its history and politics, determined not to be trapped into the sort of errors that had marred *The Christian*. He managed to avoid most pitfalls though questions of taste arose, particularly his introduction of the Pope into the story. The actions ascribed to the Pope strain credulity, though Caine's account of a visit to the Vatican suggests he knew the location well. There is a strong correlation between known facts of Roman political and high society life in the second half of the nineteenth century and the events and characters of the novel. The hero of the story, David Rossi, is accused of plotting to murder the king: in real life an Italian king was assassinated. Caine wrote a vivid account of the political repression that followed the discovery of his fictional plot. Historically, after the failure of a socialist challenge to the regime in the late 1890s there was considerable repression in Italy.

The story is, of course, a romance, with the central theme the love of Donna Roma Volonna and David Rossi. Once again the lovers turn out to have been childhood friends, as in *The Christian*, though they have been separated for years and do not at first recognise each other. There is a lively account of uproar in the Roman parliament when Rossi sets out his socialist aims and his opposition to the king's party. Caine often watched debates in the Italian parliament from the gallery as a guest of the leader of the Opposition and this chapter is like lively and accurate reportage.

Caine puts his ideas on marriage into the mouth of his heroine, Roma, views which he also often gave in newspaper articles and interviews. In a letter to Rossi, Roma says,

> The wife I call brave is a man's friend, and if she knows what that means, to be the friend of her husband to all the limitless lengths of friendship, she thinks nothing about sacrifices between him and her, and differences of class do not exist for either of them. Her pride died the instant love looked out of her eyes at him, and if people taunt her with his poverty, or his birth, she answers and says: 'It's true he is poor, but the glory is, that he was a workhouse boy who hadn't father or mother to care for him, and now he is a great man, and I am proud of him, and not all the wealth of the world shall take me away.'

When in 1908 Caine published his autobiography he dedicated it 'To My Wife, My Friend', and that is inscribed on their tomb in Maughold churchyard in the Isle of Man. He had already expressed this idea of marriage as friendship in *The Christian*. Near the end of the book Drake writes to Glory: 'You will put me under an eternal obligation if you will consent to become my wife. We should be friends as well as lovers, Glory, and in an age distinguished for brilliant and beautiful women, it would be the crown of my honour that my wife was above all a woman of genius.'

There is a passing reference in *The Eternal City* to another of the causes Caine championed. Rossi, replying to Roma, writes, 'I am back in Italy under another name, my mother's name, which is my name too, thanks to the merciless marriage laws of my country.' This—the fact that a child could never bear its father's name or inherit from him if born out of wedlock, even if the parents subsequently married—had first been brought up more forcefully and emotionally in *A Son of Hagar*.

Caine was a literary magpie. In this book he quotes Alice Meynell: 'Then she lay a long time, with eyes open and shining in the darkness, trying in vain to piece together the features of his face. But <u>in the first dream of her first sleep</u> she saw him plainly, and then she ran, she raced, she rushed to his embrace.' This is too close to the ending of Meynell's sonnet, *Renouncement*, to be mere coincidence. To anyone who knows it the source is obvious:

> I must not think of thee, and, tired yet strong,
> I shun the thought that lurks in all delight—
> The thought of thee—and in the blue Heaven's height,
> And in the dearest passage of a song.
> Oh, just beyond the fairest thoughts that throng
> This breast, the thought of thee waits, hidden yet bright;
> But it must never, never come in sight;
> I must stop short of thee the whole day long.
> But when sleep comes to close each difficult day,
> When night gives pause to the long watch I keep,
> And all my bonds I needs must loose apart,
> Must doff my will as raiment laid away,—
> With the first dream that comes with the first sleep
> I run, I run, I am gathered to thy heart.

He quoted this poem again more than ten years later in *The Woman Thou Gavest Me*. He may not have realised on either occasion that the words were not entirely his own, so deep had they become embedded in his memory. As a young man he was highly impressionable and naïve. Meynell's sonnet imprinted itself so firmly on his mind that twenty and thirty years later he was unaware the phraseology was not original. However, he used many real incidents and real people in his books, something which got him into considerable hot water from time to time, so he may have known what he was doing. In *The Christian* one of the characters says, 'Who believes what an elephant says?', quoting Rossetti talking about Fanny Cornforth when they were staying at Fisher Place.

The Eternal City ends, as do several others among his novels, with a death scene in which star-cross'd lovers are united only to be cheated of happiness by the death of one or the other, but the effect is of a three-hankie 'weepy' rather than Shakespearian tragedy. In a revealing phrase many years later Caine asserted that 'all true art is tragic'. To him his work was high art, not cheap romance. If artistic truth, or moral considerations and the necessity for sin to be punished, demanded tragedy that is how his stories would end. Unfortunately for him, his readers and publishers did not agree and demanded happy endings. The death of one or other of the lovers at the moment they finally came together was his solution to his 'problem'.

There were some vicious reviews of *The Eternal City*, all lovingly pasted into her album by Mary. The Italian critics seem to have been particularly scathing. Defying Heinemann Caine went into print to refute them. While many clergymen praised the book highly most of the literary critics panned it. Caine feigned to despise them, as in a letter to Frederic Shields, who was now living in a big house, Moraysfield, on the Kingston Road in Wimbledon. He insisted it was a Protestant book but it did not deny the true piety of the Catholic church. He himself was outside all the churches while holding to the basic tenets of the Christian faith.

> You say very truly that my book has been misconceived. The trouble is that it has been dealt with chiefly by the <u>Literary</u> critics who, speaking of them as a whole, know nothing about religious questions and very little about political ones. But there have been very clear-sighted critics of the book too... On the whole I ought to be satisfied that the message of my book is being heard. With the merely malignant abuse of the literary critics I am not much concerned. The book can take care of itself on their lines.

The preacher had got the upper hand of the storyteller.
    At the end of a lengthy letter he added,

> How long it is since our days with poor Gabriel I was made to feel very acutely a few days ago when his niece (little Olive, William's daughter, you remember) wrote to ask permission to translate my new book. She is a married woman now, and her father is seventy-two years of age. I was a youngster of twenty-six when you saw me first—how well I remember the night, and see you where you stood on the hearthrug in Gabriel's studio—and now I am forty-eight. But with all the changes I have gone through one thing remains unchanged with me—and that is the sincere affection with which I always think of you, which is a good deal oftener than I write.

The book should have come out simultaneously in New York but Appleton complained Caine had made so many corrections to the proofs that the printers could not have it ready until 6 September. They had received the copy four weeks later than promised anyway.

At the time Caine wrote to Shields three of his plays were running in Liverpool at the same time. Consultations with Bram and Sir George Lewis over two lawsuits pending against him took up his time and frayed his nerves. He was deep in plans for a magazine launch and corresponding with Viola Allen and her manager over the New York production of *The Eternal City*, still a year ahead. Ralph had left school that July, just before his seventeenth birthday. He was not particularly bright and to find something for him to do presented his father with a problem. A job was arranged for him with a firm of paper manufacturers in Edinburgh but it was not a success. Ralph had no idea of the value of money, or of how it had to be earned. He put up at a comfortable hotel and then complained that his allowance from his father was not enough to pay the bills. He earned little and got into considerable money troubles. R.M. Prescott, a solicitor friend of his father's, wrote to Caine, having tried to sort things out. Although only 17 Ralph, tall and looking older than he was, had been gambling on the Stock Exchange, 'dabbling in futures, speculating in shares on the rise or fall of the market, a most foolish and dangerous thing for an uninitiated youth to do'. Prescott had found the account still open and closed it, pointing out to the firm concerned that they were dealing with a minor and should not have done so without his father's permission. Caine could repudiate liability but if he did so would be dragged into some unpleasant publicity.

Ralph had also handed Prescott an account for money lent him by a friend in Edinburgh 'which the boy says he cannot pay'. Ralph had moved out of his expensive hotel but told Prescott it had cost him over £50. He must have been living it up because that is the equivalent of around £2500 today. His allowance was not enough for him to live in a hotel but he had no idea what else to do—with a home like Greeba Castle cheap lodgings were beyond his ken. The borrowed money had evidently been lost in share transactions. Prescott ends with 'a word in confidence'. If his father was intending to invest any money in buying an interest for Ralph in the Edinburgh business he would advise against it. Better to wait and see how Ralph went on. Prescott feared he had 'picked up acquaintances in Edinbro' whose tendency will be (unless he is very resolute about it) to lead him into extravagances'.

This was the start of continuing worries over Ralph, who became a compulsive gambler. Caine was dogged by the thought that at his death Ralph would inherit nothing because of his illegitimacy and tried repeatedly to make it up to him by setting him up in business so that he would be independent.

In the midst of all this, at a by-election in the Isle of Man on 24 October, 1901, Caine was elected MHK—Member of the House of Keys—for Ramsey.

CHAPTER TWENTY

How Caine found time to canvass for the by-election is hard to see but he spent at least one day on the stump. A photograph survives showing him in his landau in Ramsey with Mary, Derwent and Sir James Gell, then Deputy Governor. Thomas Cowley, his agent, and Dr and Mrs Marshall are also in the picture. Caine stood for Manx constitutional reform and had a majority of 267 over his Conservative opponent, substantial given the size of the constituency.

He did not actively seek to enter Manx politics, rather he was persuaded by friends because they thought his position as a famous author would help the cause of reform. It may well have done but they do not seem to have realised how little time he would be able to give to attending debates. He explained when he accepted nomination that he was 'a busy man, in active exercise of an exacting profession which sometimes demands nearly all my time and more than all my energy'. Rather than confine himself to the parochial affairs of Ramsey he would try 'to do good for the whole of the Island'. It was not long, however, before grumbles arose over his poor attendance. His backers did not know what he thought privately about the Manx parliament. On 5 December, 1901, he wrote to his old friend Theo Watts (who had changed his surname to Watts-Dunton) to thank him for his congratulations on winning the election. 'I'm afraid I did not take the matter quite as seriously as your kind words suggest, but nevertheless I do feel happy to have been selected by my own people for the highest office they could confer upon me.'

The Manx parliament sits for a fixed term of five years and he came up for re-election in November, 1903. He won again but with a smaller majority. Even those opposed to him knew how the success of his Manx novels had benefited the Island's tourist trade. The Manx National Reform League, set up a month before the election, voted Caine its first president. The moving spirit was Samuel Norris. He had arrived from Liverpool, still in his teens, in 1894, with nothing but a small tin trunk. He began work next day as the Isle of Man representative of the Liverpool *Mercury* and spent the rest of his life there. It was because of his connection with the *Mercury* that Caine took an interest in him.

Caine gave his electoral address to the voters of Ramsey on 24 October, 1901. He had radical proposals for legislative reform which he modified after talks in London with Government officials concerned with electoral reform in other parts of the Empire. He advocated nationalisation of the Isle of Man Steam Packet Company and the Island's railways (of which only a fragment now remains). His plan for renewal of the economy was based on the Island being a holiday resort.

> I take the view that the Steamship Service, which is the highroad to the Isle of Man, should be controlled by the Government as a national industry that would be run for the sole object of bringing the largest numbers of visitors and mails to our shores at the most frequent and convenient times, without respect to those questions of dividend which a private company—however excellent, enterprising and obliging—must needs regard as its first reason for existence.

They should encourage visitors not tourists, he said, because tourists did damage and were not the sort of people to benefit the Island. Although he was himself a landowner, he proposed 'a modified and practical form of the nationalisation of the land', giving the Government 'powers which would require the proper drainage, the full cultivation and the judicious tree-planting of the land of the Island'. Given the cries now for the preservation of wetlands it is amusing to read his demands for them to be drained.

He was speaking in the aftermath of the crash of Dumbell's Bank and proposed that the Island's banks be nationalised to prevent such a fearful catastrophe happening again. The population was dropping sharply as people left to find work elsewhere. The machinery of government needed reform as did the Island's legal system, which he described as 'encrusted with the hampering growth of ages'. Anything he could do as 'a man of letters' with contacts and some influence in the wider world to help the development of the Island he would do. He sat down to loud and prolonged applause.

Given the conservative nature of the Manx and that the vote was based on property it is amazing he was elected not once but twice. Perhaps the electors of Ramsey thought there was scant chance of his extraordinary proposals getting through so they were not frightened by them. Also anyone who promised to protect them from future bank collapses and improve the Steam Packet's services won their support without too much thought being given to the means to these desirable ends. He was not a popular MHK as he seldom spoke in the House. The Manx also resented his broader view. Fred Kenyon's short biography, *Hall Caine, the Man and the Novelist*, published in London in 1901, pictured him as a well-loved man of the people. It is more a hagiography than a biography. Caine insisted on scrutinising the proofs before publication.

Not long before the Ramsey by-election Caine had been asked by Lloyd George to stand for Westminister as a Liberal. He refused on the grounds that as a Man of Letters he was 'suited neither by temperament nor profession to submit to the hurly-burly of national politics'. He had refused the Liberal offer because of a stormy scene he had watched in the Italian Parliament the previous winter, when 'the leader of the House had been interrupted, howled at, laughed at, guyed at and insulted'. It took a real politician to survive such treatment and bounce back. He knew his nerves would never stand it. He felt strong enough only for the small-scale matters of the Isle of Man.

He made an emotional appeal to the electors, emphasising how Manx he was despite having been born 'across'. As a public speaker he was enormously effective. An anecdote told by Samuel Norris indicates his acting talent. Norris was present as the *Mercury*'s reporter on an occasion when Caine was asked to speak. He made a great show of reluctance, saying he was totally unprepared and had no idea he would be expected to speak. He then gave an apparently extempore speech which was word for word what he had given Norris some time before and which was already lying on his editor's desk in Liverpool!

The news of his election to the Keys was widely reported across the water. *Black and White* magazine asked for an interview. He refused but wrote a long letter which it published. In spite of the reforms of 1866, which had ended the status of self-electing oligarchy of the House of Keys, in 1901 the franchise was restricted to men and women of

*The Ramsey by-election. Caine seated in his carriage with Mary
and Derwent aged 10. Sir James Gell is behind the coachman.
Dr and Mrs Marshall are on the right of the picture.*

property and the women had to be spinsters or widows over 30—no married woman could vote. Herbert Gladstone, while deeply embroiled in the problems of Home Rule for Ireland, asked Caine what system prevailed in the Isle of Man. Caine told him it was very far from the independent Home Rule proposed for Ireland because the Legislative Council, the second chamber, was unelected and its members were salaried civil servants, representing nothing but themselves and the English Home Office, yet they could veto the wishes of the people as expressed by the elected Keys. This remained the case until 1919 and it was only in 1958 that the Island won control over its own internal finances. The description Caine gave Gladstone of the electoral system of the Isle of Man in the 1890s sounds like Dickens's description of the Eatanswill Election in *Pickwick Papers*.

Shortly after the by-election Caine left for London. One thing which was standing in the way of attending to business in the House of Keys is apparent from the letter to Watts quoted above: it is on paper headed 'Household Words. Printers, Publishers, Advertising Agents', with a Fleet Street address. For some time Caine had planned to revive Dickens's magazine. Now the first number, written almost entirely by him, was about to appear. He explained this venture to Watts: 'It may be that you have heard that my son (think of it) is now trying to conduct Dickens's old paper, and that I am making some effort to help him to his start in life. How the years go by! He was a little fellow in ringlets the day before yesterday.'

He was not such a big fellow then—only 17. Evidently the Edinburgh venture had failed. Caine was trying to kill two birds with one stone— provide Ralph with a job and fulfil his own ambition regarding *Household Words*. For years he had hankered after producing a literary magazine and with it the ambition to revive the one his hero Dickens had founded. It did Ralph no good to be pushed forward like this and it seems strange that Caine should have done so, rather than allowing the boy time to find his feet, grow up and make his own way. But Caine was convinced he could die at any time and this illegitimate son might be left penniless. When Caine kept on insisting that Ralph was the editor it only provoked mirth, behind his back at least. There was a manager, Percy Hickie, and the principal contributor was Papa.

It was Ralph's Uncle Willie who did the real work. The first edition under Hall Caine as proprietor was the special Christmas number of 1901. It contained a long article by Caine about the Pope and the private audience he had with him. The first regular edition appeared in January, 1902. It identified neither the editor nor the proprietor. *The Eternal City* was the first serial, starting in the March issue with an episode running to 57 pages. There was not much else.

During the first year of his ownership Caine contributed many signed articles. One subject he tackled was 'The Great Story of Emigration: A Protest and a Plea'. It began

> The hope of those who have raised the question [in Parliament] is that restrictions will be put on alien immigration into England, for the reason that the poor of other countries are burdening our rates for the education of their children and by severe and unfair competition making it harder for our own people to live.

He provided articles throughout the short life of the magazine, covering his favourite subjects of temperance and the Woman Question, and lighter efforts such as an account of his being mistaken for a tramp in Berlin. One has a curiously modern ring: 'Is the Novel Dying?'

They printed 50,000 copies but costs got out of control—Caine took substantial fees for his contributions. A new manager, Sutherland, was brought in to sort things out. 'What is preeminently required in this office or in any office is method', he wrote to Willie Hall Caine.

1902 was a crowded year. Caine rented a large house on Wimbledon Common, The Hermitage, and he and Mary spent a lot of time there. Between overseeing his business investments, including *Household Words*, his involvement with the staging of *The Eternal City* in London and New York and keeping tabs on his plays and books around the world he could have had little time to think of his duties in the Isle of Man. Interruptions to his work came from odd quarters but were sometimes useful. The manager at Her Majesty's, where rehearsals were about to begin for *The Eternal City*, confessed to being in serious financial trouble after losing £500 gambling at Monte Carlo. He could not pay his debts and turned to Caine for help. If he resigned his post he would be ruined and Beerbohm Tree, who was to play Baron Bonelli, considerably inconvenienced. 'To work heartily and zealously for the production is the only amends possible that I can make for the difficulty in which my act of unconsidered folly may have landed all those friends who believe in me.' Caine lent him £200 without conditions of any kind. The man thanked him 'over and over again for the friendly, delicate and sympathetic friendship which has led you to help me out of my quandary'. Caine squirrelled away this incident—and some of the man's phrases—for his next book.

This example of Caine's unpublicised generosity shows how, apart from donations to charity, he went out of his way to help people. A New York journalist who lost his job shortly after writing a damning review of *The Christian* was found a new job by Caine who also lent him money to help him get on his feet again. He never pressed for the return of such loans.

Meanwhile royalties continued to roll in. All his novels were still in print and his plays being performed. In August, 1902, Wilson Barrett took his company to South Africa for a season at the Good Hope Theatre in Cape Town with Lillah McCarthy as his leading lady. He played several of his famous parts, including *The Manxman*. It was an unmitigated disaster. He was now far too old to play Pete. 'Here was a man,' wrote one critic, 'feeble, nay almost tottering in his movements, with a haggard face, looking fifty if he looked a day [he was 56], struggling painfully to realise the strong, robust and manly hero of Mr Hall Caine's imagination.' Barrett was already ill and he died less than two years later, on 22 July, 1904. Far more successful were Leonard Rayne's productions of several Hall Caine plays at the Cape Town Opera House the following year.

Queen Victoria died in January, 1901. Edward VII's coronation was delayed by an appendix operation but when it took place on 9 August, 1902, Caine was in the Abbey and seated well enough to be able to see clearly the expression on the King's face as the heavy crown was lowered onto his head. He gained the impression that the King's strong will was struggling with 'a terrible infirmity'. To help his convalescence he and the Queen cruised in the royal yacht along the west coast. As they sailed up the Irish Sea the Queen asked if they could call at the Isle of Man. She had enjoyed Caine's Manx stories and was interested to see where the Deemster, the Bondman and Pete the Manxman had lived. There was general astonishment when the royal yacht sailed into Douglas Bay unannounced on the evening of 24 August, 1902. To the disappointment of watchers on the Promenade it sailed away again, heading north. Next morning it appeared off Ramsey. It was a Sunday and the churches ended their services early so that their congregations could line the pier and the seafront.

All that day the *Victoria and Albert* lay in the bay with its attendant destroyer. Launches went back and forth bearing deputations wanting to present loyal greetings but Lord Knollys, the Private Secretary, told them the visit was unofficial and part of His Majesty's holiday so no deputations would be received. The new Governor, Lord Raglan, had still not arrived nine months after his appointment. In the interregnum Caine's old friend Sir James Gell was Acting Governor. He and the Speaker of the Keys, A.W. Moore, were received on the yacht but no one else—with one exception. The King made it known that he and the Queen would like to see Mr Hall Caine. To the annoyance of the assembled notabilities Caine was ferried out to the royal yacht while they were left on the pierhead fuming. He was with the King for over an hour.

Next morning the Island was covered with bunting although no formal announcement had been made that the royal couple would land. A welcoming party assembled on the Queen's Pier, including Caine and Derwent. Mary, who must have been furious at missing the fun, was in London and so was Ralph. Derwent, just 11, was in his St Cyprian's Sunday suit with a straw boater. The royal party which came ashore included the King's special friend the Marquis de Soveral and his mistress, Mrs Alice Keppel, with her husband the Hon. George Keppel. They set off for Bishopscourt, the official residence of the Bishop of Sodor and Man, the Rt Revd Norman Straton, the setting of much of *The Deemster*. A group photograph was taken with Caine standing beside Queen Alexandra with a quite ineffable smirk on his face. He is holding his top hat but Derwent is wearing his boater. When his father asked him afterwards why he did not take his hat off for the photograph Derwent replied that he had looked to see what the King did. 'He kept his hat on so I did too.'

They set off again with Caine taking the place of the Marquis de Soveral in the King's carriage. On the way to Peel, Caine pointed out the sights and answered the King's questions. Only a select party was allowed to enter Peel Castle where they enjoyed a picnic lunch sent from the royal yacht. Derwent was the only child present—admitted by the King's special permission. Queen Alexandra, who had her beloved camera with her, took photos of him with his father. She explored the ruined cathedral with Caine as her guide.

Caine and Derwent photographed at Peel Castle by Queen Alexandra,
25 August, 1902.

After returning to the carriages they passed through St John's, where a crowd had gathered, certain the King would want to stop and look at Tynwald Hill, the mound where their famous outdoor Parliament met and which had the nature of a national shrine. However, Caine was quite unable to interest the King. His carriage only slowed for a moment and then speeded on up the road to Douglas. At Greeba Caine proudly pointed out his house to the royal couple. They left him there and went on to take tea with Mrs Moore, the mother of the Speaker.

The day ended with a ride by electric tram along the spectacular east coast route to Ramsey. Caine rejoined the royal party at the terminus. When he arrived the large crowd awaiting the King parted good-humouredly to let him through, though one wag shouted, 'Get your 'air cut!' Caine rode with the King and Queen in their special carriage. Before being ferried out to the royal yacht the King thanked him for all he had done to make their visit so enjoyable.

It has been said that this was the first time Caine met the King and it was from this moment that his friendship with him grew. This is clearly not so. Caine himself said it was his first opportunity for a long talk with the King, which is probably true. The hour on the yacht on the Sunday, and then most of Monday spent with the royal couple gave him a better opportunity to get to know the King than their meetings in the Beefsteak Club had done. One can see how the misapprehension arose but he did nothing to correct it. Perhaps he had an inkling of how little the visit in general and he himself in particular had really mattered to the royal couple. After their tour of the Island the King wrote a letter to the Prince of Wales without mentioning Hall Caine and the Queen said, 'We paid a visit to the Bishop, lunched near an old ruined Castle at Peel, and met Hall Caine, a curious looking man, the same as his books'!

Mary returned to Greeba with Lily soon after the royal visit but Caine went to Switzerland where he stayed for a month on his own, working on his latest novel, *The Prodigal Son*, which was not published until two years later. He was back in London for the opening of *The Eternal City* at His Majesty's Theatre on 2 October, 1902. Beerbohm Tree drew good notices as did Constance Collier as Roma. Mascagni's incidental music was much praised. The play did not cause anything like the controversy that *The Christian* had and it did rather better, running for 117 performances before going on tour. There were objections to the Pope being shown on stage and to his crucial part in the action. Caine denied that his character was a portrait of the Pope, Leo XIII. When Leo died two years later his successor, Cardinal Guiseppe Sarto of Venice, took the name Pius X—the name Caine had given his fictional pope.

A few days after the London opening Caine left for New York for the opening night there. This time Mary did not make the mistake of staying

Caine and his wife skating at St Moritz, 1902.

behind. Ralph went too. They arrived in the *Lucania* on 15 October to be met by the crowds of reporters Caine now expected as a matter of course. The papers reported that Ralph was 'the youthful editor of *Household Words*' and was in America to explore the possibility of publishing an American edition. Nothing came of that. Mary, considerably more mature and self-assured than on her previous visit, was also interviewed. She told the papers she thought the American way of bringing up girls with greater freedom than in England was best. 'I was married with my hair down my back, at least it was in a braid,' she said, 'and I was in short skirts until I married.' This was an indication of her age at the time though she did not say just how young she had been. It is no surprise that she continued to be mistaken either for Ralph's elder sister or his young stepmother.

The Eternal City had its first American performance in Washington a few days after the London opening. The Liebler Company presented it and Viola Allen was the star. She was greatly praised but the play did not have the extraordinary success of its predecessor. One night during the New York run, in the scene where Roma smashes the bust she has made of David Rossi, Viola cut her hand badly. A doctor had to be called. He stitched it and after an extended interval she carried on. The audience did not realise what had happened—they thought all the blood was fake. New York reviewers were lukewarm and the play ran for only 92 performances. When it went.on tour Caine travelled with the company, leaving Mary and Ralph with friends. He was tinkering with the script all the time, upsetting the actors who had constantly to learn fresh lines and re-rehearse some scenes. In Philadelphia Caine collapsed and seemed really ill. Mary was sent for. The stress which felled him had been caused not merely by the unenthusiastic reviews but by a back-stage crisis. Viola Allen was threatening to resign from the Liebler company, form another and continue to tour the play under her own management. Tyler, the Liebler manager, insisted he had sole rights to the play. Caine was the unfortunate pig in the middle. Eventually Viola Allen got her way and continued to present both *The Eternal City* and *The Christian* successfully. As a sop to Cerberus Caine offered Tyler the American rights to his own version of *The Manxman*. It proved a disaster and lost Tyler a great deal of money which he tried to recover from Caine.

It was a relief to get home in December and settle back into another rented Wimbledon house, but Viola Allen's letters were upsetting. Tyler's lawyer had already approached Caine about the row over rights when she wrote in February, 1903. 'What point they hope to gain I don't quite see for it is <u>certain</u> I will <u>not</u> continue under this management after this season.' In March she said, 'You were more than good and kind and just and generous to me and I appreciate it all more than I can say.' She was sure 'unpleasantness of any kind will be averted', but the legal wrangles continued. It was all complicated and unpleasant and not at all good for Caine's notorious nerves.

As usual he fled, this time to Biarritz, writing a magazine article about it to pay for the three-week holiday. Mary and Ralph went with him, leaving an aggrieved Uncle Willie in charge of *Household Words*, now in real trouble. Mary returned to London after a few days. Willie wrote to Caine and Ralph on 1 April, 1903:

I hope you are having a pleasant time of it in the sunshine. We are having a hot time one way and another... The Wheel of Fortune has stopped. I presided over a meeting of Creditors today... I am here from 9.30 till after 6 o'clock every night. Beating up debtors is a business in itself... I am looking forward to a little rest and fresh air at Easter.

Best love, Willie.

In April Caine's *Letters and Speeches on Manx Politics* was published, part of his re-election campaign. In May he was back at Greeba, shortly before the *Tatler* published a full page photograph of him titled 'Mr Hall Caine in the study of his Wimbledon home, Danmore', where Mary remained. Their continual separations led to gossip both in London and in the Isle of Man. Like all small communities the Island is a great place for rumour, known as 'skeet'. It was whispered that Caine was conducting a series of torrid love affairs, of which there is no evidence whatsoever, but many of the Manx—and some folk from further afield—thought Caine lived the love scenes and romances he wrote about. More sophisticated people noted the stream of male visitors to Greeba Castle when Mary was not present and drew other conclusions.

One can see how rumours arose in the Isle of Man. Local people did not appreciate that men such as Heinemann, Stoker, Pawling, Evans and various leading actors were at Greeba to work with Caine on his books and plays, as well as being friends. As a result they jumped to unwarranted conclusions. When Oscar Wilde, whom Caine knew personally, was tried and convicted Caine is reported as exclaiming,

To think of it! that man, that genius as he is, who you and I have seen and fêted and flattered! Whose hand we have grasped in friendship! a felon, and come to infamy unspeakable! It haunts men, it is like some foul and horrible stain on our craft and on us all, which nothing can wash out. It is the most awful tragedy in the whole of literature.

He was not alone in this reaction—Clement Scott at the *Telegraph* called for all the windows to be opened to let in fresh air and other former friends of Wilde's turned on him in the same way. If Caine has been correctly reported, however, this outburst is telling. For so many years he had suppressed the feminine side of his nature and buried memories of his youth. When Wilde was brutally pilloried it must have shaken him to the core although he had never behaved as Wilde did and never would. His letters to Mary at this time show his abiding affection for her. He insisted she was his 'best friend'. Among his many men friends were a number of known homosexuals but that is not to say he shared their proclivities. He was a deeply religious man and such behaviour would have been against his beliefs. However, when he and Mary continued to spend so much of their time apart it is not surprising that rumours continued and long outlived him.

Caine had returned to the Island to take part in an important debate in Tynwald on taxes and reform. There were no direct taxes at that time. They were often proposed only to be defeated in the Legislature. Extra revenue was needed and a tax on sugar proposed, to the fury of the Reformers. The debate began on 29 May, 1903. As the new Governor, Lord Raglan, had still not arrived Sir James Gell presided. He knew his fellow Manx well and understood every move in the Tynwald Court. He was determined to get the new tax through. Several members, including Caine, held that expenditure should be curbed rather than a tax imposed on the people's food. Caine made a long speech on the Reform Movement, what it meant to the Island and how it arose. He also reviewed the costs of the Old Age pensions and other reforms they proposed and the likely effects on the Island's economy.

His supporters were furious and accused him of abandoning the reforms he had put forward when first elected because he wanted to avoid paying tax on his own enormous income. They were even more infuriated when, as soon as he had concluded his speech, Caine left the Court and the Island without waiting for the vote. What they did not understand was that he had to catch the Steam Packet boat to Liverpool to connect with a liner sailing for New York. The unpleasant legal business with the Liebler Company had reached the point where his presence was essential.

Back in London after a hectic few days in New York he found troubles were not coming as single spies: *Household Words* was on the point of folding. Willie, unable to cope with either Ralph or the debts piling up, resigned. When the magazine collapsed Caine was left with a heavy loss on the venture and Ralph at a loose end again. Willie, now 43, had recently married and wanted to pursue his own career independently of his famous brother. His bride was a widow, Mary Elizabeth Levy. She and Willie settled in Yarmouth in the Isle of Wight with her daughter Vera, who was eight. In the summer of 1904 she had another daughter. In October Vera caught chickenpox and gave it to the baby, which died. They never had another child.

Ralph out of a job was a problem. His father got him a place with a firm of printers and was back in Greeba Castle in mid-July. Arthur Collins, the manager of the Theatre Royal, Drury Lane, travelled there to see him about the staging of *The Prodigal Son*. Though the play was not actually produced until September, 1905, Caine was already working on the dramatisation. This time he wrote the play before completing the book. As he finished each act he sent it to Mary who read it and commented before giving it to Ralph to take to the printers. The Wimbledon house had been given up to save money and she was staying with Ralph in a flat in Whitehall Court. She wrote that she was sorry 'Mr Collins has written disturbing your 3rd act... I'm afraid I don't like what he has suggested. I told Ralph it sounded just like a scene out of one of Cecil Raleigh's plays and not a bit like your own work. I'm sure it would be wrong to take the interest away from Oscar just at the top of his big scene.'

Rumours had reached his father that Ralph was 'carrying on' with a young married woman. Mary tried to smooth things over.

> I really don't think there is any harm in Ralph going about with Chris Levant. She is a very sweet girl and is very fond of her husband. It is true Ralph and she go about a good deal and yesterday they went to Windsor to lunch at the Riviera Hotel. She pays her own expenses and Ralph pays his own. Mrs Levant has a girl friend…who is the daughter of a rich merchant and lives in Clarges St W. Ralph is a little interested in her. I am trying to get her to come to tea. The boy will have girls about him so I try to find nice ones. I shall be happy to have you with me. Do come as soon as you have finished your work.

In the midst of all this Caine was busy with preparations for the arrival in the Isle of Man of Beerbohm Tree and his company with *The Eternal City*. It opened at the Grand Theatre, Douglas, on 11 August, 1903. Caine prepared the press release himself, on paper headed *Her Majesty's Theatre*. It announced that the first night in Douglas would be the 958th performance of the play in England and America. 'Three companies are now touring with the piece in the English provinces, one in South Africa, one begins in Australia in September, and one is on the road in the United States. Thus six companies are playing Mr Hall Caine's drama in various parts of the English speaking world.' He also planned the layout of the advertisement for the front page of the paper. It included a summary of the action of the play and prominently featured a picture—not of the stars of the show but of Hall Caine.

CHAPTER TWENTY-ONE

As soon as Tree's company had left Douglas Caine returned to Iceland. His new book, *The Prodigal Son*, was taking shape. Most of it was set there and as fourteen years had passed since his previous visit he needed to refresh his memory of the place. Mary, shuddering at memories of the voyage, stayed in Wimbledon. Derwent, now 12, having refused to go back to St Cyprian's for the summer term, was running wild at Greeba, staging an asthma attack whenever school was mentioned. Caine sailed from Leith, as before, taking Derwent with him. He intended to hire ponies and ride out to see more of the countryside than he had before. They were to go to Thingvellir to attend a meeting of the Althing and Caine wanted to have a good look at the site of an important scene in the book. The agent who arranged the trip told him there was a hotel 'of sorts' at Thingvellir but he would do better at a farm, Karastodum, where he would 'see more of Iceland Life and Habits'. Farmers were always good hosts and refused payment from travellers 'but it must always be given'. Caine could best study real Icelandic domestic life in the farms and small fishing villages—Reykjavik was more Danish than Icelandic. The agent reminded him to take 'three or four sixpenny boxes of Keating's Insect Powder'.

At Leith they met Jon Stefansson, who had come from Denmark to be their guide. Two years later he had still not been paid and wrote asking deferentially that as *The Prodigal Son* had been 'a pecuniary success' please could he be reimbursed for his expenses. He was Caine's adviser on both the book and the play, both of which nevertheless attracted criticism in some quarters for 'unIcelandic' matter. Perhaps residence in Denmark had 'detribalised' him.

Caine was no longer an unknown tourist in Iceland. He was welcomed now as a celebrity and everyone wanted to entertain him. He set out for Thingvellir with Stefansson and Derwent, accompanied by many of the leading citizens of Reykjavik. They stayed at the recommended farm and a scene from the end of the book almost certainly describes what Caine saw in 1903:

> Magnus and his mother were sitting in front of their farm at Thingvellir. Anna was spinning and Magnus was making a rope by a twister turned by a small boy a dozen yards away, for it was just after the wool-plucking and a little before the hay-harvest. The sun was setting behind the crags of the Almanagja, the blueberry ling was reddening over the green waters of the chasm, and

> there was no sound in the evening air save the plash of the Axe waterfall, the lowing of kine, and the cry of curlew. Then over the hum of the wheel and the wis-wis of the twister came the dull thud of horses's feet on the hollow ground and Anna stopped to listen.

This depiction of a tranquil country scene is an effective prelude to the drama and tragedy with which the story closes.

Their tour lasted about two weeks and then the party returned to Reykjavik, where, on 1 September, Caine was the guest of the Governor at a banquet. He was struck by how similar the Manx and Icelandic assemblies were. What he thought of them is reflected in the scene in *The Prodigal Son* where Helga, the evil genius of Oscar Stephensson, the prodigal of the title, mimics 'the manners of parliament, with its "Mr Speaker, permit me to rise to a point of order," and "Will the honourable and learned member explain," and all the other inanities of a legislative assembly in a little country.' This infuriated his constituents in Ramsey, who took it as a criticism of the House of Keys, and upset the Icelanders who thought he was referring to their Parliament.

Caine bought a shaggy Icelandic pony and took it home with him, as William Morris had done nearly thirty years before. This pony was a great favourite at Greeba. Caine rode it for years and it featured in several cartoons of him.

They were home by the end of September. On 3 October, his father took Derwent back to Eastbourne and St Cyprian's, finally agreeing with his mother and ignoring the fuss he made. The next day, in a letter to Shaw, Caine mentioned they had seen the Baltic Fleet off Beachy Head. Derwent had worked himself up into a 'cold state', convinced they were about to blow up the British ships and the town of Eastbourne.

Throughout that winter of 1903–1904 Caine worked on the serial, the book and the stage version of *The Prodigal Son*. There were some distractions. Tyler wrote in January, 1904, complaining of the money he had lost because of Viola Allen's defection. She herself was ill and had to abandon her tour. She wrote from the New York Eye and Ear Infirmary that she felt Caine had not wanted to keep up their correspondence 'so though I have many times wanted to reply I could not quite make up my mind that a letter would be welcome'. She was recovering but 'not allowed visitors and forbidden to think—fancy doctors believing that is possible'.

Viola was not the only one ill. On 23 March Bram Stoker wrote from Deal, where he was convalescing. He had been in bed for several weeks but was beginning to work again. Caine had invited him to Greeba. Bram would be delighted to accept as soon as he had finished the novel he was writing. 'I would be glad to see you take a holiday. You need it more than work or money. When I am free you and I will have to go away for a bit.'

In April Mary returned to England with Derwent, after spending his Easter holiday at Greeba, and took him to Eastbourne for the St Cyprian's summer term. Mary loved the Season in London and the social whirl which her husband hated. Lunches, dinners, tea parties and visits to the theatre with a circle of friends, many of them titled, filled her diary. Ascot and the Derby were high points in her year. She enjoyed a flutter on the horses but was never the compulsive gambler that Ralph became.

Meanwhile Caine set off for one final bit of research for the new book. He spent a week or two at Monte Carlo looking at the casino and observing the gambling fraternity. From there he went to Biarritz on a similar mission. After that he met William Appleton in Paris to discuss publication in America. There were problems over the serialisation there. Caine refused to use an agent, who would have sorted out such matters for him, because he grudged the commission. He had arranged dates for serialisation in Manchester that summer and for Heinemann to publish the following spring without consulting Appleton. At the same time he had placed constraints on the American magazines not to publish ahead of England. Appleton pointed out that not only would his firm lose money but Caine would get much less from America than the $10,000 he had been offered. After much argument and telegrams to Heinemann a compromise was reached—Heinemann would bring publication in London forward to November. Appleton gave Caine a cheque for $770 as an advance and they parted still on fairly good terms.

Caine returned to Wimbledon in May and Frederic Shields came to stay. For some time Caine had wanted to buy one of his paintings and now finally chose a rather sentimental and wishy-washy oil, *Mercy at the Gate*. It was sent to Greeba and hung over the drawing-room fireplace. His parents joined him there and it was clear that John Caine was failing. Mary came up from London and Lily arrived with her husband, George Day, and their little boy, Davy, now eight. John Caine died on 12 July, 1904. He was buried in Liverpool beside his son John and the two little girls. Lily and her family stayed on at Greeba to keep Mary company when Caine returned to St Moritz to write at the beginning of August. He was greatly saddened by a letter which was wrung from Lily a week or two after he had left.

She and George, who were both out of work, had no home. 'You know I am extremely anxious to get into somewhere where we can have the few things we possess round us. It is high time we got back to London and got something to do. I am naturally very dead sick of things. After many talks and talks George has decided to ask H.A. Jones for fifty pounds and I said I would ask you for the loan of the same amount.'

This would pay for a small cottage somewhere outside London. Mary was helping her to find something. 'Whatever happens,' she said sadly, 'I feel it is an absolute impossibility for me to go on much longer in this unsettled state. When I had hopes of one day being able to <u>do</u> something in acting all the unsettled part didn't trouble me. I looked upon it as a means to an end. Today the future looks <u>very</u> different to me. I feel if I look after the home part it will have to be my share—and George must do the rest.' Someone she knew had offered her the lead in a new play being tried out at Worthing for one week with three weeks of rehearsals but by the time she had paid for her dresses and lodgings she would be out of pocket. 'I am afraid of landing myself with <u>more</u> on my shoulders than I already have, which already seems too much for me at times—and it would all be on the <u>chance</u> (oh that chance!) of the play going to London.'

How Caine's heart must have bled for his sister, worn out and disappointed at 35 with a useless husband. She assured him she would repay any loan by instalments, doing everything herself in the cottage to save a servant's wages,

> as long as my health made this at all possible. Mary doesn't seem to think I could do it—but necessity is one thing and choice is another. This isn't at all the life I had mapped out for myself and I never thought I would be in the present position at my present age. Still I have the good sense to set my teeth and go on and make the best of it—which sometimes wants a bit of doing—but up to now I have managed it. It's only the <u>nights</u> that are not cheerful... You can imagine this has not been an easy letter to write—but just say what you think. George has tried hard to go on and not go to Mr Jones (one does not want strangers to know ones real position) but it must be now.

The letter is smudged in places, perhaps with tears, and she added a note: 'I have opened this to say that I know you have all sorts of "applications"—and that has made it doubly hard for me to write this. And I am quite aware that you have <u>heavy</u> expenses one way and another.' Though no record has come to light we can be sure that Caine responded as generously as he could. George Day was a drifter but his health was not good—he died only four years later. Whatever help Caine was able to give, Day came back for more. When Caine was ill in bed, something which Day very well knew, he telegraphed from London to Greeba: 'Must absolutely have hundred pounds this morning can you instruct bank am waiting here for reply.'

On 16 August, 1904, Caine wrote to Mary, 'So it is 20 years since I walked up and down the road in Hampstead when Ralph was being born!... On the whole we have had a very happy and a very prosperous twenty years... I have much to thank you for, too, and we have been very happy together.'

Celebrities Caught—And Bowled, a page from The Tatler,
7 September, 1904.

The Prodigal Son came out from Heinemann on 4 November, 1904. Caine sent an advance copy to Theodore Watts, who had discussed the story and helped with it while staying at Greeba in the summer. Caine had altered the final chapter 'for do what I would, I could not end as I intended, feeling that it was wrong ethically and artistically too. I have shed a good many tears over it, and I have so far verified the emotions it describes as to have gone through them myself.' He was delighted to hear Ernest Hodder-Williams (one of the founding partners of Hodder & Stoughton) was bringing out a biography of Watts, something he felt was long overdue. He promised to review it in the *Bookman*, as he had known Watts for so long.

He wrote to Clement Shorter, of the *Tatler*, about *The Prodigal Son*, telling him how he had brooded for years over the different versions of the story of the prodigal's return. It had taken a long time to choose between the biblical story, in which the father welcomes his son and kills the fatted calf, and others where the prodigal returns wealthy, is not recognised and is killed by father or brother for his money. Caine's story comes somewhere between. For Caine, justice demanded the death of the prodigal who had sinned but his story stopped short of murder by an unwitting relative. He went back to Greeba in good time for the copyright performance of *The Prodigal Son* at the Grand Theatre, Douglas, on 2 November.

With this novel there is a clarity in the writing and in the construction of the plot which is too often missing in the previous books. The story is easier to follow, even though it has its longeurs. He works up to a pitch of excitement only to hold up the action while the characters agonise over the morality of what they are about to do, or else with descriptive passages which may be fine in themselves but are maddening to someone who just wants to know what happens. He diverts into long descriptions of festivals, legends and landscapes until in places the novel reads likes a tourist guide.

Once again Hall Caine had done his homework and once again he got some things wrong. The account of the hero, Oscar, an untrained amateur musician, being invited through Helga's intervention to conduct at Covent Garden and achieving a huge success strains credibility, as does his subsequent triumph as a composer. An overheated account of Helga singing an anthem by Oscar while he accompanies her on the organ of Reykjavik Cathedral ends thus:

> When the anthem was over and all was still, Oscar sat quiet for some moments while the unheard echo of the music seemed to roll through the silent air; and then the lightning-flash of joy or madness which comes to every man of genius once in his life came to him also, and his heart cried out, in its delirious happiness, 'I, too, am a great composer!'

It is impossible not to speculate at which point in his career Hall Caine had felt that 'lightning-flash'.

The 'Rossetti theme' recurs in this book. The Governor's younger son, Oscar, becomes engaged to the Factor's daughter, Thora, supplanting his brother Magnus, who was going to marry her. Then her sister Helga returns from a trip to Denmark and she and Oscar fall in love. Oscar realises he only wanted Thora in order to take her away from Magnus—it is Helga he really loves. Caine had pondered what he saw as Rossetti's tragedy for years. In this book he has Oscar musing to Helga,

> 'When a man has engaged himself to a good woman he ought to be true to her. It is his duty, and whatever the consequences to himself he ought to do it. If he has to suffer he <u>must</u> suffer, Helga, and if he has to sacrifice himself…' A faint sound stopped him. Helga was crying. Her crying seemed to search his innermost thoughts, and to say, 'But have you any right to sacrifice me?'

Accounts of Rossetti's agony when his wife died are mirrored in the description of Oscar when Thora dies a few days after the birth of their daughter, Elin. This could have passed muster but Caine did worse than that: he took the story of Rossetti which he had first heard as a susceptible 17-year-old at Maughold, the story of how the poet/painter had buried his book of poems in his wife's grave. He even used the detail of how Rossetti had wrapped his wife's hair around the book. Oscar is a musician and it is the manuscript of his compositions that he places in his wife's coffin, but no one was fooled by that. The incident of Rossetti's poems was too well-known and the substitution of a musician for the poet was no disguise. As Rossetti later had his wife's body exhumed in order to retrieve the poems and publish them, so in the book Oscar, in desperate need of money to pay off gambling debts in Monte Carlo, yields to Helga's tempting and orders the exhumation of Thora's coffin so that his music can be retrieved and sold.

When the book was published, to the instant success to which Caine had become accustomed, William Rossetti's wrath was terrible. He never spoke or wrote to Caine again and nor did any of his children. Caine lost some good friends and influential acquaintances through this episode, as well as the respect of critics. It was a crass thing to do. He tried to justify himself in the papers, protesting that his story had nothing at all to do with Rossetti and his manuscript. It would have been better if he had kept quiet.

Writers must draw on their own experience and it may be facile to read too many parallels with Caine's own life into the texts but it is difficult to avoid doing so. In a later chapter, where Helga and Oscar are in London, both living in the house of Oscar's college friend Neils Finsen, one reads: 'Sometimes they supped or dined at restaurants with their new friends, who were chiefly Finsen's friends, and then brought their hosts back to Helga's rooms for cards and conversation until one, two or three o'clock in the morning. It was a reckless, irresponsible, unconventional life…though they never thought of that.' There were plenty of people who remarked on Caine's own 'unconventional life', though there was more innuendo than plain fact. However, what this scene does bring to mind is the first months in Clement's Inn with Eric Robertson and the descent of the wrathful fathers, an episode which finds more explicit use in a later novel.

There are several scenes in the book set in the French Riviera, which Caine made it his duty to visit—evidently with pleasure as he returned for holidays for years. He describes the enchantments of the place but is censorious about the life and the people, calling Monte Carlo 'a sink of iniquity and a den of thieves which ought to be closed down'. He describes Oscar at the casino finding

> the usual company gathered about the tables—all middle-class, whatever their rank and station—the middle-class financier, the middle-class millionaire, the middle-class baron, the middle-class peer, the middle-class duchess smoking her cigarettes, and then the prostitute in her feathers and the black-leg in his diamonds, as well as reputable men and virtuous women, for the gaming-house knows no distinctions of means or morality or intellect, and is the high court of the devil's democracy.

(The old meaning of 'black-leg' was a swindler or card-sharp.) This diatribe stems from Caine's unsophisticated and puritanical nature, together with his chapel upbringing, which forbade him even to enter a 'gambling hell', let alone join one of the tables.

That he had never been inside a casino was immediately clear to his more worldly readers. People commented that he had written a scene about baccarat being played at Monte Carlo when it never was. He retorted that the setting was meant to be the casino at Nice. When he produced the playscript for Drury Lane Arthur Collins and most of the cast saw that the swindle Caine described Oscar perpetrating was ridiculous and could never have worked. Collins took him on an educational trip. They went to Monte Carlo where he introduced Caine to an old lag who had done time for a gambling fraud and explained how it could be done. Solemnly Caine took notes and shook hands with his instructor, most grateful for his help and politeness and unaware of his criminal record—according to Collins. According to Caine, in a newspaper interview in America some months later, he had been perfectly well aware that he was talking to 'a man who had been banished from all the cities and all the casinos of Europe'. The truth may be that he only found this out later. Or maybe Collins could not resist enlightening him.

Caine is on record as saying he always shaped his stories so that in the end justice was done. He constantly returned to the theme of the repentant sinner. As Dan Mylrea in *The Deemster* struggled and prayed that he might atone for his sins, so Oscar 'found himself praying that he might be permitted to begin again, to put the past behind him, and to think of the lost days of his life hitherto as seed that was not dead though he had trampled it into the clay'. Oscar experienced being down and out in London. Returning from a night of dissipation, 'crossing Westminster Bridge, he stopped for a moment to look down at the houseless wretches who were still asleep on the benches of the Embankment'. Some things don't change that much in London.

One odd feature of this book is that, although it bears a biblical title and Caine himself said it was his version of the story of the prodigal son, he used quatrains from *The Rubáiyát of Omar Khayyám* as chapter headings and on the flyleaf is the verse:

> Then to the rolling Heav'n itself I cried,
> Asking, 'What Lamp had Destiny to guide
> Her little Children stumbling in the Dark?'
> And—'A blind Understanding!' Heaven replied.

The reviews were many and long. Most came to the conclusion that a) the plot was highly improbable, b) that it would be as successful as The Bondman, to which it was likened, and c) that while the author stuck to Iceland, an improbable setting for romance, and its simple people it was very fine with some excellent writing, but when the scene moved to London and Monte Carlo the more sophisticated reader would only laugh at it. Most reviewers praised his female characters, including the hard and repellent Helga. They were better drawn than the men. The Icelandic setting was the background for 'the high tragedy in which Mr Hall Caine delights,' said the *Queen*.

> Some of his finest writing has been done when he has been depicting human beings in the talons of fate... Mr Hall Caine once more shows the secret of his immense power over his public, that of weaving a story which can only be compared to a close-meshed net, in which the principal characters are helplessly entangled... Mr Hall Caine is a great dramatist. He reaches the heights of exultation and corresponding depths only conceivable to a Celtic imagination. His inspiration is the product of a cross between the Celtic twilight and the Preraphaelite Dream.

This reads as if it was written by someone who knew him, possibly Watts. Caine had learnt from Rossetti how to drum up a claque and his friends were invited to review.

After the critical battering he had taken over *The Christian* and *The Eternal City* Caine had made a deliberate choice to go back to the style of his earlier successes. The book certainly caused a great stir. Some praised the way he blended story and moral 'as warp and woof', others ridiculed the morals, saying his great strength was as a compelling storyteller and that his work would be greatly improved by leaving out the morals, something he was incapable of doing. To him the moral was the whole justification for the book; mere story-telling would have been a weak indulgence. Jerome K. Jerome chose *The Prodigal Son* as the Book of the Month for the December number of the *Review of Reviews*. Their critic, however, headed his piece, 'The Prodigal Son according to the Gospel of St Hall Caine.' He felt it would be edifying for his readers if he recast the version of the new Evangelist in the phraseology of the original Gospel. It was, he found, rather difficult 'because St Luke practised brevity whereas the new Evangelist is—well, not brief.' St Paul managed to tell the story in 22 verses while the 'new Evangelist' filled 426 pages. Caine was annoyed but kept his copy of the magazine with a slip of paper marking the page.

On 25 November, he gave a banquet for 250 of his Ramsey constituents at the Mooragh Hydro Hotel, which he owned. According to one of the local papers the guests were not just 'the toffs and top people of the town' but included young people 'and even the town's letter-carriers'. Caine took the chair and in responding to a toast to his health said he was a Republican, a Democrat and a Socialist in principle, firmly convinced that the sovereignty of the people was the only true basis of government. However, under the existing rule the monarchy in England was doing the work of democracy and the King was 'the best republican, the best democrat and the best Socialist of his age' so he, Caine, was a Royalist too. This speech was reported in the mainland papers and no less a person than the King read it. He was so pleased he sent Caine a long telegram of thanks.

Caine and Mary were in London for a few days on their way to spend Christmas, 1904, at the Palace Hotel, St Moritz. He would have liked to see Shields, who was still ill with his painful leg ulcer, but there was a 'pea-souper' fog and he could not get out to Putney. On New Year's Day he wrote him a long letter from Switzerland. 'It must be a joy to you to realise that your work at the chapel [of the Ascension] is fast (I hardly dare to say fast) attaining to the recognition it so richly deserves.' He had been sent a book, *The Gospels in Art*, for review and had used the opportunity to praise his friend's work. He hoped the certainty of how fine it was would cheer him despite the pain he had endured with his leg. 'We had to come here again,' he continued,

> for my health, though not utterly broken (as the papers said), was getting low, and I was feeling the strain of life severely. So here we are with blue skies over our heads and the white ground under our feet and the air full of sunshine. It is a strange and almost miraculous change from the dark days of a fortnight ago in London. I should have been happy indeed to hear your impressions of 'The Prodigal Son', but you must not give yourself one moment's pain to write on

that subject. The book has apparently had a generous reception—more favourable than perhaps any other book of mine... On the whole I have reason to be thankful and happy, and if the work as a whole does not cover all that I meant by it, I think it expresses more of my best self than anything I have done. You may know that it has been a subject of many sermons in many countries, and I think it has done good... There are other aspects of the book which it is less pleasant to me to think about, and one of them concerns our friend——, who has written both to and of me in a spirit that is a little painful to remember. However, I put this as far back in my mind as possible and try to think of pleasanter things.

The friend whose name is replaced by dashes was probably William Rossetti.

From St Moritz Caine and Mary went to Monte Carlo. They were there in March, 1905, when he was told of the death of Sir James Gell in a letter from Samuel Norris. 'He was the oldest of my Manx friends,' he wrote back,

and taken altogether, the best. Regarded all round I doubt if he has left anybody so good behind him in the little field of Manx public life... One by one the threads that bind me to the Island are being broken. The Isle of Man has never quite survived for me the death of T.E. Brown, and though I am grateful for my sincere and self-sacrificing friendships there I am not a little weary of some other influences.

Norris had been anxious to know if Caine would be attending the Keys debate on reform in May but Caine said he would be too busy. He did not appear in the House of Keys at all that year but kept in touch with his colleagues. He collated the results of the Reform Committee's work and edited the Petition which was sent to London. When it was presented to the Home Secretary, Herbert Gladstone, Caine was not one of the party. As he knew Gladstone personally he thought it best to keep out of the way. He had embarrassed him by proposing Ralph as a possible Liberal candidate at the age of 19. Gladstone had dealt diplomatically with both father and son. Ralph became an MP after World War I—as a Conservative.

In May, 1905, Ralph was involved in a scandal which left his father 'feeling more degraded than I have ever felt in my life'. He had been borrowing money which he could not repay. Now a summons was to be served on him at his office, meaning his employer would find out. His affairs were giving his father 'infinite trouble' and he dreaded the whole thing getting into the papers. Then his London lawyer telegraphed him that he should pay Ralph's debts 'or be prepared for publicity' as there was another case to follow the present one. 'It is horrible,' he said to Mary, telling her he had sent a cheque for £50—about £2500 at today's values—as a first instalment.

These troubles distracted Caine from a new project. Queen Alexandra was known for her charitable work and had set up the Queen's Fund for the Unemployed. Caine had suggested to her that he prepare and edit a book to be sold in aid of the Fund, a suggestion Her Majesty fell in with at once. This was *The Queen's Christmas Carol*, published towards the end of 1905 by the *Daily Mail*. It was an anthology of poems, stories, music and pictures, all given without fee. Caine contributed a story but did not otherwise allow his name to be associated with the book. It was, he said, the Queen's book and nothing must distract from that. Hoping to keep Ralph out of further trouble he involved him in the work.

Caine wrote to potential contributors. Most of them were friends, but the list included his *bête noir*, Marie Corelli. Bernard Shaw refused to take part. Sir Edward Elgar sent a 'Sketch for Pianoforte Solo'. As he was struggling for recognition in his own country this could have been a help to him. Sir Alexander Mackenzie contributed a setting of Tennyson's 'Ring Out, Wild Bells', Meredith wrote the foreword, Swinburne and Watts sent sonnets, Bram Stoker a short poem, Holman Hunt a drawing of Arabs in the desert, Shields a drawing of an angel and Louis Wain a pair of his delicious cats. Fred Pegram, the artist who had drawn Caine and Mary at Keswick, contributed a picture and there was much more. The book brought in a substantial sum of money for the Queen's Fund and the Queen was delighted. A month or two after publication someone wrote to the *Daily Telegraph* pointing out that Mr Hall Caine and his son had been responsible for it and should have some of the praise. Caine was cross.

In June he settled in Greeba Castle to produce the final stage version of *The Prodigal Son*, with Lily and his mother for company. Lily was to play Thora and Elin, the big West End break she had waited for so long, and her brother coached her in the doubled part. Mary remained in London at Whitehall Court. More and more of their time was being spent apart. Mary often wrote to her husband when he was at Greeba saying how much she missed him but seemed unwilling to join him—he must come to her. His letters at this time repeatedly said how much he missed her but he did not want to leave his beloved Greeba and go to London in summer. It began to look like just a form of words.

On 13 June he wrote, 'I am working pretty well. But all the same I wish you were here. Apart from the great expense of the flat, just when we wanted to keep down expenses, it seems a dreadful pity that you should miss all this wonderful weather. There has been hardly a cloud since I came home.' Arthur Collins had suggested a change to one of the scenes in the play. 'I have made up my mind about it, but I should like you to tell me how it strikes you quite independently... [George] Alexander thought the incident was all right as it stands.' Mary had sent a long account of her social life.

I don't wonder you were sick with two or three engagements every day. You'll be fit for nothing by the time I get down to London... Derwent is having another attack of asthma and he is quite sure it is the trees here are the cause of it. I fear I shall have to send him to the Hydro at Ramsey. The new cook is here but is very expensive. We must get a new one as soon as possible. A young housemaid (a Tweeny) comes from Greeba tonight.

He was as worried about Ralph as he was about Derwent. His mother may have tried to find 'nice girls' for him but Ralph seems to have had a penchant for married women. 'I trust Ralph keeps steady at work,' said his father,

and is never away from the office except on a business errand. Tell him he has to live down the name he unhappily earned in Edinburgh. You must judge for yourself whether it is wise that he should see quite so much of Mr Jones's young married daughter. She has the reputation of being a little flighty. It may be all right and very nice, but he should exercise common prudence.

There were problems with the New York production of *The Prodigal Son* and he told Mary he could plan nothing until he knew whether he would have to go to New York.

I would far rather not go to America on such a flying visit at the hottest part of the year, and I will only go if it is felt to be absolutely necessary. The cook is wanting to leave to go to Douglas and if she goes I don't know what we are to do. Cooks are hard to get now. The 'Tween maid was 'longing' and had to be sent home.

Derwent was now at Ramsey Grammar School as a boarder. His mother wrote to him that she was sorry about the asthma 'but I always regret that I did not have my own way and insist on your returning to Eastbourne. You never would have had an attack. I trust you are not idle but hope you are having lessons to do like other boys.' Derwent, who was nearly 14, wrote an almost illiterate reply.

Mary was again pleading for a house near London but her husband hastened to pour cold water on that idea.

The carpets have come but are not being put down. They come to over £40!! The expenses are becoming terrifying. To have a house near London would cost more than you have the least idea of. Do you reflect that I should then have to pay income tax through and through instead of the present compromise? That might be a shocking addition and make the house rent at the very least double what anybody else has to pay. Say nothing of this to anybody whatever—I don't want a dispute with the income tax commissioners again. I might get off less well next time. As long as my domicile is here we have a defence in court of law against the monstrous double taxing. But all the same I am much troubled that you have to be so much away from me... Greeba only needs you now, and all I want here is one more woman. That would have made my stay at home perfectly happy.

The suggestion that his wife was just 'one more woman' would have been unlikely to bring Mary running. She stayed in London.

In mid-August he joined her there to supervise rehearsals for *The Prodigal Son*, opening on 7 September at Drury Lane. He signed a contract for a production in Sweden. Sending the playscript to the agent he wrote, 'Whatever it may be it is at all events my best. And in this case I am a dramatist first, and not (as always before) a novelist first and a dramatist afterwards.' He could not tear himself away from Drury Lane to see the American production but had promised his American friends 'to cross the ocean as soon as we have finished in London'.

Lily Hall Caine (left and right) and George Alexander (two central figures)
in The Prodigal Son at the Theatre Royal, Drury Lane, October, 1905.

Urgent cables continued to arrive from America. 'Please cease worrying also Collins every indication colossal success Washington twentyeighth expect you Coronia or Kaiser latter quickest', read one of them. However, there was no question of his leaving before the Drury Lane opening. George Alexander played Oscar to high critical praise. Lily earned good notices, to her brother's delight. Praise for the play itself was mixed. Dobbs's *History of Drury Lane* says only, '1905 saw a play by Hall Caine, *The Prodigal Son*, notable for a specially trained flock of sheep and not much else.' It had a reasonable run of 105 performances and subsequently toured successfully. It was revived at the Adelphi in 1907 with an altered cast but with Lily still playing Thora/Elin. The *Pall Mall Gazette* carried a candid and most amusing review of what it called 'The Drama of the Heart'. Everyone must have overacted madly as it ends: 'Miss Lily Hall Caine...is the one oasis of comparative calm and pathos, and even she, now and then, catches the contagion of strenuousness and "takes the stage" with the best of them.' The *Morning Post* remarked that she 'acted admirably and spoke her lines splendidly save for an occasional excursion into the tones of Mrs Patrick Campbell', while the *Daily Mirror* wrote, 'Miss Lily Hall Caine coos softly as the good young girl who died.'

Caine was prostrate with a splitting headache after the opening night, 'when I foolishly permitted myself to be carried off to supper', as he said in a letter to Watts. He was writing in bed though in the midst of preparations 'for an almost immediate flight to America. It is with great reluctance that I go, but I realize the necessity both from the financial and artistic points of view, for I see that the Yankees are doing their best (in a way unknown to me) to ruin the last act.' As this was the crux of the whole piece, 'one wonders what they can have done to spoil it, and I must take the first steamer across to see.' At least the Drury Lane production was 'a very real success' with record takings—he always tended to judge his work by the money it made rather than by what the critics thought of it.

Derwent added to his worries, being almost out of control. Before going to London Caine had written to Mary, 'There is Derwent to settle somehow & that is a headaching business & God knows what will happen.' He was expelled from school and as his mother could not cope with him Caine took him to New York. Willie Hall Caine came too. Caine never travelled alone now. By 30 September they were ensconced in the Gregorian Hotel, their base for what Caine later called an 'unhappy visit'. Derwent went to stay with old friends in the country. 'New York is certainly no place for a boy,' said his father. Willie called on publishers trying to sell his latest books but with little success. After a brief excursion to Toronto where on the 27th he addressed a banquet at the Union Club, Caine turned his attention to rescuing his play. Even his friends agreed it was a mess. He saw the performance on 2 October and wrote to Mary next day that 'it was perfectly frightful. Dead—stone dead from first to last.' Boucicault was completely miscast in the lead. Within days he and four other actors had either resigned or been fired. Caine worked long hours rehearsing their replacements. He despaired of the New York run but managed to turn the production round before it moved on to Brooklyn, Washington and Chicago.

George Tyler, of Liebler & Co., wrote gloomily that hopes for 'a sudden jump in business' were not strong. Caine avoided meeting him, as he gleefully told Mary. As Derwent was with him it is a puzzle that Mary did not come too. Each claimed to be missing the other. Letters of Caine's in the Berg Collection of the New York Public Library, which give a detailed account of this visit, show affection for his wife but he stayed on longer than originally planned. On 30 October he gave 'a forcible address' to the young men of John D. Rockefeller's Bible class at the Fifth Avenue Baptist Church, thundering against 'the menace of great private and national wealth, with its concomitants of luxury and self-indulgence, and the necessity for the application of Christian principles to the practical side of life'. This did not go down well with the local press but he was better received when he opened a Carnegie Library a few days later. Staying with the Appletons at Oyster Bay he was taken to meet the former President Grover Cleveland. Back in New York the Appleton firm gave a dinner in his honour. He was invited everywhere, even dining with Admiral Evans of the American navy on his flagship. While in New York he received the news of Irving's death in a cable from Stoker. He wrote a long article on Irving for the *New York Herald* which was syndicated across the country.

By mid-October he was tired and depressed, feeling he had come too late to save his play. He told Mary to watch the *Telegraph* for news of his departure so that she would know when to expect him. Before they sailed on 31 October, 1905, Uncle Willie took Derwent to see the Niagara Falls. Reports that the play was doing well on tour cheered Caine. 'On the whole America has been good to me,' he wrote to Mary, '& except for the wretched worry of the play I think I should have enjoyed my stay.'

He was home in time for the publication of *The Queen's Christmas Carol* and was immediately faced by a protest from Watts who, having received the proofs, did not like the proposal for a page of facsimile signatures at the front. He and Swinburne would not sign. Caine wrote at once, in a letter marked Private with heavy underlining, that he took Watts's point but hoped he would think again. 'It was felt by many of the contributors, and I think also by the Queen (who partly suggested it) that a certain personal note would be given to the volume by the autograph signatures.' He got his way. Watts—using the new form of his name, Watts-Dunton—signed and persuaded Swinburne to do the same. Caine ended his letter, 'There will be good things in the book and other things (by famous people) that are not very good, but my responsibility is to the authors, not to the public, except so far as I have had to compile a book that shall speak to all classes—wise and ignorant alike, educated and the reverse.'

CHAPTER TWENTY-TWO

By the end of 1905 Caine was exhausted, physically, emotionally and creatively. He was now 52. Nearly five years passed before he brought out another novel but he took care not to disappear from the public eye. His plays continued to be produced around the world. Apart from the dramatisations of his books he wrote a number of plays, some for the summer seasons at the Gaiety Theatre in Douglas. A few survive as playscripts in American libraries and museums but for the most part scattered references in letters and old newspapers are all that remain. In 1903 Appleton's published *The Isle of Boy*, described as a comedy in four acts, which seems unlikely for such a humourless writer and it is not particularly funny. Whether it was produced or not is another matter. *Love and the Law*, *The Old Home* and *His Partner's Wife* are undated. In 1908 he adapted his story *Home From Home or Jan the Icelander* for the stage and signed a contract with the 17-year-old Derwent and a M. Leveaux for its production. A letter from Mary evidently written around 1905 refers to a play called *The Red Shirt* being well suited to the Douglas summer season. There were almost certainly others.

In addition Caine continued to write newspaper and magazine articles and stories, and addressed meetings and banquets. First, however, he fled the British winter for the snows of St Moritz. For once it did not suit him and he complained of not being able to sleep so he and Mary moved to the Hotel des Anglais at Nice. Early March, 1906, saw them heading for Genoa on the way to Sicily. Travelling north again they parted in Rome, Mary returning to London and Caine going to Naples, where he arrived on 1 April for a stay of three weeks at Bertolini's Palace Hotel. It was there that he had an odd encounter. Sir Osbert Sitwell, who so memorably recalled spotting Hall Caine striding through the London streets with his cloak flying behind him, tells the story in *The Scarlet Tree*.

Sir Osbert's erratic and difficult progenitor, Sir George Sitwell, had spent most of that winter based at Bertolini's, which his son describes as being then 'the most luxurious establishment of its kind, riding with mast and pennons above the city'. It was against Sir George's principles to stay there too long as it was expensive, though he enjoyed the view, so before Caine's arrival he and his valet, Henry Moat, had gone off to visit Puglie. They returned late one evening. It was now high season.

Henry, far from realising how crowded the hotel had become in the interval, did not even trouble to make enquiries at the desk, but, taking it for granted that everything was as usual, told the porters to carry the heavy luggage up in the lift and leave it outside the door of 143, the room [Sir George] had occupied all the winter. Himself had then climbed the stairs and...walked along the passage to find his trunks already waiting for him outside the door. He opened it, without turning on the light, and—for he was very strong, and knew the exact position of every piece of furniture in the room—took up my father's heavy, old-fashioned leather portmanteau and threw it on the bed. Immediately the room was filled with loud groans of pain and terror; then light flooded the room and two trained nurses dashed in from doors each side. The victim was Hall Caine... The one-time earnest young friend and embryo Boswell of Dante Gabriel Rossetti was now a man at the height of world-wide fame...a figure in each continent, his novels being translated into every language.

The famous nerves were in a poor shape after that and needed all the cossetting a luxury hotel could provide as he had also caught a chill on his liver. He had been joined by Arthur Collins who insisted on calling a doctor. His manservant Robert nursed Caine night and day. On 5 April he wrote to Mary that the worst was over but he had to stay in bed a bit longer. She must not worry—Collins would telegraph if anything more was amiss. He wished she had been able to come to Naples with him but it was 'so very fortunate that you were with Ralph when he was in such great trouble'. Again, Caine told Mary he wished he 'could get free of the House of Keys' because of his health and his family worries.

Matching his reaction to Henry Moat's assault by portmanteau, Vesuvius staged a spectacular eruption. Caine grabbed his pen and sent an account to the *Daily Telegraph*. Wherever he went he sent articles home, for the benefit of the Receiver of Revenue as much as the readers. It established that he was travelling in the course of his work and justified, in his own eyes at any rate, putting down his hotel bills and fares as legitimate expenses.

He and Collins left for home on 25 April, stopping off in Florence and Lucerne, telegraphing Mary to say they would be staying in Paris for a while. She wrote a long letter to 'My darling old Boy', surprised to get his telegram as she had been expecting him home that day. She had been shocked to read his Vesuvius article. 'If I had known you were in such danger I should have been dreadfully unhappy about you. I'm glad I wasn't there.' The great San Francisco earthquake was then filling the papers, which Mary said had 'spoilt' his Vesuvius article. 'Lady Cornwall said she thought your description of the eruption was beautiful.' Lady Cornwall, a close friend of Mary's, lived next door to the Caines at Whitehall Court, in Flat 3. Her husband, Sir Edwin Cornwall, was chairman of the London County Council and for many years the Liberal MP for Northeast Bethnal Green, in London's East End. He was Deputy Speaker of the House of Commons from 1919 to 1922. Mary often stayed with them at their country home in Surrey—Oaklands, Horley—when Caine left her on her own. The Cornwalls were regular summer visitors to Greeba Castle.

In March, 1906, the House of Keys passed a motion on Reform in the Isle of Man while Caine was in Naples. On 11 May he was at Greeba—without Mary—and made a rare appearance at a debate on the subject. The MHKs drew up a petition to the Governor—Lord Raglan, who had at last arrived—asking that the reforms agreed by Tynwald should be implemented. That autocratic old despot rejected them out of hand. The Keys appealed to the Home Secretary, Herbert Gladstone, who replied that the Governor was within his rights and there was nothing the British government could do.

Caine and Mary now lived increasingly separate lives. Mary had always disliked the Isle of Man, not least because it entailed crossing the sea to get there, and she was a real Cockney sparrow, happiest within the sound of Bow Bells. It is clear from her letters to her husband that she adored him and it is difficult to explain their increasingly lengthy times apart. A letter addressed to her husband at St Moritz, telling him how much she missed him, said, 'It is very hard to be left behind at the last minute.' She no more enjoyed being a grass widow than she had when Caine went to Russia. She remained to the end completely loyal and faithful. It was to her women friends such as Lady Cornwall that she turned when she was lonely, not to other men.

As he grew older Caine became ever more egocentric and self-important. Nothing was ever allowed to interfere with his writing and his wishes were paramount in the family. Photographs in his middle and later years often show a man looking haunted, serious, sometimes downright miserable, to the extent that one must wonder what lay behind it. No single photograph of him smiling has turned up so far. He was not entirely happy with the way his career had developed and longed to devote himself to his *Life of Christ*, which may account for the strained expression. His sensitivity to criticism probably contributed. Mary could be equally self-centred, refusing to spend more than short summer holidays at Greeba. She filled the gap in her life by a frenetic pursuit of the social round and buying clothes and hats.

The only book Caine published in 1906 was *Drink: A Love Story on a Great Question*. Heinemann refused to touch it but George Newnes brought it out in August. It was only 118 pages, based on a magazine story Caine had written about seventeen years before, and illustrated by Cyrus Cuneo, well-known in his day. The 'Great Question' was Temperance. The book was terrible and duly slated, but 125,000 copies were sold. Appleton took it up and it went well in America, as did anything with Caine's name to it. Typical of the reviews was one in the *Manchester Guardian*: 'There is no reason why novelists, however eminent, should not write tracts and no doubt Mr Hall Caine has the best of motives for his latest production. He has, however, not given us anything but a sensational magazine story which is undistinguished as literature and ineffective as a tract.' It was only 'a rather gruesome love story'.

In August Mary packed Greeba Castle with young people for Ralph's birthday on the 15th. They were all photographed assembled in the garden on the day of the party, which was widely reported as being for his 21st birthday. This is puzzling as it was in fact his 22nd. His father was not there. After many years of waiting, *The Bondman* was about to be staged at Drury Lane, produced by Arthur Collins, and Caine was in London supervising the rehearsals. It was not necessary for him to be in attendance all the time. He could quite well have returned to Greeba for Ralph's birthday but he chose not to. As usual, he was completely immersed in his own affairs. He was also interfering in the tour of *The Prodigal Son*, in which Lily was playing Thora and Elin—it was in Douglas for the last week in August.

The setting of *The Bondman* had been changed from Iceland to Sicily for the play, hence Caine's visit there earlier in the year. This gave the opportunity for Mt Etna to erupt on stage in the last act. As Mrs Patrick Campbell was playing Greeba that was hardly necessary—she was an Etna in herself. At least she did not pass the time waiting for her cue to enter by flicking chocolates at the backcloth, as she had done in another play that bored her. Arthur Collins regarded getting 'Mrs Pat' as a coup. She despised the play but needed work badly, having been in a succession of flops. On the first night she upset Caine considerably. Mrs Pat told the story in her memoirs of finding him backstage, white and trembling with nerves before curtain up. She felt instinctively sympathetic and said, 'Is this your first play?' She was accused of saying it on purpose and deliberately upsetting him but pleaded she did not. She admitted being ignorant and impulsive, 'for, had I stopped to think, I should have remembered his many successes'.

The production was notable for real cows being milked on stage and the specially trained sheep. One of the milkmaids was Mary's stage-struck eldest niece, an example of Caine's practical approach to helping people who needed money. He had sent her to Arthur Collins with a note that she should be allowed to appear in the milking scene. Her mother, Mary's sister Jennie Mandeville, had written to Mary from South Bermondsey—the letter is transcribed as written:

Dear Mary,
      would you be so kind if you have got any of your boys cloths I should be
very thankful for them or any of your boots as I have not got any to go out
with. Dear Mary I am very sorry to tell you that I have just got a nother baby
boy I did not like to tell you as I think you have a nough trubles but thank God
that I am going on all right again and I trust this will be the last as it makes six
boys and three girls it is a hard strugle to bring them up. hoping you are all
well,
      love Jennie.

This pencilled letter, in childish writing, indicates the probable level of
Mary's education at the time she went to live with Caine in Clement's
Inn. Mary's family never saw their Aunt Jennie but they did know some
of their Mandeville cousins. They became used to Mary disappearing
from time to time with large boxes of clothes and so on. Nothing was
said but they knew they went to her sister.

Though panned by the critics, *The Bondman* was a huge popular
success and had a long West End run. Critics pointed out that the play
ended not with the death of Jason, as in the book, but with his being left
on the Lonely Island, like Napoleon on St Helena. 'As a practical man,'
said the *Daily News*, 'Mr Arthur Collins favours a happy ending to a
play. The British public love a drama that brings a tear to its eyes, but it
must smile through its tears before the end is reached.'

Derwent, aged 16, made his stage début in *The Bondman*, playing a
convict, a coastguard and a farm hand. He appeared in the programme
as 'Mr Derwent', not wanting to trade on his father's name. The audience were unaware who he was until the press blew his cover, after he
had left the cast and was preparing to join a *Prodigal Son* tour. The
Daily Express reported in January, 1907: 'Only just 16, he has the manner of a middle-aged man and a deep bass voice. Slightly built and rather
delicate, the lad has always dreamed of the stage.' His ambition was to
play heroic characters.

I hope to get a good part in 'The Prodigal Son' but tomorrow I am off to St
Moritz, where I hope to cure my asthma. I was the first boy ever to descend
the big Cresta Ice-run at St Moritz. It is a mile long and has been travelled in 50
seconds. I know I did it quite unintentionally in 58 seconds because I lost control of the toboggan. Tobogganing and motor-cycling are my favourite sports
but my father so often told me of the number of accidents resulting from
motor-cycling that I was compelled in self-defence to give it up. I believe he
spent hours collecting statistics of injuries.

1906 was the year war broke out in the book trade, a dispute between
The Times Book Club and the Publishers' Association. The Book Club
sold off as second-hand, at a big discount, books which had only been
on the shelves for a month or two and were virtually new. The
Publishers' Association protested that *The Times* was breaking the Net
Books Agreement of 1899, wrecking the book trade.

Caine waded into the controversy on 10 October with a letter to the *Daily Mail* which he also published in pamphlet form. He announced he would bring out one of his own books—the text of *The Bondman* play—at 2/6d and publish the sales accounts. His argument was that the NBA kept prices up artificially and did a disservice to both authors and readers. Authors could expect to make more from selling a lot of cheap books than from fewer sold at a higher price. A.E.W. Mason said in a letter to the *Daily Mail*, 'It needed a Mr Hall Caine to seize upon the most serious crisis in which the fortunes of authors have been for many years involved to apply it to advertising himself and his play.'

The booksellers wanted *The Times* prevented from discounting books within six months of publication. The Book Club replied loftily that they would sell books as soon as members stopped requesting them, which could be in as little as four weeks. After maintaining a dignified silence for a while *The Times* joined in on Caine's side. The Publishers' Association 'remained unmoved by Mr Hall Caine's new venture' and a number of unkind cartoons appeared. The *Westminster Gazette* printed one showing Caine flying a kite with his own face on it and a tail saying '2/6d'. The title reads, 'Mr Hall Caine: Ill blows the wind that profits nobody.' Another paper carried a cartoon called 'The Boomster', of Caine banging a big drum. In his pocket are pamphlets headed 'The Secret of Success' and 'Log Rolling', while pound notes are stuck all over his jacket.

In the midst of all this the *Daily Mail* published *The Bondman Play* at 2/-, illustrated by photographs of the cast, claiming it proved Caine's contention that English books were sold to the public at prices out of proportion to the costs of their manufacture. It did nothing of the sort, being only an hour or two's reading, far shorter than the average novel. The *Sketch* printed a lofty rebuke to Caine, saying 'the modern novelist does not seem to realise that glorious sales became a thing of the past from the time when a daily newspaper found its way into every home and for a ha'penny provided enough reading matter for a family'.

A truce was reached when The Times Book Club agreed not to discount any book less than four months after publication. The row rumbled on, however. Speaking at a banquet in Bexhill on 24 November, 1906, Caine, asked when the Book War would end, said the only end he could think of was the Day of Judgement. It was another ninety years before the Net Books Agreement collapsed.

The autumn of 1906 found Caine speaking all over the country despite a series of what appear to be severe migraine attacks. In Yorkshire, opening the free library at Morley, he expressed strong views on votes for women. The *Yorkshire Evening News* quoted him as saying,

It is an anomalous and a monstrous thing that one half of the human family—
not the least important, having regard to the duties they are called upon to perform—should be excluded from the exercise of the ordinary rights of
citizenship... No words I can use would be too strong to express my feelings
of the absolute justice of the claim made on behalf of women's suffrage; but
that doesn't in the least commit me to any expression of sympathy with the
unwomanly methods employed. I object to violent suffragette demonstrations
as doing more harm than good to The Cause.

Ever since Kitchener's reconquest of the Sudan at Omdurman in 1898
and his entry into Khartoum, where General Gordon had died, Caine
had been almost obsessed by Egypt. He now planned to set his next
novel there which meant he had to see the country. He had not abandoned his *Life of Christ* and intended visiting the Holy Land as well but
before he could leave there was more trouble with his elder son. Ralph
was again in financial hot water and entangled with a young married
woman whose husband was threatening fire and fury. Ralph's employer
reported to his father that the boy was arriving late for work or not at all
and if things did not improve he would have to go. Caine responded by
removing Ralph from London and putting him under the supervision of
a retired schoolmaster at Seaford on the Sussex coast. In September this
guardian wrote to confirm he had Ralph with him.

I think he is contented and happy. We make our days long, so his uprising is
improving rapidly. 60 miles from London, he will of course never be in town.
Naturally, after so long an interval he finds work rather irksome and tedious.
However he appears interested in Thackeray. I encourage him to keep up all
possible correspondence as this makes him careful alike of writing and
spelling.

Meanwhile his mother was dealing with his debts. She wrote to his
father saying she had to meet what Ralph owed for the hire of a car. She
had told the man Ralph had been ill 'and left in a hurry'. After Ralph's
period in purdah at Seaford, Caine found him a post with the publisher,
P.F. Collier.

Early in 1907 Caine was recuperating in Rome from all these strains,
staying at the Hotel Excelsior with Mary. On 6 March they sailed from
Marseilles on an Eastern Mediterranean cruise. They travelled with the
Co-operative Cruising Ship Company and—amazingly—Caine travelled
incognito. On the 18th they arrived in Jerusalem on the first of several
visits Caine made to Palestine. It was pouring with rain and he wanted
to leave again at once but their guide begged him to stay, saying rain
never lasted long in his country. From Jerusalem they went to Egypt,
staying in Cairo at the Hotel Semiramis. For some time he had been in
touch with people working in Egypt and in his usual way had consulted
piles of books, including Government Blue Books on the country.

Ever since the Denshawai Affair a few years earlier, which both he and Bernard Shaw had denounced, Caine had been opposed to the British take-over in Egypt and understood how the ordinary Egyptian loathed and feared the British Army of Occupation. A party of British officials had gone to the neighbourhood of an Egyptian village, Denshawai, on a shooting expedition. Their quarry were pigeons, which they thought of as legitimate targets for British sportsmen but which the Egyptian farmers considered part of their livestock. Naturally they protested and mobbed the officials in an effort to prevent the shooting. The officials thought they were facing an attack by militant Islamic fundamentalists. In the mêlée which followed the wife of one of the farmers was shot dead—accidentally, as it happened, but her husband was not to know that. Understandably, he struck the official. This unleashed a violent reaction. Sure that the villagers involved were not farmers concerned for their livelihood but Islamic revolutionaries the authorities descended on this small place to bolster British supremacy and make an example of those who opposed it. In the presence of their families four men were hanged, others flogged and sent to prison for life or a long period of hard labour. The sorry affair was reported in England as the brave and romantic survival of honourable men attacked by wicked Muslims out to destroy their country and British rule. The officials thought they had knocked an insurrectionary movement on the head but in fact they had made a present to the Egyptian Nationalists who ever after only had to murmur 'Denshawai' to get the ordinary people on their side.

The true facts were ferreted out and exposed by the poet Wilfrid Scawen Blunt, whom Caine knew. As a result the imprisoned men were pardoned and released. The British Consul took a firm hand and the thing was hushed up but the damage it caused was considerable.

The Consul, Lord Cromer, was as autocratic as Lord Raglan in the Isle of Man, but he was far more enlightened and intelligent. A great statesman, diplomat and administrator, he had first gone out to Egypt in 1876 as plain Evelyn Baring. After a spell in India he had been knighted and appointed British Agent and Consul-General in Cairo in 1883. He was made Viscount Cromer in 1899 and created an earl in 1901. When Caine arrived in Cairo in April, 1907, he was about to retire. He had done much good in bringing Egypt back from bankruptcy and in protecting the Suez Canal, but to Caine's Egyptian Nationalist friends he was a foreign tyrant. Caine hoped to see him before he left for home but Cromer was too busy so Caine wrote to him instead, saying he had for some time been in close touch with 'a score of the Egyptian ruling classes as well as with many of the extremists of the nationalist movement'. He had reached the conclusion that Egypt was 'a hot-bed of conspiracy against England' and that educated Egyptians who co-operated with

Cromer were regarded by the Nationalists as no better than secret agents of a foreign power. It had been said in his presence, and perhaps for his benefit, that whatever England might do to protect the Suez Canal the revolutionary party could destroy it in a single night. He urged Lord Cromer to meet the wish of the Egyptians 'for a speedy fulfilment of England's promise to get out of Egypt as soon as it was safe to do so'. He felt strongly that it was better for Britain 'to yield to legitimate claims to national independence than to run the risk of losing the East as we lost the West'.

Lord Cromer replied on 5 April, 1907, thanking him for his kind letter and adding that he entirely agreed with Caine's ideas.

> In reality, I think the main difference of opinion between myself and the English opposition is that they want to gallop, and my belief is that the pace most suited to Egyptian requirements is a steady jog trot. I feel quite certain that any attempt at hurry could produce a reaction which would be to the detriment of all interests here, whether European or Egyptian.'

It had been a brief but important trip and Caine went home determined to return the following winter. Meanwhile he had a major project to attend to, his autobiography. He spent most of the summer of 1907 at Greeba working on it, with a few interruptions. Lady Raglan asked him to open a fête at Government House and on 31 July he presented the prizes at a gymkhana at Peel Castle. The Channel Fleet called and on 10 August dropped anchor off Peel. Caine dined aboard the flagship with the commanding officer, Lord Charles Beresford, a friend of the King whom Caine had first met in the old days in Irving's Beefsteak Room. Beresford had been one of the King's party on the 1902 visit to the Island. At the end of the Fleet's stay a banquet was given for the officers at the Palace Hotel in Douglas. At Lord Raglan's request Caine made a speech of farewell.

By this time Mary had joined him with Lady Cornwall. Lily and her husband were also staying at Greeba for the run of *The Prodigal Son* in Douglas. Lily was still playing Thora/Elin and George Day was the touring company manager. As ever, Caine was writing numerous press articles. One was on 'The Real Raisuli', a Moorish rebel who had taken some British people hostage in Morocco, while the *Daily Telegraph* asked for an article on the proposed reform of the Divorce Act. His post was always full of letters from madmen—and women—demanding he right their wrongs or get their unprintable novels or poetry published. One from a would-be poet in New York he marked for his secretary with a terse, 'Send the book back.' Many correspondents wanted him to find parts for indigent female relatives in his plays, jobs for sons, or someone to produce their own terrible plays.

He had revised *The Christian*, which was to be restaged at the

Lyceum, and was upsetting director and cast by sending last-minute alterations. Mary and Lady Cornwall left for London on 28 August to be met at Euston by Sir Edwin 'with his lovely motor car'. Mary lost no chance of praising cars in the hope Caine would buy one. The Cornwalls were taking her to Deal for a week 'in order to get some long motor runs to places round about there. We should be so happy if you could join us. A little holiday just now would do you all the world of good and I would like you to see this very lovely car.' Everyone, she said, was hoping Caine would be at the opening night of *The Christian*. The whole of London was 'painted red with beautiful posters... I just caught a sight of one, flying past in the motor.' Caine, however, was not there. Few could have been surprised when he cracked under the strain of work and worry that year. On 2 September Dr Marshall sent telegrams to the London papers reading, 'Mr Hall Caine is suffering from extreme exhaustion which may lead to a nervous breakdown unless the necessary rest is taken.' This provoked more hilarity than sympathy. An anonymous set of verses on 'Mr Hall Caine's Nerves' went the rounds and *Punch* contributed a page of cruel but funny cartoons, The Greeba Castle Pageant. The first showed the Great Haulcanosaur (or Greebatherium) appearing on the scene, 'heralded by the rolling of logs'. The second was of Caine in bed in the castle garden for the benefit of the Press, while the third showed a cart arriving with a 'Powerful Searchlight' to 'illuminate The Mighty Brows every evening from 8 till 10'. The last was of Caine on his hairy Icelandic pony 'Escaping from Observation pursued by a Corps of Mounted Sharp-shooters'.

Mary sent a long and slightly incoherent account of the play.

> You had a very brilliant success last night. I was wishing you were there, it would have done your heart good to see that great audience held almost spell-bound. I have never seen any of your plays or anybody else's, hold an audience as 'The Christian' did last night... Nobody applauded while the play was going on, and whenever they did, which was pretty often, there were shouts of 'order, order' and when they laughed at the comedy scenes, they shouted 'shut up' and 'order, order', they were so afraid of missing any of the play, but after each act the audience simply went crazy with delight... The last scene of the last act went beautifully. There was dead silence, except for the sobbing and weeping among the audience.

By six o'clock that evening the crowds converging on the Lyceum had stretched the length of the Strand. The management gave Mary the royal box. The Cornwalls were with her, also Ralph and two other friends. 'Miss Reinhold wept—a thing she has never done in the theatre before.' Arthur Collins was in a box opposite with his wife and they came round to see her between acts. She reckoned Collins was 'sick as a parrot he had not got the play. He made a big mistake in turning it down

One of a page of cartoons of Caine published in Punch, *11 September, 1907.
Dr Marshall had informed the press that Caine was too ill to attend the
opening of* The Christian *at the Lyceum. This is one of the original pencil
drawings, from the collection of the Manx Museum.*

and knew it.' The reputation of the Lyceum had declined after Irving
gave it up in 1902. It was partly demolished and rebuilt as a music hall
in 1904. Several of Caine's friends had advised him not to allow his play
to be put on there. During rehearsals the Lord Chamberlain ordered a
number of cuts. Ralph pleaded with him and got most of them restored.
Mary thought his father should 'send him a little cheque for all his hard
work'. This letter was ten pages long, becoming less and less legible as it
went on. Caine labelled the envelope, 'The Cockatoo who holds the
quill'.

Although there were 'immense audiences' for the rewritten play the
reviews were less than laudatory. 'Hall Caine has given us a wealthy
class utterly depraved as against a poorer class cruelly victimised', wrote
the *Daily Mail*, while the *People* said Hall Caine went for the emotions,
'leaving the intelligence to take its chance'. The *Pall Mall Gazette*
sneered at 'the cheap melodrama at the Lyceum', the *Observer* being of
the opinion that 'Mr Hall Caine's work has a remarkable purpose—nothing more nor less than the redemption of fallen women'. They were

close to the truth there. He was giving money regularly to the West
London Mission for that purpose.

In October, 1907, *Cobwebs of Criticism* was reissued by Routledge.
Caine was now an omnipresent phenomenon. In December *The
Bondman* was produced in Liverpool. The local papers said Caine was
'too unwell' to attend. London papers, however, reported him in court
then for every day of the trial of Robert Wood for the Camden Hill
Murder—Wood was acquitted. Caine was pictured in a drawing of the
court scene in the *Daily Chronicle* and wrote about the case, asking
that 'the generous honorarium' he had been offered should be given to a
home for fallen women and insisting the editor should publish this fact
so that Caine should not be thought to have been following the case for
pecuniary gain. The Druce Perjury Trial of January, 1908, was another
he attended. He was photographed leaving the court with Beerbohm
Tree after Druce's acquittal, both of them in top hats and fur collared
coats.

On 17 January, 1908, Caine left London with Mary on their second
visit to Egypt and Palestine. (He had asked Frederic Shields to go with
them but he was ill and aging and replied that he no longer had the
strength for travel. What energies were left him must be husbanded to
complete the last fresco in the Chapel of the Ascension.) They travelled
overland to Naples where they caught a boat to Alexandria. Thomas
Cook's had made all their tour arrangements. They were to stay for
three or four months and divide their time between Cairo and
Khartoum, which were linked by railway. Caine also wanted to go out
into the desert in the traditional way—by camel. The best organised of
holidays can go wrong, however, and before he could do anything he
went down with a bad case of 'gyppy tummy'. One of his contacts in
Cairo was an Englishman named B.L. Moseley who sent a kind note to
Mary recommending a doctor. With it he sent a book called *The Spirit of
Islam*, which he had borrowed on Caine's behalf to help with his
researches. 'I shall be happy to read to him or sit with him to relieve
you if he would like it. Pray make what use of me you like.'

Moseley was a great admirer of Caine's work and deeply interested in
his project of a novel dealing with Egypt and Islam. Caine must husband
his strength. He, Moseley, would provide all the information he wanted
'from authoritative sources. There is no reason why you should not
become the redeemer of Egypt. I mean in the moral and political sense
of the term, for you have accurately appreciated Egypt's needs and aspirations and you will be listened to at home.'

Caine and Mary reached Khartoum by the end of January. On
4 February they dined informally at the Palace with the Governor-
General of the Sudan and Sirdar of the Egyptian Army, Major-General Sir
Reginald Wingate. He had been in Egypt and the Sudan since 1884 and

would have been able to tell Caine a great deal about the country and the British occupation. He had written a book, *Mahdiism and the Egyptian Sudan*.

The following Sunday evening Caine and Mary left Khartoum for Wadi Halfa, Philae and Aswan. Caine wanted to see the great dam, designed to tame the Nile, which had been completed in 1903. They were to stay for a week before returning to Cairo but Caine fell ill again and it was well into March before they were back, this time staying at the Savoy Hotel. Moseley had been busy arranging meetings with people who could help, such as Kasim Pasha Amin who would tell Caine about the emancipation of Muslim women. Someone else sent a long dissertation on the Koranic laws on marriage and divorce. Hafiz Awad, referred to by Moseley as Hafiz Effendi, the editor of the Cairo paper *Al Minbar*, called at the hotel to talk to Caine about serialising the new book. Caine worked unremittingly, checking details of the action of his story with his advisers. He also continued to write articles for the London papers. The *Tatler* commented with a splendid cartoon by Charles Harrison, 'Caine in Egypt'. Caine, dressed as an ancient Egyptian, strides out with a box camera hung round his neck and a briefcase with four keys on it, an allusion to his position in the Isle of Man. A porter's trolley follows with a case labelled 'Press Notices' and a bundle of notebooks while in the background another Egyptian figure scatters 'pars' (paragraphs) from a bag labelled 'Publicity Department'.

Caine arrived back in the Isle of Man with Mary on 22 May, 1908. People who saw him commented that he looked 'fagged and worn'. Mary had her heart's desire: Caine had bought a car. It was a 28hp Delauney-Belville and its Isle of Man number plate was 94. According to a local paper it was a 'splendid new motor' which seated seven people comfortably. They had travelled from London 'without benefit of the train', the drive to Liverpool taking seven hours. The car had been put on the cargo boat on the Friday and Mr and Mrs Hall Caine had travelled across on the Saturday. The car caused a sensation on the Island. Concerning his new novel, the same local paper said he had 'already disposed of the serial rights for a huge sum'. About the same time the *Daily Mail* said that two million copies had been sold of his best-known novels. Another local paper called Caine 'The Uncrowned King of the Island'. Referring to the way he had bought up land and property in the chaos following the collapse of Dumbell's Bank, they reported a visitor describing a long drive with Caine. Every time he asked whose land they were passing over he was told it was either Caine's or he held a mortgage over it.

Not that his property brought him unalloyed pleasure. In July of that year he was involved in a legal dispute with a tenant who was giving up

Caine in Egypt, cartoon drawn for The Tatler *by Charles Harrison,*
19 February, 1908.

one of the farms. It concerned the value of straw and manure! His brother Willie wrote from Liverpool,

> I have read with disgust the lawsuit business. You must be irritated beyond endurance. I think you will come to think that after all there are worse things than buying India Stock at 96 and bearing 3½% with the security of the Government and the guarantee of the Secretary of State behind it... You have not the personal joy of walking upon your own territory but the bank gathers in 17/6 every quarter for every £100 of stock with the regularity of the calendar.

He had been sorting through old family papers left by their father and sent a box of them for Tom to look through when he had time.

> Don't tackle the job until you feel in such high spirits as to need a corrective. I never had a more melancholy task than one whole week amid the dead leaves of many forgotten memories. Dead leaves indeed. It was more like groping among unburned skeletons. <u>Everything</u> was kept, relics of broken promises, disappointed hopes and failed ambitions. Still it is all done and everything is now scattered to the four winds of heaven. I do not know that any harm will come to you if you cast all I have sent into the flames without a glance.

On the evidence of his archive and the many holdings of Caine's papers around the world he never consigned any paper to the flames.

That summer Bram Stoker was editing Caine's autobiography and acting as his agent. Caine had interrupted his Egyptian researches to write the preface in Khartoum. Originally he had intended the book to be 'My Story of a Great Friendship', using his *Recollections of Rossetti* as the basis. Neither Stoker nor Heinemann had liked the title or the idea so he had added a preliminary section giving an account of his early life—highly selective—and reduced the title to *My Story*. It must be the oddest autobiography ever written. More than half the book is given over to his friends, principally Rossetti. Most of what he wrote about Tennyson was cut out in the final version but he retained chapters on Ruskin, Buchanan, Blackmore and Wilkie Collins. His story of his own life is notable more for what it does not say than what it does and can at best be described as misleading.

It is dedicated 'To My Best Friend, My Wife.' He says his 'brief career' as a journalist was entirely due to Bell Scott and the article he wrote about him from Birchington in 1882. Considering he had been a freelance journalist for years before that and at the time of writing had a desk at the *Telegraph* this is moonshine. He dismisses his marriage in one brief sentence, 'By this time I had married.' When *Who's Who* was resurrected in its present form in 1897 he had been invited to contribute. He mendaciously gave the year of his marriage as 1882 instead of the actual one, 1886. Obviously he could not now contradict this. *My Story* gives the impression that he spent a large part of his childhood in the Isle of Man and went to school there, which again is not true, but was certainly what he wanted the Receiver of Revenue to believe.

Serialisation began in April in a magazine called *M.A.P.*, which stood for Mainly About People. A delighted Shields found a copy on a railway station bookstall when on his way to Lulworth Cove for a holiday and sent an appreciative postcard.

Passing through London, Caine had seen Bram Stoker about the text for book publication and ordered him to make substantial cuts. For more than ten years Stoker had addressed Caine as 'My dear Hommy-Beg' but on 23 May, 1908, he wrote to him as 'My Lord'. Obedient to Caine's command he was carrying out his orders. 'I have the necessary destruction in hand... Whilst your chariot was still winning northwards I murdered some 2000. And oh but it was sad! The poor creatures looked at me imploringly with eyes so sweet that my heart was touched. All the fell horror of murder came upon me.' He hoped that many of the precious tribes of words might later be brought back to life!

Stoker paid at least one flying visit to Greeba to discuss the book. Sending the Rossetti section for Caine to approve he said he had cut out 15,400 words as Caine wished. 'In the book there are one or two bits I think I should omit not because they are not good but because they are too intimate.' He would read the manuscript carefully again before it went to the printer. In August, when the book had reached the page proof stage, Caine still wanted changes. He could be a publisher's author from hell. When the book was printing he ordered the removal of a passage about Theo Watts-Dunton. As soon as he got the letter Stoker telephoned Adam Cranston at Collier & Co., Ralph's new employers who were publishing the book in conjunction with Heinemann's, and the change was made. It would have been easier had there been a telephone at Greeba but Caine adamantly refused to have one to the end of his life. He hated it and used telegrams instead. As late as 21 August Stoker asked Caine to confirm that *My Story* was the title he wanted. He thought it weak but Caine insisted.

In this book Caine appeared to acknowledge what many of his critics thought, that his Manx books were his best.

> The child is father of the man and what I felt nearly fifty years ago about the Isle of Man—that it was the whole world in little, that all the interests, all the emotions, all the passions, and almost all the experiences of mankind lay there on that rock in the Irish Sea—has been the motive inspiring my books... for if I have learned anything by five-and-twenty years of almost continuous travel, it is that humanity is one and the same everywhere, and that nothing I had known of our tiny Manx race was out of harmony with what I saw in races great and small at the farthest corners of the earth.

Considering the popularity of his novels and plays the autobiography did not sell particularly well, in England at least. Sales in America were better. There were fewer reviews than he was used to. The *Telegraph* said, 'Whatever else may be true about Mr Hall Caine it is very first truth about all his work that it has an indomitable power of interesting the public.' The *Daily Graphic* mused that a certain amount of egotism was as necessary as pen and ink to the writing of autobiography and Mr Hall Caine did not lack anything in that department but there was surprisingly little of it in his book, which praised his friends more than himself. Frank Harris wrote waspishly, 'Success is apt to confuse values. George Bernard Shaw succeeds and one feels he has come to his own: Mr Hall Caine succeeds and I cudgel my brain to find out what people can see in him. But the fact stands four square; his novels sell by tens of thousands; his plays draw crowded houses and the man takes his work seriously.'

CHAPTER TWENTY-THREE

One of the summer house parties for which Greeba Castle became famous assembled at the end of July, 1908, including Lily and her husband. On 7 August, Caine and Mary started out from Greeba Castle in the car with Lily and some other guests. They were going to Ramsey, where Mary was due to present the prizes at a swimming gala. The castle stands on a steep hillside and on the driveway down to the road the car's brakes failed. It crashed into a stone gatepost at the bottom. No one was hurt but Caine's nerves were so upset he could not continue. Mary had to stay with him and Lily presented the prizes in her stead, driven by Derwent in his far less opulent 8hp Rover. Caine's car was not seriously damaged but with only about 120 cars on the Island there was no one to fix it. The insurance company insisted it should be shipped to Mulliner's, the coach builders at Bootle, for repair. Ralph dealt with the business for his father.

News of the accident reached the national papers. Shields was appalled. He hated cars. London, he said, had been made 'a very vestibule of the Inferno by these horrible engines'. On hearing of the mishap at Greeba he wrote,

> A thrill of horror shook me as I read lately how nearly you had met a sudden and horrible death, like the very many reported every day in the newspapers, from a motor car. Amazement still holds me that you—you—should put your life in the grinding power of this latest hell-inspired machine. How many of our streets and roads have been soaked with the blood of its mangled victims. Surely you will never resume the deadly engine—perilous to yourself and others. Surely it shall not be applicable to you, 'Though thou bray a fool in a pestle and mortar, yet will not his folly depart from him.' For your own sake, for your family—and for the sake of all who love you, break away from the evil thing— Do! resolutely do! I forbear more, in grief and fear for injury you may already have sustained to the nervous system. With very kindest regards to Mrs Hall Caine,
>   Yours ever affectionately, Frederic Shields.

Caine did not take his advice. When invited to revise his *Who's Who* entry for the 1918 edition he removed 'Mountaineering' from his 'Recreations' and added 'travelling and the automobile'.

Mary and her house guests left for London and the actor-manager Mattheson Lang, who was to play the lead, and Ernest Carpenter, who was producing, arrived on a brief visit to discuss a rewrite of *The*

Manxman, with the title *Pete*, about to be staged at the Lyceum. In this new version Caine collaborated with Louis N. Parker, whose telegraphic address was Somnolent, London, but judging from the correspondence he was anything but and did the bulk of the work. In June he told Caine he had written a ceremony for installing the Deemster and thought they should not overload the play with 'antiquarian details'. If he had not used the exact words of the ritual, what he had written showed it was 'simple and dignified. That is what is really wanted, isn't it?' He also rewrote Caine's ending to Act II, making it more dramatic. He had a far better sense of theatre and knew what would work on stage. Caine did not like his version of Act III and told him so. Parker replied, 'You need never fear saying anything you like to me. I am in the habit of saying just what I like, whatever I feel I ought to say, to other people and I want them to do the same. We must waste no time in circumlocution. If you say "Rot" I'll say "Right" and on we go.' Parker preferred to 'err on the side of reticence'. The audience should be able to infer from the action rather than have things rammed down their throats but if Caine wanted it 'more definite' so be it. Though he demurred, Caine accepted most of what Parker did. The result was a much better play than the ill-fated Wilson Barrett version. Mattheson Lang was superb in the title role and played it for years. His wife, Hutin Britton, was Kate.

In London Stoker was keeping a watching brief. At 5.30 am on 29 August he wrote to Caine saying he had been at the dress rehearsal the night before and all had gone well. 'Mattheson Lang was really fine. The part is a noble one and he stands up to it thoroughly and sincerely. He will score by it as an actor enormously.' Hutin Britton was good 'and will be better but it is he who really shines'. He gave three pages of detailed notes in his tiny hand which is almost as bad as Caine's. He ends, 'Altogether, old chap, I congratulate you with all my heart. It is a noble play and on big broad human elemental lines. It made me cry like a baby... I shall of course go tonight and write on how it goes.' Critics, as usual, were lukewarm, audiences enthusiastic.

The public in the Isle of Man would not have been enthusiastic had they known of a little plan Caine had been hatching for some time. This was nothing less than the building of a Caine Memorial Tower some-where around Ramsey. He had asked his agent, Cowley, to look for a site. Eventually, in May, 1908, he told his employer he had found the ideal spot—a small tableland on Maughold Head. This, he thought, would be cheaper than previous plans to build on Snaefell or North Barrule, would be just as visible from land and sea, and complement the Albert Tower. The plot could be purchased cheaply because it was on the farm Baldromma over which Caine held a mortgage. It was bought in September, 1908. Mercifully the tower was never built. Putting him-self up beside royalty would have been too much. He still at this stage

Mattheson Lang as Pete.

intended to be buried on the Head. Several memorials, apart from his grave, remain in the Isle of Man. One is Hall Caine Airfield, established by Ralph and Derwent in 1933. It is a grass field in the north of the island used by private aircraft and the Island's gliding club. Another is a statue by Bryan Kneale, for which Derwent provided the money in his will. It stands in a small garden at the end of Douglas Promenade, though it was intended to go opposite the Gaiety Theatre. Passing tourists often mistake it for Shakespeare. There is a memorial plaque on one of the Greeba Castle gateposts.

At some point Caine suggested to Queen Alexandra that she should do another gift book in aid of her charities. He had spoken to Lord Burnham, the proprietor of the *Daily Telegraph*, who would be honoured to publish it. The Queen was delighted. It was her idea that this time the book should consist of her photographs. Published at the end of 1908 as *Queen Alexandra's Christmas Gift Book*, it was subtitled 'Photographs From My Camera'. She set about choosing the pictures at once. Caine was too busy to deal with the day-to-day production of the book himself, leaving it to Ralph. His letters to his father about the book throughout the spring and summer of 1908 show that while he may have been a fool over women and gambling, in business he was clear-thinking and efficient. He was becoming well versed in the printing and book trades. Charming and well mannered, he pleased Queen Alexandra with his efforts.

The book was designed by Ralph to look like a family album. The Queen provided the captions which in their informality enhanced the 'happy snaps'. A picture of her grandson, the future Edward VIII, in his naval cadet's uniform is labelled 'Edward of Wales (Little David)'. Her own family, including her father, the King of Denmark, and her sister, the Empress of Russia, are all there as well as her children, her husband and their friends. Family holidays at Sandringham, Balmoral and in Denmark all feature.

The book was successful, selling well in America and the Dominions and at home. Soon after Christmas, 1909, Ralph was invited to Sandringham for the day to present a cheque for £250 to the Queen, the first instalment of the profits on her book. In long letter to his father Ralph described how a carriage met him at Wolferton Station and he lunched with Queen Alexandra, Princess Victoria and the Prince of Wales (soon to be George V). The Queen and Princess Victoria sent their best wishes to his father. The Prince of Wales remarked that he had not met him but 'I have heard a great deal about him from the King'. They had a long conversation. 'The Prince asked me many questions about the political situation and I think I was able to give him some of the information required. Of course he is an out-and-out Tory and looks upon the Dukes and Earls as pillars of the Constitution. At the same time I think he sees the strong reasonableness of many of the points in the Budget.' The only other people present were Charlotte Knollys and Sir Dighton Probyn, who told him privately as he was leaving that 'there is a strong feeling of resentment against Lloyd George in the Royal Household'. Ralph, who hoped to stand as a Liberal candidate in the next election, was amused.

His parents stayed on in St Moritz where Caine was doing the final revision of his Egyptian novel and working on the stage version. The book had been announced in *My Story* as *The White Christ: A Novel*. Almost everyone concerned with its publication was worried by the title—the only person who liked it was Sydney Pawling. Caine floundered among choices almost equally bad. In the end the problem was settled in March of 1909 by the editor of *Strand Magazine*, who was about to start serialising it. He decided to call it *The White Prophet*. Caine agreed reluctantly. Stoker and Heinemann were both relieved and the title was used for the book as well. Unfortunately American magazines had already begun publication with the original title which caused much confusion when Americans asked for the book.

Beerbohm Tree had agreed to direct the play and take the lead. In January of 1909 rumours began to spread, inspired by some of the civil servants in Egypt who were opposed to Caine's ideas, that the book was seditious and gave an unfair picture of the country. Tree was worried and said he would go to Egypt to see for himself. This upset Caine and he asked Louis N. Parker to go with Tree on his behalf. The two of them travelled separately and met in Cairo. There they were well and truly nobbled by the anti-Caine lobby. They were overwhelmed with hospitality from colonial officials and local hostesses all anxious to put their view of Egyptian affairs. 'It was one of Tree's mysterious gifts,' Parker wrote later, 'that he seemed to look at nothing, but saw everything. During this trip he infuriated me by his apparent indifference to his surroundings: but years afterwards... I found he remembered a great deal more of the local colour than I, who had worked like a slave hunting it up. We wandered from one fashionable hotel to another, lunching, dining, tea-ing and supping, with exactly the same people one met at the Carlton or the Savoy.' They visited Luxor, Carnac and the Valley of the Kings. 'Altogether we had a gorgeous time, hobnobbing with Egyptian princesses, the very interesting Cairene Society, and the extraordinary procession from all parts of the world which passes through Shepheard's.'

Caine's supporters were angry at this circus. Both Moseley and Hafiz Effendi wrote urging him to come Egypt at once to make sure Tree and Parker saw the other side of the question. Perhaps unwisely he stayed

Beerbohm Tree, from a publicity postcard.

put in St Moritz, firing angry letters off to Egypt and London. He demanded that Tree come to see him on his way back to London but Tree and Parker went straight home. When they got to London Tree told R. Golding Bright, Caine's theatrical agent, that he was withdrawing from the contract and would not be producing *The White Prophet*. Caine was shaken. Despite his huge book sales he had always made far more money from the stage versions and this would be a financial disaster as well as a blow to his reputation. Not that he was in danger of penury. *Pete* was still running at the Lyceum and his other plays were touring the country and being performed abroad in a number of languages. The worst hurt was to his pride. A copyright performance was given at the Garrick on 27 November, 1909, but the play was never given a full production, nor has it ever been filmed.

In February he went briefly to Berlin, where Edward VII was on a state visit, reporting it for the London papers. From there he returned to Bertolini's at Naples, en route for Egypt, but it was too late to undo the damage Tree had done. Caine was not cheered by a letter from Sydney Pawling saying gloomily that booksellers reported a drop of between 25% and 30% in sales 'owing to this depression'. Heinemann's had initiated publicity for the new book but orders were far below subscriptions for *The Prodigal Son*. 'I hope Tree won't let any idea get about that there is anything anti-imperial or anti-English in your conception of the story,' he said. 'I have heard one or two rumours of the sort and we are just now passing through such a strong phase of ultra-patriotism that any such idea would have a disastrous effect.'

Rumours had indeed got about and there had been an attack on Caine in *The Bookman* the previous December. Bram Stoker wrote to his 'Dear Hommy-Beg' to tell him Adam Cranston of Collier's had asked him to respond. Of course he would and a rebuttal would come better from him because he was not personally involved. Far from being grateful, Caine sent a furious letter to Stoker, declaring he could stand up for himself and Bram should stay out of it. The long-suffering Bram replied, 'You see, old chap, your view must be different from mine. You have been assailed and are entitled to hit back as hard as you can', but he could give independent support. Caine replied angrily. Bram, hurt, answered curtly, 'I am glad you wrote and so frankly as I was really in a quandary as to what to do. As it is I leave the matter alone and the Editor may go hang for an answer!' He was glad to hear Caine had finished the first draft of the novel and only the polishing remained. 'There may be a lot of politicing but it is politicing and politicing only. Your affectionate Bram.' That he remained affectionate after Caine's treatment of him is testimony to Stoker's good nature and the strength of his feeling for Caine.

There was much public disquiet at this time about developments in Germany. At the end of May Caine heard from the former Alfred Harmsworth, now Lord Northcliffe and with a stable of newspapers which included the *Mail*, the *Mirror* and—a recent acquisition—*The Times*. He wrote from the Ritz Hotel, Paris, to say he was glad that Caine was in agreement with him. There was no fear of his papers 'going back as to the German danger'. His editors had never misunderstood the German situation. He himself had begun to understand the position some eight years previously, when he first began visiting Germany, a wonderful unknown country. Foolish people panicking about airships, he said, only caused Britain to be despised in Germany. He suggested the Germans would think more of us if we were to follow Meredith's advice and let each man arm himself instead of hiring other men to do the fighting for him. When it came to the Navy, the quicker we began to prepare the better. 'This matter should interest you particularly, as the Isle of Man is likely to feel the first force of any blow.' An odd idea. George Meredith died a few months later, another link with Rossetti gone.

In June Caine and Mary were back in St Moritz. W.P. Byrne, of the Home Office, in a personal letter, hoped they were enjoying themselves away from the wet and dreary English summer. 'Please think sometimes with sympathy of our mackintoshes and rheumatism!' A PS said he hoped Caine would be back in time to give evidence before the Joint Committee of Lords and Commons on the Censorship of Plays. 'A flood of nonsense is being written by G.B.S. and other irresponsible persons and it ought to be dammed!' He was clearly unaware that Caine's views on censorship coincided with Shaw's, as became apparent when they both gave evidence to the Committee the following September.

Greeba Castle was opened up for the family's return in July. On August Bank Holiday Monday *The Prodigal Son* opened at the Grand Theatre in Douglas. On the Tuesday the actor who played the Governor of Iceland was ill and Caine stood in for him. As invitations were issued to local notabilities, including the Governor and Lady Raglan, a thought arises that the 'illness' may have been more diplomatic than real. Caine went on without make-up or costume and carrying his script but praise and applause were rapturous. A local paper said Caine read his lines so beautifully that the applause with which he was greeted was amply justified. 'Mr Hall Caine has a delightful speaking voice and his audience was not slow to recognise its charm, and he put new life and gave fresh interest to what is really quite a minor part in the play.' He was not allowed to get on with it when he first came on stage. 'For a few minutes the play was hung up while the audience thundered its applause.' He was called on for a speech at the end and 'graciously complied'. He said it was his first—and last—stage appearance but when word got round that the author had appeared in his own play there was a demand for him to repeat the performance, which he did on the Saturday. The national press was there in force and pictures of the cast, including Caine and the 18-year-old Derwent who played Oscar, were printed in several papers and magazines. When he left the theatre, driven away in Derwent's green Rover, 'There was quite a scene', according to a local paper. 'The street was blocked with people and the eminent novelist had to bow his acknowledgements to the cheers of the crowd time after time.'

Caine on stage (centre) as the Governor General in The Prodigal Son
*at the Grand Theatre, Douglas, August, 1909. May Beatrice as Helga
Neilson (left) and Derwent Hall Caine as Oscar Stephenson (right).*

The White Prophet appeared as a book in September, 1909. The illustrator was R. Caton Woodville, whose work was well known. He had given Caine considerable help over points of military discipline and how a court martial functioned. William Heinemann used Caine's popularity to launch a new idea which seems at first glance like a return to an old one: two-volume publication. Heinemann had just been elected President of the Publishers' Association. In that capacity he used a large trade gathering to float his new idea. In his speech he attacked 'the production of worthless books and books that have been artificially spun out to bulk within covers at six shillings which contain in reality little more reading matter than the old-fashioned one shilling book contained'.

He proposed to price books according to their length. To the argument that quality not quantity should be the yardstick he replied, 'There is in the whole range of commerce no commodity for which the public is asked to pay indiscriminately one price, whether it be a pound or an ounce, that is offered.' He also insisted that quality was already ignored in fixing the price of a novel and that this damaged the publishing business. 'We must not forget that the sale of every bad and unworthy novel is a nail in the coffin of six shilling novels as a class.'

He took the considerable risk of practising what he preached and that autumn launched the Heinemann Library of Modern Fiction. To start the series he chose *The White Prophet* and because of its length opted for two volumes at four shillings each. Nine other titles followed but this attempt, much praised at the time, to fit the price of a book to its merit and length was a failure. No one else followed suit and after the first list Heinemann abandoned the idea. The circulating libraries had a part in killing it off: it was not popular with them because two volumes at four shillings were more expensive than the six-shilling one-volume novels they were used to.

As usual the new title was translated into many foreign languages. The story had been in Caine's mind since *The Scapegoat* of 1890. Indeed, it falls into the same category, with its North African setting and theme of religious bigotry and racial tension. He had returned to the theme in 1894 in *The Mahdi* (Arabic for 'The Expected One'), which reads like a study for a much longer novel. A story often recounted by Frederic Shields could have contributed to the inspiration of the Egyptian book. A Syrian carpet merchant whom Shields met on his travels told him that when the news of Gordon's death at Khartoum came through even the Muslims joined in the universal grief because 'General Gordon, he Mussulman, he Jew, he Christian—he for everyone'.

Caine intended *The White Prophet* to address the problems of colonial rule and to attempt a synthesis of the great world religions. His years of biblical studies and researches for his projected *Life of Christ*, his reading of the Koran and discussions with Jewish and Muslim teachers enabled him to propound, through the character of Ishmael Ameer, a vision of the world's great religions united. A lengthy obituary in the *Isle of Man Weekly Times* said of this book, 'It is believed to present portraits of the Mahdi and General Gordon. It gave offence at home by reason of its sympathy with the nationalistic aspirations of a section of the Egyptian people.'

For the first time in Caine's novels the romance, in which yet again two men are in love with the same woman, is not the most important element in the story. Apart from the theological arguments it is a tale of adventure which begs comparison with A.E.W. Mason's *The Four Feathers*, which had been published in 1904. Caine's is by far the stronger story, being set entirely in Egypt and the Sudan. It would make a powerful film but no one has yet attempted it.

In Egypt and the Sudan Caine had met and talked to the colonial authorities, soldiers and statesmen, and religious leaders of the Jewish, Christian and Muslim churches. He sought out the rabbis, the missionaries and the poorest Arabs. He walked the streets of the cities, sailed on the Nile and travelled in the desert, storing up impressions of the two countries which he reproduced in some of his best descriptive writing, evoking both the scenes and the atmosphere to telling effect.

Before commencing the actual novel he wrote six pamphlet-sized fictional biographies, one for each of the chief characters, so that he could keep track of who and what they were and how they reached the crises in their lives which he intended to describe. As a result the complicated story is well organised and gripping, with fewer tedious diversions into political, moral or theological arguments than many of his books. Indeed, some of these arguments are so cogent and so germane to the story that they illuminate the narrative rather than interrupt its flow. This is possibly truer today when we know less of events in Egypt at the time. We are not so well versed as Caine's contemporaries in the heroes of Empire and unsure what happened at Khartoum and Omdurman. General Gordon's name means little now: in 1908 he was a tragic hero. Numbers of boys were christened Gordon after him in the 1890s and early 1900s.

The central characters of the story are Colonel Gordon Lord, a brilliant young soldier; his fiancée, the beautiful Helena Graves; his Arab friend Hafiz; the White Prophet, Ishmael Ameer; Gordon's father, the Consul-General and ruler of Egypt, Lord Nuneham, and Helena's father, the commander-in-chief, General Graves. Caine admits to modelling Gordon Lord on General Gordon and accusations that he had based Lord Nuneham on Lord Cromer struck home. Ishmael Ameer is clearly the Mahdi in the way he begins as a purely spiritual leader of his people and then becomes involved with nationalist politics and an attempt to drive the English out.

Gordon Lord is presented as the epitome of the young empire-builder. His sympathy for the Arabs and the cause of Egyptian nationalism, however, brings him into conflict with his father. In some ways he would appear to foreshadow Lawrence of Arabia, taking to the desert disguised as a Bedouin named 'Omar Benani'. At the time the book was published T.E. Lawrence was in fact a young Army officer of about 20 or 21 stationed in Egypt.

Caine skilfully sets up the conflict which almost destroys Gordon Lord. 'On the one side,' he wrote, 'the duty to obey orders which military discipline requires of every officer, no matter how highly placed; on the other side, the overwhelming moral sense which told him that he could not obey without outraging the highest dictates of his conscience.' Added to that is the terrible conflict of father and son. The ageing and tyrannical Lord Nuneham (who resembles Lord Raglan as much as Cromer), ready to sacrifice his son in the name of army discipline and to risk a bloodbath to preserve British rule, is a cruel portrait and it is no wonder that people who saw Lord Cromer as the inspiration were up in arms when they read the book. The description of the Consul as a private person is quite different to the real official but there is some resemblance in the public life of the two. However, Cromer, though in the position of a dictator, would never have acted as Caine's fictional Lord Nuneham did.

Helena's father, a widower, is not quite so harsh as his political boss but he ends by putting his daughter in a dreadful position. He refuses to return home to England when he becomes too ill to carry on, nor will he let anyone know the doctor's verdict: that he has serious heart trouble and is no longer fit for duty. Helena herself is sympathetically drawn as a loving and beautiful girl torn between her father, whom she adores, and her love for Gordon Lord. Her father dies of a heart attack but she thinks it is murder. Inevitably the young people are separated. After an act of insubordination for which he is stripped of his medals by Colonel Graves, and an attack on a brother officer which in fact prevents a native uprising, Gordon disappears.

Much of Caine's inspiration for this book lies in the Denshawai Affair of 1904. As he wrote in a letter to his friend Bernard Shaw, the Government, in a classic cover-up situation, were running scared that the facts of the case would come out and would therefore do all they could to kill the book which they thought was going to give the show away. In *The White Prophet* Caine set out to put the Nationalist point of view and expose what lay behind the Denshawai Affair. The result was to infuriate the authorities concerned and lay him open to attacks by people who considered him little better than a traitor.

In the novel Gordon Lord, after his disgrace, hides in the Arab quarter and then, disguised as a Bedouin, travels south by camel to join Ishmael Ameer in Khartoum. He thinks Helena has gone home to England: she thinks he has fled the country. In fact, Helena, convinced that Ishmael murdered her father, has already gone to Khartoum disguised as an Indian woman. There she poses as a follower of the White Prophet and helps him with his work, seeking an opportunity to betray him to the authorities in Cairo as a seditious and fanatical leader, another Mahdi, planning an uprising which will drive the British out of Egypt. Ishmael is a widower and to protect her takes her into his house and betroths himself to her, though he promises not to exact the rights of a husband. At first he shows no interest in her as a woman but inevitably he falls in love with her and sex rears its ugly head. Helena's honour is preserved but it is a near thing. In Ishmael, Caine returns to the idea of the devout man almost succumbing to religious mania, like John Storm in *The Christian*. The words he puts into the preacher's mouth proclaim a new era of peace and love, of old religions made new, and then through the action of the story, he exposes it as an impossible dream.

Gordon arrives in Khartoum and is staggered to find Helena there, apparently Ishmael's wife. The plot is worked out through a complicated series of misunderstandings and errors. The story certainly 'grips', as Caine said any good novel should, and the ending is in doubt right to the last page. There are deaths and tragedies but eventually Gordon triumphs and is acquitted by a court martial. Ishmael, freed from prison, nobly releases Helena from her betrothal by saying, 'I divorce thee' three times, and rides off broken-hearted into the desert. Lord Nuneham resigns and returns to England leaving Gordon as his successor and about to marry Helena. This is the only Hall Caine novel with a conventional happy ending.

The book did not do well. In Hall Caine terms it nearly approached a flop. It was rumoured that Caine went round buying up copies to avoid remaindering. There was 'animated controversy' and his friend Bernard Shaw sprang to its aid, writing a long and spirited defence in the *Daily Telegraph*. This was to have been the preface to a second edition but Heinemann took fright, refusing to reprint, though he did publish Shaw's defence as a pamphlet with the title *The Critics of the White Prophet*. Some of Caine's friends protested at this. B.L. Moseley wrote to Adam Cranston that he sincerely hoped Bernard Shaw's defence would not be published. 'That literary contortionist counts for nothing with those whose judgement is of value and I should think Mr Caine would best consult his own dignity and reputation by not allowing his name to be bracketed with that Prince of paradoxical fooling.' Cranston replied saying that even if Shaw were all Moseley said, it detracted nothing from his spontaneous and able defence 'made when many who should have spoken out were silent'.

One of the friends who failed to support Caine was Lord Northcliffe. Returning the proofs to Heinemann unread, he said he was sorry he 'could not do more about Hall Caine' but he was worried by a report from Khartoum, 'an interesting description of Mr Hall Caine's visit to the Soudan... The impression left by Mr Hall Caine on the minds of the British responsible for Soudanese administration was not dissimilar to that left on the minds of Anglo-Indians by the cold-weather Parliamentary visitors to our Eastern Empire.' Mr Hall Caine doubtless believed he had been in touch with the native mind after two visits to Egypt, said Northcliffe, but men like Sir Reginald Wingate, who had studied the Eastern mind for a quarter of a century, humbly confessed how little they knew about it. He was surprised that Caine did not understand how little he could know of Egypt 'and how misleading a little knowledge may become in the hands of a master of phrase-making'. Northcliffe was worried about the book being translated into Arabic, fearing it would damage the British cause. In fact the translation had already been made and Hafiz Effendi was serialising it in his paper, *Al Minbar*. Moseley wrote that Caine's novel had 'set the Nile on fire'. Everyone, native and European, was talking about it. Hafiz Effendi was publishing it in both daily and weekly parts. The Sheikh Al Azhar was delighted.

The book anticipated by many years some of the racial, political and religious problems which wracked Egypt and India around 1930. The author was invited to defend his book by the Jewish Literary Society, whose President, Mr Baron L. Benas, took the chair. Caine's long and interesting address was published as a pamphlet, *Why I Wrote The White Prophet*, at the insistence of Benas. First printed privately and issued by Collier & Co., it was then taken up by Heinemann who printed and circulated another 30,000 copies.

A Syrian living in London wrote to Caine saying he had striven for thirty years to explain the East to the West and vice versa but 'the bulk of the people we wish to enlighten are steeped in ignorance and craft and look upon we writers simply to hold on to the cow's head for them to milk in their own way'. Another friend told Caine not to take the critics too seriously. 'True ideas are eternal and good work endures.'

In November, 1909, Caine was at Greeba, recuperating from the gut infection he had picked up in Egypt. Benas, acknowledging a copy of the pamphlet, hoped Caine was convalescent and invigorated by the fresh breezes of his Island. He called it Caine's Island because he was doing for the Isle of Man what Scott had done for Caledonia, which was to invite pilgrimage to a beautiful place whose charms had been largely ignored 'until Romance threw a ray of sunlight and made the obscure bright'. He told Caine not to be discouraged by what had happened to *The White Prophet*. His experience of John Bull was that he was a good fellow, perhaps the best of human beings, but it was difficult to get anything new into his head, and once in equally difficult to get it out again. Every new idea must go through three stages. First, 'It won't do, it is utterly unthinkable', perhaps 'unEnglish'. One could not argue with that phase, or phrase, only bide one's time until the problem surfaced again in an acute form, when one got to the second phase: 'I am not convinced it is not the right or correct solution, but it is a subject for enquiry', leading to 'a mental royal commission'. Then stage three is reached: tentative acceptance with a chorus of something like, 'Good Gracious! We should have adopted this thing years ago.' Unless one waited patiently for these stages to be gone through, 'one suffers, like the bird in a cage beating itself to death against the bars. Some day the door is left open, and the bird is free again, and the bars themselves rot away.' Benas had just reread Disraeli's *Sybil or Two Nations*, and found it was only now possible to understand it fully, nearly seventy years after it had been written. Caine's time would come and he would be seen to have written the truth.

CHAPTER TWENTY-FOUR

On 3 December, 1909, the Isle of Man Steam Packet Company's ship, the *Ellan Vannin*, was lost in the Mersey. Fourteen passengers and 21 of her crew died. The Manx accused Caine, who wrote a poem on 'The Loss of the *Ellan Vannin*', of failing to give money for the bereaved families. In fact, he headed the list of contributors to a Disaster Fund set up by the *Daily Telegraph* at his instigation.

He and Mary were on their own—apart from the nurse who now always accompanied him—for Christmas in St Moritz. Mary returned to London in February, leaving Caine to work. Once home Mary worried about propriety. 'Is it right for you to be travelling only with the nurse?' she wrote. However, losses on *The White Prophet* had to be made up and he needed a new play. He had no novel far enough advanced to draw on nor any inspiration for an original scenario. As he had often done before, he went back to old material, working up two dramas to fill the gap left by Tree's defection.

Mary stayed with the Cornwalls at Oaklands over Easter and told her Dearest Tom about 'the long motor rides' they had taken. She welcomed the arrival of each instalment of the play scripts for his secretary to type as evidence that he would soon be home. Why she did not stay with him in Switzerland is a puzzle. Derwent was playing small parts in a provincial theatre company. Perhaps they felt she must keep an eye on Ralph but the uneasy impression is given that Caine did not want her with him while he worked.

News reached him at the end of February that Frederic Shields had died, his great work at the Chapel of the Ascension completed. Caine mourned him deeply, not least because it was through Rossetti he had met him. He was back in London by the beginning of May. On the 6th King Edward died. Caine was in the crowd waiting at the palace gates, one of the first to read the bulletin announcing the King's death. He wrote a long article for the *Daily Telegraph*, headed 'King Edward, A Prince and a Great Man'. It was an informal account, based on his personal acquaintance with the King. He said very little about Edward as Prince of Wales and nothing of meeting him with Irving. It is a tactful, affectionate, portrait of the monarch he had been so proud to know. Lord Burnham, proprietor of the *Telegraph*, gave permission for the article to be reproduced as a small book, published by Collier & Co., using some of the photographs from Queen Alexandra's book. It was sold in aid of her charities.

Within days of George V's accession there was a mining disaster in the West Cumberland coalfield. Caine asked Lord Carrington to suggest to the King that he should go to Whitehaven. Carrington sent a note dated 16 May saying he would 'put Mr Caine's proposal to the King'. With crowned heads from all over Europe assembling for the funeral it was out of the question for the new king to leave London. His private secretary, Lord Stamfordham, wrote to tell Caine so but he would not take no for an answer. On the 17th Caine wrote to Stamfordham. He appreciated why the King should remain in London. 'On the other hand as a student of the world and of history, whose life's business it is to feel the pulse of the public, I humbly say that this is an hour of immense gravity to the throne, and that what I suggested to the king would have had results far beyond the expression of that deep sympathy with the Whitehaven sufferers which I am sure he feels.' He still believed that if the King could possibly

> set aside for 24 hours the tyranny of his uncle [the Kaiser] in London and go to Whitehaven and say, 'The Palace is in mourning, but the cottage is in mourning too, and I come here because king and people are at this great moment bound together by a common bond of freedom and fate'—if he could do this, he would do the greatest thing any English Sovereign has ever had the chance of doing and place himself at the absolute head for the rest of his reign.

A romantic notion but of course the King could not go. Stamfordham was a man of great tact and diplomacy and dealt kindly with Caine's emotional proposal. His standing at the palace was not damaged as on 13 July he and Mary attended the investiture of the new Prince of Wales in Caernarvon Castle at the personal invitation of the royal family. They stayed at the Royal Hotel where Mary was mistaken for Marie Corelli!

The first project Caine had worked on the previous winter had been a revised stage version of *The Eternal City*, retitled *The Eternal Question*. It might just as well have been called *The Woman Question*, because that was what it was about. He used the same plot and characters but new dialogue, employing the ideas on divorce and the sex relationship he had prepared for presentation to the Royal Commission on Divorce which met that year. It was a cast of unknowns when the play opened at the Garrick Theatre on 27 August. The incidental music Mascagni had written for the original version was played but even this did not ensure success. Critics said it was a discussion of socialism and divorce with the emphasis on the latter. Caine came on stage to the usual calls of 'Author' at the end but the applause was polite rather than rapturous. The *Daily News* said, 'shallow rhetoric masquerades as a problem play'. It was warmed-up leftovers and most of the critics did not like it. It was more sociological tract than drama. Many thought Caine should not have put new wine into old bottles. Didactics and divorce hardly gelled into a play. The *Catholic Times* objected to Caine's representation of the Pope as the hub of the action, which he had not been in the earlier version.

The other stop-gap play Caine produced that year was a rewrite of *Ben-my-Chree*, based on his first successful novel, *The Deemster*, and called *The Bishop's Son*. It was taken on tour by the Wentworth Croke management with Derwent in the cast. A copyright performance of the new version was given in Douglas on 15 August. Caine made a long speech, talking about 'the distressing case' of a love-child born to a servant-girl in Douglas which had starved to death. Judge and jury said no one was to blame—cries of 'shame!' from the audience. Public opinion, said Caine, was stronger than judges and juries. All life was sacred, no life unwanted. There were 'loud and long cheers' when he finished and he and Mary were mobbed by a delighted crowd as they left. When *The Eternal Question* was taken off after only three weeks, *The Bishop's Son* replaced it at the Garrick, opening on 28 September, 1910, with Bransby Williams, then at the start of a distinguished career, playing Dan Mylrea. Derwent had been dropped.

The Eternal Question had lost money and Ralph, who produced it, was so worried his father feared for his health. He was still worrying about him when he arrived at the Palace Hotel, St Moritz, in November 1910. He stayed there, apart from a brief visit to England in February, 1911, until the end of March. On March 1 he wrote indignantly to Mary, 'So I am not to expect a letter every day & am not to telegraph! All right, we'll see who can play longest at that game!' He was working on a new play, *The Quality of Mercy*. His next letter ended, 'I miss you more & more. I suppose you are growing fatter & fatter. I shall find out when we meet.' He was home by the end of the month.

That summer at Greeba was a busy time. Caine addressed a meeting of Boy Scouts in Peel Castle, spoke at the Wesleyan Chapel in Victoria Street, Douglas, wrote articles for papers as various as the *Isle of Man Weekly Times* and the *Westminster Gazette*. There was a strike on the railways and he publicly supported the strikers, saying he was sure everybody would when they 'realised what vast numbers of men and women had been paid starvation wages and worked unconscionable hours'. He blamed 'the silly pride' of the companies for the trouble.

On 4 September he and Mary were in Manchester for the first performance of *The Quality of Mercy* at the Theatre Royal. Set in Yorkshire, the play, based on the story of David and Bathsheba, criticised the marriage laws of the time. It was a great success in Manchester but bombed in Sheffield and was not heard of thereafter.

Mary Hall Caine in May, 1911, aged 42.

Plans were afoot for Caine's usual winter migration but this year he and Mary were to go further than before—to India. Heinemann had returned from there full of enthusiasm and urged Caine to go and see the country for himself. If he thought Caine would make a great novel out of it he was mistaken. After the mauling he had received over his Egyptian book he was in no mood to tackle an Oriental setting again and, like Russia, India seemed too vast a subject for romance.

His Cairo friend, B.L. Moseley, wrote to tell him how Egyptians had reacted to the appointment of Kitchener as Lord Cromer's successor. Kitchener was an ogre to the Egyptian Nationalists, who remembered all too well his victory at Omdurman and how many Dervishes had died there when he annihilated the Khalifa's army. They remembered it was Kitchener who had re-occupied the Sudan and taken the name of its capital, Khartoum, when he was made a Baron for his services. After his successes in South Africa during the Anglo-Boer War he had been created Viscount Kitchener of Khartoum and sent to India as Commander-in-Chief before returning to take over in Egypt. (He was given an earldom in 1914 when he joined the War Cabinet and was lost at sea when HMS *Hampshire* went down off the Orkneys on the way to Russia.)

Moseley said reactions to Kitchener's appointment had been polite, not to say servile, on the surface but deeply resented behind closed doors. Everyone was despondent and full of gloomy forebodings. They could not understand why a Government professing Liberal principles and promising to grant them fully democratic institutions had sent them 'a man of blood and iron who is more likely than not to crush out of us all spirit of independence'. In an aside at the end of the letter he said the Bahais were asking if *The White Prophet* was based on the Bahai tenets as they were identical.

Caine spent Christmas at St Moritz with Mary before going on to Rome for a short stay, sending an article, 'Woman and Marriage', to London. After that, silence until they were back in London. Derwent was with his parents when they sailed for India. It appears to be the only journey Caine ever undertook which was pure holiday and had nothing at all to do with his work. They went at the invitation of old friends, Colonel Stephen, an officer in the Indian Army and a great polo player who captained his regimental team, and his wife, Florence. Their stay had unforeseen consequences.

With Colonel and Mrs Stephen was their 17-year-old daughter, Frances Dorothy, known as Dolly. The girl was stage-struck and longed to be an actress. One can be sure Derwent spun a good yarn about his own theatrical experiences and she fell madly in love with him. When the time came for the Caine family to return to England Derwent refused to board the ship with his parents. 'When I travel on my own I'm somebody,' he told his father. 'When I travel with you I'm nobody.' He was 20 at the time. In the end Caine and Mary sailed on their own, leaving him to follow.

After a few days in Cairo seeing friends they were back in London in mid-April, 1912. Bram Stoker died a few days later. The *Daily Telegraph* published an appreciation by Caine on the 24th, headed 'Bram Stoker, the Story of a Great Friendship', exactly the same phrase as he used for his account of his friendship with Rossetti. Whether Stoker's novels were great he was not sure but 'he was truly great in one thing: a genius for friendship'. The funeral was held at the Golders Green Crematorium, Caine leading the small band of mourners. He was greatly distressed at the loss of his closest friend on whom he had depended so much. From this time on Caine, now nearly 60, was a lonely man. Although he always asserted his wife was his best friend, there was no one now to whom he could unburden himself as he had to Bram. They had known each other for 34 years. Bram had watched, and materially helped, his career for all that time. When Theodore Watts-Dunton died two years later the circle of his oldest friends was gone, his last link with Gabriel Rossetti broken. Caine turned increasingly to Robert Marshall, his doctor in the Isle of Man, who to some degree took Stoker's place as confidant, while his friendship with Robert and Marie Leighton meant more and more to him.

That same month of April, 1912, the White Star Line's *Titanic* hit an iceberg in the north Atlantic on her maiden voyage and sank. Caine wrote a *Hymn for the Survivors of the Titanic*, to the tune of *Oh God our Help in Ages Past*. It was sung throughout the country and at the City Temple's evening service on 21 April, 1912. Caine lost at least one friend in the disaster, W.T. Stead, former editor of the *Pall Mall Gazette*, and was deeply shocked.

He had barely recovered from this and Bram's death when another, if quite different blow, fell: Dolly Stephen was pregnant and Derwent was the father. There was no question but that they must be married at once and the engagement was announced. The girl's father was with his regiment in India, though her mother had travelled home with her. Caine insisted the summer wedding, in the absence of Dolly's father, should take place in the Isle of Man. Dolly arrived at Greeba with Florence and arrangements were made for her and Derwent to be married by the Bishop of Sodor and Man in his chapel at Bishopscourt. Everything was arranged, down to the detail of the marriage certificate being made out ready for signature.

There are two versions of what happened next. The first is that Derwent got cold feet and when he should have been getting ready for the wedding was waving good-bye to the Island from the deck of a Steam Packet boat. In later years he sometimes told this story himself, particularly if he had had a few drinks, and may have come to believe it. The other, and rather more credible, story is that on the eve of the wedding Derwent's ungovernable temper (he seems never to have outgrown his toddler tantrums) got the better of him. Dolly seems to have been little better. They had a shrieking row. She was standing on the half landing of the stairs at Greeba Castle, Derwent at the foot of them.

A large vase stood on a pedestal beside her and she grabbed it and threw it at him. Luckily she missed. Mrs Stephen decided on the spot that the marriage could not go ahead, despite her daughter's pregnancy. Better an illegitimate baby than a lifetime of unhappiness with a man who seemed at times on the verge of madness. After a brusque interview with Derwent's parents she packed their bags and departed for home with Dolly. It is very likely that Derwent was on the next boat out. As time went on he comfortably forgot why. With his monster ego, he would have found the reality difficult to accept, hence his version of events.

The baby, a girl, was born on 1 November, 1912, at Flo Stephen's home in Sheffield. Caine wanted the child named Elin—an Icelandic name pronounced e'*leen*, with the accent on the second syllable. Dolly and her mother agreed. With more honesty than Caine had shown when Ralph was born, Dolly registered the child herself as Stephen, not Hall Caine, giving her own name and occupation, 'A Theatrical Actress', but leaving the spaces for the father's name and occupation blank. There was much anxious discussion between Mrs Stephen and Derwent's parents about the baby's future—she would have to be adopted. Caine insisted that he and Mary would take her and bring her up as their own child. Flo Stephen agreed. After all, they were old friends.

A nanny was engaged and when the baby was about six weeks old Dr and Mrs Marshall went to Sheffield and brought her back to Greeba. Dolly handed the baby over more or less happily but refused to agree to adoption for some time so that while Caine and Mary acted as if the child's name was Hall Caine, and she grew up believing it was, it remained legally Stephen. Dolly put her career before the child. She was very young—only 18 when Elin was born—but never had any great success on the stage.

All might have been well had Caine and Mary simply said they had adopted a baby but Caine was desperate that no word of the child's true parentage should leak out. He ruthlessly enforced the fiction that Mary was the child's natural mother. Mary was a youthful 43 but nobody was fooled. The charade imposed a dreadful strain on her. She was by nature honest and open. Maintaining this absurd fiction affected her health and could have contributed to a nervous breakdown in 1918. Caine genuinely thought he was acting in the best interests of all concerned. Mary resented the child and gave the impression of being jealous of the place she took in Caine's time and affections. The child sensed this. She never felt completely happy with her mother/grandmother though she adored 'Poppa', as she called her grandfather. Mary was acutely embarrassed by the false position she was put in of having to make out she had borne another child so many years after her two sons without ever being seen by even her closest friends to be pregnant. She knew only too well how tongues would wag and realised what Caine apparently failed to see—that people would think that, while she was not the mother, he was undoubtedly the father. Stories flew round the Island that this was so and the mother variously an actress or a servant in the house.

Caine was either pig-headed or incredibly naïve, or both, in obliging Mary to assert she was the child's mother. He was determined to protect Derwent's reputation. His adored son's name must not be tarnished, whatever the cost to anyone else, himself included, and ultimately it was high. He was also concerned for Dolly—the girl was after all the daughter of personal friends, not just some unknown Derwent had picked up. He was baffled by her refusal to marry Derwent and reacted in this odd way. It is a measure of the strength of Mary's love for him that she agreed to the deception and continued to back him.

During the summer of 1912 Caine went to Germany to see Baron Tauchnitz, who had published the Continental editions of his books for nearly twenty years and was an old friend. On his return Caine wrote that for all the bellicose talk he could not believe that two such civilised countries as England and Germany, with all their ties and common interests, could ever go to war.

He was keeping to himself the theme of his latest novel, which was ready for serialisation in *Nash's Magazine* by the end of 1912. The story had been brewing since 1905, when he told a New York paper that his next novel would concern 'American money', but would be set in the Isle of Man and deal with 'the outcast woman and the outcast man'. He had outlined the story to Bram Stoker in 1908. Bram had been enthusiastic, which encouraged him to continue after the debacle of the Egyptian novel.

An amusing sidelight on his activities can be found in a number of the *Sphere* in 1912. An advertisement shows Hall Caine's head together with the heads of Sir William Bull, the MP for Hammersmith, the musician Landon Ronald, actress Ellaline Terriss and the author Eden Philpotts. Their heads are circled to form the fruit on a tree. The advertisement was for Sanatogen Nerve Tonic, said to 'calm the nerves'. The *Queen* published an advertisement on 6 April, 1912, with a picture of satisfied customers 'Signing their Declaration of Confidence in Sanatogen, The Tonic Food'. Caine is drawn in the centre of the picture. Some years previously he had featured in a picture postcard series, 'Maxims of Great Men'. His maxim was: 'I believe in luck—think you are going to be lucky and you will be lucky. A man's luck never fails him until his faith fails.'

About this time he sat next to Mrs Alice Tweedie at a dinner party. Later she gave a thumbnail sketch of him:

The Manxman is an interesting companion. His nervous intensity throws warmth and intensity into all his sayings and makes his subjects seem more interesting than they really are. There is a magnetic influence in him. Physically delicate, there is an electric thrill in all he says, in spite of the sad, soft intonation of his voice.

She commented that 'he throws his soul into his characters, himself lives all the tragic episodes and terrible moments they undergo'.

The Woman Thou Gavest Me was published in July, 1913, and caused the biggest furore of any of his novels. Proprietors of circulating libraries objected to the book's morals and refused at first to stock it. When they did, they kept it out of sight and available only on request. Both Caine and Shaw complained bitterly about censorship but it did no harm to his sales. It was reprinted five times before the end of 1913, when nearly half a million copies had been sold. This in spite of the threats from some of his readers never to read anything of his again after *The White Prophet*. It remained in print until his death in 1931, when it was in its 26th English edition and had been translated into nine languages.

The book is a literary teaser. There was considerable speculation as to who 'Martin Conrad' might be and where Caine got the matter of the book, which is largely a polemic against the divorce laws of the time and contemporary attitudes to illegitimacy. He wrote in the first person as a woman and with considerable insight into a woman's thoughts and feelings, so much so that years later he was still getting letters from women asking how it was he knew so exactly how they felt.

How much of his own life went into this book is pure speculation, though memories of boyhood holidays in the Isle of Man played their part. Caine was a literary magpie who was frequently accused of putting people he knew into his books. In a Note to the Reader he said,

How much of the story of Mary O'Neill is a work of my own imagination, and how much comes from an authentic source I do not consider it necessary to say. But as I have in this instance drawn more largely and directly from fact than is usually the practice of the novelist, I have thought it my duty to defeat all possible attempts at personal identification by altering and disguising the more important scenes and characters.

He insisted the novel did not refer to anyone living and the convent school he described did not represent any such school in Rome. As his account of it is ludicrous this is more true than he meant.

There may be a clue as to what sparked off the story in chapter 54. Mary O'Neill, now married against her wishes to the dissolute 'young Lord Raa', a marriage which she has refused to consummate, realises that she really loves her childhood friend Martin Conrad. Brought up in a convent in Rome after the death of her mother, she is deeply religious and struggles with the conflict between her heart and her marriage vows.

> I searched my Missal for words that applied to my sinful state, and every night
> on going to bed I prayed to God to take from me all unholy thoughts, all
> earthly affections. But what was the use of my prayers when in the first dream
> of the first sleep I was rushing into Martin's arms?

This is once more reminiscent of Alice Meynell's poem, which he had drawn upon before. His heroine is a married woman in love with another (unmarried) man. Having refused to let her husband near her, she loses her virginity to Martin Conrad in one night of passionate love before he goes off on an expedition to Antarctica. He promises to come back and rescue her from the awful Lord Raa, who has imported one of her old schoolfriends as his mistress and installed her in Castle Raa.

Raa, or more correctly Rhaa Mooar, is an ancient earthworks and pile of fallen stones on Maughold Head in the Isle of Man. The name means 'great fort'. Enough to give Caine, who knew the area so well, a name. Where a few years before he had planned a real tower he raised an imaginary castle. He called his fictional island in which much of the story is set Ellan, but it is the thinnest of disguises for the Isle of Man, which in Manx is called Ellan Vannin.

Mary O'Neill soon finds she is pregnant with Martin's child and flees Castle Raa for London. There she hides and struggles desperately to keep herself and the baby. Lord Raa makes a token search for her but soon gives up. There are telling vignettes of an East End sweatshop, a baby minder, the lives of the East End poor contrasted with those of the 'idle rich'. For these scenes Caine leant heavily on Beatrice Webb's investigations into the nineteenth-century Jewish sweatshops. It was one of his weaknesses that he tended to rely for much of his research on reading rather than looking for facts on the ground. Had he ever been inside a big London hospital instead of reading a rule book he would never have made the mistakes that marred *The Christian*. He talked to all kinds of people—he talked, but how much did he listen?

The book reflects Caine's interest in 'the Woman Question'. The theme obsessed the Victorians and he was no exception. He kept readers' letters, including one received in September, 1907, in which the writer referred to 'the Langham case'. A magistrate had found two women who lived alone in flats not guilty of living off immoral earnings but refused them costs, thus, Caine's correspondent asserted, proclaiming his belief that they were really guilty. The case raised the question of the freedom of women workers to live where and as they chose. The police did not worry about men living alone having women in at night. She hoped Caine would consider the matter and express an opinion.

He may or may not have done so at the time. He certainly made use of the picture that woman gave him in describing the difficulties Mary O'Neill encountered in trying to find somewhere to live and work to support herself and her child. The book is often appallingly sentimental and over-written, even ridiculous in places, and yet it is compelling. Once Mary O'Neill is brought back from her convent school in Rome and forced into a loveless marriage the story strengthens. The account of her wedding night—in her own words—is an extraordinary piece of writing in its sympathy for the woman's feelings. No wonder it caused an uproar when the 1913 public read it. Caine also hammered away at his old theme of the treatment of bastards.

Mary O'Neill thinks Martin dead but he returns, finds her and takes her and the baby home to 'Ellan' where she develops 'consumption', brought about by her privations in London. Lord Raa divorces her. Martin plans to marry her and take her to the winter quarters of his new Antarctic expedition, sure that the pure air there will cure her. 'What a glorious thing it would be,' he says, 'to escape to that great free region from the world of civilisation, with its effete laws and worn-out creeds which enslave humanity.'

Mary's priest, however, makes her see that as a good Catholic she can never marry again. Her dilemma is solved by her death the day before the proposed wedding. The description of Mary O'Neill dying of tuberculosis becomes more poignant when one recalls how Caine's brother John James died. This book is in its way as powerful a piece of writing as *The White Prophet*. Most of it is from the heroine's point of view, the rest in the form of 'Memoranda' inserted in the story by her lover, Martin Conrad. Caine over-eggs the omelette but it is still a strong story. Whether the whole thing was concocted or Caine was indeed given the original tale as he says does not really matter. There appear to be elements of reality but who knows whose life it was drawn from? One must allow for the novelist's imagination but what in this case lay behind it one would dearly like to know.

A storm of criticism and abuse broke over Caine's head when the book came out. Roman Catholics reacted with fury to his account of the love affair and excommunication of a monk and a nun, and poured scorn on his admittedly risible account of a convent school. He was attacked for writing 'pornography', though by today's standards it is mild stuff. He was also accused of undermining the sanctity of marriage and condoning adultery and illegitimacy. All of which did no harm at all to his sales and whipped up eager audiences for the film when it was made in 1919.

A review in Australia, in the *Melbourne Herald*, likened Caine to Harriet Beecher Stowe, George Eliot, Dickens, Meredith and Thackeray as being a writer of novels with a purpose. 'Hall Caine is one who is convinced that the artist and the teacher can go hand in hand.' Another critic commented, 'in one portion of the book we are rather too long in the low stop till the strain of pathos becomes almost painful'. Too true. One (woman) fan wrote, 'I cannot express my thoughts but you—how beautiful to be so gifted, with <u>such</u> a mind and the power to express. I cannot tell you what that book was to me.' Caine marked the envelope, 'Preserve.'

With both his reputation as a novelist and his fortunes restored, Caine organised a family holiday in North Africa. Christmas, 1913, was spent at the Majestic Hotel, Tunis. Ralph and Derwent were there and with them two young women. One was an actress, Lillian Digges, who was engaged to Ralph—they married in 1914. The other was Dolly Stephen. Caine had still not given up hope that she and Derwent would overcome their differences and marry, for the sake of Little Elin, as the family called her. Elin was not there, she was at Greeba in the charge of her nanny and the servants, as she was for much of her childhood.

From Tunis they moved to Biskra in Algeria. A photograph was taken of Caine and Mary sitting on a bench in the garden of their hotel. Lillian is on one side of them and Dolly on the other. At the end of January, the young people and Mary returned to London while Caine settled in at the Hotel Excelsior in Rome to begin the dramatisation of what Mary always referred to as 'the Woman book'. In February he received a shock. While they had all been in Tunis both Ralph and Derwent had touched the manager of their hotel for money. As they had not repaid it he sent the bill to their father.

Mary had finally won her battle to have a London house. While her husband worked in Rome she was beginning the task of decorating and furnishing Heath Brow, overlooking Hampstead Heath, which had been bought from Lord Iveagh. It was near Jack Straw's Castle and was destroyed in an air raid in World War II. Mary sent her husband lists of furniture, carpets and curtains and the bills for them. He gave her a free hand, regarding it as her house. His home was Greeba, and always would be.

Soon after returning to London Mary was unwell. On 15 February she relayed her symptoms to her Dearest Tom.

> Had a terrible night last night. Kept awake till 5 and sweating all the time... I felt very low in spirits this morning and sent for Dr Macnaughton. He came and massaged me all over and said I had a good deal of poison in my system...he rather thinks it is due to the change I am passing through at present... He says I am not to worry about it. The sweating is not serious. I am to keep in bed until it passes away. He is going to give me medicine to try and drive the poison away.

The 'hot flushes' put her in low spirits. She was also depressed because Ralph had not been near her since they got back from North Africa. 'How can he be so selfish. I wish this house was finished and then you could come home.'

He was home in March, brought by news that his sister was also ill. She seemed better when he arrived and he went on to Greeba. Mary wrote on 30 March, 1914, saying Lily was not so well again and she had arranged for her to go into a nursing home. 'I saw Lily yesterday after I had been to the home and I think she is quite pleased with the arrangements I have made for her. The nurse told me a misplaced kidney needs feeding up and rest. They promised to take great care of her... So everything will be all right and you need not worry.' On 11 May Mary wrote him a largely illegible note saying Lily had recovered enough to leave the nursing home. Mrs Dean, her sister-in-law, had taken her to Aldershot to stay with her and her husband, Edward Dean. 'She needs fresh country air,' said Mary, and Caine was reassured. When Lily died of pneumonia and heart failure on 31 May he was devastated. She was only 45 and her son, David Day, was 17. The Deans gave their nephew a home and Caine helped him from time to time.

After the funeral Mary travelled back to Greeba with her husband. Disappointed that his ploy of the Christmas holiday had not brought Derwent and Dolly together, Caine had one last try. He invited Dolly to Greeba and made sure Derwent was there too. A family snap shows them on the lawn with the 18-month-old Elin between them. Both the adults look awkward and self-conscious, looking neither at each other nor at the toddler holding their hands. If Caine thought that seeing her daughter would bring Dolly round he was wrong. There is no record of Derwent and Dolly ever meeting again and it was a long time before Elin saw her natural mother. Derwent never acknowledged her as his daughter or acted as a father towards her. When he died in 1971 he left her a small legacy, identifying her in his will only as 'my friend, Mrs Elin Gill'.

CHAPTER TWENTY-FIVE

When war broke out on 5 August, 1914, Caine admitted he had mis-judged the situation in general and Germany's intentions in particular. He returned to London with Mary immediately and took up his desk at the *Telegraph*. The young men would have to go and fight—the old hacks could do the writing. He was 61 and saw his way clear: he would use his fame and talents as a writer on behalf of his country. Other writers were co-opted less willingly—or took themselves less seriously. Jerome K. Jerome, who was also busy with articles about the war, wrote in *My Life and Times*, 'The newspapers had roped in most of us literary gents to write them special articles upon the war. The appalling nonsense we poured out, during those hysterical first weeks, must have made the angels weep, and all the little devils hold their sides with laughter.'

Germany's rape of Belgium, the plight of her King exiled in London, and her people, so many of them refugees, moved Caine deeply. The *Daily Telegraph* opened a Belgian Fund to help them. Caine knew what to do: he would edit another charity book. From September, 1914, he devoted his time to assembling contributions, sending letters to writers, artists, poets and musicians—Claude Debussy was one of the latter—asking for their help. In addition he wrote to the good and the great asking for messages of sympathy, which were printed with facsimile signatures—Lloyd George, the explorer Nansen, the actress Sarah Bernhardt, Kitchener, former US President William Taft, the Aga Khan, Bonar Law, Gilbert Murray and Admiral Lord Charles Beresford were among them.

He leaned heavily on his friends. Ernest Hodder-Williams, head of the publishers Hodder & Stoughton, whom he had known for some years, readily agreed to produce the book in co-operation with the *Telegraph*. Edmund Gosse, by this time Librarian to the House of Lords, was one of those who translated foreign language contributions. Ralph was co-opted to help with the basic hard work. He was 28 and quite young enough to have volunteered for the Army—conscription was not introduced until 1916—but he did not. Before the outbreak of war he had spent some time in Canada working for a firm of papermakers and had become something of an expert in the business. Eventually he became a director of papermaking businesses in Canada and South Africa. In 1914 he was a printer and bookbinder. Paper was a strategic commodity—cartridge cases were made of it and from the start of the war it was rationed. Ralph went to the Ministry of Munitions and remained there for the duration. He was resourceful in assuring supplies for *King Albert's Book*.

One person Caine turned to for a contribution was his friend of nearly twenty years' standing, Bernard Shaw. He wrote to him on 16 October, enclosing a copy of the circular sent to everyone. 'I am in a quandary about the accompanying letter,' he wrote. 'Our friends at the Daily Telegraph tell me that you are against the war. This means that if you respond, or, as usual, give rein to your never-failing sincerity, you will say something which in a book like this I dare not print.' He could not leave Shaw out, however, and hoped he would be able to express his sympathy with the Belgians and their King. Shaw evidently did, and quickly, as on the 20th Caine wrote to him again: 'Splendid! As you say, "let them boil their heads". Only if I were not in danger of a devastating shaft from your Krupp factory, I should ask you to delete one or two very short sentences in the interests of a quiet life.' He hoped to have the proof ready for Shaw to check shortly but the *Telegraph*'s printers flatly refused to print work signed by a professed pacifist. Caine had put up a long fight for the piece ever since he received it and gave Shaw details of the battle in several pages of his tiny writing. The upshot was that the disputed contribution was omitted and the book came out in time for Christmas.

Shaw took no umbrage, replying on 2 December from Ayot St Lawrence, 'My dear Hall Caine, Lord bless you, it doesn't matter. If I had known you were having any trouble about it, I should have told you at once to tell them to withdraw it if they were afraid of it, as you have no need to stand on ceremony with me, and anyhow I can easily get it published if I want to, all the more effectively if it can be headed THE ARTICLE THE DAILY TELEGRAPH FUNKED!' Even without Shaw the book sold well, raising a substantial amount for the Belgian Fund but getting Caine into hot water with the general run of booksellers and publishers who were smarting under paper rationing. Hodder & Stoughton, as the official publishers, were responsible for about a quarter of the sales. Caine organised the rest himself, canvassing friends and selling the book in offices and through shops which did not usually carry books. As so often in his career he found himself at the centre of an almighty row, branded with Hodder-Williams as destroyer of the book trade. He was furious but kept quiet. The Publishers' Association rounded on Hodder-Williams. Privately to Shaw Caine was vitriolic about 'stick-in-the-mud publishers who made no attempt to publish during the slack time'. John Murray went to Queen Mary and asked her not to give her name to a charity book again. King Albert, however, was delighted and rewarded

Photograph of the Jonniaux portrait of Caine presented to him
by the Belgian Government, 1918.

Caine by creating him an Officer of the Order of Leopold of Belgium. In 1918 the Belgian parliament commissioned the artist Alfred Jonniaux to paint Caine's portrait and presented it to him.

While his brother was seconded as a government worker Derwent, who also avoided military service, was touring his own theatrical company performing leading roles in his father's plays. In 1914 he was 23. Admittedly he had poor sight and still tended to be asthmatic but many young men whose health was just as bad persuaded the Army doctors to turn a blind eye and went to serve in France, while Alice Keppel's husband George spent his fiftieth birthday in the trenches. Caine, however, was determined to keep his sons out of the fighting. Derwent's contribution to the war effort was to perform sketches written for him by his father in aid of wartime charities, before leaving for New York, where he sat out the rest of the war.

King Albert's Book finished, Caine turned his attention to articles, mostly for the *New York Times*, aimed at persuading America to come into the war on the side of the Allies. Early in 1915 he crossed the Atlantic to give a series of lectures. He was disagreeably surprised to find he was not as well received as previously. The press misrepresented his mission, or he thought they did. He was dismayed by the amount of pro-German feeling and returned to London earlier than planned.

Concerned for his well-being now he could not winter in St Moritz or the Mediterranean, he undertook a long car tour of England with Mary 'answering the call of health', as he put it. All his life so far, whenever he felt unwell he had set off on his travels. Now in his sixties his instinct to be on the move if he did not feel 'up to the mark' remained. He set out with Mary and his chauffeur, starting in the West Country, visiting Clovelly, Barnstaple, Tavistock and Bath before heading north.

Of course this was not all a holiday. He had almost always travelled to get good copy and he did so now. Wherever he went he wrote, in articles for the *Telegraph*, about how ordinary people were helping the war effort and how the conflict had dislocated their lives. 'When I hear people say that Great Britain is not yet awake to the fact that she is at war,' he wrote, 'I wonder where they keep their eyes... Such a spirit has never breathed through our Empire during my time, or yet through any other empire of which I have any knowledge. Everybody, or almost everybody, is doing something for England, and few or none idle who are of military age except such as have heavy burdens or secret disabilities into which I dare not pry.' Presumably he hoped no one would pry into why neither of his sons had enlisted.

In September, 1915, Heinemann reprinted Caine's *Telegraph* articles, together with some of the American ones, in a small volume titled *The Drama of Three Hundred & Sixty-Five Days: Scenes in the Great War*. The frontispiece was a photograph of the Prince of Wales, who was three years younger than Derwent, in army uniform. The book was dedicated to 'the Young Manhood of the British Empire'. Caine began by paraphrasing the playwright, Maeterlinck, saying

> what we call the war is neither more nor less than the visible expression of a vast invisible conflict... Time and again we can find no reason why things happened as they have... Hence some of us are forced to yield to Mr Maeterlinck's

theory, which is, I think, the theory of the ancients—the theory on which the
Greeks built their plays—that invisible powers of good and evil, operating in
regions that are above and beyond man's control, are working out his destiny
in this monstrous drama of the war.

It was an understandable reaction from a man as religious as Caine with
a leaning towards the supernatural.

Derwent left for America in November, 1915. He had trouble gaining
admittance when he arrived but was armed with a note from his father.
'I showed your letter to the Aliens Inspector,' he wrote on 30 November,
1915, 'and after some little talk he accepted it and stamped my pass-
port.' He also carried letters of introduction to several agents and people
in the New York theatre. The first one he saw, a Mr Brooks, gave him 'a
very chilly welcome', which surprised him. Brooks was annoyed that
Derwent had come over without an invitation. 'He is generally throwing
cold water on all my propositions, and today he has turned down a new
one-act piece. He has also said that "Pete" is old-fashioned, uninterest-
ing; generally speaking a bad play.' Derwent later managed to get it
produced with himself in the title role but it was not a success. This
was not entirely due to the script. Acting, especially in America, was of
the new, more naturalistic, quiet style, as exemplified in London by
Du Maurier. Derwent was of the old-fashioned school of melodrama.
Everyone else on stage was acting in the modern style so that Derwent's
ranting performance threw the whole play.

He complained to his father that the press, to whom he had talked
freely, was printing things he had never said. They reported that he was
engaged to be married, which was news to him. Caine supplied him
with a new sketch but Brooks did not like that either so his father
cabled him £100 to tide him over. Derwent was as disconcerted as his
father had been at the extent of pro-German feeling he encountered. He
never had much success on the American stage, despite his name, but
he soon moved into the burgeoning film industry and at once had plenty
of work, beginning with Pathé. He found the film people were eager for
new scripts and interested in his father's novels. Interested to the point
of pirating some of them. Fox made unauthorised versions of *The
Deemster* and *The Bondman*. In 1914 Vitagraph filmed *The Christian*,
also without the author's permission, and re-released it in 1917.

Before leaving for the States Derwent had starred as John Storm in
The Christian, made by the London Film Company with George Loane
Tucker, an American, directing. Glory Quayle was played by Tucker's
wife, Elizabeth Risdon. By the spring of 1916 Derwent was negotiating
on his father's behalf for the sale of film rights in America. There was
much competition for *The Woman Thou Gavest Me*. Derwent suggested to his father that he get Louis N. Parker, whose work was highly
thought of in the States, to write the film script. Derwent was soon

working most of the time, prospering sufficiently to move out of a cheap hotel into an apartment with a large studio sitting-room, a bedroom, bath and kitchenette, sublet to him by a friend. He engaged an inscrutable Japanese servant as valet and cook. He had also acquired a new girlfriend, an actress called Roma June who came from a Romany family. Before he returned to London he appeared in several more films, including the authorised version of *The Deemster*.

In June, 1916, his call-up papers arrived at Heath Brow. He lay low in New York leaving his father to deal with the recruiting officer. When America entered the war he had a nasty shock: he had taken up permanent residence to escape the British call-up, now he was liable to the US draft. The exemption from British conscription his father engineered would not help. However, by this time he was having serious problems with his eyes and he escaped. In October, 1917, the Recruiting Officer in London was after him again. Caine wrote a detailed letter describing Derwent's state of health and pointing out that he had failed a medical examination before leaving for America. He was 'suffering from rupture, moving kidney, varicose veins, disease of the ear &, I regret to say, many other physical disabilities'. He was staying in California 'for his health'.

At home Caine was still in touch with Queen Alexandra. In April, 1916, the faithful Charlotte Knollys wrote from Marlborough House saying the Queen was grateful for his help with arranging for her to receive more copies of her *Christmas Carol* book 'and thanks you for all the trouble you have taken in this matter'.

The year 1916 had begun sadly for Caine with the death of his old Keswick friend, Edwin Jackson. He and his family had often been guests at Greeba Castle. His eldest daughter was named Greeba and was Caine's goddaughter. After his death Greeba wrote to her 'Dearest Godfather' to tell him how much his wonderful letter had helped her mother. When her sister Dorothy was about to be married she wrote inviting him to the wedding which would be a quiet one in Cockermouth. 'Do come if you can but I expect you are busy. It would be lovely to have you.' She had been to London and seen Ralph and 'his lovely baby', who had been christened Derek—known to the family as Derry. 'They all seem ideally happy.' The appearance of his first grandson was a joy to Caine while Mary was ecstatic over the new baby, who could cause her none of the problems Little Elin had.

A Liverpool friend still in touch was Sir William Lever, the soap manufacturer and philanthropist, later Lord Leverhulme. Caine was greatly interested in Lever's creation of Port Sunlight, a development of which he very much approved. Remembering his own childhood in the back-to-back, terraced streets of Toxteth the provision of well-designed, healthy homes for working people was a cause he championed. Lever came over to Greeba quite often and on his way to and from the Island Caine sometimes stayed with him at his Wirral home, Thornton Manor. One such visit was at the end of April, 1916. Caine used the opportunity to look in on his old Liverpool haunts, among them the Myrtle Street chapel. He still owned the South Chester Street house, having inherited it from his mother when she died in 1912. Liverpool was his home town, remembered fondly wherever he subsequently went.

Around this time Caine and his brother Willie had an epic quarrel. No one else could make out what it was about but the two brothers refused to speak to each other for years. When they had to communicate they did so through Ralph, writing terse notes. Willie and his wife lived in a house on Lord Iveagh's Ken Wood estate, quite near to Tom and Mary. In addition Willie had a holiday house in the Isle of Man, on the outskirts of Douglas. The older men's quarrel was mirrored in the rows between Tom's sons. Derwent had found out about his brother's illegitimacy as a schoolboy. He continually taunted his elder brother with being a bastard and bragged that when their parents died he would inherit everything and Ralph would have nothing. He was to be disappointed. By the time their parents died not only had the law been changed but they both left wills which scrupulously divided their estates equally between their sons. Ralph and Derwent remained at daggers drawn. 'How they hated each other', commented one of their descendants.

Caine had intended to spend much of the summer of 1916 at Greeba with Mary and Little Elin and to speak in the House of Keys on Manx taxation. However, he was called back to London at the beginning of July so his speech was published in a local paper instead. He was strongly against what he called 'the iniquity of the food taxes—wealth should pay for the war, not the people's food'. He was paying substantial income tax in London, he claimed, and was angry that his wealthy neighbours in the Isle of Man paid nothing while the poor paid a tax on sugar.

The reason for his recall to London was the offer of new work. Lord Robert Cecil (created Viscount Chelwood in 1923) had presented Asquith, the Prime Minister, with a Memorandum which became the basis of the Covenant of the League of Nations. Caine knew Cecil through his younger brother, Lord Edward, who was Under-Secretary of State in the Egyptian Government when Caine was in Cairo. He was now invited to work with Lord Robert at the Foreign Office, on the British government's proposals for the peace, when it came. Some years afterwards, in a letter to the American Judge Buffington, he said,

the first document in the earliest development of the League of Nations sent
out by the British Foreign Office to the heads of the governments of foreign
countries was drawn up by me, and a large part of the first document issued by
the League of Nations after its establishment was the joint work of Lord Cecil
and myself.

Letters from Viscount Chelwood acknowledge the importance of
Caine's contribution and say how he had enjoyed working with him.

He was able to get back briefly to the Isle of Man for an event which
excited not only the author but the whole population—the filming of
The Manxman. The London Film Company were again the producers
and George Loane Tucker directed. The popular actor Henry Ainley
played Philip. Filming had to be hurried through as he was about to join
the Army. Elizabeth Risdon again had a starring part as Kate Cregeen
while Caine's old friend John M. East was her father, Caesar Cregeen.
Pete was played by the relatively unknown Fred Groves, but he was
greatly applauded for his performance, as Caine knew he would be. The
two had been friends for more than ten years. It had always been
Caine's intention that Derwent should take the part but he dared not let
him return from America. The small part of the Bishop was played by
Ralph, who had trouble with his billowing lawn sleeves in the stiff
breeze that blew during the scene of the open-air Tynwald, filmed on
the actual location at St John's. Interviewed for a local paper he said he
had enjoyed himself but had no desire to be a professional actor like his
brother.

The film company virtually took over the Island for a fortnight, hiring
the complete railway system to move cast, technicians and extras
around the various locations. There were 110 exterior shots, something
no one had attempted before. For the famous Tynwald scene special
trains were put on from all the main towns on the Island and free tickets
issued to the eight thousand local people taking part as extras, happily
dressing up in the fashions of the 1890s. A local lawyer well known for
his usually dandified appearance was spotted boarding the special train
at Douglas kitted out as a rat catcher. Two hundred and fifty regular soldiers from the prisoner-of-war camp at Knockaloe were borrowed to
play British infantry confronting the deputation of Peel fishermen.
Rumour had it even the prisoners took part, under the eye of their
guards. Tucker set out to make an epic and succeeded. According to the
trade paper, *Bioscope*, 'Several very beautiful scenes' had been filmed of
the Manx countryside, 'and as the film is looked upon as splendid advertisement for the Isle of Man the Manx Government is lending the
London Film Company every assistance.'

When it was released in 1917 *The Manxman* drew huge crowds, not
least in America. It was not only a popular but a critical success. When
films first arrived in 1896 they ran for only a few flickering minutes—

about 60 feet of film. By 1916 four- or five-reel films were the staple of cinema programmes but *The Manxman* ran to eight. The *New York Times* said, 'Mr Caine's stories are well adapted to the picture medium because they abound in vigorous action', while the trade paper *Variety* said, 'It can be stated without fear of contradiction that this photoplay feature may be heralded by exhibitors as one of the best film entertainments ever put forward.'

It had gone way over budget but looked set to make all concerned a great deal of money when disaster struck. A fire destroyed the Twickenham headquarters of the London Film Company and with it were lost the master and most of the copies for exhibition. The copies already sent to America survived and continued to be shown well into the 1920s but London Films collapsed and George Loane Tucker went back to America to work with Sam Goldwyn. This ultimately did Caine no harm as Tucker introduced him to Goldwyn. All that now survives of this first epic version of Caine's most popular book is one still, of the Tynwald scene, in the archives of the British Film Institute in London.

Caine became involved in arguments over the film rights to his first three books which he had sold outright to Chatto & Windus. He had kept the dramatic rights and insisted that these included films, which were 'photographed drama'. Percy Spalding, Andrew Chatto's successor, did not agree and much acrimonious correspondence ensued. Spalding argued that films had not existed in the 1880s so as publishers they had the right to have the books filmed. A compromise was eventually reached but neither of the first two were ever filmed. *The Deemster* was made in America in 1917 by the Arrow Film Corporation with Derwent and the American actress Marian Swayne in the star parts.

Another small book on the war, *Our Girls: Their Work for the War Effort*, was brought out by Hutchinson's in 1916. Caine was commissioned to write it by the Ministry of Munitions and Ralph selected fifteen photographs from the Ministry's files for illustrations. Opposite the title page is printed, 'From One of Our Girls to One of Our Boys to...' and below is a space marked 'Photograph of Sender may be pasted on this space.' Designed to be sent to men 'at the Front', it gave an account of women working in the munitions factories around London and was intended to show the contribution women were making to the war effort. It is propaganda but the writing occasionally rises above it. Caine accepted the commission with alacrity as it gave him the opportunity to descant on new developments in the Woman Question brought about by the war.

The book described a visit to Woolwich Arsenal arranged by Edwin Montagu, the Minister of Munitions, who also sent him to factories making guns, rifles, cartridges, shells and bombs. He told Caine to write about them in a way that would boost the morale of both the people at home and 'Our Boys at the Front', without giving away any secrets as to location or details of what was being made.

Caine described the giant forges at Woolwich being worked by men, pointing out how vital their work was and hoping that no ignorant women would give them white feathers. He wrote enthusiastically about the work the women were doing but much of his account of Woolwich Arsenal is naïve, as if he had never been in an engineering works before, as indeed he may not have. He was surprised how well the women got on with the machines: they had 'wooed and won this new kind of male monster'. They were also doing skilled and dangerous work in the section where the finished shells and bombs were filled with high explosive.

He was crucially aware that what women were doing for the war effort, not just in the factories but as nurses and drivers of ambulances and lorries, and on the farms as Land Girls, was changing the way men saw women and perhaps more importantly how women saw themselves. The good money they were earning was giving them a status they had never had before. They also had responsibility. If the girls inspecting cartridge caps for faults skimped their work then their own brothers or boyfriends might pay the price of their carelessness and they knew it. The sight of men and women working together at machines making large calibre shells brought home to him how things were changing. 'As far as one can see the sexes get on well together,' he commented.

> Common interests and common labour seem to have brought them into friendly relations. Constant intercourse at work [we might phrase that differently today] has given the men a high opinion of women... In like manner the women seem to have come to a good understanding of the men... It looks like a brave fellowship, a fine camaraderie, and one hopes that long after the war it may continue. And let nobody suppose that to these men these women will be less desirable as wives because they have worked by their sides in soiled overalls with oily hands and even blackened faces.

Visiting a night shift in north London he experienced his first air raid and gave a highly coloured account of a Zeppelin being shot down. Summing up what he had seen of the women working on munitions, Caine came to the conclusion that 'wholesome food, regular hours, healthy workshops, animated company, human discipline, and above all, the sense of being somebody of importance in the world, doing something of consequence, have made a better woman of her'. Until then two general views of woman's relation to labour had been formed, he said, one that she should be the drudge, doing all the mean work, the other that she should be a parasite, doing no work at all. Both were damnably wrong, the one turning women into squaws, the other into houris. 'Work…is good for woman, and in this war the daughters of Britain seem to have found themselves.' He appeared oblivious to the damage to the health of some of the girls, especially those working at filling shells and bombs. He comments that most only wore their masks and protective caps when the supervisor was looking. Many of them paid a high price later, suffering as the match girls had done.

However, he was right in thinking that 'doing a national service of immense importance' gave working women a new self-respect.

> Earning substantial wages, and being free to marry or not to marry, as they please, has dealt a death-blow to that hoary old wickedness (prostitution in its various forms) which is based on the poverty of the woman and the wealth of the man… The daughters of Britain are free women, worthy of the men they are fighting for. And when our soldiers come back…they can line up and salute them.

It did not work out like that. The men needed the jobs and the women were pushed out of the factories to make room for them.

In February, 1917, Mary was taken severely ill. Whatever ailed her it lasted several months and could well have been induced by the strain of the pretence over Elin. She was not well enough to go to Greeba for the summer so Caine sent for Elin and her nanny to stay with them at Heath Brow for a month or two. What impressed the five-year-old most was the big anti-aircraft gun on Hampstead Heath just at the end of the garden. She went for a while to a local school but by mid-September she was back at Greeba while Caine took Mary to a hotel in Hove to recuperate. He was pursued by requests to give interviews, to write a regimental history, to give money for charities and individuals. There was even a letter from the editor of a Tokyo newspaper, *Hochi Shimbun*, asking for an article—one of his plays, *The Bondman*, was being produced there in Japanese.

Back in London Caine received a letter from Lloyd George, who had succeeded Asquith as Prime Minister the previous December. A National War Aims Committee had been set up to keep the public informed. This committee, said Lloyd George, 'is proposing to make as large a use as possible of the cinema in carrying on this work.' The scenario must be provided 'by a really competent hand'. As Caine had the reputation of being a Man of Letters 'your name would have been the first to suggest itself in this connection even if I had not the advantage of a friendly acquaintance with you extending over many years'.

Caine was delighted to take it on. For some time he had been convinced that the cinema was going to be of increasing importance and if so, he wanted to be part of it in any way he could. Lloyd George sent a note on 30 October thanking Caine for his prompt reply, adding, 'the

Committee are to be congratulated on securing your services'.

Work began at once and Caine was involved in constant meetings and discussions as well as writing the script. Herbert Brenon was chosen to direct what was generally referred to as the National Film. First called *The Invasion of Britain*, the final title was *Victory and Peace*. The stars were Mattheson Lang, whose good looks showed as well on film as on stage, and Ellen Terry. It was never released as the war ended before it was finished. Less than 1000 feet of it survives in the National Film Archive and only part of that in viewable condition. It was preserved only because it contained one or two of Ellen Terry's scenes.

Caine approached friends and fellow writers for contributions, as he had for his charity books. One of these was Galsworthy, who replied in May 1918 that as he might not like the film (and it was probable as he hated most films) and as he might even disapprove of it, he must refuse. He feared that mention of his name would inevitably make people think he was partly responsible 'for the *dramatic and constructional* side of the film'. Though the film was being made for patriotic purposes he still could not meet Caine's request. Rudyard Kipling sent a note that the music for the Cantata founded on his *Song of the English* had been written by Robert Bridges. If Caine wanted to use it he should approach the publishers, Novello. Kipling insisted this version must be used if Caine wanted to have it in his 'forthcoming cinema'.

Towards the end of the year another letter arrived from Downing Street. Lloyd George asked if Caine would allow his name to be put to the King for the award of a peerage. Lord Burnham, proprietor of the *Daily Telegraph*, was one among several people who suggested it. Lloyd George's secretary wrote to Burnham saying he agreed about 'Mr Hall Caine's just deserts' and he would 'see the matter is not overlooked'. What was offered was a baronetcy. This recognition of his position as a man of letters and of his work for the war effort both pleased and appalled him. A baronetcy was hereditary and Ralph was illegitimate. If he accepted, then at his death Mary and Ralph would both be publicly shamed and Derwent, who seemed to his father quite unworthy of such an honour, would be the next baronet. (Ironically, Derwent, who was knighted in 1932, was created a baronet in 1938 for political services rendered, but left no heir.) Caine could not know that before his death the law would be changed to allow the legitimisation of offspring born before the marriage of the parents. Thanks to his own perjury when he registered Ralph, and later when he gave the date of his marriage to *Who's Who* as 1882, the secret had been well kept. He agonised over the problem before finally writing privately to Lloyd George asking to be allowed to decline 'the King's gracious gift'. His friends in high places did not let the matter rest, however. If he would not accept a baronetcy,

asked Downing Street, how about a knighthood? This, not being hereditary, was accepted gratefully. A KBE—Knight of the British Empire—
was agreed on and the announcement was prepared in the form 'Sir
Thomas Hall Caine'. This he promptly rejected. His hatred of his given
name was stronger than ever and he insisted on being 'Sir Hall' instead
of 'Sir Thomas'. This looked and sounded awkward, but that was the
way he wanted it and the way he got it. It was a moment of high emotion when at the next investiture he was dubbed a knight at
Buckingham Palace by George V.

How many people knew of the offer of a baronetcy and of his reason
for refusing it can only be guessed. That Caine was deeply stirred by the
situation is certain. He retreated with Mary to the Isle of Man where
they spent Christmas and New Year at the Fort Anne Hotel, overlooking
the harbour and bay, the scene of Mary O'Neill's traumatic wedding
night in *The Woman Thou Gavest Me*.

CHAPTER TWENTY-SIX

The year 1918 began for Caine with a reminder that he was essentially a novelist. An American publisher asked if he had a war novel ready—if so, they would pay a royalty of 25%. He replied with a brief note in the negative. It was not that he had no story brewing but he had forsworn fiction until the war was won. Back in Hampstead, he continued to work on the National Film while pouring out a stream of newspaper articles. One was headed, 'Thank God for Lloyd George'. He was also working with Cecil on the proposals for a League of Nations.

The war had curtailed Mary's frenetic social life, as it had their travelling, but she still gave regular dinner parties in spite of rationing and shortage of servants. Caine was becoming an egotistic monster. He presided at the head of his dinner table and held forth. If anyone dared to say anything he would glare at the offender and continue as if nothing had happened. The more sycophantic of his admirers were happy to sit and drink in his 'wonderful talk'. Others were annoyed by the way he pontificated. A few stood up to him, particularly Shaw. As a teenager Elin was delighted by the evenings when Mr Shaw came to dinner. He and her grandfather both had red hair and fought like Kilkenny cats, 'but they always made it up afterwards'.

In March the film of *The Deemster*, made in America the previous year by the Arrow Film Corporation and starring Derwent, was about to be released in London. Caine drummed up a stellar first night audience in aid of war charities. He wrote to Lloyd George but his secretary replied that 'the seriousness of the Military situation will make it impossible for the Prime Minister to be present at the performance on Saturday, much as he would like to be there. Mr Lloyd George has asked me to convey to you his best wishes for the success of your venture.'

Caine's play *The Prime Minister* was revived the following month, unsuccessfully, and Caine, the backer, lost £600. It had first been produced in America, at Atlantic City, in 1915. The Vedrenne management staged it in London in January, 1916, under the title *Margaret Schiller*. This third presentation reverted to the original name. Another of his wartime plays, a one-acter called *The Iron Hand*, which had been the centrepiece of a variety bill at the Coliseum in 1916, was also revived. When the opening night of *The Prime Minister* came Caine was confined to the house with a heavy cold and Mary went without him.

This was the least of his health troubles that year. Failing to shake off the cold he consulted his London doctor. The local GP was not good enough for him: he summoned the King's doctor, Sir Thomas Horder, later Lord Horder. He followed the King in other things, too, buying his cigars from the King's cigar merchant in Pall Mall, Carlin's. They advised him of any particularly choice goods that came in and stored them for him. They also sold him a humidor for Greeba Castle. He merited the term 'champagne socialist'.

To return to his health, tests showed he had picked up an 'intestinal infestation', possibly in India but more probably during one of his stays in Egypt. The treatment was unpleasant but worked. Sir Thomas told him his trouble was also due to his teeth and recommended that most of them come out. 'We have to face that they are not much use to you now.'

After all this a holiday was necessary. He and Mary went to stay with Lord Leverhulme at Thornton Manor in July. Mary was also ill and depressed. She remained at Thornton while Caine and Leverhulme sailed to Stornoway, in the Outer Hebrides, where Leverhulme owned Lews Castle. There he gathered a house party of a dozen politicians and intellectuals and Caine thoroughly enjoyed himself. He was interested in his friend's plans to develop the harbour at Stornoway and help the local fishermen. The locals did not appreciate the soap magnate's efforts and his plans were ignored. On 23 August Caine wrote to Mary at Thornton Manor saying he had seen most of the island on drives with Leverhulme. 'The cottages of the crofters are certainly the most shocking human habitations I have ever yet seen in my part of the world. And yet the people on the whole seem clean and healthy.'

Mary replied asking him to tell Lord Leverhulme how much she was benefiting from her stay in his 'lovely house'. She had put on three pounds and now weighed eight stone (112 lbs)! Caine returned to Thornton Manor for another week's stay. The reason for this was that scenes for the National Film were being shot in the army barracks at nearby Chester. Work on the film had dragged on far beyond the date at which it was hoped to have it completed. Herbert Brenon, the director, wrote to Caine at Thornton Manor explaining that the delay had been occasioned by difficulties with the cast. Marie Lohr starred opposite Mattheson Lang and a number of popular actors and variety artists were included as well as a 'guest appearance' by Ellen Terry. They all had different matinée days, could come this day, couldn't come that, were ill, exhausted by two performances the night before and so on. When they were there, however, they worked well—Marie Lohr was 'a joy and delight, as is her performance; what do you think of her for "The Woman Thou Gavest Me"?' Brenon would like to do it in England as soon as the present picture was finished. Filming in England was so much cheaper than in America and he thought the actors available were good. (Hugh Ford directed it in America the following year for Famous Players with Katherine Macdonald, not Marie Lohr.)

By the end of August, 1918, the scenes with actors were finished and Brenon, having shot sequences of submarines in Portsmouth, arrived in Chester for the army ones. Caine as scriptwriter went to watch the shooting with Mary. The whole project of the National Film was impossibly grandiose and was abandoned when the Armistice meant there was no further need for propaganda. Having watched the filming for a couple of days they crossed to the Isle of Man. Caine invited Leverhulme to join them but he had no time that summer. He would like to come later, he wrote, as whenever he had been to the Island he had 'always felt—as I do in Lewis—toned up as by no other place. I have the happiest recollections of all my visits to the Isle of Man.'

Mary stayed only briefly at Greeba, returning to London on her own. In September she was very ill again and Caine went down to Hampstead to be with her. Once there he plunged back into work for the League of Nations. Sir Ernest Hodder-Williams came to see him and they discussed the proposals. Caine read him his draft memorandum, which Sir Ernest described as 'very remarkable', and asked for a copy. Thanking him for it, Sir Ernest sent a long list of other people whom he thought should see it, starting with the Archbishop of Canterbury, the Bishop of London, the Chief Rabbi and sundry lords and ambassadors, ending with H.G. Wells, Arnold Bennett and Conan Doyle. Caine took his advice and most of them responded favourably.

When peace came on 11 November, 1918, Caine's first thought was for his Island. Its thriving tourist industry had been decimated. Another royal visit would, he was sure, be the medicine to revive it. He wrote to the King suggesting one. Lord Stamfordham replied that the King had read Sir Hall's letter with great interest. 'A visit by the King and Queen to the Isle of Man is never lost sight of in prospective arrangements.' There were no firm plans and the Island had to wait a while.

There were plenty of plans, however, for the filming of more of his novels. Derwent, still in New York, was busy on his behalf and also starring with Ivy Close in *Darby and Joan*, made by Master Films. Caine had written the script, basing it on his novella of the same name of more than twenty years before. Meanwhile Famous Players were at work filming *The Woman Thou Gavest Me*. Although it drew big audiences and good reviews nothing remains of this film but some stills in the National Film Archive. Derwent, now 27, returned to London early in 1919.

Heath Brow was proving too big. They moved out and let it furnished. It was Caine's intention that a smaller house should be bought in Mary's name. She knew that with the war over her husband would return to working abroad or at Greeba for much of his time. Meanwhile she rented a house at Maidenhead where Ralph and Lillian had settled. Another attraction was that Mary's old friend Vesta Tilley, and her husband Walter de Frece, knighted in the New Year's Honours List of 1919 and about to become a Conservative Member of Parliament, also had a house there. When Vesta Tilley announced in April, 1919, that she would make a final tour before retiring, Mary was delighted at the prospect of seeing more of her. Lady de Frece was 56 and though she hated the idea of leaving the theatre she knew the time had come, for her husband's sake as well as her own. He cut himself off so completely from his former music hall connections that people who knew him called him 'Sir Altered de Frece'.

Another name in the New Year Honours was Ralph's. In October, 1918, on his return from a business trip to New York, he had written to his father saying he had heard 'on very best authority' that his name had been put forward for the New Year Honours List, though what for he did not know. He wanted his father to put in a discreet word for him. 'Without my work the newspapers would not be in half so good a position as they are. The ease of the paper position is almost entirely due to my efforts.' He was offered the CBE. Mary was furious. She wrote to his father that it was an insult to Ralph 'after all his hard work'. He should have a knighthood 'at least' and should accept nothing less. Ralph, however, accepted the CBE, though from his offhand account of the investiture he was clearly as disappointed as his mother.

Derwent was at a loose end in London, a state of affairs his father considered dangerous. He wrote a sketch for him and Derwent performed it at a 'Victory Drive' at the Coliseum which raised £2000, but that was not enough to keep him out of trouble. Derwent formed a company, backed by his father, to tour one of his father's plays with himself in the lead opposite Margaret English. Rehearsals began in June, 1919. On a visit to Greeba to discuss the play he was involved in a car accident in Douglas. He knocked a young man down outside the Peveril Hotel. The man was not badly hurt but the incident provoked a lot of anger and both Derwent and his father were attacked in the local papers. His father went back to London with him and watched a rehearsal. He was deeply shocked when Derwent rounded on his leading lady with a vicious display of bad temper. Derwent stamped out of the rehearsal and left his cast to struggle on without him for a week or more. His father returned to Greeba full of foreboding about Derwent's future. Mary wrote on 15 July telling him not to worry as 'he is now all right and rehearsing his people'. She was going with him to a private showing of the film of *The Woman Thou Gavest Me*, which Ralph had organised after problems delayed the trade showing.

Still anxious about Derwent, Caine wrote to Margaret English hoping she would influence him 'to give his company a fair and proper chance to do their work well. It is quite impossible that they should do so if the leading actor is not constantly with them.' The tour was to start in the Isle of Man 'and then if his company do not give a first-rate performance in Douglas we shall never hear the last of it, for the Manx people and the Manx newspapers are at this moment so angry with me that they will jump at any opportunity to injure Derwent and hold his company up to contumely if they possibly can'. He appears more worried on his own behalf than his wayward son's.

Despite these distractions Caine worked throughout the summer of 1919 on his first post-war novel. The story, originally titled *The Manx Woman*, had been in his mind for a long time. He had first discussed the plot with Bram Stoker before he died in 1912. Fresh impetus was given to it by the trauma of the offered baronetcy. Working in a solitary fury of composition he sought to exorcise his demons with this book, published as *The Master of Man*. He told no one the plot, not even Mary, and he did not follow his previous practice of sending her each episode as he completed it, ready for magazine serialisation. She wrote sadly, saying how strange it was not to know what the new book was about and not to be helping him with it. Hating the Island, as she now did, and knowing the new book was set there she said petulantly she wished he would drop it and 'write another Eternal City instead'.

Charley Evans, his editor at Heinemann's, visited Greeba to discuss the book in June, 1919. Later Ray Long, Caine's agent, came to discuss film contracts. *Darby and Joan* was shown in London without raising much excitement—*The Woman Thou Gavest Me* was still being delayed by contract and technical matters but did much better when it came out in 1920. After the first showing Mary telegraphed, 'Woman film a great success.' It did not reach the Isle of Man until October, 1920, when the author took a party of friends to see it. He was highly incensed to find the film was damaged and the credits missing. He wrote a stiff letter of complaint to the cinema manager.

In September of 1919 Derwent was still trying to negotiate a film deal for his father. Mary told her husband she thought he was asking too much for the film rights and as most of those on offer were not sold she was probably right. Sam Goldwyn telephoned Derwent asking to read the new book with a view to buying the film rights but was told it was not sufficiently advanced. Derwent told him his father would wish to make a play of it before it was filmed. Though a script was prepared there is no record of it being performed in a theatre apart from a copyright performance, unless it was staged under another name. Sam

Goldwyn filmed the book in 1923 as *Name the Man*, with Mae Busch and Conrad Nagel in the leading parts. Some of the scenes were shot at Woolley Firs, Ralph's house in Maidenhead.

A telephone at Greeba Castle would have made dealing with all this business much simpler but Caine was still adamant in his refusal to have one. With so much to distract him it is no wonder the new book progressed slowly. In December he retreated to St Moritz with his valet and a nurse. He stayed there until March, 1920, complaining about his health and struggling with a magazine version. Mary was at Maidenhead much of the time with Elin, who was now at school. Her cousin Derry was old enough to be company for her and his sister Mary was two.

Publication of the serial had begun in two American magazines the previous autumn and Caine had worked hard through the winter keeping up with the printers. As usual it was a big book and was not finished when he returned to London in early April, staying at the Savoy Hotel. Mary was not there to meet him. She was at the Fort Anne Hotel in Douglas, supervising the first major refurbishment of Greeba Castle since they had bought it in 1896. The drains had to be replaced and electricity was being put in. Finally the whole house was redecorated. Wherever they lived Mary took great pleasure in decorating their various homes. She had green fingers and enjoyed designing and managing the garden wherever she was. Her taste was much admired by her friends. At the end of one of her letters reporting on progress at Greeba Mary added a postscript, in tiny writing squeezed into the corner of the page as if she meant it to escape notice. It said, 'Having the telephone put in. Cost to be £9 a year including three hundred calls.' There was a roar of rage from her husband and the telephone was cancelled. Greeba Castle was only connected to the telephone system, at Dr Marshall's insistence, during Caine's last illness, when the Post Office hastily looped wires through the trees up to the house. Until then Greeba Castle remained a telephone-free zone.

Derwent had gone back to America with his girlfriend Roma June and Ralph was there on an extended business visit. Mary complained that neither had written to her. Derwent fell ill and wrote a letter to his father in St Moritz which so alarmed him he replied he would leave for New York at once. Roma wrote in haste to tell him 'Derwent's trouble is mostly mental' and his father should only come over if he really 'needed a change'. Derwent was so irritable there would only be trouble. The main cause of his irritability was a problem with his eyes—he complained of seeing 'a spot' and that he was going blind. The doctors said he was not but he was advised to give up his career in films and on the stage because the bright lights might cause further damage. His sight deteriorated no further but he wore pebble-thick glasses from then on.

The verdict threw him into an intense fit of depression, made worse by seeing his brother doing well in business and making a lot of money while his own career was at an end. He told his mother he wanted to settle in Italy and do nothing. 'I feel like laying down like a tired horse that has been in a race and saying I'm beaten, I give up.' However, he was back in London by the summer and plunging into fresh fields of business.

By mid-May Caine was at Greeba. He was supposed to be finishing the serial but he was soon complaining of being ill again and went off to Marienbad to take the waters. They do not seem to have done him much good. He got back to England at the end of June and visited Ralph and Lillian in Maidenhead—Mary was now at Greeba with Elin for the summer. He was at once embroiled in arguments over his income tax and rows engendered by some newspaper articles he had written, all of which made him feel more ill than ever.

There is evidence that his marriage was under strain again. The big gap in their ages mattered more now than it had previously. Caine was 67 and feeling older while Mary was a lively 51. He was increasingly self-centred, solitary and difficult. People who knew Mary described her as mischievous, manipulative and demanding, evidence borne out by her letters. Caine felt responsible for her as if she were still a child. He remained the centre of her world. She had adored him since she was thirteen and still loved him, whatever their arguments. He seems to have been a better lover on paper than in person. All his life he found it difficult to show affection. Mary's delight when he wrote her one of his 'love letters' is clear from one of hers in September, 1920: 'My Darling, I am so very happy to receive your naughty letter and enjoyed it very much. I too am longing for a kiss. I wonder how much longer I have to wait.' She ended, 'With all my love and longing for you. Yours only, Mary.' Caine did not want a divorce, or even a legal separation, but he did not want to live with her. It hurt. Defensively she said to friends, 'My husband and I get on so well because we don't live together.'

Caine went back to St Moritz with his valet and shut himself up there to finish the serial. His trunk got lost on the way, another aggravation. He wrote to Ralph to chase it up and asked him to see Charley Evans with a view to holding up the serial for a few months, or even stopping it altogether. He needed the pressure lifted for a while if he was ever to recover his health and get the book finished. Ralph replied that he was sorry his father still felt ill 'although at St Moritz'. He had spoken to Evans 'and we all feel you are wise to immediately lift the strain from your mind at any cost'. He advised his father to send the magazines concerned a medical certificate from his St Moritz doctor, Dr Bernhard, 'to cover the legal side'. Evans had agreed to space out the serial to give his father three months of 'the complete relief from strain that you desire'. He was back in London by 20 September, staying at the Savoy for a few days before joining Mary and Elin at Greeba.

The sudden death of William Heinemann from a heart attack on 5 October, 1920, at the early age of 57, was as much of a shock to Caine as to anyone. They had had their arguments and Caine had recently complained that Heinemann had not been doing enough to promote his books, all of which, apart from *The White Prophet*, were still in print, but they were old friends of thirty years' standing. Caine was the firm's first author and for years their best seller. While he grumbled, he had never taken his novels elsewhere. Already nervous about the reception his book would have he was thrown into a panic over what might now happen to his publishers and his work.

A memorial service for William Heinemann was held at St Peter's, Eton Square, on 8 October and Ralph went to it. 'There was a very good attendance,' he wrote to his father, 'I told the reporter I represented you as you were unable to get up to London in time. The funeral was quite private for the family only... Pawling seemed very upset.'

Someone else who was deeply shocked at the death was the American publisher F.N. (Effendi) Doubleday—Rudyard Kipling had given him his nickname. His New York firm of Doubleday, Page & Co. had been founded in 1897 and he too had been a friend of William Heinemann for thirty years. Doubleday arrived in London on 5 October with his wife and son, Nelson, looking forward to dining with Heinemann that night. He was horrified when he and Nelson arrived at the office at 21 Bedford Street to find a notice on the door saying that Heinemann had died during the night. Heinemann's death left the firm in a precarious position with Sydney Pawling, the surviving partner, holding 45% of the equity and the threat of a take-over shadowing the business, which had not recovered from the disruption of the war. Heinemann's sight had been failing and he had been far from well for some time but his death was entirely unexpected and provoked a crisis in the affairs of the firm.

Doubleday found Pawling in a state of shock. He had an option to buy Heinemann's share of the business but he did not have the money. Would it, he asked Effendi, be of any interest to Doubleday, Page? It would give them control of the business but he would be prepared to continue running it. Doubleday, who was both shrewd and far-sighted, understood perfectly well the value of what he was being offered. Running a London business from the other side of the Atlantic would be tricky but he took the chance and bought William Heinemann's shares for £25,000. It was a bargain. The new Anglo-American partnership, with Sydney Pawling promising to maintain Heinemann's character and traditions, was announced in December. Caine, who liked both Pawling and Evans, was greatly relieved. His contract would be honoured.

Charley Evans, however, was worried. Cassell made him a tempting offer and he thought seriously of accepting. 'Effendi', when he found out, had a hard time persuading him to stay but he realised how important Evans was to the firm. He promised him that if he stayed, 'you will be happy and your wife will wear diamonds'. Charley stayed, with the odd title of Secretary, though he later became Managing Director. His wife did wear diamonds when, a few years later, 'Effendi' presented her with a souvenir brooch mounted with them, but he was not happy as is clear from his correspondence with Caine. Arthur Page, who was the son of Doubleday's founding partner Walter Page, was appointed to the board. Theodore Byard, who was a friend of William Heinemann's and had only joined the firm recently, was put in overall charge as 'Resident Chairman', despite having almost no experience of publishing. Byard had private means, a weekend cottage in Surrey and a house in Venice complete with gondola. It had been his love of music and art that had drawn him and Heinemann together. He had also become friendly with Caine and invited him and Mary to parties and musical soirées at his London home. He exuded reliability and could be expected to act responsibly on his own so he made a good partner for the creative, mercurial, highly strung Evans.

The new partnership was publicly inaugurated with a dinner at the Bath Club in honour of Arthur Page, who had been a popular American ambassador in London during the war. Literary London was well represented. The guest list included Arnold Bennett, T.P. O'Connor, J.C. Squire, Sir Arthur Pinero, Arthur Rackham and two youngsters, Robert Graves and Siegfried Sassoon. Seated at the top table, as usual, was Caine, who proposed the main toast of the evening in characteristic style.

'This is a gathering of the Heinemann clan,' he began. 'Its chieftains, its captains and its soldiers. I have belonged to it for thirty-one years. Indeed, I am the oldest surviving member.'

He was not to be for much longer. The illness over many months and then the death of Sydney Pawling at 61 in December, 1922, caused another crisis. Again Doubleday's cash solved the problem: he bought Pawling's share of the firm from his widow, thus making it entirely American-controlled. Despite a damaging strike in the book trade Heinemann's survived and went on to fresh prosperity. A few of their leading authors wavered but Caine was the only one to leave.

In 1920, however, that was still in the future and Heinemann's were preparing to publish *The Master of Man*. Caine went to St Moritz as usual in December, leaving Mary and Elin at Maidenhead. He had promised to return to spend Christmas with them all but, still feeling unwell, he could not face the long, cold train journey and the ferry for just a few days. Ralph wrote to say they all understood and thought he had made the right decision. Mary, Elin and Derwent would be with them at Woolley Firs for Christmas Day and they looked forward to seeing him home in the Spring. He was home, however, in February, 1921, following a tragedy which shattered him. A lift cable snapped at his hotel. The cage plunged to the bottom of the shaft and his valet was killed.

Elin Hall Caine, aged 8. She is wearing the Moroccan costume
given to Ralph by his father.

Before leaving for Switzerland he had begun discussions with Mary about their future. She had asked for a 'definite arrangement of figures' to be decided before his return home but as he had come back early this had not been done. He did not stay in London but went straight on to

Greeba, leaving Mary at Maidenhead. The first thing to confront him was news of the failure of his appeal against an assessment for £9000 surtax. He wrote in fury to his accountant, pointing out that he was domiciled in the Isle of Man, but he had to submit to the ruling in the end. His constant whingeing and quibbling over his tax affairs finally drew an exasperated letter from the accountant.

> I am sorry to learn you are not sleeping well. I wish I could influence you not to worry over these Income Tax questions past, present, and future. You have threshed the whole problem out and have decided, knowing the cost, to accept what I agree appears inevitable, viz. residence in England. Take it philosophically and let it stop at that. Work no harder, you have enough, but be content and accept the result, viz that you will leave that much less money some day, long distant I hope, for others to spend.

Mary had found the place she wanted, Heath End House, overlooking Hampstead Heath and next to the Spaniard. Though a fair size it was not so big as Heath Brow. It is still there, divided into flats. The purchase was agreed and it became urgent to settle Mary's finances. Thanks to his previous generosity she had the capital to buy the house but he wanted her to have her own separate income to run it. Negotiations were going on for a new Collected Edition. He had paid Chatto £350 for the use of *The Deemster* but again *A Son of Hagar* was to be left out. He put in train arrangements for the collected edition to be published on Mary's behalf and she was to receive the proceeds. He wrote her a detailed letter on 28 February, 1921, setting out exactly what she would get and what would be due to him, both from the collected edition and the new book. On the back of an old envelope he worked out what *The Master of Man* would bring in at different levels of sales, at home and abroad. His payment to Chatto went into the calculations as well. The letter is a long and complicated document which illustrates the grasp of business and finance which had made him the wealthy man he was. The letter begins, as many did over the years, 'My dear Darling,' but, oddly and perhaps significantly, it ends, 'With kind regards, Hall Caine.' Though perhaps that was a slip of the pen after setting out so many business details.

That these negotiations were a strain on both of them is shown by the way they both fell ill at this point. Mary, driven into what looks like a nervous breakdown, demanded her husband's presence. He went but took her back to Greeba with him early in May. In June Sidney Walton wrote to say he hoped there was 'better news of Lady Caine' and referring to 'the deep black shadow that has been upon you all these months'. At the same time, in the course of a long letter mainly about business, Ralph wrote that he was glad Dr Marshall had been consulting with Horder over his mother's 'gastritis'. Ralph was sorry the attacks had been so frequent, leaving her very weak. He evidently understood her well for he added, 'I certainly think that if she is anxious to return to England and to London, you should enable her to do so, because I am sure that the mental effect has something to do with it, and she was as right as possible during the time she was at the Savoy Hotel.'

In July, 1921, Heinemann's brought out *The Master of Man*. Charley Evans arranged for a newsreel company to go to Greeba and film an interview with the Great Author. Elin and her friend Yvonne were included, dancing around the garden in white frocks. Evans was delighted with the result which was excellent publicity. This novel effectively rounds off the Hall Caine canon. As so often before, he was undecided over what to call it almost to the last minute. Ray Long wrote urging him to drop the title, *The Manx Woman*. 'I am convinced that the title *The Master of Man* has a ring to it like the chimes of Big Ben—something that stirs one to the utmost, and arouses every element of curiosity.'

Although he is not explicit as to dates, as with most of his other books, from internal evidence the action is set in 1910-1912. The mind set is definitely Edwardian rather than 1920s. Below the title is the quotation which supplied the moral of the book: 'Be sure your sin will find you out.' As his own sin of living with Mary and begetting a child out of wedlock had caught up with him. This maxim is hammered home. The climax of the story is supposed to be the resurrection of the young man's soul. The subject is dramatic in that it is the story of a judge who is called to sit in judgement on his own victim. The germ of the story can be traced back to a letter Caine received in September, 1908, enclosing a petition and asking him to sign it. With it was a letter about Daisy Lord, aged 21, who had given birth alone in her room to a baby girl and then 'in a fit of insanity' killed it. She had struggled back to work next day as if nothing had happened. Three weeks later she was arrested and tried for murder. At her trial she said, 'I thought I would put an end to it so that it should not have the trouble I have had.' She was sentenced to death. Three weeks later this was commuted to penal servitude for life. The writer of the letter thought the girl had suffered enough punishment 'for what is the fault of our sex' and should now be released. After seeing a performance of *The Christian* he thought Caine might be sympathetic. He signed the petition and returned it, keeping the letter and mulling over the case of Daisy Lord for years. Eventually her story became the core of *The Master of Man*.

Initially the book had more success than many of its predecessors: the first printing of 100,000 was sold out in a matter of days and it appeared simultaneously in translation in several countries. It went well in America, where Caine had sold it outright to Lippincott for $17,000— about £180,000 at 1990s values. It was old-fashioned: Caine had not changed with the times. One reviewer referred to 'this Victorian author'—reviews were mixed. The story has an intensity and a passion which recall the work of his prime but it had nothing like the success of *The Christian* or *The Manxman*. When it appeared he was disagreeably surprised to find it did not automatically top the best-sellers list for weeks on end. What he regarded as his position by right was taken almost immediately by A.S.M. Hutchinson with *If Winter Comes*. Hutchinson, who was praised by critics as being 'among the artists' and a writer of great novels, has disappeared even more completely than Hall Caine. Ralph, in New York on business, wrote that *If Winter Comes* was top of the best-seller list there as well, with sales of 300,000 so far. Second was an American novel while his father's book was only third. He had been told sales were around 160,000.

A comparison of Hutchinson's book with Caine's is interesting. They both begin in the period immediately before the war. Hutchinson takes his characters through the war years, showing vividly how they and their circumstances were changed, while Caine's story ignores the war. He ignored it also in his style, which remains the same—high Victorian, with bosoms heaving. Hutchinson's book, on the other hand, is recognisably twentieth-century in tone and style. Melodrama and preaching were out of fashion. Caine's book is written as if it is a contemporary story while conveying the feel of an earlier age. The only clue as to the date of the action is a vivid description of Douglas Promenade lit by electric fairy lights. This was not done regularly until after the publication of the book but it had been staged for the 1914 Douglas Carnival, just before the outbreak of war, when he was on the Island and must have seen the illuminations.

He announced that this would be his last novel. Even at the end of a long and successful career as a romancer he seemed oddly unsure of himself. As he had done so often before, he turned to friends for advice and criticism. He agonised once more over 'the problem of the happy ending'. To him the book was a tragedy and should end as such but friends and his publisher insisted the public would demand a happy ending. This he provided by the device of having the hero and heroine married in the prison chapel, Victor returning to his cell afterwards to complete his sentence. Many applauded this but one or two astute critics told him it did not ring true and that the book would have been better had it ended with the pair reunited at the castle gate when Victor was finally released. As it stands the last scene reads awkwardly and the author was clearly uncomfortable with it. The suggested ending would have allowed the book to finish on a high note, but his fixation with sin and justice ensured that Victor must be seen to be fully punished. Had the author had his way Victor would have lost his Fenella.

Ahead of publication he sent presentation copies of the book to friends asking for their comments. The longest and most appreciative reply came from his old friend, Robert Leighton, who had earned a solid reputation as a writer of boys' adventure stories. Addressing him as 'My Very Dear Caine', Leighton heaps praise upon praise and calls the book 'your supreme achievement...the greatest and most perfect thing you have done. It seems to me you know human nature with absolute sureness.'

Most of the other recipients acknowledged the book briefly and politely. The Bishop of London wrote that he had finished it, 'appropriately, late on a Sunday night after a long day's work. I say "appropriately," for its end is better than the best sermon.' The book had inspired him with 'fresh conviction to preach the great Gospel of Sacrifice'. Sir Edward Hulton, on the other hand, was merely 'very pleased with it'. J.A. Steuart thought the book 'a big, big thing... In the emotional passages there is tremendous power.' The end worried him. The book, he says, is a tragedy and yet it ends with wedding bells, thus vindicating the author's own feelings about it. The replies were set up in type and a limited edition of one hundred copies of the book printed with the letters bound in at the back. These were given to members of his family and his closest friends. One was inscribed, 'For Elin, to read when she grows up.'

Set entirely in the Isle of Man, the plot is at many points hard to believe. That a young man of 27 or 28 could be made a Deemster (Judge) almost as soon as he had passed his final law examinations seems so unlikely as to vitiate the story at its central point. Victor Stowell and his friend Alick Gelling, first seen as schoolboys at King William's College, the school in Castletown which Ralph attended and which still exists, are well drawn and contrasted. Victor's seduction of Bessie Collister some years afterwards, and the birth of their illegitimate baby, recall *The Manxman*, but the plot of this book is more convoluted. Bessie kills the baby, accidentally it seems, as soon as it is born and hides the body. She is arrested and tried for infanticide in Victor's court and as her judge he pronounces sentence of death on her. Haunted by what he has done, and the fact that he was the cause of her crime, he helps her escape from Castle Rushen, which was in those days the Island's prison, and hands her to Alick, with whom she is in love and who wants to marry her. The two board a tramp steamer in Castletown harbour and escape to Ireland and thence to America.

All along Victor has been in love with Fenella Stanley, daughter of the Governor of the Island. Fenella represents sacred love and Bessie profane love. Victor confesses to prison-breaking and is himself flung into Castle Rushen. Fenella stands by him and engineers their marriage in the castle chapel. She has taken the job of Lady Wardress at the prison and swears she will stay near him until his two-year sentence is up.

The book is written at white heat and with a passionate fervour that carries the unlikely story along. It is in many ways an extraordinary production. The old faults of religiosity and sentimentality are still present but some of the scenes are dramatic and powerfully written. There is a scene where Fenella, desperately seeking a clergyman who will consent to marry her to Victor and risk the wrath of the bishop and her father, goes to see Parson Cowley. She notices on the mantelpiece 'a photograph in a mourning frame of a young man in sailor's costume with the fell stamp of consumption in his eyes and cheeks'. The old parson is not too happy with Fenella's request and asks his wife what she thinks.

'The old lady did not reply immediately and pointing to the photograph on the mantelpiece the parson said, "If it had been John James's case, eh?" ' A touching tribute to Caine's long-dead brother, to immortalise him thus in a story.

As the book rises to its climax Victor torments himself over Fenella. He wants to confess what he has done but how could he do such a thing to her? And his friend Alick, what was he going to suffer when he found out who the father of Bessie's baby was? His urge to confess must be set against the hurt it would do to others whom he loved. But,

> it was a lie to say that a sin could be concealed. An evil act once done could never be undone; it could never be hidden away. A man might carry his sin out to sea, and bury it in the deepest part of the deep, but some day it would come scouring up before a storm as the broken seaweed came, to lie open and naked on the beach.

As had the corpse in *The Deemster*.

How many of his friends reading this knew or guessed from what recesses of the author's soul it came? Mary must have known but there is no record of her reaction to the book.

The Master of Man is a *roman à clef*, sufficiently strewn with clues for anyone who had even a hint of the truth to have seen what the author was getting at. When Dan Collister turns up on Victor's doorstep to demand that Alick Gell, whom he takes to be the father of Bessie's child, should make an honest woman of his stepdaughter, echoes resound of the traumatic night in Clement's Inn in 1882 when the two fathers turned up demanding that Caine and Robertson marry their daughters. There are passionate paragraphs on the tragedy of a child born out of wedlock—no new theme for this author.

There are other echoes from the 1880s. Among a few touching scenes is one where Bessie has been hidden away with two old sisters, retired governesses, Victor having decided the girl must be educated if she was to be a fit wife for his friend, the young advocate Alick Gell. The scene where Bessie is sitting up in bed late at night, working hard at learning her spelling and grammar until the candle is burnt right down, so that she might be a good wife to such a gentleman as Alick, has the ring of truth about it. As we have seen, Caine put Mary to school in Sevenoaks when she first came to live with him. Bessie could be read, at least in part, as a portrait of the young Mary Chandler, working to improve herself to be the wife of the toff with rooms in Clement's Inn.

CHAPTER TWENTY-SEVEN

The publication of *The Master of Man* did not mean that Caine could relax. In August, 1921, he was raising funds for the relief of the terrible famine in Russia after the Revolution. His old friend Sidney Low, now Sir Sidney, congratulated him on the numerous well-argued articles he had contributed to the papers. It may have been Derwent who involved him. Ralph wrote to their father on 28 July saying Derwent 'has now conceived an idea for work & it appears there is a chance of getting support for a scheme to feed the starving people of Russia'. A Russian friend of their father's, Alexis Aladin, would be writing about the plan. 'At any rate,' Ralph concluded, 'I beg you to give the idea consideration & write Derwent enthusiastically about it if you feel you can. I am sure in work & interest lies Derwent's salvation.' In that Ralph and his father would have been at one.

That summer Derwent started a new concern: he founded the Readers Library Publishing Company. At least he always claimed to have had the idea and founded the business, while Ralph asserted it was him. Whichever of the two was initially responsible they were first in the field with 'the book of the film', aiming to bring out a book a month at a popular price. The first title was *The Hunchback of Notre Dame*, then a successful silent film. The books were printed and produced by the Greycaine Book Manufacturing Company. This was a firm of printers and bookbinders founded by Ralph with Frank Grey some years before. Ralph's father was a major shareholder. The firm did work for William Heinemann who praised it highly. When the Readers Library was set up Derwent was appointed Managing Director. Ralph was put out as his company had provided most of the capital and held a controlling share. He refused to go onto the board of Readers Library in a position junior to his younger brother and appointed his partner Frank Grey and another of his directors to watch Greycaine's interests as board members.

At first, despite the friction between the two brothers, the arrangement for the Readers' Library seems to have worked well to their mutual benefit. Their mother took a great interest in the business, telling her husband of a visit to the Greycaine factory to help choose the binding for the Readers Library books. It is notable that whenever she had something useful to do such as this, or helping her husband deal with agents and film directors, or getting his manuscripts typed, she was brisk and happy and in good health. She needed useful occupation as much as Derwent.

Caine remained an Isle of Man magistrate after the war and sat on the Peel bench whenever he was available. His only relaxation was his weekly At Home. From the early years at Greeba, whenever he was in residence he kept open house on Sunday afternoons and anyone was free to drop in. Apart from his friends on the Island—men such as Dr Marshall, Reginald Farrant and Ramsey Moore and their wives— American tourists, actors playing the Gaiety Theatre in Douglas, and notabilities visiting the Island in their yachts, made their way up the steep drive to the house to be welcomed with tea, cakes and conversation.

By the early 1920s Elin, 'a sweetly pretty little girl' according to one guest writing to thank Sir Hall and Lady Mary for their hospitality, was usually on show. Caine removed the child from Maidenhead in March, 1922, and brought her back to Greeba where she had few friends of her own age (six), though she went to dancing classes which she thoroughly enjoyed. She delighted Caine by showing a facility for making up rhymes. He invented a limerick based on her name and she quickly picked up the idea and the rhythm. Where she could not think up a rhyme 'she invented strange words of her own to suit her needs', according to her doting grandfather.

She had become a bone of contention between her adoptive parents. She was a beautiful and sweet-natured child and Mary enjoyed showing her off. A tug-of-war began. Mary wanted her to go to school in Hampstead but her husband was not happy, feeling Elin was not learning enough there. Though he did not say so to Mary, he was justifiably worried that his wife was too unstable and her health too precarious for her to be responsible for a young child. Her rackety social life was another factor. It was a strange upbringing. Elin's grandparents continued to argue over her education, an argument which ended only when she went to boarding school. Back at Greeba the much-loved nanny was dismissed and a governess, Miss Reilly, installed. She had been Mary's lady's maid and was good with her needle, though how this qualified her to be a governess is difficult to understand. Worse than that, she was cruel to the child who suffered mental agonies under her rule. She never said anything to her parents—she was still under the impression Caine and Mary were that and called them Mama and Poppa. Puzzled that people she loved and who she believed loved her could leave her with this dragon, it never occurred to the child to complain about Miss Reilly. Loving as they were in their different ways her adoptive parents were both distant and Mary at least showed little open affection to her. She was left alone at Greeba for much of the time with Miss Reilly and the servants while her grandfather travelled abroad and her grandmother pursued her busy social life in London.

Mary wrote regularly to Dolly Stephen, Elin's natural mother, reporting on her progress. As soon as the child could sign her name she too wrote to 'Dear Dolly', once choosing and signing a photograph of herself to be sent, but having no idea who Dolly was. Dolly did not write back until Elin was 21. It may indeed have been a condition placed on her when she handed the baby over.

Elin's tormentor, Miss Reilly, had some charming devices. One favourite trick was to send the child out to play, then as soon as she had climbed the long flight of steps to the back garden above the house, call her to tidy her toys. Often she would wait until the child was asleep at night and then wake her on the same pretext. She insisted on sleeping in the same room so there was no escaping her. One night she routed Elin out of bed to look for a needle she had lost. She followed the sleepy, tearful child around, goading her to find the needle which she had already found herself. The child's memory of sitting on the stairs, cold and in tears, was indelible.

Despite all this it is clear that Caine loved the child dearly. He fussed over her so that she had only to sneeze and he wanted to take her temperature and put her to bed. The deaths of his two little sisters while he was himself only a child had left a searing mark. Little girls, to his thinking, were fragile and liable to be carried off suddenly, therefore the utmost care must be taken of this lovely child so miraculously given to him late in life. His over-protectiveness hedged her existence. One example was the Sunday School outing. She was longing to go with the other children but when her grandfather found they were to be taken on the picnic in a 'roundabout'—a type of Manx horse-drawn cart—he said it was far too dangerous, she might fall off and be injured, even killed. So she had to stay at home and the party went on without her. Needless to say all the children returned home quite safely. She adored her 'Poppa' but the loss of that outing rankled for a long time. Both his granddaughters remembered Caine as a loving man, kind and gentle, though they were sometimes intimidated by him, a dramatic figure in his black cloak and hat. Ralph's little girl Mary, a shy child, loved to be with him as he always made a fuss of her. Her brother, on the other hand, found his grandfather distant and severe and stood in considerable awe of him.

Mary seems not to have cared much for her granddaughters at all, though she spoilt Derek as she did Derwent. She often said, 'all girls should be drowned at birth'. She said this to Lillian, Ralph's wife, in Mary's hearing when the child was about four, adding, 'The boy is so handsome he will break all the girls' hearts when he grows up, but, my dear, the girl is so plain you will never get her off your hands.' This thoughtlessly cruel and silly comment not only angered Lillian, it marked the child for life. No wonder Mary's granddaughters disliked her.

Caine's work was sacred. None of the household dared enter the study while he was writing and Mary impressed on everyone that he must in no circumstances be disturbed. The only one who could enter the sanctum was Elin. If Mary wanted to get a message to her husband while he was writing she would send the child. Cautiously she would open the door and peer round. If Caine held up his hand, palm towards her with the gesture of a traffic policeman, she would back out and quietly close the door before reporting the failure of her mission. If, however, her grandfather nodded ever so slightly—without looking at her—she would go and stand by his chair until he stopped writing and looked up to ask what she wanted.

Negotiations for the sale of Heath Brow and purchase of Heath End House were long and complicated. Mary divided her time between Maidenhead and the Savoy, increasingly restless and longing to have her own home again. Except when Greeba Castle needed redecorating she seems not to have been much interested in it and never regarded it as home. The tenant moved out of Heath Brow without paying the rates. Mary, when she heard, got in a state over the furniture, which was hers, afraid the bailiffs would distrain on it. She rushed to tell the authorities that it was hers and they must not touch it. This made matters considerably worse and her husband found himself liable for the rates owed by the defaulting tenant.

Mary resorted to being ill and demanding her husband's presence in January, 1922. He went to see her but she did not improve. Their usual rooms were booked in St Moritz but she insisted she was too ill to travel. When Caine wrote to cancel the booking the manager replied that Derwent was occupying the rooms. Ralph had just returned home after eight months in Canada. He had an interest in a Canadian paper-making company and wanted to settle there but his wife and parents did not agree so he reluctantly gave up the idea.

Back in the Isle of Man with Elin, Caine stayed for about six weeks at the Fort Anne Hotel as further work was being done at Greeba. Before leaving London he had had a long talk with Horder about Mary's health and how her constant demands were wearing him down and interfering with his work. In a personal letter of April, 1922, Horder said he thoroughly understood Caine's feelings and the position he was in.

> Much as I should like, in cold, calculated reason, to oppose the tendency your wife shows to have you so constantly involved in the scheme of her own health, I realise how very difficult it is for you to break the habit of so many years. The problem is, of course, largely a psychological one, as you so fully appreciate, and I am compelled to bow to your generous and loyal solution of it.

The solution was a de facto separation, though not a legal one, with Mary set up in a house of her own with her own income. Caine could never have broken with her completely but neither could he live with her. He would not subordinate his wish to live in the Isle of Man to hers to live in London. Both of them were basically selfish. The agreement, which was to include his use of her house whenever he visited London, does not seem to have been fully understood by Mary at first. She took the income settled on her as an increase in her dress allowance, unaware she was meant to use it to keep herself and run her own home. By June, 1922, she had gone through it all and had 'an upsetting letter' from the bank informing her of the size of her overdraft. She sent it to her husband demanding he 'see the bank and put things right'.

A clue to what lay behind the separate lives they had in fact lived for some time lies in Caine's constant quest for intellectual conversation, as if trying to recreate the wonderful evenings with Rossetti so many years before and the later ones with Irving and Bram Stoker. Bright and lively as she was, her best friends would not have described Mary as intellectual and she was never as serious-minded as her husband, hence their increasing incompatibility. He had always preferred male company anyway. On the eve of one of his visits to St Moritz he wrote to Ramsey Moore, 'I must do my best to get some sort of an intellectual companion', as if it never occurred to him his wife might fill the role. No one else was as congenial as Robert Marshall but he was often too busy to leave his patients. Reginald Farrant went to Switzerland with Caine at least once. On another occasion Caine's brother Willie provided the intellectual conversation.

The summer of 1922 brought increasing problems. Once the purchase of Heath End House was agreed Mary could not see why she should not immediately go ahead with alterations such as installing central heating—and a telephone. To the horror of her solicitor she put in a builder who started removing an internal wall. The contract was not signed and the solicitor ordered her to stop, pointing out there were still important matters concerning the property to be settled. Mary replied that she intended to buy, building work would take some time and must be started. To protect himself the solicitor wrote to Caine saying he could not be responsible for controlling 'a client as wilful and headstrong as Lady Hall Caine'.

His trials were not over. When the contract to purchase arrived Mary signed it and sent it straight back without consulting him. Again he ordered her to stop the building work, telling her there were legal points yet to be agreed and he had instructed the vendor's solicitor not to exchange contracts until they were. Mary replied that she intended the work to continue. The solicitor told the builder he was not to touch anything until instructed by Sir Hall or himself. He lunched with Mary at the Savoy and explained things to her. He thought he had made everything clear but when he went to the house next day he found the builder digging to look at the foundations. It was an old house and in a poor state of repair.

Exasperated, he wrote to Caine on 24 July, 1922,

> I agree with you that your wife is in the midst of worries. Unfortunately they are nearly all of her own making. She is so impetuous, self-willed and determined to have her own way, that my attempted guidance by advice has I am afraid little influence with her... There has not been one hour's delay on the part of any of her advisors in trying to get the purchase completed and carry out her wishes but difficulties have arisen at every step.

To start with the vendor's solicitors could not find the deeds. When they turned up the plans of the property were obviously wrongly drawn, leading to problems as to where the boundaries were. The vendor had told Mary verbally she could do what she liked in the house. 'Your wife thinks this is sufficient to justify her architect and builders taking up boards, knocking off plaster, stripping roofs.' He was evidently appalled at what was going on and afraid he would be blamed. In his opinion it would be very much better for Mary if she stayed away from both Heath Brow and Heath End House until the legal problems were sorted out 'but she does not think so, and while she is there nobody can save her from constant worry'.

For a number of years Caine had found his extensive property holdings in the Isle of Man were taking up too much of his time and energy. In 1922 he made up his mind to sell everything except Greeba Castle and the adjacent farm. The decision was triggered by a letter from one of the banks he used in London saying he was overdrawn. He responded with a furious blast. The manager tried to placate him, protesting that they had not meant to give offence by suggesting he might sell some of his War Loan to meet the debt. They 'regretted this breach in our previously smooth relations over many years'. Most people wanted to know if they were overdrawn but if Sir Hall 'felt humiliated by their letter', would he please nominate someone in London to whom they could write. There was no question of dishonouring his cheques, 'even up to as much as £1000'.

Charley Evans, whom Caine had told about the land sale though not about the spat with the bank, wrote that he was 'interested in what you tell me about your Manx estate. It must be a blow to you to sever in this way the associations of a life-time. But you are never going to sell Greeba are you? That beautiful house ought to remain associated with you and your family directly.' The new regime at Heinemann's had not settled down and office politics were making life difficult, said Evans,

Caine (right) with his friend Reginald Farrant in Switzerland,
at Wengen, in the 1920s.

especially in his dealings with Pawling—'I wish I knew his nature'. Byard, who had been away in Europe for six weeks, was back 'and the undercurrents are flowing again'.

In the midst of worrying about his Manx affairs, Mary and Heath End House caused Caine more concern. After a row with her daughter-in-law

Mary decamped to Hampstead. She stayed with friends while seeing her builder. Caine, worried about mounting costs, told her she must do nothing without a full estimate. When she had the figures she told her husband the central heating would be £282.14.0 but she was afraid to tell him what the building work would cost, which did nothing to ease his anxiety. 'I will not worry you with all the terrible disappointments I have had during the week which so upset me,' she wrote on 23 July, the day before her solicitor wrote to her husband. 'I was feeling so ill with it all, I find I cannot go on any longer without your help... God knows if the house will ever be finished at the rate they have been going on. I haven't the health or the strength to do all there is to be done by myself.' She had a car now, which was 'very useful', and the chauffeur she had engaged was a careful driver. So careful that when Derwent accompanied her on a Sunday visit to friends in Surrey he thought they were going backwards, the man drove so slowly. 'But I find the little car very light and it shakes me up a good deal,' Mary continued, hoping her husband would take the hint and provide her with a larger one more suited to her station in society as she saw it. 'I am glad to hear you intend trying to take a real rest,' she ended, 'but it doesn't seem like it when you are still writing these articles.' Rest was not on the agenda while Mary was around. The next day she sent a telegram: 'Not well would like you to come and help me wrote yesterday.'

Apart from the dispersal of his Manx estates, the big event of 1922 was Caine's acquisition of the *Sunday Illustrated* newspaper. Derwent was appointed Editor and Managing Director with Ralph on the Board. About this time Caine seems to have made things up with their Uncle Willie, who was now living at the Old Farm House on the Kenwood Estate, but his sons were bitterly jealous of each other. Both wrote to their father complaining about the way the other was trying to run the paper.

It had first been published by Odhams's Press on 3 July, 1921, the founder and editor being Horatio Bottomley, MP. In September 1923, it was sold to the *Sunday Pictorial* and incorporated with it. The paper was retitled the *Sunday Mirror* in 1963. Horatio Bottomley was notorious in his day. He was a journalist, financier and politician. Born in Bethnal Green, he was by turns an errand boy, a solicitor's clerk and a shorthand writer in the Supreme Court. He became a brilliant journalist and a persuasive speaker but had a dubious reputation as a financier, with an all-consuming desire for a life of luxury. By 1900 he had promoted nearly fifty companies involving capital of 20 million pounds, an astronomical sum at the time. In 1891 and again in 1909 he was charged with fraud but acquitted. In 1906 he became MP for South Hackney and founded the weekly paper, *John Bull*. In 1911 he went bankrupt and applied for the Chiltern Hundreds, ceasing to be an MP. In 1918 he was discharged from bankruptcy and re-entered Parliament. During World War I he received subscriptions worth £900,000 for various projects and charities, but in 1922 he was found guilty of fraudulent conversion and sent to prison, when Caine picked up the paper for a song. Bottomley died in poverty in 1933, his name a byword for fraud and double dealing.

The first Sunday picture newspaper was the *Sunday Pictorial*, founded by Sir Edward Hulton in 1915. *The Sunday Herald*—later the *Sunday Graphic*—appeared soon afterwards. These papers, together with the *Sunday Illustrated*, had their roots in Victorian sensationalism, featuring details of scandalous cases and lurid murders. Caine determined to improve the tone of the paper but the shrewder and less idealistic Derwent knew what sold. His father wrote regularly for it, his name a big selling point. Mary thought he was wasting his time. 'I'm afraid you will get nothing done of your own work if you give all your time to the Sunday Illustrated', she wrote on 1 July, 1922. She had been to Derwent's office and found he had received two long articles from his father. Derwent, she said, 'has been successful in getting "If Winter Comes" for the serial', news which did not please his father. Her letter is plastered with small red stickers, reading 'Is England in Danger? See the *Sunday Illustrated* next Sunday.' She had been to 'all the Stores' and stuck them in several departments. 'Derwent is sticking them all over London.'

She was struggling with her finances and referred to a visit from the accountant. 'He says he wants all my bank books to see what the whole of my income is. I tell him they are so mixed up with your money and Derwent's and my own he would never be able to make them out... He also wants my deposit a/c books. Do you think I should let him have the whole lot?' Her letter ends, 'You have been gone a week today and already it seems like a month.' Two days later she wrote again. Derwent was having girlfriend trouble, as usual. She was sorry her husband had not liked the last edition of the *Sunday Illustrated* but Ralph and Derwent thought it good. 'The shop kind of girl' liked it but she knew their father 'would never lower himself to write trash for that kind of person'.

He had written an article, 'The Wreckers of Ireland', which appeared in the *Sunday Illustrated* of 2 July, 1922, and attracted a lot of attention. Sinn Fein, who wanted an independent republic, had swept the board in the south in the general election of 1918 but lost in the six counties of the north. Sinn Fein would not accept the result and set up their own Dail with Eamon de Valera as president. Some of its members, under Michael Collins, started a terrorist campaign against the British security forces and those Irish civilians who served the Crown. In 1920 the

British government partitioned the country by the Government of Ireland Act which established two separate Home Rule parliaments and also provided facilities for eventual union, or reunion. A peace treaty was signed in 1921 and the following year the Irish Free State was officially proclaimed, having the same status as Canada, Australia and South Africa. De Valera signed but Michael Collins repudiated the treaty and continued the terrorist campaign which led ultimately to his assassination.

The first Southern Irish elections were held successfully and an official Dail constituted under the leadership of de Valera. Michael Collins and his followers opposed him and continued the fight. When Caine wrote his article the new state was being put in jeopardy by the terrorists, particularly by the murder of Field-Marshal Sir Henry Wilson. Lloyd George's government in London, which appears to have seen the division of Ireland as only a temporary compromise until peace was restored, responded with an effective counter-terror whose instruments were the Auxiliaries and the 'Black and Tans'. 'The gunmen,' Caine wrote in his article, referring to the Sinn Feiners, 'are the minority of Irish people, and they know it. But although they have lost at the polls they are determined to force their will on the majority.' The people had voted for 'the Treaty and peace with Great Britain' but the gunmen wanted 'the republic and war'. The man arrested for Wilson's murder was thought to be an Irish-American, so who was it who was out to wreck Ireland? Caine suggested it might be neither Sinn Fein nor the Irish-Americans but the Communists. The government ought to investigate whether the gunmen were not 'members of the Third International'. This was the Comintern, the revolutionary organisation founded by Lenin in 1919 to bring about Communism throughout the world.

All else was put aside, however, when Caine heard of the death of his old friend, Lord Northcliffe, on 13 August, 1922, at 57. He wrote a 'character sketch' of him for the *Sunday Illustrated*. It began,

> The fall of Northcliffe in little more than the meridian of man's life is a spectacle of tragic significance... In the thirty-odd years in which I knew him, neither his heart nor his brain knew rest. Both were sixty horse power engines which never stopped. They ran generally in their highest gear from first to last. His unresting spirit made the very air about him vibrate. It wore out strong men. He was a strong man himself, but it wore him out also. It is hard to realise that the hitherto irresistible human torrent that was Northcliffe has been arrested in its headlong course. He used to say that he was above all else a journalist. It was true, but only because he had gathered nearly the whole range of the possible activities of man into one journalistic life.

He also wrote an article on divorce and marriage for the paper, which evoked a long letter to the editor headed 'The Catholic Clergy and Sir Hall Caine'. A number of the Catholic clergy were angry with him and had written to tell him so. For twenty years, Caine replied, he had numbered Catholic priests in all levels of the hierarchy as his friends in Italy, England and America,

> But I have always known that no men were more impatient or even intolerant of criticism, and that to whisper so much as a word that cast a doubt upon the infallibility of the doctrines of their Church or the wisdom of its administration was to incur their grievous displeasure. In my recent article I whispered many such words and hence I am not taken unawares by their present condemnation.

He set out the Catholic idea of what made a valid marriage and added his own long-held beliefs. At the same time he made himself even more unpopular in the Isle of Man than he already was by writing a strong condemnation of the TT races in which several young men had been killed.

In November of 1922 he was made a Companion of Honour. He stayed at the Savoy for the investiture before he and Mary went to Maidenhead for Christmas with Ralph and the family.

Caine had a final and tremendous row with Doubleday over publicity methods and his percentage. As a result he took himself off to Cassell's, who had approached him after Heinemann's death. The loss of their first author and his popular romances which sold literally in millions was a commercial disaster. Doubleday was unworried. In his autobiography 'Effendi' wrote of Caine:

> Of all the bores and thick-headed idiots I ever knew, he took the palm. His books were entirely out of key with the whole Heinemann business, but they had been very successful and the profits, I think, induced Heinemann with his thrifty mind to keep on with Hall Caine, especially as poor Pawling had to do all the dirty work. I had several interviews with Caine, and Nelson did some talking, and we were both convinced that his material would be less valuable as time went on, and in any event would not add to the dignity or the quality of our list.

Cassell's were delighted and brought out the new Collected Edition. Newman Flower, the partner in charge of its production, was invited to Greeba in the spring of 1923. During his stay he came across a manuscript—he says by accident. Caine insisted he had no intention of publishing it. He had written it 'solely for the relief of his own feelings at thought of the present lamentable condition of the world'. He said he had dreamed the essentials of the story during a restless night the previous December, but when he looked at what he had written he saw it contained several incidents which had actually occurred during the war. He felt he could not publish it—he was sufficiently unpopular in the Isle of Man already without inviting more coals of fire on his head. Flower read the story and insisted it must be published, and at once. Cassell's brought out *The Woman of Knockaloe* before the summer was over. 'I am asking my Publisher to send you an advance copy of a little book I am shortly to publish,' Caine wrote to Bernard Shaw on 29 August. 'Rightly or wrongly I did my best for the war, and now, as you see, I am trying…to do my best for the peace.'

It was 'the first of the war stories', according to an obituary, which could be correct as it was published ahead of *All Quiet on the Western Front.* It sold more than 500,000 copies and was filmed by Paramount in 1927 as *Barbed Wire* with Pola Negri and Clive Brook starring.

'I read it with very deep emotion,' said Newman Flower in an Editorial Note. Praising the book lavishly, he said it illustrated eternal truths. To soothe their author's anxiety as to its reception Cassell's added a note, 'The Publishers wish it to be understood that nothing in this book is intended to refer to real-life persons in the Isle of Man or elsewhere.' This disclaimer, however, failed to avert the storm of abuse heaped on Caine by the Manx for daring to suggest, even in fiction, that a Manx girl could have fallen in love with a German prisoner of war.

The Woman of Knockaloe is a coda to Caine's oeuvre. It is quite different to the novels that went before and is also shorter. By the time he wrote this last story he was thoroughly disillusioned over the war and the Treaty of Versailles. For more than three years he had gone round the country speaking at meetings on the League of Nations, often sharing a platform with Cecil, now Viscount Chelwood, but this was not the world that he had striven for. Reality was at odds with his Christian Socialist ideals. He was dismayed by the coming to power of Mussolini and his Fascists in Italy and was unhappy about the British Mandate over Palestine, which had been immediately rejected by the Arab congress at Nablus. The British had at last recognised the Kingdom of Egypt under King Fuad but then the country had been handed back to Britain by a League of Nations Mandate. Perhaps worst of all, the Liberals had lost the 1922 election and his friend Lloyd George had had to give way as Prime Minister to the Conservative Bonar Law. Ralph was the new Conservative member for East Dorset.

May, 1923, saw his 70th birthday, heralded by all the papers with many column inches on 'Hall Caine at 70', and bringing in letters and greetings from all over the world. A newsreel company interviewed him—a snippet of the film survives in the National Film Archive. He had outlived many of his friends and felt an old man. It was to be expected that he would think everything was going to the dogs and nothing was as it had been in the golden days of his youth. That would not be quite fair. He had, after all, grown up in the back streets of Liverpool and that experience, as much as anything, had made an idealistic socialist of him. He had worked all his life for a better world, for an end to injustice and hatred. He had endured a shattering world war, the convinced pacifist never completely submerged in the propagandist. His final war article, written on Armistice Day, 1918, said that while the price paid for the victory of the Allied cause had been a terribly bitter one it had been justified, inasmuch as it 'had killed warfare and so banished for ever the greatest scourge of mankind'.

By 1923 it was clear how wrong he and others who agreed with him had been. He now saw that the seeds of another world war had been sown at Versailles. He was appalled at the treatment of Germany, whatever it had done, and in despair over the chaos at home, the conflict everywhere of separate and selfish interests. He now thought the Great War, far from abolishing war for ever, had 'inflamed and strengthened the spirit of it'. He had not been prepared for the aftermath. He saw, or thought he saw, the ruination of everything he had worked for, the failure of his ideals. Racial hatred, which he had fought and preached against for so long, was still rampant. At the close of the new story it drove the star-cross'd lovers to bind themselves together and jump over a cliff as the only solution to their predicament: that she was Manx and he was German and they were rejected by both sides.

Essence of Hall Caine. A still from the film of The Prodigal Son
*shot in Iceland in 1923. Edith Bishop as Thora (left), Stewart Rome
as Magnus (centre) and Henry Victor as Oscar (right).*

What, Newman Flower asked in his Note at the front of the book, would the public of Britain, France, Belgium and America, still mourning their war dead, think of a writer who asked them to shake hands with the Germans? He praised Caine for agreeing to publication, saying that he had 'consented to risk temporary misrepresentation and perhaps serious personal hostility for the sake of what he believes to be the Truth and the Right'. Despite his war record, for which he had been honoured, Caine was in danger of being accused of lack of patriotism, in those days a serious matter for a popular writer. In fact, while it did not set the Thames on fire the book was successful and sold particularly well in America. There were readers who thought as he did and were ready to accept what he said. Perhaps things had indeed changed in some ways more than he realised.

The style is quite different to anything he had written previously. The dream in which the story came to him had, he said, remained with him so strongly on waking that he had written it down briefly, in haste, and in the present tense. It was this first draft which Newman Flower had seen. It was a parable and contained, Caine said, 'feelings which had long oppressed me on seeing that my cherished hope of a blessed Peace that should wipe out war by war and build up a glorious future for mankind, had fallen to a welter of wreck and ruin'.

In working the story up into a novel he retained the urgent present tense, giving it a simplicity and directness which is so notably missing in much of what went before. Knockaloe (pronounced 'Knock*ay*loe') is a large farm on the west coast of the Isle of Man just south of Peel. It is now the Manx Government's Experimental Farm but during the First World War it was in fact used as a German prisoner-of-war camp as the author describes.

The book is of course basically a love story but its theme is the wickedness and destructiveness of racial hatred. At the start of the story Knockaloe is being farmed by Robert Craine, a widower, helped by his son, Robbie, and daughter Mona—the 'woman' of the title. The farm is commandeered by the authorities and a prisoner-of-war camp built on it. Robbie goes off to the war and is killed in action, Mona remaining with her father. Prisoners come each morning to collect milk from Mona in the dairy. She falls in love with one of them, Oskar Heine, and he with her. Both fight what is happening to them but, as the quotation on the title page from the Song of Songs says, 'Love is as strong as death: jealousy is cruel as the grave. Many waters cannot quench love, neither can the floods drown it.'

When Mona's father finds out he has a stroke and dies. Mona's friends and the people of Peel get wind of the love affair and revile her. Oskar tells her that when the war is over he will take her to Germany and his mother will welcome her. That idea is shattered when his mother writes an angry letter saying that if he intends bringing home an English bride he is no longer her son and she will slam the door in their faces. Mona then says bravely they can stay on the farm but it is sold over her head— she has only inherited a tenancy. When the sale looms the lovers say they will go to America, where surely no one will care whether they are English, German or anything else. However, claims are trumped up against Mona so that after the sale she is left penniless and they cannot afford the fare. In this predicament, hounded on all sides by hatred and jealousy, they take the only way out they can see—joint suicide.

The straightforwardness of the story, the single strand with a limited cast of characters, the unity of place, the relative lack of purple patches and preaching, make this last novel in many ways more accessible to modern readers than any of its predecessors but it is still as forgotten as the rest. This was Caine's swansong, the last of his romances.

CHAPTER TWENTY-EIGHT

Caine made his first broadcast on 11 November, 1923, at 9.45 p.m. He gave an address on 'Peace' which the BBC sent out from all stations. No script has come to light. Broadcasts in those days were live and not recorded so we do not know what he said, but that it was impressive is indicated by the letters he received afterwards.

The sale of the *Sunday Illustrated* towards the end of 1923 freed him from the necessity, as he saw it, of writing regular articles. He had never entirely stopped working on his *Life of Christ* and now, with his career as a novelist rounded off, he turned to it again. When he was in London there were long talks about the book over dinner with his brother, who lived nearby. They discussed Old Testament prophets endlessly until both Mary and Elin were fed up with the subject. Willie continued to write books which few people read then and no one has heard of now.

His wife had died in 1919. Although he occasionally brought what Mary described as 'ladyfriends' to see them he never remarried. He had a housekeeper, Bertha Blacker Bailey. His brother's family thought she was his mistress, though when they visited she acted as a servant, eating her dinner alone, not with the family. After Willie Hall Caine's death she said she had been 'his friend, companion and nurse for many years'. It looks as if she expected Willie to marry her. When he did not it turned her bitter and vindictive. As part of the reconciliation with his brother Caine had bought Willie a small, two-bedroom house on the Kenwood estate, the Old Farmhouse. Willie called it The Piggery, maintaining the man who looked after the farm's pigs had lived there. One evening there was an urgent telephone call from Miss Bailey—something awful had happened, would they come over at once. All three trooped across and were shown into Willie's bedroom. He was sitting up in bed, his arms defiantly crossed over his chest, glaring at his brother with an expression which plainly said, 'Look at the pigsty you have put me in': the legs at the head of his brass bed had gone through the floorboards. Mary and Elin had a struggle not to howl with laughter.

Ralph and Derwent were far from being without occupation when the *Sunday Illustrated* passed from their control. Apart from the Readers Library both had other business interests and both were deeply involved in politics. They stood in the 1922 election. Ralph had tried for years to be adopted as a Liberal candidate with his father's backing but without success before being accepted by the Conservatives. His father's feelings when he won must have been mixed. Derwent stood for Labour at Reading and lost. He was actually far to the right of his brother in his political views but set up in opposition to him as much out of sheer bloody-mindedness as anything. However, he had met and become friendly with Ramsay Macdonald's son Malcolm, which could have had something to do with it. In addition he had a new girlfriend, Eirane Naismith, who was politically minded and an ardent Labour supporter. Work was continuing at Heath End House when Caine wrote to thank Mary for agreeing to all the arrangements he had proposed, including his use of the house when he came to Town. 'It is early days yet to be thanking me,' she replied, 'I should be very happy to have you.' She moved into Heath End House that summer of 1923. Ralph sent his mother a bill for £285.4.0 'for your long stay at Woolley Firs', the cheque to be made out to his wife, Lillian. His father paid.

British politics were in a state of flux. In January, 1924, Baldwin resigned and Ramsay Macdonald became the first Labour prime minister. He headed a minority government able to function only in coalition with the Liberals. It survived barely ten months. In the ensuing General Election Ralph defended his East Dorset seat for the Conservatives while Derwent stood for Labour in Clitheroe. Their father, holed up in Greeba, wrote election addresses for both of them. Not surprisingly, after this schizophrenic endeavour he was ill again. Mary scolded him once more for wasting his time and energy. Ralph got back, Derwent was defeated. Their father was depressed when the Conservatives won and the Liberals were reduced to a rump of only 40 seats.

Apart from a few excursions to London Caine was at Greeba for most of 1923. On 5 July he not only attended Tynwald but was seated near the Governor at the top of the mound. One little boy was mesmerised by the weird figure with piercing eyes and white beard, dressed in a flowing black cloak and black, wide-brimmed 'artist's' hat. He could not take his eyes off him. 'Who's that?' he asked his mother, 'Hush, dear, that's Sir Hall Caine, the Famous Writer.' Seventy years later he clearly recalled 'Hall Caine at Tynwald'.

Mary enjoyed giving 'little dinner parties' at Heath End House, 'all *ladies*', she assured her husband after one of them. She now had her own nurse and her letters were full of her ill-health. She constantly complained of her 'dreadful palps', palpitations, which she was sure presaged an imminent heart attack whatever her doctor said to the contrary. The house was nearly to rights. 'You can come and stay with me if Greeba gets too much for you.' Lots of love and kisses were sent to Elin. Mary had a fur coat made for her—which the child hated. Ralph was 'too busy with parliament' to come to her dinner parties but Derwent was often there, with or without girlfriend. Mary still spoilt him rotten. He was very much a mother's boy and before long moved into Heath End House to live. Eirane helped Derwent with his campaign and sometimes stayed with Mary. She ran classes in elocution for children in the poorer part of Derwent's latest constituency, Tottenham, explaining in a letter to his father how important it was for the children to learn to speak well if they were to get good jobs. She expected the mothers to vote Labour in appreciation of her efforts. Mary described to her husband how she had 'dressed Eirane up in scarlet, very bright, and she looked lovely. She has an appearance of her own at a Music Hall in Tooting tonight.' Eirane and Derwent had been to the Labour Party conference together. Both were keen on cars and entered rallies and concours d'élégance. When at Bournemouth Eirane won with her car while Derwent's was not placed he gave a disgraceful show of petulance and bad temper. Mary thought his car was 'vulgar' and 'just an advertisement for paint' and he should have been pleased for Eirane. But that was not in his nature. Even as a grown man he would throw a tantrum if crossed or thwarted. His young nephew was shocked, on one occasion at Heath End House, to see his uncle lying on the drawing room floor drumming his heels, screaming with rage and biting the carpet.

Caine spent a lot of time going through the many letters he had accumulated. He was either preparing to write another volume of his autobiography or else putting material in order for a biographer. Years before he had declared that he wanted no biography written of him but he appears to have changed his mind in his seventies. He had a mass of papers at Greeba and was making heavy weather of sorting them out. 'What has been the matter with you lately? Your last two letters have been awful, you seem to have had a fit of the Blues,' Mary wrote. 'The papers you speak of in the trunk were sorted out about fifteen years ago by Miss Wood, & some of them placed in the Cabinet.' This was a green filing cabinet in the hall and the letters concerned were neatly, though sometimes incorrectly, labelled with filing cards. They were all from the more famous of his friends, such as Christina Rossetti, Edmund Gosse, and Lloyd George. 'You make hard work of it. I could sort out the papers and find what you want in less than a day. All the scrapbooks had better be sent here. They are no use over there,' said Mary.

Despite having a resident nurse Mary wanted someone always with her in the house. Greeba Jackson, now married, spent a few weeks with her and after that a friend called Dora, but she wanted her husband there. 'Do you feel like returning?... If you are not coming back I must try & get someone else to stay with me... I expect Elin is longing to come back to look at the shops.' Her husband was worried about who would live in Greeba Castle and look after it when he was away. 'It is foolish to say the Christians will not live in the house and take care of the place,' Mary answered. 'Thank God I have never let a servant get the better of me yet.' Indeed she had not. She was hard on her servants and unkind to the point of occasional cruelty. As a result they hated her and did not stay long. 'Cheer up & write one of your nice love letters to your jealous little wife,' she ended.

He joined her for one of the great evenings in London's theatrical history, the opening night of Shaw's *St Joan*, with Sybil Thorndike as Joan of Arc. By the final curtain Caine was overwhelmed, exhausted both physically and emotionally. Mary insisted they go straight home. The play had moved and impressed him so deeply he could not go to bed. He felt an urgent need to tell Shaw how he felt. Overcoming his phobia about the telephone, he tried to ring him. He tried until one in the morning, unable to get through, and then sat down to write a note to his friend.

> Splendid! I don't know whether I enjoyed most the play or the playing. Both were wonderful. Every word came through perfectly clearly and every sentence went home... I could not go to bed without telling you that you had had a magnificent success. But like a wise man you had taken off your receiver, as your telephone would have been ringing until morning.

In a postscript he added, 'I cannot expect you to read all this screed. Nobody can read much of my handwriting these days. But you will understand that I join the multitude who wish to thank you for the best 50 minutes one has had for a very long time. Now I know why your plays are acknowledged as better than anybody else's.' Which 50 minutes of the play he was referring to is not clear, any more than his writing.

He returned to Greeba but was back with Mary for Christmas, 1924, taking Elin with him. He again broadcast to the nation, this time on Christmas Eve. Radio programmes began at seven o'clock in the evening on 2LO, the BBC's London station. Caine opened the Christmas Eve programme with a talk, 'A Dream of Christmas Day', which as before went out from all stations and again no record remains. He was followed by 'A Light Orchestral Programme of Christmas Fare' given by the Wireless Christmas Orchestra conducted by Sir Dan Godfrey, the famous conductor of the Bournemouth Symphony Orchestra.

For the next three years Caine published almost nothing. Instead he concentrated on biblical researches for his *Life of Christ*. The work became his refuge from an age that had left him behind and with which he was out of tune. He was increasingly lonely as his circle of friends and acquaintances dwindled—Leverhulme died in 1925, as did Rider Haggard. He shared less and less in his family's everyday life. When Mary and the others were laughing and chatting together he would retreat to his study and work on the *Life of Christ*, unable to understand in the

OCTOBER 27, 1926.] PUNCH, OR THE LONDON CHARIVARI. 473

LORD of the Isle that breeds the tailless cats,
  'Tis his to teach—and ours to learn who can—
"The proper study of mankind," and that's
  The Masterpiece of Man.

MR. PUNCH'S PERSONALITIES.

XXVIII.—SIR HALL CAINE.

Hall Caine drawn by Bernard Partridge for the second time, October 1926.

least what they found so amusing. The last traces of a vestigial sense of humour had disappeared.

In 1926 the simmering row between Derwent and Ralph over the Readers Library broke out in full flood. Ralph wrote to his father putting his side of the matter. Something he said brought an outraged reply. On 30 September he wrote again,

> I am very sorry that you should think my letter of last Sunday an improper letter for me to write… You must however understand that ever since I had that unfortunate difference with Derwent over Readers Library matters I have been practically cut out from all relation to an important branch of the activities of my own firm & I feel this very deeply.

He had tried to keep clear of anything to do with Derwent's affairs. He had only become involved when his appointees on the board of Readers Library appealed to him. Derwent had accused these two men of plotting to get him removed as managing director. Ralph pointed out to his father that this was nonsense as they could not act without his, Ralph's, agreement and signature. 'I have not the smallest idea how you got hold of the story,' he said to his father, perhaps unwisely. He thought his father was implying he had been plotting to 'dislodge Derwent' but disclaimed knowledge of any plot and was angered by his father's suggestion that he felt more loyalty to his own directors than to his brother. He had been 'sidetracked on Readers Library matters' because his brother was managing director and resented the position he had been put in.

The row carried on with their father apparently siding all the time with Derwent. Fresh trouble blew up when Derwent sacked a long-serving member of the firm without notice and without pay in lieu so that the rest of the staff threatened to resign. Ralph thought that ordinary decency dictated that Derwent, whatever the legal position, should have 'parted on generous terms' with the man, adding, 'These Socialists are hard masters when they have to do with labour', perhaps forgetting momentarily that his father had been an ardent Socialist all his life. It provoked a furious wire from Greeba, again accusing Ralph and his nominees of conspiring to throw Derwent out. Ralph retorted that he had kept well away from this

> atmosphere of intrigue… I am not in the least surprised at this fighting in Great Queen Street but I am astonished that you should have mixed yourself up in it or listened for one moment to such suggestions. You may take it they are absolutely untrue and unfounded & unless you wish to sift to the bottom who has exposed you to this mare's nest I should dismiss the whole matter from your mind.

The affair simmered down and there were family holidays which included Ralph, Lillian and their children. They went more often to the

South of France than to Switzerland. Mary was convinced she had high blood pressure, in spite of constant reassurances from her doctors that it was normal, something she admitted to her husband. However, she insisted that though she would love to go to St Moritz she did not dare 'because I am sure to get blood pressure if I go up so high again'. During one family holiday in Monte Carlo Ralph gambled heavily at the casino. When they were due to return home he admitted he was bankrupt and unable to pay his losses. They all had to stay on while his father telegraphed his London bankers for money to settle Ralph's debts. Later Caine and Mary had a holiday together in Rome. She thoroughly enjoyed it, saying it was 'like another honeymoon, and we have had so many'.

One summer about this time, driven by his devoted chauffeur and valet, Brind, Caine took Mary and Elin on a tour of the Lake District. In Keswick they went to look at Hawthorns. Caine stumped up to the door and told the surprised owner, 'I used to live here. Can I look round?' He was gone some time while his wife and granddaughter, too embarrassed to join him, sat in the car feeling silly.

Arguments over Elin and her upbringing continued. She was fourteen and had outgrown her unsuitable governess. Miss Reilly was pensioned off and set up in a dressmaker's business in Douglas, where she did well. Apparently without consulting Mary, Caine arranged for Elin to go to a boarding school at Chislehurst, in Kent. The news almost unhinged Mary. 'Please accept a little line today. After receiving your letter this morning I had a very bad attack of palp which has left me feeling weak and exhausted. I will not tell you why because you surely ought to know yourself. We have never agreed about Elin's schooling & I expect we never shall.'

Elin's letters home were affectionate in tone but those to her 'Dearest Papa' were more relaxed and easy than those to 'My dearest Mother'. She settled in well at the school though at first she had trouble with 'Mademoiselle' whom she feared and who reduced her to tears. A friend spoke up for her and afterwards Mademoiselle was kind and understanding. 'She said I was difficult to deal with because I was so different from the other girls,' she told her grandfather. This is understandable, given her strange childhood on top of the famous name.

It began to look as if Derwent was going to marry at last. Caine bought a house with a large garden at Totteridge—The Priory—intended for Derwent and Eirane after their marriage. Mary threw herself enthusiastically into decorating the place and restoring the neglected gardens which included a tennis court. The invoices, naturally, went not to Derwent but to his father. 'The enclosed bill for The Priory is too high for me to pay out of my housekeeping money. I have just paid for a

*Mary Hall Caine (second left) in the garden of her Hampstead home
in 1928 with Lady de Frece (the former Vesta Tilley), Sir Walter de Frece
(left) and her elder son, Ralph Hall Caine (right).*

petrol lawn mower which cost £32,' said Mary in a long letter that June.
Derwent and Eirane played tennis there on fine evenings and had tennis
parties for their friends at weekends. They never lived in the house,
however. They parted company and The Priory was sold. Yet another
girl had found she could not cope with Derwent's temper. The house

came in handy, however, for Caine's 75th birthday in May, 1928: he was filmed there by Empire News for their Bulletin No. 214.

How Mary had time to see to the Totteridge house in the midst of her hectic social life is a puzzle. Two visitors at Heath End House that summer were Sir Walter and Lady de Frece. They were all photographed in the garden, Mary with her arm round the shoulders of the now white-haired Vesta Tilley. Lunches at the Savoy with Lady This, evening receptions with Lady That—her diary was full for weeks ahead. She suffered recurring bilious attacks but still kept her engagements most of the time. She and a friend went to Ascot on a wet day, enjoying themselves in spite of the weather. 'I had very bad luck and so did Mrs Syrett. Ralph won £20 but I hear he lost today.' Dr Marshall was in London to see a consultant. His daughter told Mary he had been feeling very ill for some time and was to go into a nursing home. 'I trust all will go well for him. He has been such a wonderful friend to us for such a long time we cannot afford to part with him yet awhile.' (He made a good recovery.) 'Trust you are not feeling too lonely without me. I should love to be there sometimes to torment you. It is good for you.'

He did not need tormenting—he was busy checking proofs. 1928 was the centenary of Gabriel Rossetti's birth and Cassell's had asked him to provide a new edition of his *Recollections of Dante Gabriel Rossetti*. He did better than that. Re-titled *Recollections of Rossetti*, it was almost completely rewritten and differed substantially from the 1882 version. In what at first sight looks like a typographical error or a revealing slip, he dedicated it 'to the memory of a great friendship 1879-1928', but that could well have been what he meant. Rossetti had been his dearest and greatest friend and he never forgot him.

Charley Evans wrote in June about a great depression in the book trade, affecting all kinds of works. Novels by well-known authors were all anyone wanted and if Caine were to announce one it would sell, but nothing else unless it was sensational. Evans had never known it so difficult to sell serious books. Rossetti, he said, was 'dead to the public at large'. He had heard that Evelyn Waugh's recent book on him had met with no success. He had considered a definitive life of Rossetti but had rejected it. Caine replied in pique or despair that he would withdraw the book if that was the attitude of the public. Evans wrote reassuringly on 25 June, 1928, that he understood and sympathised with Caine's indignation, but how could anyone expect a generation which got its music from the wireless and the gramophone, its drama from the cinema, and its literature from a daily paper, to appreciate the work of a poet such as Rossetti. As a young man he had known *The Blessed Damozel* by heart but he doubted if many schoolboys in the 1920s had even heard the name of that once-popular poem. The nerves of the new generation were on edge, he said. 'Our lives are fevered & we have laid aside the things that are excellent. My own amazement at the condition of things grows daily.' Caine had quoted Hugh Walpole on 'that mass of pathological filth, Ulysses. Is it conceivable that critics...would have hailed such an outpouring of a diseased mind as "a renaissance of literature" when we were young?' Rossetti's fame, however, was secure. He advised Caine not to withdraw his book but 'let it take the chances of the time'.

Caine set out to counteract 'the many evil things that have been said and written about Rossetti'. He gave a much fuller account than previously of their stay in the Lake District in the autumn of 1881. In particular, there is no mention in the earlier work of 'the nurse' who had accompanied them or of the long train journey back to London during which Rossetti told Caine things about his marriage and his wife's death which he had told no one else. However, Caine is still not explicit as to what Rossetti told him.

Comparing the two versions of the *Recollections*, the difference in style is striking. The 1882 book is turgid and heavy with Victorian circumlocutions: for example he says that Rossetti 'went to his pillowed place'. In the 1928 version of the book he says simply, 'Rossetti went to bed'. The whole book is far easier to read than most of his work. Mary received it rapturously, writing at once to say she had read it straight through almost at a sitting. When Derwent received his copy he was more measured in his praise. He thought it well and tastefully produced but his father should not expect his usual sales from it as it would have only a limited appeal. 'Your usual reading public, or rather the larger part of them, will not, I fear, go into raptures over the story of a writer whom, however well known he may be in literary circles throughout the world, is quite unknown to the young reader of this generation.' Mary's comment that the book reads easily is fair enough—it does—but 'like a poem' is over-doing it a bit.

Reading the two versions one can see how the legend arose that when Caine became acquainted with Rossetti he had never been to London and was a completely raw provincial from Liverpool: he was responsible for it himself. It has been held as the central truth concerning Caine that he was brought to London by Rossetti and that it was entirely due to Rossetti's friendship that he got to know anyone in London or in the literary and artistic life of the time. Without doubt Rossetti was of the utmost importance to him and opened doors which otherwise might have remained closed but it is not the whole story. Caine's reason for creating this false impression could have been his adoration of his benefactor. He well knew how much he owed to Rossetti and this was his way of acknowledging it.

Judging by the number of letters thanking him for autographed books the profits on the first printing must have gone on presentation copies.

One recipient wrote, 'It is like a breath from one's youth to be mingling again with Rossetti and Morris and Swinburne. And don't these fiery spirits make our modern taste seem very much under proof!'

As always, Caine involved himself actively in marketing his book. He drafted a press advertisement. Newman Flower sent it back, suggesting he cut it as it would have to be printed so small it would defeat its end. Professional that he was, he cut it to size. Even so it is wordy by today's advertising standards. It begins,

> This book is beautifully written and is as fascinating to read as almost any novel; it proves that the friendship and affection between two men can be as tender and strong as the love between a man and a woman; it is a vivid human drama which shows for the first time that the shadow which hung so long over its unhappy subject was due to nothing less than the deepest personal tragedy that can enter into a man's life.

That phrase about friendship and affection between two men is more revealing than he probably intended but it reflects accurately the strong homoerotic strain in late nineteenth-century England, the days of his youth, particularly in London. By 1928 the scandal of Oscar Wilde had receded and in a mellower old age Caine was able to express his affection for Rossetti, certain it could not be misunderstood—or not even aware that it might be.

Caine sent an advance copy of the new book to Bernard Shaw, who was out of the country. On his return he 'immediately seized your Rossetti and read it straight through'. The book, said Shaw, added 'something to the record that nobody else could supply'. Shaw had never met Rossetti but Socialism had brought him into contact with Morris and through him he met Watts ('I never could fit Dunton onto him') and Swinburne.

> The truth is, Morris was so enormously bigger than most of the old Pre-Raphaelite set, and Socialism seemed then so far above their literary and pictorial enthusiasms, that to us they were only figures of fun except when they called Morris Topsy, which made us feel that the insects were going too far. You too had outgrown them sensationally and become a centre instead of a satellite; and this was why, though your friendship with Rossetti was well known, we never thought of you as one of that lot.

Shaw went on to say that Caine had not lost anything by not talking to Mrs Morris. He said she was

> a wonderful figure at first sight; for she existed until then as an invention of Rossetti's; and when you saw the picture live and walk the effect was supernatural. But you did not hear it talk. She maintained her strong horse sense through all the adoration of that circle, and let the men talk and adore. I remember only two sentences of hers, completing a whole dialogue. It was at a meal at Hammersmith. SHE. 'Have some more pudding?' GBS. 'Thank you: I will, I can't resist it.' And then, when I had finished, SHE. 'That will do you

good: there is suet in it.' All her sensible contempt for the duped vegetarian
came out in her tone.

It was the chloral, he told Caine, which had made Rossetti uninterest-
ing to him as a man and the exhumation of the manuscript had revolted
him. 'I like sane people, and loathe drunk people, drugged people, crazy
people. Your book has therefore done me good in making me take
Rossetti more seriously as a man, even though I know that you have left
out all the shadows except the ones that give dignity and tragic beauty
to the portrait.' Shaw apologised for 'a ridiculously long letter' but Caine
received it with delight. He valued his friendship with Shaw all the more
as he got older and lost other friends. Gosse, whom he had known since
1882, died that year, Jerome K. Jerome had died the year before. He
replied to Shaw at once with an even longer letter.

He wrote in pencil on 24 September, 1928, explaining he was only
just getting over an attack of bronchial pneumonia, and it was a little
easier to write with a pencil than a pen. He recognized 'some straight
blows' in his friend's letter but thought some of them might come from
second-hand knowledge. 'But you shall judge for yourself and lay me flat
if you think me worth it.' About what he called 'the tumultuous side' of
Rossetti's life, he thought he knew 'nearly all there was to know, but
what was the good of telling what seemed to one non-essential?' Over
many pages he filled Shaw in on some of the things he had refrained
from saying publicly. Referring to Rossetti's marriage to Elizabeth Siddal
he said, 'Ruskin did Rossetti an ill turn with a high intention when he
persuaded him to go on with the marriage, which he recognized as a
duty. A stronger man than Rossetti, having done the woman one wrong
would not, at any outside appeal, have gone on to do her another. He
would have stopped, if necessary, at the church door.' He discussed the
other women in Rossetti's life and what he knew of them. Though he
had not named her, Fanny Cornforth was, he said, 'really all over the
book' and he wondered how Shaw had missed her: she was 'the nurse'
who went with them to Cumberland. He told Shaw in detail what happened there and when they got back to Chelsea. So many of Rossetti's
friends over a number of years had tried to get rid of her, 'and then a
young fellow of 26 out of the country bundled her out of doors. That
was myself.'

Now he knew the whole story he thought Shaw would agree he had
said all that was necessary about the 'dark shadow' that hung over
Rossetti. 'As to Rossetti's delusions I certainly do know more than I have
told, but then I think I know the chief cause of them.' It was not the
chloral but years of sleeplessness, after the death of his wife. He, Caine,
had suffered all his life from insomnia and knew the toll it took.
The urge to take drugs was almost overpowering 'and to yield to the

temptation is to produce the secondary (not the primary) cause of delusions'. He implied that he resisted the temptation and after seeing what
it had done to Rossetti he probably had no difficulty.

In response to Shaw's comment that Rossetti's behaviour drove his
friends away, he assured him that

> he never (as far as I can remember) said one ill word about any of them.
> Certainly never about Morris, and when he called him Topsy it was always
> when his heart seemed warming to him. I don't think he liked Swinburne at
> all. After his death I found letters and books from Swinburne which Rossetti
> had never opened.

He knew Rossetti had not liked him going to see Swinburne.

> I conclude by telling you that at some time during my Rossetti period I heard
> for the first time of a tremendously if not damnably clever young fellow with
> red hair and wearing nearly always a flannel shirt who was to be met with at
> Morris's... Sick as I have been it has really done me good to write to you—oth-
> erwise to talk to you—for an hour or so.

Mary, wrapped up as always in her own health and concerns, had not
realised just how ill her husband was. Her 'attacks' and her 'palps'
engrossed her but did not interfere much with her social life. 'Lady
Leggett is having a garden party on the 3rd. Lady Spielman gives a lun-
cheon on the 4th. I must be careful with food—no strawberries or
champagne.' Elin was coming home by train at the end of the summer
term—her report was 'the best yet'. A succession of nurses fussed over
Mary but never stayed long. When visiting friends in nursing homes, if
she liked the look of one of the nurses she would tempt her from her
post to come to her. In July she was busy engaging a new secretary for
her husband to go to Greeba in August. Her choice was disastrous and
caused an unholy row. For a while he shared a secretary, Paddy Gurton,
later Mrs Dixon, with Ramsay Macdonald. The best secretary he ever
had was Rose de Bear, sister of Archie de Bear of the Co-optimists, a variety troupe, who had first worked for him in 1918. He wanted her to
work part-time but she needed a full-time job and left. On 14 July, 1928,
she wrote to him as 'the wisest man I know'. She had been working
with the Maharaja of Kashmir's staff. She had been asked to go with
another ruling prince and his suite to Geneva and 'may even be invited
to return to Kashmir!' India sounded 'so exciting' but should she go? 'I
trust...your films will be a great success—they should be, under your
personal supervision: if you are able to convince the producers that
your point of view must be the correct one.' After the upset caused by
the secretary Mary sent him, and urged on by Rose de Bear's threat to go
off to Geneva and even India, he asked her to come back, though still
only part-time.

'Don't work too hard on your big book,' Mary wrote at the beginning of August, meaning the *Life of Christ*. 'I notice whenever you work too closely on it you have liver attacks & no doubt it must be very depressing work... I shall be glad when I feel a bit stronger, this attack has pulled me down. Have to lead a quiet life.' She went to see Horder who told her she was fitter than she had been for years. 'He chaffed me a good deal and said I would never look my age... In fact my body was a very healthy one & there was nothing wrong.' He might have saved his breath as she continued to moan about how ill she was. In mid-July she complained of the 'excessive heat which has affected my heart'. She had not been able to leave the house by day for a week. She constantly exaggerated her symptoms and wrote to her friend Mrs Duryea, the former Viola Allen, who was living in Paris, saying she had had a heart attack, causing Viola much anxiety. Another time Mary told her she had had 'an awful motor accident' when it was only a very minor bump. These pleas for sympathy indicate her unhappiness at her state, neither widow nor fully a wife.

Elin was at Greeba for her summer holidays: had she told him, Mary asked, that she wanted to leave school at Christmas and go abroad to learn French? 'It has been a terrible disadvantage to all of us not speaking a word of French or Italian.' This is a prime example of Mary's manipulativeness. Elin had said nothing at all about either leaving school or learning French. It was never discussed with her and she knew nothing of Mary having asked Viola Duryea to look at a finishing school in Paris which Mary fancied for Elin.

When it finally got through to Mary in early September, as a result of a letter from Elin, how ill her husband was she wrote that she was 'dreadfully upset' at the news. 'I have been ill myself and was distressed to feel I could not get to you.' She had spent a weekend with friends in Eastbourne and had returned feeling better. 'Sorry to say my health has been bad lately. I cannot get back to my old self. Perhaps it is being too much alone.' Ignoring the fact that her husband was barely convalescent, she said in a letter of 29 September,

> I want you to arrange to send me the Frederic Shields picture. It will look and be far more suitable for the large drawing-room here. A beautiful old mirror will be and look better in the drawing-room at Greeba. The Shields picture is out of keeping with all those small pictures in the room.

Mary miscalculated. The picture was *Mercy at the Gate*, which Caine had bought from the artist more than twenty years before and treasured as a memento of his old friend from his time with Rossetti. Her next letter said, 'Your letter about the wretched "Mercy" picture upset me dreadfully. I had palpitations the whole day long after it.' Which goes to show how little she understood her husband of so many years.

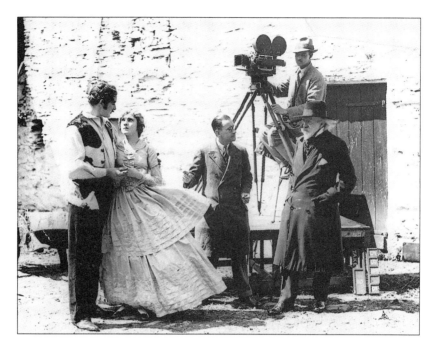

*Caine talking to the director Herbert Wilcox filming on location
in the Isle of Man for* The Bondman, *July 1928. The actors are
Norman Kerry and Frances Cuyler.*

Hard on the heels of Herbert Wilcox another film company arrived in
the Island. This time it was British International Films, about to embark
on a new version of *The Manxman*. Caine had sold the rights but the
director, Alfred Hitchcock, paid a courtesy visit to Greeba Castle taking
along Carl Brisson, who was to play Pete. He was a matinée idol with
typical film star good looks, though he had once been an amateur box-
ing champion. Elin, who was nearly seventeen, was bowled over by
him. Afterwards she begged her grandfather to get her a signed photograph. Brisson obliged.

Relations with Hitchcock were difficult. Whenever he felt well
enough Caine struggled out to see what the company were up to. He
objected to the popular Anny Ondra being cast as Kate. 'She doesn't
look a bit like a Manx girl,' he thundered. It had been Hitchcock's intention to shoot all the outdoor scenes on the Isle of Man but when only
one or two had been completed he could take no more interference
from the irascible author and removed himself and his company to
Cornwall, where Polperro stood in for Peel. In the finished film only a
shot of Pete and Kate sitting on some rocks gazing out to sea and

another of Pete striding through Cregneish village as if on his way home show identifiable Manx settings.

In an attempt to placate the old man the film company wrote inviting him to their studios at Elstree to watch a few of the interior scenes being shot. Caine was still in the Isle of Man and not well enough to go so Mary went instead. She wrote an excited account of her day, noting that she had been photographed with Carl Brisson.

As soon as he felt sufficiently strong Caine went down to London to consult Horder. The journey proved too much for him. As soon as he reached Heath End House he suffered a serious relapse. He was in bed for nearly a month with Horder in attendance. Word got out and on 7 November the *Daily Express* carried headlines that he was dangerously ill and might not be able to complete his *Life of Christ*. Horder was furious as his patient was beginning to recover. Caine sent a pencilled note to Ramsey Moore: 'Dear Attorney-General, Don't be too much alarmed at the headlines this morning which have apparently frightened some of my Editor and Publisher friends.' The pneumonia had returned, giving him a racking cough at night, but the most worrying aspect of his illness, he told Moore, was that he had severe memory loss. Horder did not think it would last long, provided he could get his strength back enough to go away for a holiday. 'The truth is that loss of memory is not unusual with a great nervous collapse,' he assured his friend. He wanted to get to St Moritz and rooms were booked but he was not up to the journey. He wrote again to Ramsey Moore saying sadly, 'As a result of my really bad time I have done very little work indeed. Just as I had begun, as I thought, vigorously, and written a few chapters to my satisfaction, I was completely bowled over.' He continued to write to Moore in pencil, discussing the character of Christ, the works of Paul and the lives of the Old Testament prophets. It seems he now realised he would not be able to finish it himself.

CHAPTER TWENTY-NINE

Caine did not go to St Moritz that winter. He set his heart on one last trip to the Holy Land but would not go without Dr Marshall. In February, 1929, when Horder told him he was well enough to travel, he and Mary, accompanied by Dr and Mrs Marshall and Elin, went overland to the south of France. Mary, Elin and Mrs Marshall stayed in Monte Carlo while Caine and the Doctor went by sea from Marseilles to Palestine. They covered the whole country, including Jerusalem, Galilee, Bethlehem and Nablus, and had a look at the River Jordan. Photographs were taken wherever they went, showing Caine bald, stooped and dressed in a dark suit with a double-breasted waistcoat, often an over-coat, in the brilliant sun. The journey was an intense spiritual experience. Though he feared he might not be able to finish his *Life of Christ* he was a deeply religious man, with a simple, Bible-based faith, and this last visit to Palestine was of overwhelming importance to him. His aim was to show Jesus as a real man in his historical setting. It was as important to him to visit the places connected with Jesus as it had always been for him to go to the countries in which he set his novels.

On the way back they rejoined the rest of the party in Rome. They all spent a few days at the Italian lakes before setting off home. Caine remained with Mary at Heath End House while the Marshalls returned to Douglas. Hitchcock's version of *The Manxman* was about to open at the Hippodrome. For the performance they sat in a box. Caine was infuriated by what had been made of his story and by the unsuitability of Anny Ondra for the part of Kate Cregeen. It was his own fault: he had insisted on selling the film rights without reservation, despite the warnings of Derwent and his agent, because he was paid more that way, but it meant he lost control of the film. He was so outraged by what had been done to his book that he stalked out half way through, followed by his wife, leaving Elin to watch to the end. When it finished a spotlight shone on Hitchcock's box. He acknowledged the applause and gestured towards Caine's box. There were shouts of 'Author! Author!' The spotlight swung across but there was no one there but Elin, cowering at the back.

Caine had ordered Brind to fetch them when the film was due to end but of course as he came out early the car was not there. Wherever he went he always took a red rubber hot water bottle. Mary lovingly

A page from Caine's manuscript of The Life of Christ.

crocheted a woolly cover for it. He had it with him that night and when
Elin came out she found him standing on the pavement holding it by the
top of the cover, which was stretching and stretching, nearly to the
pavement. She was as embarrassed as only a teenager in the company of
an eccentric parent can be. She tried to ignore the hot water bottle, pretending she had nothing to do with the old man attracting curious
glances.

*Caine with Dr Robert Marshall (right) beside the River Jordan
during their visit to Palestine in February, 1929.*

The Manxman was Hitchcock's last silent film and is still screened
from time to time. A critic in 1984 called it 'an old oaken bucket of a
melodrama alleviated by some evocative directorial touches'. It was
already old-fashioned in 1929 but at that stage of his career Hitchcock
had little control over the material he had to work with. In an interview
with François Truffaut in 1968, 'Hitch' called it 'a very banal picture'.

The original reviews ruffled Caine's feathers, not least when they
praised the film. When it reached the Isle of Man he objected to what
one of the local papers said and wrote to protest, in part because the
critic had been too kind! In reply the journalist said he had praised the
first part but criticised the second half because he thought the producer
had completely failed to comprehend the 'motif' of that part of the
story, and consequently of the story as a whole: *The Manxman* was not
a story of Kate's sin or Philip's acceptance of punishment but of Pete's
forgiveness. The critic sympathised with the author's feelings of outrage
that the film had turned Philip's noble self-denunciation into the
extorted confession of a criminal who had been found out. He had
described the scene as 'unjustifiably garbled'.

If Caine saw some of the American reviews he would probably have
been even more upset. One trade paper said, 'Antiquated adaptation of
best seller of another day, first error. Lustreless performance by this all-
British cast plus usual foreign direction and editing, the second. English
locale about the only asset for a pancake. Story is unfolded in a stupid
elementary way.' The newspapers were not much kinder.

Immediately after the film première Caine returned to Greeba. At the
beginning of July Charley Evans came to stay for a few days but Caine

was feeling too ill with an upset stomach to enjoy his friend's visit as much as usual. Mary wrote saying she was sorry to hear of his 'stomach attacks'. She would send Dr Marshall the prescription for a mixture which had helped her to see if it was suitable for him. 'I am afraid you are eating the wrong kind of food now I am not near to watch what you are eating.' She signed her letter, as she always had, 'With all my love & kisses, yours only, Mary.'

*Caine's study at Greeba Castle showing the mantelpiece copied from
one in Rossetti's home. The casket holding the scroll of Caine's
Freedom of Douglas stands in the centre of it.
The sofa came from Rossetti's studio.*

The previous autumn, while Caine was recuperating from pneumonia, he had been offered the Freedom of Douglas. He had replied that he was not well enough to leave the house and would be grateful if the presentation ceremony could be put off until he felt stronger. Now Mary joined him for the delayed event in Douglas Town Hall. It was packed for the occasion. A specially installed public address system relayed the speeches to the large crowd on the stairs, in the foyer and in the street outside. A parchment scroll was presented to Caine in a silver gilt casket adorned with enamelled scenes of Douglas. He was the third Freeman— the first was the Earl of Derby and the second Alderman J.T. Faragher, founding father of the Corporation (who was on the platform that day).

The Mayor gave a speech in which he referred to Caine as 'the greatest living Manxman in the field of literature, the greatest whom we have amongst us now, and the greatest we have had for many years'.

In reply, Caine apologised for speaking seated, explaining he was still weak from his illness. His speech has a curiously modern ring—he talked about how the fishing industry had declined and remarked that the tourist industry was going the same way because potential visitors were finding it too expensive to travel to the Island: they were going to the Continent instead.

Mary returned to London the next day, leaving her husband at Greeba. Her left eye was painful and weeping, with disturbed vision. A London specialist told her the symptoms were serious and he must deal with it. 'It was a very painful operation,' she wrote to her husband in a barely legible scrawl a couple of weeks later, 'which upset all my nerves. I had to go to bed and keep the eye covered but there is no more pain now.'

The problem of secretarial help was still not solved. Mary wrote to Rose de Bear and asked her to come back. She said she would like to, she did not like her present job, but she still needed full-time work. She would help with typing in her spare time if that was any use. In the end she returned to Caine and was with him until his death. She was one of the few who could read his writing. Another was his friend, James Douglas, who wrote in July, 1928, 'I read your letter with ease and delight. I think I possess the gift of divination so far as your marvellous calligraphy is concerned!'

Another winter closed in. Caine worried about his chest, though Mary told him it was 'only catarrh'. Requests for articles and interviews still came in, even invitations to lecture although those were refused. The papers said he was 'very busy despite his ill-health'. It was not in his nature to sit about doing nothing. He did no more broadcasts or filmed interviews and his vast correspondence dwindled but he was never without occupation: his life's work, his 'Jesus' book, absorbed him completely. It was the work he hoped to be remembered by and if he could not finish it himself he was determined to leave it ready for his successors to edit and publish. To the end he could not resist tinkering with it.

He had hoped that one or both of his sons would be writers. When it was clear they would not he encouraged his grandson to write a weekly page or two and send it to him, but there were to be no further authors bearing the Hall Caine name—Derek went into the Army.

Elin turned seventeen in November, 1929. Finishing schools seem to have been forgotten. She was her grandfather's almost constant companion. When she met a young man from Douglas whom she liked she wanted to invite him home but was too nervous about her grandfather's possible reaction. Brind, who knew his employer so well, insisted she must ask the young gentleman to the house. It would be hard to tell which of the party was the most nervous when Charles Gill came to tea. The next day he plucked up courage to ask if he could take Elin for a drive and gracious permission was granted. When he called for her Caine handed him a long list of instructions. This so amused him he kept it for years. It detailed how he was to conduct himself, including not driving at more than 30 miles an hour and bringing Elin home by nine o'clock.

This was no bar to an early engagement. Caine liked the young man and raised no objection although Elin was so young. Her fiancé came from a prominent property-owning family in Douglas and Caine knew he was handing his loved granddaughter over to a young man who would be well able to take care of her. His judgement was vindicated as the marriage has lasted happily for more than 65 years.

However, in 1930 chickens looked like coming home to roost once more and it seemed his sins, of omission as much as commission, would find him out again. Bishop Stanton-Jones, who had been appointed Bishop of Sodor and Man the year before and was a regular visitor at Greeba, agreed to marry the couple in his chapel at Bishopscourt, but said he could only perform the ceremony in her legal surname, Stephen. She was with her adoptive parents at Heath End House when this bombshell dropped. Caine turned for help to Ramsey Moore. As Attorney-General of the Isle of Man and a close friend he knew all the pertinent facts and was the only person Caine trusted to help. Moore drew up the necessary papers and travelled to Hampstead.

Elin was called to the drawing-room to meet him. Her grandparents left her alone with Mr Moore, which surprised her. There were papers on the table. 'Now Elin,' he said. 'You know me, you've known me all your life. You know I would never ask you to sign anything that was not for the best for you.' He showed her where to put her name and she signed, without reading the documents or being told what they were. She thought it was something to do with the marriage settlement her grandfather—whom she still believed to be her father—had said he would make for her. In fact, they were her adoption papers, legally changing her name to Hall Caine. It did not occur to her to question the proceedings or to ask what she had signed. It seems extraordinary now that a girl of seventeen should have been so kept in the dark but her grandparents were Victorians. They had never told her anything or discussed family affairs with her. She did not expect to be allowed to ask questions or to be given any answers.

The wedding, on 5 November, 1930, in the Bishopscourt chapel, was called 'an imposing ceremony' by the local papers. The bride was eighteen years and four days old. The chapel was packed with all the leading members of the Island community, headed by the Governor, Sir Claude

Hill, but Mary was not there. She was ill. Caine, 'looking well despite his 77 years of active life', as the *Isle of Man Examiner* said, led his beautiful daughter up the aisle in a designer gown of white satin with a gold coronet set with seed pearls holding her long tulle veil in place.

When everyone was assembled at Greeba for the reception Caine spoke: 'I must say how much I regret the absence of my dear wife. She is in Brighton very unwell and strictly forbidden by her physician to attempt to cross to the Island at this season of the year.' Doubtless merely the thought of the Irish Sea in November was enough to make her feel ill. Neither of his sons were there either. Ralph sent his love and best wishes in a telegram to Elin but Derwent only wrote a curt note claiming pressure of parliamentary business as his excuse for not turning up. Wild horses would not have got him there. Elin did not like him much but he seems to have hated her. She must have personified his bad conscience. Both he and Ralph were jealous of the place she had in their father's affections and the money spent on her wedding and everything that went with it. Neither young man was missed by a crowd of friends.

For the reception Caine had laid out the leather-bound volumes of his manuscripts on the grand piano. Throughout the afternoon he led guests up to them, inviting their interest and admiration. 'A great treat', the paper tactfully called it. He was quite unable to step back and let anyone else take the limelight, not even his granddaughter on her wedding day. Elin was amused and did not mind a bit but many of the guests were cross and thought the exhibition was in bad taste.

Caine had bought the couple a house. It was called Santa Rosa and was in the part of Douglas known as Little Switzerland which had been largely built by Charles Gill's grandfather, Alexander Gill. His father, also Charles, was an MHK. He and his wife lived in one of the original Little Switzerland houses.

Charles and Elin had no sooner returned from their honeymoon in Torquay and at Heath End House when, early in the New Year, Caine carried them off to St Moritz where they enjoyed skiing. Mary, however, could not stand the altitude and for her sake they all moved down to Monte Carlo. The young couple were bored, longing to get back to Douglas and begin life in their new home. This they did by the beginning of April while Caine remained at Heath End House with Mary. Charles put a parcel on the boat to them containing 'our first spring lamb'.

Leaving Mary in Hampstead as usual Caine returned to the Isle of Man at the end of May and stayed at Santa Rosa for two or three weeks. When he went back to Greeba he was lonely and asked Charles and Elin to keep him company for the summer. They were with him for more than two months. He was still plagued with stomach pains and upsets but happy that the young people were there. On 22 August, a Saturday, Ralph arrived. He was worried to find his father greatly aged and looking frail and weak. However, on the Monday he seemed better and Ralph took him for a drive round the Island. They had tea with Dr and Mrs Marshall on the way home. Ralph had intended to stay a short while and then escort his father to London. However, his father would only say, 'I want to stay here—and die here.'

He seemed well when he went to bed that night but at three the next morning was taken acutely ill with violent stomach pains. Marshall came at once. The patient worsened and was delirious from time to time. Ralph telephoned his mother and she crossed to the Island on the Thursday with Derwent. With this influx and with Dr Marshall sleeping in the house there was no room for Charles and Elin and they returned to their own home. Part of the trouble was Derwent. He would never speak to Elin, and if she came into a room where he was he would leave or turn his back on her. Once, at his mother's insistence, he had given her a lift in his car from London to Brighton and spoken not one word for the whole drive. All this made it difficult for her to be in the same house with him.

Mary, far from well herself, was distraught to find her beloved Tom so ill and barely aware she was there. She scarcely left his side. Elin visited her grandfather daily, more and more fearful. On the Sunday he seemed briefly better. He talked to his family, but later he relapsed with pain and delirium. Marshall called in Dr Pantin, the senior doctor on the Island, and together they had a telephone consultation with Horder in London. A bowel blockage had been diagnosed and the three doctors were agreed that there was nothing that could be done.

On the Monday morning Caine was weak but awake when Elin came to see him, and knew both her and Mary, but soon after Elin left he worsened and it was clear he was critically, even dangerously, ill. Mary sat beside him all day, occasionally chafing his cold hands. When Bishop Stanton-Jones called at about five in the afternoon Caine did not recognise him. During the evening Elin rang anxiously to ask if she could see him, grateful that Dr Marshall had insisted the week before on the telephone being put in. As gently as he could Marshall told her that her grandfather had slipped into a coma and would not know her—it was best she stayed where she was. Hall Caine died that night, 31 August, 1931, at 10.50. He was 78. His poor old heart had given out under the strain. 'Cardiac syncope' was what Dr Marshall put on the death certificate when he registered the death in Douglas next day, signing it as 'present at the death'.

Afterwards rumours arose that there had been a rift between Elin and her grandfather after her marriage and that she had refused to go and see him in his last illness when he asked for her. It is difficult to understand how this got about as it does not fit with recorded facts.

The newspapers had got wind of Caine's illness at the weekend and reported that he had either pneumonia or heart trouble. Messages of concern and sympathy had begun to arrive on the day he died, from Lord Beaverbrook. *The Times* must have had their obituary already in type because it appeared next day, 1 September. As it is largely accurate it seems to have been written by someone who knew him well, probably Robert Leighton. The two had remained close friends to the last. After describing the painstaking research that went into all Caine's books, the obituary writer continued,

> This characteristic earnestness, which in personal matters made him an easy prey to the irresponsible American interviewer, often raised his work to a fine fervour; at its worst, it robbed him of his sense of proportion and fitness, and of his sense of humour. His work gives the impression that he took himself very seriously. In reading him it was rarely possible to forget that he had chosen an axe to grind, and wished to be regarded as writing with a political or moral mission.

This balanced view remains valid. 'He never forgot his responsibility to the huge public which looked to him for information and advice on religion, morals and politics, finding in his work at once a brave show of independence and a due regard for its own opinions.' The public responded and with his most popular novels 'he won a popularity in which he was equalled only by another didactic novelist of the period, Miss Marie Corelli'. It is doubtful whether Caine would have been pleased to be bracketed with her, or she with him (she had died in 1924). Other obituaries appeared around the world, mostly less accurate in recording the famous author's life.

Within hours of his death telegrams and letters of sympathy were pouring into Greeba Castle for Mary. One of the first was from King George V and Queen Mary. Others were from the Governor of the Isle of Man, Sir Claude Hill, Arthur Pinero, Baroness Orczy, Mattheson Lang, Bransby Williams, Sir Walter de Frece and the erstwhile Vesta Tilley, Willie Hall Caine (who was ill himself), and many more. One from the Prime Minister, Ramsay Macdonald, was addressed to Derwent. It read, 'So very grieved but you have as an inheritance both the pride and distinction of his great career. Malcolm joins me.'

There was a call in the Isle of Man for Caine to be buried in the ruined cathedral within the walls of Peel Castle. The last burial there had been in 1864. The Manx government, who owned the castle, would not give permission. Mary wanted him to be buried in the grounds of Greeba Castle but it was explained to her that it would take too long for the ground to be consecrated. Her sons reminded her that only weeks before their father had bought a grave plot in Maughold churchyard, and

One of the last photographs to be taken of Hall Caine.

before that he had wanted to be buried on Maughold Head, the spot on the Island he loved the best, perhaps even more than Greeba. Maughold churchyard was chosen and the plot he had himself selected.

The funeral took place on Friday, 4 September. A huge crowd from the surrounding area waited at the gates of Greeba Castle to see Hall Caine's simple coffin of unpolished oak with silver fittings carried down to the waiting hearse. Business in Douglas came to a standstill for an hour as the cortège passed slowly through the town, along the Promenade and onto the Mountain Road. It was the same when it reached Ramsey and all the way out to Maughold Church. The chief mourners (as listed in the local papers) were Ralph and Derwent, accompanied by two cousins, one representing Willie who was still not well enough to travel. Behind them came Elin's father-in-law Charles Gill MHK and his son, with Dr Marshall and Attorney-General Ramsey Moore, Percy Cowley, Brind, his devoted chauffeur and valet, and the two nurses who had looked after him. Also there was Robert Leighton, the last survivor of his Liverpool friends. Elin stayed with Mary, as was the custom.

A slate obelisk was erected over the grave, designed by the Manx artist Archibald Knox, famous for his work for Liberty's. It was decorated with traditional Celtic patterns in low relief. Characters from the novels were carved on the plinth with the inscription 'Slumbering in the deep solitude of the hills he loved so much'. It is a strikingly handsome monument.

A memorial service was held in London at St Martin's-in-the-Fields on 8 September, reported in *The Times* and in the *Daily Telegraph*. Hundreds of people crowded into the church. Mary led the mourners, escorted by Ralph and Derwent, with Lillian and her children Derek and Mary. The Prime Minister and Lloyd George were represented and the Vice-Chamberlain of the Royal Household was there. Among old friends were Viscount Burnham, Lord Beaverbrook, Sir Arthur Pinero and Newman Flower. The London Manx turned out in force, as did representatives of the many charities Caine had supported, including Sister Mildred from the West London Mission. The curate of St Martin's took the service and the address was given by a very old friend of Caine's, Canon R.J. Campbell. A Londoner, he had entered the Congregational Ministry in 1895 and was pastor of the City Temple from 1903 to 1915. In 1907 he had startled the evangelical world by publishing an 'advanced' *New Theology*. In 1916 he had caused a fresh upset by moving over to the Anglican church. Whatever Caine's literary reputation might be in the future, he said, he would always be remembered for his association with the Isle of Man. He never forgot that it was his novels about the Island which had made him famous. Canon Campbell likened him to Burns, Wordsworth, Hardy and Arnold Bennett, who had each hymned their own country. He ended by saying that 'for all time to come the genius of that little self-contained kingdom, the Isle of Man, would be associated with the name of Hall Caine'.

There was considerable speculation in the press as to the size of Caine's estate. Whatever the exact figure he would have been a millionaire at today's values. It was widely assumed in the Isle of Man that Caine would leave his famous home to the nation. Why they thought this when he had children and grandchildren is hard to see. Having at long last honoured their famous son the Islanders now complained he had left nothing, neither money nor house, to the Manx nation.

After the funeral Mary returned to Heath End House with Derwent. It was nearly fifty years since Tom Hall Caine had taken responsibility for the thirteen-year-old Mary Chandler. Without him she was lost, the mainspring of her life broken. For a while her determination to see her husband's last book published kept her going. Robert Leighton came to her assistance, agreeing to edit the book. Assisted by Rose de Bear, who had worked on the manuscript with Caine, he sat down to the three million word manuscript of the *Life of Christ*, moving into Heath End House for a time to be able to devote himself to it completely. He had first discussed the subject with Caine in about 1898. Caine had been invited to contribute the Preface to a book by the Congregationalist divine, Dr Joseph Parker, whose original and fervid sermons at the City Temple drew big congregations. He sent the Preface to Leighton for his comments. Leighton returned it saying,

> It seems to me certainly that Dr Parker's book is not the best place for the expression of these thoughts. I have read your manuscript very carefully and can see much—very much—beyond what you have written. It is too condensed. I strongly advise you to expand it and make a book of it, in two contrasting sections—the Christ of Galilee and the Christ of today. You have, I know, been meditating deeply upon this subject, and the results of your meditation would, I am very certain, be gladly accepted and widely appreciated by the world.

Caine continued to discuss his *Life of Christ* with Leighton at intervals for the rest of his life. Whether or not he actually asked Leighton to edit it after his death, he would have approved of his doing it.

Mary followed the progress of the book eagerly, reading each chapter as it was typed, but she did not have the strength to go on. On 3 March, 1932, only six months after her adored husband's death, Mary Hall Caine died of pneumonia. Her nurse, Edith Hawkins, was with her at the end. There was a problem when no birth certificate could be found. Nurse Hawkins, who registered the death, guessed her age at 64. In fact, she was 62. Acceptable proof of her date of birth, perhaps baptismal or

Sunday School certificates, must have turned up because that is the date which is carved on the monument over the grave.

They took her back to the Isle of Man to lie beside her Tom in Maughold churchyard. It was the sort of tempestuous weather she hated, which had given her neuralgia so many years before. It was wet and windy as Ralph and Derwent followed their mother's coffin off the boat, through Douglas and along the winding coast road to Maughold. Rose de Bear was with them. She had brought a wreath made in the shape of an open book. 'Lady Hall Caine was working on the manuscript of her husband's Life of Christ not long before she died,' she told one of the reporters, 'so I thought that was what she would like.' Perhaps due to the awful weather there were no crowds for Mary's funeral, just a small group of family and friends.

Derwent inherited Heath End House and allowed Leighton to continue his work on the *Life of Christ* there. Leighton managed to reduce the vast manuscript to a rather more manageable 750,000 words but was not able to finish the job to the point of seeing it through the press. He died in 1934. Somehow Ralph and Derwent sank their differences sufficiently to oversee final production. Hall Caine's *Life of Christ* was published by Collins in 1938. An Introductory Note signed by both sons makes no mention of Robert Leighton's work. The last paragraph reads,

> We have followed his words without alteration, even though occasionally some passages restate an idea, and although there may be lines which had he lived he might have altered. But in general we have preferred to be faithful to his text and to present this great work of scholarship and inspiration without undue editing.

This reads far more like Robert Leighton than either of his sons.

Caine said at one time that he had first conceived his Life of Christ in 1888. Over the years he made a number of half-hearted attempts to publish it. For instance, his archive contains a letter dated 20 February, 1896, from the editor of the *Churchman*, in New York, acknowledging a letter from him about it. They would like to discuss serialising it in America once it was finished. Other letters indicating that Caine had put out feelers for publication bear dates right through to 1928. In some cases he was approached by editors or publishers who had heard the work was in progress and wished to put in a bid for it, but as has been shown a number of his friends were completely against the project, although Leighton had supported him all along. By the time he had finished his career as a romantic novelist he no longer had the strength to finish it.

Over a period of twenty years Caine made at least three visits to Palestine. He claimed to have explored all the available published material on the subject and to have had many ancient documents in museums and literary collections translated for his use. His sons said he never wanted to publish it during his lifetime because he felt right to the end that his research must go on and on. The realisation that he would never be able to complete it was thought by some people to have hastened his death—impossible to say now. He was after all approaching 80 with serious stomach trouble. Elin had another explanation: 'He never wanted to finish it. It was his refuge. Whenever things bothered him he retreated into his study to work on it. It was something that was always there, something he could fall back on when other things failed.'

His own Foreword to the book begins

> The principal object of this book is to tell, as simply as I can, and in the order I think best, the true story, as far as my knowledge goes, of the life of a Jewish working man, who lived in Palestine, under the rule of the Roman Empire, chiefly in the reign of Tiberius Caesar, nearly 2,000 years ago, and probably hundreds of thousands of years after the creation of the world and man.

He followed the school of thought which traced the idea of a Messiah to the beginning of history (Genesis, Chapter 1). This view is not now in favour with scholars, but in support of it he wrote what turned out to be a history of the Jews as told in the historical books of the Old Testament. He gave his story-telling powers full play and the sweep of the narrative is the outstanding feature of the book. He worked through the Old Testament prophets for traces of the Messianic expectations of the Jews. While a number of his references show they looked for a personal Messiah, others which he quotes are rather far-fetched and are discounted by modern scholarship. However, this first section of the book makes an impressive introduction to the second, the account of Jesus' life and crucifixion. The third gives the story of the resurrection and what followed, the growth of the legends of Jesus, the life of the early church and the writing of the Gospels.

What is abundantly clear is that Caine had a detailed and impressive knowledge of the Scriptures. He must have read every word of the Bible over and over again. The great weakness of his book, however, is that it entirely fails to take account of the work of scholars since about 1860 in elucidating the Bible, particularly the Old Testament. He claimed to have read all the authorities but there is no sign he was aware of researches made during his lifetime which had, for instance, corrected the chronology of the Bible. Nor does he seem to have consulted contemporary translations of the Greek Old Testament, based on a Hebrew manuscript and more accurate than the one on which our Old Testament translation was based. Of all this he apparently knew nothing, which is a pity as he could have put the book on a much more scholarly basis. However, it remains a great achievement and for beauty of style and vividness of presentation it possibly surpasses any other Life of Christ written in modern times.

When it was published it aroused little or no interest and quickly disappeared. Hannen Swaffer, a prolific journalist who claimed to have known Caine well and last interviewed him in 1926, had written a preview in the *Daily Herald* a couple of weeks earlier, when he asked, 'Why is it that Officialdom may thunder disapproval and that the masses may yet acclaim it?' In the event neither happened. The Revd C.F. Stockwood, dealing with the book in the *Isle of Man Examiner* on 21 October, 1938, said, 'This is a difficult book to review, not only because it is far too long, but also because one is never quite sure what the author himself really believes. Two voices struggle for mastery: Hall Caine the Bible critic and Hall Caine the devout, mystical and devotional Celt.' Which sums it up neatly.

Caine's brother William, the last of the children of John and Sarah Caine, died of a cerebral thrombosis at Kenwood Farm House on 14 January, 1939. Ralph continued as a Conservative MP until after World War II and died in London in 1962. Derwent, who lost his seat in the 1931 election, was knighted in 1932 and created a baronet 'for political services' in 1938. Shortly afterwards he went to live in America and died in Nassau, Bahamas, in 1971. He left a large sum of money in his will to be distributed to Isle of Man charities as his trustees saw fit. It was divided into so many small donations no one realised that some of Caine's money had returned to benefit the Island. Derwent's money also provided the statue of his father which stands in Douglas.

The mystery of Hall Caine remains. How was it that a man so famous in his own time, so enormously popular and successful as a writer, has been for so long almost entirely forgotten? Marie Corelli is no more read now than Hall Caine and yet people know of her. 'Hall *who?*' is apt to be the reaction to the mention of his name. The answer may lie in the way he dissipated his creative energies. He wanted to be teacher, preacher, writer and statesman in one. Had he concentrated on storytelling, instead of spending so much time on politics and newspaper articles, he might have produced a body of work to compare with the best of his time or even his idol, Dickens, who can be just as sentimental and given to propagandising. However, Dickens's characters are mostly diamond-clear: Caine's are frequently fuzzy at the edges and too often the same—as are his plots. Nowhere in his work do we find anything to compare with Sam Weller, Sarey Gamp or Mr Pickwick. The essential difference between them lies in his one fatal flaw: he was entirely lacking in a sense of humour. Dickens created wonderfully comic characters and situations, Shakespeare had his fools and his rude mechanicals as well as Lear and Hamlet, but in Caine's books all was deadly earnest. He took himself and his writing with intense seriousness. His stories can be riveting, passionately romantic or sad to the 'three-hanky weepie' level but he almost never makes us laugh. It is an omission posterity has found it hard to forgive.

APPENDIX I

The Letters of Dante Gabriel Rossetti and Hall Caine

The correspondence between Rossetti and Hall Caine held in the Manx Museum in the Isle of Man and in the Angeli Collection at the University of British Columbia in Canada is incomplete. There are a few letters and cards from Rossetti in Hall Caine's personal archive in the Manx Museum but there is no clue as to where other missing documents may be, if they still exist. As filed in the two archives—Rossetti's in the Isle of Man and Caine's in British Columbia—the documents are not in sequence. This becomes apparent when one puts the two sets together. As both writers, particularly Rossetti, were casual about dating their letters, often noting just the day of the week, it is only when one reads them on a letter/reply basis that one sees how they should go. The content of some of them makes it clear they are misplaced and where gaps remain.

Caine's letters to Gabriel cease abruptly in the early summer of 1881 while those from Rossetti continue to September of that year. There are some to and from William Rossetti after that date. When Gabriel died in April, 1882, Caine retrieved his own letters from Tudor House. Later William demanded them back. Caine took his time and only finally handed them over in 1902. They were left to Helen Rossetti Angeli, William Michael's granddaughter, and on her death found a final resting place in British Columbia. It seems that Caine did not return all of them, only a selection which William had picked out, and this could account for the shortfall. There is also a strong possibility that Caine destroyed some letters before William could see them.

APPENDIX II

Hall Caine (1853-1931): A Select Bibliography

Compiled by Vivien Allen

Note: An incomplete bibliography was compiled for the Manx Museum by G. Fred Clucas, who was making a catalogue of works relating to the Isle of Man in 1913. He wrote to Caine asking for his assistance. On 27 October, 1913, Caine replied that he could not help as he had never kept track of his books and the many editions, English and foreign, they had run through, nor did he have any record of the huge amount of newspaper and magazine articles and stories he had written. Today the task is impossible. What follows is based on the Manx Museum bibliography with additions from the author's researches.

1879 7 December, Caine wrote to Rossetti saying an unnamed publisher would shortly bring out 'a small 200 page volume' containing 7 of his papers. These were: 1 on restoration of old buildings; 1 on Rossetti's poetry; 4 on Shakespearean subjects; 1 on Keats. No copy has come to light so far.

1880 'Politics and Art'; a lecture delivered at the Royal Institution, Liverpool. Notes & Queries Society, Royal Institution, Liverpool.
'The Supernatural Element in Poetry', Notes & Queries Society, Royal Institution, Liverpool. This essay originally appeared in *Colbourne's Magazine*, August, 1879.

1882 *Sonnets of Three Centuries: An Anthology* (ed. Hall Caine; London: Elliott Stock). 50 de luxe copies on handmade paper were part of an edition of 1000.
Recollections of Dante Gabriel Rossetti (London: Elliott Stock; reissued in amended form in 1928).

1883 *Cobwebs of Criticism: A Review of the First Reviewers of the 'Lake', 'Satanic' and 'Cockney' schools* (London: Elliott Stock; reissued by Routledge in 1907). Facsimile of the Stock edition (New York: AMS Press, 1974).

1885 *The Shadow of a Crime* (Chatto & Windus).
She's All the World to Me: A Manx Novel (New York: Harper & Brothers). Paperback in Harper's Handy Series, No. 13, New York. Later reissued with *A Son of Hagar* in Volume III of *Hall Caine's Best Books* (New York: P.F. Collier & Son, no date).

1886 *A Son of Hagar* (Chatto & Windus).

1887 *Life of Samuel Taylor Coleridge* (Walter Scott). No. 2 in the Great Writers series edited by Eric Robertson.
The Deemster: A Romance in 3 Vols. (Chatto & Windus). 4th edn published in one vol. Up to the 1921 edition, published by Eveleigh Nash & Grayson, London, there had been 52 editions in English and it had been translated into French, German, Dutch, Danish, Swedish, Russian, Spanish, Finnish and Bohemian. Later editions carried an introduction by Bram Stoker, dated 11 June, 1905.

1888 *The Prophet*, a play written for Henry Irving but never staged. Originally titled 'Mahomet'.

1889   Play: *The Good Old Times*, produced at the Princess's Theatre, Oxford Street by Wilson Barrett.

1890   *The Bondman: A New Saga* (Heinemann). In 3 vols., January 1890, in 1 vol. October 1890. Translated into eleven languages. A new preface was included in the 1903 edition. First published in serial form by the *Isle of Man Times* between June and November, 1889.
        The Scapegoat: A Romance (Heinemann, 2 vols., September, 1890). Published simultaneously in Europe, America and Canada. 1-vol. edn May, 1892.

1890   *The Prophet* published as a novella 'mainly to preserve the title'.

1891   *The Little Manx Nation* (Heinemann).

1892   *The Fate of Fenella*. 3 vols., illustrated. Publisher unknown but likely to have been American. No record of UK publication.
        'Scenes on the Russian Frontier', Lecture to Jewish Working Men's Club, Liverpool.

1893   *Cap'n Davey's Honeymoon*; *The Last Confession*; *The Blind Mother* (Heinemann). Novellas published in one volume and dedicated to Bram Stoker.

1894   *The Manxman* (Heinemann). Serialised in the *Queen*. By 1913 it had sold half a million and been translated into 12 languages. Published simultaneously in New York by D. Appleton & Co. in 1894. 1st edn dated 3 August, 1894, reprinted 17 August and 1 September, 1894.
        The Little Man Island: Scenes and Specimen Days in the Isle of Man. A paperback guide to the Island written for and published by the Isle of Man Steam Packet Company, Douglas, 50 pp. Republished by S.K. Broadbent, 1899.
        The Mahdi: or Love and Race, A Drama in Story (London: James Clarke & Co.). Reprinted from the Christmas number of the *Christian World* for private circulation. Print run 100.

1895   'Graih my Chree, a Manx Ballad', published on St Valentine's Day. Printed in *Lyra Celtica* (no date available) and in *London Home Monthly*, March 1895.

1896   *Jan the Icelander or Home, Sweet Home, A Lecture Story* (Harrison and Sons).

1897   *The Christian* (Heinemann). Serialised in the *Windsor Magazine* and *Munsey's Magazine* January–June 1896 and in 1897. Initial print run 50,000 in August, reprinted again that month and in October, thereafter almost annually up to the edition of 1927. Translated into 12 languages—continental editions by Tauchnitz, American by Appleton.

1901   *The Eternal City* (Heinemann). Serialised in the *Lady's Magazine*. A 'theatre edition', 1902. Initial print run 100,000, August 1901, reprinting by December. By 1926 had run through 26 editions. Translated into 13 languages.
        'Unto the Third and Fourth Generation', short story, *Windsor Magazine*.

1903   'Passive Resistance', Supplement to the *Isle of Man Examiner*, 15 August.
        The Isle of Boy: A Comedy (New York: Appleton & Co.): play in 4 acts.

1904   *The Prodigal Son* (Heinemann). 500,000 of the English editions alone sold by 1913. Translated into 13 languages.

1905   *The Prodigal Son*: a drama in 4 acts, printed for private circulation and the use of the actors only.
        The Queen's Christmas Carol (ed. Hall Caine, though not named). Published in aid of the Queen's charities by the Daily Mail.
        The Prodigal Son: A Novelised Version of Mr Hall Caine's Play by S.R. Squires (Derby: Bacon & Hudson).

1906   *Drink: A Love Story on a Great Question* (George Newnes). Illustrated by Cyrus Cuneo.
        The Bondman, play. Script illustrated by photos of the cast. Hardback. *Daily Mail*, London.

My Story (Heinemann). Autobiography, incorporating much of the material in *Recollections of D.G. Rossetti* (q.v.). First appeared in English Writers of Today series, no. 4.

1908   *Queen Alexandra's Christmas Gift Book* (ed. Hall Caine, though not named). *The Daily Telegraph*, London, in aid of the Queen's charities.

1909   *The White Prophet* (2 vols.; Heinemann), illustrated by R. Caton Woodville (war artist for the *Illustrated London News*). Translated into seven languages.

1910   *King Edward: A Prince and a Great Man* (Collier & Co.), repr. from the *Daily Telegraph* by permission of the proprietors. Illustrated with photographs of the Royal Family. Hardback, 43 pp.

1913   *The Woman Thou Gavest Me* (Heinemann). Published in July, reprinted twice in August and again in September, October and November. 475,000 sold by the end of 1913. Translated into nine continental languages.

1914   *King Albert's Book, A Tribute to the Belgian King and People from Representative Men and Women throughout the World* (ed. Hall Caine, though not named). The *Daily Telegraph*, in conjunction with the *Daily Sketch*, the *Glasgow Herald* and Hodder & Stoughton.

1915   *The Drama of 365 Days: Scenes in the Great War* (Heinemann). Reprinted from the *Daily Telegraph* with additions. Hardback, 127 pp.
       30 October. Article for the *Daily Sketch* on the death of Edith Cavell, headed 'Daughter of England, you have taught us how to die. Edith Cavell's noble lesson to the people of her race'.

1916   *Our Girls: Their Work for the War* (London: Hutchinson & Co.). Small format hardback illustrated by 15 photographs provided by the Ministry of Munitions.
       Play: *The Prime Minister*.
       One-act Play: *The Iron Hand*.

1917   'August' and 'October', articles in the *Daily Chronicle* on 'The Coming of Peace, Three Years of War, Reprisals and Manpower in the Field'.

1918   'Thank God for Lloyd George', the *Sunday Pictorial*.
       'Should we Teach German?', the *Observer*.
       'Victory and Peace', scenario for propaganda film.

1919   Film script: *Darby and Joan*.

1921   *The Master of Man: The Story of a Sin* (Cassell & Co.).
       100,000 printed in July, reprinted in November. American, Canadian and Continental editions came out simultaneously and translations in Holland, Sweden, Denmark, Finland, Norway, Bohemia, Poland and France. First published in serial form in *Nash's Magazine*. A privately printed edition containing letters from various notabilities was circulated among family and friends.

1923   *The Woman of Knockaloe: A Parable* (Cassell & Co.).

1928   *Recollections of Rossetti* (Cassell & Co.). A note says 'Some portions of this book were published in 1882; other portions of it in 1908; much of it is now new. It is first published as a completed book at the Centenary of Rossetti's birth, 1928.'

1938   Posthumous publication: *Life of Christ* (London: Collins), foreword by his sons Ralph and Derwent Hall Caine.

Three Collected Editions of the novels were published, two by Heinemann, in 1905 and 1921, and one by Cassell in 1923.

APPENDIX III

Caine Family Tree

Ralph Hall m. Mary ? (b. 1803 d. 1875)
Stonemason, b. Whitehaven 1799
d. Liverpool 20.1.1870

Sarah Hall
b. 1829 d. 1912

William Caine of Ballaugh, IoM
d. 1844
m. Isabella Clarke 18.6.1811

10 children inc. John Caine
Baptised 23 January, 1821,
at Ballaugh, d. at Greeba, 1906

m.

Thomas Henry Hall
b. 14.5.1853
d. 31.8.1931
m. 1886 Mary Chandler
(25.5.1869–3.3.1932)

John James
b. 21.9.1855
d. 2.4.1877

Sarah Jane
b. 21.1.1858
d. 16.3.1863

Emma
b. 7.4.1862
d. 27.6.1863

William Ralph Hall
b. 5.2.1865
d. 14.1.1939
m. 1904 Mary
Elizabeth
w. of John Levy

Vera (stepdaughter)
m. Layton

Elizabeth
Ann (Lily)
b. 13.12.1869
d. 31.5.1914
m. George David Day
5.3.1896

David Day

Ralph Hall
b. 15.8.1884
d. 26.6.1962
m. i Lilian

Derek   Mary

Derwent
b. 12.9.1891
d. 2.12.1971
m. Yvonne c. 1940
(d. c. 1942)

Elin b. 1.11.1912
m. 1930 Charles Gill

1 daughter

m. ii Dorothy Sara who survived him for a short time

BIBLIOGRAPHY

Apart from Hall Caine's own books and standard reference works, these are the principal books consulted:

Angeli, Helen Rossetti, *Dante Gabriel Rossetti: His Friends and Enemies* (London: Hamish Hamilton, 1949).

Appelbaum, Stanley (ed.), *The New York Stage: Famous Productions in Photographs* (New York: Dover Publications Ltd, 1976).

Belford, Barbara, *Bram Stoker: A Biography of the Author of Dracula* (London: Weidenfeld & Nicolson, 1996).

Benzie, William, *Dr F.J. Furnivall: A Victorian Scholar Adventurer* (Oklahoma: Pilgrim Books, 1983).

Bingham, Madeline, *Henry Irving and the Victorian Theatre* (London: George Allen & Unwin, 1978).

Bonham-Carter, Victor, *Authors by Profession: A History of Writing* (London: Society of Authors).

Booth, John Bennion, *London Town* (London: T. Werner Laurie, 1929).

—*Sporting Times: The Pink 'Un World* (London: T. Werner Laurie, 1938).

—*The Days we Knew* (London: T. Werner Laurie, 1943).

—*Palmy Days* (London: Richards Press, 1957).

Bosman, F.C.L., *Drama en Toneel in Suid-Afrika*, II (Cape Town: 1856-1912).

Brandon, Ruth, *The New Women and the Old Men* (New York: W.W. Norton & Co., 1993).

Bratton, J.S. (ed.), *Music Hall: Performance and Style* (Buckingham: Open University Press, 1986).

Burnham, Lord, *Peterborough Court: The Story of the Daily Telegraph* (London: Cassell, 1955).

Cecil, Lord Robert (Viscount Cecil of Chelwood), *A Great Experiment* (London: Jonathan Cape, 1941).

—*All the Way* (London: Hodder & Stoughton, 1949).

Clarke, William M., *The Secret Life of Wilkie Collins* (London: Allison & Busby, 1988).

Crosby, Christina, *The Ends of History: Victorians and 'The Woman Question'* (New York and London: Routledge, 1991).

Davis, Tracy C., *Actresses as Working Women, their Social Identity in Victorian Culture* (London and New York: Routledge, 1991).

De Frece, Lady M.A., *Recollections of Vesta Tilley* (London: Hutchinson & Co., 1934).

Cumberland, Gerald, *Set Down in Malice* (London: Richards, 1919).

Dobbs, Brian, *Drury Lane: Three Centuries of the Theatre Royal 1663-1971* (London: Cassell, 1972).

Dobbs, Brian, and Judy Dobbs, *Dante Gabriel Rossetti: An Alien Victorian* (London: Macdonald & Jane's, 1977).

Evans, Stewart, and Paul Gainey, *The Lodger: The Arrest & Escape of Jack the Ripper* (London: Century, 1995).

Fredeman, William, ' "Fundamental Brainwork": The Correspondence Between Dante Gabriel Rossetti and Thomas Hall Caine' (Paper delivered in Canada, October, 1977).

Gaunt, William, *The Pre-Raphaelite Tragedy* (London: Cape, 1975).

Gifford, Denis, *Books and Plays in Films 1896-1915: Literary, Theatrical and Artistic Sources of the First Twenty Years of Motion Pictures* (London: Mansell, 1991).

Grylls, Rosalie Glynn, *Portrait of Rossetti* (London: Macdonald, 1964).

Hake, T., and A. Compton-Rickett, *The Life and Letters of T. Watts-Dunton* (London: T.C. & E.C. Jack, 1916).

Holroyd, Michael, *Bernard Shaw* (4 vols.; London: Chatto & Windus/Penguin).

Hueffer, Ford M., *Ford Madox Brown* (London: Longmans, Green & Co., 1896).

Jerome, Jerome Klapka, *My Life and Times* (London: Hodder & Stoughton, 1926).

Kernahan, Coulson, *In Good Company* (London: John Lane, 1957).

Leatherdale, Clive, *Dracula: The Novel and the Legend* (Brighton: Desert Island Books, 1993).

Leighton, Clare, *Tempestuous Petticoat* (London: Victor Gollancz, 1948).

Lindop, Grevel, *A Literary Guide to the Lake District* (London: Chatto & Windus, 1993).

Ludlam, Harry, *A Biography of Dracula: The Life Story of Bram Stoker* (Cippenham: Foulsham & Co., 1962).

McCarthy, Lillah, *Myself and my Friends* (London: Butterworth, 1933).

Marsh, Jan, *Christina Rossetti* (London: Cape, 1994).

Member of the Aristocracy, A, *Society Small Talk: What to Say and How to Say It* (London: Warne & Co., 1879).

—*Manners and Tone of Good Society; Party Giving On Every Scale; The Management of Servants* (London: Warne & Co., 1882).

Mills, Ernestine (ed.), *The Life and Letters of Frederic Shields* (London: Longmans, Green & Co., 1912).

Morris, William, *Journals of Travel in Iceland, 1871 and 1873* (London: Longmans, Green & Co., 1911).

Norris, Samuel, *Two Men of Manxland* (Douglas, Isle of Man: Norris Modern Press, 1947).

—*Manx Memories and Movements: A Journalist's Recollections* (1938; repr; Douglas, Isle of Man: Manx Heritage Foundation, 1994).

Parker, Louis N., *Several of my Lives* (London: Chapman & Hall, 1928).

Pearson, Hesketh, *Modern Men and Mummers* (London: George Allen & Unwin, 1921).

Peters, Margot, *Mrs Pat: The Life of Mrs Patrick Campbell* (London: The Bodley Head, 1984).

Rossetti, Dante Gabriel, *Family Letters* (2 vols., with Memoir and commentary by William Michael Rossetti; London: Ellis & Elvey, 1895).

Rossetti, William Michael, *Dante Gabriel Rossetti as Designer and Writer* (London: Cassell & Co., 1889).

—*Some Reminiscences* (London: Brown Langham & Co., 1906).

—*Dante Gabriel Rossetti: His Family Letters with a Memoir* (London: Ellis & Elvey, 1895).

St John, John, *William Heinemann: A Century of Publishing 1890-1990* (London: Heinemann, 1990).

Scott, William Bell, *Autobiographical Notes of the Life of William Bell Scott* (2 vols.; ed. W. Minto; London: James R. Osgood, McIlvaine & Co., 1892).

Sharp, William, *Dante Gabriel Rossetti* (London: Macmillan & Co., 1882).

Thwaite, Ann, *Edmund Gosse: A Literary Landscape 1849-1928* (London: Secker & Warburg, 1984).

Sitwell, Osbert, *The Scarlett Tree* (London: Macmillan, 1946).

Stephens, Frederick G., *Dante Gabriel Rossetti* (London: Seely & Co., 1894).

Stoker, Bram, *Personal Reminiscences of Henry Irving* (2 vols.; London: Heinemann, 1906).

Stone, Lawrence, *Road to Divorce* (Oxford University Press, 1990).

Truffaut, François, *Hitchcock* (London: Secker & Warburg, 1968).

Waugh, Evelyn, *Rossetti: His Life and Works* (London: Duckworth, 1928).

Wearing, J.P., *The London Stage* (1976).

Wood, Esther, *Dante Rossetti and the Pre-Raphaelite Movement* (London: Sampson Low, 1894).

INDEX

A Life Poem 234
A Son of Hagar 164, 172, 179, 181-84, 232, 258, 278, 379
Abbé Liszt 163
Aberleigh Lodge 172, 177, 178, 185, 187, 191
Abraham, G.F. 218
Abrey, Mrs 134, 138, 139, 141, 143, 145, 150
Academy 114, 117, 175
Adler, Dr Herman 209, 214, 215, 246
Aga Khan, the 356
Ainley, Henry 363
Albert of Belgium 357
Al Minbar 341
Alexander, George 306, 308
Allen, Viola 259-61, 264, 268, 274, 280, 291, 296, 413
Althing 194, 195, 295
America 241, 243, 256, 257, 264, 297, 326, 359-61, 363, 369, 371, 380, 398, 430
Anti-Scrape Society, the 62, 80
Antiquary 102
Anti-Semitism 209, 211
Appleton, William 243, 244, 267, 271, 277, 280, 297, 310, 311, 314
Architect 55
Arnold, Matthew 110, 162
Arrow Film Corporation 364, 369
Arts and Crafts movement 32, 247
Asquith, Herbert Henry 362
Athenaeum 78, 117, 138, 167, 171, 182, 206
Author 245
Authors' Club 231
Authors' Syndicate 214
Autobiography 319, 325, 327
Aveling, Edward 50, 51, 159
Awad, Hafiz 323

Bailey, Philip James 60
Balcombe, Florence 65
Baldwin, Stanley 401
Balestier, Wolcott 198-200, 249

Baptist 102
Barbed Wire 396
Baring, Evelyn 318 *see also* Lord Cromer
Barr, Robert 234
Barrett Browning, Elizabeth 77
Barrett, Wilson 165-67, 188, 189, 191, 192, 199, 235, 236, 252, 267, 287, 329
Barrymore, Lionel 277
Bear, Rose de 412, 420, 427, 428
Beaverbrook, Lord 424, 426
Beefsteak Room 163, 164, 217, 238, 243, 289, 319
Beerbohm, Max 256
Belgium 356, 358
Ben-my-Chree 188, 190-92, 199, 268, 345
Benas, Baron L. 341, 342
Beresford, Lord Charles 319, 356
Berlin 221, 334
Bernhardt, Sarah 356
Besant, Annie 50, 208
Besant, Walter 214, 261
Bevan, Sofia 254
Bexley Heath 172
Biograph and Review 80
Bioscope 363
Birchington 138, 139, 141, 148, 150
Birmingham Daily Post 55
Bishop's Son, The 345
Black and White 217, 284
Blackmore, R.D. 162, 179, 208, 266, 271, 272, 325
Blathwayt, Raymond 217-19
Blind, Mathilde 76
Boer War 269, 347
Bondman, The 21, 176, 194, 199, 200, 202-204, 206, 211, 216, 314-16, 322, 366
Bookman 300
Borrow, George 167
Bottomley, Horatio 392, 393
Brenon, Herbert 367, 370, 371
Bright, Henry Arthur 58, 78, 161, 219, 266
Bright, R. Golding 219, 334
Brisson, Carl 414

British Architect 55, 78
British Film Institute 364
British International Films 414
Britton, Hutin 237, 329
Bromley & Son 30, 43, 55, 69, 112, 120
Bromley, Israel 30, 53, 56
Bromley, James 30, 53, 56, 61-63, 103, 112, 116, 117
Brook, Clive 396
Brown, Revd. Hugh Stowell 187
Brown, T.E. 130, 187, 212, 213, 219, 240, 249, 264, 305
Browning, Robert 162
Buchanan, Robert 69, 98, 126, 137, 165, 174
Builder 24, 55, 64, 72, 80, 105
Burne-Jones, Edward 129, 135, 145, 148
Burnham, Lord 331, 343, 367, 426
Busch, Mae 374
Byard, Theodore 377, 391

Caine, Derek Hall 387, 420, 426
Caine, Derwent 216, 217, 241, 253, 258, 265, 272, 282, 288, 295, 297, 307, 309, 310, 315, 328, 331, 336, 343, 345, 347-50, 354, 355, 358-63, 367, 369, 371-74, 378, 385, 388, 392, 393, 400-402, 405-407, 409, 416, 422, 423, 426-28
Caine, Elin 349, 355, 362, 366, 369, 374-78, 380, 386-88, 401-403, 406, 412-14, 416, 417, 420-23, 429
Caine, Elizabeth Ann 20 *see also* Lily Caine
Caine, Emma 16, 17
Caine, Isabella 16, 20
Caine, John 15-17, 20, 27, 69, 241, 246, 253, 255, 257, 258, 265, 274, 297
Caine, Mrs John 246
Caine, John James 16, 24, 32, 43, 48, 50, 54, 353, 383
Caine, Lily 24, 55, 109, 138-44, 148, 149, 165, 167-69, 177, 178, 199, 206, 213, 218, 219, 221, 246, 252, 256, 258, 261, 269, 274, 289, 297, 306, 308, 309, 319, 328, 355
Caine, Mary Hall 188, 191, 194, 195, 205, 206, 209, 213, 216, 218-21, 225, 229, 237, 238, 240, 241, 243, 244, 246, 253, 256, 257-59, 261, 263-66, 271, 272, 275, 279, 282, 286, 288-92, 294, 295, 297, 298, 304, 307, 310, 313, 317, 319, 320, 323, 328, 343-47, 349, 350, 354, 359, 361, 362, 366, 369-80, 384-86,
388-93, 401, 402, 406, 408, 409, 412, 413, 415, 416, 419, 420, 422, 424, 426, 427 *see also* Mary Chandler
Caine, Mary Hall (daughter of Ralph Hall Caine) 426
Caine, Mary (Elizabeth) Hall 387
Caine, Ralph Hall 171, 177, 181, 184, 188, 191, 194, 205, 206, 213, 216, 218, 240, 241, 243, 244, 253, 256, 258, 280, 281, 285, 288, 290, 291, 293, 294, 298, 305-307, 312, 314, 317, 321, 331, 354, 357, 361-64, 372, 373, 375, 378, 379, 381, 382, 385, 388, 392, 393, 395, 400, 401, 405, 406, 422, 423, 426, 428
Caine, Sarah Jane 16, 17, 194, 205, 246
Caine, William Ralph Hall 20, 24, 55, 109, 149, 155, 168, 170, 174, 177, 206, 216, 221, 246, 257, 265, 285, 291-93, 309, 310, 325, 362, 392, 400, 424, 430
Caine, William 16
Calamus 56
Campbell, Canon R.J. 426
Campbell, Mrs Patrick 309, 314
Cap'n Davey's Honeymoon 217, 222-24
Carlyle, Thomas 128
Carpenter, Ernest 328
Carroll, Lewis 126
Cassell 377, 395
Castletown, Isle of Man 212, 253
Catholic Times 345
Cecil, Lord Robert 362, 396 *see also* Viscount Chelwood
Chamberlein, Joseph 241
Chandler, Jenny 213 *see also* Jenny Mandeville
Chandler, Mary 153, 154, 158-60, 167-72, 176, 177, 181, 182, 184 *see also* Mary Hall Caine
Chapel of the Ascension 304, 322, 343
Chapman & Hall 238
Charlie the Cox 234
Chatto & Windus 175, 179, 187, 199, 200, 364
Chatto, Andrew 175, 176, 178, 183, 187, 188, 199, 200, 364, 379
Chelwood, Viscount 363
Cheyne Walk 69, 87, 90-92, 96, 114, 118, 121, 125, 137, 138, 148-50, 205
Christian World 238
Christian, The 169, 246, 251-59, 263, 264, 266, 267, 269, 274, 275, 277-79, 289, 291, 319, 320, 352, 360, 380, 381

Christian, William 212
Clegg, John 19
Clement's Inn 153, 154, 159, 162, 165, 169, 383
Cleveland, President Grover 243, 310
Close, Ivy 371
Close, John 49, 50
Cobwebs of Criticism 105, 161, 162, 167, 322
Cockermouth, Keswick and Penrith Railway 127
Colbourne's New Monthly 70, 71
Coleridge, Derwent 186
Coleridge, Hartley 161, 186
Coleridge, Samuel Taylor 23, 44, 45, 150, 151, 161, 162, 168, 185-87, 197, 216, 266
Collier & Co. 334, 341, 343
Collier, Constance 277, 289
Collier, P.F. 317
Collins, Arthur 199, 293, 302, 306, 312, 314, 315, 320
Collins, Michael 393, 394
Collins, Wilkie 179, 180, 189-91, 266, 325
Comintern 394
Communism 25, 30, 219, 394
Connor, Marie 200
Conway, Martin 261
Copyright 164, 189, 200, 241, 244, 250, 251, 256, 267, 300, 334, 373
Copyright Bill 241, 245
Copyright Conference 245
Corelli, Marie 234, 239, 258, 306, 344, 424, 430
Cornforth, Fanny 124, 127-31, 133, 144, 145, 279, 411
Cornwall, Lady 312, 313, 319, 320, 343
Cornwall, Sir Edwin 312, 320, 343
Cowley, Peter 426
Cowley, Thomas 274, 282, 329
Cowper, T.C. 29
Crabtree Watching the Transit of Venus 142, 152
Cranston, Adam 334, 340
Crawfurd, Oswald 217, 231, 238
Crisis of the White Prophet, The 340
Cromer, Lord 318, 319, 338, 339, 347 *see also* Evelyn Baring
Cumberland, Gerald 249
Cumbria 61, 125, 127, 251, 266
Cuneo, Cyrus 313

Daily Express 315, 415
Daily Graphic 215, 327
Daily Herald 430
Daily Mail 306, 316, 321, 335
Daily Mirror 309, 335
Daily News 344
Daily Telegraph 271, 306, 310, 325, 326, 331, 340, 343, 347, 356, 357, 359, 367, 426
Danny Fayle 164
Dante's Dream of the Death of Beatrice 107, 109, 110, 118, 119, 133
Darby and Joan 371
Day, David 258, 297, 355
Day, George David 246, 274, 297, 298, 319
Debussy, Claude 356
Deemster, The 165, 187-89, 199, 200, 202, 243, 268, 288, 302, 345, 361, 364, 369, 379
Demon Lover, The 238
Denshawai Affair 318, 339
Dhone, Illiam 212, 213
Dickens, Charles 180, 238, 285, 430
Digges, Lillian 354, 372, 375, 387, 405, 426
Divorce 351
Divorce Act 319
Dixon, Revd R.W. 76
Doubleday, F.N. (Effendi) 376, 377, 395
Doubleday, Nelson 376
Doubleday, Page & Co. 376
Douglas, Isle of Man 274, 373, 381
Douglas, James 420
Dowden, Edward (later Sir Edward) 56-59, 61, 68, 73, 80, 82, 89, 93, 138
Dowden, Ernest 66
Dracula 67, 223, 249
Drama of Three Hundred & Sixty-Five Days: Scenes in the Great War, The 359
Dreyfus Affair 245
Drink: A Love Story on a Great Question 313
Drury Lane 199, 308, 314
Duke of Edinburgh 240
Duke of York's Theatre, Liverpool 269
Dumbell's Bank 272, 283, 323
Dunn, Henry Treffry 87, 98, 114, 121, 124, 150
Duryea, Viola 413 *see also* Viola Allen

Earl of Derby 419
East, Charles 192
East, John M. 192, 252, 363
Edinburgh 184
Edinburgh Philosophical Society 237
Edward VII 287, 289, 304, 334, 343
Effendi, Hafiz 332, 341
Egypt 178, 238, 317-19, 322, 332, 334, 338, 339, 341, 347, 370, 396
Elementary Education Act 20
Elgar, Sir Edward 306
Eliot, George 128
Ellan Vannin 343, 352
Elliott, Rowland 23
English, Margaret 372, 373
Eternal City, The 267, 269, 271, 274, 275, 277-79, 285, 286, 289, 291, 294, 344
Eternal Question, The 277, 344, 345
Evans, Charley 275, 292, 373, 375, 377, 380, 390, 408, 418
Expulsion of the Danes, The 105

Famous Players 371
Faragher, Alderman J.T. 419
Farrant, Reginald 59, 260, 386, 389
Farrar, Dean 255
Festus: A Poem 60
Feuillet, Octave 182
Film 360, 367, 370, 371, 373, 396, 408, 414
Film rights 200, 360, 373
Finland 268, 269
Fisher Place 113, 117, 118, 120, 127, 130, 133, 174, 237
Fleshly School of Poetry, The 126, 165
Flower, Newman 395, 396, 398, 410, 426
Fors Clavigera 26
Fox Studios 360
Franzos, Karl Emile 220
Frece, Lady de 408
Frece, Walter de 271, 372, 408, 424
French Revolution 186
Frohman, Charles 259, 260, 267
Funeral 426
Furnivall's New Shakespere Society 58
Furnivall, Frederick James 57, 61
Fürst, William 263

Gaiety Theatre, Douglas 311
Galloway 110
Galsworthy, John D. 367
Garrick Theatre 344, 345

Gell, James Stowell 260
Gell, Sir James 187, 260, 282, 287, 293, 305
George V 344, 368, 424
Geraldine 44, 81
Germ 61, 63
Germany 221, 245, 335, 350, 356, 397
Ghosts 139
Gill, Alexander 422
Gill, Charles 421-23, 426
Gill, Elin 35 *see also* Elin Caine
Gill, George 18
Gladstone, Herbert 263, 285, 305, 313
Gladstone, William 22, 81, 202, 256, 257, 263
Goldwyn, Samuel 364, 373, 374
Good Old Times 192, 199
Gordon, General 317, 337, 338
Gorky, Maxim 222
Gosse, Edmund 111, 112, 156, 222, 245, 356, 402, 411
Governor of the Isle of Man 335
Graih my Chree 238
Granby Steet Board School, Liverpool 168
Grand Theatre, Douglas 256, 294, 300, 335
Grand Theatre, Leeds 235
Graphic 178, 208
Greeba Castle 225, 229, 240, 245, 247, 251, 253, 263, 266, 268, 274, 275, 292, 293, 306, 314, 326, 328, 335, 341, 345, 348, 355, 361, 370, 373, 374, 386, 388, 390, 402, 414, 422, 424, 426
Greeba Towers 229
Grey, Frank 385
Greycaine Book Manufacturing Company 385
Grossmith, George 234
Grossmith, Weedon 234
Groves, Fred 363
Guild of St George 26
Gurton, Paddy 412

Haggard, H. Rider 175, 188, 193, 208, 403
Hake, George 126
Hall, Mary 15, 20, 109
Hall, Ralph 15, 20, 24, 25, 130
Hall, Sarah 15
Halliwell-Phillipps, James 89, 97
Hampstead 169, 172, 213, 238, 366, 386
Handwriting 217
Hardy, Thomas 208, 222

Harmsworth, Alfred 214, 335 *see also* Lord Northcliffe

Harte, Brett 238

Hawthorns 178, 193, 196, 197, 204, 205, 217, 218, 222, 225, 229, 237, 406

Health 36, 82, 113, 217, 265, 304, 312, 359, 370, 374

Heath Brow 354, 366, 371, 388

Heath End House 379, 388, 389, 391, 401, 402, 415, 422, 427, 428

Heckford, Sarah 218

Heinemann, William 33, 176, 183, 199, 200, 202, 203, 211, 212, 215-23, 231, 234, 239, 249-51, 255, 256, 258, 275, 277, 280, 292, 297, 300, 313, 325, 326, 332, 334, 336, 337, 340, 341, 346, 359, 373, 376, 377, 380, 390

Her Majesty's Theatre 286

Hill, Sir Claude 421, 422, 424

Hirsch, Baron 220

His Majesty's Theatre, London 277

Hitchcock, Alfred 414, 416, 418

Hodder & Stoughton 300, 356, 357

Hodder-Williams, Ernest 300, 356, 357, 371

Holman Hunt, William 151, 180, 239, 240, 306

Holroyd, Michael 183

Home Rule for Ireland 285

Home, Sweet Home 250

Hommy-Beg 16, 67, 223, 326, 334

Hope Street British Schools 18, 20

Hope, Anthony 234, 238

Hopkins, Gerard Manley 76, 119

Horder, Sir Thomas (later Lord Horder) 370, 379, 388, 413, 415, 416, 423

Houghton, Lord 58, 78, 93, 162, 266, 268 *see also* Richard Monkton Milnes

House of Keys 260, 284, 285, 296, 305, 313, 362

Household Words 180, 238, 285, 286, 290, 291, 293

Hulton, Sir Edward 393

Hutchinson, A.S.M. 381

Hutchinson's 364

Ibsen, Henrik Johan 256, 268

Iceland 193, 194, 200, 202, 295, 303

Icelandic sagas 63, 193, 195, 202

Idler, The 219, 234

Illustrated London News 215

India 341, 346, 347, 370

Ireland 394

Irving, Henry 34, 35, 50, 51, 56, 59, 61, 64, 65, 93, 163, 164, 166, 176, 184, 188, 199, 204, 205, 214, 217, 238, 239, 243, 244, 250, 310, 321, 343, 389

Irving-Aveling Mystery, The 50

Islam 322

Isle of Boy, The 311

Isle of Man 15-17, 20, 24, 88, 176, 187, 188, 194, 202, 212, 213, 216, 225, 229, 231, 234, 240, 243, 246, 251, 258, 263, 266-68, 271, 272, 276, 278, 284-87, 292, 294, 313, 323, 325, 326, 329, 331, 335, 341, 348, 350, 351, 362, 363, 368, 371, 373, 379, 382, 386, 388, 390, 395, 398, 414, 418, 422, 424, 426-28, 430

Isle of Man Examiner 422, 430

Isle of Man Steam Packet Company 231, 258, 267, 283, 343

Isle of Man Times 200, 233

Isle of Man Weekly Times 337

Isle of Wight 168, 178

Jackson, Edwin 50, 167, 178, 191, 193, 196, 361

Jackson, Greeba 402

Jackson, W.W. 32, 33

Jameson, Dr Leander Starr 245

Jerome, Jerome K. 214, 219, 234, 237, 239, 304, 356, 411

Jewish Literary Society 341

John Bull 392

Jones, Henry Arthur 237

Jonson, Ben 235

June, Roma 361, 374

Kenyon, Fred 283

Keppel, Alice 288, 359

Keppel, George 288, 359

Keswick 60, 71, 113, 167, 178, 181, 191, 193, 196, 197, 212, 217, 218, 220, 225, 361, 406

Keswick Museum 229

Khartoum 322, 323, 337, 338, 340, 347

King Albert's Book 357, 359

King William's College, Castletown 253, 255, 382

Kinnish, John 233

Kipling, Rudyard 234, 367, 376

Kitchener, Lord 245, 317, 347, 356

Kneale, Bryan 331

Knickerbocker Theatre, New York 264

Knockaloe 363, 398
Knollys, Charlotte 332, 361
Knox, Archibald 426
Kruger, Paul 245

Lady's Magazine 274
Lake District 26, 59, 88, 127, 131, 167, 191, 243, 406
Lake Poets 161
Lang, Mattheson 237, 328, 329, 367, 370, 424
Lange, Marie 47-50, 52-54, 74, 84
Last Confession, The 222
Law, Andrew Bonar 356, 396
Lawrence, T.E. 338
Laxey Mills 26
Laxey, Isle of Man 26
League of Nations 362, 363, 369, 371, 396
Leaves of Grass 56, 57
Leighton, Marie 348
Leighton, Robert 180, 200, 201, 219, 255, 348, 382, 424, 426-28
Letters and Speeches on Manx Politics 292
Leo XIII 289
Lever, Sir William 361 *see also* Lord Leverhulme
Leverhulme, Lord 370, 371, 403
Levy, Mary Elizabeth 293
Levy, Vera 293
Lewis, Sir George 179, 267, 274, 280
Leyland, Frederick 145, 147, 148
Library, Museum and Arts Committee 68, 108, 109, 118
Liebler & Company 260, 263, 291, 293, 310
Life of Christ 218, 219, 313, 317, 337, 400, 403, 413, 415, 416, 427, 428
Life of Samuel Taylor Coleridge 33, 185, 186
Limericks 95
Little Man Island: Scenes and Specimen Days in the Isle of Man, The 231
Little Manx Nation, The 212
Liverpool 15, 19, 21-23, 29, 58, 62, 63, 76, 77, 81, 108, 109, 113, 114, 116, 121, 130, 131, 133, 134, 149, 155, 170, 174, 180, 182, 212, 216, 244, 249, 257, 269, 284, 322, 361, 362, 396
Liverpool *Courier* 30
Liverpool Free Library 21, 23, 67, 68, 118
Liverpool Lantern 55

Liverpool Mail 43
Liverpool Mercury 112, 149, 155, 163, 164, 170, 174, 178, 180, 182, 206, 282, 284
Liverpool Shakespeare Society 58
Liverpool *Town Crier* 35
Lloyd George, David 283, 366, 367, 369, 394, 402
Lohr, Marie 370
London Film Company 360, 363, 364
London Library 183
Long, Ray 373, 380
Longfellow, Henry Wadsworth 128
Loveday, Henry 34, 65
Lovell, John 112, 149, 150, 163, 164, 168, 169, 174, 175, 206, 266
Low, Sir Sidney 385
Lyceum Theatre, London 34, 163, 164, 204, 320, 321, 329, 334
Lyric Opera House, Hammersmith 192

Macdonald, Katherine 371
Macdonald, Malcolm 401
Macdonald, Ramsay 401, 412, 424
Mackenzie Bell, H.T. 183, 192, 213, 214, 246
Mackenzie, Sir Alexander 217, 306
Macleod, Fiona 111 *see also* William Sharp
Madox Brown, Emma 88, 110
Madox Brown, Ford 87-90, 95, 105-107, 110, 114, 127, 129, 132, 134, 142, 145, 146, 148, 152, 156, 162, 165, 266
Madox Brown, Oliver ('Nolly') 88, 110, 156
Maeterlinck, Maurice 359
Magazine of Arts 114
Magnusson, Erikur 193
Mahdi, The 209, 213, 245, 337
'Mahdi: A Story of Love and Race, A Drama in Story, The' 238
Mahomet 199, 203, 204, 214, 218
Malmberg, Aino 268, 269
Manchester Evening Mail 215
Manchester Evening News 231
Manchester Guardian 55, 314
Manchester Town Hall frescos 87-89, 105-107, 142
Mandeville, Jennie 314
Manx Museum 176
Manx National Reform League, The 282

Manxman, The 27, 33, 192, 229, 231, 233-35, 237, 244, 257, 266, 269, 287, 291, 329, 363, 364, 381, 414, 416, 418
Marbury, Elizabeth 244
Margaret Schiller 369
Marriage 184, 278, 325, 375
Marriage Law Reform 239
Marriage Law Reform Association 240
Marshall, Dr John 133-35, 138, 143, 145
Marshall, Dr Robert 27, 260, 261, 272, 275, 282, 320, 348, 349, 374, 379, 386, 389, 408, 416, 423, 426
Marshall, Mrs Robert 282, 349, 416, 423
Marston, Philip Bourke 77, 102, 134, 135
Marx, Eleanor 50, 159
Mascagni, Pietro 277, 289, 344
Mason, A.E.W. 316, 337
Master Films 371
Master of Man, The 53, 160, 373, 377, 380, 383
Maudsley, Dr Henry 135
Maughold 21, 24, 27, 329, 352, 424, 428
Maurier, George du 234, 360
McCarthy, Lillah 261, 287
Melbourne Herald 353
Member of the House of Keys (MHK) 281, 422, 426
Memoir of Dante Gabriel Rossetti 156
Memorial service 426
Mercy at the Gate 297, 413
Meredith, George 91, 165, 180, 183, 186, 216, 306, 335
Meynell, Alice 77, 279, 352
Millais, Sir John Everett 219
Milnes, Richard Monkton 58 *see also* Lord Houghton
Moore, A.W. 187, 287
Moore, Arthur 260
Moore, Ramsey 386, 415, 421, 426
Morning Post 309
Morocco 209, 211, 214, 215
Morris & Co. 62, 249
Morris, Janey 79, 80, 125, 126, 128, 129, 132
Morris, William 32, 46, 61-63, 68, 79, 80, 86, 91, 93, 125, 129, 162, 172, 187, 193, 195, 205, 247, 296, 410
Moseley, B.L. 322, 323, 332, 340, 347
Munsey's Magazine 251
Murray, Gilbert 356
Murray, John 22, 24, 29, 30
My Story 20, 21, 153, 325, 326

Mylchreest, Joe ('The Diamond King') 233
Myrtle Street Chapel 17, 30, 257, 362

Nagel, Conrad 374
Naismith, Eirane 401, 402, 407
Name the Man 374
Nash's Magazine 350
National Film 367, 369-71
National Film Archive 367, 371, 396
Negri, Pola 396
Nelson, Thomas & Son 183
Net Books Agreement 1899 315, 316
New Court, Lincoln's Inn 169, 170, 192
New York 234, 241, 243, 256, 260, 289, 293, 296, 307, 309, 350, 359, 381
New York Public Library 310
New York Times 359, 364
New York theatre 360
Newnes, George 313
Newton, A.S. 253
Nielson, Julia 261
Nineteenth Century 72
Noble, James Ashworth 51, 52, 58, 111
Norris, Samuel 282, 284, 305
Northcliffe, Lord 214, 335, 340, 341, 394
  see also Alfred Harmsworth
Notes & Queries Society 30, 32, 55, 58, 61-63
Nowell, William 228, 229

Observer 321
Omdurman (Sudan) 317, 338, 347
Ondra, Anny 414, 416
Orczy, Baroness 424
Our Girls: Their Work for the War Effort 364

Padereweski, Ignace Jan 243
Page, Arthur 377
Palestine 209, 317, 322, 396, 416, 428
Pall Mall Gazette 55, 309, 321, 348
Pantisocracy 186, 187
Paramount 396
Parker, Louis N. 166, 237, 261, 329, 332, 334, 360
Partridge, Bernard 257
Pawling, Sydney 239, 251, 255-57, 275, 292, 332, 334, 376, 377
Peel, Isle of Man 176, 229, 233, 237, 240, 241, 247, 276, 288, 319, 345, 363, 424
Pegramm, Fred 306
People 321

Personal Reminiscences of Henry Irving 67

Pete 237, 329, 334

Pierce, William 19, 38, 46, 47, 180

Pinero, Sir Arthur Wing 237, 268, 424, 426

Pines, Putney Hill, The 116, 132, 162, 185

Pius X 271, 277, 285, 289, 345

'Poetry of Pre-Raphaelitism, The' 67

Poland 214

Pre-Raphaelite Brotherhood 60, 61, 68, 86, 102, 105, 127, 133, 135, 151, 165, 180, 410

Price Hughes, Hugh 254

Price, Nancy 277

Prime Minister, The 369

Prince of Wales 344, 359

Prince of Wales (Edward) 164, 179, 240, 289 *see also* Edward VII

Prince of Wales (George) 331, 344, 359 *see also* George V

Princess Victoria 331

Princess of Wales 164

Probyn, Sir Dighton 332

Prodigal Son, The 289, 293, 295, 296, 300, 304, 306-308, 314, 315, 334, 335

Prophet, The 204, 218

Protection of Minors Act 155

Publishers' Association 315, 316, 336, 357

Punch 188, 257, 320

Quality of Mercy, The 345

Queen Alexandra 234, 288, 289, 303, 305, 310, 331, 344, 361

Queen Alexandra's Christmas Gift Book 331

Queen Mary 424

Queen Victoria 168, 179, 287

Queen magazine 229, 231, 246, 350

Queen's Christmas Carol, The 306, 310

Queen's Fund for the Unemployed 306

Quiller Couch, Arthur 234

Rae, George 86, 118, 119

Raglan, Lady 319, 335

Raglan, Lord 287, 293, 313, 339

Rambler 34, 50

Ramsey Grammar School 253, 272, 307

Ramsey, Isle of Man 304

Rathbone, Philip 68, 98, 108

Rayne, Leonard 287

Readers Library Publishing Company 385, 400, 405

Recollections of Dante Gabriel Rossetti 60, 91, 93, 95, 127, 128, 150, 325, 408

Red House 172

Reform Committee 305

Reform Movement 293

Review of Reviews 256, 304

Rhodes, Cecil 245

Risdon, Elizabeth 360, 363

Robertson, Eric 153, 154, 159, 162, 185, 383

Robinson, John 228

Rome 272, 275, 277, 354, 406

Rose, George 26, 27, 29, 30, 32, 33

Rosebery, Lord 234

Rossetti's letters 158

Rossetti's poetry 63

Rossetti, Christina 52, 76, 77, 104, 115, 121, 132, 136, 143-45, 150, 151, 155, 157, 160-62, 165, 183, 402

Rossetti, Dante Gabriel 60, 61, 66, 69-75, 77-88, 90, 91, 93, 94, 96-106, 108, 109, 111, 113-18, 120, 121, 123-28, 130-38, 140-44, 147-52, 155, 156, 158, 165, 174, 180, 181, 186, 187, 205, 237, 247, 249, 263, 266, 277, 279, 280, 301, 303, 312, 325, 335, 348, 389, 408-12

Rossetti, Elizabeth 91, 131 *see also* Elizabeth Siddal

Rossetti, Lucy Madox 103, 115, 146, 152, 155-57, 165

Rossetti, Maria 136

Rossetti, William Michael 61, 63, 69, 70, 72, 76, 87, 91, 93-96, 103, 104, 115, 120, 124, 127-29, 132-34, 136, 139, 145-47, 149-51, 155-58, 161, 165, 301, 305, 322

Royal Commission on Divorce 344

Royal Institution 30, 58, 212

Royal Literary Fund 183

Royal Lyceum Theatre 64, 65

Ruskin Severn, Joan 222

Ruskin, John 26, 32, 62, 89, 124, 151, 222, 223, 238, 266, 325, 411

Russia 178, 202, 211, 214-17, 219, 221, 222, 268, 347, 385

Russo-Jewish Committee 214, 215

Saintsbury, George 138, 161

Samuelson, Alderman Edward 68, 108-10, 133

Saturday Review 126, 127, 138, 175

Scapegoat, The 208, 209, 211, 215, 216, 252, 337
Scawen Blunt, Wilfred 46, 318
Scott, Clement 192, 292
Scott, Laetitia Bell 136
Scott, Walter 46, 277, 341
Scott, William Bell 76, 102, 115, 125, 132, 136, 145, 149, 165, 325
Sevenoaks 159, 160, 167
Shadow of a Crime 169, 174, 176, 178, 179, 190, 237
Shaftesbury Theatre 235
Shakespeare, William 430
Sharp, William 111, 132, 142, 148, 151-53, 158, 162, 165, 170, 171, 186, 191, 213 *see also* Fiona McLeod
Shaw, George Bernard 132, 145, 182, 183, 222, 236, 257, 268, 296, 306, 318, 327, 335, 339, 340, 351, 357, 369, 396, 403, 410-12
She's All the World to Me 164, 178, 188
Shelley, Percy Bysshe 197
Shields, Frederic 71, 95, 116, 123, 126-28, 132, 134, 136, 137, 142, 145-49, 162, 165, 180, 247, 253, 280, 297, 304, 306, 322, 326, 328, 343, 347
Shorter, Clement 300
Siddal, Elizabeth 124, 181, 411 *see also* Elizabeth Rossetti
Sitwell, Sir George 311
Sitwell, Osbert 275, 311
Sketch 21
Sladen, Douglas 258
Society for the Protection of Ancient Buildings, the 62
Society of Authors, The 214, 241, 245, 250, 261
South Africa 245, 257, 269, 287, 347
Southey, Robert 186, 197
Sovreal, Marquis de 288
Spalding, Percy 364
Speaker 234
Spedding, J.J. 197, 225
Sphere 350
St Cyprian's school 272, 296, 297
St Joan 403
Stamfordham, Lord 344, 371
Standard 236
Stanton-Jones, Bishop 421, 423
Stead, W.T. 256, 348
Stephen, Colonel 347

Stephen, Dolly 348-50, 354, 355, 387 *see also* Frances Dorothy Stephen
Stephen, Florence 347-49
Stephen, Frances Dorothy 347 *see also* Dolly Stephen
Stephens, Frederick G. 86, 87, 90
Stevenson, R.L. 208
Stock, Elliot 102-106, 112, 114, 115, 137, 150, 151, 161, 167
Stockwood, Revd C.F. 430
Stoker, Bram 65, 67, 164, 176, 179, 180, 184, 187, 199, 203, 204, 214, 216-19, 223, 231, 233, 238, 239, 243, 244, 249, 250, 261, 267, 274, 275, 280, 292, 296, 306, 310, 325, 326, 332, 334, 347, 350, 373, 389
Stoker, Florence 203, 219
Strand Magazine 332
Straton, Rt Revd Norman 288
Sudan 317, 338, 340, 347
Suez Canal 318, 319
Sunday Graphic 393
Sunday Herald, The 393
Sunday Illustrated 392-94, 400
Sunday Mirror 392
Sunday Pictorial 392, 393
Swaffer, Hannen 430
Swayne, Marian 364
Sweden 202
Swinburne, Algernon 46, 104, 111, 116, 121, 124, 126, 129, 138, 145, 162, 165, 306, 310, 410, 412
Swinnerton, Frank 275

Taft, President William 356
Tangier 213, 214, 223
Tatler 292, 300, 323
Tauchnitz, Baron 350
Teare, Adelaide 25, 246
Teare, Alfred 25
Teare, Catherine 21, 24, 25
Teare, James 21, 24, 25, 27
Teare, Mona 25
Teare, Reuben 25
Telford, Thomas 197, 229
Tennyson, Alfred Lord 46, 138, 168, 222
Terry, Ellen 34, 154, 163, 250, 259, 367, 370
Terry, Fred 261
Theatre Royal, Drury Lane 293, 345
Thorndike, Sybil 403
Tilley, Vesta 271, 372, 408, 424

Tillotson's Newspaper Literature 179, 200, 203, 214, 229

Times Book Club, The 315, 316

Times, The 202, 222, 316, 335, 424, 426

Tirebuck, Maggie 23, 49

Tirebuck, William 18, 23, 24, 29, 30, 32-34, 36, 43-50, 54, 71, 80, 107, 151, 180, 266

Titanic 348

Tolstoy, Count Leo Nikolayevich 215, 221, 222, 268

Toxteth 16, 32

Toynbee Hall 254

Tree, Beerbohm 277, 286, 289, 294, 322, 332, 334, 343

TT Races, Isle of Man 395

Tucker, Arthur 218

Tucker, George Loane 360, 363, 364

Tudor House 91, 101, 123, 124, 132, 139, 144, 247

Tumblety, Francis 37-40, 42, 46

Turgenev, I.S. 136

Twain, Mark 218

Tyler, George 263, 264, 291, 296, 310

Tynwald 194, 195, 232, 293, 313, 363, 364, 401

Tynwald Day 240

Tynwald Hill 289

Valera, Eamon de 393, 394

Vaughan Wilkes, Cicely 272

Vaughan, Cardinal 269, 271

Vesuvius 312

Victory and Peace 367

Vitagraph 360

Votes for women 212, 316

Wain, Louis 306

Wainwright, Albert 29, 30, 44

Walker Art Gallery, Liverpool 107, 133

Walpole, Hugh 409

Warner, Charles 246

Waterbury, Florence 27

Watson, William 78, 84, 111

Watts, G.F. 154

Watts, Theodore 71, 75-77, 95, 98-100, 111, 115-17, 121, 130, 132-34, 137, 142, 144-46, 149, 156, 159, 162, 164, 165, 167, 175, 178, 180, 182, 185, 186, 191, 282, 285, 300, 303, 306, 310, 410 *see also* Theodore Watts-Dunton

Watts-Dunton, Theodore 282, 310, 326, 348 *see also* Theodore Watts

Waugh, Evelyn 408

Webb, Beatrice 352

Wells, H.G. 222

West London Mission 254, 322, 426

Westcliffe Bunglow 141, 150

Westminster Gazette 316

Westminster Review 56, 72

Weyman, Stanley 238

White Prophet, The 178, 332, 334, 336, 337, 339, 341, 343, 347, 351, 353, 376

Whitehall Court 229, 239, 293, 306

Whitehall Review 182

Whitman, Walt 56, 66

Why I Wrote The White Prophet 341

Wilcox, Herbert 414

Wilde, Oscar 38, 65, 111, 112, 268, 292

Williams, Bransby 345, 424

Wimbledon 297

Windsor Magazine 251

Windus, Edward 225

Windus, Mrs 225, 228, 229, 245, 247

Windus, William 188, 225

Wingate, Major-General Sir Reginald 322, 340

Woman Question, The 254, 255, 344, 352

Woman Thou Gavest Me, The 272, 279, 351, 360, 368, 371, 373

'Woman and Marriage' 347

Woman of Knockaloe, The 396

Women's University Settlement 254

Woodville, R. Caton 336

Wordsworth, Gordon 222

Wordsworth, William 161, 162, 222, 235

Yorkshire Post 107

Zangwill, Israel 209, 246

Zionism 209, 220